Intelligent, Adaptive and Reasoning Technologies:

New Developments and Applications

Vijayan Sugumaran
Oakland University, USA & Sogang University, South Korea

Information Science
REFERENCE

Senior Editorial Director:	Kristin Klinger
Director of Book Publications:	Julia Mosemann
Editorial Director:	Lindsay Johnston
Acquisitions Editor:	Erika Carter
Development Editor:	Hannah Abelbeck
Production Editor:	Sean Woznicki
Typesetters:	Keith Glazewski, Natalie Pronio, Milan Vracarich, Jr., Deanna Zombro
Print Coordinator:	Jamie Snavely
Cover Design:	Nick Newcomer

Published in the United States of America by
Information Science Reference (an imprint of IGI Global)
701 E. Chocolate Avenue
Hershey PA 17033
Tel: 717-533-8845
Fax: 717-533-8661
E-mail: cust@igi-global.com
Web site: http://www.igi-global.com

Library of Congress Cataloging-in-Publication Data

Intelligent, adaptive and reasoning technologies: new developments and applications / Vijayan Sugumaran, editor.
    p. cm.
  Includes bibliographical references and index.
  Summary: "This book is a comprehensive collection of work from researchers in related fields such as information systems, distributed AI, intelligent agents, and collaborative work that explores and discusses various aspects of design and development of intelligent technologies"--Provided by publisher.
  ISBN 978-1-60960-595-7 (hbk.) -- ISBN 978-1-60960-596-4 (ebook) 1. Management information systems. 2. Expert systems (Computer science) 3. Intelligent agents (Computer software) 4. Web services. 5. Artificial intelligence--Industrial applications. I. Sugumaran, Vijayan, 1960-
  T58.6.I5778 2011
  658.4'038011--dc22
                              2011013008

British Cataloguing in Publication Data
A Cataloguing in Publication record for this book is available from the British Library.

All work contributed to this book is new, previously-unpublished material. The views expressed in this book are those of the authors, but not necessarily of the publisher.

Table of Contents

Section 1
Semantics and Reasoning

Chapter 1

Cecil Eng Huang Chua, University of Auckland, New Zealand
Roger Hsiang-Li Chiang, University of Cincinnati, USA
Veda C. Storey, Georgia State University, USA

Chapter 2

Manoj Thomas, Virginia Commonwealth University, USA
Richard Redmond, Virginia Commonwealth University, USA

Chapter 3

Dhavalkumar Thakker, Press Association, UK
Taha Osman, Nottingham Trent University, UK
David Al-Dabass, Nottingham Trent University, UK

Chapter 4

Joerg Leukel, University of Hohenheim, Germany
Vijayan Sugumaran, Oakland University, USA & Sogang University, Korea

Chapter 5

Fergle D'Aubeterre, Flint Transfield Services Ltd (FT-SERVICES), Canada
Lakshmi S. Iyer, The University of North Carolina at Greensboro, USA
Richard Ehrhardt, The University of North Carolina at Greensboro, USA
Rahul Singh, The University of North Carolina at Greensboro, USA

Section 2
Agent-Based Systems

Section 3
Intelligent Technologies

Detailed Table of Contents

Section 1
Semantics and Reasoning

Chapter 1

Cecil Eng Huang Chua, University of Auckland, New Zealand
Roger Hsiang-Li Chiang, University of Cincinnati, USA
Veda C. Storey, Georgia State University, USA

Search engines are ubiquitous tools for seeking information from the Internet and, as such, have become an integral part of our information society. New search engines that combine ideas from separate search engines generally outperform the search engines from which they took ideas. Designers, however, may not be aware of the work of other search engine developers or such work may not be available in modules that can be incorporated into another search engine. This research presents an interoperability architecture for building customized search engines. Existing search engines are analyzed and decomposed into self-contained components that are classified into six categories. A prototype, called the Automated Software Development Environment for Information Retrieval, was developed to implement the interoperability architecture, and an assessment of its feasibility was carried out. The prototype resolves conflicts between components of separate search engines and demonstrates how design features across search engines can be integrated.

Chapter 2

Manoj Thomas, Virginia Commonwealth University, USA
Richard Redmond, Virginia Commonwealth University, USA

As e-commerce applications proliferate the Web, the cognitive load of sifting through the copious volumes of information in search of relevance has become formidable. Since the nature of foraging for information in digital spaces can be characterized as the interaction between internal task representation and the external problem domain, we look at how expert systems can be used to reduce the complexity of the task. In this chpater, we describe a conceptual framework to analyze user interactions in an e-commerce environment. We detail the use of the ontology language OWL to express the semantics of the representations and the use of SWRL rule language to define the rule base for contextual reasoning. We illustrate how an expert system can be used to guide users by orchestrating a cognitive fit between the task environment and the task solution.

Chapter 3
Dhavalkumar Thakker, Press Association, UK
Taha Osman, Nottingham Trent University, UK
David Al-Dabass, Nottingham Trent University, UK

Web service development is encouraging scenarios where individual or integrated application services can be seamlessly and securely published on the Web without the need to expose their implementation details. However, as Web services proliferate, it becomes difficult to matchmake and integrate them in response to users requests. The goal of our research is to investigate the utilization of the Semantic Web in building a developer-transparent framework facilitating the automatic discovery and composition of Web services. In this chapter, we present a Semantic Case Based Reasoner (SCBR) framework that utilizes the case based reasoning methodology for modelling dynamic Web service discovery and composition. Our approach is original as it considers the runtime behaviour of a service resulting from its execution. Moreover, we demonstrate that the accuracy of automatic matchmaking of Web services can be further improved by taking into account the adequacy of past matchmaking experiences for the requested task. To facilitate Web services composition, we extend our fundamental discovery and matchmaking algorithm using a light-weight knowledge-based substitution approach to adapt the candidate service experiences to the requested solution before suggesting more complex and computationally taxing AI-based planning-based transformations. The inconsistency problem that occurs while adapting existing service composition solutions is addressed with a novel methodology based on the Constraint Satisfaction Problem (CSP).

Chapter 4
Joerg Leukel, University of Hohenheim, Germany
Vijayan Sugumaran, Oakland University, USA & Sogang University, Korea

Product-related information can be integrated with the help of a product ontology, which can provide consensual definitions of concepts and inter-relationships relevant in a product domain of interest. A product ontology is either given by a third party or results from ontology engineering. In both cases, the problem is how to assess its quality, and then select the "right" ontology. This chapter: (1) proposes a metrics suite for product ontology evaluation based on semiotic theory, and (2) demonstrates the feasibility and usefulness of the metrics suite using a supply chain model. The contribution of this research is the comprehensive metrics suite that takes into account the various quality dimensions of product ontology.

Fergle D'Aubeterre, Flint Transfield Services Ltd (FT-SERVICES), Canada
Lakshmi S. Iyer, The University of North Carolina at Greensboro, USA
Richard Ehrhardt, The University of North Carolina at Greensboro, USA
Rahul Singh, The University of North Carolina at Greensboro, USA

In the context of a customer-oriented value chain, companies must effectively address customers changing information needs during the process of acquiring a product or service to remain competitive. The ultimate goal of semantic matchmaking is to identify the best resources (supply) that fully meet the requirements (demand); however, such a goal is very difficult to achieve due to information distributed over disparate systems. To alleviate this problem in the context of eMarketplaces, the authors suggest an agent-enabled infomediary-based eMarketplace that enables semantic matchmaking. They extend and apply the exact, partial, and potential match algorithms developed in Di Noia et al. (2004) to show how partial and potential matches can become full matches. Specifically, the authors show how multi-criteria decision making techniques can be utilized to rank matches. They describe mechanisms for knowledge representation and exchange to allow partner organizations to seamlessly share information and knowledge to facilitate the discovery process in an eMarketplace context.

Jeffrey A. Schiffel, The Boeing Company, USA

Inserting the human element into an Information System leads to interpreting the Information System as an information field. Organizational semiotics provides a means to analyze this alternate interpretation. The semantic normal forms of organizational semiotics extract structures from natural language texts that may be stored electronically. In themselves, the SNFs are only canonic descriptions of the patterns of behavior observed in a culture. Conceptual graphs and dataflow graphs, their dynamic variety, provide means to reason over propositions in first order logics. Conceptual graphs, however, do not of themselves capture the ontological entities needed for such reasoning. The culture of an organization contains natural language entities that can be extracted for use in knowledge representation and reasoning. Together in a rigorous, two-step process, ontology charting from organizational semiotics and dataflow graphs from knowledge engineering provide a means to extract entities of interest from a subject domain such as the culture of organizations and then to represent these entities in formal logic reasoning. This chapter presents this process, and concludes with an example of how process improvement in an IT organization may be measured in this two-step process.

Prior research on negotiation support systems (NSS) has paid limited attention to the information content in the observed bid sequences of negotiators as well as on the cognitive limitations of individual negotiators and their impacts on negotiation performance. In this paper, we assess the performance of human subjects in the context of agent-based NSS, and the accuracy of an exponential functional form in representing observed human bid sequences. We then predict the reservation values of negotiators based on their observed bids. Finally, we study the impact of negotiation support systems in helping users realize superior negotiation outcomes. Results indicate that an exponential function is a good model for observed bids.

Despite the importance of resource availability, the inclusion of availability awareness in current agent-based systems is limited, particularly in decision support settings. This article discusses issues related to availability awareness in agent-based systems and proposes that knowledge of resources' online status and readiness in these systems can improve decision outcomes. A conceptual model for incorporating availability and presence awareness in an agent-based system is presented, and an implementation framework operationalizing the conceptual model using JADE is proposed. Finally, the framework is developed as an agent-based decision support system (DSS) and evaluated in a decision making simulation.

The reliable execution of a mobile agent is a very important design issue to build a mobile agent system and many fault-tolerant schemes have been proposed. Hence, in this article, we present an evaluation of the performance of the fault-tolerant schemes for the mobile agent environment. Our evaluation focuses on the checkpointing schemes and deals with the cooperating agents. We derive the Fault-Tolerant approach for Mobile Agents (FANTOMAS) design which offers a user transparent fault tolerance that can be activated on request, according to the needs of the task. We also discuss how a transactional agent with different types of commitment constraints can commit. Furthermore, this article proposes a solution for effective agent deployment using dynamic agent domains.

Multi-agent paradigms have been developed for the negotiation and brokering in B2C e-commerce. Few of the models consider the mental states and social settings (trust and reputation) but rarely any model depicts their combination. In this chapter, a combined model of belief, desire, intention (BDI) for agent's mental attitudes and social settings is used to model their cognitive capabilities. The mental attitudes also include preferences, commitments, along with BDI. These attributes help to understand the commitment and capability of the negotiating agent. In this work, we present three mathematical models. First, a cognitive computational model is used for the computation of trust, and then index of negotiation, which is based on trust and reputation. The second computation model is developed for the computation of business index that characterizes the parameters of some of the business processes, which match the buyer's satisfaction level. On the basis of index of negotiation and business, we calculate SI (selection index) to select a seller agent with the highest value of SI. The third computation model of utility is used for negotiation between seller and buyer to achieve maximum combined utility increment (CUI), which is the difference of marginal utility gain (MUG) of buyer and marginal utility cost (MUC) of seller.

This study investigates user perceptions and employment of interface agents for email notification to answer three research questions pertaining to user demographics, typical usage, and perceptions of this technology. A survey instrument was administered to 75 email interface agent users. Current email interface agent users are predominantly male, well-educated and well-off innovative individuals who are occupied in the IS/IT sector, utilize email heavily and reside in an English-speaking country. They use agents to announce incoming messages and calendar reminders. The key factors why they like to use agents are perceived usefulness, enjoyment, ease of use, attractiveness, social image, an agent's reliability and personalization. The major factors why they dislike doing so are perceived intrusiveness of an agent, agent-system interference and incompatibility. Users envision 'ideal email notification agents' as highly intelligent applications delivering messages in a non-intrusive yet persistent manner. A model of agent acceptance and use is suggested.

Section 3
Intelligent Technologies

This article proposes a neural network based traffic signal controller, which eliminates most of the problems associated with the Traffic Responsive Plan Selection (TRPS) mode of the closed loop system. Instead of storing timing plans for different traffic scenarios, which requires clustering and threshold calculations, the proposed approach uses an Artificial Neural Network (ANN) model that produces optimal plans based on optimized weights obtained through its learning phase. Clustering in a closed loop system is root of the problems and therefore has been eliminated in the proposed approach. The Particle Swarm Optimization (PSO) technique has been used both in the learning rule of ANN as well as generating training cases for ANN in terms of optimized timing plans, based on Highway Capacity Manual (HCM) delay for all traffic demands found in historical data. The ANN generates optimal plans online to address real time traffic demands and thus is more responsive to varying traffic conditions.

The authors present their work in the conceptualization, design, implementation, and application of "lean" information integration systems. They present a new data integration approach based on a schema-less data management and integration paradigm, which enables developing cost-effective large scale integration applications. They have designed and developed a highly scalable, information-on-demand system called NETMARK, which facilitates information access and integration based on a theory of articulation management and a context sensitive paradigm. NETMARK has been widely deployed for managing, storing, and searching unstructured or semi-structured arbitrary XML and HTML information at the National Aeronautics Space Administration (NASA). In this paper the authors describe the theory, design and implementation of our system, present experimental benchmark evaluations, and validate our approach through real-world applications in the NASA enterprise.

A large sample (initially 33,000 cases representing a ten percent trial) of university alumni giving records for a large public university in the southwestern United States is analyzed by Formal Concept Analysis. This likely represents the initial attempt to perform analysis of such data by means of a machine learning technique. The variables employed include the gift amount to the university foundation as well as traditional demographic variables such as year of graduation, gender, ethnicity, marital status, etc. The foundation serves as one of the institution's non-profit, fund-raising organizations. It pursues substantial gifts that are designated for the educational or leadership programs of the giver's choice. Although they process gifts of all sizes, the foundation's focus is on major gifts and endowments. Association Analysis of the given dataset is a two-step process. In the first step, FCA is applied to identify concepts and their relationships and in the second step, the association rules are defined for each concept. The hypothesis examined in this paper is that the generosity of alumni toward his/her alma mater can be predicted using association rules obtained by applying the Formal Concept Analysis approach.

Chapter 15

KStore is a computer data structure based on the Phaneron of C. S. Peirce (Peirce, 1931-1958). This structure, called a Knowledge Store, KStore or simply K, is currently being developed as a storage engine to support BI data queries and analysis (Mazzagatti, 2007). The first Ks being constructed handle nominal data and record sequences of field/record data variables and their relationships. These rudimentary Ks are dynamic allowing real-time data processing, ad hoc queries and data compression, to facilitate data mining. This paper describes a next step in the development of the K structure, to record into the K structure, meta data associated with the field/record data, in particular the column or dimension names and a source indicator.

Chapter 16

As 80-85% of all corporate information remains unstructured, outside of the processing scope of enterprise systems, many enterprises rely on Information Systems that cause them to risk transactions that are based on lack of information (errors of omission) or misleading information (errors of commission). To address this concern, the fundamental business concept of monetary transactions is extended to include qualitative business concepts. A Transaction Concept (TC) is accordingly identified that provides a structure for these unstructured but vital aspects of business transactions. Based on REA (Resources, Events, Agents) and modelled using Conceptual Graphs (CGs) and Formal Concept Analysis (FCA), the TC provides businesses with a more balanced view of the transactions they engage in and a means of discovering new transactions that they might have otherwise missed. A simple example is provided that illustrates this integration and reveals a key missing element. This example is supported by reference to a wide range of case studies and application areas that demonstrate the added value of the

TC. The TC is then advanced into a Transaction-Oriented Architecture (TOA). The TOA provides the framework by which an enterprise's business processes are orchestrated according to the TC. TOA thus brings Service-Oriented Architecture (SOA) and the productivity of enterprise applications to the height of the real, transactional world that enterprises actually operate in.

Chapter 17

It is suggested that the use of the semiotic ladder, together with a supportive trust agent can be used together to better explicate "soft" trust issues in the context of Grid services. The contribution offered here is intended to fill a gap in current understanding and modelling of such issues and to support Grid service designers to better conceptualise, hence manage trust issues. The semiotic paradigm is intended to offer an integrative viewpoint within which to explicate "soft" trust issues throughout the Grid life-cycle. A computationally lightweight trust agent is described that can be used to verify high level trust of a Virtual Organisation. The potential benefits of the approach that is advocated here include the reduction of risk and potential improvements in the quality and reliability of Grid service partnerships. For these benefits to accrue, explicit "soft" as well as "hard" trust management is essential as is an integrative viewpoint.

Preface

In this global economy, companies are increasingly using intelligent and adaptive technologies to improve their efficiency, deliver high quality products quicker and cheaper to the market place, innovate, and gain competitive advantage. With the advent of the Web and other enabling technologies, there is a growing trend in the convergence of information and communication technologies in a number of sectors. Broadly speaking, the notion of technology convergence refers to the synergistic amalgamation of conventional industry, IT (Information Technology), and communication technology. With respect to the development of novel and innovative applications, cutting-edge technologies are used to create new products that can improve the quality of life. Thus, Intelligent, Adaptive and Reasoning Technologies (IART) that facilitate product innovation and efficiency are integrated with traditional approaches. This convergence, referred to as IART convergence, results in businesses being more agile and nimble and be able to respond to changes in the market place by offering new products and services that will meet user needs.

One major area of application of IART convergence is the area of Knowledge Management (KM) and Business Intelligence (BI). These domains have been active areas of research within the Information Systems (IS) community. Prior research on knowledge management has primarily focused on factors that impact the creation, capture, transfer, and use of knowledge in organizations as well as different forms of knowledge and their usage. While there is some initial success, knowledge management has not been widely adopted and practiced due to lack of appropriate tools and technologies to foster knowledge creation, reuse, and exchange within and among different communities. Similarly, business intelligence systems have been hampered with numerous technical and managerial challenges. Lack of data standardization and semantics has affected the interoperability of data between various data sources and systems. With the recent developments in semantic technologies and services and the IART convergence, there is renewed interest in KM and BI. The underlying goal of semantics and services based approach to KM and BI is to foster knowledge and data exchange through mediation. For example, each community within a network can create a local ontology and metadata that captures the syntactic and semantic aspects of data and knowledge relevant to this community. These ontologies and the metadata from multiple communities can then be integrated to create a global ontology and meta-schema. This is used to provide interoperability between the multiple community networks and facilitate broader collaboration.

With the advent of Semantic Web and service orientation, there is considerable research underway in semantic technologies and service oriented architectures for developing intelligent systems and applications that can understand the semantics of the content in Web resources. They help manage, integrate, and analyze data, i.e., individual information elements within a single document or from multiple data sources. Semantic technologies help add meaning to characterize the content of resources. This facilitates the representation of Web content that enables applications to access information autonomously using common search terms. A fundamental building block in the semantic technology is an ontology. Ontologies express basic concepts and the relationship between concepts that exist in a domain. They form the backbone for the Semantic Web and are used to reason about entities in a particular domain as well as knowledge sharing and reuse. Ontologies can be used to specify complex constraints on the types of resources and their properties. OWL (Web Ontology Language) is the most popular ontology language used by applications for processing content from a resource without human intervention. Thus, it facilitates machine interoperability by providing the necessary vocabulary along with formal semantics.

Insofar as reasoning is concerned, rule languages are used to write inferencing rules in a standard way that can be used for automated reasoning in a particular domain. A rule language provides kernel specification for rule structures that can be used for rule interchange. This facilitates rule reuse and extension. Querying Web content and automatically retrieving relevant segments from a resource by an application is the driving force behind Web query languages. They provide a protocol for querying RDF graphs via pattern matching. They support basic conjunctive patterns, value filters, optional patterns, and pattern disjunction. Logic and reasoning are also an integral part of the Semantics Web. A reasoning system can use one or more ontologies and make new inferences based on the content of a particular resource. It also helps identify appropriate resources that meet a particular requirement. Thus, the reasoning system enables applications to extract appropriate information from various resources. Logic provides the theoretical underpinning required for reasoning and deduction. First order logic, Description Logic, et cetera, are commonly used to support reasoning.

Ontologies and reasoning mechanisms as well as IART convergence can have a direct impact on the design and deployment of knowledge management and business intelligence systems. The convergence of these intelligent technologies facilitates the easy access and processing of large amount of data and information to generate actionable "intelligence" that can be used by humans and applications to gain competitive advantage. It also improves the efficiency of knowledge creation and dissemination across different groups and domains. Issues related to interoperability of knowledge sources are minimized with the use of ontology-based mediation. The objective of this book is to encourage and renew research on IART convergence with respect to KM and BI technologies and systems with a fresh perspective of semantics and services. For example, using the service oriented paradigm, one can create data and knowledge services that can promote adaptability, reusability, and interoperability of data and knowledge from a variety of sources. The purpose of this book is to provide a forum for academics and practitioners to identify and explore the issues, opportunities, and solutions that improve knowledge management and provide business intelligence, particularly from the view point of semantics, services, and IART convergence. In other words, in the era of Service Oriented Architecture (SOA), Web Services, and Semantic Web where adaptivness, reuse, and interoperability are paramount, how can IART based KM and BI be taken to the next level using these technologies to achieve large scale adoption and usage?

BOOK ORGANIZATION

This book is organized into three sections. The first section discusses semantic technologies and their applications as well as automated reasoning for Semantic Web services composition and knowledge management. The second section discusses issues related to intelligent agent and multi-agent systems and their use. The third section delves into intelligent technologies and their applications related to business intelligence, intelligent search engines, trust in virtual organizations, etc.

Section 1: Semantics and Reasoning

In the first section, there are six chapters related to semantics and reasoning. The first chapter is titled "*Improving Domain Searches through Customized Search Engines,*" contributed by Cecil Eng Huang Chua, Roger Hsiang-Li Chiang, and Veda C. Storey. They emphasize that search engines are essential, ubiquitous tools for seeking information from the Internet. Prior research has also demonstrated that combining features of separate search engines often improves retrieval performance. However, such feature combination is often difficult, because developers don't consider other developers when building their software. To facilitate the development of search engines, they propose a customized search engine approach to integrating appropriate components from multiple search engines. This chapter presents an interoperability architecture for building customized search engines. To achieve this, the authors analyze existing search engines and decompose them into self-contained components that are classified into six categories. They have developed a prototype called Automated Software Development Environment for Information Retrieval (ASDEIR), which incorporates intelligent features that detect and attempt to resolve conflicts between components.

The second chapter is titled "*A Framework to Analyze User Interactions in an E-Commerce Environment,*" written by Manoj Thomas and Richard Redmond. As e-commerce applications proliferates the Web, users are often overwhelmed by the task of sifting through the copious volumes of information. Since the nature of foraging for information in such digital spaces can be characterized as the interaction between internal task representation and the external problem domain, the authors look at how expert systems can be used to reduce complexity of the task. They describe a conceptual framework to analyze user interactions based on mental representations. They also detail an expert system implementation using the ontology language OWL to express the semantics of the representations and the rule language SWRL to define the rule base for contextual reasoning. This chapter illustrates how an expert system can be used to guide users in an e-commerce setting by orchestrating a cognitive fit between the task environment and the task solution.

The third chapter is titled "*Semantic Web Services Composition with Case Based Reasoning,*" by Dhavalkumar Thakker, Taha Osman, and David Al-Dabass. With the rapid proliferation of Web services as the medium of choice to securely publish application services beyond the firewall, the importance of accurate, yet flexible matchmaking of similar services gains importance both for the human user and for dynamic composition engines. In this chapter, the authors present a novel approach that utilizes the case based reasoning methodology for modeling dynamic Web service discovery and matchmaking, and investigates the use of case adaptation for service composition. Their framework considers Web services execution experiences in the decision making process and is highly adaptable to the service requester constraints. This framework also utilizes OWL semantic descriptions extensively for implementing both the components of the CBR engine and the matchmaking profile of the Web services.

The fourth chapter is titled "*Semiotic Evaluation of Product Ontologies,*" authored by Joerg Leukel and Vijayan Sugumaran. In recent years, product ontology has been proposed for solving integration problems in product-related Information Systems such as e-commerce and supply chain management applications. A product ontology provides consensual definitions of concepts and inter-relationships being relevant in a product domain of interest. Adopting such an ontology requires means for assessing their suitability and selecting the "right" product ontology. In this chapter, the authors (1) propose a metrics suite for product ontology evaluation based on semiotic theory, and (2) demonstrate the feasibility and usefulness of the metrics suite using a supply chain model. The contribution of this chapter is the comprehensive metrics suite that takes into account the various quality dimensions of product ontology.

The fifth chapter is titled "*Discovery Process in a B2B eMarketplace: A Semantic Matchmaking Approach*," by Fergle D'Aubeterre, Lakshmi Iyer, Richard Ehrhardt, and Rahul Singh. In the context of a customer-oriented value chain, companies must effectively address customers' changing information needs during the process of acquiring a product or service to remain competitive. The ultimate goal of semantic matchmaking is to identify the best resources (supply) that fully meet the requirements (demand); however, such a goal is very difficult to achieve due to information distributed over disparate systems. To alleviate this problem in the context of eMarketplaces, the authors suggest an agent-enabled infomediary-based eMarketplace that enables semantic matchmaking. Specifically, the authors show how multi-criteria decision making techniques can be utilized to rank matches. They describe mechanisms for knowledge representation and exchange to allow partner organizations to seamlessly share information and knowledge to facilitate the discovery process in an eMarketplace context.

The sixth chapter is titled "*Organizational Semiotics Complements Knowledge Management: Two Steps to Knowledge Management Improvement*," by Jeffrey A. Schiffel. The semantic normal forms of organizational semiotics extract structures from natural language texts that may be stored electronically. In themselves, the SNFs are only canonic descriptions of the patterns of behavior observed in a culture. Conceptual graphs and dataflow graphs, their dynamic variety, provide means to reason over propositions in first order logics. Conceptual graphs, however, do not capture the ontological entities needed for such reasoning. The culture of an organization contains natural language entities that can be extracted for use in knowledge representation and reasoning. Together in a rigorous, two-step process, ontology charting from organizational semiotics and dataflow graphs from knowledge engineering provide a means to extract entities of interest from a subject domain such as the culture of organizations and then to represent these entities in formal logic reasoning. This chapter presents this process, and concludes with an example of how process improvement in an IT organization may be measured in this two-step process.

Section 2: Agent-Based Systems

The second section contains five chapters dealing with intelligent agent and multi-agent systems and their applications. The seventh chapter is titled "*Negotiation Behaviors in Agent-Based Negotiation Support Systems*," by Manish Agrawal and Kaushal Chari. Prior research on negotiation support systems (NSS) has paid limited attention to the information content in the observed bid sequences of negotiators as well as on the cognitive limitations of individual negotiators and their impacts on negotiation performance. In this chapter, the authors assess the performance of human subjects in the context of agent-based NSS, and the accuracy of an exponential functional form in representing observed human bid sequences. They then predict the reservation values of negotiators based on their observed bids. Finally, they discuss the impact of negotiation support systems in helping users realize superior negotiation outcomes. Their results indicate that an exponential function is a good model for observed bids.

The eighth chapter is titled "*Agents, Availability Awareness, and Decision Making*," by Stephen Russell and Victoria Yoon. Despite the importance of resource availability, the inclusion of availability awareness in current agent-based systems is limited, particularly in decision support settings. This chapter discusses issues related to availability awareness in agent-based systems and proposes that knowledge of resources' online status and readiness in these systems can improve decision outcomes. A conceptual model for incorporating availability and presence awareness in an agent-based system is presented, and an implementation framework operationalizing the conceptual model using JADE is proposed. Finally, the framework is developed as an agent-based decision support system (DSS) and evaluated in a decision making simulation.

The ninth chapter is titled *"Evaluation of Fault Tolerant Mobile Agents in Distributed Systems,"* by Hojatollah Hamidi and Abbas Vafaei. The reliable execution of a mobile agent is a very important design issue to build a mobile agent system and many fault-tolerant schemes have been proposed. This chapter presents an evaluation of the performance of the fault-tolerant schemes for the mobile agent environment. This evaluation focuses on the check-pointing schemes and deals with the cooperating agents. The authors propose a Fault-Tolerant approach for Mobile Agents (FANTOMAS) design which offers a user transparent fault tolerance that can be activated on demand, according to the needs of the task. This chapter also discusses how a transactional agent with different types of commitment constraints can commit. Furthermore, this chapter proposes a solution for effective agent deployment using dynamic agent domains.

The tenth chapter is titled *"Cognitive Parameter Based Agent Selection and Negotiation Process for B2C E-Commerce,"* by Bireshwar Dass Mazumdar and R. B. Mishra. Multi-agent paradigms have been developed for negotiation and brokering in B2C e-commerce. Few of the models consider the mental states and social settings (trust and reputation), but no model depicts their combination. This chapter presents three mathematical models. First, the cognitive computational model, a combined model of belief, desire, and intention (BDI) for agents' mental attitudes and social settings, is discussed. This is used for the computation of trust and then the index of negotiation, which is based on trust and reputation. The second computation model is for the computation of business index that characterizes the parameters of some of the business processes, which match the buyer's satisfaction level. The third computation model of utility is used for negotiation between the seller and buyer to achieve maximum combined utility increment (CUI), which is the difference between the marginal utility gain (MUG) of a buyer and the marginal utility cost (MUC) of a seller.

The eleventh chapter is titled *"User Perceptions and Employment of Interface Agents for Email Notification: An Inductive Approach,"* by Alexander Serenko. This chapter investigates user perceptions and employment of interface agents for email notification to answer three research questions pertaining to user demographics, typical usage, and perceptions of this technology. A survey instrument was administered to 75 email interface agent users. Current email interface agent users are predominantly male, well-educated, and well-off innovative individuals who are employed in the IS/IT sector, utilize email heavily, and reside in an English-speaking country. They use agents to announce incoming messages and calendar reminders. The key factors why they like to use agents are perceived usefulness, enjoyment, ease of use, attractiveness, social image, an agent's reliability, and personalization. The major factors why they dislike doing so are perceived intrusiveness of an agent, agent-system interference, and incompatibility. Users envision "ideal email notification agents" as highly intelligent applications delivering messages in a non-intrusive yet persistent manner. A model of agent acceptance and use is discussed in this chapter.

Section 3: Intelligent Technologies

The third section of the book deals with intelligent technologies and contains five chapters. The twelfth chapter is titled "*Traffic Responsive Signal Timing Plan Generation Based on Neural Network,*" by Azzam ul-Asar, M. Sadeeq Ullah, Mudasser F. Wyne, Jamal Ahmed, and Riaz ul-Hasnain. This chapter proposes a neural network based traffic signal controller, which eliminates most of the problems associated with the Traffic Responsive Plan Selection (TRPS) mode of the closed loop system. Instead of storing timing plans for different traffic scenarios, which requires clustering and threshold calculations, the proposed approach uses an Artificial Neural Network (ANN) model that produces optimal plans based on optimized weights obtained through its learning phase. Clustering in a closed loop system is the root of the problems, and therefore, it has been eliminated in the proposed approach. The Particle Swarm Optimization (PSO) technique has been used both in the learning rule of ANN as well as generating training cases for ANN in terms of optimized timing plans, based on Highway Capacity Manual (HCM) delay for all traffic demands found in historical data. The ANN generates optimal plans online to address real time traffic demands and thus is more responsive to varying traffic conditions.

The thirteenth chapter is titled "*Intelligent Information Integration: Reclaiming the Intelligence,*" by Naveen Ashish and David A. Maluf. The authors present their work in the conceptualization, design, implementation, and application of "lean" information integration systems. They present a new data integration approach based on a schema-less data management and integration paradigm, which enables developing cost-effective, large scale integration applications. They have designed and developed a highly scalable, information-on-demand system called NETMARK, which facilitates information access and integration based on a theory of articulation management and a context sensitive paradigm. NETMARK has been widely deployed for managing, storing, and searching unstructured or semi-structured arbitrary XML and HTML information at the National Aeronautics Space Administration (NASA). In this chapter, the authors describe the theory, design, and implementation of their system, present experimental benchmark evaluations, and validate their approach through real-world applications in the NASA enterprise.

The fourteenth chapter is titled "*Association Analysis of Alumni Giving: A Formal Concept Analysis,*" by Ray Hashemi, Louis A. Le Blanc, Azita A. Bahrami, Mahmood Bahar, and Bryan Traywick. They have analyzed a large sample of university alumni giving records for a public university in the southwestern United States using Formal Concept Analysis (FCA). This represents the initial attempt to perform analysis of such data by means of a machine learning technique. The variables employed include the gift amount to the university foundation as well as traditional demographic variables such as year of graduation, gender, ethnicity, marital status, et cetera. The foundation serves as one of the institution's non-profit, fund-raising organizations. It pursues substantial gifts that are designated for the educational or leadership programs of the giver's choice. Although they process gifts of all sizes, the foundation's focus is on major gifts and endowments. Association Analysis of the given dataset is a two-step process. In the first step, FCA is applied to identify concepts and their relationships and in the second step, the association rules are defined for each concept. The hypothesis examined in this chapter is that the generosity of alumni toward his/her alma mater can be predicted using association rules obtained by applying the Formal Concept Analysis approach.

The fifteenth chapter is titled "*KStore: A Dynamic Meta-Knowledge Repository for Intelligent BI,*" by Jane Campbell Mazzagatti. KStore is a computer data structure based on the Phaneron of C. S. Peirce (Peirce, 1931-1958). This structure, called a Knowledge Store, KStore or simply K, is currently being developed as a storage engine to support BI data queries and analysis. The first Ks being constructed handle nominal data and record sequences of field/record data variables and their relationships. These rudimentary Ks are dynamic, allowing real-time data processing, ad hoc queries, and data compression to facilitate data mining. This chapter describes a next step in the development of the K structure, to record into the K structure, meta data associated with the field/record data, in particular the column or dimension names, and a source indicator.

The sixteenth chapter is titled "*A Transaction-Oriented Architecture for Structuring Unstructured Information in Enterprise Applications*," by Simon Polovina and Simon Andrews. It is known that 80-85% of all corporate information remains unstructured. As such, many enterprises rely on Information Systems that cause them to risk transactions that are based on lack of information (errors of omission) or misleading information (errors of commission). To address this concern, the fundamental business concept of monetary transactions is extended to include qualitative business concepts. A Transaction Model (TM) is accordingly identified that provides a structure for these unstructured but vital aspects of business transactions. By highlighting how unstructured information can be integrated into transactions, the TM provides businesses with a much more balanced view of the transactions they engage in or to discover novel transactions that they might have otherwise missed. A simple example is provided that illustrates this integration and reveals a key missing element. This discovery points to a transactions pattern that can be used to ensure that all the parties (or agents) in a transaction are identified, as well as capturing unstructured and structured information into a coherent framework. In support of the TM as a pattern, more examples of its use in a variety of domains are given. A number of enterprise applications are suggested such as in multi-agent systems, document text capture, and knowledge management.

The seventeenth chapter is titled "*Virtual Organizational Trust Requirements: Can Semiotics Help Fill the Trust Gap?*" by Tim French. It is suggested that the use of the semiotic ladder, together with a supportive trust agent can be used together to better explicate "soft" trust issues in the context of Grid services. The contribution offered here is intended to fill the gap in current understanding and modeling of such issues and to support Grid service designers to better conceptualize, hence manage trust issues. The semiotic paradigm is intended to offer an integrative viewpoint within which to explicate "soft" trust issues throughout the Grid life-cycle. A computationally lightweight trust agent is described that can be used to verify high level trust of a Virtual Organization. The potential benefits of the approach that is advocated here include the reduction of risk and potential improvements in the quality and reliability of Grid service partnerships. For these benefits to accrue, explicit "soft" as well as "hard" trust management is essential as is an integrative viewpoint.

Considerable advancements are being made in IART convergence, and novel approaches and applications are emerging as a result of this convergence in different domains. Efficient use of intelligent systems is becoming a necessary goal for all, and an outstanding collection of latest research associated with advancements in intelligent, adaptive, and reasoning technologies is presented in this book. Use of intelligent applications in the context of IART convergence will greatly improve efficiency, effectiveness, and productivity in a variety of domains including healthcare, agriculture, fisheries, manufacturing, and telecommunication.

Vijayan Sugumaran
Oakland University, USA & Sogang University, South Korea

Acknowledgment

Dr. Sugumaran's research has been partly supported by Soang Business School's World Class University Program (R31-20002) funded by Korea Research Foundation

Vijayan Sugumaran
Oakland University, USA & Sogang University, South Korea

Section 1
Semantics and Reasoning

Chapter 1
Improving Domain Searches through Customized Search Engines

Cecil Eng Huang Chua
University of Auckland, New Zealand

Roger Hsiang-Li Chiang
University of Cincinnati, USA

Veda C. Storey
Georgia State University, USA

ABSTRACT

Search engines are ubiquitous tools for seeking information from the Internet and, as such, have become an integral part of our information society. New search engines that combine ideas from separate search engines generally outperform the search engines from which they took ideas. Designers, however, may not be aware of the work of other search engine developers or such work may not be available in modules that can be incorporated into another search engine. This research presents an interoperability architecture for building customized search engines. Existing search engines are analyzed and decomposed into self-contained components that are classified into six categories. A prototype, called the Automated Software Development Environment for Information Retrieval, was developed to implement the interoperability architecture, and an assessment of its feasibility was carried out. The prototype resolves conflicts between components of separate search engines and demonstrates how design features across search engines can be integrated.

1. INTRODUCTION

Arguably, the most important driver in the growth of the Internet and e-commerce is the existence

DOI: 10.4018/978-1-60960-595-7.ch001

of easy to use and effective search engines. This makes search engines an integral part of the world economy. Unfortunately, there is no single best search engine for all contexts. Algorithms suited for a domain such as medical research (Mao & Tian, 2009) are not effective for searching the Semantic Web (Li, Wang, & Huang, 2007). Similarly, algorithms optimized for the Semantic Web are not as efficient for searching blogs as specialized blog search algorithms (Thelwall & Hasler, 2007). It is also costly to develop new search engines for emergent domains from scratch. However, certain aspects of search engines are shareable across domains. For example, search interfaces for blogs and semantic search can be similar. Unfortunately, search technologies developed by one researcher cannot be easily combined with technologies developed by another, resulting in wasted efforts when developing advanced search technologies.

The objective of this research is to propose an interoperability architecture to help developers build customized search engines by combining existing and developing technologies (Papazoglou & van den Heuvel, 2007). There are two tasks involved. The first is to analyze and decompose existing search engines into a set of self-contained components, and to create a meaningful set of categories in which to classify them. This is consistent with many engineering disciplines that exploit how various parts of distinct tools perform the same task (Bucchiarone, Pelliccione, Polini, & Tivoli, 2006). For example, in Google, the vector query interface, the content repository of billions of web pages, and the PageRank search algorithm (Brin & Page, 1998; Page, Brin, Motwani, & Winograd, 1998) can all be self-contained search engine components. The second task is to craft an interoperability architecture as the basis for building customized search engines.

The contribution of this research is to enable search engine developers to identify and integrate self-contained search engine components based on the search needs of a particular domain, instead of building a domain-specific search engine from scratch. Component integration must be achieved with the support of intelligent interfaces to bridge components.

Software architecture is usually validated via a case study (Dashofy, Hoek, & Taylor, 2005;

Hayes-Roth, Pfleger, Lalanda, Morignot, & Balabanovic, 1995; Xu, Yang, & Huang, 2004). This research, however, tries to demonstrate how the architecture can be designed and implemented, and how the deliverable can simulate and behave like existing software artifacts (customized search engines). In this way, the evaluations performed on search engines developed using the proposed architecture share performance characteristics of more traditional search engines. The contributions of the research are both the creation and evaluation of the proposed architecture. The evaluation of the proposed architecture is based on the following.

- *Feasiblity*: the architecture can be applied and used to build customized search engines;
- *Robustness*: the architecture encompasses a wide range of search engines and demonstrates that components of existing search engines can be easily assembled to build a customized search engine; and
- *Usefulness*: the customized search engines built improve retrieval accuracy.

The research is carried out in three stages.

1. **Componentization of Search Engines.** Existing search engines are analyzed and decomposed into a set of self-contained components. Section 2 presents a classification taxonomy of these self-contained search engine components.
2. **Interoperability Architecture.** The interoperability architecture for building customized search engines is developed. This involves identifying the relationships between search engine components, and proposing mechanisms to resolve incompatibilities. Section 3 presents the proposed architecture.
3. **Prototype and Evaluation Experiments.** A prototype is developed to evaluate the interoperability architecture. The prototype

demonstrates that the proposed architecture is feasible (can be implemented), robust (applicable to diverse kinds of search engines), and useful (retrieval performance of search engines built with our architecture mirrors traditional search engines). Section 4 presents evaluation experiments and assesses the limitations of the architecture.

2. COMPONENTIZATION OF SEARCH ENGINES

This research strives to componentize search engines to achieve interoperability. The problem of componentizing a technology domain is not a new one (Bucchiarone, et al., 2006). Other researchers have examined the same problem for chat software and groupware (Mørch, et al., 2004), digital libraries (Eyambe & Suleman, 2004), and audio-visual equipment (e.g., TVs and DVD players) (van Ommering, 2002). Much research in service-oriented architectures examine ways of using components within and across organizations (Medvidovic & Taylor, 2000; Papazoglou & van den Heuvel, 2007; Zhou, Pakkala, Perala, & Niemela, 2007).

Within the search engine literature itself, there is a growing realization that no particular search engine component is suitable for all search tasks. Indeed, much of the recent work on web search has focused on specialized tasks. Specialized search domains include ad retrieval (Bendersky, Gabrilovich, Josifovski, & Metzler, 2010), news articles (Demartini, Saad, Blanco, & Zaragoza, 2010; McCreadie, 2010), and blogs (Jiang, Pei, & Li, 2010). Other research examines search where the exact nature of the target document is unclear, but where tangential information may be available. For example, the document could have been copied by the searcher into a (now deleted) e-mail on a previous date (Chau, Myers, & Faulring, 2008). Other work has examined collaborative search (Amershi & Morris, 2008),

peer review information (Hu, Lim, Sun, Lauw, & Vong, 2007), best results from a query with poor matches (Wang, Fang, & Zhai, 2007), web services (Zhang, Zheng, & Lyu, 2010), the Semantic Web (Li, et al., 2007); and search in languages other than English (Ahmed & Nürnberger, 2010; Ishita, Agata, Ikeuchi, Yosuke, & Ueda, 2010). It would, therefore, be useful to develop ways in which developers can quickly configure new search engines to facilitate search in specialized domains.

The scope of this research is restricted to the searching of textual data. Search is a generic problem that can be applied to many non-textual areas. For example, there is a growing need to search for music (Bainbridge, Novak, & Cunningham, 2010; Dang & Shirai, 2009; McNab, Smith, Bainbridge, & Witten, 1997) and graphics (Eitz, Hildebrand, Boubekeur, & Alexa, 2010; Kogler & Lux, 2010; Li & Wang, 1997), and most importantly, for relevant textual documents. This research focuses on textual search, because the basic principles of textual search are more mature. It is, therefore, easier to obtain consensus on the basic components and techniques associated with textual search (Arasu, Cho, Garcia-Molina, Paepcke, & Raghavan, 2001).

Furthermore, it is well-recognized that when searching textual documents, combining techniques from multiple streams of research often results in better query performance (Bartell, Cottrell, & Belew, 1994; Croft, 2000; Lee, 1995; Yang, 2002). However, combining techniques is a difficult and laborious process, largely because techniques developed by one researcher are not designed to be compatible with the work of others.

A four-step approach was used to study this problem. First, we began with the classification scheme proposed by Arasu et al. (2001). Second, we reviewed the literature to identify whether there were components that did not fit well with the classification scheme. Simultaneously, we collapsed some elements of the classification scheme. The classification scheme in Arasu et al. (2001) was then selected as a framework to review search engine technologies because, to our knowledge, it provides the most comprehensive framework for defining search engine components.

Third, we refined the framework of Arasu et al. (2001) from two perspectives. First, the original framework was employed as one for literature review. We needed an engineering framework to effectively design customized search engines. Second, Arasu et al. (2001) focused on web search engines, but our framework focused on text search. Thus, we had to adapt the framework to our domain.

Finally, we attempted to establish a standard set of both input and output interfaces for each category. Arasu et al. (2001) created a framework to facilitate their review of the literature comprising six separate categories: (1) query engine, (2) ranking, (3) collection analysis module, (4) indexer module, (5) crawl control, and (6) page repository. The review suggested three additional aspects of search. These arose mainly because iteration and learning, and user interface design were less prevalent in web search than in text search. The three aspects were the original query interface, the result interface, and search expansion. In addition, certain distinctions made in the original framework did not make sense from an engineering perspective. Specifically, crawl control, the indexer module, and the page repository all appeared to address aspects of documents stored in the search engine. Crawl control focuses on document collection, the page repository on the data, and the indexer on access to the data. For the purpose of our research, we considered these to be the same engineering component. Similarly, the query engine and ranking are done by a single component as ranking implies the exclusion of irrelevant documents.

Thus, our final framework comprises six categories of search engine components. Figure 1 presents the major components identified. The following sections describe each category in detail.

2.1 Query Interface

The query interface allows the user to communicate his or her search intention to the search engine by translating it into a search engine processable representation (Agichtein, Lawrence, & Gravano, 2001; Bruza, McArthur, & Dennis, 2000; Chui, 1999; Leake & Scherle, 2001; Meier, 2002; Muramatsu & Pratt, 2001). The most common query interfaces employ keywords, or Boolean logic arguments, although more sophisticated interfaces exist such as one where the user can draw a Venn diagram (Chui, 1999).

Almost all query interfaces translate queries into either a vector or boolean-based form (Yang, 2002).

- **Boolean:** A boolean-based query represents the search intention so that, given a query, every article in the document corpus/content repository can be identified as 'true' or 'false.' SQL and XPath/XQL are examples of boolean-based query representations. In some search engines, fuzzy-boolean representations are employed where a document has a probability of being true (Callan, Croft, & Harding, 1993). These are treated as boolean-based in this research.

- **Vector:** In the vector representation, the query is represented as a set of (possibly weighted) keywords. The vector model does not have the expressive power of the boolean model. However, because keywords can be weighted, this representation allows for better retrieval accuracy (Salton, Buckley, & Fox, 1983).

Also, some search engines include relevance feedback, e.g., search engines that incorporate query expansion or learning-based search algorithms (Bast, Majumdar, & Weber, 2007; Leung, Ng, & Lee, 2008). Previous queries are applied to change the way a search engine responds to

Figure 1. A conceptual framework of search engines (adapted from Arasu et al., 2001)

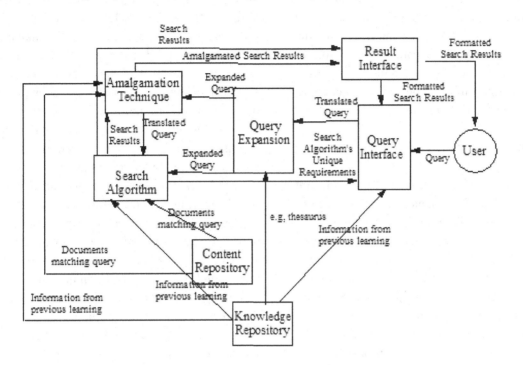

current queries. In this chapter, the ability to learn (i.e., intelligence) is modeled as either data stored in a content repository, or results from a result interface that are fed back into the search engine instead of to the user. Furthermore, the search algorithm often requires certain kinds of user input. For example, Google PageRank (Brin & Page, 1998) has two variables that must be assigned values to function, c (the weight of backlinks), and $E(u)$ (a zeroing constant) (Wang, Tao, Sun, Shakery, & Zhai, 2008).

Thus, in order to interact with other components of search engines, a query interface receives input from four different types of components: (1) the user, (2) the result interface, (3) the knowledge repository, and/or (4) the search algorithm. The user communicates and specifies his or her search intentions as a query. The result interface and content repository provide input on a user's previous

queries. Query interfaces forward the queries to the query expansion algorithm.

2.2 Query Expansion

In most cases, users do not fully utilize the query interface to properly communicate and specify their search intentions. For example, most users specify only one or two keywords (Jansen, Spink, Bateman, & Saracevic, 1998; Leung, et al., 2008; Silverstein, Henzinger, Marais, & Moricz, 1999). Query expansion resolves this problem by intelligently inducing users' search intentions, and expanding the boolean or vector-based representation according to those intentions (Xu & Croft, 1998).

In addition to the query representation produced by the query interface, some query expansion algorithms require additional pre-existing information, such as a thesaurus stored in the content repository (Greenberg, 2001; Mandala,

Tokunaga, & Tanaka, 1999). Thus, the query expansion algorithm may need to obtain additional information from the query interface and the content repository. The expanded search queries will be sent to either the search algorithm or the meta-search algorithm. Some search engines have no query expansion algorithms.

2.3 Search Algorithm

The search algorithm searches and ranks relevant documents stored in the content repository according to the search query representation received. Some search algorithms generate a score that indicates how relevant each document is to the query (Faloutsos & Oard, 1996). Others simply rank order retrieved documents, or produce all supposedly relevant documents unranked.

There are four kinds of search algorithms, each of which requires distinct information: (1) text-based, (2) link-based, (3) cue-based, and (4) learning-based search algorithms (Faloutsos & Oard, 1996). Text-based algorithms such as Inquery (Callan, et al., 1993) rely on the grammatical relationship between terms in the documents. Link-based algorithms such as Google PageRank (Brin & Page, 1998) rely on the link structure between hypertext documents. Cue-based algorithms such as Okapi (Robertson, Walker, Jones, Hancock-Beaulieu, & Gatford, 1993) or SMART (Singhal, Choi, Hindle, Lewis, & Pereira, 1998) use quantifiable parameters of the document text such as the frequencies in which particular terms appear in the document (term frequency), and the frequencies in which terms appear in documents in general (document frequency). Learning-based algorithms refine their parameters based on the results of prior queries (Chen, 1995).

2.4 Meta-Search Amalgamation

Search algorithms often generate different results for a given query, making it beneficial to synthesize the results from multiple search algorithms (i.e.,

meta-search amalgamation) (Croft, 2000; Melnik, Vardi, & Zhang, 2007; Meng, Yu, & Liu, 2002). Like search algorithms, meta-search amalgamation algorithms produce a sequence of documents ranked from the most to least relevant. Similar to search algorithms, some meta-search amalgamation algorithms produce a ranking score.

The key distinction between meta-search amalgamation and search algorithms is that meta-search amalgamation obtains information, not only from a content repository, but also from search algorithms. Some meta-search amalgamation algorithms supplement search algorithms with information directly accessed from content repositories (Mishra & Prabhakar, 2000). Many meta-search amalgamation techniques incorporate weighting schemes to identify search algorithms that are more relevant to a particular query. These weights can be pre-defined (Meng, et al., 2002; Tsikrika & Lalmas, 2001), or learned (Dreilinger & Howe, 1997; Glover, Lawrence, Birmingham, & Giles, 1999; Meng, Wu, Yu, & Li, 2001) and stored in the knowledge repository.

2.5 Content Repository

The content repository represents the information and documents stored in the search engine, and the tools used to retrieve, but not process, the relevant documents. In the classification scheme of Arasu et al. (2001), the content repository category consists of four components: the text corpus, the index, the knowledge repository, and the crawler/spider.

The text corpus is the set of documents available to be searched and retrieved.

The index comprises a set of document organizational structures on top of those documents to facilitate the search of relevant documents. The knowledge repository captures additional information about the search process such as the number of times a query identified a specific document. The crawler/spider is a tool for automatically expanding the text corpus with more documents

(Hansen & Shriver, 2001; Meng, et al., 2001; Tsikrika & Lalmas, 2001).

The content repository provides the content (text documents) and their descriptions, the structure and organization of these documents, and the access information along with the tools to process these documents.

2.6 Result Interface

The result interface presents query results (i.e., relevant documents) to the user, or feeds query results back to the search engine to help refine the results. A result interface, in effect, returns a list of documents that the search engine predicts will address the user's query.

The main distinction among result interfaces is how results are displayed, and whether the result interface allows the user to refine the original query. For example, whereas most result interfaces present a sorted list of results, others cluster results based on particular categories. In this research, the main role of the result interface is the presentation of information.

3. INTEROPERABILITY ARCHITECTURE

There are two main issues in the design of an interoperability architecture. The first is what the interfaces actually are. Addressing this issue involves identifying the critical information flows that must be transmitted and received between components of the architecture. Much of the discussion in Section 2 focused on this issue. Doing so has provided the main theoretic contribution of this research.

The second concern is how information flows are enabled. This focuses on the implementation of the interface in an artifact. The broad strategy of 'how' to design an interoperability architecture has been addressed by other researchers. Our main contribution, therefore, is the adaptation of generally understood principles to the domain of search engine interoperability.

The modern practice for enabling standard information flows is to define a flow schema, represented in the form of (often XML) tags. A database is then constructed that represents these tags. Each category of the framework is represented in the database. New components must be created according to the framework. Each new component is represented by appending database entries where values are assigned to each tag. When a user or system requires a component, it consults the repository to learn how the component should be invoked. This practice is used in many XML business process standards, for example, in OASIS (www.oasis-open.org/).

In our work, each category of component is represented as a well-defined object interface (e.g., Java interface). After the component is constructed, it is registered in a component registry (the database) that a search engine consults before using the component. Fundamentally, the component registry has the design presented in Figure 2.

Detailed functional specifications about each component are captured and stored in the registry. For example, the component registry will capture that the PageRank link analysis search algorithm (Brin & Page, 1998): (1) supports only vector-based query representations, (2) has variables that require threshold values, and default thresholds values, (3) requires backcitations from the content repository, (4) generates a score, and (5) refers to a particular XML tag to identify linking text. When a developer needs to build a customized search engine by integrating available self-contained components, he or she can examine and select components from these six categories by referring to the functional specifications stored in the registry. To ensure that a customized search engine can be built automatically, the proposed interoperability architecture performs two tasks.

First, the architecture queries the registry to determine whether the chosen search engine com-

Figure 2. Contents of the component repository

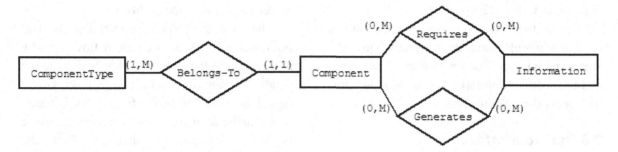

ponents fit together. To enable interoperability, two key facts are stored in the registry. (1) The registry stores the kinds of information the component can provide. For example, a traditional text corpus content repository can only provide documents. However, one that also stores links between documents can provide backcitation information. (2) The registry stores the kinds of information the component requires. For example, PageRank requires backcitation information. When a developer assembles components to form a search engine, the system checks if the requested information matches the information the components of the search engine can provide (Brinkmeier, 2006).

Second, the architecture identifies other components required to integrate the specified components. Components fit together if every component can obtain required information from other components the developer chooses. In some cases, incompatible components are reconciled by incorporating translation algorithms between them. A translation algorithm takes an existing piece of information generated by a component and intelligently transforms it into a piece of information required by another component. For example, if a query expansion algorithm requires a boolean representation of a query, but the query interface outputs a vector-based query, then a vector-to-boolean translator (e.g., (Salton, et al., 1983) is incorporated.

Currently, the architecture only supports single level transformations. For example, if a search algorithm requires vector-based keywords, but the interface provides Boolean keywords, the system searches for a translator that converts vector-based keywords to boolean keywords.

Interoperable mechanisms have been developed to intelligently resolve incomplete information among components. For example, meta-search amalgamation algorithms are designed to integrate the results of multiple search algorithms, so they are often robust, and, therefore, highly interoperable. However, some meta-search amalgamation algorithms require that search algorithms score each returned document. Unfortunately, not every search algorithm produces such scores. When the ranking score is not available, the proposed architecture considers that there is equal distance between documents. Thus, each document from a search algorithm is assigned a score of $\frac{1 + (d - p)}{d}$ where d is the number of documents retrieved, and p is the position of the specific document in the ranking.

A customized search engine built according to the interoperability architecture can run in two modes: operational and learning. In the operational mode, the user inputs a query and receives a response from the search engine. In the learning mode, the search engine maintains and refreshes intelligent knowledge repositories and learning algorithms. Search engines that incorporate no learning, of course, have no learning mode. The information transmitted and received between component categories is summarized in Table 1.

Table 1 should be interpreted in conjunction with Figure 1. The table represents the types of information originating and terminating at each category of component, whereas the figure represents the movement of the information. They should be interpreted as follows. The intent of the user is to obtain documents that match a certain query. The user expresses the query at the query interface. That expression comprises two parts - a query written either as a boolean or vector representation, and a set of settings/other options the interface provides. These two kinds of information are passed to the query expansion algorithm, which generates an expanded query. The expanded query along with user information is transmitted either to a search algorithm, or a meta-search amalgamation algorithm, which passes it to a set of search algorithms. The (one or more) search algorithms use the expanded query and user information to retrieve documents from the repository. These documents are then ranked by the algorithm. The ranked documents and user information are either passed back to the meta-search amalgamation component or result interface. If they are passed to the meta-search amalgamation component, the meta-search amalgamation component combines them into a single ranked search to be passed to the result interface. The result interface presents the results to the user.

Table 1. Information transmitted and received between component categories

Category	Input/Source	Output/Destination
query interface	1. highly variable/user	1. boolean or vector query representation/ query expansion or query transformation 2. user specified modification variables/ any
query expansion	1. boolean or vector query representation/query interface or query transformation 2. user specified modification variables/ any	1. boolean or vector query representation/ meta-search amalgamation or search algorithm
search algorithm	1. boolean or vector query representation/query expansion 2. available information/ index, content repository, or knowledge repository 3. results of queries/index or content repository 4. user specified modification variables/ any	1. ordered list of relevant documents/ meta-search amalgamation or result interface 2. document score/meta-search amalgamation or result interface 3. information required from documents/index, or content repository 4. alternate search algorithm/ search algorithm
meta-search amalgamation	1. boolean or vector query representation/query expansion 2. ordered list of relevant documents/ search algorithm 3. scores of relevant documents/ search algorithm 4. user specified modification variables/ any	1. ordered list of relevant documents/ meta-search amalgamation or result interface
index/content repository	1. query/search algorithm 2. information available in documents/search algorithm 3. user specified modification variables/ any	1. data corresponding to query/ search algorithm 2. set of available queries
result interface	1. ordered list of documents/ search algorithm or meta-search amalgamation 2. user specified modification variables/ any	1. compiled results

A search algorithm may be highly interdependent with some search engine components and incompatible with others. For example, the search algorithm PageRank is unable to operate without backcitation information (Brinkmeier, 2006). The TIPSTER content repository employed in the Text Retrieval (TREC) conferences does not have this information and, thus, is incompatible with PageRank (Linguistic Data Corporation, 1993). Every piece of information requested by a component is flagged as critical, or optional. If all interfacing components cannot provide a piece of critical information, the search components have some kind of incompatibility.

There are two kinds of incompatibility. Severe incompatibility occurs when a component lacks some specific information and, therefore, cannot execute. Minor incompatibility occurs when the lack of some specific information will reduce the accuracy of the search. Our system attempts to resolve incompatibility by employing the following rules. (1) If an incompatibility is detected, determine whether an intelligent routine exists that can transform existing information into the required information. (2) If not, determine whether the search engine can function with degraded performance (minor incompatibility). (3) If not, there is a severe incompatibility and a component will have to be swapped out. For example, Google can function with TIPSTER - the lack of backcitation information in the TIPSTER database simply means all retrieved documents have the same score.

4. EVALUATION EXPERIMENTS

In traditional software architecture research, a software architecture is usually validated via a case study (Dashofy, et al., 2005; Hayes-Roth, et al., 1995; Xu, et al., 2004). This research, however, creates the software architecture, uses it to build an artifact, and then tests the artifact built by the architecture. Specifically, traditional

search engine evaluation criteria are applied to the customized search-engine built according to the software architecture. Three evaluation metrics were applied to demonstrate the value of the interoperability architecture.

4.1 Feasibility

The Automated Software Development Environment for Information Retrieval (ASDEIR) is a prototype of the proposed interoperability architecture. It has been developed to show 'proof of concept' and for evaluation purposes. The prototype was developed in Java, using Microsoft Access as the underlying database management system for both the registry and the knowledge repository. The component categories are implemented as Java interfaces and Java implementations. Communication between components is via Java RMI calls. Java RMI was selected, because Java enables cross-platform compatibility without requiring the overhead necessary to manipulate large chunks of text (i.e., XML formatted arguments).

Every component takes as input and output a list of variable name/variable value pairs. Some variable name/variable value pairs are "expected" by all components in a component category. For example, all query expansion algorithms expect a variable with the name "query input" that denotes the query the user keyed in. Some variable name/variable value pairs are specific to a particular component. For example, "pagerankEU" is a variable name that only PageRank, or one of its variants would search for. Each component reads the appropriate variable name/variable values from the list and adds the results of its processes to the list. The list is then passed to the next component down the chain.

Six text corpii were chosen and integrated by the prototype. These were selected for two reasons. (1) They were publicly available. (2) They have been used elsewhere for testing search engines. These six corpii are the (1) national propulsion laboratory (NPL) (Salton & Buckley, 1990), (2) cystic fibrosis (CFC) (Shaw, Wood, Wood, & Tibbo, 1991a), (3) Time Magazine (Merkl & Rauber, 1999), (4) California (Kleinberg, 2002b), (5) Environmental Protection Agency (Kleinberg, 2002a) and (6) Associated Press (AP) (Linguistic Data Corporation, 1993) corpii. NPL is a collection of abstracts about jet engines. CFC is the subset of the MedLine medical articles content repository dealing with Cystic Fibrosis. Time Magazine is a collection of abstracts for Time Magazine articles from 1963. The California and EPA content repositories are used for testing link-analysis algorithms. The California content repository is a collection of websites about California. EPA is a collection of websites that link to the US Environmental Protection Agency. AP is a subset of the TIPSTER Test Collection. The eXist (Meier, 2002) XML database engine was employed to store the documents.

4.2 Robustness

To demonstrate that our architecture could be used to assemble components, we developed components originally implemented across several search engines and attempted to assemble them together. Search engine components from four existing search engines (Okapi, Rocchio-Cosine, Google, and Inquery) and one meta-search engine (KhojYantra) were constructed based on descriptions in published documents. These search engines were chosen to reflect the diversity in multiple streams of search engine research. Our ability to assemble components from these incongruous search engines demonstrates that our proposed interoperability architecture is applicable to build a variety of customized search engines and is thus robust. In each case, we reverse-engineered each search engine component based on published reports. Table 2 presents the search engine components implemented in the prototype. ASDEIR will then build the search engine according to the selected search engine components. Figure 3 presents the configuration menu of ASDEIR. The following discussion describes each search engine and highlights their differences.

Okapi (Robertson, et al., 1993). We selected two components from Okapi. One is the vector search interface. The second is the Okapi search algorithm. The Okapi search algorithm is representative of cue-based search engines and is the most popular TREC search engine. The search algorithm we implemented was $\sum_{T \in Q} W_q \times W_d$, where T refers to terms in the corpus, and Q to the set of query terms.

W_q represents the weight of the term in a query, which is calculated as follows:

Table 2. Classification of components of search engines built by ASDEIR

Part	Okapi	Rocchio	Google	Inquery	KhojYantra
Query Interface	Vector	Vector	Vector	Boolean/ Natural Language	Vector
Query Expansion	None	Semi-Automated	None	None	None
Search Algorithm	Cue-Based	Cue-Based	Link-Based	Text-Based	None
Meta-Search Amalgamation	None	None	None	None	Unbiased/ Ranked
Index	Term/ Document statistics	Term statistics	Backlinks	Term statistics	Term statistics
Content Repository	Varies	Varies	Proprietary	Varies	Varies
Result Interface	TREC format	TREC format	Ranked documents	Scored documents	Ranked documents

*A serifed font identifies a component used to create the customized search engine

Figure 3. Search engine configuration menu

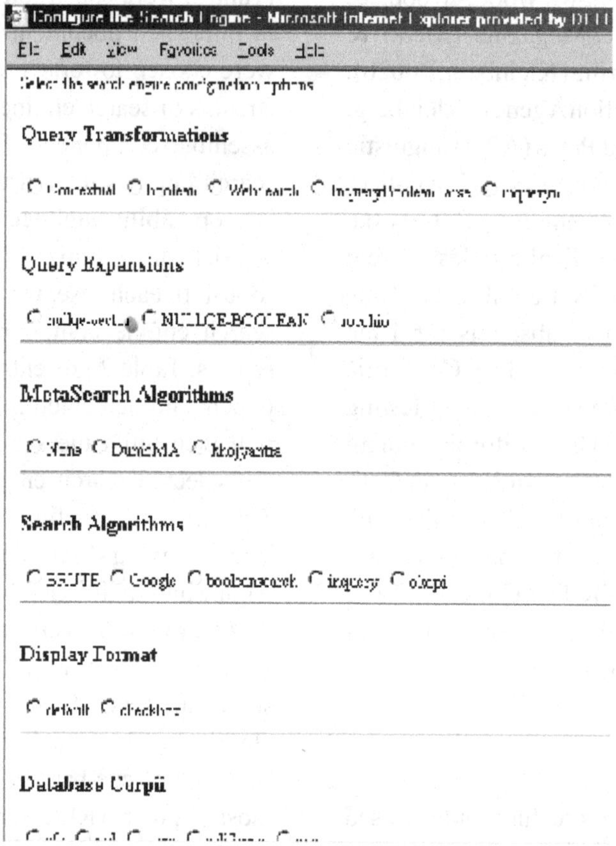

$$\log \frac{(r+0.5)\,/\,(R-r+0.5)}{(n-r+0.5)\,/\,(N-n-R+r+0.5)}$$

$$\frac{(k_1+1)t(k_3+1)q}{k_1(1-b)\left(b\dfrac{d}{a}\right)k_3+q}$$

R is the number of relevant documents in the corpus. In TREC, this number is already known. In most circumstances, however, this number is estimated. N is the number of documents in the corpus, and n is the number of documents that contain the query terms. r is the number of relevant documents that contain the query terms.

W_d is the weight of the document, calculated as follows:

t refers to the term frequency (i.e., the number of times a term appears in a document), and q refers to the number of times a term appears in the query. d is the document length in bytes, and a is the average document length. k_1, b, k_3 are weights, and are normally set at 1.2, 0.75, and 7 respectively.

Rocchio. We extracted two components from the Rocchio search engine (Lewis, Shapire, Callan, & Papka, 1996), (1) Rocchio's query expansion algorithm, and (2) Rocchio's search algorithm.

Rocchio's search expansion operates as follows. The user inputs a vector string of keywords. Rocchio then identifies the documents that match those keywords and presents the first X matching documents to the user. The user selects the relevant documents from this set and the search engine scans the user-identified documents to identify common terms. These common terms are compared to terms in the non-relevant documents. Keywords that are common only to the relevant documents are retained, and added to the vector string (i.e. query expansion).

The Rocchio search algorithm we implemented uses the cosine coefficient formula:

$$\frac{\sum_{T \in r} t \times \log N / d}{\sqrt{\sum_{T \in r} t^2 \times \sum_{T \in r} \log(N / d)^2}}$$

Where T refers to the term being evaluated, r refers to the relevant documents, t refers to the number of times the term appears in the document, and d refers to the number of documents that have the term. For a more in-depth discussion of Rocchio see Chen and Zhu (2000).

Google. The PageRank search algorithm from the Google search engine (Brin & Page, 1998) was implemented. The PageRank algorithm is:

$$R(u) = c \sum_{v \in B_u} \frac{R(v)}{N_v} + E(u)$$

where $R(u)$ is the rank of the document u, B_u identifies the webpages that link to u, and N_v refers to the number of webpages v links to. The constants c and $E(u)$ are normally set at 0.15 and 0, respectively (Brin & Page, 1998).

Inquery. Four components from Inquery (Callan, et al., 1993) were implemented: two interfaces, the search algorithm, and an indexing algorithm. There were two interfaces from Inquery: (1) a boolean text search interface, and (2) a natural language interface. Users can type in English sentences that Inquery parses to generate a query. The Inquery search algorithm weighs documents based on the extent to which they satisfy a boolean query. For example, when Inquery processes the instruction #and (fibrosis,levin), it identifies all documents that contain either term, but weights the documents that contain both more heavily. Finally, we implemented an indexing algorithm to count the frequency of words in the document repository. Inquery uses such an index to speed up search.

KhojYantra. KhojYantra's (Mishra & Prabhakar, 2000) meta-search amalgamation technique was also implemented. KhojYantra was selected because it uses multiple types of information, such as the rankings produced by the search engines it employs, the URLs of retrieved documents, and the titles of the web pages. The KhojYantra meta-search amalgamation technique is useful for demonstrating the flexibility of our architecture. KhojYantra sorts returned web pages (documents) into three groups: (1) web pages where the domain name of the web page contains a keyword, (2) web pages where the URL contains a keyword, and (3) other web pages. Each of these groups is subdivided by the number of keywords in the URL, title, and main text.

To demonstrate that the prototype can build customized search engines, we created a customized search engine with the following features: (1) Inquery's Natural Language parser, (2) Google's PageRank, and (3) Rocchio's query expansion features. Our goal in building this search engine was to assess how well ASDEIR could support the construction of search engines that spanned different search engine classifications.

Only the object classes developed to recreate the search engines from the published documents were employed in the customized search engine. There was no additional coding (e.g., to bridge the components). The components in Table 2 that were used to create the customized search engine are identified with a serifed font and presented in Figure 4. Other combinations are also possible.

4.3 Usefulness

To demonstrate that the interoperability architecture can be employed to build customized search engines to improve retrieval accuracy, an evaluation experiment was performed that compared the performance of the Rocchio and Okapi search engines against a customized search engine that merged the query expansion feature of Rocchio with the Okapi search algorithm. The experiment was patterned after the procedure used to test both Okapi and Rocchio in the Text Retrieval (TREC) conferences (Broglio, Callan, & Croft, 1994; Lewis, et al., 1996; Robertson, et al., 1993).

The Associated Press (AP) subcollection of the TIPSTER data set, which is the standard TREC data set, was used for testing. The AP subcollection consists of 164,597 articles from the Associated Press. Each file was represented in SGML, an XML compatible format. Because of the size of the content repository, article content information (i.e., text encapsulated by <TEXT></TEXT> tags) was not employed. Information contained in the article titles, byline, keywords, etc. were retained. Rocchio has a learning-based algorithm, so Rocchio and the customized search engine were allowed a maximum of four learning cycles on each query as per standard practice (Magennis & Rijsbergen, 2000; Ruthven, 2003).

To control for experimenter bias, topics 51-100 were used to test the performance of the search engines. TREC queries are called topics. These queries were originally employed for TREC-2 and TREC-3. Each TREC topic is an SGML-formatted description of the kinds of document that fits the query, and the matching TIPSTER documents. All concepts (i.e., anything encapsulated in the <con> tag) from the topics were used as keywords for search engine testing. For example, for Topic 51, the keywords employed were 'Airbus Industry, European aircraft consortium, Messerschmitt-Boelkow-Blohm GmbH, etc.' Topics 51-100 were selected because they are both publicly available, and the earliest (and, thus, most well understood) queries employed in TREC.

To improve retrieval accuracy for the three search engines tested, the queries and documents were word stemmed (Porter, 1980), i.e., transformed into roots, enabling a search engine to retrieve relevant documents when words do not exactly match. For example, 'excellence' will retrieve documents containing 'excellent,' and 'excel.'

Three measures of retrieval accuracy were employed, (1) precision, (2) recall, and (3) the sign test (van Rijsbergen, 1979). Table 3 and Figure 5 show the average precision and recall tradeoffs for the search engines employed in the experiment, and demonstrates that the customized search engine outperformed the two traditional ones.

To overcome known statistical problems associated with precision and recall (van Rijsbergen, 1979), a more rigorous analysis of the data was required using the sign test.[1] Every document relevant to a query was assigned a score based on its sort order. The ranks assigned by the customized search engine were then compared to the

Figure 4. Components in the customized search engine

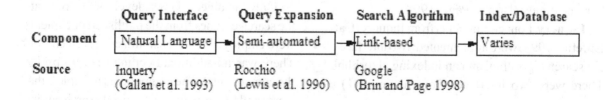

Component	Query Interface	Query Expansion	Search Algorithm	Index/Database
	Natural Language	Semi-automated	Link-based	Varies
Source	Inquery (Callan et al. 1993)	Rocchio (Lewis et al. 1996)	Google (Brin and Page 1998)	

ranks assigned by Rocchio and Okapi, respectively. If the customized search engine had a lower rank/higher/equal rank, the result was scored with a '-,' '+,' and '0,' respectively. Table 4 provides an excerpt of the analysis for topic 51.

The sign test ascertains whether a result is significantly skewed away from 0 based on the difference between the number of '-' and '+' scores. Table 5 presents the results which strongly suggest that a search engine combining features of Okapi and Rocchio outperforms a search engine only incorporating features of one search engine. When the Okapi search algorithm was added to Rocchio, about 70% of the relevant articles improved in their ranking (i.e., 4194/5987 relevant articles). When the Rocchio query expansion algorithm was added to Okapi, almost 80% of the relevant articles improved in the ranking (i.e., 4692/5987 relevant articles). Furthermore, the Rocchio/Okapi combination is the outermost of the three precision/recall tradeoff curves, demonstrating that it is the best performing search engine of the three.

This experiment demonstrates the usefulness of the architecture by demonstrating that, for at least one situation (i.e., Rocchio/Okapi on the TIPSTER AP subcollection), the architecture can make a noticeable difference. The results parallel that of others who demonstrate that combining features of search engines often means that retrieval accuracy is improved (Bartell, et al., 1994; Croft, 2000; Lee, 1995; Yang, 2002). For example, the benefits of adding query expansion to Okapi was demonstrated during one of the earliest TREC conferences (Efthimiadis & Biron, 1993) where recall improved from 0.5790 to 0.7264. Lee (1995) demonstrated that combining features could improve recall performance by up to 18%.

4.4 Limitations

The interoperability architecture and corresponding prototype were developed to demonstrate that the componentization and customization of search engines are achievable. However, the prototype has two main limitations.

Weak Mapping Between Tags. It was assumed that each field, tag, or attribute of a document represents a unique piece of information and that the translation of syntax between documents is straightforward. However, this assumption may not be valid. For example, the cystic fibrosis content repository (Shaw, Wood, Wood, & Tibbo, 1991b) captures bibliographic information on cystic fibrosis. The content repository also captures information on citations between articles within the <reference> tag which means that backlinks

Table 3. Tradeoffs between precision and recall across search engines

	Precision		
Recall	Rocchio	Okapi	Combined
10	99.9	70.1	100.0
20	99.4	53.9	99.8
30	98.4	44.5	99.6
40	94.7	34.3	98.0
50	86.8	23.8	92.2
60	69.4	13.1	78.2
70	45.9	2.7	52.7
80	2.2	0.0	1.1
90	0.0	0.0	0.0
100	0.0	0.0	0.0

(and therefore a corresponding PageRank) can

Table 4. Excerpt of analysis for topic 51

	Rank of Document			Compare	
DocNo	Rocchio	Okapi	Combined	Rocchio	Okapi
1	17	31	1	-	-
2	91	870	2	-	-
3	92	870	3	-	-
4	141	2065	6	-	-
5	142	2333	7	-	-

Figure 5. Tradeoffs between precision and recall across search engines

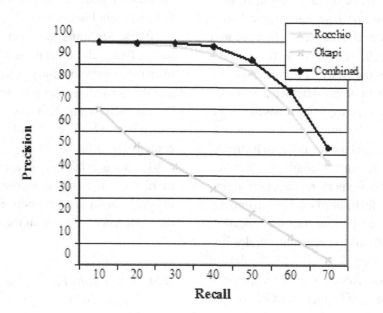

Table 5. Sign test results

	No. -	No. +	No. 0	Z-score	*p*-value
Combined vs. Rocchio	4192	532	1261	-53.254	<0.001
Combined vs. Okapi	4692	170	1125	-64.838	<0.001

be established. However, each reference provides full bibliographic information about each article, including the author name, article title, journal name, etc., instead of an identifier pointing to another article in the CFC content repository. Thus, whereas a human could manually establish backlinks, it was not feasible to have ASDEIR do so. Developing generic rules for resolving this issue is outside the scope of our research. Schema reconciliation between XML documents is a complex problem on its own (dos Santos-Mello & Heuser, 2001; Schmitt & Saake, 1996). For our project, we employed substring search, mapping the titles of each article against the bibliographic entry, and replacing the entries when a match was found.

Limited Error Control. ASDEIR allows for arbitrary combinations of search engine com-ponents, so it does not incorporate strict error checking controls. As a result, errors generated by a faulty component are propagated through the system. For example, the California (Kleinberg, 2002b) and EPA (Kleinberg, 2002a) corpii were originally collections of HTML documents. Unlike XML, HTML was designed with few error check-ing rules. When these documents were converted to XML, numerous errors were incorporated that were ignored by the XML content repository. ASDEIR will process these documents, but often cannot display them due to errors - a problem prevalent in most loosely coupled technologies. For example, many modern programming lan-guages allow for weak type checking and type conversions to encourage flexibility. As a result, compilers often do not detect inappropriate type conversions. For testing purposes, when this problem arose, we displayed the XML output as text, rather than using a result interface with an XML engine.

5. CONCLUSION AND FUTURE RESEARCH

This research has presented an approach to customizing search engine development, through the componentization of search engines. An interoperability architecture was developed based upon an analysis of existing search engines and their development processes. The architecture is intended to facilitate the integration of self-contained search engine components to build customized search engines. Doing so simplifies the task of selecting appropriate search engine components to assemble a personalized, or domain specific, search engine.

The research results should be especially useful because most search engine components achieve high relevance in a small number of domains. Using the architecture, it is both possible and feasible to build a customized search engine by integrating existing components, thereby improving the retrieval accuracy and reducing the development efforts required to construct new search engines as they might be needed.

The architecture is feasible and robust. Feasibility was demonstrated by implementing the architecture in a prototype system. Robustness was then demonstrated by reengineering five distinct search engines employing separate kinds of search engine components to conform to the architecture, and building a customized search engine by combining existing search engine components.

The results of the assessment suggest that the architecture can be employed to create any arbitrary combination of components with two caveats. First, the major limitation to the use of components lies in the data in the repository. If the data is not defined to provide information that

components need, then the components cannot be used. Second, as search engine research matures, components that do not fit into the identified categories are likely to evolve. However, it will not be possible to model them with our architecture.

Further research is needed to investigate ways to facilitate the development of the software. Other efforts will focus on applications to new applications and an assessment of scalability. Principles from this research are also applicable to other domains. For example, the central principle behind this research is that data from one module can be transformed for use in another. Such data transformation can be employed (for instance) to facilitate the search for music, where the stored music is a transposition (i.e., played in a different musical key) from that which the searcher remembers.

REFERENCES

Agichtein, E., Lawrence, S., & Gravano, L. (2001). *Learning search engine specific query transformations for question answering.* Paper presented at the Tenth International World Wide Web Conference.

Ahmed, F., & Nürnberger, A. (2010). *Multi searcher: Can we support people to get information from text they can't read or understand?* Paper presented at the ACM Special Interest Group of Information Retrieval (SIGIR) Conference, Geneva, Switzerland.

Amershi, S., & Morris, M. R. (2008). *CoSearch: A system for co-located collaborative Web search.* Paper presented at the Computer and Human Interaction Conference, Florence, Italy.

Arasu, A., Cho, J., Garcia-Molina, H., Paepcke, A., & Raghavan, S. (2001). Searching the Web. *ACM Transactions on Internet Technology, 1*(1), 2–43. doi:10.1145/383034.383035

Bainbridge, D., Novak, B. J., & Cunningham, S. J. (2010). *A user-centered design of a personal digital library for music exploration.* Paper presented at the ACM/IEEE-CS Joint Conference on Digital Libraries, Surfer's Paradise, Australia.

Bartell, B. T., Cottrell, G. W., & Belew, R. K. (1994, 3-6 July). *Automatic combination of multiple ranked retrieval systems.* Paper presented at the 17th Annual International ACM-SIGIR Conference on Research and Development in Information Retrieval, Dublin, Ireland.

Bast, H., Majumdar, D., & Weber, I. (2007). *Efficient interactive query expansion with CompleteSearch.* Paper presented at the Conference on Information and Knowledge Management, Lisbon, Portugal.

Bendersky, M., Gabrilovich, E., Josifovski, V., & Metzler, D. (2010). *The anatomy of an ad: Structured indexing and retrieval for sponsored search.* Paper presented at the World Wide Web Conference, Raleigh, NC.

Brin, S., & Page, L. (1998). *The anatomy of a large-scale hypertextual Web search engine.* Paper presented at the Seventh International World Wide Web Conference.

Brinkmeier, M. (2006). PageRank revisited. *ACM Transactions on Internet Technology, 6*(3), 282–301. doi:10.1145/1151087.1151090

Broglio, J., Callan, J. P., & Croft, W. B. (1994). *INQUERY system overview.* Paper presented at the TIPSTER Text Program (Phase I).

Bruza, P., McArthur, R., & Dennis, S. (2000). *Interactive Internet search: Keyword, directory, and query reformulation mechanisms compared.* Paper presented at the 23rd Annual International ACM SIGIR Conference on Research and Development in Information Retrieval.

Bucchiarone, A., Pelliccione, P., Polini, A., & Tivoli, M. (2006). *Towards an architectural approach for the dynamic and automatic composition of software components.* Paper presented at the 2nd International Workshop on the Role of Software Architecture in Testing and Analysis Portland, Maine.

Callan, J. P., Croft, W. B., & Harding, S. M. (1993). *The INQUERY retrieval system.* Paper presented at the International Conference in Database and Expert Systems Applications.

Chau, D. H., Myers, B., & Faulring, A. (2008). *What to do when search fails: Finding information by association.* Paper presented at the Computer and Human Interaction Conference, Florence, Italy.

Chen, H. (1995). Machine learning for information retrieval: Neural networks, symbolic learning, and genetic algorithms. *Journal of the American Society for Information Science American Society for Information Science, 46*(3), 194–216. doi:10.1002/(SICI)1097-4571(199504)46:3<194::AID-ASI4>3.0.CO;2-S

Chen, Z., & Zhu, B. (2000). *Some formal analysis of Roccio's similarity-based relevance feedback algorithm.* Paper presented at the International Symposium on Algorithms and Computation.

Chui, M. (1999). *Pattern, procedurality and pictures: Factors affecting Boolean query interface design for the Web.* Paper presented at the SIGIR Conference.

Croft, W. B. (2000). *Combining approaches to information retrieval. Advances in information retrieval: Recent research from the Center for Intelligent Information Retrieval* (pp. 1–36). Kluwer Academic Publishers.

Dang, T.-T., & Shirai, K. (2009). *Machine learning approaches for mood classification of songs toward music search engine.* Paper presented at the International Conference on Knowledge and Systems Engineering.

Dashofy, E. M., Hoek, A. d., & Taylor, R. N. (2005). A comprehensive approach for the development of modular software architecture description languages. *ACM Transactions on Software Engineering and Methodology, 14*(2), 199–245. doi:10.1145/1061254.1061258

Demartini, G., Saad, M. M., Blanco, R., & Zaragoza, H. (2010). *Entity summarization of news articles.* Paper presented at the ACM Special Interest Group of Information Retrieval (SIGIR) Conference.

dos Santos-Mello, R., & Heuser, C. A. (2001). *A bottom-up approach for integration of XML Sources.* Paper presented at the Workshop on Information Integration on the Web.

Dreilinger, D., & Howe, A. E. (1997). Experiences with selecting search engines using metasearch. *ACM Transactions on Information Systems, 15*(3), 195–222. doi:10.1145/256163.256164

Efthimiadis, E. N., & Biron, P. V. (1993). *UCLA-Okapi at TREC-2: Query expansion experiments.* Paper presented at the Text REtrieval Conference.

Eitz, M., Hildebrand, K., Boubekeur, T., & Alexa, M. (2010). *Sketch-based 3D shape retrieval.* Paper presented at the ACM Special Interest Group on Graphics (SIGGRAPH) Conference, Los Angeles, CA.

Eyambe, L., & Suleman, H. (2004). *A digital library component assembly environment.* Paper presented at the South African Institute for Computer Scientists and Information Technologies.

Faloutsos, C., & Oard, D. W. (1996). *A survey of information retrieval and filtering methods.* University of Maryland College Park.

Glover, E. J., Lawrence, S., Birmingham, W. P., & Giles, C. L. (1999, 1999-11). *Architecture of a metasearch engine that supports user information needs.* Paper presented at the Eighth International Conference on Information and Knowledge Management (CIKM'99), Kansas City, MO.

Greenberg, J. (2001). Automatic query expansion via lexical-semantic relationships. *Journal of the American Society for Information Science and Technology, 52*(5), 402–415. doi:10.1002/1532-2890(2001)9999:9999<::AID-ASI1089>3.0.CO;2-K

Hansen, M. H., & Shriver, E. (2001). *Using navigation data to improve IR functions in the context of Web search.* Paper presented at the Conference on Information and Knowledge Management.

Hayes-Roth, B., Pfleger, K., Lalanda, P., Morignot, P., & Balabanovic, M. (1995). A domain-specific software architecture for adaptive intelligent systems. *IEEE Transactions on Software Engineering, 21*(4), 288–301. doi:10.1109/32.385968

Hu, M., Lim, E.-P., Sun, A., Lauw, H. W., & Vong, B.-Q. (2007). *On improving Wikipedia search using article quality.* Paper presented at the Web Information and Data Management Conference, Lisbon, Portugal.

Ishita, E., Agata, T., Ikeuchi, A., Yosuke, M., & Ueda, S. (2010). *A search engine for Japanese academic papers.* Paper presented at the ACM/IEEE-CS Joint Conference on Digital Libraries.

Jansen, B. J., Spink, A., Bateman, J., & Saracevic, T. (1998). Real life information retrieval: A study of user queries on the Web. *ACM SIGIR Forum, 32*(1), 5–17. doi:10.1145/281250.281253

Jiang, D., Pei, J., & Li, H. (2010). *Search and browse log mining for Web information retrieval: Challenges, methods, and applications.* Paper presented at the ACM Special Interest Group of Information Retrieval (SIGIR) Conference.

Kleinberg, J. (2002a). *Local approximation of centrality measures.* Pages linking to www. epa.gov. http://www.cs.cornell.edu/Courses/cs685/2002fa/data/gr0.epa

Kleinberg, J. (2002b). *Pages matching the query "California".* Retrieved from http://www.cs.cornell.edu/ Courses/cs685/2002fa/data/gr0.California

Kogler, M., & Lux, M. (2010). *Bag of visual words revisited - an exploratory study on robust image retrieval exploiting fuzzy codebooks.* Paper presented at the 10th International Workshop on Multimedia Data Mining Washington, DC.

Leake, D. B., & Scherle, R. (2001). *Towards context-based search engine selection.* Paper presented at the International Conference on Intelligent User Interfaces.

Lee, J. H. (1995). *Combining multiple evidence from different properties of weighting schemes.* Paper presented at the ACM SIGIR Conference on Research and Development in Information Retrieval.

Leung, K. W.-T., Ng, W., & Lee, D. L. (2008). Personalized concept-based clustering of search engine queries. *IEEE Transactions on Knowledge and Data Engineering, 20*(11), 1505–1518. doi:10.1109/TKDE.2008.84

Lewis, D. D., Shapire, R. E., Callan, J. P., & Papka, R. (1996). *Training algorithms for linear text classifiers.* Paper presented at the 19th Annual International ACM SIGIR Conference on Research and Development in Information Retrieval.

Li, J., & Wang, J. Z. (1997). Automatic linguistic indexing of pictures by a statistical modeling approach. *IEEE Transactions on Pattern Analysis and Machine Intelligence, 25*(9), 1075–1088.

Li, Y., Wang, Y., & Huang, X. (2007). A relation-based search engine in Semantic Web. *IEEE Transactions on Knowledge and Data Engineering, 19*(2), 273–282. doi:10.1109/TKDE.2007.18

Linguistic Data Corporation. (1993). *TIPSTER complete text corpus.*

Magennis, M., & Rijsbergen, C. J. v. (2000). *The potential and actual effectiveness of interactive query expansion.* Paper presented at the Twentieth Annual International ACM SIGIR Conference on Research and Development in Information Retrieval.

Mandala, R., Tokunaga, T., & Tanaka, H. (1999). *Combining multiple evidence from Different types of thesaurus for query expansion.* Paper presented at the 22nd Annual International ACM SIGIR Conference on Research and Development in Information Retrieval.

Mao, Y., & Tian, W. (2009). *A semantic-based search engine for traditional medical informatics.* Paper presented at the Fourth International Conference on Computer Sciences and Convergence Information Technology.

McCreadie, R. M. C. (2010). *Leveraging user-generated content for news search.* Paper presented at the ACM Special Interest Group of Information Retrieval (SIGIR) Conference.

McNab, R. J., Smith, L. A., Bainbridge, D., & Witten, I. H. (1997). The New Zealand digital library MELody inDEX. *d-Lib Magazine, 3*(5), 288-301.

Medvidovic, N., & Taylor, R. N. (2000). A classification and comparison framework for software architecture description languages. *IEEE Transactions on Software Engineering, 26*(1), 70–93. doi:10.1109/32.825767

Meier, W. M. (2002). *eXist open source database.* Retrieved from http://exist.sourceforge.net/

Melnik, O., Vardi, Y., & Zhang, C.-H. (2007). Concave learners for Rankboost. *Journal of Machine Learning Research, 8*(1), 791–812.

Meng, W., Wu, Z., Yu, C., & Li, Z. (2001). A highly scalable and effective method for metasearch. *ACM Transactions on Information Systems, 19*(3), 310–336. doi:10.1145/502115.502120

Meng, W., Yu, C., & Liu, K.-L. (2002). Building efficient and effective metasearch engines. *ACM Computing Surveys, 34*(1), 48–89. doi:10.1145/505282.505284

Merkl, D., & Rauber, A. (1999). *Uncovering associations between documents.* Paper presented at the International Conference on Artificial Intelligence.

Mishra, R. K., & Prabhakar, T. V. (2000). *KhojYantra: An integrated MetaSearch engine with classification, clustering, and ranking.* Paper presented at the International Database Applications and Engineering Symposium.

Mørch, A. I., Stevens, G., Won, M., Klann, M., Dittrich, Y., & Wulf, V. (2004). Component-based technologies for end-user development. *Communications of the ACM, 47*(9), 59–62. doi:10.1145/1015864.1015890

Muramatsu, J., & Pratt, W. (2001). *Transparent queries: Investigating users' mental models of search engines.* Paper presented at the Twenty-Fourth Annual International ACM SIGIR Conference on Research and Development in Information Retrieval.

Page, L., Brin, S., Motwani, R., & Winograd, T. (1998). *The PageRank citation ranking: Bringing order to the Web.* Stanford University.

Papazoglou, M. P., & van den Heuvel, W.-J. (2007). Service oriented architectures: Approaches, technologies and research issues. *The VLDB Journal, 16*(3), 389–415. doi:10.1007/s00778-007-0044-3

Porter, M. (1980). An algorithm for suffix stripping. *Program, 14*(3), 130–137.

Robertson, S., Walker, S., Jones, S., Hancock-Beaulieu, M., & Gatford, M. (1993). *Okapi at TREC-2.* Paper presented at the Second Text REtrieval Conference (TREC).

Ruthven, I. (2003). *Re-examining the potential effectiveness of interactive query expansion.* Paper presented at the Twenty-sixth Annual International ACM SIGIR Conference on Research and Development in Information Retrieval.

Salton, G., & Buckley, C. (1990). Improving retrieval performance by relevance feedback. *Journal of the American Society for Information Science American Society for Information Science, 41*(4), 288–297. doi:10.1002/(SICI)1097-4571(199006)41:4<288::AID-ASI8>3.0.CO;2-H

Salton, G., Buckley, C., & Fox, E. A. (1983). Automatic query formulations in information retrieval. *Journal of the American Society for Information Science and Technology, 34*(4), 262–280. doi:10.1002/asi.4630340406

Schmitt, I., & Saake, G. (1996). *Schema integration and view generation by resolving intensional and extensional overlappings.* Paper presented at the 9th ISCA Int. Conf. on Parallel and Distributed Computing Systems (PDCS'96), Dijon, France.

Shaw, W. M., Wood, J. B., Wood, R. E., & Tibbo, H. R. (1991). The Cystic Fibrosis database: Content and research opportunities. *Library & Information Science Research, 13*(4), 347–366.

Silverstein, C., Henzinger, M., Marais, H., & Moricz, M. (1999). *Analysis of a very large Altavista query log.* Paper presented at the ACM SIGIR Forum.

Singhal, A., Choi, J., Hindle, D., Lewis, D. D., & Pereira, F. (1998). *AT&T at TREC-7.* Paper presented at the Seventh Text REtrieval Conference (TREC-7).

Thelwall, M., & Hasler, L. (2007). Blog search engines. *Online Information Review*, *31*(4), 467–479. doi:10.1108/14684520710780421

Tsikrika, T., & Lalmas, M. (2001). *Merging techniques for performing data fusion on the Web*. Paper presented at the Conference on Information and Knowledge Management.

van Ommering, R. (2002). *Building product populations with software components*. Paper presented at the International Conference on Software Engineering.

van Rijsbergen, C. J. (1979). *Information retrieval* (2nd ed.). Butterworths.

Wang, X., Fang, H., & Zhai, C. (2007). *Improving retrieval accuracy for difficult queries using negative feedback*. Paper presented at the Conference on Information and Knowledge Management, Lisbon, Portugal.

Wang, X., Tao, T., Sun, J.-T., Shakery, A., & Zhai, C. (2008). DirichletRank: Solving the zero-one gap problem of PageRank. *ACM Transactions on Information Systems, 26*(2), 10:11-10:29.

Xu, G., Yang, Z., & Huang, H. (2004). A basic model for components implementation of software architecture. *ACM SIGSOFT Software Engineering Notes, 29*(5), 1–11. doi:10.1145/1022494.1022522

Xu, J., & Croft, W. B. (1998). Corpus-based stemming using cooccurrence of word variants. *ACM Transactions on Information Systems, 16*(1), 61–81. doi:10.1145/267954.267957

Yang, K. (2002). *Combining text-, link-, and classification-based retrieval methods to enhance information discovery on the Web*. Unpublished PhD Thesis, University of North Carolina-Chapel Hill, Chapel Hill, NC.

Zhang, Y., Zheng, Z., & Lyu, M. R. (2010). *WS-Express: A QoS-aware search engine for Web services*. Paper presented at the Proceedings of the IEEE International Conference on Web Services.

Zhou, J., Pakkala, D., Perala, J., & Niemela, E. (2007). *Dependency-aware service oriented architecture and service composition*. Paper presented at the IEEE International Conference on Web Services.

ENDNOTE

[1]   It is not strictly correct to employ an ANOVA or paired sample t-tests to analyze search engine results, because such results are not normally distributed. Non-parametric tests such as the sign test are therefore superior.

Chapter 2

A Framework to Analyze User Interactions in an E-Commerce Environment

Manoj Thomas
Virginia Commonwealth University, USA

Richard Redmond
Virginia Commonwealth University, USA

ABSTRACT

As e-commerce applications proliferate the Web, the cognitive load of sifting through the copious volumes of information in search of relevance has become formidable. Since the nature of foraging for information in digital spaces can be characterized as the interaction between internal task representation and the external problem domain, we look at how expert systems can be used to reduce the complexity of the task. In this chpater, we describe a conceptual framework to analyze user interactions in an e-commerce environment. We detail the use of the ontology language OWL to express the semantics of the representations and the use of SWRL rule language to define the rule base for contextual reasoning. We illustrate how an expert system can be used to guide users by orchestrating a cognitive fit between the task environment and the task solution.

INTRODUCTION

Digital domains on the Internet exist in different forms serving different purposes. They range from e-commerce storefronts to digital libraries, offering goods and services, and serving as store houses of information that are rich in content. Visitors to these information spaces rely on navigational aids (e.g., hyperlinks, menu structures, keyword search, etc.) to find the information content of interest and to evaluate their relevance (e.g., feedback forms, reviews, ranking, testimonials, etc.). Users of these information spaces almost often have uniquely different information needs. While one might

DOI: 10.4018/978-1-60960-595-7.ch002

search the Amazon website (www.amazon.com) for reviews on a specific book, another person might use the extensive drill-down capabilities of Bizrate website (www.bizrate.com) to determine the specifications and best price of a certain brand of LED high definition TV. Ironically, it is the navigational aids that provide effective information search and enhance the consumer experience. But, they are almost always passive facilitators.

There is no shortage of information on the World Wide Web today. In our efforts to find what we need on the web, we often end up playing the guessing game of making the right choice from a finite set of juxtaposed options (links, search results, etc.). The passive navigational aids at our disposal are often not adept in leading the user in the right direction nor are they designed to reflect the cognitive process of the individual user who ultimately use them. Since browsing information spaces involve cognitive actions of the user, it is only natural to assume that navigational aids should be in agreement with, and adjusts in an anticipatory manner based on the perceived user intentions.

We undertake different types of tasks during our interaction with information spaces. We can refer to these as *task environments* (Newell et al., 1972). The activities of individuals in these task environments are situated in the social and physical setting in which they occur (Klahr et al., 1989; Newell et al., 1972). This applies to both physical and digital worlds, where consciously or subconsciously we engage, interact and converse with the environment before directing an action. Even today, existing information processing models fail to adequately address this *situated character* of activity (Suchman, 1987). For effective interaction with the environment, an individual's knowledge structure must incorporate detailed understanding of the structural features of the environment (Klahr et al., 1989). Unfortunately, this becomes a far-fetched expectation, especially in instances where representations fail to provide any form of guidance prior to the decision to act.

Simon (1996) argues that the complexity of the environment rather than the complexity of the mechanism governs the actions of the decision maker. However, the complexity of the external environment is not the only input or stimuli that determine a person's ability to successfully (or optimally) complete a task. The situated actions are also driven by the internal representation of the task (Khatri et al., 2006; Shaft et al., 2006; Vessey, 1991; Zhang et al., 1997). Problem solving involves human thinking that is governed by arranging simple information processes into orderly, complex sequences that are responsive to and adaptive to the task environment where clues are extracted from the environment as the sequences unfold (Newell et al., 1972; Simon, 1996). In other words, the activities of an individual in a task environment involve processing of information distributed across the internal mind as well as the external environment. The role of information perceived from external representations and the information retrieved from internal representations, and the interwoven relationship between them that leads to a decision to act is not a radical new way of thinking in this world. In this chpater we limit ourselves to the digital realm, and we use ontologies to model and discover user intentions, which in turn serves as a facilitator to guide a user through a digital information space.

The chpater is presented as follows. Based on literature review we first summarize prevailing techniques for managing information overload. We then present an overview of existing theories of cognition from related disciplines. The conceptual model that is used to describe the user dynamics in an e-commerce environment is then outlined. The ensuing section then describes the ontology development process and the architecture that relies on expert systems for providing mediating assistance in an e-commerce environment. The chpater concludes by summarizing the strengths and limitations of the approach, including opportunities for future research work.

RELATED WORK

Activities associated with assessing, seeking and handling information sources is characterized as information foraging (Pirolli et al., 1999). Foraging for information is an activity undertaken to find information by making optimal use of available knowledge required to support a decision making task. Almost always, the search is an adaptive cognitive activity that is based on internalized user goals and contextualized to the source of information. For instance, a cytogeneticist searching the genomic library for a match on a detected chromosome aberration or the house electrician looking to verify a specific safe installation code in the National Electrical Code handbook are respectively examples of complex and generic information foraging activities. Users in the information space need help to find their way to the right information. Often, they also need help to determine if what they found is relevant to complete the decision task. Information foraging is thus a combination of contextualized exploration and internalized exploitation tasks.

Exploratory search can take many forms and is aided by variety of methods (Fox et al., 2006). Kuntz (2005) summarizes three broad categories for indexing and systematic access to stored information. The systematics based approach hierarchically catalogues content based on topic, author, date, etc. to create a navigable structure. This approach borrowed from librarianship is too rigid and requires a high degree of pre-editing before use. Conventional full-text search on the other hand is a highly popular approach, as it makes no assumptions regarding structure and semantic relationships of terms. But queries that are too generic will retrieve inordinate volumes of results even with advanced retrieval systems such as Google. The approach that is currently gaining momentum is the one that aims to retrieve information based on semantic relevance of the content (Berners-Lee et al., 2006). Information foraging substantiated on semantics is possible when knowledge spaces are enhanced with ontologies and knowledge structures are created as a semantic web (Berners-Lee et al., 2006; Ding et al., 2002; Kalfoglou et al., 2003; Uschold et al., 1996). The task of enhancing the content with semantic vocabulary is arduous and requires extensive human intervention. But benefits present themselves in the form of high quality outcomes from knowledge queries since results produced are based on matches against ontological terminology.

The information content in digital spaces is constantly subjected to change as organizations add new information, change existing information or remove stale information. The underlying linking structures, layout maps, drill-down menus and other navigational aids designed to help the user also change to reflect the transformations on the information space. An expert or the domain owners may rely on their expertise or body of knowledge to circumvent changes to the information models, whereas a person who is nescient about the domain will easily lose hope in the face of transition. We regularly observe this around ourselves – the ease with which an expert programmer can switch IDEs (Interactive Development Environment) to work with a different programming language being an example of the former; the elderly refusing to upgrade operating systems on their computers or use cell phone based text messaging are examples of the latter. Such is the necessity to adjust to the changing digital environment, it is rumored that major search engines like Google and Yahoo incur huge computational overheads to ensure that their PageRank vectors reflect this constant fluctuation in the information content of the web.

To effectively use an information space, it is essential that the navigational aids combine the semantic attributes of the situated character of activity and the internal representation of the task with the spatial attributes of the external representations (Dillon, 2000; Suchman, 1987; Zhang et al., 1994). Creating a cognition based model will allow the creation and maintenance of a dynamic information space that can facilitate better user interaction by providing spatial cues (layout, image placement, text highlights, window size, navigation icons etc.) which are coupled to semantic inferences based on relevance and meaning of individual user action. The system will continually seek to apply asserted and inferred knowledge to improve effectiveness in the information foraging activity with every step of the situated action.

LITERATURE REVIEW

A review of literature reveals many forms of user-centric semantics based adaptation approaches. Vector space models, Probabilistic relevance models (Kuntz, 2005; Wang, 2006), Artificial Neural Networks (Lin, 1997), Lexical Chaining based on linguistic factors (Green, 1998) and Pathfinder Network Scaling (Chen, 1999) are some examples. Utilities such as Spatial Co-Citation Maps (Chen, 1999), Fisheye View (Janecek et al., 2002), and the Spatial Paradigm for Information Retrieval and Exploration (SPIRE) (Hetzler et al., 1998) are often attached to these methods to provide visualization of the semantic structures.

Intelligent human-computer interaction (Duric et al., 2002) is a four-stage computational cognitive model that uses raw sensory-motor input (e.g., pupillary responses, eye fixations, keystroke force) to understand the current cognitive state. The perceptual, behavioral and cognitive states in this approach are inferred from nonverbal information captured by complex input sensors that monitor keystroke choices, strength of keystrokes, mouse gestures and pupillary changes. Adaptive web (Dolog et al., 2003) is an approach that employs RDF based ontologies to standardize description formats of document metadata to reason over facts described in the metadata. Other variations of this approach have also been proposed, such as separation of adaptation rules from metadata to enable reasoning over the widely distributed metadata on the web.

All these adaptive approaches, including those that come close to using semantically supported information foraging techniques are mostly passive facilitators. They rely on post hoc interaction history analyzed from server logs, client side cookies or persistent session data. Gajos et al. (2008) examines the influence of accuracy and predictability of adaptive interfaces on utilization and user satisfaction rating. They conclude that machine-learning algorithms that can predict a user's next action may have the potential to improve user satisfaction.

RETHINKING THE EXTENDED COGNITIVE FIT MODEL

The Extended Cognitive Fit Model (Shaft et al., 2006) provides a preliminary footing for the framework proposed in this chpater. This model was an extension of the Theory of Cognitive Fit (Vessey, 1991), which suggested that performance (measured along the objective dimensions of accuracy, time and interpretation accuracy) on a task will be enhanced when there is cognitive fit between information emphasized in the problem representation and that required by the type of problem-solving task. For tasks that require processing of information available from the environment, transformations are required to form the mental representation of the task (Vessey, 1991). The Extended Cognitive Fit Theory suggests that the internal representation of the problem domain and the external problem representation are two integral factors that drive the transformation required to create the mental representation of task solution (Shaft et al., 2006). Here, the internal representations are the knowledge structures in the problem solvers' mind and the external representations are the knowledge structures in the environment. Furthermore, the Extended Cognitive Fit model suggests that, it is the cognitive fit between the internal representations and the external representations and the interactions between them that contribute to the development of mental representations for task solution (Khatri et al., 2006; Shaft, 2006). The extended model of cognitive fit has been applied and studied in the context of various domains such as Geospatial-temporal applications and software modification tasks. However, it is important to point out one fundamental commonality that stands out in the application areas where the theory has been tested - that is, the mental representation of the problem solver is based on interpretations of explicitly stated tasks or clearly narrated problem statements. The task definition need not always be explicit for a user in a digital space. With a little astute thinking and objective use of philosophical footing from other disciples, information structures developed by redefining this framework can help orient a user towards a finely determined subset of relevant information within the very large set of possibilities in the vast information space. Keeping in mind the well-recognized limitations of passive navigational aids and coordination mechanisms, such a facilitator could moderate interventions in a way that, as Schön (1983) says, would orient action to change the present situation into one closer to what is desired.

For the sake of clarity, consider the classic consumer decision-making process as it applies in an e-commerce setting. The decision making process is a time consuming effort that can be characterized as a sequence of five stages. They are need recognition, alternative search, alternative evaluation, purchase decision and post-purchase evaluation (Engel et al., 1995). Every stage in the buyer behavior involves different cognitive tasks, reasoning, and decision-making challenges that reside in the consumer's mind rather than being explicitly stated. The structure of this task hierarchy will also most probably be different and unique from one user to another and is dependent on the objective of the consumer. The objective may be a simple exploratory exercise (learn how the 3:2 pull-down ratio enhances picture quality on a 1080p progressive scan television), an im-

pulsive purchase or the completion of an intended purchase (buy the cheapest HD-DVD player based on convincing user reviews). No matter how simple or complex the objective, the user at each stage creates a mental representation of the task solution based on the internal representation of the task and the perception of the external domain representation. A cognitive fit shows agreement, which in turn reasons to action, that moves the user to the next task in the hierarchy. At each stage of the task, if we can identify the representational properties of the perceptual and intuitive operations, we then can present the user with cues that are likely to provide more accurate guidance resulting in quicker completion of the task. Since the representational properties for individual users will be contextual, we need a flexible means to express the differences and isomorphic similarities (Zhang et al., 1994). The representations can be decomposed into its component level and can be expressed using ontologies (Thomas et al., 2005).

An important question then is, how the extended cognitive fit model can be refined to depict the user dynamics in digital information spaces. Additionally, we need a means to express the internal, external and mental representations. Ontologies have recently amassed rapidly growing adulations as the preferred formal means to model shared conceptualizations.

ONTOLOGIES

An ontology is a formal explicit description of concepts in a domain of discourse (or classes). They include properties of each class that describe the various concepts, relationships between the concepts, and restrictions on the properties and relationships (Noy et al., 2001). Ontology has emerged as an attractive sub-discipline in the field of knowledge engineering to enable uniform representation of data and their association with the domain of interest. Berners Lee et al. (2001) portrayed the semantic web model as an extension of the web from its current form, with enhanced capabilities made possible through explicit representation of the semantics underlying the data on which software agents can carry out sophisticated goal-oriented tasks (Embley, 2004). As a key element for the successful implementation of the semantic web model, ontology enables content-based access, interoperability and communication at a level that was unattainable in the traditional hyper-text markup based web environment. By using ontology as the primary structuring model for information presented on the web, information foraging activities can retrieve facts more effectively and conveniently because of the semantically shared understanding of the underlying structure. Conceptual terms can be used for finding query matches based on domain knowledge instead of the traditional approach of matching on strings and substrings as per operational knowledge.

Web Ontology Language (OWL) is the commonly used computational language to express ontologies. OWL can provide relatively easy human readability, context representation and reasoning capabilities, knowledge sharing, and meta-language definitions (Chen, 2004). OWL is developed as part of the Semantic Web initiatives from W3C and has evolved as the popular open standard for semantic knowledge representation. As a knowledge representation language for defining and instantiating ontologies, OWL describes the class, properties of attributes in the class and restrictions on properties using normative RDF/XML format. The next section details a conceptual model that uses ontologies for information processing in an e-commerce setting and presents an architecture for rule based inferences from the ontologies.

THE COGNITIVE INFORMATION MODEL

To illustrate the Cognitive Information Model (CIM), we use the hierarchy of tasks in a consumer decision-making process as it applies in a typical e-commerce setting. For the purpose of this research, we use the hierarchy of tasks proposed by Engell et al. (1995) that consists of five phases - need recognition, information search, alternative evaluation, purchase decision and post-purchase evaluation.

Theories of social action and cognitive science show that creating a mediating structure of information based on the cognitive fit between the internal task representation and the external problem representation may lead to better task completion performance. The theoretical basis of this effort originates from the notion suggested by Vessey (1991) that complexity in the task environment will be effectively reduced when problem solving problem aids support task strategies (methods and processes) required to perform the task. The extended cognitive fit model makes the argument that, when the decision maker's mental representation of the problem and the mental representation of the task match, problem-solving performance is likely to be more accurate and quicker than would otherwise be the case (Shaft et al., 2006). A closer analysis reveals that this philosophical position can be re-conceptualized to enhance the effectiveness of the extended cognitive fit model to express user intentions in a digital information space. This enhanced notion is portrayed in CIM as shown in Figure 1.

The decision making process in an e-commerce environment is a higher-level decision task that can be decomposed into elementary subtasks at each of the five phases. Cognitive fit in this context implies that the internal representation of the subtask matches contextual problem representation perceived from the environment. Intuitive operations on the internal environment and the perceptual operations on the external environment

Figure 1. The cognitive information model

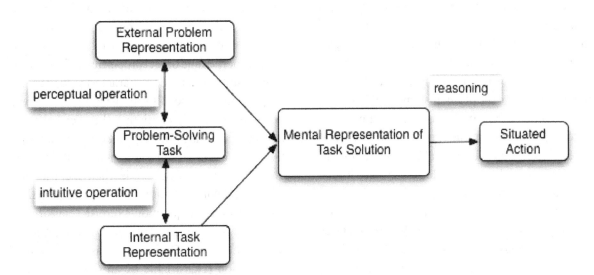

together help to find new and unexpected meaning and to direct response to such discoveries. To use Schön's jargon (1983), this 'reflective conversation' with the situation guides the response (an action) leading to the next subtask in the consumer decision-making process. The intuitive operation on internal representation influence the rational and emotional behavior (for example, the justifiable need to conform with changes in computing platforms as *sufficing* or a long overdue software upgrade considered as *satisfying*) and hold an equally important position with the automated operations of perception (Kahneman, 2003). Intuitive operation are slower, effortful, more likely to be consciously monitored or deliberately governed (Kahneman, 2003). Information from the internal representation is retrieved by intuitive processes and is influenced by three main factors: look-ahead, biases and learned knowledge (Zhang, 1997). The external representation provides a holistic view of the domain in context of the task and is processed by perceptual mechanisms, which is, of course, internal (Zhang, 1997). In the digital information space, the perceptual operations may be sequential or parallel as far as

the spatial representation of the information space is concerned. Perceptual operations also have direct impact on look-ahead capabilities. When complete look-ahead is impractical, as is the case with most information rich digital space today, we rely on percepts or biases to help narrow the decision on action in hopes of leading to a situation closer to what is desired (Schön, 1983; Zhang, 1997). The interplay between the intuitive and perceptual operations creates the mental representation of the task solution. This is cognitive fit.

ONTOLOGIES AND THE FRAMEWORK

To operationalize the internal, external and mental representations as computational models, we use three different ontologies. We call the ontology for internal task representation as the 'User Ontology' since the task representation is contextual to an individual user and should therefore allow for variations in interpretation and nuances in meaning relegated by that user. The external problem representation is the problem domain or the information space in context and is referred as the 'Domain Ontology'. Lastly, the mental representation of the task solution is the 'Cognitive Fit Ontology.'

Ontology development is an iterate process and requires the researcher to gain a thorough understanding of the problem domain. It is a common practice to verify the suitability of existing ontologies by testing against well-defined use cases (Chen, 2004; Firat et al., 2004). Available ontologies can also be extended or new ontologies can be created. For developing User Ontology and Domain Ontology, we start by examining the existing ontology models such as the Generic User Model Ontology (Dominik et al., 2005) and the Organization ontology for modeling enterprises (Fox et al., 1997). Concepts in the ontology should be a close representation of the objects and their relationship with the domain of interest (Noy et al., 2001). Intuitive operations on internal representations are represented in Cognitive Fit Ontology. The Domain Ontology encompasses representational vocabulary that expresses the semantics of the task environment – in this case, the e-commerce setting. The taxonomic structure depicts the classification of concepts starting with the most generic categorization of items available from the e-commerce store. Perceptual operations of sequential and parallel processing are nominally defined in the Domain Ontology.

In an e-commerce environment, potentially every user has a different goal. The goals may also be isomorphic in nature, for which each user possibly constructs a different mental model (Figure 2). The User Ontology is the internal task representation that takes into consideration the contextual variations in individual tasks (Consumer A and B in Figure 2), classifiable as phases in the consumer decision-making process. It reflects the position of the customer's behavior in the digital space based on situational influences that direct their action. The interaction of a specific consumer in the e-commerce environment is translated into specific instantiations of the classes in the User Ontology. Assuming that satisficing is localized optimization within the constraints of domain bounds and complete (or partial) information, data properties and object properties defined in the User Ontology is used to characterize the current and reasoned phase of the consumer in the buyer behavior model. Instantiating the user behavior as members of the ontology *classes* is a daunting task. For example, an elementary task such as an individual viewing the detailed specification of a particular television may be interpreted as an information acquisition exercise (classifiable as an OWL instantiation of *Information Search phase* in the User Ontology) or as evaluation of information (classifiable as an OWL instantiation of *Alternative Evaluation phase* in the User Ontology). To address this challenge, a rule set is developed to conceive the various different possibilities. The rules are generated by the knowledge engineer and implemented in SWRL (Semantic Web Rule Language); an Expert System Shell is used to interpret the rules (Figure 3). JESS (Java Expert System Shell) is a popular rule engine that uses the Rete algorithm based pattern matcher to deductively (forward chaining) or inductively (backward chaining) reason inferred facts from available data and inference rules (Forgy, 1982; Peuschel et al., 1992). Only those matching SWRL rules are fired by the Expert System to reason about OWL individuals that are semantically asserted as instances of OWL classes defined in the ontology.

The Cognitive Fit Ontology maintains the recognition of the variance in individual task and the information needs specific to the task. The hierarchy of concepts and class properties described in the Cognitive Fit Ontology consists of two main subsets – *CurrentState* and *ReasonedState*. The rules for asserting the context, the individual states and their re-classification within the knowledge base are defined using SWRL rules. For example, the given SWRL rule

Figure 2. Ontological mapping of contextual variations in the individual tasks using the cognitive information model

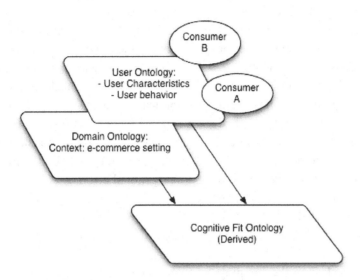

```
AddToCart(?a) ∧ TV(?t) ∧
itemInCart(?a, ?t) ∧ D_
PurchaseDecision(?pd)
→ machineState(Checkout_
Static,"reasoned") ∧ CurrentNode(?a)
∧ CurrentPhase(?pd) ∧
behaviorState(D_PurchaseDecision_
Static, "current")
```

is triggered by the expert system shell when the antecedent (the consumer adds an item to the shopping cart) condition is encountered (the situated user action). The rule consequent re-classifies the ontology instances and the properties of existing instances to represent this task and to update the machine state with the newly inferred knowledge. A reasoner engine like Pellet or Racer Pro then validates the consistency and integrity of asserted

Figure 3. Implementation architecture

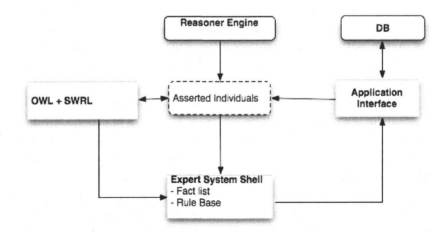

and inferred individuals. This is to ensure that the semantic updates resulting from rule execution preserve the references of their component terms and the truth of assertions in the domain where they are carried out. The architecture for implementing the model is shown in Figure 3.

For the consumer in the e-commerce environment, the ontology mapping will link local variations in individual user actions (described in the User Ontology) with the task environment (Domain Ontology). The resulting cognitive fit aligns the interpreted user context with specific concepts of the domain ontology. The objective is to represent the outcomes of thought, action and reflection in action that will help to change the present situation to one closer to the desired state. In general, a SWRL rule Φ, is the mapping from knowledge base and the known fact list to semantic expression in first order descriptive logic. If Φ preserves the truth of assertion for the given domain, the expert system shell will reclassify the asserted individuals as an instance of the *Reasoned State*, as well as tag the next predicted consumer decision-making phase and the information space of consequence. The *Reasoned State* may guide (or misguide) the user to the next sub-task in the consumer decision-making process. Since assistive aids to guide situated actions will reduce complexity in the task environment (Vessey, 1991; Pirolli et al., 1999), determining the context and the subtask of a given user from the Cognitive Fit Ontology will allow creation of active representations in the form of content highlighting, notification icons, image positioning, adaptive navigational structures and interactive tools. By including the known characteristics of situated activity in creating the knowledge representations, the asserted individuals in the ontology will be sufficiently informed with a general knowledge about the consumer decision making process and specific knowledge about domain orientation.

The main focus of the implementation architecture is to provide a contextually rich representation of the external environment that will lead towards better problem solving performance, irrespective of whether the person is a new customer or an experienced user. By coordinating a fit between the internal task representation and the external stimuli, the expert system updates the application interface with cues and navigational aids pertaining to user's task solution. Updates to the application interface resulting from the expert systems firing the SWRL rules provide effective guidance to the user by constructing semantically rich target pages and by reducing ambiguity in the navigational efforts.

CONCLUSION

The framework proposed in this chpater aims to provide the ability to analyze user interaction with the external space and build digital information spaces from knowledge bases that are represented as ontologies. The proposed implementation architecture will help to proactively examine the contextual nature of the task performed by the user and to customize the problem-solving aids (tools, navigational aids, menu structures, etc.) required to perform the task.

To develop the model proposed in this study, we relied on well-established literature to identify the factors that influence the intuitive operations and perceptual operations. The model does not include all known factors that influence problem solving performance. For instance, the role of illusion or curiosity is not included. Since the SWRL rules in essence reflect the espoused theories of action (Argyris et al., 1992) of a user, concerns may be raised over how changes can be made to the rule base to accommodate variations observed in user's theories of action. The dilemma of inconsistency (progressive incompatibility of governing variables of the theory-in-use) and effectiveness (deterioration of rule sequence reaching a point at which the SWRL rules fail or fall outside allowed bounds) can only be understood through a longitudinal study of the artifact. Any necessary adjustments to the rule base will require manual intervention followed by additional regression testing.

This chpater describes the Cognitive Information Model to help guide situated actions in information spaces. The architecture relies on expert systems for triggering application interface updates based on semantic inferences from known facts stored in ontologies and SWRL rules. The model can be used by domain owners (e-commerce owners and managers) to analyze the relevance of information content and to improve organization of information on the website. It will enhance the user's (consumers) ability to explore and exploit information presented on information space. Application areas of this framework range from e-commerce domains and digital libraries to organizational knowledge stores, large database repositories and even help desk systems. Combined with the newer web presentation tools such as Windows Presentation Framework, Asynchronous JavaScript And XML (AJAX) and Adobe Flex ActionScript, we can envision the prospects of molding semantically informed digital information spaces adorned with jaw dropping interface designs and interactivity features.

REFERENCES

Argyris, C., & Schön, D. A. (1992). *Theory in practice: Increasing professional effectiveness.* Jossey Bass Higher and Adult Education Series.

Berners-Lee, T., Hall, W., Hendler, J. A., O'Hara, K., Shadbolt, N., & Weitzner, D. J. (2006). A framework for Web science. *Foundations and Trends in Web Science, 1*(1), 1–130. doi:10.1561/1800000001

Berners-Lee, T., Hendler, J., & Lassila, O. (2001). The Semantic Web. *Scientific American, 284,* 34–43. doi:10.1038/scientificamerican0501-34

Chen, C. (1999). Visualising semantic spaces and author co-citation networks in digital libraries. *Information Processing & Management, 35,* 401–420. doi:10.1016/S0306-4573(98)00068-5

Chen, H. L. (2004). *An intelligent broker architecture for pervasive context-aware systems.* PhD Thesis, University of Maryland.

Dillon, A. (2000). Spatial semantics and individual differences in the perception of shape in information space. *Journal of the American Society for Information Science American Society for Information Science, 51*(6), 521–528. doi:10.1002/(SICI)1097-4571(2000)51:6<521::AID-ASI4>3.0.CO;2-5

Ding, Y., & Foo, S. (2002). Ontology research and development part 1 – a review of ontology generation. *Journal of Information Science, 28*(2), 123–136.

Dolog, P., Henze, N., Nejdl, W., & Sintek, M. (2003). *Towards the adaptive Semantic Web.* First Workshop on Principles and Practice of Semantic Web Reasoning, (pp. 51-68).

Dominik, H., Schwartz, T., & Brandherm, B. Schmitz, M., & Wilamowitz-Moellendorff, M. V. (2005). Gumo – the general user model ontology. *Proceedings of The 10th International Conference on User Modeling,* Edinburgh, Scotland, UK, (pp. 24-29).

Duric, Z., Gray, W. D., Heishman, R., Li, F., Rosenfeld, A., & Schoelles, M. J. … Wechsler, H. (2002). Integrating perceptual and cognitive modeling for adaptive and intelligent human-computer interaction. *Proceedings of the IEEE, 90*(7), 1272–1289.

Engel, J. F., Blackwell, R. D., & Miniard, P. W. (1995). *Consumer behavior* (8th ed.). Fort Worth, TX: Dryden Press.

Firat, A., Madnick, S. E., & Grosof, B. (2004). *Contextual alignment of ontologies for semantic interoperability.* Retrieved from http://papers.ssrn.com/sol3/papers.cfm?abstract_id=612472

Forgy, C. L. (1982). Rete: A fast algorithm for the many pattern/ many object pattern match problem. *Artificial Intelligence, 19,* 17–37. doi:10.1016/0004-3702(82)90020-0

Fox, M. S., Barbuceanu, M., Gruninger, M., & Lin, J. (1997). An organization ontology for enterprise modelling. In Prietula, M., Carley, K., & Gasser, L. (Eds.), *Simulating organizations: Computational models of institutions and groups* (pp. 131–152). Menlo Park, CA: AAAI/MIT Press.

Gajos, K. Z., Everitt, K., Tan, D. S., Czerwinski, M., & Weld, D. S. (2008). Predictability and accuracy in adaptive user interfaces. *Proceedings of the 28th Annual SIGCHI conference on Human Factors in Computing Systems,* (pp. 1271-1274).

Green, S. J. (1998). Automated link generation: Can we do better than term repetition? *Proceedings of the 7th International World-Wide Web Conference,* Brisbane, Australia.

Hetzler, B., Whitney, P., Martucci, L., & Thomas, J. (1998). Multi-faceted insight through interoperable visual information analysis paradigms. *Proceedings of IEEE Information Visualization '98.*

Janecek, P., & Pu, P. (2002). *A framework for designing fisheye views to support multiple semantic contexts.* In the 6th International Working Conference on Advanced Visual Interfaces, Trento, Italy.

Kahneman, D. (2003). A perspective on judgment and choice. *The American Psychologist, 58*(9), 697–720. doi:10.1037/0003-066X.58.9.697

Kalfoglou, Y., & Schorlemmer, M. (2003). Ontology mapping: The state of the art. *The Knowledge Engineering Review, 18*(1), 1–31. doi:10.1017/S0269888903000651

Khatri, V., Vessey, I., Ram, S., & Ramesh, V. (2006). Cognitive fit between conceptual schemas and internal problem representations: The case of geospatio-temporal conceptual schema comprehension. *IEEE Transactions on Professional Communication, 49*(2), 109–127. doi:10.1109/TPC.2006.875091

Klahr, D., & Kotovsky, K. (1989). *Complex information processing. The impact of Herbert A. Simon.* New Jersey: Lawrence Erlbaum Associates Publishers.

Kuntz, C. (2005). An integrated approach for semantics-driven information retrieval. *Proceedings of the 11th International Conference on Human-Computer Interaction,* Las Vegas, Nevada, USA, (pp. 22-27).

Lin, X. (1997). Map displays for information retrieval. *Journal of the American Society for Information Science American Society for Information Science, 48*(1), 40–54. doi:10.1002/(SICI)1097-4571(199701)48:1<40::AID-ASI6>3.0.CO;2-1

Newell, A., & Simon, H. A. (1972). *Human problem solving.* New Jersey: Prentice Hall, Inc.

Noy, N. F., & McGuinness, D. L. (2001). *Ontology development 101: A guide to creating your first ontology,* (pp. 1-25). (Stanford Knowledge Systems Laboratory Technical Report KSL-01-05).

Peuschel, B., & Schafer, W. (1992). Concepts and implementation of a rule-based process engine. *Proceedings of the 14th International Conference on Software Engineering,* Melbourne, Australia, (pp. 262-279).

Pirolli, P., & Card, S. (1999). Information foraging. *Psychological Review, 106*(4), 643–675. doi:10.1037/0033-295X.106.4.643

Schön, D. A. (1983). *The reflective practitioner: How professionals think in action.* Basic Books.

Shaft, T. M., & Vessey, I. (2006). The role of cognitive fit in the relationship between software comprehension and modification. *Management Information Systems Quarterly*, *30*(1), 29–55.

Simon, H. A. (1996). *The sciences of the artificial* (3rd ed.). Cambridge, MA: MIT Press.

Suchman, L. (1987). *Plans and situated action.* New York, NY: Cambridge University Press.

Thomas, M., Redmond, R., Yoon, Y., & Singh, R. (2005). A semantic approach to monitor business process performance. *Communications of the ACM*, *48*(12), 55–59. doi:10.1145/1101779.1101809

Uschold, M., & Grüninger, M. (1996). Ontologies: Principles, methods, and applications. *The Knowledge Engineering Review*, *11*(2), 93–155. doi:10.1017/S0269888900007797

Vessey, I. (1991). Cognitive fit: A theory-based analysis of the graphs versus tables literature. *Decision Sciences*, *22*(2), 219–240. doi:10.1111/j.1540-5915.1991.tb00344.x

Wexelblat, A. D. (1999). *Footprints: Interaction history for digital objects*. PhD Thesis, Massachusetts Institute of Technology.

Zhang, J. (1997). The nature of external representations in problem solving. *Cognitive Science*, *21*(2), 179–217. doi:10.1207/s15516709cog2102_3

This chapter is an enhanced version of the article "Using Ontological Reasoning for an Adaptive E-Commerce Experience" by Manoj Thomas, Richard Redmond, and Victoria Yoon, published in issue 5(4) of the International Journal of Intelligent Information Technologies.

Chapter 3
Semantic Web Services Composition with Case Based Reasoning

Dhavalkumar Thakker
Press Association, UK

Taha Osman
Nottingham Trent University, UK

David Al-Dabass
Nottingham Trent University, UK

ABSTRACT

Web service development is encouraging scenarios where individual or integrated application services can be seamlessly and securely published on the Web without the need to expose their implementation details. However, as Web services proliferate, it becomes difficult to matchmake and integrate them in response to users requests. The goal of our research is to investigate the utilization of the Semantic Web in building a developer-transparent framework facilitating the automatic discovery and composition of Web services. In this chapter, we present a Semantic Case Based Reasoner (SCBR) framework that utilizes the case based reasoning methodology for modelling dynamic Web service discovery and composition. Our approach is original as it considers the runtime behaviour of a service resulting from its execution. Moreover, we demonstrate that the accuracy of automatic matchmaking of Web services can be further improved by taking into account the adequacy of past matchmaking experiences for the requested task. To facilitate Web services composition, we extend our fundamental discovery and matchmaking algorithm using a light-weight knowledge-based substitution approach to adapt the candidate service experiences to the requested solution before suggesting more complex and computationally taxing AI-based planning-based transformations. The inconsistency problem that occurs while adapting existing service composition solutions is addressed with a novel methodology based on the Constraint Satisfaction Problem (CSP).

DOI: 10.4018/978-1-60960-595-7.ch003

1. INTRODUCTION

The last decade has witnessed an explosion of application services delivered electronically, ranging from e-commerce and Internet information service, to services that facilitate trading between business partners, better known as B2B relationships. Traditionally these services are facilitated by distributed technologies such as RPC, CORBA, RMI, and more recently Web services. The application of automatic composition of Web services has received a great deal of attention from the industry and research groups as the composition of services adds a new dimension to Web services advantages. Web service composition refers to the technique of composing arbitrarily complex services from relatively simpler services available over the Internet (Chakraborty, 2001; Maigre, 2010). Web services composition technology is ever increasingly being adopted by the industry (Yen, 2009; Zhang, 2008). Large software houses such as Microsoft, IBM and Sun have implemented Web services protocol stack as part of their main computing platforms (http://java.sun.com/javaee/, http://www.microsoft.com/NET/, http://www-01. ibm.com/software/websphere/).

As Web services are being increasingly adopted as the distributed computing technology of choice to securely publish application services beyond the firewall, the importance of composing them to create new, value-added service is increasing. Thus far, the most successful practical approach to Web services composition is based on the Business Process Execution Language (BPEL) (Andrews, 2007). Largely endorsed by the industry, this approach borrows from business processes' workflow management theory to achieve the formalization necessary for describing the data and control flow in the composition process. The BPEL specification solves the immediate problems that the IT industry is facing regarding the use of Web services for enterprise application integration. However, in its present form the specification overlooks the possibility of integrating applica-

tion services and performing flow management on the fly, hence it only specifies how the service composer can perform both activities manually.

One of the solutions to this problem are the hybrid approaches attempting to enrich the BPEL specification with machine processible semantic descriptions. However as demonstrated by Mandell (2003), Osman (2005), and Traverso (2004), enriching BPEL specification with semantics achieves limited level of automation. Generally in order to automate Web services composition, two problems have to be resolved: automatic discovery and selection of Web services and automatic compilation of flow management for the selected services (Thakker, 2005). These hybrid approaches address the Web service discovery problem, but rely on the flow management provided by the BPEL process model and hence on the understanding of the service composer to design the flow management; therefore human developers are still largely involved in the Web services composition task.

The root of the problem is related to building the process model on top of WSDL, which is an XML grammar. XML cannot define concepts or relations between concepts, which is the most important factor for the intelligent reasoning required for the automation. The issue related to the current discussion is the use of non-semantic grammar for the composition specification. For the composition engine to provide automatic discovery and flow management, the process model needs to have the consideration of the semantics in the specification. The addition of semantics within an XML centric standard like BPEL will not achieve the sought-after automation as that would require an intelligent reasoner that can interpret the semantic description.

The second approach to Web services composition aspires to achieve more dynamic composition by semantically describing the process model of a Web service and thus making it comprehensible to reasoning engines or software agents. Our approach builds on this premise and proposes an intelligent semantic-web based reasoner based on the AI theory of Case Based Reasoning (CBR).

1.1. Motivation

We believe that despite the evident popularity of Web services as a distributed computing paradigm and the value-added dimension that composition contributes to it, there are complexity problems restricting the practical adoption of the technology to its potential. The main thesis of this research work is based on the theory that assistance with the facilitation of the composition process to the service providers and the composers plays a major role in encouraging the adoption of the Web services composition technology.

The facilitation to be provided to the service developers and providers can be considered in terms of the minimum effort they have to make to subscribe their services to composition schemes. This effort is manifested in two chief scenarios:

- The application service is not yet published as a Web service, in which case a blue-print is required to build a Web service wrapper that plugs the application to the composition interface.
- The service provider has exposed the application as Web service that has a specification and format conceptually similar but syntactically different from what the composition interface expects. Ideally here the service provider should not be required to re-write the Web service, but some work-around is suggested to overcome the mismatch.

The composition techniques can be judged based on how seamlessly they allow the service providers to take part in the composition for the above scenarios. For the service composer, who can either be a human developer or an intelligent program/software agent, the facilitation constitutes automating as many steps as possible

in order to build the composition logic. These steps include:

- Matchmaking services to the required solutions;
- Implementing the execution flow management of the match-maked services, i.e. the composition workflow;
- Automatic integration of alternative services;
- Overcoming mismatches in the service descriptions which are the result of disparate implementations of the same service, as transparently as possible.

The literature in the area of Web services composition reflects the fact that in search of automation the focus of the research and development effort has shifted from giving priority to the composition participants to the application of various existing formal methodologies to solve composition problem, often at the expense of the practicality of the solutions. Hence, the aim of this work is to pursue a pragmatic vision of contributing towards the efforts of making the composition process as transparent as possible to all the composition participants. This should allow developers and users to perform everyday chores using Web services without being worried about behind the scene technical details.

1.2. Case Study

To highlight the type of problems we are aiming to address and the facilitation required in solving such problems, we present a Web service composition case study based on the travel agent problem (Osman, 2005). We believe that travel agent is an ideal application of Web services composition where a travel agent has to deal with a number of sub-domains under the travel domain such as bus, rail, airline, hotel, etc. Moreover, there are numerous existing travel domain applications that can be published as Web services and subsequently benefit from the dynamic discovery and composition mechanism. Here we present a scenario that illustrates the role of service participants and depict how dynamic Web services composition benefits each of them.

The service requestor initiates the service request. We assume that in addition to the request parameters (input), the user also would like to provide constraints and preferences on the expected results (outputs) as described below:

Inputs (*Name, Expected Departure Date, Expected ArrivalDate, No of Passengers, Departure City, Arrival City*)

Constraints & Preferences:

Provision of a travel package with Airline and Hotel

Output currency must not be USD.

Output currency must be in GBP.

The execution speed of the service must be 3 seconds.

I do not particularly like British Airways.

I get sick in bus, so please do not include bus in the results.

Outputs *(Price, Currency)*

The service provider may want to participate in the composition process by providing their service to the composer using a generic travel service registry.

The composer represents a travel agency that takes requestor's request and finds suitable service(s). In a dynamic Web services composition scenario, rather than having a fixed list of Web services that travel agency always accesses, the agency would like to instead dynamically discover Web services at each transaction. This allows the travel agency to avoid having a pre-negotiated agreement with each Web service. The ultimate goal of the intelligent framework is to satisfy user request and facilitate each of the participants in the process of achieving required results.

1.3. Semantic Case Based Reasoner (SCBR) for Web Services Composition

The accuracy of service selection is critical to the success of the composition process and largely relies on assessing the capability of a service in accordance with the service composition request. The existing approach to address this problem is to consider the semantic representation of service(s) against the semantic representation of the search problem descriptions. We classify this approach under the category of approaches that perform "comparison of static behaviour of services". For example, semantic approaches based on planning techniques (such as Mcilraith, 2002; Wu, 2003) rely on OWL-S profile for discovery and compare service descriptions of the service request and existing services in the registry in terms of whether they have similar inputs and outputs (i.e. have similar data or object types). These approaches can satisfy coarse-grained service requests that consist of a simple singleton query such as book purchase, airline booking, or sensor reading services; however they cannot satisfy fine-grained service requests such as finding a book purchase service that charges in USD or finding an airline that travels from Milan and charges in EUR or finding a sensor service that has reliability of 0.9. We demonstrate this using an example.

Figure 1 exemplifies the above argument regarding the limitation of comparing the static behaviour of Web services. As shown in Figure 1 (A) for a new service request, the descriptions (service parameters) are matched with the available service descriptions. For instance, to find a service that provides flight to the German city Bonn and charges in USD, approaches in this category match service descriptions of (OutputCurrency, To_City) with the existing services in the service registry. Although for the candidate Web services it is highly likely that service descriptions are semantically similar, the run-time behaviour of the service can vary significantly. For instance, the service might be a travel service but may not provide a flight to Bonn or might not be able to complete the transaction in USD. This variation (cities serviced) is expressed in the values for functional and non-functional parameters that constitutes domain-specific knowledge. This domain-specific knowledge depicting run-time behaviour of a service can provide valuable guidance for the decision-making process regarding the service adequacy for the task.

In this research, the concept of considering "runtime behaviour of services" to improve the accuracy of Web services discovery is proposed. For example, as illustrated in Figure 1 B, in addition to functional parameters (OutputCurrency, To_City), the current service description also includes non-functional parameters such as QoS. This enables comparing services in registry with their execution values such as it describes: "there exists a past run-time experience with Easyjet where the service transaction is in USD, the des-

tination city for travel was Bonn and QoS of the service was 1.5". We believe that taking into account the adequacy of such past matchmaking experiences for the requested task can significantly improve the accuracy of the Web services matchmaking process, therefore we claim that there is a need for a methodology that uses domain-specific knowledge representation for capturing the Web services execution experiences and reason based on those experiences. Case Based Reasoning (Aamodt, 1994) provides such methodology as its fundamental principle is that an experience formed in solving a problem situation can be applied for other similar problem situations. An added benefit of reasoning about past execution experiences can be the analysis of aggregate service behaviour over a period of time. For instance, more precise conclusions can be drawn about the service reliability by analyzing its QoS execution experiences over a period of time.

Figure 1. Matching service descriptions v/s run-time behaviour of Web services

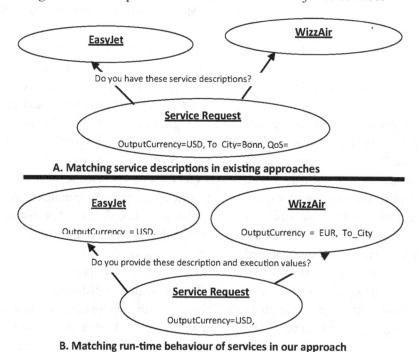

The chapter begins with the overview of the theory of CBR. Section 3 explains how we model Web services matchmaking using CBR. In section 4 we discuss the design of our matchmaking algorithm. The implementation of the framework is described in section 5. Finally we investigate how case adaptation can further extend our matchmaking algorithm to cater for service composition and review related work.

2. OVERVIEW OF CASE BASED REASONING

The Case-Based Reasoning technology was developed in 1977 based on the research effort of Schank and Abelson. They proposed that our general knowledge about situations is recorded in the brain as scripts that allow us to set up expectations and perform inferences (Aamodt, 1994). The processes involved in CBR can be represented by a schematic cycle comprising three phases (Schank, 1979):

I. Case Representation

A case is a core component of a CBR system and can be defined as a contextualized piece of knowledge representing an experience. A case records knowledge at an operational level by capturing experiences in terms of a problem situation and the solution involved. It contains the problem, a description of the state of the world when the case occurred, and the solution to this problem.

II. Case Storage and Indexing

A case worthy of storage contributes to the reasoning process by representing a potential base solution for new problem situations. Such cases need to be indexed and stored in the case library or case base, so that the reasoner can retrieve them for reasoning. The process of searching the entire case library is computationally expensive; hence indexing the cases using a specific categorization system improves the efficiency of the search process by limiting the search cases' pool.

III. Case Search and Evaluation

Whenever a new problem needs to be solved, the case library is searched for the cases that can provide a potential solution. The first phase of the search is case retrieval, which uses indexing to retrieve cases that are contextually similar to the new problem. The next phase is matchmaking where the retrieved contextually similar cases are further investigated to verify if a solution to prior problem situations can be applied to the problem in-hand. If the system does not find an adequate match, then the combined contextual knowledge of relevant cases is applied to solve the problem, this phase is called adaptation. On success, the adapted cases are entered in the case library. On failure, the situation leading to failure is entered in the case library, which serves as a case and guides the CBR reasoner to avoid future failures in similar problem situations. The inconsistencies encountered during the evaluation are recorded as cases and are termed "case revision".

3. UTILISATION OF CASE BASED REASONING FOR WEB SERVICES MATCHMAKING

3.1. Modelling Web Services Discovery and Composition Problem into CBR Problem

CBR maps naturally into the Web services composition problem as it is possible to model the search and adaptation methodology in CBR as Web services discovery and composition mechanism. Figure 2 illustrates how CBR modelling can be applied to the problem of Web services discovery and composition. In the proposed SCBR framework, Web services execution experiences are modelled as cases, where the cases are the functional and non-functional domain-specific Web services' properties described using semantics. In our model, the case library will be the storage place for such execution experiences and is identical to Web service registries in that it stores Web services references, but unlike registries, case libraries also describe the services' runtime behaviour.

The process of case search is divided into matchmaking and retrieval sub-processes. The retrieval process is similar to the Web services discovery problem in that both mechanisms seek to find potential Web services for the current problem. The case matchmaking process is similar to Web services matchmaking as both processes attempt to select acceptable Web services from those retrieved at the retrieval phase. The process of case adaptation which is applicable when the available cases cannot fulfil the problem requirements and the process is carried out by adapting available cases is similar to Web service composition, as the composition is applied when available services are not sufficient in meeting the requirement for the problem.

The apparent compatibility argued above confirms the thesis of this research that the CBR methodology is well suited to build automatic Web services composition frameworks.

3.2. The Framework Architecture

In the SCBR framework, there are two main roles: the case administrator, who is responsible for case library maintenance by entering or deleting cases from the library, and the case requestor, who searches the case library to find a solution for the Web services composition problem. Figure 3 illustrates the schematic diagram of the framework.

The framework allows the Web service requestor to specify the problem description and then search for Web service that meets the problem requirements. The dynamics of the framework operation is as follows:

1. Initially, the administrator populates the repository with semantic case representation formats for a specific application domain. This representation is used to semantically

Figure 2. Mapping Web services composition problem to CBR

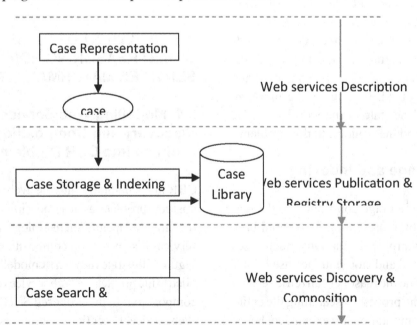

annotate both the user requests for suitable services and the execution experiences of Web services for the specific domain.

2. The SCBR interface is the first entry point for the Web service requestor, who can use the interface to input the problem requirements, and also receive the resultant Web service references (solution). After receiving the problem description, the SCBR interface starts the search process for suitable services that matches the request.

3. At this stage, the search engine passes the new problem description and the custom semantic case representation format to the Semantic Description generator module, which annotates the new problem according to the representation format

4. The annotated problem is then passed to the indexing module, which computes the suitable index for the new problem and passes the index to the Case retrieval module.

5. The case retrieval module queries the case library for cases with similar indexes. The output of this stage is the cases that have a similar index to the current problem. These retrieved cases are then passed to the next stage.

6. The case matchmaking module receives the retrieved cases and the annotation of problem description from the semantic description generator module, processes the cases further and then outputs matched cases that are a small proportion of the retrieved cases.

7. The SCBR interface receives these matched cases and extracts the Web services details from the solution part of the case.

8. The SCBR interface returns Web services details to the service requestor.

3.3. The Benefits of Utilizing Semantics for Service Discovery

One of the main features of the SCBR framework is the extensive utilization of semantic web technologies in describing the problem parameters and in the implementation of the core components of the framework described in the previous section: representation, indexing, storage, matching and

Figure 3. SCBR matchmaking framework

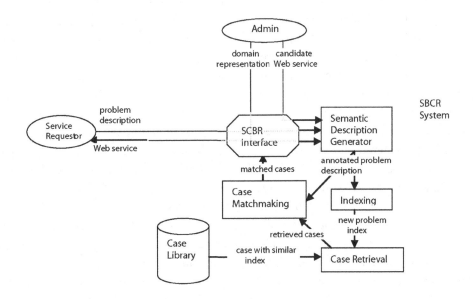

retrieval. The Web Ontology Language (OWL) is utilized for constructing ontologies in this framework.

From a computer science point of view, an ontology represents an area of knowledge that is used by people, databases, and applications that need to share domain information. Ontologies include computer-usable definitions of basic concepts in the domain and the relationships among them.

Applied to Web services retrieval, the semantic annotation of Web services creates a conceptual understanding of the domains that the services represent, thus enabling software agents to make more intelligent decisions about the relevance of the services to a particular service request. For example, when searching the jUDDI free-text based Web services search engine (http://ws.apache.org/juddi) for some travel Web services relevant to London, it seems relevant to use keywords 'travel service to London'. However, the jUDDI search engine returns one service out of possible ten relevant services, with returned results including *London Underground Web service*, primarily because the string "London" is part of the service name.

The use of the semantic web in Web services retrieval is likely to improve the computer's understanding of the domain objects and their interactions. The goal is to make the machine understand that "London" is a city and that it is capital of the "United Kingdom" and that there are numbers of transport mediums available departing from and arriving to the city of London.

The ontology relating "London" to the "City" concept should be able to retrieve all the services execution experiences where the departure city is London. To attain such expanded results, a taxonomy is required that allows search engines to infer that the "City" concept is affiliated to the "Travel" domain as a "Departure" and "Arrival" points.. The semantic web is capable of providing such taxonomy that integrates concepts and inter-entity relations from different domains, such

as "City", "Travel", and "Transport" in relation to the query above.

3.4. Semantics for Case Representation and Storage

The most common use of ontologies is the reconciliation between syntactically different terms that are semantically equivalent. Applied to CBR case descriptions for Web services, ontologies can be used to provide a generic, reasoner-independent description of their functional and non-functional parameters. Moreover, ontologies can also be used to further index and structure cases with key domain features that increase the efficiency of the matchmaking process. For instance, we can add a feature to the travel domain ontology to indicate whether a trip is domestic or international. Web services Quality of Service QoS parameters can also indexed using ontologies to further improve the accuracy of case matchmaking.

In our framework, ontologies are also used to describe the rules of the CBR reasoning engine, which not only streamlines the intercommunication between the Web service, user request, and the case library, but also promotes exploring the collaboration at the reasoning level between different composition frameworks.

To achieve these objectives, we require a generic case representation schema which will prove the applicability of our approach for heterogeneous domains/services by catering for the situations where services with different descriptions from the composers can exist. Figure 4 outlines partial view of such representation scheme.

We use the Web Ontology Language (OWL) for constructing ontologies and Semantic Web Rule Language (SWRL) (Horrocks, 2004) for defining rules. Some of the properties and descriptions are similar to OWL-S descriptions, as the intention is to extend OWL-S descriptions for fulfilling the objectives of building domain-independent case representation format. OWL-S has been a significant semantic web based Web ser-

Figure 4. Generic case representation

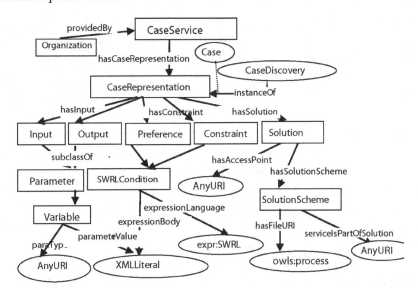

vices standard and this work provides backward capability with OWL-S descriptions. OWL-S specification provides grounding in WSDL hence the service providers with existing services can utilize OWL-S specification for semantically annotating their Web services. Similarly, service providers will be able to use this case representation schema that extends OWL-S description to semantically decribe non-functional parameters and in providing elements to support the service requestor in searching for Web services.

The ontology in Figure 4 for case representation has a *CaseRepresentation* class that is the upper class with ObjectProperties including: *hasInput, hasOutput, hasConstraint, hasPreference* and *hasSolution*. These properties have value range *Input, Output, Preference, Constraint* and *Solution. Input* and *Output* classes are grounded in *Variable* class while *Preference, Constraint* are grounded in *Condition* class, and *Solution* in *SolutionScheme* class respectively.

The *CaseRepresentation* class has two instances: *Case* and *CaseDiscovery. Case* is used for describing various Web service execution experiences, while *CaseDiscovery* is used while

searching for cases that fulfil user requirements from the case repository. Both use different components of *CaseRepresentation*: *Case* uses *Input, Output, Feature, Solution* and *Feedback* to store execution experiences. While *CaseDiscovery* uses *Input, Output, Constraint, Preferences* and *Feature* to formalize a search request.

The variable classes *Input* and *Output* are subclasses of the *swrl:Variable* class that achieves variable status by defining parameters using a resource URI as a *ParameterType* and XML Literal as *ParameterValue*. Other variable classes are *Constraint* and *Preference* on search and their variable status is achieved by defining them as *SWRLCondition* using SWRL as description language and *XMLLiteral* to encode such condition. We here re-used the publicly available semantic descriptions with namespaces *swrl* and *expr*. Our framework currently supports conditions defined only in Semantic Web Rule Language (SWRL).

Solution and *Feedback* concepts have fixed semantics. *Solution* contains an object property *hasAccessPoint* that points to the access point of a Web service, which could be a WSDL file or a Web based access point for the service. To formalize the detail of the solution, the SCBR framework uses a pointer to an OWL-S process file as the result of *hasSolutionScheme*. *serviceIsPartOfSolution* is an important part of the *Solution* class as it contains the domain based URI for the candidate solution services.

3.5. Case Vocabulary

In CBR theory, the first step towards formalizing the search problem is to define all the elements contained in a case and the associated vocabulary that represents the knowledge associated with the context of a specific domain. For instance, the generic case representation for the "travel domain" can be modelled as follows:

1. Functional parameters represent the service input (e.g. the travel details), and the service output (e.g. the travel itinerary). Input corresponds to the request of the user (e.g. date or city of departure) whereas output corresponds to the response given to the user (e.g. price, flight number).
2. Non-functional parameters are the constraints imposed by the user (e.g. exclusion of a particular travel medium) or preferences over certain specific parameters (such as Price range or Quality of Service expected). In addition, runtime experiences stored in the case library should also include the solution (i.e. Web services effectively used), and a notion to specify if the solution was acceptable for the end-user using feedback. Features that characterise the domain are extremely useful for top-level indexing and can also be included as non-functional parameters.

3.6. Case Indexing and Retrieval

The cases can be indexed based on vocabularies, which should allow the retrieval of appropriate cases during the search procedure. For indexing the cases, the framework uses "partitioning case library" method, which is a variation of the "flat memory indexing" technique (Kolodner, 1993). In this indexing method, the case library is partitioned based on certain vocabularies and the new problem is recognized based on identical vocabularies in order to decide which partition the problem falls into. The indexing is performed based on identifying combinations of features of a case that describe the circumstances in which a reasoner might find the case useful during reasoning (Kolodner, 1993). In the travel domain case study exemplified in this chapter, cases are stored based on the vocabulary element *Features,* which corresponds to the *hasFeatures* property from the CaseRepresentation ontology class. The possible values for this vocabulary are either *Domestic* or *International* (pre-defined instances from the *TravelRegion* class), hence indexing will partition the case library into two parts corresponding to the relevant travel region.

Whenever a new Web service needs to be searched, the problem description involving the functional parameters and non-functional parameters is encoded using the case representation frame structure, i.e. as an instance of CaseRepresentation ontology. The framework identifies the new problem based on the partition it falls into and then the rest of the matching is applied to cases from that partition only. This corresponds to using *hasFeatures* property value to reason whether the new problem falls under *Domestic* or *International* travel region. Based on the outcome of reasoning, the cases associated with a particular partition are further investigated.

3.7. Case Matchmaking and Ranking

The case retrieval procedure fetches the Web services that are a potential solution to the new problem. The matching process narrows down the retrieved cases to present an acceptable solution(s). The framework utilizes the k-weighted Nearest-Neighbour Matching and Ranking method (Remind, 1992). This method operates as follows:

1. Measure the similarity between the properties of the new problem and that of the retrieved cases. The method used for comparison depends on the type of property.
2. Quantify the weight of the similarity. A ranking is assigned to each property in accordance with its importance. To improve the accuracy of matchmaking process, a spectrum of functional and non-functional parameter based matchmaking criteria are employed, thus requiring such quantifying mechanism to measure these parameters individual contribution to the overall of Aggregate Degree of Match (ADoM).

For each retrieved case, the similarity degree is computed and the case with the highest score corresponds to the best match. Similarity takes values between 0 and 1, which is attributed to each property for each retrieved case. The similarity comparison depends on the type of the dimension: data or object.

Object Property Comparisons

For semantically matching the object property value of the new problem and the retrieved cases, the algorithm compares the instances. If the instances match, then the degree of match is 1. Otherwise, the algorithm traverses back to the super (upper) class that the instance is derived from and the comparison is performed at that level.

The comparison is similar to traversing a tree structure, where the tree represents the class hierarchy for the ontology element. The procedure of traversing back to the upper class and matching instances is repeated until there are no super classes in the class hierarchy, i.e. the root node of the tree is reached, giving a degree of match equal to 0. The degree of match (DoM) is calculated according to the following equation:

Equation 1. Degree of Match (DoM)

$$DoM = \frac{MN}{GN}$$

where the *MN* is Total number of matching nodes in the selected traversal path, and *GN* is Total number of nodes in the selected traversal path.

Data Type Property Comparisons

To compare data type properties such as the price range or the value of QoS (e.g. execution time), we use the qualitative regions based measurement method (Kolodner, 1993). The closer the value in a retrieved case is to the value in the request higher the similarity coefficient is.

For each data type property, the comparison formula used is:

$$|V_r - V_c| \leq X. |V_r|$$

where V is the value of the property in the request **r** or in the retrieved case **c** and X the factor of tolerance. Thus, a factor of tolerance of 0.9 means the value of the retrieved case should be in ±10% region in relation to the value of the request. The optimum tolerance value is determined by the administrator and can be calculated heuristically.

Computing the Overall Similarity Value

Overall similarity is evaluated by computing the aggregate degree of match (ADoM) (Remind, 1992) for each retrieved case according to the following equation:

Equation 2. Aggregate Degree of Match (ADoM)

$$ADoM = \frac{\sum_{i=1}^{n} W_i \times sim(f_i^N, f_i^R)}{\sum_{i=1}^{n} W_i}$$

where n is the number of ranked dimensions, W_i is the importance of dimension i, sim is the similarity function for primitives, and f_i^N and f_i^R are the values for feature f_i in the new problem and the retrieved case respectively.

The evaluation function sums the degree of match for all the dimensions as computed in the object and data type comparison step (I and II) and takes aggregate of this sum by considering the importance of dimensions.

The accuracy of Web services discovery and matchmaking is dependent on the right combination of indexing, ranking and the existence of adequate cases in the case library.

Although the chosen case study for this work is from the travel domain, the modular, ontology-driven design of framework makes it application-independent and allows its seamless reuse for other application domain.

4. EXTENDING THE SCBR MATCHMAKING FRAMEWORK TO FACILITATE WEB SERVICES COMPOSITION

The SCBR framework elaborated in section 3 addresses the problem of automatic Web services discovery and matchmaking by annotating Web services runtime behaviour and storing them into a case base. The search considers domain-specific criteria and user preferences to find a Web services execution experience that solved a similar problem in the past. However, the framework assumes that the case library contains suitable cases for every

possible problem. This assumption is not always satisfied considering the vast number of problems and problem parameters. For example, a new problem might contain constraints and preferences that were not evaluated in existing cases, therefore requiring further evaluation of existing cases to adapt them to the new constraints and preferences. Moreover, the framework also needs to deal with situations where the aggregate degree of match (ADoM) is below the domain-specific expected degree of match set by the domain administrator or to deal with negative user feedback, where the matched services are not acceptable to the user. The following section addresses these limitations and presents a novel approach to case adaptation (Hammond, 1986.) as an extension to the SCBR framework for solving the problem of Web services composition. This novel approach is characterized by knowledge based substitution and planning based transformation of existing cases.

4.1. Introduction to Case Adaptation

Case adaptation is termed as the REVISE phase in CBR theory and is applicable when the available cases cannot fulfil the problem requirements, so matchmaking is attempted by adapting available cases. Adaptation looks for prominent differences between the retrieved case and the current case and then applies formulae or rules that take those differences into account when suggesting a solution (Watson, 1994).Case adaptation can be defined by the following formula:

Equation 3. Case Adaptation

$$C' = \alpha(C)$$

where, C' = new case, C = old case(s) and α indicates adaptation operator.

The adaptation operator indicates the process of identifying and substituting or transforming an existing solution to fit new situations and is used in knowledge-based substitution adaptation.

4.2. Knowledge Based Substitutions

In CBR's matchmaking process previous cases cannot be always reused without making some adaptation to the existing solutions. The reasoning about these changes requires general and domain specific knowledge *(K)* to mould case adaptation. Under this circumstance, Equation 3 can be reformulated as:

Equation 4. Knowledge based Substitution

$C'=\alpha(C,K)$

In our SCBR framework, we advocate a new, knowledge-exhaustive approach to automate the process of adaptation in the CBR-inspired Web services discovery and composition solution. Web services composition is an extremely complex task to autonomously undertake by a software agent, therefore to avoid involving human intelligence in the loop, software agents need all the relevant domain specific and independent knowledge to be at their disposal. Our approach is novel as existing approaches focus primarily on semantic descriptions of Web services but are oblivious to the fact that the process of Web services matchmaking might invalidate the consistency of the constrains imposed by the problem description as several autonomous Web services are composed to deliver the solution.

In Equation 4, *K* indicates the influence of general or domain specific knowledge that is used for the following purposes:

1. Targeting situations where an exact match is neither available nor possible.
2. To help the reasoner in operating more efficiently by ignoring the unnecessary search and exploration.

3. To make absolutely sure that the only possible solution is transformation (which is an expensive operation involving AI planner or some sort of ultra-intelligent, resource expensive exercise). For example, if for the current problem *P*, the available cases in the case library are

$C_1 \; (S_1+S_2, \; F_1)$,

$C_2 \; (S_2+S_3, \; F2)$

$C_3 \; (S_1)$,

$C_4 \; (S2)$

$C_5 \; (S_1+S_2, \; F5)$

The interpretation of this formalism as follows: $C_1 \; (S_1+S_2, \; F_1)$ indicates a case that has services S_1 and S_2 as a solution under circumstances defined by F_1. These circumstances could be service description, problem description, constraints and preferences in the problem request P_1.

The successful knowledge based substitution should solve a new problem with *P* with a possible solution $(S_1 + S_2, F_3)$ by exploring the matching cases C_1 and C_5 first before transforming C_3 and C_4 to find a solution from scratch.

After identifying the criteria and expectations from knowledge based substitutions (KBS), the following section formalizes how knowledge can be represented using semantic web technologies.

4.3. Representing Knowledge Using Semantic Web Technologies

The semantic web provides a rich knowledge representation which allows a domain expert to encode the knowledge required to model the required knowledge based substitution. The knowledge can be represented in terms of concept relationships defined by ontologies. For the benefit of the discussion, we believe it is necessary to revisit the following components of semantic web formalism:

Taxonomy Relationships (TR)

Taxonomy is the concepts' classification system facilitated by the semantic web. *Class* and *Individual* are the two main elements of this structure where a class is simply a name and collection of properties that describe a set of individuals. Examples of relationships between concepts at the taxonomy level are *class, subclass, superclass, equivalent class, individual, sameAs, oneOf, disjointWith, differentFrom, AllDifferent*.

For example, we anticipate description discrepancies due to the possibility of heterogeneous service and case representations in our framework. In these circumstances, *TR* could be used to encode a heuristic with explicit knowledge that a particular class or property in one ontology is equivalent to a class or property in a second ontology. In this situation, a casual model can be developed which states these facts. For instance:

$O1 \cdot \text{TravelDomain} \equiv O2.\text{Travel}$

Where $\equiv$ represents *equivalentClass* and *O1* and *O2* are two different ontologies.

Similarly a *TR* element *sameAs* can equate two individuals.

O1.Cities.Paris=O2.City.Paris

Where = represents *sameAs, O1* and *O2* are two different ontologies, Paris (City) and Paris (City) are part of ontology *O1* and *O2* respectively.

Similarly *TR* could be used to describe knowledge that is not explicit but requires some level of reasoning to derive inference and relationship between two components of semantic descriptions, where matching the value *M* will be:

$M=Dist(S,D)$

Where *Dist* is the function which finds the semantic distance between source *(S)* and destination *(D)* concepts.

To evaluate implicit relationships and the matching distance *M*, we use *subsumption* and *classification* to perform semantic tree traversal and compare concepts with respect to the semantic network tree as detailed in our retrieval algorithm in section 3.7.

Rules Based Relationships (RR)

Semantic Web Rule Language (SWRL) defines rule based semantics using a subset of OWL with the sublanguages of Rule Mark-up Language (RuleML) (Horrocks, 2004).

The use of rules to define complex concept relationships is highlighted with the following example. Let's assume that there is a service provider adhering to a different version of taxonomy than that expected by the composer, and subscribes to the category *LicencedTaxi*. While matchmaking, the composer will fail unless there is a casual model or heuristic bridging the gap between categories of the service *LicencedTaxi* and the categories that the composer is aware of. If a rule such as the one described below exists, then the composer will be able to infer indirect subclass relationship between *Taxi* and *LicencedTaxi* and assigns matching factor of *M*, where $M = o1.LicencedTaxi \subset o2.Taxi = \frac{1}{2} (0.5)$.

Taxi (? t) ^ Licence (? l) ^ hasLicence (? t,? l)
-> LicencedTaxi (?t)

After identifying how knowledge is represented in the semantic web, in the following section we formalize the levels at which this knowledge is applied to achieve knowledge based substitution.

4.4. Applying Knowledge Based Substitution (KBS) to the Matchmaking Framework

Applied to the current framework, when the existing Web services experiences in their original form (case description) are not sufficient to satisfy current request, the framework uses KBS for relaxing the case restrictions under which a solution is acceptable. The following section explains the process of utilizing KBS in the existing system. In our set up, we anticipate application of KBS at two levels:

I. Description Level

In this category, using the available domain-specific and domain-independent knowledge, modification is made to the new problem and the old case descriptions to prepare the SCBR framework for the new problem request. For example, if the new problem request adheres to a case description D_1 and there is no case with similar descriptions in the case library but there is a case with description D_2 that is potentially similar to the description D_1 then the framework uses the knowledge base *(KB)* to verify if D_1 and D_2 are equivalent. On success, the framework employs routine matchmaking algorithm to find a respective case which matches to new problem request.

II. Solution Level

In this category using the available domain-specific and domain-independent knowledge, modification is made to the solution part of an existing case to adapt the solution for the new problem request. This adaptation is required if for instance on one hand the solution is satisfactory because the problem description matches the case representation in the case library or if they do not match but the description level step is successful in resolving discrepancies, but on the other hand the resultant highest degree of match is below the domain specific average or the result presented to the user is rejected by them.

In our efforts to implement case adaptation at the solution level we came to a similar conclusion as the authors of (Watson, 1994) that modification is a complex process since the local solutions typically exhibit inconsistencies when modified and merged with other solutions. This is one of the most complex problems of implementing CBR systems and precisely the reason why the majority of composition approaches bypass adaptation entirely by building advisory systems that human users rely on to perform the adaptation themselves thus denting the automation of the composition process.

To illustrate the problems in adaptation we will take an example of a travel trip problem where the system needs to find a solution, satisfying constraints on variables such as price, travel domain, currency. While, adapting a solution which already satisfies currency and price but not travel domains, then the challenge is to find a service that satisfies travel domain constraint while not violating already satisfied constraints of price and currency.

The fact that the variable currency depends on the travel domain instance, hence change in airline will affect the output currency, needs to be documented. This observation raises a new challenge of encoding variable dependency as the framework should use such dependency relationships to make sure that while adapting existing solution for the new problem request it does not violate any of the previously satisfied constraints. Therefore, some mechanism is necessary to maintain the integrity and consistency of the framework in order to prevent scenarios where contradicting constraint causes inconsistency as described with the aforementioned example while applying knowledge base substitution.

In our framework, we have designed a novel methodology based on Constraint Satisfaction Problem (CSP) to address this challenge and handle the inconsistency problem with a CSP inspired Domain Dependency Module (DDM). Our approach allows defining the dependency between the variables of the domain and ensuring the consistency of solutions by maintaining the dependency constraints between these variables whenever a solution is adapted.

4.5. Defining Variable Dependency in the SCBR Framework

The constraint satisfaction problem (CSP) (Freuder, 1978) is a powerful and extensively used AI paradigm. Solving the constraint satisfaction problem involves finding values for variables subject to restrictions on which combinations of values are acceptable. Formally speaking, CSP is defined by a set of variables $Z=\{X_1, X_2, ..., Xn\}$, and a set of constraints $C = \{C_1, C_2, ..., C_m\}$. Each variable X_i has a nonempty domain D_i of possible values. Each constraint C_i involves some subset of the variables and specifies the allowable combinations of values for that subset. A state of the problem is defined by an assignment of values to some or all of the variables, $\{X_i = v_i; X_j = v_j ...\}$. An assignment that does not violate any constraints is called a consistent or legal assignment. A complete assignment is one in which every variable is mentioned, and a solution to a CSP is a complete assignment that satisfies all the constraints.

CSP problem can be modelled as a graph called CSP graph. CSP graph is a representation of CSP where the vertices are variables of the problem and the edges are constraint between variables. Vertices are referred to as *nodes* and edges are called *arcs*. A *Node* represents the domain variables and an *arc* represents the relationship between variable nodes. These relationships could be of type dependent →, independent ⇕, incremental etc and can be formalized using different constraint operators.

Commonly used techniques to solve CSP problems examine two types of consistency to solve problems.

a. Node Consistency
b. Arc Consistency

Node consistency ensures that every component or variable satisfies its domain constraint. Hence, for every variable X, values $x \in Domain[X]$, that x satisfied constraint on X. For example, region variable w in a colouring problem should have values from red, green or blue.

In order to maintain Arc consistency, for every variable X, $x \in Domain[X]$ and for all variables Y (Kumar, 1992), there needs to be a value $y \in Domain[Y]$, such that relationship C(X, Y) is satisfied by $\{X \leftarrow x, Y \leftarrow y\}$ and such value Y is called support for x. If X does not receive support from one of its neighbours then X is inconsistent.

We term such definition of variables and their dependency in our framework as the Domain Dependency Module (DDM).

Semantic Description for the Domain Dependency Module

Figure 5 illustrates a partial view of the DDM description for the exemplified travel domain case study where the dependency relationship between domain variables currency, solution, QoS and domain are described. The arrows in the graph describe dependency directions, for instance *currency* is dependent on *solution* variable and *solution* variable is dependent on the *domain* variable.

When applied to the Web services composition problem where the framework requires a formal methodology to describe the constraint on the variables and a way to formalize the consistency criterion on variables, the definition of CSP is modelled as follows (travel domain exemplified):

Figure 5. DDM for travel domain

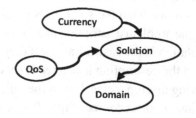

The variables are $Z = \{w = currency, x = solution, y = domain, z = QoS\}$

The domain for the variables is $Dw = \{Any\ currency\ apart\ from\ P\}$

$D_x = \{Any\ solution\ apart\ from\ Q\}$
$D_y = \{Any\ travel\ domain\ apart\ from\ R\}$
$D_z = \{Any\ double\ but\ at\ least\ S\}$

The constraints on the variables are $C = \{w{\to}x, x{\to}y, z{\to}x\}$

Category of Constraints

The types of constraints defined using CSP are broadly classified as illustrated in Figure 6, which are termed constraint behaviour.

Our survey of relevant literature revealed that there are no semantic descriptions that provide ontology for describing CSP problem. Hence we have created an ontology for the CSP descriptions which covers *Functional, Resource, Reliance,* and *Precedence* behaviours applicable in various domains and also modelled this ontology in generic fashion making it amenable for extension and reuse.

In our research work we are only concentrating on the *Reliance* behaviour of CSP in order to address the dependency relationship between domain variables and explore this particular constraint behaviour in detail.

Reliance

Arc constraints are considered as *Reliance* constraints when the variables in the systems have relationship $X{\to}Y$, implying that if values of X changes then value of Y also changes. The DDM ontology section related to handling the *Reliance* constraint behaviour is illustrated in Figure 7. The figure highlights our approach to encode *Reliance* concept as OWL ontology where the concept is implemented as an OWL class with an object property *dependsOn* which relates two variables as a dependency (reliant) relationship.

After formalizing domain dependency module to define and solve variable dependency using CSP, in the following section the *ApplyKBS with DDM* algorithm is described, which takes advantage of DDM to overcome consistency problems while applying KBS for Web services composition.

4.6. ApplyKBS with DDM: DDM Inspired Knowledge Based Substitution in SCBR

In the application of available knowledge at the solution level, modification is made to the solution part of an existing case to adapt the solution to the new problem request. This adaptation is required if for instance on one hand the solution is satisfactory because the problem description

Figure 6. Constraint behaviour definition in DDM

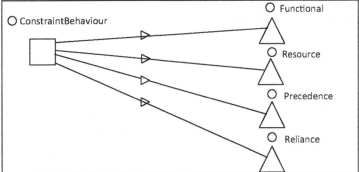

Figure 7. DDM reliance: An optional module

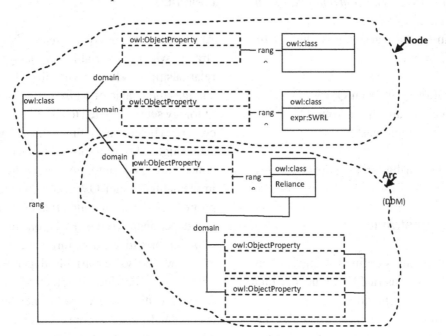

match the case representation in the case library or if they do not match but the description level step is successful in resolving discrepancies, but on the other hand the resultant highest degree of match is below the domain specific average or the result presented to the user is rejected by them. In this scenario, let's say P a represents a new adaptation problem that has the following specifications:

$P(R, c_e, S_e, C)$, where c_e is the existing case with S_e as solution that has the highest $ADoM$ as a result of the matchmaking process for the request R. However, the solution violates the problem constraint cs that is based on variable v. Lets say, S_e is a solution composed of a finite set of service instances $I(i_1, i_2, \dots i_n)$ and C is the case base which contains finite set of cases in case library $(c_1, c_2 \dots c_e \dots c_n)$ then problem P is to discover a case C_d with atomic solution S_d with service instance i_d which replaces the contradicting solution instance i_c in S_e consistently and satisfies request R.

Our approach using DDM is described as follows:

To assist the reasoner in finding a solution, let's assume that there exists an acyclic CSP graph (DDM) G that depicts relationship between the domain variables V. Then following steps are performed:

1. Retrieve the initial state of the problem. This is achieved through creating a tree from the CSP graph G and finding the root of the violated variable v assuming the tree representation of the graph. The variable is stored in the path of variable v including the root variable; let's say that these variables are a set V_1. Next retrieve the variables from this set that are dependent on the root variable using dependency relationships; let's say these variables are $V - V_1 = V_2$.

2. Start with the initial state. Vary the value of the root variable while applying node and arc consistency on the variable sets V_1 and V_2 to observe consistency. For Web services composition this corresponds to finding other service instances I_d from the same or related domains using TR and RR relation-

ships. Next retrieve the cases that contain these atomic services. These cases will be considered ball park cases B and will be scrutinized further.

3. Exclude any case from the ball park cases B which still violate constraint cs for variable v.

4. Apply node and arc consistency on ball park cases for the variables set V_1, where node consistency will be measured against request R for finding cases with maximum value, giving a set of cases that are least violating the constraints in the request. Repeat the same process with arc consistency while measuring it against relationships in V_1. Resultant qualified cases from both sets of consistency are called plausible cases L.

5. Apply node and arc consistency on plausible cases for the variables set V_2, where node values will be compared against execution values e in S_e for finding cases with maximum value, giving a set of cases that are least violating the existing parts of solution. Similarly arc consistency will be measured against relationships in V_2. The resultant qualified case is called solution cases C_d.

6. Retrieve replacement service instance I_d from the solution case C_d and modify the existing solution S_e to replace the violating instance i_e with the new concept I_d. Apply the following algorithm *modifyOWLS (S_e, i_e, i_d)* to create a new OWL-S description file. Finally save new case with this new file as a solution.

Algorithm ModifyOWLS

Assuming that there exists an OWL-S process which satisfies problem P and the process is assumed to be a composite process of services S_1 and S_2. If there is a mechanism in place to verify that service S_3 is similar in functionality and semantic descriptions to S_1, then following is the list of main components that need to be modified in order to

create a new process with composition of S_2 and S_3 which will also be able to solve problem P.

1. Replace *Import* URLs of S_1 with S_3
2. Replace atomic process belonging to S_1 with the functionally similar atomic process of new service S_3
3. Bindings of old service S_1 have to be replaced with functionally and semantically similar bindings from the new service S_3.

5. IMPLEMENTATION AND EVALUATION

5.1. Overall Architecture of the SCBR Framework

A context diagram of the SCBR framework components is given in Figure 8. SCBR allows service participants to perform their publishing, composition and discovery tasks in a transparent manner, where the framework components work as a black box that dynamically matches service requests with published service definitions.

The CBR controller module is the first point of entry for the framework users and provides matchmaking and ranking of existing services to service request and also performs lightweight knowledge-based substitutions of service descriptions if the resultant solution is unsatisfactory.

The indexer module is responsible for assisting the controller in effective discovery of Web services using indices to index cases in the case library. The adaptation engine module performs substitutions of service solution components if the controller fails in finding satisfactory results and generates new executable composition schemes using the case adaptation process.

The execution engine allows enacting existing or newly generated composition schemes. The case library and knowledge base store assist the framework in finding relevant results by supplying the knowledge that is stored in terms of cases and heuristic rules. The error reporting and recovery

Figure 8. SCBR framework modules

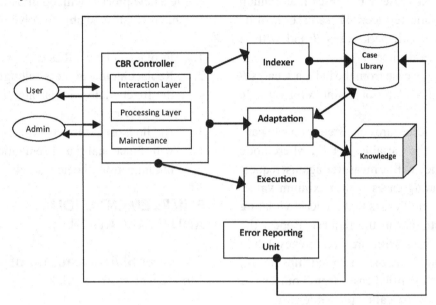

unit stores any errors and exceptions occurring during the framework operations into the case library to avoid redundant error processing.

5.2. Evaluation of the SCBR Framework

This section presents the result of the experiments that were carried out to evaluate the precision and recall of Web services discovery and composition using the SCBR framework.

Experiments Design

For the implementation of the SCBR framework, OWL was the ontology language of choice and Pellet (Sirin, 2007), a Java based OWL reasoner, as the ontology engine in favour of the more popular Jena (McBride, 2002) as it supports user-defined simple types. Pellet was used to load and verify (type and cardinality) ontology class instances of user requests and candidate cases.

The frameworks which are analyzed and compared with our own approach are an implementa-

tion of OWL-S matchmaker and jUDDI (Cooper, 1997), which is a private UDDI registry.

The main motivation behind selecting these tools for comparison is to evaluate our framework against two diverse approaches which are widely adopted by industry and academia.

The experiments were performed on closely coupled workstations within our departmental LAN, the connection speed of which is 100 Mbit/se. The Web services are developed using Apache Axis 1.2 and are hosted on Web services container provided by Apache Tomcat server 5.5. The hardware configuration for the end user is a PC with AMD Athlon XP processor (2.01GHz), 1 GB of RAM and 100 Mbit/sec connection speed running on Windows XP platform.

In the developed test bed, there are 150 Web services with variety of sub-domains from travel industry and 250 cases involving these Web services in the case library.

R-Precision for Ranking Based Web Services Discovery and Matchmaking

For evaluating frameworks for fine-grained queries the widely used measures of precision and recall are insufficient as these measurements are set-based measures, i.e. measuring the performance of frameworks is based on the number of correct documents retrieved as opposed to the number of correct documents retrieved in the correct rank order with the most relevant on the top (Codd, 1970). R-precision provides an alternative to these measures and provides a methodology that relies on measuring the performance of frameworks based on the ranked retrieval.

Following is the definition of R-Precision when applied to the Web services discovery and matchmaking problem:

Equation 5. R-Precision of Web services search engine

$$R\text{ - }precision = \frac{r = Relevant\ Web\ services\ from\ Top\ R\ number\ of\ results}{R = Relevant\ Web\ services\ to\ request}$$

R is the number of relevant services to a request and *r* is the number of relevant services from the top *R* results of a framework, then R-Precision for this framework will be *r/Rel*. For example, a query

"Bus service with payment in currency USD" has 5 relevant service, and a particular framework's response to the query with top 5 results has 3 relevant services then the *R-Precision* for such framework will be 3/5 = 0.6.

We perform 10 fine-grained queries on jUDDI and SCBR framework to find out the average R-Precision for both the frameworks. As jUDDI only supports matchmaking and has no provision for composition, to evaluate on fair ground we turn off the adaptation phase in SCBR framework. Figure 9 charts result of the experiments for comparing R-Precision for jUDDI and SCBR frameworks.

The average R-Precision for SCBR is 0.672 compared to 0.124 in jUDDI. The support for high-granularity in case representation to describe service requests make it possible for SCBR to allow specifying fine-grained queries and interpret them semantically. However, the precision performance depends on the availability of knowledge in terms of cases, hence as high as 100% precision was recorded for the request 4 and request 6 while precision for the request 5 was a low 20%.

For experimenting with jUDDI, we compose as many random queries as possible and retrieve results from the registry and for each request we take mean value of these results.

Figure 9. Comparison using R-Precision

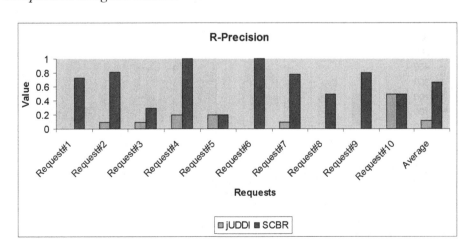

5.3. Performance Study

The performance of framework is not the main concern of the result of our research as our research mainly focuses on the presentation of Web services by semantic languages and the design of a general framework for service discovery and composition instead of the development of new semantic reasoner.

Figure 10 shows the result of performance study on frameworks. The measured time is inclusive of external factors such as background threads served by CPU. As shown in the graph, an average request is answered by jUDDI in 98.84 sec, by OWL-S matchmaker in 212.82 seconds and by SCBR framework in 370.94 seconds. The results are indicative rather than conclusive as there are various optimization techniques employed by a mature implementation such as jUDDI, while the other implementations use basic optimization techniques. However, these results highlight the fact that the reasoning in OWL-S and SCBR framework is slower than a database search methodology adopted by frameworks such as jUDDI registries. The difference in the execution time

of OWL-S matchmaker and SCBR highlights the fact that the addition of knowledge consideration in SCBR on top of OWL-S functional parameter matchmaking has considerable overhead.

These results confirmed our objective of using Case Based Reasoning with semantic web for Web services discovery and composition to improve the precision and recall of Web services search with acceptable level of performance.

6. RELATED WORK

Semantic descriptions are increasingly being used for exploring the automation features related to Web services discovery, matchmaking and composition. In Zhang (2003) such semantic-based approach is described. The authors use ontology to describe Web services templates and select Web services for composition by comparing the Web service output parameters with the input parameters of other available Web services. A constraint driven composition framework in Aggarwal (2004) also uses functional and data semantics with QoS specifications for selecting Web services.

Figure 10. Performance study

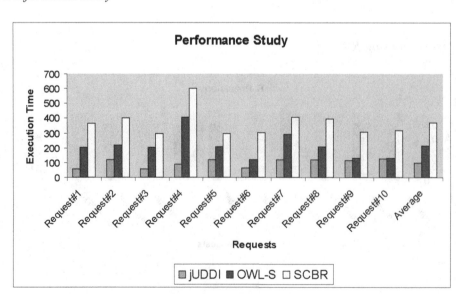

In similar spirit, DARPA's OWL-S (Ontology Web Language for Web services) is the leading semantic composition research effort. OWL-S ontologies provide a mechanism to describe Web services functionality in machine-understandable form, making it possible to discover, and integrate Web services automatically. An OWL-S based dynamic composition approach is described in (Sirin, 2004.), where semantic description of the services are used to find matching services to the user requirements at each step of composition, and the generated composition is then directly executable through the grounding of the services. Other Approaches use Artificial Intelligence planning techniques to build a task list to achieve composition objectives: selection of services and flow management for performing composition of services to match user preferences. Mcilraith (2002) uses Golog – AI planning Reasoner for automatic composition, while in a similar spirit some other approaches such as Wu (2003) have used the paradigm of Hierarchical Task Network (HTN) planning to perform automated Web service composition. These approaches use semantic technologies for automatic Web services discovery, but they overlook the Web service run-time behaviour in the decision-making process.

Experience based learning using CBR is a relatively old branch of Artificial Intelligence and cognitive science and is being used (Hammond, 1986) as an alternative to rule-based expert system for the problem domains, which have knowledge captured in terms of experiences rather than rules. However, case based reasoning for Web services was initially documented in (Limthanmaphon, 2003), where the developed framework uses CBR for Web services composition. In their approach, the algorithm for Web services discovery and matchmaking is keyword based and has no notion for semantics. This affects the automation aspects for Web services search and later for composition. A similar approach is described in Diaz (2006), which proposes an extension of the UDDI model for Web services discovery using category-

exemplar type of CBR, where Web services are categorized in domains and stored as exemplar of particular domain. Their implementation of CBR reasoner facilitates UDDI registry by indexing the cases based on the functional characteristics of Web services. However, the approach does not take into consideration the importance of non-functional parameters in service selection and the use of semantics at CBR level is peripheral as they primarily use the UDDI based component for service discovery. The UDDI registry based publication and discovery is text-based leaving little scope for automation. The SCBR framework consumes semantics extensively and achieves the automation required for Web service discovery and matchmaking. Use of ontologies also makes framework extensible and reusable.

The application of CBR, semantic web and Web services are common technologies in our research effort and the efforts by Agre (2005), albeit with different objectives. Their work is based on consuming these technologies to assist the procedure of semantic Web services creation using CBR approach, while our main concern is services composition. The authors present INFRAWEBS project to implement Semantic Web Unit (SWU) which is a collaboration platform and interoperable middleware for ontology-based handling and maintaining of semantic Web services. The framework provides knowledge about a specific domain and relies on ontologies to structure and exchange this knowledge to semantic Web services development process.

There are also a number of existing approaches which apply CBR for workflow modelling. Madhusudan (2004) propose an approach to support workflow modelling and design by adapting workflow cases from a repository of process models where workflow schemas are represented as cases and are stored in case repositories. The cases are retrieved for a problem which requires similar business process to solve the problem. The description and implementation language of the framework is based on XML and main focus is on assisting workflow designer in creating business process flows.

In similar spirit, Cardoso (2005) presents adaptive workflow management system based on CBR and targets highly adaptive systems that can react to different business and organization settings. The adaptation is achieved through CBR based exception handling, where the CBR system is used to derive an acceptable exception handler. The system has the ability to adapt itself over time, based on knowledge acquired about past execution experiences that will help solve new problems. The approach discussed in this chapter concentrates on Web services as a unit of computation to take advantage of highly accessible and loosely coupled nature of Web services technologies. The focus is on utilising service execution experiences to best serve user requirements and encode the framework with semantics.

Recent work on Web services discovery by Zaremba (2007) have drawn similar conclusion about considering run-time behaviour of services. They realize the limitation of matching static behaviour of services in semantic and non-semantic approaches and propose that service discovery that operates on abstract descriptions of services needs to be further elaborated in order to return results of concrete services satisfying concrete goals. For this purpose they utilize instance data using data-fetching algorithm from the service provider at discovery-time. The authors use abstract state machine formalism (Gurevich, 2000) to model the interface allowing scalable interactions with a service provider for specific discovery sessions. However a drawback of interacting with a service during the discovery phase can be a significant communication overhead and in circumstances where the service provider does not provide interface for data-fetching services or does not provide such service at all. In contrast, the SCBR framework chiefly relies on existing service and service interface to capture the knowledge required to evaluate the run-time behaviour of services.

7. CONCLUSION

Semantic description of Web services' profiles paves the way for automating the discovery and matchmaking of services since it allows intelligent agents to reason about the service parameters and capabilities. However, the accuracy of such automatic search mechanism largely relies on how soundly formal methods working on such semantic descriptions consume them.

In this chapter, we argued for the importance of considering the execution values for semantically described functional and non-functional Web services parameters in decision making regarding Web service adequacy for a certain task. While the static behaviour of a service can be measured in terms of whether the service has a similar description to the problem in terms of functional and non-functional parameters, the run-time behaviour of a service is the result of service execution and how the service will behave under different circumstances, which is difficult to presume prior to service execution. We implemented a Semantic Case based Reasoner (SCBR), which captures Web service execution experiences as cases and uses these cases for finding a solution for new problems. We have experimented with this implementation and demonstrated that the accuracy of automatic matchmaking of Web services can be further improved by taking into account the adequacy of past matchmaking experiences for the requested task.

A central theme of our approach to the problem of automated Web services discovery and composition is to explore existing solutions before devising a full-fledged solution from scratch. To achieve this we apply case adaptation process by adapting local solutions from previously solved problems to create a globally consistent solution for the new problem.

While investigating case adaptation we discovered that the process of modifying existing solutions is more complex than reported in the literature. When individual service instances are composed, they might compromise the consistency of the solution primarily because they originate from different solution sets. We have designed a methodology based on investigating the Constraint Satisfaction Problem (CSP) to address this challenge and address the inconsistency problem with a CSP inspired Domain Dependency Module (DDM). Our approach allows defining dependency between variables of the domain and ensuring the consistency by maintaining dependency constraints between these variables whenever a solution is adapted.

We carried out quantitative analysis of our framework where we have performed experiments to evaluate the effectiveness of SCBR framework using the R-precision measurements and have used execution time for measuring efficiency. The results of the experiments have shown that SCBR has higher precision compared to UDDI and OWL-S albeit there are performance penalties in developing a higher level semantic web based tool such as SCBR. It is feasible to believe that this performance shortcoming will steadily improve, as processing costs decrease and the need for more intelligently and automatically integrate services increases. Hence, the presented results demonstrate the effectivness of our composition methodology. The results also reveal that the incurred overheads are acceptable since the developer has the opportunity to balance the performance against the application requirements giving the indicator of applying SCBR approach to Web services discovery and composition.

8. REFERENCES

Aamodt, A., & Plaza, E. (1994). Case-based reasoning: Foundational issues, methodological variations, and system approaches. *AI Communications*, *7*(1), 39–59.

Aggarwal, R., Verma, K., Miller, J., & Milnor, W. (2004). *Constraint driven Web service composition in Meteor-S*. IEEE International Conference on Services Computing. Shanghai, China, September 15-18, 2004. IEEE Computer Society, (pp. 23-30).

Agre, G., Atanasova, T., & Nern, H.-J. (2005). *Case-based Semantic Web service designer and composer*. Euromedia 2005. Toulouse, France, April 11-13, 2005. Springer Verlag, (pp. 226-229).

Andrews, T., Curbera, F., Dholakia, H., Goland, Y., Klein, J., Leymann, F., et al. Weerawarana, S. (2007). *Business process execution language for Web services*, version 1.1. Retrieved from http://www-128.ibm.com/developerworks/library/wsbpel/

Cardoso, J., & Sheth, A. (2005). *Adaptation and workflow management systems*. International Conference WWW/Internet, Lisbon, Portugal, 19-22 October, 2005. (pp. 356-364).

Chakraborty, D., & Joshi, A. (2001). *Dynamic service composition: State-of-the-art and research directions*. (Technical Report TR-CS-01-19, 2001), Department of Computer Science and Electrical Engineering, University of Maryland, Baltimore County, Baltimore, USA.

Codd, E. F. (1970). A relational model of data for large shared data banks. *Communications of the ACM*, *13*(6), 377–387. doi:10.1145/362384.362685

Cooper, W. S. (1997). *On selecting a measure of retrieval effectiveness* (1st ed.). San Francisco, CA: Morgan Kaufmann Publishers Inc.

Diaz, O. G. F., Salgado, R. S., Moreno, I. S., & Ortiz, G. R. (2006). *Searching and selecting Web services using case based reasoning*. Workshop on Ubiquitous Web Systems and Intelligence (UWSI 2006) In Conjunction with Computational Science and Its Applications (ICCSA 2006). Glasgow, UK, May 8-11, 2006. (pp. 50-57). Berlin/ Heidelberg, Germany: Springer.

Freuder, E. (1978). Synthesizing constraint expressions. *Communications of the ACM, 21*(11), 958–966. doi:10.1145/359642.359654

Gurevich, Y. (2000). *Abstract state machines: Theory and applications* (1st ed.). Berlin, Germany: Springer. doi:10.1007/3-540-44518-8

Hammond, K. (1986). *Learning to anticipate and avoid planning problems through the explanation of failures*. Fifth Conference on Artificial Intelligence, AAAI86. Philadelphia, USA, August 11-15, 1986. Morgan Kaufmann, (pp. 556-560).

Horrocks, I., Patel-Schneider, P. F., Boley, H., Tabet, S., Grosof, B., & Dean, M. (2004). *SWRL: A Semantic Web rule language combining OWL and RuleML*. W3C member submission. Retrieved on June 10, 2007, from http://www.w3.org/Submission/SWRL/

Kolodner, J. (1993). *Case-based reasoning* (1st ed.). San Mateo, CA: Morgan Kaufmann.

Kumar, V. (1992). Algorithms for constraint satisfaction problems: A survey. *AI Magazine, 13*(1), 3–44.

Limthanmaphon, B., & Zhang, Y. (2003). *Web service composition with case-based reasoning*. The Fourteenth Australasian Database Conference on Database Technologies. Adelaide, Australia, February, 2003. ACM International Conference Proceeding Series, (pp. 201–208).

Madhusudan, T., Leon Zhao, J., & Marshall, B. (2004). A case-based reasoning framework for workflow model management. *Data & Knowledge Engineering, 50*(1), 87–115. doi:10.1016/j.datak.2004.01.005

Maigre, R. (2010). *Survey of the tools for automating service composition*. ICWS, (pp. 628-629). 2010 IEEE International Conference on Web Services

Mandell, D., & McIlraith, S. (2003). Adapting BPEL4WS for the Semantic Web: The bottom-up approach to Web service interoperation. In *Proceedings of the 2nd International Semantic Web Conference* (ISWC2003), Sanibel Island, Florida, 2003.

McBride, B. (2002). Jena: A Semantic Web toolkit. *IEEE Internet Computing, 6*(6), 55–59. doi:10.1109/MIC.2002.1067737

Mcilraith, S., & Son, S. (2002). *Adapting Golog for composition of Semantic Web services*. The 8th International Conference on Principles of Knowledge Representation and Reasoning. Toulouse, France, April 20-22 2002. Morgan Kaufmann. (pp. 482-496).

Osman, T., Thakker, D., & Al-Dabass, D. (2005). Bridging the gap between workflow and Semantic-based Web services composition. In the *Proceedings of the Workshop on WWW Service Composition with Semantic Web Services 2005* (wscomps05*), the 2005 IEEE/WIC/ACM International Joint Conference on Web Intelligence (WI 2005) and Intelligent Agent Technology (IAT 2005)*, Compiègne, France, September 19, (pp. 13-23). ISBN 2-913923-18-6

Purvis, L., & Pu, P. (1995). *Adaptation using constraint satisfaction techniques*. The First International Conference on Case-Based Reasoning Research and Development. Springer, (pp. 88-97).

Remind. (1992). *Developer's reference manual, cognitive systems*. Boston.

Schank, R., & Abelson, R. (1979). Scripts, plans, goals, and understanding: An inquiry into human knowledge structures. *The American Journal of Psychology, 92*(1), 176–178. doi:10.2307/1421499

Sirin, E., & Parsia, B. (2004). *Planning for Semantic Web services*. In Semantic Web Services Workshop at the 3rd International Semantic Web Conference. Florida, USA, November 8-10, 2004.

Sirin, E., Parsia, B., Grau, B., Kalyanpur, A., & Katz, Y. (2007). Pellet: A practical Owl-Dl reasoner. *Web Semantics: Science, Services and Agents on the World Wide Web*, *5*(2), 51–53. doi:10.1016/j.websem.2007.03.004

Thakker, D., Osman, T., & Al-Dabass, D. (2005). Web services composition: A pragmatic view of the present and the future. In the *Proceedings 19th European Conference on Modeling and Simulation*, (pp. 826-832). ISBN 1-84233-112-4

Traverso, P., & Pistore, M. (2004). Automated composition of Semantic Web services into executable processes. In *Proceedings of Third International Semantic Web Conference* (ISWC2004), November 9-11, 2004, Hiroshima, Japan, (pp. 380-394).

Watson, I., & Marir, F. (1994). Case-based reasoning: A review. *The Knowledge Engineering Review*, *9*(4), 355–381. doi:10.1017/S0269888900007098

Wu, D., Parsia, B., Sirin, E., Hendler, J., & Nau, D. (2003). *Automating DAML-S Web services composition using SHOP2*. The 2nd International Semantic Web Conference (ISWC2003). Florida, USA, October 21-23, 2003. IEEE computer society, (pp. 195-210).

Yen, V. (2009). Trends of Web services adoption: A synthesis. In Al-Hakim, L. (Ed.), *Business Web strategy: Design, alignment, and application* (pp. 134–144). Hershey, PA: Idea Group Publications. doi:10.4018/978-1-60566-024-0.ch007

Zaremba, M., Vitvar, T., & Moran, M. (2007). *Towards optimized data fetching for service discovery*. The European Conference on Web service. Halle, Germany, November 26-28, 2007. IEEE Computer Society, (pp. 191-200).

Zhang, L. J. (2008). EIC editorial: Research innovations in service-oriented solutioning. *IEEE Transactions on Services Computing*, *1*(3), 129. doi:10.1109/TSC.2008.21

Zhang, R., Budak, I., & Aleman-Meza, B. (2003). *Automatic composition of Semantic Web services*. The International Conference on Web Services, ICWS '03. June 23 - 26, 2003, Las Vegas, Nevada, USA. CSREA Press 2003, (pp. 38-41).

Chapter 4
Semiotic Evaluation of Product Ontologies

Joerg Leukel
University of Hohenheim, Germany

Vijayan Sugumaran
Oakland University, USA & Sogang University, Korea

ABSTRACT

Product-related information can be integrated with the help of a product ontology, which can provide consensual definitions of concepts and inter-relationships relevant in a product domain of interest. A product ontology is either given by a third party or results from ontology engineering. In both cases, the problem is how to assess its quality, and then select the "right" ontology. This chapter: (1) proposes a metrics suite for product ontology evaluation based on semiotic theory, and (2) demonstrates the feasibility and usefulness of the metrics suite using a supply chain model. The contribution of this research is the comprehensive metrics suite that takes into account the various quality dimensions of product ontology.

INTRODUCTION

Product-related information is of paramount importance in many inter-organizational applications, since it concerns goods and services being procured, manufactured and sold to customers. Due to the involvement of multiple organizations, there is a need for integrating product-related information, e.g., by standardization or mediation. In the past years, *product ontology* has attracted

both industry and academia because of its potential contribution to solving integration problems. Major fields of application are e-commerce (Shim & Shim, 2006), product engineering (Yoo & Kim, 2002), and product life-cycle management (Matsokis & Kiritsis, 2010). A product ontology provides, at least to some extent, consensual definitions of concepts and inter-relationships between these concepts in a product domain of interest. Most product ontologies define a hierarchy of product classes and respective properties for describing product instances. Such ontologies may support

DOI: 10.4018/978-1-60960-595-7.ch004

finding and comparing products being offered by multiple suppliers and described in distributed data sources, or allow for benchmarking the procurement activities of organizational units (Doring et al., 2006). Ontology users are required to annotate their product instance data accordingly.

Product ontologies have already emerged in diverse industries and for various tasks. However, assessing the quality and suitability of a given product ontology, i.e., to what degree it actually meets user requirements, remains a critical question for potential ontology adopters. This question is the focus of *ontology evaluation*, which aims at providing metrics reflecting the ontology's quality and suitability. There is great difficulty in determining what elements of quality to evaluate. In other words, what factors should be considered in evaluating product ontology quality? Current research yields a number of approaches, metrics, and tools for automatically evaluating ontologies; for an overview, see (Vrandecic, 2009). However, most of this research originates from the Semantic Web arena, and therefore relies mainly on the expressiveness of ontology languages such as DAML (DARPA Agent Markup Language) and OWL (Ontology Web Language); hence their scope is constrained by these languages and does not take the specific setting of product ontology into account.

Very often, an ontology is regarded as an artifact used by a community as a common vocabulary without considering the organizational properties of the respective community and thus the interrelations within the community (Zhdanova et al., 2007). For example, a community that often uses product ontologies is made of entities belonging to a supply chain. A supply chain is a system of entities participating in producing, transforming, and distributing goods and services from supply to demand. A single product ontology is thus used within supply chains and determining its quality and suitability has to consider the supply chain characteristics, e.g., by distinguishing different roles such as manufacturer and distributor. A major

trend affecting supply chains is individualization, caused by customers demanding individualized products, which are tailored to their specific needs (e.g., custom-made products) (Coates, 1995) (Kirn, 2008). For instance, enabling customers to order custom-made shoes via an e-commerce application does not only concern the e-commerce firm but also the stakeholders in the respective supply chain (e.g., manufacturer and its suppliers). Here, a product ontology may help provide a common terminology and means of describing products along the entire supply chain.

In the context of supply chain and individualization, a product ontology should emphasize the importance of quality metrics that allow the assessment of product complexity in terms of richness of product description and product structure, and how the final product is composed of individual parts. Current evaluation metrics do not take these factors into account: Domain-independent metrics are not able to exploit the domain characteristics (e.g., Yao et al., 2005), whereas domain-specific evaluation metrics regard products as single and atomic items without considering existing interrelations that arise due to supply chain structures and customer requirements (e.g., Hepp et al., 2007). To overcome this limitation, we address product ontology evaluation on a broader scale by taking a semiotic perspective. Semiotics studies the properties of signs; for our purposes, it can provide a theoretical basis for distinguishing generic categories of quality. We define evaluation metrics based on Stamper's et al. (2000) semiotic framework and adopt the domain-independent semiotic metrics suite proposed by Burton-Jones' et al. (2005).

The objectives of this research are to: (1) develop a semiotic set of metrics that allow for assessing the quality of product ontologies, and (2) apply the metrics to two commonly available product ontologies to demonstrate the feasibility and usefulness of the metrics suite. The contribution of this research is the comprehensive metrics suite that takes into account the various quality dimensions of product ontologies. A preliminary study of semiotic metrics for product ontology evaluation can be found in (Leukel & Sugumaran, 2007). The contribution of this research is that the current work adapts the metric suite developed by Burton-Jones et al. (2005) to the product domain in the context of supply chain management to determine which metrics are applicable and how they relate to the existing work in the product ontology domain. We map the metrics developed in both streams of research and develop a unified set of metrics for the product ontology domain.

The rest of the chapter is organized as follows. The next section reviews related work. After that, we define the basic model of supply chain and product ontology. The subsequent section presents our semiotic metrics suite. In the section that follows, we provide a preliminary validation of the metrics. Finally, we draw some conclusions and outline avenues of future research.

RELATED WORK

The related work can be grouped into two major areas: product ontologies and ontology evaluation. Despite the former's importance, it is rather a specialized field which attracts interest from communities such as knowledge engineering (e.g., Fensel et al., 2001), data management (e.g., Beneventano et al., 2004), e-commerce (e.g., Leukel, 2004), and certainly product data management. While the phrase 'product ontology' is often used to stress the formal specification aspect, other widely used terms, though not equal in meaning, are 'product classification standard' or 'product classification system'. The quality and suitability of such artifacts, however, have rarely been the focus of dedicated research. Many researchers take these ontologies for granted and do not further investigate their structure and content.

To the best of our knowledge, only the work by *Hepp et al.* provides product ontology metrics as well as results of extensive quantitative evalu-

ation (Hepp et al., 2007). While these metrics analyze product ontologies to a great extent and their rationale reflects a lot of domain expertise, they are confined only to the product ontology. Thus, they do not investigate the relationship between the ontology and, for instance, its users, the ontology language, or other ontologies. With regard to semiotics, Hepp et al.'s metrics concern the pragmatic dimension only.

Ontology evaluation in general aims at assessing the relevance of diverse types of ontologies. There is a growing research community which develops methodologies, models, and tools for ontology evaluation, e.g., EON Workshop Series (Garcia-Castro et al., 2007). Studying the ontological quality is made difficult by a number of factors. Contrary to Information Retrieval, for instance, one cannot easily define the metrics 'precision' and 'recall', since these require a clear set of items – here concepts, inter-relations, and properties – being relevant in the respective domain of interest (Brewster et al., 2004). Ontology evaluation can be classified using attributes, for instance as described in (Hartmann, 2004) and (Brank et al., 2005). For the purpose of our work, we focus on one attribute which distinguishes functionality and structure.

The *functionality* of an ontology describes how suitable and appropriate it is for its intended usage in an information system. There are two major approaches. First, one could relate the ontology directly to requirements of the respective task. In this case, such requirements need to be elicited, formalized, and then mapped to elements of the ontology. Second, one could select a particular ontology and compare it to a reference ontology. The shortcoming of both approaches is that both requirements and the reference ontology for the domain of interest can be incomplete, wrong, lacking, and if available, subjective. This is in particular true for broad product ontologies such as UNSPSC[1], eOTD[2] and eCl@ss[3], which all aim at becoming the first reference and global standard. Thus comparing them to another reference ontology is not feasible.

The *structure* of an ontology is formed by its elements and inter-relations. A major stream of research is rooted in the Semantic Web arena and its approaches rely on ontology languages such as OWL and its predecessor DAML+OIL. By systematically checking the actual usage of language features such as classes, properties, axioms, instances etc., one can determine the structural characteristics. For instance, complexity metrics are defined in (Yang et al., 2006); they include number of concepts, relations and paths, and the mean of relations and paths per concept. Similar metrics can be found in (Huang & Diao 2006), which defines metrics for assessing how balanced a taxonomy is. However, both proposals represent only a limited subset of the entire ontology language features and respective structural aspects.

A more elaborate set of metrics describing cohesion can be found in (Yao et al., 2005). Based on graph theory, these metrics determine the degree of relatedness of concepts in an ontology. Though mathematically sound, the results of such metrics cannot easily be interpreted in terms of quality. The same is true for many structural metrics. For instance, whether a big, nested ontology is better than a smaller one depends primarily on the domain of interest. This point of criticism complements the fact that structural metrics in general rely on the expressiveness of ontology languages (thus on what can be described formally). Consequently, these metrics should be regarded as a component of a broader evaluation framework.

The most comprehensive framework for ontology evaluation is proposed by Vrandecic (2010). This framework is itself specified in an ontology. It consists of six aspects, which determine the subject of evaluation: vocabulary, syntax, structure, semantics, representations, and context. These aspects are then related to concrete evaluation criteria and applicable evaluation methods (i.e., formal procedures). It differs from our approach in that Vrandecic has analyzed the criteria found in five research papers and summarized them into a super-set, while we ground the evaluation on semiotic theory.

The review of related work points out that (1) generic ontology evaluation limits its scope by respective ontology languages and thus cannot fully exploit the quality of domain ontologies, in particular product ontologies which rather rely on size and deepness than on formal complexity, and (2) domain ontology evaluation requires not only extensive domain expertise, but also an ontological foundation to arrive at both suitable and well-defined metrics. Most current research exploits the pragmatic quality dimension only without taking into account the setting of an ontology. By employing semiotics theory, the proposed metrics suite aims at overcoming these deficits.

BASIC MODEL OF SUPPLY CHAIN AND PRODUCT ONTOLOGY

A supply chain model is a representation of entities participating in producing, transforming and/or moving goods or services from suppliers to customers (Steven, 1989; Supply-Chain Council, 2007). Such a model thus includes both products and organizations which we call actors. The inter-relations between actors are constituted by the flow of products. We define the supply chain model as a directed graph $S=(A,F)$ using the following notions.

A: set of actors
a: element of A
F: set of flows of products with $F \subseteq A \times A\text{-}1$
f: element of F connecting two actors, $f = (a_i, a_j)$

To allow for distinguishing the specific role of each actor within a supply chain, we define five generic roles: 1) OEM, 2) N-tier supplier, 3) distributor, 4) retailer, and 5) customer. These roles represent the generic types of participants in a supply chain. A specific supply chain may include several instances of each of these roles. Typically, a supply chain is made of two major parts being separated by the original equipment manufacturer (OEM). The left hand side role of n-tier suppliers describe how the product is made from parts (thus it focuses on procurement and manufacturing) with n denoting the number of supply chain stages. For instance, by assigning the 1st tier supplier role to different actors each supplying a different part of the final product, one can represent the product structure in the supply chain model. 2nd tier suppliers provide products to the 1st tier supplier etc. The right hand side roles participate in distributing the product from the OEM across one or more stages which are: distributor and retailer. Respective actors do not apply manufacturing assets but change the product with regard to location (e.g., by moving), time (e.g., by storing at warehouses), and quantity (e.g., by bundling and unbundling) until the product reaches the final customer. The sequence of roles can be regarded as the reference structure of many real-world supply chains, as shown in Figure 1. Note that this simple model contains only one actor for each role whereas in reality multiple actors exist for almost any supply chain stage.

Product ontology evaluation focuses on the ontology constructs that are used in this type of ontology. Product ontology relies essentially on providing an often broad and deep hierarchy of product classes based on is-a relationships, while other relationship types play a minor role. Having reviewed current product ontologies, we define product ontology *PRO* as a 6-tuple *PRO=(PC,RC,PP,RP,PV,RV)* as defined in Table 1.

The relationship between supply chain and product ontology model is two-fold. First, since the arrows (F) connecting two actors in the supply chain model represent flows of one or more products, each such arrow (f) has to be mapped to at least one respective product class $pc \in PC$ in the ontology; otherwise the ontology would not be able to cover the respective part of the supply chain model. Figure 2 shows an example how product flows can be annotated with references to product classes (pc) to describe the product structure along the supply chain stages (e.g., wheels being assembled from tires and rims).

However, this type of relationship does not reflect how well the product class represents the semantics of the product flow. For instance, choosing rather abstract product classes would allow for describing many different product flows, but lose the actual semantics (e.g., by replacing all classes in Figure 2 with a generic class for automotive parts). Therefore, a second relationship has to be considered, which reflects the richness

Figure 1. Reference structure of supply chains

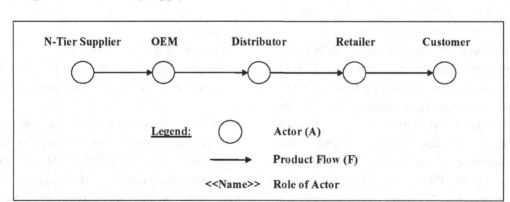

Table 1. Elements of product ontology

Element		Definition
PC	set of product classes	A product class *pc* represents the product concept and often consists of, besides the class name, natural language definition and some data management information (e.g., identifiers, version etc.).
RC	set of relations between product classes	Is-a relations build a hierarchy of product classes with $RC \subseteq PC \times PC$; often a taxonomy with top-level classes $CT \subseteq PC$ for separating domains (e.g., automotive, chemical, textile etc.).
PP	set of product properties	A product property *pp* is a template for describing product instances; consists of property name, a natural language definition, data type, and unit of measurement.
RP	set of class-property relations	Maps properties of *PP* to classes *PC* with $RP \subseteq PC \times PP$; the semantics of such relations can range from loose recommendation to mandatory.
PV	set of property values	Values *pv* for properties besides standard data types such as integer, float, and string. Used for expressing a narrower domain, e.g., for colors, shapes, materials etc.
RV	set of property-value relations	Maps values of *PV* to properties PP with $RV \subseteq PV \times PP$.

Figure 2. Example: Relationship between supply chain and product ontology

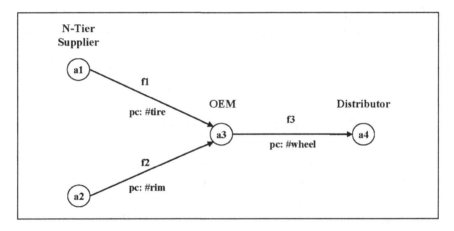

of the product class. Thus, additional information from the product ontology is used to specify a product flow in greater detail. In the example shown in Figure 2, it is not specified whether the wheels are for cars, trucks, or both. If the product ontology contains more specific classes, one could, for instance, describe the supply chain of a specialized OEM which produces wheels for trucks only more precisely.

PROPOSED METRICS SUITE

In this section, we propose a metrics suite for product ontology evaluation based on semiotic theory (Stamper et al. 2000) and earlier work by Burton-Jones et al. (2005). First, we introduce the semiotic approach to ontology evaluation and define the basic metrics. Then we define five categories of semiotic metrics.

Semiotics

Stamper et al. (2000) present a general theoretical semiotic framework derived from linguistics that includes general elements of quality for evaluating signs. It includes pragmatic issues to develop a metrics suite that is widely applicable yet can be tailored to the needs of specific applications. They provide a 6-level semiotic framework to support the analysis of signs: a) physical, b) empirical, c) syntactic, d) semantic, e) pragmatic, and f) social. There is a strong relationship between the successive levels, i.e., each level contributes to the next level. The physical level deals with representation of signs in hardware, components, etc. and the empirical level is concerned with communication properties of signs including channel capacity, noise, and entropy. Since these levels are very implementation specific, they may not be highly relevant to quality assessment (Burton-Jones et al. 2005). The remaining levels are considered in developing the metrics suite for quality assessment.

Based on these levels, Burton-Jones et al. (2005) have developed a metric suite that consists of syntactic, semantic, pragmatic, and social qualities. As mentioned above, they do not include physical and empirical quality since they correspond to implementation aspects. With regard to product ontology, these two stages can also be omitted because signs do exist (physical in terms of explicit concepts) and can be seen (empirical in terms of a formal representation of the concepts). For our purposes, their metric suite can provide a theoretical basis for developing metrics, because (1) the general semiotic framework takes the various dimensions of the meaning of signs into account, and (2) it has been proven to be applicable and valuable for ontology evaluation.

Metrics

The metrics suite originally proposed by Burton-Jones et al. (2005) is adapted for the product ontology domain. While the metrics themselves and their constituent parts are applicable to product ontologies, additional constructs specific to the product ontology domain are identified and added to the overall metric suite. In particular,

we consider the work of Hepp et al. (2007) in identifying additional constructs and create a unified set of metrics by explicating the similarities and differences between the two sets of metrics discussed in the literature.

The overall quality Q of an ontology is computed using a weighted function of its syntactic (S), semantic (E), pragmatic (P), and social (O) qualities (Burton-Jones et al. 2005):

$$Q = b_1 \times S + b_2 \times E + b_3 \times P + b_4 \times O$$

The weights sum to unity. In the absence of pre-specified weights, the weights are assumed to be equal. Since the numerical values of these relative scores could exceed one for any given ontology, the scores for these metrics are normalized so that the values of all metrics vary between zero and one prior to calculating the overall ontological quality. According to Burton-Jones et al. (2005), the values for a given ontology will depend on external benchmarks such as the metric's average value across all ontologies in the ontology library. With respect to product ontology, the small size of the respective ontology library may prevent using such a benchmark.

Syntactic Quality

Syntactic Quality S measures the quality of the product ontology according to the way it is written. It consists of *Lawfulness,* the degree to which an ontology language's rules have been complied, and *Richness,* the proportion of features in the ontology language that have been used in an ontology. Lawfulness is entirely domain-independent because one would require that any given product ontology complies with the syntax of the ontology language used. Otherwise the ontology cannot be processed. The interpretation of richness, however, must consider the requirements of the product domain with respect to expressiveness. For instance, if a highly expressive language based on description logic is used but the domain does not require much reasoning support, the richness metric would have quite a low value.

Semantic Quality

Semantic Quality E evaluates the meaning of terms in the product ontology. Three attributes are used in this metric: interpretability, consistency, and clarity.

Interpretability refers to the meaning of terms in the ontology (e.g., names of product classes and product properties). Meaning could be determined by checking whether the terms used can be found in the product domain of interest, for example, by searching the standards and references. *Consistency* is whether terms have a consistent meaning in the ontology. The appearance of the same term in more than one concept could indicate inconsistency. *Clarity* is whether the context of terms is clear. For example, if a product ontology claims that class "Chair" has the property "Material", an application must know that this describes furniture, and not academics.

Pragmatic Quality

Pragmatic Quality P refers to the product ontology's usefulness for users, irrespective of syntax or semantics. Three criteria are used for this metric, namely, accuracy, comprehensiveness, and relevance.

Accuracy is whether the claims about products an ontology makes are "true." In general, it can only be determined by domain experts, or by reasoning if the product ontology defines respective relationships between concepts. *Comprehensiveness* is a measure of the size of the ontology. Larger product ontologies are more likely to be complete representations of their domains, and provide more knowledge to the user. Size could indicate both how well the product domain is covered and to which degree of detail it is represented by explicit concepts. However, one has to be careful since sometimes, simply considering the total number

of concepts and relationships may lead to false assessments. *Relevance* is whether the ontology satisfies the user's specific requirements. It could be calculated by checking against a set of explicit requirements articulated for a particular scenario.

Social Quality

Social quality O reflects the fact that users and product ontologies exist in communities. It consists of two attributes, namely, authority and history. The *authority* is the number of other ontologies that link to it. More authoritative product ontologies signal that the knowledge they provide is accurate or useful. The *history* is the number of times the ontology is accessed, and more precisely how often its concepts are used in actual product-related information systems. It is assumed that ontologies with longer histories are more dependable.

For the purpose of evaluating product ontologies in the context of supply chain management, comprehensiveness can be used as an indicator for both coverage of supply chains and richness of the product concepts (as defined in the basic model section). Therefore, we extend the comprehensiveness metric at this level by integrating the work of Hepp el al. (2007), which proposes an elaborate set of pragmatic metrics for product ontology evaluation. We select the relevant metrics and transform their definition into our notation of product ontology. The result is shown in Table 2, which depicts the following four aspects of product ontology quality: (1) amount of ontology content, (2) hierarchical order and balance of scope, (3) class-specific property sets, and (4) ontology growth and maintenance.

Based on our analysis of the product categorization standards work by Hepp et al. (2007), it is evident that there is some commonality between the metrics identified by Hepp et al. (2007) and Burton-Jones et al. (2005). Table 3 summarizes the integrated product ontology metrics The initial set of metrics identified by Burton-Jones et al. (2005) are still applicable for the product domain

Table 2. Determination of pragmatic metrics of Hepp et al. (2007)

Aspect	Metric	Determination
Amount of content	M11: Number of classes	Number of elements in PC, i.e., $M11 = |PC|$
	M12: Number of properties	Number of elements in PP, i.e., $M12 = |PP|$
	M13: Number of enumerative data types	Number of elements in PV, i.e., $M13 = |PV|$
Hierarchical order and balance of scope	M21: Number of classes per top-level class $CT_i \subseteq PC$	Number of elements in PC which are subclass of CT_i
	M22: Services ratio	(Number of elements in PC representing services) / (number of elements in PC)
	M23: Distribution properties of metric M21	Minimal value, maximal value, mean, median, first quartile, third quartile, interquartile range, standard deviation, and coefficient of variation of M21
	M24: Percentage of content in the three biggest top-level classes CT	(Number of subclasses of the three biggest classes CT) / M11
	M25: Size of the biggest top level class vs. median of M21	(Number of subclasses of the biggest class CT) / median of M21
	M26: Number of descendents per subordinate class CO_n	Number of elements in RC with CO_n superclass of CO_m
Class-specific property lists	M31: Specific property lists ratio	(Number of elements in PC with a specific property list in RP) / M11
	M32: Distribution of specific property lists per top-level class CT_i	(Number of elements in PC which are subclass of CT_i and have a specific property list in RP) / M21
	M33: Property usage in property lists	Minimal value, maximal value, mean, median, standard deviation, and coefficient of variation of {number of elements in RP with PP_i}
	M34: Semantic weight of property PP_i	1 / (number of property lists in RP including PP_i)
	M35: Semantic value of property lists	Sum of M34 for each property PP in property list of class PC_i
Growth and maintenance	M41: Number of new classes per month	((Number of elements in PC in the current version of PRO) – (number of elements in PC in the former version of PRO)) / (number of months between publication of the current and former version of PRO)
	M42: number of new classes per top-level class CT_i	M41 for CT_i

ontology, however, the pragmatic quality metric *P* is extended with some additional metrics.

PRELIMINARY VALIDATION

In this section, we provide a preliminary validation of the proposed semiotic metrics suite. We apply the metrics suite to a supply chain scenario and demonstrate its relevance and usefulness. We describe the experimental design, report the results, and discuss the findings.

Validation Scenario

The purpose of the experiment is to demonstrate the feasibility and usefulness of the metrics suite in the specific setting of product ontology. In the context of individualization or mass customization in supply chains, we consider the following 5-tier supply chain model in the IT industry (Figure 3): The ultimate goal of the supply chain is to deliver custom-made desktop computers to end customers. The supply chain consists of a retailer, distributor, OEM, and three 1st tier suppliers with $S=(A, F)=(\{a1,a2,a3,a4,a5,a6,a7\}, \{f1,f2, f3,f4,f5,f6\})$.

Product flows *f1, f2,* and *f3* represent parts, whereas *f4* and *f5* represent both parts and computers; *f6* is computers only. This supply chain model enables different options for individualization. For instance, both the distributor and retailer can create a new bundle of computers and parts and offer it as individualized computers.

In the above supply chain scenario set up for individualization, we study the use of two ontologies:

- eCl@ss which is available in both an OWL representation called eClassOWL (Hepp, 2006) and in simple comma-separated value files. The eCl@ss is originally an international classification scheme for goods and services, and thus is of practical importance in many industries and countries (eCl@ss, 2008).
- UNSPSC, the United Nations Standard Products and Services Code, which is also an international classification scheme; it is only available in a spreadsheet format and lacks product properties. However, this ontology is widely used in inter-organizational information systems and thus relevant (UNSPSC 2010).

We conduct different levels of validation. First, we pre-check each metric whether it can be applied and what results can be expected. Then, we apply those metrics and evaluate how well the product ontology can be used to support individualization in the supply chain scenario. In

Table 3. Product ontology metrics [adapted from Burton-Jones et al. (2005)]

Metric	Definition
Overall Quality (Q)	$Q = b_1 \cdot S + b_2 \cdot E + b_3 \cdot P + b_4 \cdot O$ where: $b_1,..,b_4$: weights
Syntactic Quality (S)	$S = b_{s1} \cdot SL + b_{s2} \cdot SR$ where: *SL*: Lawfulness *SR*: Richness
Semantic Quality (E)	$E = b_{e1} \cdot EI + b_{e2} \cdot EC + b_{e3} \cdot EA$ where: *EI*: Interpretability *EC*: Consistency *EA*: Clarity
Pragmatic Quality (P)	$P = b_{p1} \cdot PO + b_{p2} \cdot PU + b_{p3} \cdot PR$ where: *PO*: Comprehensiveness *PU*: Accuracy *PR*: Relevance
Social Quality (S)	$O = b_{o1} \cdot OT + b_{o2} \cdot OH$ where: *OT*: Authority *OH*: History

particular, we focus on the metrics that are the most relevant for our purposes, namely, *Interpretability*, *Consistency*, *Clarity*, and *Relevance*, since they refer to semantics and pragmatics. The results of our analysis are discussed in the next section.

Results

Table 4 summarizes the results of pre-checking of each metric. This assessment of eCl@ss and

Figure 3. Supply chain model used in validation

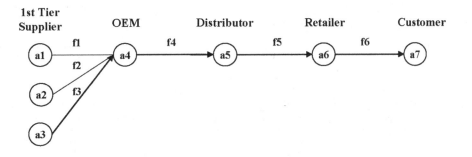

UNSPSC ontology shown in Table 4 does not relate to the supply chain model yet, but provides the general findings.

Next, we report on applying the individual metrics to the supply chain scenario. Specifically, we highlight our findings with respect to *Interpretability, Consistency, Clarity,* and *Relevance* metrics using a snapshot of eCl@ss and UNSPSC. We choose a sample of 100 classes from the fourth level from eCl@ss; the relevant *segment 19* is entitled 'Information, communication and media technology'. From UNSPC, we choose 100 classes from the fourth level of its *segment 43* ('Information Technology Broadcasting and Telecommunications').

Lawfulness and Richness. In a supply chain context, participants exchange product information. If the participants use different descriptions, ontologies can be used to resolve differences. To automate this process, ontologies should be machine processable. The eClassOWL representation has been checked by OWL tools and it is syntactically correct, however, the spreadsheet version contains several data errors. With respect to Richness, the eClassOWL uses only a few OWL language features (missing, e.g., unionOf, intersectionOf, inverseOf). Unlike eClassOWL, UNSPSC is provided in a spreadsheet format only, which would first require a conversion into an ontology language. Thus, lawfulness is restricted to the very generic syntax of spreadsheets. Richness is also lower, because the ontology is actually only a taxonomy, constructed from is-a relationships.

Interpretability of the terms used in eCl@ss and UNSPSC is checked by searching for respective entries in WordNet. For eCl@ss, WordNet returns respective entries for 97 out of 100 terms (which correctly refer to IT). The three missing terms can be explained by typos and not separating words correctly (i.e., 'computersystem', 'mainmemory', and 'harddrive'); these probably could have been retrieved by using a more capable stemmer. The result for UNSPSC is very much the same, with retrieving 97 entries correctly. There

Table 4. Applicability and results of metrics for eClassOWL and UNSPSC

Metric	Applicability and Results
Lawfulness (SL)	eClassOWL is syntactically correct and has been checked formally by respective OWL tools. Its spreadsheet version contains several data errors though; see Hepp et al. (2007). UNSPSC is provided in a spreadsheet format which is not an ontology language; therefore this metric is not applicable.
Richness (SR)	eClassOWL uses rather few OWL language features (missing, e.g., unionOf, intersectionOf, inverseOf). UNSPSC is only a taxonomy, thus a conversion into an ontology language would use very few language features (e.g., only class and subClassOf).
Interpretability (EI)	The meaning of terms used in eClassOWL and UNSPSC can be checked by searching for entries in a reference dictionary
Consistency (EC)	Inconsistencies can occur if is-a relationships are used falsely; here, cross-checks with reference dictionaries could help identify those.
Clarity (EA)	Interpreting terms at the lowest level of the taxonomy should consider the scope or context defined by its super classes.
Comprehensiveness (PO)	All detailed metrics can be applied; see Hepp et al. (2007) for results.
Accuracy (PU)	Whether a claim made is true or false can only be determined by domain experts. Reasoning cannot help, because there are is-a relationships only.
Relevance (PR)	Whether eClassOWL and UNSPSC provide the knowledge required by an application could at least partly be answered by querying the ontology based on explicit requirements.
Authority (OT)	No ontology in the public ontology repositories link to eClassOWL or UNSPSC yet.
History (OH)	Accesses to eClassOWL can be recorded by the ontology provider only. eCl@ss is mostly used in non-public applications, thus acceptance can hardly be determined. The same holds true for UNSPSC.

are two instances of compound spelling ('motherboards' 43201513, 'daughterboards' 43201507). Surprisingly, WordNet does not know the word 'expander' at all, which is used as a designator of class 43201605.

This result shows quite a high interpretability of the terms used in eCl@ss and UNSPSC; we did not search for too technical or new terms (such as acronyms of interface standards) because WordNet has not been designed for technical domains. We thereby acknowledge that the results of the interpretability metric also depend on the quality of WordNet, which is used as the reference dictionary. We assume that the share of equal terms is lower in specific product domains (e.g., chemical domain) than in broader ones.

Consistency relates to the correct usage of is-a relationships. We examined the same sample of 100 product classes and made the following observations:

- The general layout of the eCl@ss taxonomy is consistent with separating computer systems from parts. The former is classified into notebook, PDA, server, PC etc.; the latter into graphic card, cooler, drive etc. Thus, the rationale is to arrive at increasingly specialized product classes.

- The structure of UNSPSC follows the same rationale. The differences relate to width and depth of the class hierarchy, resulting in a higher level of detail (the number of classes at the fourth level is about four times higher).

- In eCl@ss, this rationale is, however, violated by inserting six generic product classes for both computer systems and parts (12 inconsistent classes in total). These classes represent 'other' goods (that do not belong to any other class), 'parts' (in the most generic sense), 'accessories,' 'assembly,' 'maintenance service' and 'repair.' The usage of such generic product classes cannot only be observed in the sample, but in the entire eCl@ss ontology.

Clarity of the terms used in eCl@ss relates to both product classes and properties, while in UNSPSC only to product classes. The classes are exclusively part of a four-level taxonomy. Therefore, the context of each term in the sample is already defined by the name of the top-level segment, and on the lower levels by names of classes on levels 2 and 3. In eCl@ss, some terms at lower levels make the context explicit by extending the class name. For instance, the class 'Mouse (computer input device)' is a sub class of 'Input device for computer'; such an extension is made only for improving interpretation by human readers and not machines. With regard to product properties, there are some generic properties (e.g., 'manufacturer name', 'supplier product number') which are assigned to every single class, whereas other properties are specific and used in few or even one class only. We can state that clarity is high for all properties in the sample due to how properties are used in eCl@ss in general. While eCl@ss adds to some class names keywords (for searching) and a short description (for reading), clarity in UNSPSC must be related to class names only. In general, these names tend to have a higher length. For instance, 'Asynchronous transfer mode ATM telecommunications interface cards' (43201501) resolves the abbreviation ATM. Another observation is that some class names break the rule of plural nouns (in 8 out of 100 classes), though this can be handled by stemming.

Comprehensiveness and Accuracy metrics are typically computed based on domain expert's feedback. For the subsets of eCl@ss and UNSPSC under consideration, all detailed metrics can be applied. For eCl@ss, Comprehensiveness and Accuracy rank high. This is demonstrated by Hepp et al. (2007) in their analysis.

Relevance of the domain knowledge in eCl@ss and UNSPSC can be studied by example queries. This metric also ties the ontology to the supply chain model. We define 5 queries each testing whether the two ontologies provide respective elements, thus being able to represent the required product. Note that these queries relate to the entire ontology, not just the snapshot. The queries and assessments are shown in Table 5.

Authority and History metrics rank very low for the eClassOWL ontology because no ontology in the public ontology repositories links to eClassOWL yet. Similarly, accesses to eClassOWL and UNSPSC can be recorded by the respective ontology provider only. Both ontologies are mostly used in non-public applications, thus acceptance cannot be easily determined.

Implications

The semiotic metrics suite has several implications for users of product ontologies as well as its creators. In particular, applications such as agent-based systems can use the metrics suite to compare and select the most appropriate ontology to be used in a particular task. Ontology evaluation generally ignores specific requirements of a particular organization. Our metrics suite allows the ontology evaluation in the context of a set

of products available from an organization in a supply chain. In other words, our framework helps us take into account the context in which the ontology is used in an organization. Since the metrics go beyond pragmatic dimensions such as comprehensiveness, they can help detect weak points in a given product ontology (e.g., lack of interpretability, inconsistencies, and irrelevant concepts).

Existing tools do not adequately support ontology searching and selection. Our proposed metrics suite provides a framework for evaluation of product ontologies and possibly selecting appropriate ontologies for supporting seamless e-commerce activities. The metrics can also be used by product ontology creators such as industry associations or standardization bodies as a means for analyzing the ontology and generating quantitative information about the various quality dimensions, as defined by the metrics suite.

Table 5. Example queries for assessing the relevance of eCl@ss and UNSPSC

Query	Assessment
Q1: Customer a7 searches for a thin client with specific technical features (i.e., dimensions).	eCl@ss: 'thin client' is linked to the 'personal computer' class by a keyword; requirements can be described using 25 class-specific properties. UNSPSC: a class 'Thin client computers' (43211506) is returned directly; no class-specific properties exist.
Q2: Retailer a6 asks distributors for laptop computers with no software installed in order to create a bundle by himself.	eCl@ss: 'laptop computer' class allows specifying whether software is included or not by the Boolean property 'software included'. UNSPSC: search must use 'notebook' to find the class 'Notebook computers' (43211503); no details about software installed can be expressed.
Q3: Retailer a6 searches for similar offerings from multiple distributors using the product number of the OEM a4.	eCl@ss: All product classes possess, besides the supplier product number, manufacturer name and manufacturer product number, thus enabling respective search beyond the previous stage in the supply chain. UNSPSC: Due to missing property, a search is not possible.
Q4: Distributor a5 searches for a replacement of TFT monitor by plasma monitor.	eCl@ss: The classes for 'TFT monitor' and 'plasma monitor' share the same superclass 'monitor'. However, the two lists of properties are completely different, which prevents supporting the replacement decision. UNSPSC: Two respective classes exist, entitled 'Liquid crystal display LCD panels or monitors' (43211902, LCD instead of TFT) and 'Plasma display panels PDP' (43211904).
Q5: OEM a4 searches for suppliers a1-a3 which can deliver modem cards for all desktop computers.	eCl@ss: The product class for PCs contains a suitable property indicating whether a modem card is present or not; however, this property is not linked to the corresponding class 'telecommunication card' because of limitations of the eCl@ss ontology model which defines is-a relationships only. UNSPSC: The ontology provides a respective class 'Modem cards' (43201403).

CONCLUSION

This chapter proposed a metrics suite for product ontology evaluation based on semiotic theory and demonstrated the feasibility and usefulness of the metrics suite using a supply chain model. The contribution of our research is the comprehensive metrics suite that takes into account the various quality dimensions of product ontology.

Our approach also incorporates the specific setting of product ontologies. This setting is mainly determined by supply chains in which such ontologies are used. Thus, our work has studied supply chains based on a general supply chain model, which allows us to distinguish different roles of actors. In particular, we have addressed the individualization of supply chains which no longer makes it feasible to consider only a small snapshot of a supply chain. For instance, reducing the problem to the relationship between supplier and customer arrives at two-tier supply chain models.

However, finding a suitable product ontology for a particular industry is non-trivial because these ontologies are implemented using a variety of languages, methodologies, and platforms. Assessing their quality and selecting a particular ontology is difficult because of the heterogeneity. We have presented a semiotic set of product ontology metrics that allow for assessing the syntactic, semantic, pragmatic, and social quality, and showed how these metrics could be used for evaluating a real-world product ontology. This metric suite can be used by applications and decision makers to assess the quality of available ontologies in a particular domain. The semiotics based approach sheds light on creating various categories of quality and provides a systematic way to develop quality metrics.

Our proposed product ontology evaluation approach has some limitations. First, it does not provide explicit guidelines for determining the optimal weighting scheme of the various quality dimensions. Second, product ontologies evolve over time and the metric suite does not yet take into account this dynamic nature (Hepp, 2007). Third, it does not include any learning mechanism to update the evaluations based upon feedback from external users. Finally, empirical testing of the approach is needed to validate the relationship between an ontology's internal attributes reflected in its metrics and its external attributes such as its usefulness for supporting an application. Our future work involves: (1) testing our metrics suite in more realistic and comprehensive usage scenarios, (2) developing a tool for automated ontology quality assessment, and (3) applying it to ontologies in other domains.

ACKNOWLEDGMENT

The work of the second author has been partly supported by Sogang Business School's World Class University Program (R31-20002) funded by Korea Research Foundation.

An earlier version of this chapter appeared in the *International Journal of Intelligent Information Technologies*, Vol. 5, No. 4, pp. 1 – 15.

REFERENCES

Beneventano, D., Guerra, F., Magnani, S., & Vincini, M. (2004). A Web service based framework for the semantic mapping amongst product classification schemas. *Journal of Electronic Commerce Research*, 5(2), 114–127.

Brank, J., Grobelnik, M., & Mladenic, D. (2005). A survey of ontology evaluation techniques. *Proceedings of the Conference on Data Mining and Data Warehouses (SiKDD 2005)*.

Brewster, C., Alani, H., Dasmahapatra, S., & Wilks, Y. (2004). Data driven ontology evaluation. *Proceedings of the International Conference on Language Resources and Evaluation (LREC-2004)*.

Burton-Jones, A., Storey, V. C., Sugumaran, V., & Ahluwalia, P. (2005). A semiotic metrics suite for assessing the quality of ontologies. *Data & Knowledge Engineering, 55*(1), 84–102. doi:10.1016/j.datak.2004.11.010

Coates, J. (1995). Customization promises sharp competitive edge. *Research in Technology Management, 38*(1), 6–7.

Doring, S., Kiebling, W., Preisinger, T., & Fischer, S. (2006). Evaluation and optimization of the catalog search process of e-procurement platforms. *Electronic Commerce Research and Applications, 5*(1), 44–56. doi:10.1016/j.elerap.2005.08.004

eCl@ss. (2008). *International standard for the classification and description of products and service*, V8.0. Retrieved September 30, 2010, from http://www.eclass-online.com

Fensel, D., McGuinness, D. L., Schulten, E., Ng, W. K., Lim, E.-P., & Yan, G. (2001). Ontologies and electronic commerce. *IEEE Intelligent Systems, 16*(1), 8–14. doi:10.1109/MIS.2001.1183337

Garcia-Castro, R., Vrandecic, D., Gomez-Perez, A., Sure, Y., & Huang, Z. (2007). *Evaluation of ontologies and ontology-based tools.* Retrieved from http://km.aifb.uni-karlsruhe.de/ws/eon2007

Hartmann, J. (2005). *Methods for ontology evaluation.* (Knowledge Web Deliverable D1.2.3). Retrieved from http://knowledgeweb.semanticweb.org

Hepp, M. (2006). *eClassOWL 5.1. Products and services ontology for e-business, user's guide.* Retrieved from http://www.heppnetz.de/eclassowl

Hepp, M. (2007). Possible ontologies: How reality constrains the development of relevant ontologies. *IEEE Internet Computing, 11*(1), 90–96. doi:10.1109/MIC.2007.20

Hepp, M., Leukel, J., & Schmitz, V. (2007). A quantitative analysis of product categorization standards: Content, coverage, and maintenance of eCl@ss, UNSPSC, eOTD, and the RosettaNet technical dictionary. *Knowledge and Information Systems, 13*(1), 77–114. doi:10.1007/s10115-006-0054-2

Huang, N., & Diao, S. (2006). Structure-based ontology evaluation. *Proceedings of the IEEE International Conference on e-Business Engineering (ICEBE 2006)* (pp. 132-137).

Kirn, S. (2008). *Individualization engineering.* Goettingen, Germany: Cuvillier.

Leukel, J. (2004). Standardization of product ontologies in B2B relationships – on the role of ISO 13584. *Proceedings of the 10th Americas Conference on Information Systems (AMCIS 2004)* (pp. 4084-4091).

Leukel, J., & Sugumaran, V. (2007). Evaluating product ontologies in e-commerce: A semiotic approach. *Proceedings of the 6th Workshop on e-Business (WeB 2007)* (pp. 240-249).

Matsokis, A., & Kiritsis, D. (2010). An ontology-based approach for product lifecycle management. *Computers in Industry, 61*(8), 787–797. doi:10.1016/j.compind.2010.05.007

Shim, J., & Shim, S. S. Y. (2006). Ontology-based e-catalog in e-commerce: Special section. *Electronic Commerce Research and Applications, 5*(1), 1. doi:10.1016/j.elerap.2006.01.001

Stamper, R., Liu, K., Hafkamp, M., & Ades, Y. (2000). Understanding the role of signs and norms in organisations – a semiotic approach to information systems design. *Behaviour & Information Technology, 19*(1), 15–27. doi:10.1080/014492900118768

Stevens, G. (1989). Integrating the supply chain. *International Journal of Physical Distribution & Materials Management, 19*(1), 3–8.

UNSPSC. (2010). *The United Nations Standard Products and Services Code.* Retrieved September 30, 2010, from http://www.unspsc.org

Vrandecic, D. (2009). Ontology evaluation. In Staab, S., & Studer, R. (Eds.), *Handbook of ontologies* (pp. 293–313). Berlin, Germany: Springer. doi:10.1007/978-3-540-92673-3_13

Vrandecic, D. (2010). *Ontology evaluation.* Doctoral dissertation, Karlsruhe Institute of Technology. Retrieved September 30, 2010, from [INSERT FIGURE 001]http://www.aifb.kit.edu/web/Phdthesis3008/en

Yang, Z., Zhang, D., & Ye, C. (2006). Evaluation metrics for ontology complexity and evolution analysis. *Proceedings of the IEEE International Conference on e-Business Engineering (ICEBE 2006)* (pp. 162-169).

Yao, H., Orme, A. M., & Etzkorn, L. (2005). Cohesion metrics for ontology design and application. *Journal of Computer Science, 1*(1), 117–113.

Yoo, S. B., & Kim, Y. (2002). Web-based knowledge management for sharing product data in virtual enterprises. *International Journal of Production Economics, 75*, 173–183. doi:10.1016/S0925-5273(01)00190-6

Zhdanova, A. V., Krummenacher, R., Henke, J., & Fensel, D. (2005). Community-driven ontology management: DERI case study. *Proceedings of the 2005 IEEE/WIC/ACM International Conference on Web Intelligence* (pp. 73-79).

ENDNOTES

[1] http://www.unspsc.org
[2] http://www.eccma.org
[3] http://www.eclass-online.com

Chapter 5
Discovery Process in a B2B eMarketplace:
A Semantic Matchmaking Approach

Fergle D'Aubeterre
Flint Transfield Services Ltd (FT-SERVICES), Canada

Lakshmi S. Iyer
The University of North Carolina at Greensboro, USA

Richard Ehrhardt
The University of North Carolina at Greensboro, USA

Rahul Singh
The University of North Carolina at Greensboro, USA

ABSTRACT

In the context of a customer-oriented value chain, companies must effectively address customers changing information needs during the process of acquiring a product or service to remain competitive. The ultimate goal of semantic matchmaking is to identify the best resources (supply) that fully meet the requirements (demand); however, such a goal is very difficult to achieve due to information distributed over disparate systems. To alleviate this problem in the context of eMarketplaces, the authors suggest an agent-enabled infomediary-based eMarketplace that enables semantic matchmaking. They extend and apply the exact, partial, and potential match algorithms developed in Di Noia et al. (2004) to show how partial and potential matches can become full matches. Specifically, the authors show how multi-criteria decision making techniques can be utilized to rank matches. They describe mechanisms for knowledge representation and exchange to allow partner organizations to seamlessly share information and knowledge to facilitate the discovery process in an eMarketplace context.

DOI: 10.4018/978-1-60960-595-7.ch005

INTRODUCTION

In the context of a customer-oriented value chain, companies must effectively address customers changing information needs during the process of acquiring a product or service to remain competitive. In order to satisfy those information needs, companies must integrate heterogeneous and dispersed information and knowledge resources that span across multiple organizations, it is essential that integrative technologies supply effective standardizations and adaptability to support the transparent exchange of information and knowledge in a value chain.

Implementing and managing the integration of value chain activities over distributed and heterogeneous information platforms such as the Internet, is a challenging task with large potential benefits. Although technical integration of systems is essential, a common language to express context specific constructs and relevant business rules to assist autonomous system entities and decision makers to solve specific business problems is essential (Stal, 2002). Disparate technical systems need the ability to share data, information, and knowledge. A common and shared understanding of the domain-specific concepts and the relations between them is critical for creating integrative views of information and knowledge in eBusiness processes. However, there is paucity in research on distributed information and knowledge sharing that provides a unifying process perspective to share information and knowledge (Oh and Park, 2003).

In this context, the Semantic Web vision provides the technical foundation to support the transparent flow of semantic knowledge representation to automate, enhance and coordinate collaborative inter-organizational eBusiness processes (Singh et al., 2005). The Semantic Web vision comprises *Ontologies* for common semantics of representation and ways to interpret ontology; *Knowledge Representation* for structured collections of information and inference rules for automated reasoning in a single system; and *Intelligent Agent* to collect content from diverse sources and exchange data enriched with semantics (Berners-Lee et al., 2001). This vision provides the foundation for the semantic framework proposed in this research. Semantic technologies incorporate knowledge representation and intelligent software agents to integrate heterogeneous systems across organization.

The ultimate goal of semantic matchmaking is to identify the best resources (supply) that fully meet the requirements (demand); however, such a goal is very difficult to achieve due to information distributed over disparate systems. To alleviate this problem in the context of eMarketplaces, we suggest an agent-enabled infomediary-based eMarketplace that enables semantic matchmaking. In this article, we use a process perspective to integrate knowledge of resources involved in a process with process knowledge including process models and workflows used in process automation. We develop theoretical conceptualizations using ontological analysis that will be formalized using description logics (DL). The ontology will support a common vocabulary for transparent knowledge exchange across inter-organizational systems. DL forms the basis for developing machine interpretable ontologies and knowledge representation using standardized knowledge representation languages such as OWL-DL. We describe mechanisms for knowledge representation and exchange to allow partner organizations to seamlessly share information and knowledge to facilitate the discovery process in a B2B eMarketplace context. We extend and apply the exact, partial, and potential match algorithms developed in Di Noia et al. (2004) to show how partial and potential matches can become full matches. In this context, it is important to note that ranking of exact matches involves the use of multiple criteria and selecting a satisfying solution (Ramesh and Zionts, 1997). Although multi-criteria decision making (MCDM) techniques have been applied in various decision making environments (Slowinski and Zopounidis, 1995; Jacquet-Lagreze, 1995; Weistroffer et al., 1999), to our knowledge, they have not been used in eMarketplace matchmaking. In this article, we show how MCDM techniques such as preemptive priorities, Pareto optimality and Analytic Hierarchy Process (Saaty et al. 2000; 2003) can be used to rank matches.

We describe the setting of our research with a discussion of related work in Section 2, including the role of infomediaries in the eMarketplace; semantic matchmaking; and semantic web technologies. In Section 3 we describe how knowledge can be represented in the semantic web using ontologies and description logics so that intelligent software agents can coordinate resources and execute transactions in business processes. We continue the development of the model in Section 4, where we propose a semantic matchmaking scheme for the discovery process in an infomediary based eMarketplace. We close the article with a summary and suggestions for future research in Section 5.

BACKGROUND

eMarketplace and Infomediary

Electronic marketplaces (eMarketplace) are defined as interorganizational information systems that facilitate the exchange of information about price and product offerings between buyers and sellers that participate in the marketplace (Bakos, 1998). Choudhury et al. (1998) identified the following examples of electronic marketplaces: airline reservation systems (CRSs) such as SABRE and APOLLO (Copeland and McKenney, 1988); American Gem Market System (Lee and Clark, 1996) in the precious stones industry; and TELCOT in the cotton industry (Lindsey et al, 1990). Recently, Amazon.com and eBay.com have become some of the most popular electronic

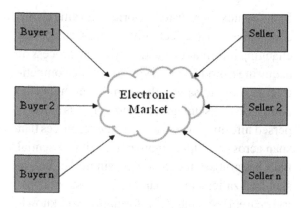

Figure 1. Electronic market (adopted from Choudhury et al., 1998)

marketplaces. Figure 1 depicts the structure of a typical electronic marketplace.

In a decentralized market afforded by the Internet, coordination costs are higher than in a centralized market because decentralized market requires that each buyer communicates with all possible suppliers. The infomediary role in the eMarketplace is to reduce the coordination costs and vulnerability costs of buyer and supplier organizations (Malone, 1987). An eMarketplace is a mechanism that adds value by streamlining information flows within supply chains and rebalancing information asymmetries (Zhu 2002). The main roles of an eMarketplace (Bakos 1998) are:

- *Discovery* – of buyers and suppliers that meet each other's requirements for a potential matchmaking,
- *Facilitation* – of transactions to enable information flows leading to the flow of goods and services among buyers and suppliers, and
- *Support* – of decision processes leading to the development of collaborative relationships between eMarketplace participants.

Infomediaries are vital resources of knowledge about the nature of exchanges in the eMarketplace. The infomediary business model can also add value by providing valuable information to matchmaking decision processes through its role as the repository of experiential knowledge of transactional histories for both buyers and suppliers (Grover and Teng, 2001).

An Infomediary-based eMarketplace is an advanced eBusiness exchange where infomediaries manage information and knowledge exchange to support required eBusiness processes (Grover and Teng, 2001). Knowledge management in the eMarketplace provides critical input to the supplier discovery and selection decision problem while reducing the transaction and search costs for the buyer organization. Infomediaries coordinate and aggregate information flows to support eBusiness processes and provide value-added services to enhance the information processes of the eMarketplace by deciphering component knowledge of products and transactions in the eMarketplace. Infomediaries play a vital role in the exchange of knowledge and information in these knowledge networks embedded within inter-organizational value chains. The transparent flow of information and problem specific knowledge across collaborating organizations, over systems that exhibit high levels of integration, is required in order to enable such inter-organizational eBusiness process coordination (Singh et al., 2005).

Sycara et al. (1999) discuss the role of intelligent agents in dynamic matchmaking through the comparison of features expressed in standardized knowledge representation. Li and Horrocks (2004) describe matchmaking using Semantic Web Technology and discuss the mechanisms for matching in DL-based knowledge representation. Singh et al. (2005) describe the agent communications required for an agent-enabled e-marketplace. This model requires information transparency in the flow of information to allow organizations to coordinate supply chain interactions efficiently in dynamic market conditions. This article highlights the use of emerging technologies and standard business ontologies to facilitate the discovery process as the first step toward creating intelligent

e-marketplaces. Singh et al. (2005) indicate the need for knowledge representation languages that are unambiguously computer-interpretable and amenable to agent interoperability and automated reasoning techniques, such as OWL-DL. They develop the information flows and agent architecture, including agent communications. However, they do not develop the critical knowledge representation needed for intelligent infomediary-based eMarketplaces. The Agent communications in an intelligent-agent infomediary-based B2B eMarketplace is shown in Figure 2.

In this article, we provide standard knowledge representation and apply a semantic matchmaking approach to facilitate the discovery process, which is a critical eBusiness process required for an intelligent infomediary-based B2B eMarketplace. Analysis of the infomediary business model shows that individual buyers and suppliers seek distinct goal oriented information from the infomediary, providing decision parameters through their individual demand or supply functions. This discovery process is essentially a matchmaking activity where buyers and suppliers search for a match of their requirements and preferences through infomediaries. Here, we are interested in the application of semantic matchmaking algorithms and mechanisms to implement the discovery process. In the next section, we discuss related work in the area of Semantic matchmaking and our plans for extending that work in an eMarketplace.

Semantic Matchmaking

Matchmaking is the process of discovering a qualified provider based on a set of desired capabilities specified by a requester (Sycara et al., 2002). Figure 3 shows the process of matchmaking. In such process, three types of collaborating agents, namely Provider, requester, and matchmaking agents, are involved.

Li and Horrocks (2004) define matchmaking as " a process that requires a repository host to

Figure 2. Agent communications in an intelligent agent infomediary-based B2B eMarketplace (Adopted from Singh et al. 2005)

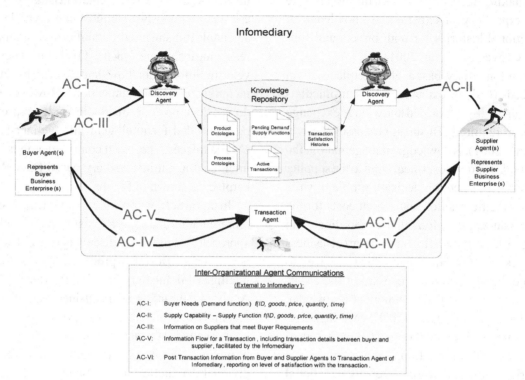

take a query or an advertisement as input, and to return all the advertisements that may satisfy the requirements specified in the input query or advertisement ". Interestingly, Di Noia et al. (2006) make a distinction between matchmaking and semantic matchmaking. They define *matchmaking* as "an information retrieval task whereby queries (a.k.a. demands) and resources (a.k.a. supplies) are expressed using semi-structured text in the form of advertisements, and task results are ordered (ranked) lists of those resources best fulfilling the query". This definition is similar to the one provided by Li and Horrocks (2004), but it includes the semantic ranking of the resulting list

Figure 3. Matchmaking process (adopted from Sycara et al., 2002)

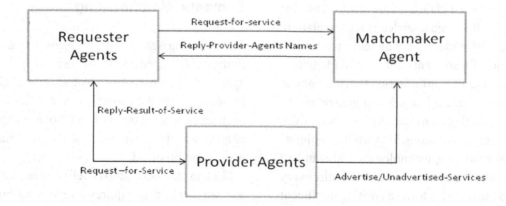

items. On the other hand, they define *semantic matchmaking* as "a matchmaking task whereby queries and resources advertisements are expressed with reference to a shared specification of a conceptualization for the knowledge domain at hand, i.e., an ontology". Semantic matchmaking allows for a dynamic and transparent representation of suppliers and buyers needs. In this article, we are interested in the conceptualization of an architecture that enables *semantic matchmaking* in the context of an agent-enabled infomediary-based eMarketplace.

Several matchmaking systems have been proposed in the literature. For instance, RETSINA (Reusable Task Structure-based Intelligent Network Agents) is a multi-agent infrastructure that relies on service matchmaking. It consists of three different agents: a service provider agent, a service requester agent, and a middle agent that communicate with each other using an agent capability description language called LARKS (Language for Advertisement and Request for Knowledge Sharing). RETSINA implements distributed infrastructural services that facilitate the interactions between intelligent agents. LARKS matchmaking process performs both syntactic and semantic and allow for specification of local ontologies via a concept language. LARKS matchmaking uses five different filters: context matching, profile comparison, similarity matching, signature matching and constraint matching (Sycara et al., 2002). The reader is referred to Sycara et al. (1999) and Sycara et al. (2002) for a comprehensive explanation about RETSINA. Li and Horrocks (2004) describe a software framework for matchmaking based on semantic web technology. They develop a service matchmaking prototype using a DAML-S web service ontology and a description logic reasoner. The prototype exhibits advertising, querying, modifying/withdrawing, and browser matchmaking functionalities.

However, those matchmaking systems do not provide a clear ranking of the resulting matches. To enable semantic matchmaking with ranked results, we focus on applying the *exact, partial, and potential match* algorithms developed in Di Noia et al. (2004) to an infomediary-based eMarketplace model. Di Noia et al. (2004) explain that i) *exact matches* occur when all needs in demand exist in supply (or vice versa); ii) *potential matches* occur when some needs in demand are not specified in supply leading to further inquiry or refinement; and iii) *partial matches* arise when some needs in demand are in conflict with supply leading to not further action (retract).

It is important to note that the exact matching algorithm of Di Noia et al. (2004) does not provide a mechanism to rank exact matches. Ranking of exact matches involves the use of multiple criteria. For instance, products' characteristics, such as a price, quality, color, and quantity can be used to select and rank the resulting exact matches. This type of task is treated by the field of multi-criterion decision making (MCDM), which and be defined as selecting a satisfying solution in the presence of multiple objectives (Ramesh and Zionts, 1997). To the best of our knowledge, multiple-criterion techniques have been successfully applied in various decision making environment including credit cards assessment (Lam et al., 1996), business failure prediction (Slowinski and Zopounidis, 1995), R&D project evaluation (Jacquet-Lagreze, 1995), portfolio selection and management (Nakayama and Kagaku, 1998; Doumpos et al. 2000), and tax planning (Weistroffer et al., 1999). However, MCDM techniques have not been used to select and rank exact matches. Here we show how the use of two multiple-criterion techniques namely the preemptive priorities, as used in the literature of goal programming (Lee, 1972; Winston and Albright 2007), and (2) Pareto optimality, which identifies all choices that are not "dominated" by any others (Winston and Albright 2007) can be used to rank exact matches. We also discuss how the techniques of the Analytic Hierarchy Process (Saaty, et al, 2000, 2003) can be used to develop and compare rating scores for different decision alternatives and criteria.

The ultimate goal of semantic matchmaking is to identify the best resources (supply) that fully meet the requirements (demand); however, such a goal is very difficult to achieve. To alleviate this problem in the context of eMarketplaces, we suggest an agent-enabled infomediary-based eMarketplace that enables abductive inferences; so that, partial and potential matches can become full matches.

Semantic Web, Ontologies, Description Logics, and Intelligent Agents

The Semantic Web is an extension of the current Web in which information is given "well-defined meaning" to allow machines to "process and understand" the information presented to them (Berners-Lee et al., 2001). Ontologies provide a shared and common understanding of specific domains that can be communicated between disparate application systems, and therein provide a means to integrate the knowledge used by online processes employed by organizations (Klein et al., 2001). Ontology describes the semantics of the constructs that are common to the online processes, including descriptions of the data semantics that are common descriptors of the domain context. Ontology documents can be created using standardized content languages like BPEL, RDF, OWL, and DAML to generate standardized representations of the process knowledge (Thomas et al. 2005; Sivashanmugam et al., 2004). We refer the reader to Kishore et al. (2004) for more comprehensive discussion of ontologies in information systems. The use of standardized ontologies, message content, and message protocols of the semantic web could make e-commerce interaction more flexible and automated (Li and Horrocks, 2004).

The structure of ontology documents are based on the Description logics (DL) formalisms for knowledge-representation (Li and Horrocks, 2004). DL provides formal linear syntax to express descriptions of top-level concepts in a problem domain, their relationships and the constraints on the concepts and the relationships imposed by pragmatic considerations in the domain. DL supplies the language to build composite term descriptions from primitive concepts. A DL contains a T-BOX, with terminology of the problem domain built through declarations that describe general properties of concepts; and an A-Box, with contains extensional knowledge specified by individuals in the problem domain (Baader et al., 2003). The terms include primitive and derived concepts, similar to classes or templates to categorize individual instances; and roles or binary relationships between concepts. In addition to an inheritance hierarchy of primitive and derived concepts, hierarchies of relationships can describe specialized relationships between derived concepts that are specializations of more general relationships between primitive concepts.

Ontologies are domain specific; therefore, to craft useful ontologies, it is important to identify the purposes of them. Noy and McGuinness (2002) identified the following as the major purposes of ontologies:

1. Enable and shared understanding of structure of information among people and agents,
2. Enable information reuse in applications,
3. Make the assumptions underlying an IS implementation explicit and well-understood,
4. Specify the knowledge embodied in an ontology at an appropriate level of granularity (universe, bounded universe, domain, operational), and
5. Apply the ontological structures at different stages of IS development: analysis, conceptualization, and design (Kishore et al., 2004).

Jasper and Uschold (1999) identify that ontologies can be classified into: a) ontology for knowledge reuse; b) ontology as specification; c) ontology as a provider of common access of heterogeneous information; and d) ontology as a search mechanism. In this research, we develop ontologies to knowledge reuse, share, and representation and to provide a common vocabulary to integrate knowledge resources across inter-organizational business process.

We use SHIQ-DL (Li and Horrocks, 2004) for its expressive power. In addition, OWL-DL, is based on the SH family of DL. OWL is the W3C standardized approach for semantic web ontologies using description logic as its fundamental knowledge representation mechanism. Ontological analysis results in ontology descriptions that are presented formally through description logics for theoretical soundness; and in machine readable format using OWL-DL to provide practicality for the model. In addition, software reasoners, such as Racer, support concept consistency checking, T-Box reasoning and A-Box reasoning on DL models translated into OWL-DL using tools such as Protégé. Sycara et al. (2002) emphasize that in order for any advertisement, request or even matchmaking can occur, a common language to express agent capabilities is required. We develop DL-based semantic knowledge representation for activity resource coordination in semantic eBusiness processes. These provide the basis for developing machine-interpretable knowledge representation and computational ontologies in OWL-DL format to support knowledge integration in collaborative inter-organizational business processes.

Intelligent agents can be used for knowledge management to support semantic activities. The agent abstraction is created by extending an object with additional features for encapsulation and exchange of knowledge between agents to allow agents to deliver knowledge to users and support decision-making activity (Shoham, 1993). Agents work on a distributed platform and enable the transfer of knowledge by exposing their public methods as Web services using Simple Object Access Protocol (SOAP) (W3C) and XML. DL-based knowledge representation provides the formalism to express structured knowledge in a format amenable for normative reasoning by intelligent software agents. An intelligent agent is "a computer system situated in some environment and that is capable of flexible autonomous action in this environment in order to meet its design objectives" (Jennings and Wooldridge, 1998). Newell (1982) provides a functional view of knowledge as "whatever can be ascribed to an agent, such that its behavior can be computed according to the principle of rationality". This provides the basis for functional knowledge management using agents through explicit, declarative knowledge represented using standard knowledge representation languages. A fundamental implication is that knowledge must be available in formats that allow for processing by software agents. OWL documents represent domain ontologies and rules, and allow knowledge sharing among agents through the standard Web services architecture (Iyer et al., 2005). Web services technology provides the envelope and transport mechanism for information exchange between software entities. Knowledge exchange architectures use Simple Object Access Protocol (SOAP—www.w3.org/TR/soap/) messages to carry relevant semantic knowledge between agents, as OWL documents. Agents work on a distributed platform and enable the transfer of knowledge by exchanging messages through FIPA compliant agent communication languages through Web services using SOAP and XML. These technologies provide the knowledge representation and exchange mechanisms to allow for knowledge integration, which enable collaborating organizations to seamlessly share information and knowledge to coordinate eBusiness processes.

In the next section, we discuss mechanisms for knowledge representation and exchange to allow partner organizations to seamlessly share information and knowledge to facilitate the discovery process in an eMarketplace context.

eBUSINESS PROCESS CONCEPTUALIZATION

In executing processes across inter-organizational systems, human and software agents perform activities, such as matchmaking, which require transparent access to organizational knowledge resources. Here, *knowledge transparency* refers to *the dynamic, on-demand and seamless flow of relevant, machine-interpretable knowledge across inter-organizational systems*. Current systems integration models suffer from a lack of knowledge transparency (Singh et al., 2005). A process view of knowledge integration incorporates management of *component knowledge* and *process knowledge*, as defined below, for integrated inter-organizational systems that exhibit knowledge transparency. It is essential that integrative technologies supply effective standardizations and adaptability to support the transparent exchange of information and knowledge to inter-organizational eBusiness Processes.

We focus on two specific types of knowledge in this research:

i. *Component knowledge* includes descriptions of skills, technologies, tangible and intangible resources, consumer and product knowledge, and is amenable to knowledge exchange (Hamel, 1991; Tallman, et al., 2004).

ii. *Process knowledge* is typically embedded in the process models of workflow management systems or exists as coordination knowledge among human agents to coordinate complex processes.

Component and process knowledge are central to activities of human and software agents in inter-organizational eBusiness processes. Newell (1982) provides a functional view of knowledge as *"whatever can be ascribed to an agent, such that its behavior can be computed according to the principle of rationality"*. This view forms a basis for functional knowledge management by agents (human and/or software) when using standards-based knowledge representation languages that can be processed via reasoning mechanisms to reach useful inferences. Our emphasis in this study is to illustrate the process knowledge, including workflow composition and business processes views, of an infomediary-based B2B e-Marketplace to support the discovery process.

In an eBusiness process, a human or software agent represents a business enterprise and performs activities on its behalf. Agents perform the individual business activities that comprise the eBusiness process. Business activities require access to resources of the organization in order to perform business activities in the eBusiness Process. Activities are operations performed by agents on individual resources owned by a business enterprise. Resources, owned by various owner organizations or business enterprises, coordinate activities that are performed on them. In the eBusiness process universe of discourse (see Figure 4), *information* and *knowledge* are central resources. They are used by actors in business enterprises to perform their assigned tasks (activities) in order to accomplish their goals. In this article, we utilize a pragmatic definition of knowledge that is explicit and declarative enough to be represented by a standards-based knowledge representation language or formalism. Additionally, we constrain this declarative knowledge as amenable to being processed through some reasoning mechanism to reach useful inference.

The essential set of concepts fundamental to model eBusiness Processes are: *business enterprise, agent, business activity, resource, coordination, information* and *knowledge*. These concepts are similar to those proposed by Malone and

Figure 4. The eBusiness Process universe of discourse for an intelligent infomediary-based B2B eMarketplace.

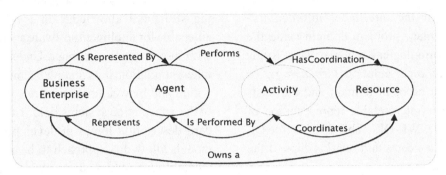

Crowston (1994). The conceptualization of the eBusiness Process universe of discourse for an intelligent infomediary-based B2B eMarketplace is described as:

In an eBusiness process, a Business Enterprise is represented by an Agent to perform Activities which are coordinated by resources.

Resources coordinate the Activities performed by Agents representing Business Enterprises, engaged in an eBusiness Process.

Description Logic Model Knowledge Representation for eBusiness Process Universe of Discourse

The elementary descriptions of the atomic concepts and relationships in the intelligent infomediary-based B2B eMarketplace problem domain are described in Table 1.

Information and knowledge are the primary resources pertinent to the problem domain we consider in this article. We utilize the concept definitions:

Resource $\subseteq$
  Information
  Knowledge

Here, if R is a relationship between two concepts in the problem domain, then R^{-} denotes the inverse of the relationship R. Description logic derives its descriptive power from the ability to enhance the expressiveness of the atomic descriptions by building complex descriptions of concepts using concept constructors. These *terminological axioms* make statements about how concepts or roles are related to each other. This develops a set of terminologies, comprise of definitions, which are specific axioms which define the inclusions ($\subseteq$) or the equivalence ($\equiv$).

Given the atomic concepts and relationships for the eBusiness Process universe of discourse,

Table 1. Atomic concepts and relationships in the eBusiness Process Universe of Discourse

Essential Atomic Concepts include	**Essential Atomic Relationships include**
Business Enterprise (BE) *Agent (Ag)* *Business Activity (Ac)* *Resource (Rs)*	*Represents (≡ IsRepresentedBy -)* *Performs (≡ IsPerformedBy -)* *Coordinates(≡ HasCoordination -)*

we can begin to define the relationships between the concepts in the domain. Here, we define the terminology for the intelligent infomediary-based eMarketplace problem domain using the following terminological axioms. This forms the knowledge representation *terminology, or T-BOX,* for the problem domain and the basis for the machine-interpretable representation of the ontology in OWL-DL. Table 2 shows the DL for the atomic concepts and relationships of the universe of discourse.

These complex descriptions of concepts, built from atomic descriptions, describe classes of objects in the problem domain and their interrelationships. The terminological axioms presented above make statements about how concepts and relationships are related to each other. The set of terminological axioms, including definitions, provide the terminology, or the *TBox,* for a problem domain. In the following sections, the Discovery eBusiness process in the context of an infomediary-based eMarketplaces is provided to illustrate the process knowledge and the discovery

process. We utilize Description Logics as the knowledge representation formalism for expressing structured knowledge in a format that is amenable for intelligent software agents to reason with in a normative manner. Understanding the inherent relationships among business processes within and between organizations is a key topic of the information systems field. The use of standard description logics in developing semantic models allow this approach to be a truly implementable framework using W3C's OWL (Web Ontology Language) and OWL-DL without losing theoretical robustness.

ONTOLOGICAL ENGINEERING FOR INFOMEDIARY ENABLED BUYER/ SUPPLIER DISCOVERY PROCESS

Using the atomic concepts from the universe of discourse, we describe the buyer // supplier discovery process as follows. Buyer agents present buyer needs to the eMarketplace by communicating the

Table 2. DL for the Atomic Concepts and Relationships in the eBusiness Process Universe of Discourse

Atomic Concept	Description	Description Logics
Business Enterprise (BE)	A *Business Enterprise (BE)* concept is defined as a *Thing*, the top concept in OWL-DL, which is represented by at least one *Agent (Ag)* in the problem domain.	*BusinessEnterprise* $\subseteq$ $(\geq 1\ IsRepresentedBy \cdot Agent) \wedge$ $(= 1\ HasID \cdot StringData) \wedge$ $(\geq 1\ HasAddress \cdot Address) \wedge$ $(\geq 1\ HasReputation \cdot StringData) \wedge$ $(\geq 1\ Has\ TransactionSatisfactionHistory \cdot StringData)$
Agent (Ag)	An *Agent (Ag)* concept is defined as a Thing that represents a *Business Enterprise* and performs activities for the *Business Enterprise*.	*Agent* $\subseteq$ $(= 1\ HasID \cdot StringData) \wedge$ $(= 1\ Represents \cdot BusinessEnterprise) \wedge$ $(\geq 1\ Performs \cdot BusinessActivity)$
Activity(Ac)	A *Business Activity* defined as a Thing that is performed by an *Agent,* has a coordination relationship with *Resources*, and has a *Begin Time* and an *End Time*.	*Business Activity* $\subseteq$ $(= 1\ hasLabel \cdot StringData) \wedge$ $(\geq 1\ isPerformedBy \cdot Agent) \wedge$ $(\geq 1\ hasCharacteristics \cdot StringData) \wedge$ $(\geq 1\ HasDescription \cdot StringData) \wedge$ $(\geq 1\ HasCoordination \cdot Resource) \wedge$ $(= 1\ hasBeginTime \cdot DateTimeData) \wedge$ $(= 1\ hasEndTime \cdot DateTimeData)$
Resource (Rs)	Each Resource is defined as a Thing that is owned by exactly one *Business Enterprise* and coordinates *Business Activities*.	*Resource* $\subseteq$ $(= 1\ hasID \cdot StringData) \wedge$ $(= 1\ hasOwner \cdot Business Enterprise) \wedge$ $(\geq 1\ Coordinates \cdot BusinessActivity)$

Figure 5. Use-case diagram for Supplier discovery based on buyer needs

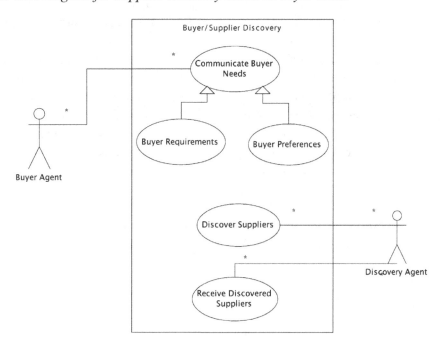

buyer requirements and buyer preferences. The discovery agent uses the buyer needs to discover a set of suppliers that are able to meet buyer requirements and match the buyer preferences. The set of discovered suppliers are communicated to the buyer enterprises through the buyer agent. Figure 5 shows the Use-case diagram for Supplier discovery based on buyer needs.

An eMarketplace supports the process of discovery of buyers and suppliers for its participants. A typical workflow for the supplier discovery eBusiness process is shown in Figure 6.

The Buyer Needs resource abstracts the specialized buyer requirements and buyer needs as shown in Figure 7. Buyer requirements are characteristics or features that the supplier must have.

Buyer preferences are characteristics that are not required, but if present would enhance the value of the supplier. In other words, they are not required but would be nice to have.

BuyersNeeds ⊆ (Resource)
(= 1 hasCharacteristics · ProductName) ∧
(= 1 hasCharacteristics · ProductType)

Buyer Requirements are buyer needs that specify buyers' demand function; while Buyer Preferences specify buyer preferences of suppliers and additional preference criteria for the buyer enterprise. (Table 3)

This inheritance hierarchy of buyer needs, which may be specialized into the Buyer require-

Table 3.

BuyersRequirements ⊆ (BuyerNeeds)	BuyerPreferences ⊆ BuyerNeeds
(= 1 hasCharacteristics · Price) ∧	(≥ 1 hasCharacteristics · PreferredPrice) ∧
(= 1 hasCharacteristics · Quantity) ∧	(≥ 0 hasCharacteristics · PreferredDeliveryMethod) ∧
(= 1 hasCharacteristics · Quality) ∧	(≥ 1 hasCharacteristics · AllowedLeadTime) ∧ (≥ 0 hasCharacteristics ·
(= 1 hasCharacteristics · NeedByDate)	PreferredSupplierReputation)

ments and the Buyer Preferences, provides a basis to utilize the supplier discovery workflow using either type of the buyer needs resource. The hierarchy illustrates the ability to specify meta-knowledge of processes and instantiate the individual workflows using multiple types of resources that inherit from the same parent resource used in the process knowledge specification.

Supplier Capabilities are characteristics and features that specify the suppliers' supply function.

SupplierCapabilities $\subseteq$ (Resource)
(≥ 1 isPerformedBy · SupplierAgent) $\wedge$
(≥ 1 isCoordinatedBy · SupplierCapabilities) $\wedge$
(≥ 1 hasCharacteristics. SupplierID) $\wedge$
(≥ 1 hasCharacteristics · ProductName) $\wedge$
(≥ 1 hasCharacteristics · Price) $\wedge$
(≥ 1 hasCharacteristics · Quantity) $\wedge$
(≥ 1 hasCharacteristics · Quality) $\wedge$
(≥ 0 hasCharacteristics · DeliveryMethod) $\wedge$
(≥ 0 hasCharacteristics · MinPrice) $\wedge$

Figure 6. A typical workflow for the supplier discovery eBusiness process in an infomediary-based eMarketplace

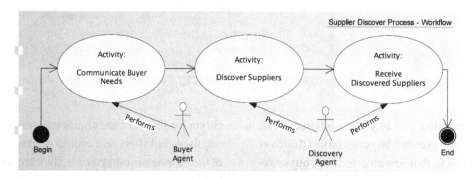

Figure 7. Buyer needs is an abstraction for the buyer requirements and buyer preferences involved in the supplier selection eBusiness Process

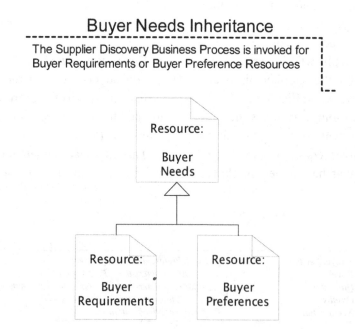

($\geq$ 0 hasCharacteristics · MaxPrice) $\wedge$
($\geq$ 0 hasCharacteristics · LeadTime)

Buyer activities when a buyer agent communicates buyer's demand to a discovery agent assigned to the buyer agent by the infomediary. Concurrently, Supplier activities are initiated when a supplier agent communicates its supplier's supply capability to the infomediary. The representation of buyers demand and suppliers supply conforms to the ontology described above to ensure interoperability of agent interactions. A semantic map that conforms to the DL-based

conceptualizations of the eCommerce process knowledge presented earlier for the supplier discovery eCommerce process is shown in Figure 8.

The DL descriptions to represent the buyer's needs, including buyer requirements and buyer preferences, and supplier capabilities are presented above. It is important to highlight that these demand requirement characteristics are intended to serve as examples and they are not exhaustive.

Buyers communicate their needs to the eMarketplace using standardized ontology for specifying the buyer needs.

Figure 8. Semantic activity-resource coordination in the supplier discovery eBusiness process

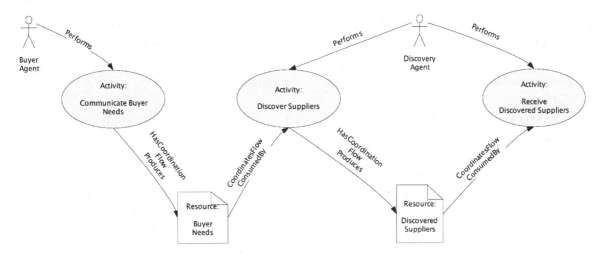

Table 4.

CommunicateBuyerNeeds $\subseteq$ *(BusinessActivity)* $\wedge$ *(= 1 IsPerformedby.BuyerAgent)* $\wedge$ *(= 1 HasCoordinationFlowProduces.BuyerNeeds)*	*SupplierCapabilities* $\subseteq$ *(Resource)* $\wedge$ *(= 1 hasCharacteristics. SupplierID)* $\wedge$ *(= 1 CoordinatesFlowProducedBy. CommunicateSupplierCapabilities)*

Table 5.

CommunicateSupplierCapabilities $\subseteq$ *(BusinessActivity)* $\wedge$ *(= 1 IsPerformedby. SupplierAgent)* $\wedge$ *(= 1 HasCoordinationFlowProduces. SupplierCapabilities)*	*DiscoverSuppliers* $\subseteq$ *(BusinessActivity)* $\wedge$ *(= 1 IsPerformedby.DiscoveryAgent)* $\wedge$ *(= 1 HasCoordinationFlowConsumes.BuyerNeeds)* $\wedge$ *(= 1 HasCoordinationFlowConsumes. SupplierCapabilities)* $\wedge$ *(= 1 HasCoordinationFlowProduces.DiscoveredSuppliers)*

BuyerNeeds ⊆ (Resource) ∧

(= 1 hasCharacteristics. BuyerID) ∧

(= 1 CoordinatesFlowProducedBy. CommunicateBuyerNeeds) ∧

(= 1 CoordinatesFlowConsumedBy. DiscoverSuppliers)

The buyer agent communicates Buyer needs to the eMarketplace to coordinate the supplier discovery activity. Communicating Buyer Needs by the Buyer Agent has a coordination flow relationship with the Buyer Needs resource by producing the Buyer Needs to the Discovery Agent. Suppliers communicate their capabilities to the eMarketplace using standardized ontology for specifying the supplier's capabilities. (Table 4)

Communicating Supplier Capabilities by the Supplier Agent has a coordination flow relationship with the Supplier Capabilities resource by producing the Supplier Capabilities. The discovery agent performs the Discover Suppliers activity. (Table 5)

Di Noia et al. (2004) extend a basic semantic matchmaking scheme into exact, potential and partial matchmaking mechanisms. We develop these mechanisms to support the discovery process in an eMarketplace, using the hierarchy of the buyer's needs to establish what is critically needed by a buyer (i.e: *BuyerRequirements* Resource), and what a buyer would additionally prefer (i.e.: *BuyerPreferences* Resource). The following paragraphs discuss the application of

matchmaking algorithms in the Discover Suppliers activity of the eMarketplace. A sample set of buyer's needs and supplier's capabilities are listed in Appendix A. These are used below to demonstrate the semantic matchmaking approach. A summary of characteristics in the sample set is presented in Table 6.

EXACT Match: An Exact match occurs when all the attributes of the demand requirements are present in the supply function. The result of the exact match would be a set of suppliers, each of whom fulfills all the buyer's requirements, and that could be ranked using the values specified in the buyer's preferences. This represents an extension to the referenced existing matchmaking algorithm which does not include a method to rank exact matches. All exact matches are considered to be equally appealing in Di Noia et al. (2004).

Based on the buyer needs resource described earlier, there are two possible cases where exact matches could arise.

- *Case 1:* All buyer's requirements find a direct match in the supplier's capabilities, and no preferences are specified.

This first case takes place when a buyer provides all its requirements without specifying any preferences at all. Therefore, an exact match will occur when all buyer's requirements (i.e.: *BuyerRequirements* Resource) exist, without any conflicts, in the supplier's capabilities (i.e.: *Sup-*

Table 6. Sample set of buyer's needs and suppliers capabilities

	Price	Quantity	Quality	Delivery Method	Lead Time
Buyer Requirements	<=105	10	>=2		<=7
Buyer Preferences	<105		>2	"Ground"	
Supplier 1	100	50	3	"Ground"	7
Supplier 2	90	50	2	"Ground"	7
Supplier 3	80	30	2	"Air"	7
Supplier 4	110	30	3	"Air"	14
Supplier 5	115	30	3	"Air"	21

plierCapabilities Resource). Under this scenario the absence of preferences prevents any ranking of exact matches. It should be noted that some of the values of the requirements may have an inherent directionality of preference, e.g., a lower price is always preferred to a higher price. Other requirements, however, may not have this property, e.g., "Ground" vs. "Air" shipment. If any of the values of the requirements do have an inherent directionality of preference, then this should be described as buyer's preferences.

- *Case 2:* All buyer's requirements and some buyer's preferences find a direct match in the supplier's capabilities.

This second case occurs when a buyer specifies requirements and some preferences (i.e.: *BuyerRequirements* and *BuyerPreferences* Resources). An exact match will occur when all buyer's requirements exist, without any conflicts, in the supplier's capabilities. Under this scenario, exact matches would be ranked based on the degrees to which the various preferences are satisfied. There are many possible ways in which preferences may be described:

- Quantifiable with clear directionality, e.g., price.
- All-or-nothing, e.g., inclusion of a desired but inessential feature.
- Quantifiable without clear directionality, e.g., a preferred set of equivalent availability dates within a required range.
- Nonquantifiable, e.g., color.

The second category can be transformed into a preference of the first type by using a $\{0,1\}$ indicator variable. The third and fourth categories may be considered equivalent in that they specify membership in a set of preferred but equivalent alternatives. Therefore, we confine our attention to preferences of two types: (1) quantifiable with clear directionality, and (2) membership in a finite set.

Comparing suppliers with more than one differing characteristic falls under the field of multiple-criterion decision making. Many multiple-criterion techniques have been proposed for various decision-making environments. We illustrate preference ranking by using (1) the concept of preemptive priorities, as used in the literature of goal programming (Lee, 1972; Winston and Albright, 2007), and (2) the concept of Pareto optimality, which identifies all choices that are not "dominated" by any others (Winston and Albright 2007).

This approach is by no means the only reasonable way to rank suppliers according to multiple preference criteria. A technique known as the Analytic Hierarchy Process (AHP) (Saaty et al 2000, 2003) can be used to compute importance weights for the various preference characteristics through a series of pair-wise comparisons among them. AHP then guides the decision maker in generating a set of normalized scores for each choice (supplier, in our case) when compared according to each preference characteristic. The software products and professional support for applying AHP include Expert Choice (www.expertchoice.com) and the Decision Lens Suite (www.decisionlens.com). It must be noted, however, that a number of technical issues must be resolved in order to apply AHP comprehensively in our semantic matchmaking environment. These will be reserved for future research.

We assume that BuyerRequirements and BuyerPreferences have the following properties.

1. BuyerRequirements may be specified by means of set membership (Color = "Red" or "Green") or by a bound (Price<=105). Any supplier that satisfies all requirements is classified as an Exact Match.
2. BuyerPreferences may be specified by means of set membership (DeliveryMethod

= "Ground") or as a preference order (Price<105), in which case preference is always given to a supplier whose characteristic is further in the preferred direction.
3. BuyerPreferences are grouped into preemptive Priority classes. Any preference in a lower Priority class is considered only for breaking ties among suppliers that are equivalent according to the higher Priority classes.

The discovery agent creates the *Discovered-Suppliers* resource including the ranking of the resulting matches. After the buyer agent selects the best supplier, the buyer can go to the contractual agreement formation activity.

When the match is made using the buyer's requirements, only suppliers 1, 2 and 3 represent exact matches. However, when the buyer's preferences are considered Supplier 3 dominates Supplier 2 because it has the same Quality and a better Price. The efficient frontier (Pareto optimal choices) for the first Priority class is then Suppliers 1 and 3. When the second Priority class of preferences is considered, no further refinement is possible because Suppliers 1 and 3 are not equivalent, despite the fact that neither dominates the other.

Table 7 shows the ranking results obtained after running the exact match algorithm.

Many variations of this scheme are possible. For example, if there are many exact matches it may be prudent to relax the definition of "efficient frontier" to include all first and second place finishers in each of the preference characteristics within a Priority class. Another possible approach is to use the pair-wise comparison method of the Analytic Hierarchy Process to compute normalized weights for each characteristic and a normalized score for each exact match, and then use a weighted average to select the best supplier.

POTENTIAL Match: A potential match will occur when at least one of the buyer's requirements (i.e.: *BuyerRequirements* Resource) does not match the supplier's capability (i.e.: *SupplierCapabilities* Resource); therefore, further refinement or inquiry is needed. Potential matches can arise under two circumstances.

- *Case 1:* First, it is possible that one of the buyer's requirements (e.g.: price) does not match the supplier capabilities; however, by using the buyer's preferences (e.g.: maximum price), the discovery agent can produce the *DiscoveredSuppliers* resource, which contains suppliers that closely satisfy the buyer requirements. Once the buyer agent selects one of the resulting suppliers, the buyer can move forward to the contractual agreement formation activity. Table 8 shows the ranking results obtained after running the potential match algorithm.

Table 7. Ranking results for the Exact Match Algorithm (the lower the ranking score, the better)

Match	Rank
BuyersNeeds,BuyersRequirements,BuyerPreferences, SupplierCapabilities1	1
BuyersNeeds,BuyersRequirements,BuyerPreferences, SupplierCapabilities3	1
BuyersNeeds,BuyersRequirements,BuyerPreferences, SupplierCapabilities2	3

Table 8. Ranking results for the potential match algorithm (the lower the ranking score, the better)

Match	Rank
BuyersNeeds,BuyersRequirements,BuyerPreferences, SupplierCapabilities4	1
BuyersNeeds,BuyersRequirements,BuyerPreferences, SupplierCapabilities5	2

Table 9. Ranking results for the Potential Match Algorithm (the lower the ranking score, the better)

Match	Rank
BuyersNeeds,BuyersRequirements,BuyerPreferences, SupplierCapabilities4	1
BuyersNeeds,BuyersRequirements,BuyerPreferences, SupplierCapabilities5	2

Suppliers 4 and 5 represent potential matches because their offered prices are higher than the buyer's requested price, and their delivery method are different from the preferred buyer's delivery method. However, when we analyze the supplier 4's minimum price, it matches with the buyer's requested price, which makes it a better option than supplier 5.

An algorithmic approach for resolving this kind of semantic conflict has been proposed in (Colucci, el al, 2005), where "strict constraints" and "negotiable constraints" parallel our requirements and preferences. They define a "Concept Contraction Problem" as finding a pair of concepts G (for Give up) and K (for Keep) which represent which preferences may be traded/retained to initiate a transaction. Their algorithm entitled *contract* computes a minimal G (and a maximal K) so that a demand and supply may be satisfiable. Although their algorithm is rigorous, their approach is limited to preference of the set-membership type. In other words, they do not treat preferences that are quantifiable with clear directionality.

- *Case 2:* Second, if some of the buyer's requirements and some of the buyer's preferences cannot be matched with the suppliers' capabilities, the resulting potential matches might lead the buyer toward two options: i) the buyer agent could pick one of the resulting suppliers and then move forward to the contract formation; or ii) the buyer refines its requirements and preferences, which implies starting a new discovery process.

This, of course, it is the worst scenario, because the buyer needs to start over and cannot move forward to the contract formation and the execution of the transactions. Table 9 shows the raking results obtained after running the potential match algorithm.

Suppliers 4 and 5 represent potential matches because their offered prices are higher than the buyer's requested price, their delivery method are different from the preferred buyer's delivery method, and their lead time are higher than the buyer's allowed lead time. Here, the buyer has two options: It could select supplier 4 and move forward to the contra ctual agreement formation or it could refine its requirements and then start over the discovery process; so that a new set of supplier are selected.

In this case a Concept Contraction Problem as defined in (Colucci, et al, 2005) could be solved to identify which requirements (strict constraints, in their terminology) must be altered in order to initiate a transaction.

PARTIAL Match: We note that partial matches will never occur under the proposed infomediary-based e-marketplace. A partial match occurs when an attribute in the demand function of the buyer does not exist in the supply function of the supplier. This creates a semantic conflict in the ontologies for the demand and supply function which would prevent semantic inter-operability resulting in consequent loss of the transparent flow of information across the buyer, the infomediary and the supplier organizations (Pollock and Hodgson, 2004). This is due to the fact that all buyer's needs and supplier's capabilities must be represented using the ontology provided by the infomediary. Buyers and Suppliers are not allowed to alter the product or process ontologies that reside in the infomediary knowledge repository. By imposing this constraint, we avoid ontology conflicts, which have been recognized as being one of the biggest barriers to fully realizing semantic interoperability and at the same time we guarantee that buyer's needs are not in conflict

Table 10.

DiscoveredSuppliers ⊆ *(Resource)* *(≥ 0 hasCharacteristics. SupplierID)* *(≥ 0 hasCharacteristics. Rank)* ∧ *(= 1 CoordinatesFlowProducedBy. DiscoverSuppliers)* ∧ *(= 1 CoordinatesFlowConsumedBy. ReceiveDiscoveredSuppliers)*	*ReceiveDiscoverdSuppliers* ⊆ *(BusinessActivity)* ∧ *(= 1 IsPerformedby. BuyerAgent)* ∧ *(= 1 HasCoordinationFlowConsumes. DiscoveredSuppliers)*

with supplier's capabilities and vice-versa (Ram and Park, 2004).

Continuing with the activity-resource coordination eBusiness process in the supplier discovery eBusiness process, the Discover Suppliers activity produces a set of discovered suppliers that meets buyer needs. The Discovered suppliers resource is produced by the discover suppliers activity and coordinates *thereceivediscoveredsuppliers* activity of the buyer agent. (Table 10)

SUMMARY AND DIRECTIONS FOR FUTURE RESEARCH

To facilitate the discovery process in a B2B environment, we proposed a semantic matchmaking approach. The ultimate goal of semantic matchmaking is to identify the best resources (supply) that fully meet the requirements (demand); however, such a goal is very difficult to achieve due to information distributed over disparate systems. We first presented ontological engineering and knowledge representation for distributed knowledge management in inter-organizational eCommerce processes and developed the central concepts to model eCommerce Process. Our primary focus is on knowledge representations and semantic architecture for knowledge management for automated inter-organizational eCommerce processes over seamlessly integrated systems. Our general framework in this article uses description logic as the theoretical basis. We then show a description logic model knowledge representation of the intelligent infomediary-based eMarketplace as an illustrative example. We also suggest the use

of multiple criteria decision making techniques to rank matches during the discovery process in the eMarketplace context.

Future research includes the evaluation of the utility and efficacy of the proposed semantic matchmaking approach. In addition, we plan to allow for assigning weights to buyers' preferences; so that the discovery agent might use those weights to rank the resulting suppliers. Here, we plan to use Analytic Hierarchy Process (AHP) to compute importance weights for the various buyer preference characteristics. Finally, we plan to apply the proposed approach to a B2C environment, where the amount of information about products and services is overwhelming.

REFERENCES

Baader, F., Calvanese, D., McGuinness, D., Nardi, D., & Patel-Schneider, P. F. (2003). *The Description Logic Handbook: Theory, Implementation and Applications*. Cambridge: Cambridge University Press.

Bakos, Y. (1998). The emerging role of electronic marketplaces on the Internet. *Communications of the ACM, 41*(8), 35–42. doi:10.1145/280324.280330

Berners-Lee, T., Hendler, J., & Lassila, O. (2001). The Semantic Web. *Scientific American, 284*, 34–43.

Choudhury, V., Hartzel, K., & Konsynski, B. (1998). Uses and Consequences of Electronic Markets: An Empirical Investigation in the Aircraft Parts Industry. *MIS Quarterly, 22*(4), 471–507. doi:10.2307/249552

Coluccia, S., Di Noia, T., Di Sciascio, E., & Donini, F., &Mongiell0, M. (2005). Concept abduction and contraction for semantic-based discovery of matches and negotiation spaces in an e-marketplace. *Electronic Commerce Research and Applications, 4*(4), 345–361. doi:10.1016/j.elerap.2005.06.004

Copeland, D. G., & McKenney, J. L. (1988). Airline Reservation Systems: Lessons from History. *MIS Quarterly, 12*(3), 353–372. doi:10.2307/249202

Di Noia, T., Di Sciascio, E., Donini, F., & Mongiello, M. (2004). A System for Principled Macthmaking in an Electronic Marketplace. *International Journal of Electronic Commerce, 8*(4), 9–37.

Doumpos, M., Zopounidis, C., & Pardalos, P. M. (2000). Multicriteria sorting methodology: Application to financial decision problems. *Parallel Algorithms and Applications, 15*(1-2), 113–129.

Grover, V., & Teng, J. (2001). E-Commerce and the information market. *Communications of the ACM, 44*(4), 79–86. doi:10.1145/367211.367272

Hamel, G. (1991). Competition for Competence and Inter-Partner Learning with International Strategic Alliances. *Strategic Management Journal, 12*, 83–103. doi:10.1002/smj.4250120908

Iyer, L. S., Singh, R., & Salam, A. F. (2005). Collaboration and Knowledge Management in B2B eMarketplaces. *Information Systems Management, 22*(3), 37–49. doi:10.1201/1078/45317.22.3.20050601/88744.6

Jacquet-Lagreze, E. (1995). An application of the UTA discriminant model for the evaluation of R&D projects. In: Pardalos, P.M., Siskos, Y., Zopounidis, C. (Eds.), *Advances in Multicriteria Analysis* (pp. 203-211). Dordrecht: Kluwer Academic Publishers.

Jasper, R., & Uschold, M. (1999). A Framework for Understanding and Classifying Ontology Applications. *Proceedings of the IJCAI-99 Workshop on Ontologies and Problem-Solving Mehtods,* Stockholm, Sweden.

Jennings, N. R., & Wooldridge, M. (1998). *Agent Technology: Foundations, Applications, and Markets,* Springer, London.

Kishore, R., Sharman, R., Zhang, H., & Ramesh, R. (2004). Computational Ontologies and Information Systems: I. Foundations. *Communications of the Association for Information Systems, 14*, 158–183.

Klein, M., Fensel, D., van Harmelen, F., & Horrocks, I. (2001). The Relation Between Ontologies and XML Schemas," *Electronic Transactions on Artificial Intelligence (ETAI), Linköping Electronic Articles in Computer and Information Science, 6*(4).

Lam, K. F., Choo, E. U., & Moy, J. W. (1996). Minimizing deviations from the group mean: A new linear programming approach for the two-group classification problem. *European Journal of Operational Research, 88*, 358–367. doi:10.1016/0377-2217(95)00183-2

Lee, H. G., & Clark, T. H. (1996). Impacts of the electronic marketplace on transaction cost and market structure. *International Journal of Electronic Commerce, 1*(1), 127–149.

Lee, S. (1972). *Goal Programming for Decision Analysis.* Philadelphia, PA: Auerbach.

Li, L., & Horrocks, I. (2004). A Software Framework for Matchmaking Based on Semantic Web Technology. *International Journal of Electronic Commerce, 8*(4), 39–60.

Lindsey, D., Cheney, P. H., Kasper, G. M., & Ives, B. (1990). TELCOT: An Application of Information Technology for Competitive Advantage in the Cotton Industry. *MIS Quarterly, 14*(4), 347–357. doi:10.2307/249781

Malone, T., & Crowston, K. (1994). The Interdisciplinary Study of Coordination. *ACM Computing Surveys, 26*(1), 87–119. doi:10.1145/174666.174668

Malone, T. W. (1987). Modeling Coordination in Organizations and Markets. *Management Science, 33*(10), 1317–1332. doi:10.1287/mnsc.33.10.1317

Nakayama, H., & Kagaku, N. (1998). Pattern classification by linear goal programming and its extensions. *Journal of Global Optimization, 12*(2), 111–126. doi:10.1023/A:1008244409770

Newell, A. (1982). The Knowledge Level. *Artificial Intelligence, 18,* 87–127. doi:10.1016/0004-3702(82)90012-1

Noy, N. F., & McGuinnss, D. L. (2002). *Ontology Development 101: A Guide to Creating Your First Ontology*. Stanford University, Stanford, CA, Stanford Medical Informatics Report SMI-2002-0880.

Oh, S., & Park, S. (2003). Task-role-based Access Control Model. *Information Systems, 28*(6), 533–562. doi:10.1016/S0306-4379(02)00029-7

Pollock, J., & Hodgson, R. (2004). *Adaptive Information: Improving Business Through Semantic Interoperability, Grid Computing, and Enterprise Integration*, Hoboken, NJ: John Wiley & Sons, Inc.

Ram, S., & Park, J. (2004). Semantic Conflict Resolution Ontology (SCROL): An Ontology for Detecting and Resolving Data and Schema-Level Semantic Conflicts. *IEEE Transactions on Knowledge and Data Engineering, 16*(2), 189–202. doi:10.1109/TKDE.2004.1269597

Ramesh, R., & Zionts, S. (1997). Multicriteria Decision Making. In Gass, S. & Harris, C. (Eds.), *Encyclopedia of Operations Research* (pp. 419-425). Operations Research Society of America.

Saaty, T., & Vargas, L. (2000). *Methods, Concepts and Applications of the Analytic Hierarchy Process*. Boston, MA: Kluwer Academic Publishers.

Saaty, T., Vargas, L., & Dellmann, K. (2003). The allocation of intangible resources: the analytic hierarchy process and linear programming. *Socio-Economic Planning Sciences, 37*(3), 169–185. doi:10.1016/S0038-0121(02)00039-3

Shoham, Y. (1993). Agent Oriented Programming. *Journal of Artificial Intelligence, 60*(1), 51–92. doi:10.1016/0004-3702(93)90034-9

Singh, R., Iyer, L. S., & Salam, A. F. (2005). Semantic eBusiness. *International Journal on Semantic Web and Information Systems, 1*(1), 19–35.

Sivashanmugam, K., Miller, J. A., Seth, A. P., & Verma, K. (2004). Framework for Semantic Web Process Composition. *International Journal of Electronic Commerce, 9*(2), 71–106.

Slowinski, R., & Zopounidis, C. (1995). Application of the rough set approach to evaluation of bankruptcy risk. *International Journal of Intelligent Systems in Accounting Finance & Management, 4*(1), 27–41.

Stal, M. (2002). Web services: beyond component-based computing. *Communications of the ACM, 45*(10), 71–76. doi:10.1145/570907.570934

Sycara, K., Lu, J., Klusch, M., & Widoff, S. (1999). Dynamic Service Matchmaking among Agents in Open Information Environments. [Special Issue on Semantic Interoperability in Global Information Systems]. *SIGMOD Record, 28*(1), 47–53. doi:10.1145/309844.309895

Sycara, K., Widoff, S., Klusch, M., & Lu, J. (2002). LARKS: Dynamic Matchmaking Among Heterogeneous Software Agents in Cyberspace. *Autonomous Agents and Multi-Agent Systems, 5,* 173–203. doi:10.1023/A:1014897210525

Tallman, S., Jenkins, M., Henry, N., & Pinch, S. (2004). Knowledge, Clusters, and Competitive Advantage. *Academy of Management Review*, *29*(2), 258–271.

Thomas, M., Redmond, R. T., Yoon, V., & Singh, R. (2005). A semantic approach to monitoring business process performance. *Communications of the ACM*.

Weisteoffer, H. R., Wooldridge, B., & Singh, R. (1999). A Multi-criteria Approach to Local Tax Planning. *Socio-Economic Planning Sciences*, *33*, 301–315. doi:10.1016/S0038-0121(99)00015-4

Winston, W., & Albright, S. (2007). *Practical Management Science* (3rd ed.). Mason, OH: Thomson South-Western.

Zhu, K. (2002). Information Transparency in Electronic Marketplaces: Why Data Transparency May Hinder the Adoption of B2B Exchanges. *Electronic Markets*, *12*(2), 92–99. doi:10.1080/10196780252844535

APPENDIX

Demand Function

```
BuyersNeeds ⊆ (Resource)
(= 1 hasCharacteristics · ProductName="Computer") ∧
(= 1 hasCharacteristics · ProductType="Office Equipment")
BuyersRequirements ⊆ (BuyerNeeds)
(= 1 hasCharacteristics · Price<=105) ∧
(= 1 hasCharacteristics · Quantity=10) ∧
(= 1 hasCharacteristics · Quality>=2) ∧
(= 1 hasCharacteristics · NeedByDate="09/03/2007")
BuyerPreferences ⊆ BuyerNeeds
(= 1 hasCharacteristics · PreferredPrice<105) ∧
(= 1 hasCharacteristics · PreferredDeliveryMethod="Ground") ∧
(= 1 hasCharacteristics · AllowedLeadTime=7) ∧ (= 1 hasCharacteristics · Pre-
ferredQuality=3) ∧
(= 1 hasCharacteristics · PreferredSupplierReputation=3)
```

Supply Function: Suppliers Capabilities

```
SupplierCapabilities1 ⊆ (Resource)
(≥ 1 isPerformedBy · SupplierAgent) ∧
(≥ 1 isCoordinatedBy · SupplierCapabilities) ∧
(≥ 1 hasCharacteristics. SupplierID =10) ∧
(≥ 1 hasCharacteristics · ProductName="Computer")) ∧
(≥ 1 hasCharacteristics · ProductType="Office Equipment") ∧
(≥ 1 hasCharacteristics · Price=100) ∧
(≥ 1 hasCharacteristics · Quantity=50) ∧
(≥ 1 hasCharacteristics · Quality=3) ∧
(≥ 0 hasCharacteristics · DeliveryMethod="Ground") ∧
(≥ 0 hasCharacteristics · MinPrice=100) ∧
(≥ 0 hasCharacteristics · MaxPrice=110) ∧
(≥ 0 hasCharacteristics · LeadTime=7)
SupplierCapabilities2 ⊆ (Resource)
(≥ 1 isPerformedBy · SupplierAgent) ∧
(≥ 1 isCoordinatedBy · SupplierCapabilities) ∧
(≥ 1 hasCharacteristics. SupplierID =20) ∧
(≥ 1 hasCharacteristics · ProductName="Computer")) ∧
(≥ 1 hasCharacteristics · ProductType="Office Equipment") ∧
(≥ 1 hasCharacteristics · Price=90) ∧
(≥ 1 hasCharacteristics · Quantity=50) ∧
(≥ 1 hasCharacteristics · Quality=2) ∧
(≥ 0 hasCharacteristics · DeliveryMethod="Ground") ∧
```

```
(≥ 0 hasCharacteristics · MinPrice=90) ∧
(≥ 0 hasCharacteristics · MaxPrice=100) ∧
(≥ 0 hasCharacteristics · LeadTime=7)
SupplierCapabilities3 ⊆ (Resource)
(≥ 1 isPerformedBy · SupplierAgent) ∧
(≥ 1 isCoordinatedBy · SupplierCapabilities) ∧
(≥ 1 hasCharacteristics. SupplierID =30) ∧
(≥ 1 hasCharacteristics · ProductName="Computer")) ∧
(≥ 1 hasCharacteristics · ProductType="Office Equipment") ∧
(≥ 1 hasCharacteristics · Price=80) ∧
(≥ 1 hasCharacteristics · Quantity=30) ∧
(≥ 1 hasCharacteristics · Quality=2) ∧
(≥ 0 hasCharacteristics · DeliveryMethod="Air") ∧
(≥ 0 hasCharacteristics · MinPrice=70) ∧
(≥ 0 hasCharacteristics · MaxPrice=90) ∧
(≥ 0 hasCharacteristics · LeadTime=7)
SupplierCapabilities4 ⊆ (Resource)
(≥ 1 isPerformedBy · SupplierAgent) ∧
(≥ 1 isCoordinatedBy · SupplierCapabilities) ∧
(≥ 1 hasCharacteristics. SupplierID =40) ∧
(≥ 1 hasCharacteristics · ProductName="Computer")) ∧
(≥ 1 hasCharacteristics · ProductType="Office Equipment") ∧
(≥ 1 hasCharacteristics · Price=110) ∧
(≥ 1 hasCharacteristics · Quantity=30) ∧
(≥ 1 hasCharacteristics · Quality=2) ∧
(≥ 0 hasCharacteristics · DeliveryMethod="Air") ∧
(≥ 0 hasCharacteristics · MinPrice=100) ∧
(≥ 0 hasCharacteristics · MaxPrice=120) ∧
(≥ 0 hasCharacteristics · LeadTime=14)
SupplierCapabilities5 ⊆ (Resource)
(≥ 1 isPerformedBy · SupplierAgent) ∧
(≥ 1 isCoordinatedBy · SupplierCapabilities) ∧
(≥ 1 hasCharacteristics. SupplierID =50) ∧
(≥ 1 hasCharacteristics · ProductName="Computer")) ∧
(≥ 1 hasCharacteristics · ProductType="Office Equipment") ∧
(≥ 1 hasCharacteristics · Price=115) ∧
(≥ 1 hasCharacteristics · Quantity=30) ∧
(≥ 1 hasCharacteristics · Quality=3) ∧
(≥ 0 hasCharacteristics · DeliveryMethod="Air") ∧
(≥ 0 hasCharacteristics · MinPrice=110) ∧
(≥ 0 hasCharacteristics · MaxPrice=120) ∧
(≥ 0 hasCharacteristics · LeadTime=21)
```

Chapter 6
Organizational Semiotics Complements Knowledge Management:
Two Steps to Knowledge Management Improvement

Jeffrey A. Schiffel
The Boeing Company, USA

ABSTRACT

Inserting the human element into an Information System leads to interpreting the Information System as an information field. Organizational semiotics provides a means to analyze this alternate interpretation. The semantic normal forms of organizational semiotics extract structures from natural language texts that may be stored electronically. In themselves, the SNFs are only canonic descriptions of the patterns of behavior observed in a culture. Conceptual graphs and dataflow graphs, their dynamic variety, provide means to reason over propositions in first order logics. Conceptual graphs, however, do not of themselves capture the ontological entities needed for such reasoning. The culture of an organization contains natural language entities that can be extracted for use in knowledge representation and reasoning. Together in a rigorous, two-step process, ontology charting from organizational semiotics and dataflow graphs from knowledge engineering provide a means to extract entities of interest from a subject domain such as the culture of organizations and then to represent these entities in formal logic reasoning. This chapter presents this process, and concludes with an example of how process improvement in an IT organization may be measured in this two-step process.

DOI: 10.4018/978-1-60960-595-7.ch006

INTRODUCTION

How might an ontology be used to measure improvements in the management of organizational knowledge? And might that ontology be derived from natural language, and then translated into a formal reasoning system? The answers can be applied readily to any subject involving measurement of activities otherwise hard to quantify. The point of departure is the observation that organizational semiotics and knowledge management are opposite sides of the same coin.

Collaborating members of an organization share a culture. Effectively improving competitiveness is a goal of knowledge management. Improving organizational knowledge thus requires changing the organizational culture to leverage the collective knowledge of collaborating groups of workers. Knowledge management is intimately tied to corporate culture and values – and organizational semiotics models corporate culture through its processes and artifacts. The subject domain to be examined here is software process improvement in a large IT department.

Like knowledge management, those involved in process improvement must possess an appreciation of the organization's culture. The improvement framework to be demonstrated here is the Capability Maturity Model from the Software Engineering Institute. The preceding description suggests a two-step procedure of semantic norming and conceptual graph reasoning that take into account both the prevailing software engineering environment and an imposed improvement framework. Both steps require developing a different semantic net in each step. One is an ontology chart from organizational semiotics. The second is a conceptual graph from the knowledge representation branch of artificial intelligence. We may wish a well-defined and organized structure of entities that make up the domain of the problem at hand, but first we must be able to capture those relevant concepts before we can reason about the situation. The means involves systematic methods to extract and organize the concepts and relations, and then to transfer the resulting ontology construct into a formal, logical reasoning system. Two complementary methods are required. The first is drawn from organizational semiotics, permitting the extraction concepts and relations into an ontology chart, and then building a set of semantic normal forms. The second method then transfers the semantic normal forms into a knowledge representation realized in the dataflow graph version of conceptual graphs. The case study to be presented draws data from the CMM and software engineering procedures of an information technology group, an ontologically structured analysis of natural language artifacts found in organizational culture, translated to semantic normal form, and transformed into the dataflow form of a conceptual graph. Measurements of quality improvement steps take by the IT group over several years are then computed into comparative metrics by the dataflow.

Organizations may improve efficiency by improving the flow and use of that information. Efficiency arises from using and creating information to solve organization problems. This applies corporate knowledge to speed cycle time, reduce costs, or increase competitiveness. (Public services increase abilities to deliver services, rather than increase competitiveness.) Since computers store and process information and make it available to organizational users, data and information must be put into some logical form to be computable. Underlying logical forms for computation rely on some form of first order logic, along with other syntax, predicates, and quantifiers. These computer data constructs have meaning only in the self-contained world of the computer system. They do not provide meaning in the real world of the organization. Communication is not explained by encodings, transmissions and decodings in computer systems, but as mental constructs (Pietarinen, 2010). That is this role of organization members, who provide the human element to produce and interpret the facts in the computer and turn those facts into useful knowledge. It follows that to understand meaning is to understand how the computer systems reflect organizational practices.

This chapter will show that organizational semiotics is a way to give form to the information flow – and thereby the implied knowledge held – in an organization to bridge between people and their cultures to the computerized systems that support them; and examines the underlying difficulty in making mental sense of the world as the problem of meaning. The organization of this chapter is as follows. *Culture, Organization, and Shared Knowledge* lays the groundwork for the effect from organizational culture and observable patterns of behavior on the ontology of organizational entities. Subsections will briefly investigate *Knowledge Management and Knowledge Engineering*. The next major section then turns to *Organizational Semiotics*, providing an overview of *Signs and Semiosis*, the building blocks of *Norms and Affordances*. The section *Semantic Networks* presents the two kinds of semantic nets used in the argument of this chapter: ontology charts to represent natural language entities, and conceptual graphs for logical formulation of those entities. *Ontology Charts and Semantic Normal Form* expands on ontology charts, leading to a case study, *An Example of SNF Development*. Similarly, the section *Conceptual Graphs* is a preamble for the extension of the example in A*n Example of Dataflow Graphs Derived from SNF*. The chapter concludes with a *Summary*.

CULTURE, ORGANIZATION, AND SHARED KNOWLEDGE

Culture is the vehicle by which ideas, customs, and material objects are created (Bennett, 1970). It is the collective programming of the mind that distinguishes one group of people from another (Schiffel, 2008). Culture only manifests itself through social action that always takes place in a changing context. Individuals experience a variety of cultures – national, regional, community, social order, workplace, and so forth. For this chapter, "culture" will refer primarily to organizational culture, which inherits and may adapt the attributes of national and occupational cultures. For communication to take place, individuals must have a shared interpretation of the signs that are exchanged, and which point to the signified entities in the world. Culture, the repeatable action of signs and interpretations, is observed through social interactions taking place in changing contexts (Hofstede, Pedersen, and Hofstede, 2002), 41). To interact, to work together, and to communicate, collaborating groups share a culture (Hofstede, 1997, p. 260). Groups of individuals develop cultural norms in the form of patterns consisting of shared meanings on shared goals and concepts. The means by which the minds of individuals in the group share meaning forms such behavioral patterns (Bateson, 1979).

Cultures may have subcultures; organizations may have suborganizations. In addition to self-generated cultural patterns, there can also be external influences, such as legal obligations, professional standards, and adopted methodologies. A culture is formed by common understanding, not the same understanding. Behavioral patterns are not identically understood, but are similarly understood. Individuals interpret and adjust patterns according to their own mental outlooks.

When a behavior pattern is recognized as being culturally useful – how the implications of the pattern can be put to work – the pattern becomes knowledge. Patterns that represent knowledge have completeness to them that data or information alone do not contain. Patterns reflect the collectively held knowledge of the organization, and are derived from the cultural context. Culture is the basis for knowledge. It is the values, norms, practices, and information involving people, processes, and tools and technology. Organizational culture contains the values, norms, practices, and information involving people, processes, and tools and technology. Sharing a culture leads to sharing knowledge.

Polanyi (1966) and Nonaka and Takeuchi (1995) described the tacit knowledge formed in minds, and on transforming tacit knowledge and capturing it in the explicit form. O'Dell and Grayson pointed out those attempts to reify collective knowledge into discrete, capturable elements fail to appreciate that knowledge is more than a discrete set of elements subject to codification. Orlikowski (2002) pointed out, however, that such taxonomic attempts to reify collective knowledge into discrete, capturable elements fails to appreciate that knowledge is more than a discrete set of elements subject to codification.

Because knowledge is information used in problem solving, it is contextual. The mind assimilates data and information; individuals in a group wish to solve problems collaboratively. Consequently, because knowledge and culture are intertwined, knowledge is thus valuable mainly in terms of its underlying organizational culture, which consequently creates the need for knowledge sharing.

Values permeating organizational culture guide decision-making and provide a basis for measurement (Keeney, 1994). Knowledge is key to evaluation and decision-making: a higher quality of knowledge and more shared knowledge lead to better decision-making (Kaner & Karni, 2004). Knowledge management is thus intimately tied to corporate culture and values, to strategy, and to competitive advantage. Like other asset management, usefulness of knowledge management is tied to asset utility as measured by the results of applying knowledge. A possible solution to the difficulty in evaluating culture entities and casting behavioral patterns into formal structures may be found in organizational semiotics, discussed in the later section, *Ontology Charts and Semantic Normal Form*. First, however, knowledge management will be discussed.

Knowledge Management and Knowledge Engineering

Knowledge management is an applied field derived from organizational studies, a branch of management theory. Knowledge management and process improvement are the opposite sides of the same coin of competitiveness and process efficiency. Knowledge management attempts to increase the rate or quality of knowledge use and knowledge formation. Process improvement removes external impediments to information flow. In practice, successful process improvement among knowledge workers improves efficiency in individual and group problem solving. This yields increased organizational competitiveness (Kreiner, 2002; McElroy, 1999; O'Leary, 1998). Unfortunately, knowledge management has too often become associated with information technology, as a grab bag of management techniques applied to knowledge workers (Malhotra, 2004; Pepper, 2000). Vendors in the enterprise software market re-label supply chain, benchmarking, and database access systems as knowledge management systems in attempts to make "Information Systems" into "knowledge management" systems and business process reengineering (Bertels & Savage, 1998, p. 7; Wilson, 2002). Here, however, the original definition and purpose of knowledge management is used.

In contrast to knowledge management, knowledge engineering is applied artificial intelligence – especially drawn from the conceptual structures branch – intended to formalize explicit knowledge into well-defined ontologies based in logics (Brachman & Levesque, 2004, pp. 31-32; Fagin, 1999; Sowa, 2000, p. 132; Turban & Aronson, 2001, p. 467ff).

Tacit knowledge is knowledge held in the mind (Kreiner, 2002; Polanyi, 1966). Advancements in knowledge representation suggest that tacit knowledge can be represented in technology. For example, software agents have been used to develop learning agents and knowledge repositories to create communities of knowledge. A limitation, however, is that software agents do not easily capture or convey context. Only human agents do. Context has not been completely integrated into agent systems because it is difficult to map learning into inference (Edmonds, 2002). The position held by researchers like Brown and Duguid (2001), Lesser and Storck (2001), and Senge (1990) is that collective knowledge is contained in how organizational processes are executed. Collective knowledge is indeterminate in nature, blurring any boundaries between tacit and explicit knowledge.

A difficulty in applying formal conceptual structures based in logic directly to a real-world problem is that first an ontology must be derived from natural language. Because an *ontology* is "an explicit specification of a conceptualization" (Gruber, 1992), it is an organized collection of defined entities and logical relations among them that describe how the entities are organized, representing those entities of some domain of interest. It describes what exists that is of interest to the situation at hand. Its form may be entity-relation diagrams, frames, Unified Modeling Language diagrams, or other constructions involving mathematical forms such as lattices. The specifications for the problem addressed in this chapter are semantic normal forms and conceptual graphs, defined in later sections.

Information systems should mirror the organization. These systems should be analogous to how the organization wishes to use its data and information to support business processes. From the viewpoint of an organizational semiotician, the systems should capture the way signs are exchanged, how meaning is generated from signs, and how knowledge emerges and is managed. Computers and databases do not have meaning, but only the ability to process sign symbols that represent norms and affordances. That is the subject of the next major section.

ORGANIZATIONAL SEMIOTICS

Organizational semiotics is the study of how signs are used in social groups that give meaning to the signs. It provides an ontology of organization structures and the interactions within the group expressed in their formal and informal work processes (such as published reports and discussions in meetings) The semantics of the signs, sign transformations, and exchanges arises from the shared ontology. That is, the cultures of the organization and the society containing it allow for a shared semantics that leads to a shared ability to give meaning to the signs. As used here, "ontology" is merely the commitment to what exists. It is not necessarily written down as some formalized structure, but arises from the prevailing cultures. An organization's culture gains existence from the collective processes and goals. It also encompasses parts of professional, national, and ethic cultures, which color it. This chapter proposes that the part of organizational culture related to informatics can be captured and expressed logically by applying organizational semiotics. Meaning and intent of information can thereby be computerized. Greater efficiency results. In short, meaning is central to the definition of an Information System (Clarke, 2001).

Because organizational semiotics examines the use of signs, texts, documents, sign-based artifacts and communications, it uses ideas from psychology, economics, management science, and Information Systems science (Gazendam, 2004). It examines human information and communications systems from the viewpoint of organizations (Codeiro & Filipe, 20004). While physical artifacts such as documents, databases, and emails have independent existence, organizations only exist in the mind (Shishkov, Dietz & Liu, 2006). They are social constructs derived from people's shared understanding of a culture. Objects of perception – how and why they are perceived – is an invariant collection of behaviors. The behaviors arise uniquely in a given culture. Organizational semiotics encompasses the processes of creating, transforming through exchange, and consuming signs – in short, the production and use of knowledge. This notion will be explored later in this chapter.

An *information field* is a shared set of norms (social, organisational or legal) in an organization or society. A community that shares sets of norms constitutes an information field; their norms define their organised behaviour and determine their information needs. Gazendam elaborated the information field as

Information field based organizational semiotics (the Stamper school of organizational semiotics) is based on the idea of an information field (Stamper, 1973, 2001; Liu, 2000). Humans are seen as agents. Agents act influenced by the forces that are present in an information field. These forces originate from the norms that are shared in an organization or social community. An information field consists of physical affordances and social affordances, and the norms attached to them. Physical affordances are physical objects, physical spaces, and other physical agents that afford certain behaviour by a species. Physical affordances correspond to behaviour patterns, and are defined in terms of these behaviour patterns. In the Stamper school of organizational semiotics, it is said that affordances are behaviour patterns.

Stamper, the originator of information-based organizational semiotics, developed MEASUR (Methods for Eliciting, Analysing and Specifying User's Requirements) from 1971 to 1994 to improve the design of Information Systems. MEASUR advances the theory of Information Systems by replacing information flow modeling with information field analysis (Stamper, 2004). The common knowledge of organizations is held by people, documents and messages, and computer information and decision systems. This suggests that rather than viewing computer systems as the usual model of information flows, an alternative

interpretation as an information field introduces the human elements of culture and organizations.

Information fields consist of agents, affordances, and norms. An *agent* is the responsible person or organisation involved in the system under study (Tan & Liu, 2004). Humans are agents who are influenced by the forces that are present in an information field. Similarly, the organizations created by humans are also agents. Forces on agents originate from the norms that are shared in an organization or social community. An information field consists of affordances and norms. *Affordances* are the things involved and the behaviors afforded by the agent. Physical affordances are artifacts, computer screens, writings, conference rooms, etc.; social artifacts are derived from culture. Affordances enable certain behaviors by agents. *Norms* are the patterns of behavior. Norms determine the information needs. This changes the information flow emphasis from merely technical analysis to an information field emphasis extending to include the human aspects of a system under development. Before continuing the discussion of norms and affordances, some definitions of signs and semiosis are necessary.

Signs and Semiosis

Signs are the basic unit of meaning. They are therefore the basic unit of analysis in organizational semiotics. Peirce (CP2.78) defined a sign to have three parts. The parts are the sign proper, which is a signifier of some object, the object signified by the sign, and an interpretant. Signs are of three types: a) icons (a portrait is the person), symbols (smoke is a sign of fire), and indexes ("Toto" is the index for Dorothy's dog). The key to a sign is not the sign as a whole, but that part that is interpreted as being significant. Peirce also at times named the interpretant as the representamen. It will be apparent later in this chapter that Stamper identifies the Peircean interpretant/representamen as a Gibsonean affordance (Gazendam, 2010). Signs allow interactions to exchange of information (Sadowski, 2010). Information results from changes in the physical states of some system. Sadowski related sign types to systems from the implications of state changes: An index is a physical change produced in the environment by an agent is called an index of that agent. An icon is a change in the environment that perceptually resembles some attribute of another agent. A symbol is the result of a system change that bears no perceptual resemblance to agents or entities.

Other traditions of sign analysis exist, principally that of Saussure (2001). The Saussure method of semiotics has been adopted into other disciplines. Among them are linguistics; literary criticism; Bahktin's social signs, leading to Social Semiotics; feminism; and art and film criticism. The Peirce tradition, however, is more closely grounded in formal logic, and is more useful for the needs of organizational semiotics. For our purposes, a) signs arise in the prevailing culture (a Kansas rancher reads more into cloud patterns that a New Yorker, but the New Yorker knows "instinctively" down which streets not to stroll); b) the exchange of signs is the method to communicate – to implant one's thoughts in another mind, more or less precisely; and c) interpreting one or more signs gives rise to secondary, tertiary, etc. signs. This last element is the process of *semiosis*.

Norms and Affordances

The notion of affordances was coined by the Gestalt psychologist Gibson, who defined, "affordances of things are what they furnish, for good or ill, that is, what they **afford** the observer" (1971, p. 403). Affordances are properties of objects, substances, places, events, animals, and artifacts. These properties are not phenomenological, but are relative to the person in terms of their culture; an affordance is determined by its utility in society. We perceive affordances as possibilities for action, such as a surface providing a place for walking, or a ladder affording a way to climb. Affordances may also be social, as in telephones, television,

trademarks and logos, and Information System artifacts for communication and information-sharing. These are the semiotic aspects of the tools. In a posting to the Ontolog on-line forum, Stamper (2008) illustrated affordances this way

Building on Gibson's work, we see that all knowledge of the world depends a) on an agent to do the knowing and b) the agent's behaviour that embodies the invariants we treat as perceived things. This suggests a syntax:

```
agent affordance
John upright
```

By realising or making available a repertoire of behaviour, the agent modifies itself, so that recursively we can say:

```
(agent affordance) affordance
(John upright) jump
```

Some affordances depend for their existence on two, coexisting antecedent affordances:

```
(agent (affordance while affordance))
affordance
(John (paper while pencil)) draw
```

When we move from direct knowledge to knowledge shared by Society through the use of information, we need to treat Society as the root agent, for example:

```
Society (person while person)
marriage
Society (John while Mary) marriage
```

But suppose they are not married; someone, perhaps John, can use a sign that stands for the marriage when he wants to propose:

```
Society (John, "(John, Mary)
marriage" propose
```

where the quotes indicate that we are talking about a sign that stands for a marriage that does not yet exist, a sign that John employs to propose.

Such patterns of perceptions are cultural interpretations: they are norms. They are the rules and regulations in an information field that regulate the manner in which agents communicate. Norms influence agents in their join behaviors to reach organizational goals. A shared mental construct, they are realized by the way business procedures and policies are used (Tan & Liu, 2004). Norms are the shared culture interpretation of affordances. In terms of Information Systems, an affordance is the property of the data, user interface, or data access that fulfills information users' motivational needs (Jung, Schneider, & Valacich, 2010).

There is no knowable reality without perception. Humans are agents of perception who discover reality in the flow of events, and causes and events. Agents act influenced by the forces that are present in an information field. These forces originate from the norms that are shared in an organization or social community. An information field consists of physical affordances and social affordances, and the norms attached to them. Agent perceptions in the information field forms an invariant interpretation shared with other agents.

Organizational semiotics as developed by Stamper developed around the information field, consisting of physical and social affordances and their norms (Stamper, Liu, Hafkamp, & Ades, 2000). Information users are agents, that act based on the norms shared by the organizational culture.

Semantic Networks

A *semantic network* is a spatial depiction in the form of a directed graph used in knowledge representation. Semantic networks are a representational format to illuminate the semantics of words and word relationships (Quillian, 1968, p. 216). (While it is commonly assumed that Quillian introduced the term, Richens (1956) coined the term "semantic net" a decade earlier,

during investigations into the requirements for machine translation from base texts to other natural or formal languages.) Semantic net are useful for the conceptual analysis of language, can be transformed into some variety or subset of first-order logic, and enable inference through an interpreter agent designed to manipulate formal representations (Hartley & Barnden, 1997). Knowledge relationships displayed in graphs are easy to construct and are easy for human readers to approach than other forms of knowledge representation, such as controlled natural language based on special rules, or the symbolic notation of first order logics. Like any abstraction, the obfuscated meaning in graphs may have more to do with poor design than with the ability of graphical depictions to convey meaning (De Angeli, Coventry, Johnson, & Renaud, 2005; Weber, 2003), leading to incorrect representation and reasoning (Rodhain, 1999; Gaifman, 2002). Parsons and Cole (2005) stated that a modeling technique should be chosen based on the nature of independent and dependent variables, experimental procedures, and the participants (developers and readers). Dau (2004) observed that carefully designed diagramming methods can support a number of logically rigorous and complete formal systems.

Brachman (1985) defined five interrelated levels of representation commonly seen in semantic net, the a) linguistic – arbitrary concepts, words, and expressions; b) conceptual -- semantics or conceptual relations, primitive objects and actions; c) "epistemological" (structural) – concept types, conceptual sub-pieces, inheritance and structuring relations; d) logical – propositions, predicates, and logical operators; and e) implementational – atoms and pointers. His intent was to demonstrate the structure of communication from the syntactical and grammatical, and building to the formal and semantic. This represents the relative level of problem-solving intentions of the semantic net designer, rather than a hypernomic taxonomy. The form of a semantic net will therefore be related to the intent of the designer.

Semantic net underlie most graphical techniques used in the capture of knowledge relationships. The solution posed in this chapter requires two different kinds of semantic nets. Ontology charting allows concepts and relations to be extracted from natural language and cast into semantic normal form – corresponding to the upper levels Brachman defined. Dataflow graphs coordinate the semantic normal forms into well-structured, processable units for reasoning. The first, the ontology chart, is a simple and intuitive visual form of knowledge representation. This is a surface structure, representing phrases that constitute a categorization of linguistic phrases (Chomsky, 2006, p. 92). It is simple in the sense that there are few symbol types, a basic syntax, and a loose structure. The second kind is a conceptual structure. Formalized logically or mathematically, this kind of semantic net may be take the form of a conceptual graph, specifically employed here in the dataflow graph variety – corresponding to Brachman's lower levels. The aim is to develop a useful connection between the two.

Ontology Charts and Semantic Normal Form

Knowledge sharing is a continuing exchange of signs among participants. The signs are semiotic signs, contained in oral exchanges and in written documents, and in drawings and images. The implied meanings, however, are subject to slightly different interpretations among individuals (Gazendam, 2004).

Organizational semiotics is a means to analyze and codify the results of semiosis in an organization. Signs – words, images, and other signifiers – are the meaning assigned to symbols by the individuals interpreting the symbols in the world. The shared understanding of signs and their use are the norms of the organizational culture. Norms are the patterns of behavior that provide guidance individuals. Since the norms describe propositional attitudes, an individual may or may not choose to follow a norm in a given situation, but overall, organizational behavior is governed by shared norms. Semiotic analysis of an organization models the meaning of information and rules flowing through it. That is, it models the use of organizational knowledge.

The norm analysis method uncovers the relationship among organizational entities formed as a result of semiosis. These extracted concepts and relations can then be further refined into semantic normal form. Semantic analysis of phrases and rules extracted from the organization is first graphed as an ontology chart. This is an intermediate step toward the desired semantic normal forms.

The usual three steps in developing a text into semantic normal form consists of a) text extraction to identify and construct a lexicon of concepts and relationships, b) development of an ontology chart from the lexicon, and c) building the basic semantic normal forms and joining them into a structure suitable for electronic storage (Salter, 2001). The three steps are now outlined.

1. *Text extraction.* Using inspection, or standard tools such as concordancers, a lexicon of terms is compiled from textual material. The material consists of natural language text, and can include standard procedure documents, interview notes, operations documentation, and so forth. The semantic elements – the extracted words – are then assigned an ontological type and a potential link to another semantic unit (if any). Ontological types are described in the next section.

2. *Develop ontological chart.* In organizational semiotics, the name *ontology chart* is the name given to a three-part, cyclic, semantic net consisting of three kinds of semantic units and three kinds of associations. Semantic units may be agents, affordances, or determiners. Associations are simple, homonymic, or meronymic. Rules for developing ontology charts are simple:

○ An agent is an actor, a person or thing of relevance in the culture under examination. Agents may take on hyponymy (is-a) role relationships to other agents. Agents, usually nouns or noun phrases, are depicted graphically as named ovals. By convention, an organization, or society, is an agent node designated as the root node. The root node can be an invented concept used as an upper bound. The graph is usually read left-to-right. There is only one root node. "Society" is the root node, since it is the primary antecedent. All subsequent, direct or indirect semantic units depend on the cultural aspects of "society" for their existence.

○ An affordance is a pattern of behavior, an action an agent may undertake. It is a collection of properties in the culture that enables or disables activities by actors. They may be further defined as universal or local affordances. Affordances are usually verb or verb phrases, but may include nouns that imply action. They are depicted as named rectangles.

○ A determiner is a property (an attribute) of and agent or affordance that differentiates the semantic unit from another. A determiner may be composite, containing other dependent determiners in a meronyn (part-of) relationship. Determiners are text prefixed by #.

○ Of the three kinds of relationships, simple associations are bidirectional and are drawn as lines without arrows. Role relationships are lines that are labeled with the role in a half-circle. Part-of relationships are lines with a dot over top.

○ The construction rules for the ontology chart are straightforward. Generally, agents connect to affordances, affordances to agents. Determiners can connect to agents or to affordances. Part-of relationships connect agents to agents, or affordances to affordances, or determiners to determiners (in which case the dot is omitted from the association line). Is-a relationships refine agents or affordances. As refiners, they connect agents to role-playing agents, or affordances to sub-affordances.

3. *Semantic normalization.* Semantic normalization results in a precisely formulated list of agents and affordance as a semantic normal form. An SNF can be specified in several different ways, depending on contextual need (Gazendam & Liu, 2004). Salter, for example, defines a consisting of a <condition, triggering state, agent, deontic operator, and action to be taken> (2001). Where time is a modeling need, a format such as <action, antecedents, time start, time stop> may be better suited. In the following Example 1, Part 1, the SNF format is <predecessor agent, affordance, successor agent>. The successor agent may be empty.

For any SNF format chosen, the relationships of the ontology chart guides development of the SNF instances derived from the agents and affordances table. The following example serves to illustrate the process of textual extraction, ontology chart drawing, and semantic normal form development.

AN EXAMPLE OF SNF DEVELOPMENT

Authentic process improvement, a kind of knowledge management, must start with the study of the cognitive phenomena inside an organization.

The following example for an IT department of a large, Midwestern aerospace manufacturer illustrates how semantic normalization proceeds from text extraction, to ontology chart drawing, and to generation of semantic normal forms. The SNFs that are extracted from the engineering and process improvement culture reflect how the IT department collectively shares knowledge practices for their process improvement goals. The SNF creation process is adapted from (Salter, 2001; Stamper, Liu, Hafkamp, & Ades, 2000).

Example, Part 1

In response to internal and external competitive pressures, IT management decided to adopt the CMM to improve the software engineering practices infrastructure of the IT department. One of the goals was to increase customer satisfaction with software systems, as measured by the number of software defects that escaped from the development arena into production. CMM adoption for process improvement required an acclimatization of the engineering culture through a shared knowledge of, and participation in, improving methods. Consider the following two elements of to be modeled in an ontology chart. The first is part of the CMM standard from the Software Engineering Institute that IT department adopted. That adoption commenced the integration of the CMM into the software engineering culture. The second element is the management direction to the engineering staff, which became a goal for the software engineers, and therefore also part of their culture.

1. The Capability Maturity Model stated the goals, activities, measurements, and verification methods for peer reviews (Paulk, Weber, Curtis & Chrissis, 1994, pp. 270ff). (The SEI is superseding the CMMI by the Capability Maturity Model – Integrated, but the data for this example dates from before that change began. In either model, the peer

review process is essentially the same for software engineering.) Among other model requirements, it calls for

○ Goal 2: Defects in software work products are identified and removed.

○ Measurement 1: Measurements are made and used to determine the status of peer reviews.

2. Management intent for the IT department.

○ Software engineering teams conduct peer reviews to remove defects before product release to customers. Defects are reported periodically to management. Management directs process improvement in software product quality through defect removal before delivery to customers. Management reviews reported defect numbers periodically.

Examination of the CMM element and the management intent element returned the following table of agents and affordances:

From Table 1 the ontology chart of Figure 1 can be drawn. Observe that the usual root node, "society," is omitted. In this particular chart "organization" is only direct successor element. "Society" is assumed.

The next step of this semantic analysis is to write the semantic normal forms. This will result in a precisely formulated list of agents and affordance as semantic normal forms. A semantic normal form can be specified in several different ways, depending on contextual need (Gazendam & Liu, 2004). Salter (2001), for example, defines a consisting of a <condition, triggering state, agent, deontic operator, and action to be taken>. Where time is a modeling need, a format such as <action, antecedents, time start, time stop> may be better suited. In this example, the SNF format is <predecessor agent, affordance, successor agent>. The successor agent may be empty. For any SNF format chosen, the relationships of the ontology

Figure 1. Ontology chart for the software engineering example

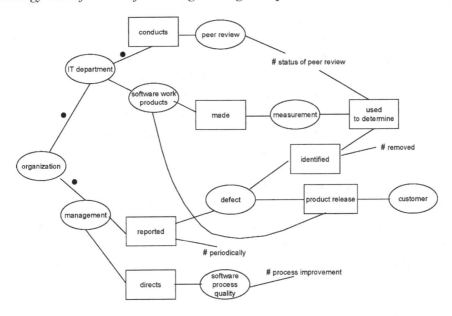

chart guides development of the SNF instances derived from the agents and affordances table.

As will be seen in Example 2, which will continue Example 1, the SNF instances used for conceptual graphs may also become the basis for the concepts, concept relations, and actors used in dataflow graphs. Before that example, however, a review of conceptual graphs is presented.

Conceptual Graphs

In comparison with the ontology charts of organizational semiotics, conceptual graphs are well known, and thus are only briefly reviewed here. More thorough treatments may be found in (Amati & Ounis, 2000; Chein & Mugnier, 1992; Schärfe, Petersen, & Øhrstrøm, 2002; Sowa, 2000). A *conceptual graph* is a two-part graph with concept vertexes that are either concepts or conceptual relations.

Conceptual graphs and dataflow graphs are used to represent the meanings of sentences. Adding constraints to natural language from which the graphs are to be extracted allows the graphs also to represent formal conceptual structures.

The difficulty, however, is in first identifying and isolating the concepts in expressed by natural language so they may be cast as conceptual graphs. By themselves, conceptual graphs do not offer a means to perform this function. A means to define the relevant concepts is needed. This will be shown in the next section, *"An Example of Dataflow Graphs Derived from SNF,"* which continues Example, Part 1.

The notation for conceptual graphs is rich, allowing expression of the meanings of sentences. By adding constraints to natural language, these graphs can also represent formal conceptual structures. Concept boxes consist of a concept type and a referent that instantiates the type. Unnamed edges joining the vertexes are simple, two-directional lines. A single line links exactly one concept to exactly one conceptual relation. Since conceptual graphs are based in first order predicate logic, they syntax contains quantifiers; relations (i.e., the conceptual relation boxes); designators for literals, numerals, and references exist. Conceptual graphs can accommodate simple first order logic, lambda formulations, or other versions such as typed first order logic. A graphical form and a linear form exist. A simple conceptual graph for the sentence "The cat is on the mat," often encountered in the literature, is shown Figure 2, in both graphical and linear form.

The linear form is slightly more difficult to read but has the advantage that it can be parsed by computer software into a schema for a knowledge base. The linear form shown may be represented in first order logic as $(\exists x)(\exists y)$ Cat(x) $\wedge$ Mat(y) $\wedge$ On(x,y).

The use of logical joins to unify conceptual graphs from two or more already existing graphs allows discovery or extraction of further domain knowledge (Nguyen & Corbett, 2006). The dataflow graph – conceptual graphs with actor nodes – allows otherwise static conceptual graphs to model dynamic behavioral and state relationships. For example, consider the sentences, "There is a situation where a group of employees use a process to produce a product. There is a proposition that measurements of the process are metrics. There is a proposition that measurements of the product are metrics." Figure 3 depicts the joined graphs of this idea. Agnt (agent) and Use are relations; Measure is an actor, which calculates metric sets mprod{*} and mproc{*}. Concepts such as Employee have as referents variables such as the set *w{}. The actor GenSpace calculates a metric space from the individual metrics. Finally, the concepts Situation and Proposition have conceptual graphs as referents.

AN EXAMPLE OF DATAFLOW GRAPHS DERIVED FROM SNF

Example, Part 2

Part 2 continues the Example, Part 1. The SNF instances previously developed are classifications of the external cultural patterns. To put these to use for reasoning – in this case, for calculation of metrics – the SNFs are internalized for use in dataflow graphs.

Table 2 modifies the table of agents and affordances. It adds the names of concepts, concept relations, and actors to the table. Since the task at hand is only defect measurement, and not the entire content of the ontology chart, those rows from Table 1 needed for the dataflow graph are brought forward.

A dataflow graph constructed from the elements of the table allows for this to be drawn, shown in Figure 4.

IT software engineering teams reported data for five consecutive years. While not germane to this demonstration, the IT department also collected data to show improvement in labor hours expended, cycle time for system development,

Figure 2. Conceptual graphs of "The cat is on the mat"

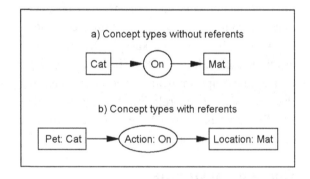

Figure 3. Joined conceptual and dataflow graphs

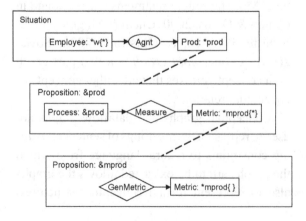

Table 1. Agents, affordances, and potential links

Entity	Type	Potential Links
defect	agent	
software work product	agent	
identified and recorded	affordance	
measurement	agent	
made	affordance	
used to determine	affordance	
status of peer review	affordance	determiner (of peer review)
peer review	agent	
software engineering team	agent	
conducts	affordance	
remove	affordance	determiner (of identified)
remove	affordance	determiner (of identified)
product release	affordance	
reported	affordance	
periodically	affordance	determiner (of reporting)
management	agent	
process improvement	agent	
directs	affordance	
defect removal	affordance	
reviews	agent	
software process quality	agent	
IT department	agent	

and customer satisfaction, but only software quality is described here. A desired quality metric was the average number of defects escaping into production. The raw data was reported monthly. For demonstration of the dataflow diagram of Figure 4, only year-end data is used. The process to execute the dataflow graph with this data is as follows.

The procedure by the IT department to collect the raw data is show in the *Situation* concept. *Situation* contains an embedded conceptual graph. The concept *ITDept* has as referent the individual members *members*. The conceptual relation *Conduct* connects the *ITDept* to the *PeerRev*, with referent *SWProd*. This is may be read, "the IT department members conduct peer reviews over software products," which also may be referenced in the ontology chart. In like fashion, the results of the peer review are passed through agent *Determine* to the concept *Defect*, collected in the referent *count*, a number. The data in *count* is shown as passing from the concept *Situation*, by the referent pointer &count, to *Proposition*. Agent *Report* processes defect counts into an array shown as *count{ }* in *SPQual*. This is, "defect counts are measured and placed into the counting array for reporting of software process quality." Results are shown in Table 3, portraying that the software engineering process was improved, and CMM knowledge was brought into the engineering culture.

SUMMARY

From the observation that culture and knowledge are opposite sides of the same coin, this chapter examined organizational culture from the organizational semiotics point of view. The resulting ontology chart provides a static view of the information field that incorporates human elements into Information Systems. Organizational semiotics analyzes natural language to extract semantic normal forms that capture the essential behavioral patterns. These are found in the cultural context that creates the natural language artifacts. The ontology charts and semantic normal forms model the structure of the pattern links. These are not, however, sufficient for formal reasoning. The dynamic model was then built from the dataflow diagram form of a conceptual graph. Conceptual graphs and dataflow graphs are graphical forms of first order logic. They are formal graphical structures. The limitation, however, is that no means to derive the concepts and relations is part of their formalization.

Table 2. Dataflow names derived from SNF

Entity	Type	Dataflow Graph Abbreviation
defect	agent	Defect: *count
software work product	agent	SWProd
used to determine	affordance	Determine
peer review	agent	PeerRev: SWProd
software engineering team	agent	*members
conducts	affordance	Conduct
reported	affordance	Report
software process quality	agent	SPQual
IT department	agent	ITDept: *members

Figure 4. Joined conceptual graph and dataflow graph

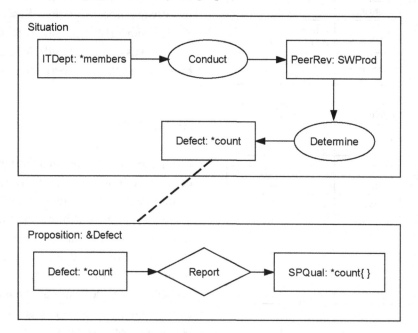

Table 3. Year-end CMM progression data for defect escapes

	Production Defect Escapes Detected
1998	2.3
1999	0.7
2000	0.6
2001	0.3
2002	0.2

This chapter demonstrated a possible way to move from natural language to first order logic, while preserving a rigorous semantics from the cultural context to the logic arena. This maps the "meaningful" semantics of natural language into the "meaningless" symbols of symbolic logic. This consisted of a two-step approach that 1) transferred relevant culture entities and behavioral patterns into semantic normal forms, then 2) applying the semantic normal forms as the concepts and relations in diagrammatic logic.

This two-step approach overcame the obstacle in finding the concepts in expressed by natural language to construct conceptual graphs. Used in succession, ontology charts and semantic normal forms drawn from organizational semiotics allow entities and relations to be defined as the concept types and other required elements to be used in dataflow graphs. This results in a coordinated approach to turn cultural entities and patterns into well-structured reasoning units.

REFERENCES

Amati, G., & Ounis, I. (2000). Conceptual graphs and first order logic. *The Computer Journal*, *43*(1), 1–12. doi:10.1093/comjnl/43.1.1

Bateson, G. (1979). *Mind and nature: A necessary unity* (1st ed.). New York, NY: Dutton.

Bennett, J. (1970). Culture. In Schindler, S. (Ed.), *Encyclopedia international* (Vol. 5, pp. 395–397). New York, NY: Grolier, Inc.

Bertels, T., & Savage, C. (1998). Tough questions on knowledge management. In von Krogh, G., Roos, J., & Kleine, D. (Eds.), *Knowing in firms* (pp. 7–25). London, UK: Sage Publications.

Brachman, R. (1985). On the epistemological status of semantic networks. In Brachman, R., & Levesque, H. (Eds.), *Readings in knowledge representation* (pp. 91–215). Los Altos, CA: Kaufmann.

Brachman, R., & Levesque, H. (2004). *Knowledge representation and reasoning*. San Francisco, CA: Elsevier, Inc.

Brown, J. S., & Duguid, P. (2001). Knowledge and organization: A social-practice perspective. *Organization Science*, *12*(2), 198–213. doi:10.1287/orsc.12.2.198.10116

Chein, M., & Mugnier, M.-L. (1992). Conceptual graphs: Fundamental notions. *Revue d'Intelligence Artificielle*, *6*(4), 365–406.

Chomsky, N. (2006). *Language and mind* (3rd ed.). Cambridge, UK: Cambridge University Press. doi:10.1017/CBO9780511791222

Clarke, R. (2001). Studies in organisational semiotics: An introduction. *Australasian Journal of Information Systems*, *8*(2), 75–82.

Cordeiro, J., & Felipe, J. (2004, July 19-20). *The semiotic pentagram framework - a perspective on the use of semiotics within organisational semiotics*. Paper presented at the 7th International Workshop on Organisational Semiotics, Escola Superior de Tecnologia, Setúbal, Portugal.

Dau, F. (2004). Types and tokens for logic with diagrams. In K. E. Wolff, H. Pfeiffer, & H. S. Delugach (Eds.), *12th International Conference on Conceptual Structures: Lecture Notes in Computer Science, 3127* (pp. 62-93). Berlin, Germany: Springer-Verlag.

De Angeli, A., Coventry, L., Johnson, G., & Renaud, K. (2005). Is a picture really worth a thousand words? Exploring the feasibility of graphical authentication systems. *International Journal of Human-Computer Studies*, *63*(1-2), 128–152. doi:10.1016/j.ijhcs.2005.04.020

Edmonds, B. (2002). Learning and exploiting context in agents. *First International Joint Conference on Autonomous Agents and Multi-agent Systems: Proceedings Part 3* (pp. 1231-1238). New York, NY: ACM Press.

Fagan, M. E. (1976). Design and code inspections to reduce errors in program development. *IBM Systems Journal*, *15*(3), 182–211. doi:10.1147/sj.153.0182

Gaifman, H. (2002). *Vagueness, tolerance and contextual logic* (Philosophy Dept., unpublished paper). New York, NY: Columbia University. Retrieved November 6, 2010 from http://www.columbia.edu/~hg17/VTC-latest.pdf

Gazendam, H. (2004, March 23). Organizational semiotics: A state of the art report. *SemiotiX*, 1. Retrieved July 5, 2010 from http://www.semioti-con.com/semiotix

Gazendam, H. (2010, April 11-12). *From subject databases to flow of responsibility*. Paper presented at 11th International Conference on Informatics and Semiotics in Organisations, IFIP WG8.1 Working Conference. Reading, UK.

Gazendam, H. W. M., & Liu, K. (2004). The evolution of organisational semiotics. In J. Filipe, & K. Liu (Eds.), *7th International Workshop on Organisational Semiotics: Proceedings* (pp. 1-11). Setubal, Portugal: INSTICC Press.

Gibson, J. J. (1982). A preliminary description and classification of affordances. In Reed, E. S., & Jones, R. (Eds.), *Reasons for realism* (pp. 403–406). Hillsdale, NJ: Lawrence Erlbaum Associates, Inc.

Gruber, T. (1993). A translation approach to portable ontology specifications. *Knowledge Acquisition*, *5*(2), 199–220. doi:10.1006/knac.1993.1008

Hartley, R., & Barnden, J. (1997). Semantic networks: Visualizations of knowledge. *Trends in Cognitive Sciences*, *1*(5), 169–175. doi:10.1016/S1364-6613(97)01057-7

Hofstede, G. (1997). *Cultures and organizations: Software of the mind*. New York, NY: McGraw-Hill.

Hofstede, G. J., Pedersen, P., & Hofstede, G. (2002). *Exploring culture: Exercises, stories and synthetic cultures*. Yarmouth, ME: Intercultural Press.

Jung, J. H., Schneider, C., & Valacich, J. (2010). Enhancing the motivational affordance of Information Systems: The effects of real-time performance feedback and goal setting in group collaboration environments. *Management Science*, *56*(4), 724–742. doi:10.1287/mnsc.1090.1129

Kaner, M., & Karni, R. (2004). A capability maturity model for knowledge-based decisionmaking. *Information Knowledge Systems Management*, *4*(4), 225–252.

Keeney, R. (1994). Using values in operations research. *Operations Research*, *42*(5), 793–814. doi:10.1287/opre.42.5.793

Kreiner, K. (2002). Tacit knowledge management: The role of artifacts. *Journal of Knowledge Management*, *6*(2), 112–123. doi:10.1108/13673270210424648

Lesser, E. L., & Storck, J. (2001). Communities of practice and organizational performance. *IBM Systems Journal*, *40*(4), 831–841. doi:10.1147/sj.404.0831

Malhotra, Y. (2004). Why do knowledge management systems fail? Enablers and constraints of knowledge management in human enterprises. In Koenig, M. E. D., & Srikantaiah, T. K. (Eds.), *Knowledge management lessons learned: What works and what doesn't* (pp. 87–112). Silver Spring, MD: American Society for Information Science and Technology Monograph Series, Information Today Inc.

McElroy, M. (1999, October). The second generation of knowledge management. *Knowledge Management Magazine*, 86-88.

Nguyen, P., & Corbett, D. (2006). A basic mathematical framework for conceptual graphs. *IEEE Transactions on Knowledge and Data Engineering*, *18*(2), 261–271. doi:10.1109/TKDE.2006.18

Nonaka, I., & Takeuchi, H. (1995). *The knowledge-creating company: How Japanese companies create the dynamics of innovation*. New York, NY: Oxford University Press.

O'Leary, D. (1998). Enterprise knowledge management. *Computer*, *31*(3), 54–61. doi:10.1109/2.660190

Orlikowski, W. (2002). Knowing in practice: Enacting a collective capability in distributed organizing. *Organization Science, 13*(3), 249–273. doi:10.1287/orsc.13.3.249.2776

Parsons, J., & Cole, L. (2005). What do the pictures mean? Guidelines for experimental evaluation of representation fidelity in diagrammatical conceptual modeling techniques. *Data & Knowledge Engineering, 55*(3), 327–342. doi:10.1016/j.datak.2004.12.008

Paulk, M., Weber, C., Curtis, B., & Chrissis, M. B. (1994). *The capability maturity model: Guidelines for improving the software process.* Reading, MA: Addison-Wesley Longman, Inc.

Peirce, C. S. (1931-1958). Vol 2, paragraph 228. In C. H. vols. 1-6, P. Weiss; & A. W. Burks vols. 7-8 (Eds.), *The collected papers of C. S. Peirce.* Cambridge, MA: Harvard University Press.

Pepper, S. (2000). The Tao of topic maps. *XML Europe 2000, Paris: Palais des Congres, Paris, June 12-16: Proceedings.* Retrieved November 5, 2010, from http://www.gca.org/papers/xmleurope2000/papers/s11-01.html

Pietarinen, A.-V. (2009, July 19-21). *On the conceptual underpinnings of organizational semiotics.* Paper presented at 11th International Conference on Informatics and Semiotics in Organisations, IFIP WG8.1 Working Conference. Beijing.

Polanyi, M. (1966). *The tacit dimension.* Garden City, NJ: Doubleday and Company, Inc.

Quillian, M. R. (1968). Semantic memory. In Minsky, M. (Ed.), *Semantic information processing* (pp. 216–270). Cambridge, MA: MIT Press.

Richens, R. H. (1956). Preprogramming for mechanical translation. *Machine Translation Archive, 3*(1), 20–25.

Rodhain, F. (1999). Tacit to explicit: Transforming knowledge through cognitive mapping - an experiment. In R. Agarwal & J. Prasad (Eds.), *1999 ACM SIGCPR Conference on Computer Personnel Research: Proceedings* (pp. 51-56). New York, NY: ACM Digital Library.

Sadowski, P. (2010). Towards systems semiotics: Some remarks and (hopefully useful) definitions. *Semiotix, 1.* Retrieved November 5, 2010, from http://www.semioticon.com/semiotix/issues/2010-issue-2011/

Salter, A. (2001). *Semantic modelling and a semantic normal form.* (School of Computing Technical Report SOCTR/01/01): Staffordshire University.

Saussure, F. (2001). *Course in literary theory: An anthology.* Hoboken, NJ: Blackwell Publishers.

Schärfe, H., Petersen, U., & Øhrstrøm, P. (2002). On teaching conceptual graphs. In Priss, U., Corbett, D., & Angelova, G. (Eds.), *Conceptual structures: Integration and interfaces: Lecture Notes in Computer Science 2393* (pp. 285–298). Heidelberg/ Berlin, Germany: Springer. doi:10.1007/3-540-45483-7_22

Schiffel, J. (2008). *Improving knowledge management programs using marginal utility in a metric space generated by conceptual graphs.* ProQuest-Theses: Doctoral Dissertation, Nova Southeastern University, Fort Lauderdale.

Senge, P. (1990). *The fifth discipline: The art and practice of the learning organization.* New York, NY: Currency Doubleday.

Shishkov, B., Dietz, J. L. G., & Liu, K. (2006, May 23-27). *Bridging the language-action perspective and organizational semiotics in SDBC.* Paper presented at the Eighth International Conference on Enterprise Information Systems, Paphos, Cyprus.

Sowa, J. (2000). *Knowledge representation: Logical, philosophical, and computational foundations.* Pacific Grove, CA: Brooks/Cole.

Stamper, R. (2004, July 18). *MEASUR – Semiotic tools for IS development*. The 7th International Workshop on Organisational Semiotics. Retrieved July 15, 2010, from http://www.orgsem.org/sedita.htm

Stamper, R. (2008). *Posting to Ontolog forum on October 6, 2008*. Retrieved October 6, 2008, from http://ontolog.cim3.net/forum/ontolog-forum/2008-10/msg00044.html

Stamper, R., Liu, K., Hafkamp, M., & Ades, Y. (2000). Understanding the roles of signs and norms in organizations – a semiotic approach to Information Systems design. *Behaviour & Information Technology, 19*(1), 15–27. doi:10.1080/014492900118768

Tan, S., & Liu, K. (2004, April 14-17). *Requirements engineering for organisational modelling*. Paper presented at the 6th International Conference on Enterprise Information Systems, Porto, Portugal.

Turban, E., & Aronson, J. (2001). *Decision support systems and intelligent systems*. Upper Saddle River, NJ: Prentice-Hall, Inc.

Weber, R. (2003). Conceptual modelling and ontology: Possibilities and pitfalls. *Journal of Database Management, 14*(2), 1–20. doi:10.4018/jdm.2003070101

Wilson, T. D. (2002). The nonsense of knowledge management. *Information Research, 8*(1), paper no. 144.

Section 2
Agent–Based Systems

Chapter 7
Negotiation Behaviors in Agent–Based Negotiation Support Systems

Manish Agrawal
University of South Florida, USA

Kaushal Chari
University of South Florida, USA

ABSTRACT

Prior research on negotiation support systems (NSS) has paid limited attention to the information content in the observed bid sequences of negotiators as well as on the cognitive limitations of individual negotiators and their impacts on negotiation performance. In this paper, we assess the performance of human subjects in the context of agent-based NSS, and the accuracy of an exponential functional form in representing observed human bid sequences. We then predict the reservation values of negotiators based on their observed bids. Finally, we study the impact of negotiation support systems in helping users realize superior negotiation outcomes. Results indicate that an exponential function is a good model for observed bids.

INTRODUCTION

Negotiation is a form of decision-making where two or more agents who cannot make decisions independently, must make concessions to achieve a compromise (Kersten, Michalowski, Szpakowicz and Koperczak 1991). As observed by Raiffa (1982, pg 358), negotiators often fail to reach an agreement when in fact agreement was possible based on the preferences of the negotiators. Much remains to be done in creating effective negotiation aids to automate the bidding process and to facilitate the development of agent-based environments where agents can act as surrogates for human negotiators.

This article addresses the emerging environment where agents act as surrogates for human principals in a fully automated agent-based environment. For example, in emerging electronic markets for perishable goods and services, where transient market opportunities may require buyers and sellers to reach agreement quickly (Kambil and Heck 1998), or in emerging e-procurement systems where buyer agents could negotiate with supplier agents. In some of these environments, there are no alternate channels for communicating justifications of bids that could be expected in traditional negotiations involving human negotiators. The only inter-agent communication is a sequence of bids for all issues being negotiated. We use experiments with human subjects to test the applicability of an exponential function to model observed negotiation bids. We then examine the impact of a software-agent-based NSS platform in helping users overcome their limitations in realizing superior negotiation outcomes. A distinguishing feature of the NSS is that it can estimate opponent characteristics.

We make the following contributions in this article: (1) model human negotiation bid sequences, (2) investigate the impact of NSS in assisting users to overcome their limitations in achieving superior negotiation outcomes, and (3) predict reservation values of negotiators based on the observed bids. The results in this article can help in the development of next generation NSS.

This article is organized as follows. Section 2 provides an overview of the agent-based NSS and relevant literature. The various research hypotheses are presented in Section 3. The experimental setup to test the various hypotheses is described in Section 4. Results from the experimental study are presented in Section 5. The article concludes with a discussion of the results in Section 6. An appendix contains a brief description of the Hybrid agent used in the experiments.

AGENT-BASED NSS

Empirical research suggests that a NSS can improve outcomes, particularly when there are opportunities for integrative solutions, i.e., when the two negotiating parties have different priorities for the various issues under negotiations, and therefore there are opportunities for expanding the pie (Raiffa 1982). For example, Rangaswamy and Shell (1997) have reported that in an integrative situation, a simple NSS that provides a structured negotiation process and enables negotiators to analyze their own preferences improves the likelihood of agreement from 11% in case of face-to-face negotiations to 43% using the NSS.

Many agent systems have been developed for automated/semi-automated negotiations. The Kasbah agent system uses simple negotiation heuristics based on pre-defined price decay or increment functions (Chavez and Maes 1996). Kasbah agents do not learn and therefore cannot adapt to the negotiation environment. Faratin et al. (1998), use families of polynomial and exponential functions to model opponent concession behaviors during negotiations. The three canonical behaviors modeled are Boulware, conceder and imitative behaviors. These behaviors are then combined using weights via human intervention to create a composite negotiation strategy. The Inspire project provides negotiators with a communication platform and analytical tools to analyze the negotiation scenario (Vetschera, Kersten and Koeszegi 2006). Agents developed in the Bazaar project (Zeng and Sycara 1998) use Bayesian update rules from historical data to learn and form beliefs about the opponent's reservation values. However, as pointed out before, estimating multitude of probabilities accurately is not always practical in many situations.

To summarize the above research, we find that the various prior NSS are generally incapable of learning and estimating opponent characteristics based on the observed bid sequence in an automated fashion. In prior research (Chari and

Agrawal 2007), we developed an agent-based NSS heuristic, referred to as multi-issue learning heuristic (MILH) for estimating opponent reservation values and for automating bidding. In this article, we use an agent-based NSS that uses this heuristic, as a platform to study human negotiations behavior, and explore how a NSS can improve negotiation outcomes. The ability of the agent-based NSS to estimate opponent information from the current bid sequence, and to use this information in making automated bids, distinguishes this NSS from existing NSS in the literature (Rangaswamy and Shell 1997; Kersten and Noronha 1999; Lim 2000; Neumann, Benyoucef, Bassil and Vachon 2003).

We use software agents based NSS developed using Aglets (Lange and Oshima 1998), as the platform for the current experimental study. The software agents provide the user interface as well as different levels of bidding support to their human principals during negotiations. The bidding support levels include the following: 1) *Unassisted and self-assisted Cases*: Negotiators have to enter their bids based on their own estimates of opponent characteristics; 2) *NSS Estimated Case*: NSS provides an estimate of opponent reservation values; 3) *Automated Case*: NSS agents compute bids automatically without giving any opportunity to their human principals to overwrite it.

RESEARCH QUESTIONS

The application of agent technology in cognitively demanding tasks such as negotiations poses many interesting research questions. Three research questions are explored in this article in the context of an agent-based environment. First, can we model the observable information such as bid sequences using a functional representation as in (Faratin, Sierra and Jennings 1998)? Second, can agent-based NSS assist negotiators in realizing superior negotiation outcomes? Third, can we predict reservation values from observed bids? If

the answers to these questions are in the affirmative, then it would be feasible and beneficial to deploy agents as surrogates for humans during negotiations. The following sections describe each of these research questions in detail.

Modeling Negotiation Behaviors

We call the series of bids made by a negotiator for one negotiation issue in the current negotiation as a bid sequence. Reasoning models such as in (Faratin, Sierra and Jennings 1998) allow for combining time dependent and imitative reasoning by generating bids based on the time remaining in negotiations and imitation of the opponent bids. Much needs to be done in terms of developing reasoning models based on actual human bidding patterns.

Functional forms with desirable properties (twice-differentiability, continuity) have been used in prior literature for representing bidding behaviors (Faratin, Sierra and Jennings 1998), because they can capture a wide range of bidding behaviors. However, to our knowledge, the accuracy of these functions in modeling negotiation behavior has not been verified using actual human bid sequence data. Such verification is useful because such a model is the basis for all estimates made by the NSS used in this research. We are therefore interested in exploring the accuracy of a functional representation for modeling the observed bid sequences of human negotiators. Thus we hypothesize that

H1: *In agent-based negotiation environments, bid sequences of human negotiators can be represented using an exponential functional representation.*

Cognitive Biases of Human Negotiators

An important potential of negotiation agents is their ability to eliminate the effects of human cognitive biases. Tversky and Kahnemann found that the limitations in human cognitive capacity made human judgments susceptible to errors and biases (Tversky and Kahnemann 1974). Anchoring and framing are important biases and the effects of using NSS to overcome these biases during negotiations are discussed next.

Anchoring

Anchoring biases are well-known imperfections in human negotiators (Northcraft and Neale 1987; Kahneman 1992; Bazerman, Curhan, Moore and Valley 2000; Kristensen and Garling 2000; Galinsky and Mussweiler 2001). Prior research has shown that encouraging negotiators to focus on opponent reservation values (RV) is a useful strategy to improve negotiation outcomes (Galinsky and Mussweiler 2001). This focus serves to counter the anchoring effect whereby the first offer made by any side in a negotiation serves as a standard for *both parties* for the rest of the negotiations. One of the most useful pieces of information to counter the effects of an opponent's initial offer is the opponent's reservation value for the various negotiation issues. The opponent's initial offer is likely to be extremely favorable to the opponent. Focusing on the opponent's least acceptable bids can highlight information inconsistent with the opponent's projected expectations. In the absence of such considerations, subjects are likely to become pessimistic about their own prospects upon receiving the opponent's first bid.

Based on the above, subjects who focus more on opponent reservation values are expected to achieve superior negotiation outcomes compared to other subjects. To obtain an objective measure of the extent to which subjects focus on information to counter the anchoring effect of initial offers, we use the accuracy of subjects' estimates of opponent reservation values. This is because if everything else is equal, subjects who focus more on the opponent's reservation values are expected to make superior estimates of these

values. This could help subjects craft bids that not only counter anchoring effects, but are also likely to be accepted.

Our goal is to verify that estimating opponent RV is indeed a fruitful approach to improve negotiation outcomes. Hence

H2(a): *In agent-based negotiation environments, subjects who make better estimates of their opponent's reservation values will achieve superior negotiation outcomes compared to subjects with less accurate estimates.*

MILH NSS Support to Counter Anchoring Effects

Accurate estimation of opponent RVs is difficult to achieve because of the cognitive complexities associated with estimating multiple values in the presence of uncertainty. Since MILH NSS is not expected to suffer from cognitive limitations (subject to the capabilities of the computer system used), it has the potential to provide superior estimates of opponent reservation values based on the opponent bid information available.

To the extent that anchoring effects hurt negotiator performance, any improvements in estimating opponent reservation values is expected to counter the adverse consequences of anchoring and improve negotiation outcomes. If a NSS can serve to deliver such improvements in estimation, it would be "extremely useful" in real world negotiations. We therefore hypothesize the following.

H2(b): *MILH NSS will make superior estimates of opponent reservation values compared to human subjects*

Framing

Kahnemann and Tversky found that subjects framing a problem in loss terms exhibited risk-taking behavior whereas subjects who framed the same problem in terms of gains showed risk-averse behavior (Kahneman and Tversky 1979). A consequence of framing effects is that subjects in the loss frame are expected to be very aggressive in their negotiating behavior leading to fewer successful negotiations, but superior outcomes for successful negotiations. On the other hand, subjects in the gain frames are expected to make more concessions with the hope that these concessions would lead to agreement. Framing differences will be significant to NSS design because they can specify problem contexts where a NSS is likely to be more useful. The distinction between subjects in the two problem frames leads to the following hypothesis:

H2(c): *In agent-based negotiation environments, subjects in loss frames are expected to achieve superior outcomes in successful negotiations than subjects in gain frames.*

Comparing Human Negotiators to MILH Negotiating Agents

MILH automated agents are capable of completely automating the negotiation process. Their ability to be competitive with human negotiators is an important requirement for the development of fully automated agent-based negotiation environments. Since MILH agents are not expected to be affected by the cognitive limitations and biases of human negotiators, they are likely to make superior estimates of opponent reservation values and make bids that are free from human biases. As a result, they should outperform human negotiators in both gain and loss frames. This is given by the following hypothesis.

H2(d): *The performance of a MILH NSS will be superior to the performance of human negotiators in both the gain and loss frames in agent-based negotiation environments.*

Reservation Values and Observed Bids

Since our experiments with human subjects have provided us data on the real bidding patterns of human negotiators, it gives us the opportunity to explore relationships between opponent reservation values and bid sequences using regressions over actual data for human negotiations. This information can be leveraged to improve estimates, as the MILH is refined further.

The bidding behaviors of negotiators are typically guided by an attempt to push negotiation outcomes in their favor to the greatest extent possible, and to hold on to such a posture for as long as possible. However, typically the only reference point available to negotiators while computing bids and evaluating counter-offers is their own reservation values. Once negotiators invest their time and effort in a negotiation, they are increasingly likely to get concerned about the likelihood of negotiation failure because negotiation failures are expensive in terms of time, effort and other variables. Later bids are therefore likely to be related to the reservation values more than the initial bids. However, if there are significant relationships between observed bids and reservation values early in the negotiations, they could be extremely useful in generating the next generation of NSS since another approach would be available for estimating or verifying opponent reservation values. Hence we propose the following hypothesis.

H3: *Reservation values of negotiators are related to observed bids even in early phases of negotiations.*

EXPERIMENTAL SETUP

To test the various hypotheses, we used the buyer-seller problem that had been used in many multi-issue negotiation experiments in prior research

(Neale and Northcraft 1986). During initial subject briefings, the negotiation problem of buying and selling a home lot based on price, interest rate and closing cost discount was described to set the context for the experiments.

In real-world negotiations, negotiators agree on many issues either during initial discussions or as a result of common practice. They then draw up a short-list of issues on which agreements have not yet been reached. Successful negotiations require agreements on all unresolved issues. It is common for both sides to have different priorities for the various negotiation issues (for example, a buyer may be more interested in keeping interest rates low, while a seller may be more interested in maximizing the sale price). These differences create opportunities for integrative or win-win negotiations (Raiffa 1982; Rangaswamy and Shell 1997). The experimental scenario preserved all the salient features of real-world negotiations and enabled us to compare the performance of agents and humans. Though negotiations typically involved exchanges of complete or partial offers complemented with arguments and counterarguments, our initial agent-based NSS only allowed communication in the form of complete offers.

Although a specific scenario was used to brief subjects about the negotiation context, the negotiation issues were given alphabetical labels such as- A, B and C during negotiations. This was done to prevent negotiators from over-riding experimental manipulations based on their personal priorities for various issues (Smith 1976). To generate differences in preferences, which lead to opportunities for integrative negotiations, issue B was set as the most important issue for the buyers while issue A was set to be the most important issue for the sellers.

A repeated measures factorial experimental design as shown in Table 1 was used to test various hypotheses presented in Section 3. Forty subjects participated in the experiments and were randomly assigned to either the gain frame or the loss frame (thus twenty subjects were in the gain frame and twenty subjects were in the loss frame). Each subject performed fifteen negotiations of which five negotiations were informal training negotiations. The five training negotiations were interleaved with ten formal negotiations. The results from the ten formal negotiations were

Table 1. Experiment configuration

Risk-Frame	Gain	Cell 1	Cell 2	Cell 3	Cell 4	Cell 5	Cell 6	Cell 7	Cell 8
	Loss	Cell 9	Cell 10	Cell 11	Cell 12	Cell 13	Cell 14	Cell 15	Cell 16
Buyer		Human Buyer (preceded by 2 rounds of training in buyer role) →	Human Buyer (preceded by 2 rounds of training in buyer role) →	Human Buyer →	Human Buyer →	MILH Automated Buyer	MILH Automated Buyer	MILH automated Buyer	MILH Automated Buyer
Seller		Hybrid Seller	Hybrid Seller	MILH Automated Seller	Hybrid Seller	Human Seller (preceded by 1 round of training in seller role)	Hybrid Seller (same RVs as in Cell 1/9)	Hybrid Seller (same RVs as in Cell 2/10)	Hybrid Seller (same RVs as in Cell 4/12)
Opponent's RV Estimation Procedure		RV not considered (Unassisted)	RV estimated by negotiator (Self-estimated)	RV estimated by negotiator (Self-estimated)	MILH agent provided estimates of RV (NSS estimated)	RV estimated by negotiator (Self-estimated)			
Bid Generation Procedure		Human Bidding (performed by subjects in sequence shown by arrows)					Agent Bidding (performed by authors)		

used for statistical analysis. In the first twelve negotiations (that included four training negotiations), subjects played the role of buyers. In the last three negotiations (that included one training negotiation), subjects played the role of sellers. In all cases, buyers made the first offer.

Human subjects were drawn from the pool of graduate students and upper level undergraduate students at the authors' university. On average, these subjects had more than 5 years of education beyond high school and 6 years of work experience, of which more than one and a half years in a supervisory position. The mean age was 26 years, 29 of the 40 subjects were male. Experimental results presented later indicate that these subjects also exhibited diversity in negotiation styles such as concession behavior. Subjects were paid $20 for participation and could earn up to $1 for each negotiation based on performance during negotiations. Since each subject participated in ten formal experiments, individual rewards could potentially reach $30. Furthermore, the best performer in the

negotiation experiments also received a $50 prize. Subject participation was voluntary and monetary compensation was the only incentive for subjects to participate in these experiments. Subjects used the graphical user interface (GUI) shown in Figure 1 to negotiate. As mentioned earlier, the NSS was developed using the Aglet toolkit. The GUI was created using AWT GUI elements in Java 1.3 and the system ran on Windows XP desktops. The NSS was extensively tested for user feedback and the subjects did not report any difficulty in using any information presented to them through the NSS. The GUI for the NSS-assisted mode is shown in Figure 1.

Subjects placed their bids in the new bids column. Only complete bids were allowed, which meant that subjects had to bid on all the three issues before the bid could be sent to the opponent. Agreement on all three issues was necessary for a successful negotiation. Subjects could recant from previous offers on an issue even if agreement was reached between the two parties on that

Figure 1. Graphical user interface of NSS

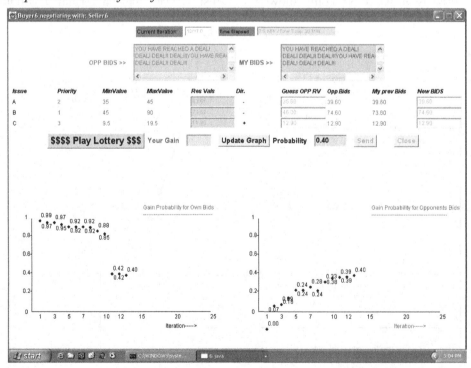

issue. Estimates of opponent RVs were shown in the *Guess Opp RV* column. The prior history of the opponent and self bids were available. Before submitting each bid, subjects could click on the *update graph* button to get a graphical history of utilities from their own bids and from the opponent bids. If a negotiation ended in an agreement, then the two negotiators clicked on the *Play Lottery* button, and the NSS determined the outcome of the lottery for that subject. The results of the lottery and bid histories were saved to persistent storage at the end of the negotiation.

Upon arriving in the laboratory, an experimenter briefed subjects about the negotiation scenario. The subjects then completed one training negotiation in the unassisted case. At the end of the first negotiation, subjects were given a questionnaire to verify that they clearly understood the meaning of reservation values, the best possible bids from their perspective and the distinction between issues where higher values were preferred (*Increasing issues)* to those issues where lower values were preferred (*Decreasing issues*). Any errors in the questionnaire were clarified and the subjects performed one more training negotiation. After these two initial rounds of training negotiations, subjects performed two rounds of actual negotiations in the unassisted case.

To maintain consistency throughout the experiments and to conserve human subjects, we used Hybrid agents (described in the appendix) as opponents. MILH agents were used as opponents only when it was absolutely necessary for the verification of a hypothesis. Hybrid agent bidding characteristics could be defined as needed for experimental control purposes in order to facilitate comparison of human and MILH performance. After the completion of two actual rounds of negotiations in the unassisted case (Cell 1 or Cell 9 in Table 1), subjects were alerted to the importance of opponent reservation values. Subjects were asked to fill in their estimates of their opponent's reservation values in a field specially marked for this purpose in a new NSS

graphical user interface. Subjects were told that they could use these estimates in any manner they chose and could update these values when appropriate. Subjects then performed two training negotiations where they estimated opponent reservation values. In the two training rounds, subjects encountered one Hybrid agent opponent and one automated MILH agent in random order. After two training rounds, subjects performed four rounds of actual negotiations where they entered their estimates of opponent reservation values (we call this the *self-assisted* case). In these four rounds, the opponents were two Hybrid agents and two automated MILH agents presented in random order.

The NSS was then set to the NSS-assisted case and the subjects performed two negotiations where they received estimates of the opponent's reservation values from MILH agents. The bids were still made by the subjects, and they were free to use or discard the NSS estimated reservation values. Opponents in the NSS estimated case were again Hybrid agents. Finally, subjects were asked to perform the role of sellers and after one training round, performed two actual negotiations as self-assisted sellers against MILH buyers. Although a time limit of 30 minutes was imposed on each experiment to prevent unnecessary delays, time was not a factor of interest in the experiments and all subjects completed all the negotiations long before the time limit.

The negotiation configurations and the sequence in which subjects performed the experiments are shown in Table 1. Each subject progressed through the cells in the human bidding column from left to right till the role of seller (cells 1 – 5 for subjects in the gain frame or cells 9 – 13 for subjects in the loss frame). After subjects completed their experiments, the authors performed negotiations for MILH automated buyer cases where both buyers and sellers were automated agents (cells 6 – 8 in the gain frame and cells 14 – 16 in the loss frame). These experiments were performed to obtain observations for comparing MILH agents to human negotiators. In the gain frame, Cell 1 vs. Cell 2 and Cell 1 vs. Cell 4 enabled testing for anchoring effects using the self-assisted and NSS-assisted cases. Cell 8 vs. Cell 4 facilitated examination of improvements in the automated case compared to the NSS-assisted case. Cell 6 vs. Cell 1 enabled comparison of the automated case with the unassisted case. Finally, Cell 3 vs. Cell 5 facilitated head-to-head comparisons of automated agents versus humans. Similar comparisons were made in the loss frame.

Inducing Utilities

We induced subjects to exhibit specified preference structures using a two-stage binary-lottery preference-induction procedure (Berg, Daley, Dickhaut and O'Brien 1986; Rietz 1993). This procedure is based on the induced value theory introduced by Smith (Smith 1976) and has been validated experimentally in prior research (Berg, Daley, Dickhaut and O'Brien 1986; Rietz 1993). According to the induced value theory, as long as subjects were assumed to be non-satiated (prefer more money to less) and maximizers of expected-utility, they could be induced to display any arbitrary preference structure through appropriate reward mechanisms. In experiments, this preference was carried out through a two-stage lottery procedure.

In the first stage of the binary lottery procedure, subjects performed the actual experiments and were awarded points that were directly proportional to their dollar gains from trade. These points were then used to calculate their probabilities of earning a reward in a binary lottery, based on a pre-defined utility behavior that was desired from subjects. Since the experimenters desired to induce risk-averse behavior, which is typical of most individuals, the probability of winning a reward was a concave function of the points earned in the first stage. If subjects succeeded in reaching an agreement, they played a lottery in the second

stage. In the second stage, a random number was drawn from a uniform distribution between 0 and 100 and if the number fell below the winning probability, subjects earned the reward. Since subjects were allowed to play the lottery only if they succeeded in reaching an agreement, subjects who reached agreements were always better off than those who did not complete negotiations.

The priorities of various issues, points awarded to subjects for each of the three negotiation issues, bid ranges for the issues and the utility functions used to compute reward probabilities as a function of points earned are shown in Table 2 through Table 4. The maximum points P_{maxk}, achievable for any issue k, is based on the maximum number of points that could be earned (P_{max}) and the importance of that issue to the negotiator. For the specific issues considered in the experiments, P_{max} was 10 and the maximum points for each issue are given in Table 2. From Table 2, the issue point weight w_k for each issue was calculated so that a negotiator achieved P_{maxk} for issue k if she was able to reach an agreement at the most favorable end of the allowed range of bids. w_k is given by the following equation.

$$w_k = P_{maxk} / diff_k \tag{1}$$

where $diff_k$ is the difference between the most favorable allowed bid and the subject's own reservation value for issue k.

For each negotiation, the reservation values for buyers and sellers were generated from a

Table 2. Importance of issues and points achievable by negotiation issue

Issue	Priority		$P_{\max k}$	
	Buyer	Seller	Buyer	Seller
Lot Price (issue A)	2	1	3.0	4.5
Interest Rate (issue B)	1	2	4.5	3.0
Closing Cost Discount (issue C)	3	3	2.5	2.5

Table 3. Reservation values for the two parties

Lot Price (Issue A)		Interest Rate (Issue B)	
Buyer	**Seller**	**Buyer**	**Seller**
RV: U[$40,500- $44,000]	RV: U[$36 - $39,500]	RV: U[70 – 85 Basis Points]	RV: U[50 – 65 Basis Points]
Range ($35,000 - $45,000)		Range (45 – 90 Basis Points)	
Display Range: 35 – 45		Display Range: 45 – 90	
Closing Costs Discount (Issue C)			
Buyer	**Seller**		
RV: U[$1,000-$1,300]	RV: U[$1,500 - $1,900]		
Range ($950 - $1,950)			
Display Range: 9.5 – 19.5			

Table 4. Utility as a function of points

Frame	Concave Utility Function
Gain	$\text{Probability(Gain)} = \dfrac{(1-e^{-\gamma*p})}{(1-e^{-\gamma*P_{max}})}$
Loss	$\text{Probability(Loss)} = \dfrac{(-1+e^{\gamma*(P_{max}-p)})}{(-1+e^{\gamma*P_{max}})}$
γ is the absolute index of risk preference (set as 0.2) $P_{max} = 10.0$	

uniform distribution in the range of values shown in Table 3. Generating RVs from a distribution prevented learning effects within and across subjects. However, since the dependent variable was measured with respect to RVs, the procedure did not adversely affect results compared to using fixed RVs. The RVs selected ensured that every negotiation was potentially capable of ending in agreement because there was always a range of mutually agreeable values for each issue. The points p_i for computing the utility for negotiator i in Table 4 was calculated as the weighted sum of points for all three issues as given by (2).

$$p_i = \sum_{k \in I} w_k * (x_{i,k} - r_{i,k}) + \sum_{k \in D} w_k * (r_{i,k} - x_{i,k})$$

if successful 0 if not successful   (2)

In (2), $x_{i,k}$ is the final agreement value for issue k; $r_{i,k}$ is the reservation value for issue k of negotiator i; I is the set of increasing issues (issues

A and B for the seller); D is the set of decreasing issues (issue C for the seller). The concave utility function in Table 4 was used to compute reward probabilities using a coefficient of risk-aversion of 0.2. Utility values from Table 4 are plotted in Figure 2.

Normalizing Bid Sequences

When exploring the relationship between bid sequences and reservation values, we used normalized values of bids. This facilitated the generalization of results across negotiation contexts. The normalization procedure converted the observed bids to normalized values within the specified bid bounds as described below.

n-tuple *T* consisted of normalized reservation value (*RV*) and *n-1* normalized bids $x_1,..,x_{n-1}$ of a human negotiator for iterations *1* through *n-1* for an issue during negotiations and was given by

$$T = (RV, \ x_1,..,x_{n-1}) \qquad (3)$$

The normalization was done as follows. Let *issueMin* and *issueMax* be the minimum and maximum possible values (i.e., bounds) that a given issue could take in its domain; RV^a be the actual reservation value of a negotiator for that issue; x^a_j be the actual bid of a negotiator for the issue at iteration j. Then for increasing issues, i.e., when the utility was non-decreasing with

Figure 2. Utilities as computed in Table 4

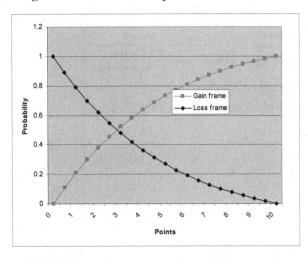

RESULTS

Categories of Negotiation Behaviors and their Relationships to Outcomes

Modeling Bid Sequences

Human subjects exhibited a wide range of negotiation patterns with varied bid sequence lengths. The distribution is shown in Figure 3.

There were three issues in negotiations. Therefore, each negotiation consisted of three bid sequences, one for each issue. Success in the negotiation required agreements on all the three issues. The available data allowed us to test for the validity of a functional form to represent bid sequences. Such a functional form could be useful in anticipating opponent behavior in automated negotiations. In order to estimate such a functional form as in (4), we had to distinguish between sequences where subjects conceded to RV (i.e., within 1% of RV) and those where they did not. This was because $t_{max\,k}$ in (4), which is defined as the iteration where the negotiator conceded to RV, was only known in the former case. Of the 1197 bid sequences (one for each issue in each negotiation), negotiators reached to within 1% of their reservation values in 96 sequences. For all practical purposes, we viewed these 96 sequences to have reached their respective reservation values. As a specific instance of a functional form with desirable mathematical properties and generalizability over a wide range of negotiation behaviors, we used the general exponential functional form adapted from (Faratin, Sierra and Jennings 1998) and given by (4). This form represented a wide variety of behaviors including concave and convex concession patterns, based on the value of β_k.

an increase in the issue values, the normalized reservation value $RV = (issueMax - RV^a)*100/(issueMax - issueMin)$ and the normalized bid $x_j = (issueMax - x^a_j)*100/(issueMax - issueMin)$; For decreasing issues, i.e., when the utility of a negotiator was non-increasing with an increase in the issue values, normalized reservation value $RV = (RV^a - issueMin)*100/(issueMax - issueMin)$ and normalized bid $x_j = (x^a_j - issueMin)*100/(issueMax - issueMin)$.

Dependent Variables

In the existing literature on negotiations, two variables are commonly used to measure negotiation performance. The first variable is the percentage of negotiations that result in agreements, while the second is the quality of negotiation outcomes. Since the second variable measures the degree to which negotiation outcomes are favorable, we only used the second variable to measure negotiation performance. Negotiation outcomes that were more favorable lead to higher reward probabilities in the experiments, as specified by the utility induction procedure. Hence, in this research, the dependent variable for negotiation performance was operationalized as the *reward probability achieved by a negotiator in successful negotiations.*

$$x_{j,k} = mn_k + \alpha_{j,k}(mx_k - mn_k) \text{ when } k \text{ is a decreasing issue;}$$
$$else\, mn_k + (1 - \alpha_{j,k})(mx_k - mn_k) \text{ when } k \text{ is a increasing issue}$$

Figure 3. Frequency distribution of bid sequence lengths

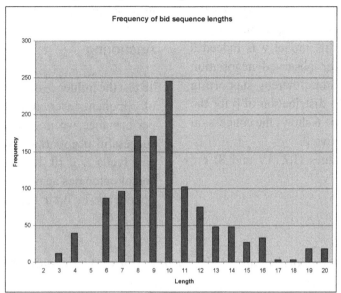

where

$$\alpha_{j,k} = e^{(1-\frac{\min(j,t_{\max_k})}{t_{\max_k}})^{\beta_k} \cdot \ln(\xi_k)} \qquad (4)$$

where $x_{j,k}$ is the bid on issue k at the jth iteration, mn_k is the minimum value a negotiator would take for issue k and is equal to the reservation value if the issue is an increasing issue; mx_k is the maximum value a negotiator would take for issue k, and is equal to the reservation value if issue k is a decreasing issue; β_k determines the concession behavior for issue k; $t_{\max_k}$ is the length of the bid sequence for issue k (at which point, a negotiator is assumed to have conceded to RV for issue k (Fatima, Wooldridge and Jennings 2004)); ξ_k is the fraction of $mx_k - mn_k$ added to mn_k to represent the starting bid. Using human bids $x_{1,k}, ..., x_{j,k}$ available at the jth iteration for issue k, parameter estimates $\hat{mn}_k, \hat{mx}_k, \hat{t}_{\max k}$ and $\hat{\xi}_k$ are determined by fitting (4) over the j offer points. It may be noted that $\beta_k = 0$ represented the special case of a linear function.

For the case where $t_{\max k}$ could be estimated (i.e., in 96 bid sequences), we first calculated the best β (the subscript k is henceforth dropped) for each bid sequence. The best β minimized the mean squared errors (MSE), and was determined using limited enumeration, where the value of β was varied in the range: 0 to 70 in steps of 0.1. Since normalized values were used, $\hat{mn}_k = 0$ and $\hat{mx}_k = 100$, while ξ_k could be estimated using the first bid. Using these parameter values, estimated bids for a sequence were generated using (4). Then the estimated bids (dependent variable) were regressed against actual bids and the resulting R-square obtained was used as a measure of goodness-of-fit. Of the 96 bid sequences, model verification was possible in 88 cases (in the other cases, subjects conceded to reservation value in the first or second bid and the calculation of R^2 was not possible with less than three data points). The mean R-square for these 88 bid-sequences was 81%, and the R-square exceeded 60% in 76 cases. This indicated a high goodness of fit for the model in (4) with data from human subjects. Note that for the remaining cases where the negotiators did not reach RV, we did not have adequate information (i.e., $\hat{t}_{\max k}$) to fit a model. In Figure 4, we show examples of actual bid sequences and the fitted exponential curve with normalized data for some bid sequences where negotiators conceded to RV. The high goodness-of-fit bid between the actual human bid data and the exponential model in (4) suggested that this model was indeed a good representation for observed negotiation bids by human negotiators, thereby supporting H1. Figure 5 shows the distribution of β for the 96 bid sequences. Figure 6 shows the concession patterns for representative β.

Behaviors for β values (1.7, 4.7 and 8) are shown in Figure 6.

Cognitive Biases of Human Negotiators

Anchoring

To test the influence of the accuracy of estimation of opponent reservation values on negotiation performance, we used observations pertaining to successful negotiations from the self-estimated case (cells 2, 3, 10, 11). This enabled a comparison of outcomes against both Hybrid and MILH opponents in both the gain and loss frames.

Figure 4. Example of actual and predicted bids for three different bid sequences

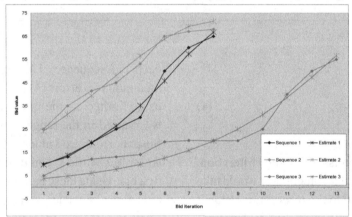

Figure 5. Distribution of bid sequences by β when bid sequences conceded to RV

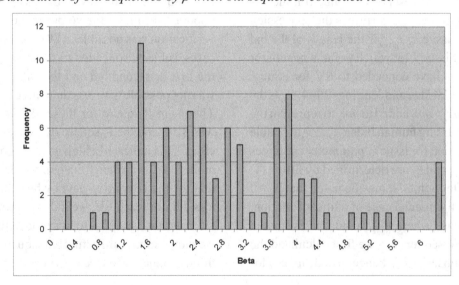

Figure 6. Bid patterns for decreasing issues

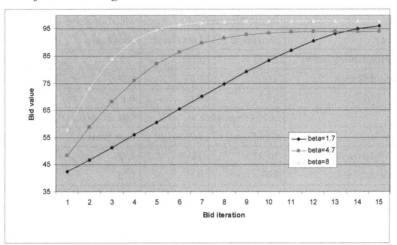

Estimation accuracy was defined as opponent's normalized actual reservation value – opponent's normalized final estimated reservation value. Each bid sequence was classified on the basis of estimation accuracy of reservation values into two categories: High accuracy and Low accuracy. In the High accuracy category, we included observations (corresponding to successful negotiations) in which the estimation accuracy for an issue was within the range centered on the normalized actual reservation value and extending in either direction to one-half standard deviation of the accuracy for that issue in the entire dataset. The Low accuracy category included all other observations corresponding to successful negotiations. The effect of estimation accuracy of opponent reservation values by human subjects (self-estimated case) on negotiation outcomes (i.e., reward probability) was tested using a t-test with pooled variances to compare the negotiation performance of subjects in the two categories. The results are presented in Table 5. In Table 5, mean difference represents the mean of negotiation outcome (i.e., reward probabilities) for High accuracy category – mean of negotiation outcome for Low accuracy category; significance levels of t-statistic in **bold** indicate cases where highly accurate sequences led to superior negotiation outcomes.

Table 5 shows that subjects who made more accurate estimates of opponent reservation values for issue B achieved significantly better negotiation outcomes. For the other two issues, there were no significant impacts of estimation accuracy on negotiation outcomes. We therefore found partial support for H2(a). It may be noted that issue B was the most important issue for the subjects.

MILH NSS Support to Counter Anchoring Effects

In order to evaluate the usefulness of *NSS support* in the form of MILH estimates of opponent reservation values, all observations (successful as well as unsuccessful negotiations) were used from cells 2, 4, 10 and 12 for ANOVA. Using ANOVA we compared the accuracy (as defined in Section 5.2.1) of human and NSS estimates of opponent reservation value. Results in

Table 6 show that apart from issue C, estimates of humans were superior to that of NSS. Therefore, H2(b) was not supported.

Pooling gain and loss frames, statistics for failures in the negotiations are reported in Table 7.

The relationship between estimation accuracy and likelihood of negotiation success was tested using logistic regression. Results after pooling

Table 5. Influence of accuracy in estimating opponent RV on winning probability for self-estimated bids

	Hybrid Opponent		MILH Opponent	
Issue A	Gain Frame	Loss Frame	Gain Frame	Loss Frame
N (High/Low Accuracy)	14/ 23	13/ 21	7/ 27	0/ 33
Mean difference	0.01	0.07	0.15	*
Sig. level	0.8	0.1	0.1	*
	Hybrid Opponent		MILH opponent	
Issue B	Gain Frame	Loss Frame	Gain Frame	Loss Frame
N (High/Low Accuracy)	10/ 27	14/ 20	5/ 29	9/ 24
Mean difference	0.09	0.1	0.22	0.19
Sig. level	**0.05**	**0.01**	**0.05**	**0.05**
	Hybrid Opponent		MILH Opponent	
Issue C	Gain Frame	Loss Frame	Gain Frame	Loss Frame
N (High/Low Accuracy)	16/ 21	17/ 17	5/ 29	9/ 24
Mean difference	0.03	0.09	0.19	0.13
Sig. level	0.3	**0.05**	0.1	0.1

Table 6. Accuracy of estimating opponent RVs

Issue		Self-assisted	NSS-estimated	Sig.
A	Mean	**-7.3**	**-19.9**	**33.4 (0.01)**
	N	80	80	
B	Mean	**-8.2**	**-15.3**	**13.6(0.01)**
	N	80	80	
C	Mean	-7.8	-11.9	2.61 (0.1)
	N	80	80	

Table 7. Comparison of failure rates

Agent type	Opponent type	Number of negotiations	Failures	Failure rate
Human	Hybrid	160	24	15%
Self-assisted	Hybrid	80	9	11.25%
Heuristic estimated	Hybrid	160	33	20.64%

gain and loss frames, but separating the cases of over-estimation and under-estimation are provided in Table 8.

The only group for which the extent of estimation error significantly affected the likelihood of negotiation success was the case of heuristic-estimated where the heuristic underestimated opponent RV. This reduced the probability of negotiation success.

Framing

The influence of problem frame on negotiation outcomes was tested by comparing outcomes in the two problem frames for successful negotiations

in unassisted and self-assisted cases. ANOVA Results are presented in Table 9. In each case, the mean outcome (i.e., reward probabilities) for subjects in the gain frame was comparable to the outcome of subjects in the loss frame. Results indicated that the F statistics for all the models were insignificant, suggesting that hypothesis H2(c) was not supported.

Comparing Human Negotiators and MILH

To compare human negotiators to automated MILH agents (automated case), we performed experiments where automated MILH agents negotiated against the same Hybrid sellers as faced

Table 8. Impact of estimation accuracy of RV on likelihood of negotiation success

		Likelihood	Pr > Chi sq
Self-estimated	Over-estimates	-0.17	0.0551
	Under-estimates	N.A (all successful)	N.A.
Heuristic- estimated	Over-estimates	0.016	0.83
	Under-estimates	**-0.25**	**0.01**

Table 9. Impact of problem framing (gain or loss) on negotiation outcomes (measured as reward probabilities)

	Unassisted (cells 1 and 9)		Self-assisted against Hybrid opponent (cells 2 and 10)		Self-assisted against MILH opponent (cells 3 and 11)	
		N		N		N
F (Sig. F)	1.06 (0.3)		0.01 (0.94)		0.00 (0.95)	
R^2	0.01		0.00		0.00	
Gain Frame	0.63	35	0.60	37	0.38	34
Loss Frame	0.60	39	0.60	34	0.37	33

by human subjects in the unassisted, self-assisted and NSS-estimated cases. The performance of humans and MILH was then compared using a paired-sample t-test. Results are presented in Table 10. Significant values for the t-statistic in a column indicated significant differences between the mean outcomes (i.e., reward probabilities) for human negotiators and MILH. Results are presented separately for the two problem frames and also after combining both the frames.

From Table 10, it can be seen that in the loss frame, automated MILH agents consistently outperformed human subjects while negotiating against the same hybrid opponents. In the gain frame however, MILH agents outperformed human subjects only for the case of self-assisted subjects. Also, when observations in the gain and loss frames were combined, MILH agents outperformed human subjects in all cases. We therefore found support for H2(d). Within the problem frames, we found partial support for H2(d) in the gain frame and full support in the loss frame.

We also compared the mean negotiation outcomes (i.e., reward probabilities) of human

subjects when negotiating head-to-head against fully automated MILH agents (cases 3, 5, 11 and 13) using ANOVA. Human subjects were in the self-assisted case while negotiating with fully automated agents. Results in Table 11 showed that fully automated NSS agents consistently outperformed human subjects.

Relating Reservation Values to Observed Bids

We explored the possible existence of a simple relationship between reservation values and observed bids by regressing normalized reservation values to the normalized bids of subjects. The regressions revealed that the reservation values were highly correlated with the 3rd bid, 4th bid and so on, for the bid sequences where subjects reached their RVs. For reference, results of regression between reservation values and 5th bids are presented in Table 12. Table 13 presents the regression results for the cases where subjects did not concede to their reservation values.

We conclude from the above that when subjects reached RV, their 5th bid was a good predictor for

Table 10. Comparison of MILH agents against human negotiators

	Unassisted		Self-Assisted		NSS-Estimated	
	Gain Frame	Loss Frame	Gain frame	Loss Frame	Gain frame	Loss Frame
	Cell 6 vs. 1	Cell 14 vs. 9	Cell 7 vs. 2	Cell 15 vs. 10	Cell 8 vs. 4	Cell 16 vs. 12
N	26	30	26	25	27	25
Mean of (MILH outcome – Human outcome)	0.02	**0.07**	**0.05**	**0.05**	0.02	**0.1**
T	0.9	**3.31**	**2.07**	**2.52**	0.88	**2.47**
Sig	0.38	**0.01**	**0.05**	**0.05**	0.39	**0.05**
	Unassisted		**Self-Assisted**		**NSS-Estimated**	
N	56		51		52	
Mean of (MILH outcome – Human outcome)	**0.05**		**0.05**		**0.06**	
T	**2.99**		**3.21**		**2.53**	
Sig.	**0.01**		**0.01**		**0.05**	

Table 11. Head-to-head comparison of human subjects and MILH agents

	Gain Frame	Loss Frame	Combined Gain and Loss Frames
Mean MILH outcome	0.59	0.63	0.61
Mean human outcome	0.42	0.38	0.40
N	138	134	272
F	**23.2**	**63.2**	**78.1**
sig.	0.01	0.01	0.01

Table 12. Relationship between RVs and 5th bids when bids reached RV

	Increasing issues	Decreasing issues
N	39	54
Adjusted R^2	0.37	0.27
F	**22.9 (< 0.001)**	**21.1 (<0.001)**
Intercept	50.5 (< 0.001)	47.9 (<0.001)
5th bid	**0.29 (< 0.001)**	**0.28 (<0.001)**

Table 13. Relationship between RVs and 5th bids when bids did not reach RV

	Increasing issues	Decreasing issues
N	423	630
Adjusted R^2	0.01	0.04
F	**4.7 (0.05)**	**30.3 (<0.001)**
Intercept	75.8 (< 0.001)	67.9 (< 0.001)
5th bid	**0.06 (< 0.05)**	**0.13 (< 0.001)**

RV, and that the 5th bid explained a high proportion of the variance in the reservation value. For sequences where subjects did not reach RV, their 5th bid was still a good predictor of RV, however, the 5th bid only explained a small part of the variance in RV. The significance of all the β coefficients in Table 12 and Table 13 supported H3.

CONCLUSION

There were three goals in this research. The first was to empirically validate a functional representation for modeling negotiation bid sequences of human negotiators. The second goal was to investigate the benefits of NSS support to human negotiators and the third was to explore the relationship between reservation values and observed bids of negotiators.

Based on the data collected from human subjects during negotiation experiments, we found that negotiation bid sequences could be modeled using an exponential function as suggested in the literature. Negotiation outcomes were measured as the utility of negotiation outcomes for the negotiator. In the multi-issue negotiations considered in this article, the impact of estimation accuracy was not uniformly distributed across all issues.

We found evidence that accurate estimates of opponent reservation values for the issue most important to subjects helped improve negotiation outcomes in successful negotiations. Thus, only the accuracy in the case of issue B significantly affected negotiation outcomes. The lack of significance of any relationship between the estimation accuracy for other issues and negotiation outcomes deserves further attention. It appeared that subjects were unable to identify the relative priorities of issues for the opponent. Therefore they were unable to leverage their superior estimates of important issues for the opponent into a negotiation advantage. This could be an important area for further research and for the potential role of NSS.

We found no evidence of framing effect. Subjects in gain and loss frames performed comparably. Since this effect has been observed fairly consistently in other experiments, we speculate various reasons for the observation. First, it is possible that the reward mechanism could not sufficiently discriminate between gain and loss scenarios. Second, it was also possible that the reward amounts were not large enough to elicit the differences in behaviors. In typical research studies where there were explicit attempts to identify the consequences of framing, subjects typically responded to questions that involved large sums of money – say 1,000 dollars or more (Kahneman and Tversky 1979). However, since the reward sums in our experiments were real and not "imaginary" dollars, we could not afford to provide these large rewards. The automated bids made by the MILH agents outperformed human subjects against the same set of opponents when the problem was framed in loss terms. In the gain frame, automated bids only outperformed human subjects in the self-estimated case. Further investigation is necessary to identify the causes of these differences in negotiation outcomes between gain and loss frames.

We found that human subjects made superior estimates of opponent reservation values for issues A and B compared to the NSS. This suggested

that the estimation heuristic could be improved further. It is surprising that although subjects made superior estimates of opponent reservation values than the NSS, the automated bids by the NSS outperformed self-estimated subjects in both the gain and loss frames. This suggested that notwithstanding the edge that human subjects had in estimating opponent reservation values, the bidding behavior of the automated NSS was superior and more than made it up for the inferior estimates of opponent reservation values. The results indicated that improving the estimation heuristic of the NSS had the potential to improve negotiation outcomes.

Finally, we found that the reservation values for each issue were correlated with observed bids. These correlations were stronger when subjects conceded to reservation values, probably because the reservation values played a stronger role as anchors in these bid sequences. The correlations were also more consistent when subjects did not concede rapidly in the early stages of the negotiation. These results could be useful in improving NSS estimation of opponent reservation value by leveraging information content in the early bids made by negotiators.

Negotiators hoping to get reciprocal concessions on some issue could not yield more on an issue than what was offered by their opponents, and effects of prior relationships, reputation effects, as well means to provide justifications for offers were not considered. These could be some limitations of this research. Further, while testing for framing effects, it may be necessary to develop a manipulation that could not be converted into an equivalent representation in gain terms. One way to address this is by giving subjects in the loss frame, a real endowment of dollars upon their arrival in the lab and taking away their losses at the end of each negotiation, in contrast to giving the total dollars earned by the subject at the end of all the experiments. Although the experimenters ensured that subjects were aware of the role of opponent RVs and informed subjects about the availability of such information in the NSS, there is no assurance that subjects actually utilized that information.

The experiments were also constrained by budget requirements to reward subjects for participation. For example, we were forced to gather repeated observations from each subject. This had the potential to introduce training effects whereby a subject's performance improved with experience in using the NSS.

The results from this article could help in the development of next generation NSS that empowered humans to negotiate better. The success of fully automated MILH agents in outperforming human subjects, particularly in loss frames was extremely encouraging and had the potential to spur the development of industrial strength agents for automated negotiations.

REFERENCES

Bazerman, M. H., J. R. Curhan, D. A. Moore and K. L. Valley (2000). "Negotiation." *Annual Review of Psychology 51*: 279-314.

Berg, J. E., L. A. Daley, J. W. Dickhaut and J. R. O'Brien (1986). "Controlling preferences for lotteries on units of experimental exchange." *Quarterly Journal of Economics 101*(2): 281-306.

Chari, K. and M. Agrawal (2007). "Multi-issue automated negotiations using agents." *INFORMS Journal on Computing 19*(4): 588-595.

Chavez, A. and P. Maes (1996). *Kasbah: an agent marketplace for buying and selling goods.* First International Conference on the Practical Applications of Intelligent Agents and Multi-Agent Technology, London, U.K., Practical Application.

Faratin, P., C. Sierra and N. R. Jennings (1998). "Negotiation decision functions for autonomous agents." *Robotics and Autonomous Systems 24*(3-4): 159-182.

Fatima, S. S., M. Wooldridge and N. R. Jennings (2004). "An agenda-based framework for multi-issue negotiation." *Artificial Intelligence 152*: 1-45.

Galinsky, A. D. and T. Mussweiler (2001). "First offers as anchors: The role of perspective-taking and negotiator focus." *Journal of Personality and Social Psychology 81*(4): 657-669.

Kahneman, D. (1992). "Reference points, anchors, norms and mixed feelings." *Organizational Behavior and Human Decision Processes 51*: 296-312.

Kahneman, D. and A. Tversky (1979). "Prospect theory: An analysis of decision under risk." *Econometrica 47*(2): 263-292.

Kambil, A. and E. V. Heck (1998). "Reengineering the Dutch flower auctions: a framework for analyzing exchange organizations." *Information Systems Research 9*(1): 1-19.

Kersten, G., W. Michalowski, S. Szpakowicz and Z. Koperczak (1991). "Restructurable representations of negotiation." *Management Science 37*(10): 1269-1290.

Kersten, G. E. and S. Noronha (1999). "WWW-based negotiation support: design, implementation and use." *Decision Support Systems 25*: 135-154.

Kristensen, H. and T. Garling (2000). "Anchor points, reference points and counteroffers in negotiations." *Group Decision and Negotiation 9*: 493-505.

Lange, D. and M. Oshima (1998). *Programming and Deploying Java Mobile Agents with Aglets.* Reading, MA, Addison-Wesley.

Lim, J. (2000). "An experimental investigation of the impact of NSS and proximity on negotiation outcomes." *Behavior and Information Technology 19*(5): 329-338.

Neale, M. A. and G. B. Northcraft (1986). "Experts, amateurs and refrigerators: Comparing expert and amateur negotiators in a novel task." *Organizational Behavior and Human Decision Processes 38*: 305-317.

Neumann, D., M. Benyoucef, S. Bassil and J. Vachon (2003). "Applying the Montreal taxonomy to state of the art e-negotiation systems." *Group Decision and Negotiation 12*(4): 287-310.

Northcraft, G. B. and M. A. Neale (1987). "Experts, amateurs and real estate: An anchoring-and-adjustment perspective on property pricing decisions." *Organizational Behavior and Human Decision Processes 39*: 84-97.

P.Faratin, C. Sierra and N. R. Jennings (1998). "Negotiation decision functions for autonomous agents." *Robotics and Autonomous Systems 24*(3-4): 159-182.

Raiffa, H. (1982). *The Art and Science of Negotiation*. Cambridge, MA, Harvard University press.

Rangaswamy, A. and G. R. Shell (1997). "Using computers to realize joint gains in negotiations: toward an "electronic bargaining table"." *Management Science 43*(8): 1147-1163.

Rietz, T. A. (1993). "Implementing and testing risk-preference-induction mechanisms in experimental sealed-bid auctions." *Journal of Risk and Uncertainty 7*: 199-213.

Smith, V. L. (1976). "Experimental economics: induced value theory." *American Economic Review 66*(2): 274-279.

Tversky, A. and D. Kahnemann (1974). "Judgment under uncertainty: heuristics and biases." *Science 185*: 1124-1131.

Vetschera, R., G. Kersten and S. Koeszegi (2006). "User assessment of Internet-bases negotiation support systems: An exploratory study." *Journal of Organizational and End User Computing 16*(2): 123-148.

Zeng, D. and K. Sycara (1998). "Bayesian learning in negotiation." *International Journal of Human-Computer Studies 48*: 125-141.

APPENDIX

Hybrid Agents

Hybrid agents are non-learning agents whose bids are obtained by combining the bids generated from four exponential functions and four polynomial functions taken from (Faratin, Sierra and Jennings 1998). The parameters for the polynomial and exponential functions are chosen such that overall bidding behavior of the Hybrid agent is complex and not easy to predict. The bids of a Hybrid agent are obtained by combining the bids of Type1 through Type 8.

Type 1- Exponential-Boulware. This type exhibits Boulware behavior on all the three issues and its behavior was generated by the exponential function of the form presented in (4). β_k values were continuously uniformly generated in [0, 1) for all issues.

Type 2- Exponential-Conceder. This type exhibits conceder behavior on all the three issues and its concession behavior was generated by the exponential function of the form given in (4). β_k values were continuously and uniformly generated in [1, 10) for all issues.

Type 3- Exponential-Boulware-Conceder. This type exhibits Boulware behavior on issues A, B, and a conceder behavior on issue C. Its concession behavior was generated by the exponential function of the form given in (4). β_k values were continuously and uniformly generated in [0, 1) for issues A, B, and in [1, 10) for issue C.

Type 4- Exponential-Conceder-Boulware. This type exhibits conceder behavior on issues A, and B, and Boulware behavior on issue C. Its concession behavior was generated by the exponential function of the form given in (4). β_k values were continuously and uniformly generated in [0,1) for issues A and B, and in [1,10) for issue C.

Type 5- Polynomial - Boulware. This type exhibits Boulware behavior on all issues and its concession behavior was generated by the polynomial function in (Faratin, Sierra and Jennings 1998) and given below

$$x_{2jk} = \{ mn_k + \alpha_{jk} (mx_k - mn_k) \text{ when } k \text{ is a decreasing issue;}$$
$$else \ mn_k + (1 - \alpha_{jk})(mx_k - mn_k) \text{ when } k \text{ is an increasing issue}$$
$$where \qquad \alpha_{jk} = k_k + (1 - k_k)(min(j, t_{maxk})/t_{maxk})^{1/\beta k}$$

β_k values were continuously and uniformly generated in *[0, 1)* for all issues.

Type 6- Polynomial-Conceder. This type exhibits conceder behavior on all issues and its concession behavior was generated by the polynomial function of the form presented above. β_k values were continuously and uniformly generated in *[1, 10)* for all issues.

Type 7- Polynomial-Boulware-Conceder. This type exhibits Boulware behavior on issues A and B, and a conceder behavior on issue C. Its concession behavior was generated by the polynomial function presented above. β_k values were randomly generated in the following ranges as follows. β_k values were continuously and uniformly generated in [1, 10) for issues A and B, and in [0, 1) for issue C.

Type 8- Polynomial-Conceder-Boulware. This type exhibits conceder behavior on issues A and B, and Boulware behavior on issue C. Its concession behavior was generated by the polynomial function presented above. β_k values were continuously and uniformly generated in $[0,1)$ for issues A and B, and in $[1,10)$ for issue C.

Hybrid Agent Bid. The bid for the Hybrid agent are generated by a weighted combination of offers that are generated by Types 1,...,8 as follows:

$$x_{2,j,k} = \{ \sum_{t=1,...,8} \pi_{t,j} \, x^t_{j,k} \; for \; j=1;$$
$$\min(\sum_{t=1,...,8} \pi_{t,j} \, x^t_{j,k}, \, x_{j,k-1}) \; for \; j>1, \, k \text{ is an increasing issue;}$$
$$\max(\sum_{t=1,...,8} \pi_{t,j} \, x^t_{j,k}, \, x_{j,k-1}) \; for \; j>1, \, k \text{ is a decreasing issue} \}$$

where $x^t_{j,k}$ denotes the offer for issue k of type t at the jth iteration
$\pi_{t,j}$ is the weight associated with a type t offer, such that $\sum_{t=1,...,8} \pi_{t,j} = 1, j \geq 1$.

This work was previously published in International Journal of Intelligent Information Technologies, Volume 5, Issue 1, edited by Vijayan Sugumaran, pp. 1-23, copyright 2009 by IGI Publishing (an imprint of IGI Global).

Chapter 8
Agents, Availability Awareness, and Decision Making

Stephen Russell
George Washington University, USA

Victoria Yoon
University of Maryland, Baltimore County, USA

ABSTRACT

Despite the importance of resource availability, the inclusion of availability awareness in current agent-based systems is limited, particularly in decision support settings. This article discusses issues related to availability awareness in agent-based systems and proposes that knowledge of resources' online status and readiness in these systems can improve decision outcomes. A conceptual model for incorporating availability and presence awareness in an agent-based system is presented, and an implementation framework operationalizing the conceptual model using JADE is proposed. Finally, the framework is developed as an agent-based decision support system (DSS) and evaluated in a decision making simulation.

INTRODUCTION

Context aware computing has gotten a great deal of attention in recent years as mobile computing and pervasive computing technologies have advanced. The scope of context aware computing is broad and covers a variety of subject areas including location awareness, environment awareness, preference awareness, and usability. In computing, context refers to the physical and social situation where a computing device is being used. Context aware computing strives to acquire and utilize information about the context of devices and their users in order to provide computational services that are appropriate for the user, place, time, and environment. This concept of context extends to intelligent agent-based systems (Moran et al. 2001). Agent interactions take place in a rich context of previous actions, individual beliefs, invisible states and different perspectives about which agents must reason in order to interpret the

DOI: 10.4018/978-1-60960-595-7.ch008

settings in which they find themselves (Benerecetti et al. 2001).

As with most modern computer systems, intelligent agent-based systems are increasingly being utilized to support human decisions making processes. Today, nearly every type of information system supports some aspect of Simon's (1960) decision making phases. The intensifying dependency on systems to support all types of decisions, from critical medical decisions, to business decisions, to commonplace personal decisions, has made context awareness increasingly crucial. In support of this fact, several management and behavioral studies have indicated that the context and environment in which decisions are made affect decision outcomes (Beach et al. 2005; Goll et al. 1997; Simon 1959).

Intelligent agent systems inherently operate in and interact with decision makers' environment. Subsequently, intelligent agent research has invested a great deal of attention in approaches that enable or utilize context awareness. As a result, many agent systems employ some form of context awareness (Payton et al. 2004; Plaza et al. 2001). However, few of these systems deliver this context information directly to the user. More specifically, context information is commonly used by agents to tailor decision makers' system experiences without users' direct knowledge of the details. The reason for this may be explained by the fact that much of context awareness research tends to concentrate on environmental conditions such as location and lighting, user characteristics such as preference and interests, or computing device characteristics such as screen size or mobile orientation. All of these things describe context about which the system user is consciously or subconsciously aware.

This raises the question, what about the context information of which a decision maker is unaware? As noted above, context can affect decision outcomes, which by extension implies that context can affect the support provided by agent-based decision support systems (DSS). Moreover, in many cases agents within a system fulfill the role of a decision maker, making decisions as a proxy for users (Ajenstat 2004). In a decision support scenario, context-related information that is not directly known may be valuable when provided to the decision maker. Particularly in agent systems where the resources necessary to provide support are distributed around a network, extending contextual information about the system may improve decision outcomes. The availability of distributed elements of the system, which is contextual information, may have direct impacts on the support provided by the system and therefore, the decision outcomes.

Consider the implications if the data needed by a data-driven DSS was not available within sufficient time to make the system useful for the decision maker or if the data was not available at the time of the initial request, but would be should the decision maker wait a few moments. How would this change the decision maker's behavior? How would having information about when the data would be available affect the decision outcome? In this example, the data can be considered a resource and the concept of resource could be generalized to any distributed element of the system. Knowledge of resource availability information could have a dramatic impact on the performance of the system and the outcomes of decisions they support. From a systems perspective, this same availability information could be equally vital for agents' resources and agent-to-agent interactions. Despite the potential benefits of making availability information obtainable to decision makers, little attention has been given to examining the effects of agent, data, and system availability on decision outcomes and agent-based DSS.

The objective of this article is twofold. The first objective is to propose an agent framework that can provide online status (presence awareness) and readiness (availability awareness) information to system users regarding agents and their data sources. The second is to answer the general research question: does raising decision makers' awareness of data's availability affect decision outcomes? This article examines what is necessary to enable this capability in an agent-based DSS and what quantitative effect it will have on decision outcomes. In the following section, a discussion of prior work and background on presence and availability awareness is provided. Section 3 illustrates agent presence and availability awareness in a decision making context and presents a theoretical model that incorporates these concepts as part of an agents functional components. In Section 4, the theoretical model is mapped to the operational framework that will be evaluated in an experiment testing the effects of presence and availability awareness on decision making. Section 5 explains the experiment evaluating the model and framework. Section 6 presents the results of this experiment; finally concluding with a summary in Section 7.

BACKGROUND AND RELATED WORK

Schilit and Theimer (1994) first introduced the term "context aware," referring to context as location and identities of nearby people and objects, and changes to those objects. Brown et al. (1997) define context as location identities of the people around the user, the time of day, season, temperature, and other environmental conditions. Dey (1998) defines context as the user's emotional state, focus of attention, location and orientation, date and time, objects, and people in the user's environment. As a general definition, from a user's perspective, concepts that fall under context awareness include changes in a user's physical state and location, workflow, preferences, or resource interests. Despite the breadth of context awareness concepts, according to Abowd et al. (1999), there are certain types of context-related information that in practice are more important than others: location, identity, activity and time. This article

does not address all of the issues considered under the context awareness umbrella. Instead, the focus is on presence and availability awareness, in terms of decision makers, agents, and data.

Because presence and availability awareness are specific aspects of context awareness it is important to provide a working definition. In this article presence awareness is defined as knowledge of whether agents, data, or system resources are online and connected for communication. In this sense, presence and availability awareness implicitly touch on the context information identified by Abowd et al. Presence awareness provides knowledge of state, in terms of connectivity; implying location and identity. Presence awareness is the basis for availability awareness, since knowing if an agent or its resources are online is the first step in determining availability for use. Availability extends presence awareness by putting presence in the context of activity and time. Succinctly, within the scope of this article availability awareness is knowledge of an agent's or its resources' readiness to be used.

The concepts of presence and availability awareness are grounded in location awareness research. Much of the research in this area concentrates on collaboration (Griswold et al. 2003; Holmquist et al. 1998) and commerce/service provisioning (Crow et al. 2003; Yu-Chee et al. 2001; Zeidler et al. 2003). Knowing where a user or system is located and whether they are available for interaction can be particularly useful for these activities. The work of Hong and Landay (2001) extends this notion of location awareness to focus on data necessary for communication or assimilation. While location or proximity is not a direct issue for availability awareness, it can allude to the quality of the connectivity between a user and remote data or computing component resources. Similarly, knowing the location context information can provide an indication when data, an agent, or a computing device will be available for interaction (Dey et al. 2000). In this manner, availability awareness implies online state or presence.

Practical implementations of presence and availability awareness specifically find their basis in real-time communication applications such as instant messaging (IM). All IM clients incorporate a form of presence awareness so that users can be made aware of when a potential communication partner, or "buddy," is online. Many of IM clients also include availability awareness using techniques such as keyboard and screen saver monitoring. From a research standpoint, most of the studies on IM have been on its utility as a communications medium (Griss et al. 2002; Kwon et al. 2006; Wang et al. 2004) and not its availability awareness capabilities as applied to decision support.

Favela's (2002) research, which utilizes IM, differs from the main body of IM related research. Favela's group investigated using instant messaging as a presence and availability awareness tool in agent-based systems by creating AIDA, an instant messaging and presence awareness client for handheld devices. What is unique about Favela's efforts is his treatment of network resources, such as scanners and printers, as presence aware resources. By extending the notion of presence availability to documents and other computing components, AIDA offers new opportunities for casual encounters in a community of co-authors. For instance, when a user notices that a document is in use, he/she might send a relevant message or even join his/her colleague in a synchronous collaborative authoring session. In contrast to the work in this article, Favela's work, while innovative and unique, does not focus on decision making. His application of presence awareness concentrates on location contexts (i.e. proximity to resources and basic online-offline status of resources). His work does not examine how knowledge of presence and availability would affect decision outcomes; rather his group studied the implications of a hybrid software-hardware

architecture supporting document management and collaboration.

In the decision support domain Kwon's (2004) work attempts to address context issues with an agent-based mobile DSS that includes context awareness called ubiDSS. Kwon explains that the ubiDSS is characterized by its ability to identify decision makers even though they are moving, and to allow them to get solutions through any portable devices, in any workplace. The ubiDSS model implemented by Kwon is specifically focused on context awareness, but Kwon's context awareness subsystem is user-centric and only delivers context information related to a users' location. It also does not include presence or availability awareness with regard to resources needed for decision making.

Burstein et al. (2005) integrate context awareness, mobile software agents and decision support concepts by proposing a real-time DSS for the emergency healthcare domain. This work proposed an integrated framework including client server components that interact with mobile devices located on an ambulance or emergency medical personnel. Context awareness was accomplished by connecting the mobile PDA device to a web server, where the web server provides an interface to the underlying federated multi-agent architecture. In this research, there are only two mobile nodes, the remote PDA in the ambulance and the hospital assistant. A significant limitation of Burstein's system is seen in the fact that the context information was manually provided from the end user. Moreover, the agents did not provide any feedback on the status of themselves or their resources.

In contrast to Burstein's work, Aneiba et al. (2006) take a different perspective on mobile agent-based DSS and emphasize data retrieval, by researching a multi-agent DSS to support wireless information management. Wireless information management involves the capture, digitization, organization, transformation, and presentation of information over a wireless link. Aneiba's efforts developed a decision support model called Wireless Information Decision Agent (WIDA) whose decision support objectives are to reduce the waste of wireless resources (e.g. bandwidth, memory, and power), increase revenue opportunity by using resources as efficiently as possible, use the communication time more efficiently, and improve user satisfaction with network usage. While Aneiba's work improved the availability of data for retrieval, it lacks presence or availability awareness and does not deliver availability information to the decision maker.

Unlike the sparsity of presence and availability awareness related research in the literature, agents have been researched extensively as components in decision support systems. Recent approaches using agent architectures have employed the agents in roles such as simulations, communications, information retrieval, and support functions (Ajenstat 2004; Labrou et al. 1999; Luo et al. 2002; Mistry 2003). Additionally, several projects integrate agents, DSS, and web-based interfaces (Dong et al. 2001; Power 2002; Wooldridge 2002). This previous work shows the utility of agents in decision support applications and indicates an increasing trend towards agent-based decision support systems whose components and data sources are distributed. However few agent-based DSS have incorporated presence and availability awareness.

The research in this article builds on this previous work and seeks to address the gap in the current literature that exists with regard to presence and availability awareness and agent-based DSS. Previous work has not investigated how awareness of data's availability would affect decision making supported by agent-based DSS. For decision problems, particularly time-sensitive decision opportunities, providing availability related information to the decision maker can change the course of the decision maker's actions and subsequently, their interaction with a DSS. In contrast to previous work, the research described in this article differentiates itself from previous efforts by examining how knowledge of agents' and their resources' (specifically data) availability can affect decision outcomes. Rather than addressing the issues that cause agent or data availability problems such as network outages or high processing loads, a method for incorporating availability awareness in an agent-based DSS is proposed.

CONCEPTUAL MODEL

In a decision making context, the effects of presence and availability awareness introduce additional choices in the decision making process. Consider the following example where a business decision maker must make a decision within a short period of time. At the outset of this process the decision maker has an initial choice to seek support or not. If the decision maker chooses to use support, that support and any necessary resources may or may not be available. If the support/resources are unavailable, then the decision maker has a second choice: to wait or not to wait for them to become available. It is the uncertainty in this second choice that presence and availability awareness addresses. If the decision maker has insight to how long the support or resources will be unavailable, then the decision maker can make an informed choice about how to proceed.

These same "inter-decision" choices extend to intelligent agents. Albeit their choices are decided programmatically a priori, which may be a worse condition in the absence of presence and availability awareness. In the same manner that the example decision maker was subjected to the unavailability of necessary resources or support, an intelligent agent must also contend with system interruptions, such as network congestion, processing load, and user-based delays. This is a particularly critical issue in federated agent systems, because of the centralized control and potential inter-agent dependencies.

The conceptual model shown in Figure 1 proposes that agents need to incorporate more than simple presence awareness; they need to have availability awareness and provide this information to the user, as well as utilize this information themselves. This capability is even more important when decisions are time constrained and necessary resources may not be local to the system. Typical agent systems are programmed a priori to handle unavailable users, system interruptions, and outages with error messages or system failures; thereby limiting the assistance provided by the system when unanticipated interruptions occur. By including presence and availability awareness as an agent behavior, resource contention, delays, and unavailability can be dealt with in real-time when the impact of these events have the highest cost. The model shown in Figure 1 includes presence and availability awareness as a functional part of an agent's internal behavior.

Resource Sensing Behavior

Many agent designs include behaviors that enable agent functionality and these behaviors define the re-useable actions that agents possess and execute (Allbeck et al. 2002; Decker et al. 1997). Figure 1 illustrates an agent enabled with a resource sensing behavior, in addition to its core task behaviors. The resource sensing behavior monitors software and hardware such as network interfaces, the system processor, or other components accessible beyond the agent's immediate hardware interface. Information (shown as arrows in the figure) gained from this behavior's activity is provided to system users and the agent community appropriately depending on the agent's primary core behaviors. While not shown explicitly in the conceptual model, the core task behaviors may utilize the hardware component interface to support its activities if necessary.

The conceptual model includes a data store (e.g. memory, file, database, etc.) to track the dynamics of the monitored resource's availability. The data store is shown in Figure 1 as a cylinder attached to the resource sensing behavior. Over

Figure 1. Agent with presence and availability awareness

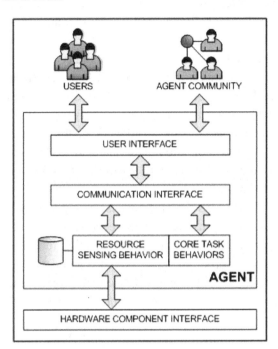

time, availability data identifying when and for how long the monitored resource was unavailable or under load is collected by the agent. As it is acquired, this data is housed in the data store. By capturing availability data over time, the agent could begin to identify the likelihood of unavailability or even predict the duration of an interruption using machine learning, operations research methods, or other algorithms. The data contained in the store could also be transmitted to a central location, aggregated, and used for service composition or other higher-order system level purposes.

Availability Data Acquisition

As discussed above, the resource sensing behavior needs to provide more than simple presence (online/offline) status information. The resource sensing behavior should provide information about if and/or when the resource will be available. The obvious question is: how is the availability data obtained? If computing resource availability is considered from the perspective of three categories (hardware, software, and users), research from other domains provides answers to this question. The first domain is high-availability computing. Research in this area has already identified methods to monitor and evaluate hardware related statuses such as power (Chakraborty et al. 2006; Rahmati et al. 2007), network characteristics (Roughan et al. 2004; Shahram et al. 2006), and computer components (Brown et al. 1999; Weatherspoon et al. 2005).

The second domain provides status of resources that can be considered software services. Software services provide a layer of abstraction for a full range of programmable functions and data. Research in the area of web service composition and quality of service (QoS) can provide agents with knowledge of these types of resources. Quality of service is often defined as the probability that a network or service will meet a defined provision contract. This probability could be used by agents to forecast the likelihood of resource interruption as well as potentially quantitatively predict outage durations. There is a significant amount of research studying applications using QoS and QoS monitoring for service level agreements, adaptation to changing system conditions, and web service composition (Ali et al. 2004; Loyall et al. 1998; Menasce 2004; Thio et al. 2005). Web service composition is a particularly active research area, rich with solutions for service availability, because of the critical nature of this information for process scheduling and execution planning (Peer 2005; Pistore et al. 2004).

A third domain provides availability information on humans or users of a decision support system. From the perspective of "users as a resource," human computer interaction research has provided several availability-oriented solutions. Most of the efforts have focused on detecting *if a user is* and not necessarily *when the user will become* online and available (Begole et al. 2004; Danninger et al. 2006; Muhlenbrock et al. 2004). However, there are probabilistic models that can track and predict humans' presence and availability. Horvitz et al. (2002) developed a prototype service intended to support collaboration and communication by learning stochastic models that foresee users' presence and availability.

Because the research conducted in these other domains provides viable solutions for obtaining quantitative data about different types of resource availability, the model and framework proposed in this article does not focus on this issue. Instead, the conceptual model and framework presented in the next section provide the basis for integrating presence and availability into agent-based systems generally and agent-based DSS specifically. Moreover, this article examines the effects of availability awareness on decision outcomes when using agent-based DSS with and without awareness capabilities.

AGENT AWARENESS FRAMEWORK

As a practical implementation of the conceptual model, a FIPA (2003) compliant Java Agent Development Framework (JADE) (Telecom Italia Lab 2007) architecture is adopted. JADE is a software framework that simplifies the implementation of multi-agent systems through a middle-ware that complies with the FIPA specifications. As defined in the theoretical model, the awareness capabilities of the framework are implemented as agent behaviors. Figure 2 illustrates the agent framework.

The bottom portion of the Figure 2 shows the significant framework elements and the top is a zoomed view of the operational agent portion of the framework. While shown at the foundation of the block diagram, the Microsoft.Net framework is employed as the "glue" for the agent internals. This approach allows other agent components to be developed in heterogeneous languages that provide the most appropriate capabilities for that component. The ability to utilize a language ag-

Figure 2. Presence and availability aware agent framework

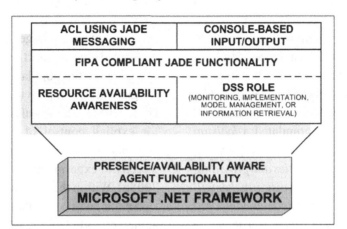

nostic as well as a platform agnostic development environment, provided by the Microsoft.Net platform, gives the framework a significant advantage over existing decision support and multi-agent architectures, which are commonly developed using one language such as JAVA (Russell et al. 2005). The work of Russell et al. (2005) further explains the benefits of this JADE-.Net approach and the agent framework shown in Figure 2 builds on these prior efforts.

By implementing the resource availability awareness as a behavior using the .Net framework it is possible to "plug in" many of the existing solutions as modules that could be integrated at a source code level or dynamically loaded during run-time execution. Furthermore, this approach allows a single agent to support more than one awareness capability or functionality. The .Net framework also provides a significant amount of "out-of-the-box" system awareness functionality in its library integration with performance counters (Gunderloy 2007) and simple network management protocol (SNMP) interfaces (Crowe 2002). The Microsoft performance counters provide detailed monitoring data for system components such as CPU utilization, disk utilization, and memory consumption. It also provides extensions for applications such as web servers, SQL databases,

and other application software (Microsoft 2003). SNMP provides similar capabilities for other non-Microsoft platforms (Teegan 1996). Additionally, the language agnostic nature of the .Net platform allows the development of other QoS and monitoring components in the programming language that is most suitable for the task.

Within this framework and its extension to the research experimentation, the agent utilizes a modified XML-based ACL that is transported over the intrinsic JADE messaging protocol. However, the modified XML-based ACL could be replaced with user-defined ACLs transported using other FIPA compliant protocols. Similarly, while Figure 2 shows the user interface as console-based, this too could be replaced with web-based, desktop-based, or other interface styles.

EXPERIMENTATION

This study raises the research question: does the awareness of when or if data will be available, for use by an agent-based DSS, affect decision making outcomes? As mobile and pervasive computing environments increasingly become the norm and system components and data resources become more likely to be distributed (e.g. computing grids and distributed databases) the relevance of this research will be progressively more significant. Systems in these environments will be relied on to provide decision makers with guidance and advice for not only essential, time-sensitive, business decisions, but also commonplace, frequently-made, personal decisions. Based on the above discussion, the following hypothesis is formulated: a *decision maker using an agent-based DSS incorporating availability awareness capabilities and providing availability information to the decision maker will have more accurate decision outcomes compared to decisions made by a decision maker using an agent-based DSS without these capabilities.*

To evaluate this hypothesis, a decision making experiment was conducted. This experiment operationalized the conceptual model from Figure 1 using the framework presented in Section 4. Two agent-based DSS were developed; one having network availability sensing capabilities and the other without. To evaluate the effects of availability awareness, a time constrained decision problem with a quantitative outcome was constructed. The problem objective is the selection of a stock to be purchased each day from the list of Standard & Poor's 500 stocks (S&P 500). The two agent-based DSS are employed to aid decision makers in this process.

In equity trading, there is the notion that trading volume precedes price (Fontanills et al. 2001) and this is the purchasing strategy for the experimental decision. In this context, stocks with the highest volume are viewed as the preferable choice. Because volume is a quantitative numeric value, this measure can be used to objectively quantify the outcome of the experimental decision. Both DSS implement the capability to identify, from the list of 500, which stock has the highest volume and this was the advice provided. The experimental design limited the amount of time in which to choose the stock to 5 minutes and utilized an Internet service that provided each stock's volume data.

To execute the experiment a simulation was constructed that would exercise both DSS. Simu-

lation can be used to gather pertinent data and conduct comparative DSS analyses. Additionally, since an extremely large number of trials can be performed in a very short period of time, simulation can generate the population information needed for generalization (David et al. 2001; Forgionne et al. 2008a). The simulation approach provides for explicit control of experimental variables and enables the ability to trace improvements directly to experimental factors (Forgionne et al. 2008b). Within the experiment, a simulated decision maker was coded that would always take the advice provided by the DSS, if it was available. While human subjects may ultimately be preferable, using a simulated decision maker allows the model and framework to be evaluated in a stringently controlled environment. A secondary consideration in this regard is that the simulated decision maker would also closely model, from a programmatic coding perspective, agents that make decisions.

In each DSS there are two agents: 1) an interface agent whose responsibility is to identify the high volume stock and communicate with the decision maker and 2) an information retrieval agent responsible for contacting an Internet resource that will provide information about the trading volumes for all 500 stocks for a given day. Figure 3 illustrates the two experimental cases that were evaluated. In one case, the decision-maker has no knowledge of when or if data will be available (control) and in the second case, the agent has knowledge regarding the availability of the resource that provides the stock volumes for the day (treatment). For both cases the Internet volume data randomly may be available immediately, become available after a period of time, or be completely unavailable.

As shown in Figure 3, each DSS has access to a stock volume data resource that exists on the Internet. The control DSS *does not* have an agent with network sensing behavior and cannot provide any availability information to the decision maker. The treatment DSS's information retrieval agent *does* have a network sensing behav-

Figure 3. Experimental implementation

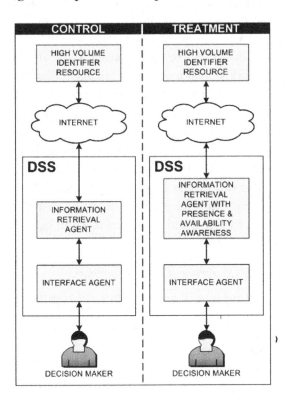

ior and is aware of the occurrence and duration of the volume data resource's unavailability. Consistent with the conceptual model, this agent provides the availability information back to the decision maker through the interface agent.

The two experimental cases have five variables that determined the conditions of the scenario, as shown in Table 1. All of these values were ran-domly generated for each run of the experiment. It was assumed that each input value would fol-low a standard normal distribution with a mean of 0 and a standard deviation of 1. To incorporate the diversity of inputs from a population of users and scenario conditions, each variable was as-sumed to follow a standard normal distribution with a mean of 0 and a standard deviation of 1. The choice of a normal distribution was based on the Central Limit Theorem, which roughly states that all distributions approach normality as the number of observations grows large (Barron 1986; Davidson 2002).

In the simulation, if the DSS cannot provide advice because the resource is not available within the allotted 5 minutes, the decision maker randomly selects (using a normal distribution) one of the 500 stocks for that day. Figures 4 and 5 show flow diagrams of the simulations for the control and treatment runs. For both, the process is essentially the same with the exception of the awareness component, which is seen the top center of the flow diagrams. In the control run shown in Figure 4, the decision maker has the "inter-decision" of whether to wait or not. In the treatment run diagram (Figure 5), information about the duration of the delay is provided to the decision maker. Subsequently, the "inter-decision" is resolved by the actual availability of the data; eliminating the need for the decision maker to have address this additional uncertainty.

Table 1. Simulation scenario variables

VARIABLE	FUNCTION
Data_Avail	This is a 1 or 0 value determining if the data is immediately available. If 1 then the data is available, 0 it is not. In the control case, if this is 0 then the DM-Wait and Delay_Amt values are used.
DM_Wait_YN	This is a 1 or 0 value determining if the decision maker waits for the data to become available or decides to choose a value before it becomes available. This variable only applies to the control case.
DM_Wait	Decimal value between 0 and 5 minutes that determines how long the DM waits. This variable only applies to the control case.
Delay_Amt	Decimal value between 0 and 10 minutes that determines how long the data will be unavailable. This data is sensed by the treatment agent.

The experiment was run 100 times; once a day, for 100 days. Each day there was only one stock with the highest volume and the volume of the stock (as well as its name) was recorded for each run. The stock volume quantity was selected as an objective measure of the quality of the DSS advice. Since the decision maker always takes the advice, the total volume can be used to determine whether the decision outcomes over all the runs are improved, quantitatively testing the hypothesis.

RESULTS

The results of the experiment were analyzed using SPSS and the hypothesis was tested. Table 2 shows a summary of the experiments' results. The table describes 4 measures for each run group (availability *known* and *unknown*): number of correctly identified stocks (*correct*), defined as the stock with the highest volume for the day; total volume (*total vol.*), the sum of the volume for all 100 days; average volume (*avg. vol.*), the average

volume per day; and the total square error (*total sq. err*), the sum of the error between the selected volume and the maximum for each day. From this it can be seen that the runs with an availability awareness enhanced agent that provides awareness information to the decision maker, have more correct decisions, higher total and average volumes, and a lower mean square error (difference between the possible maximum volume and the volume of the chosen stock).

To evaluate the hypothesis, the control and treatment runs were compared using paired t-tests for volume and square error. Table 3 shows

Table 2. Experiment results summary

	AVAILABILITY KNOWN	AVAILABILITY UNKNOWN
CORRECT CHOICE	79/100	66/100
TOTAL VOLUME	7.63E+09	6.13E+09
AVERAGE VOLUME	7.63E+07	6.13E+07
TOTAL SQUARE ERROR	1.80E+17	4.27E+18

Figure 4. Simulation flow diagram for the control runs

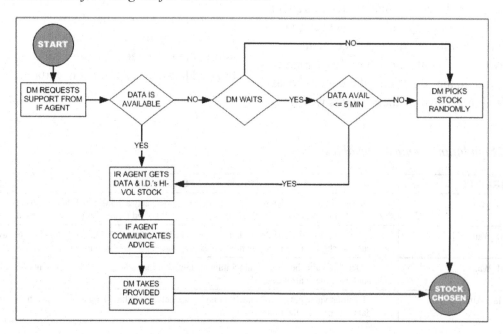

Figure 5. Simulation flow diagram for the treatment runs

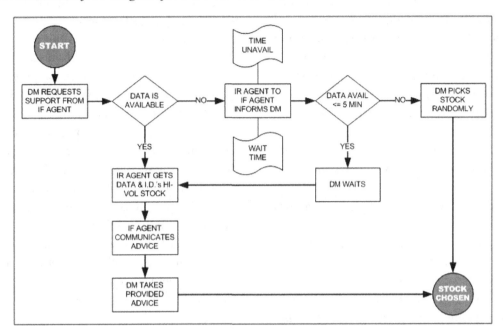

the results of the t-tests. The awareness-enabled agent outperformed the "unaware" agent with higher total volume and lower square error. For both measures, the t-test results were significant with alphas lower than.05, supporting a rejection of the null hypothesis.

The results demonstrate a significant improvement in decision outcome, measured quantitatively by volume. In summary, the results show that the availability aware agent provided better advice, leading to better outcomes.

IMPLICATIONS AND DISCUSSION

The results of this study show that knowledge of resource availability provided by an agent-based DSS can affect specific decision outcomes. Additionally, the study demonstrates that the proposed agent framework is capable of supporting availability aware decision support activities. Knowledge of the data's availability yielded a 15% improvement in accuracy that provided a 20% increase in the objective outcome measure: total stock volume. While more research may

Table 3. Hypothesis testing

	Paired Differences							
				95% Confidence Interval of the Difference				
	Mean	Std. Deviation	Std. Error Mean	Upper	Lower	t	df	Sig. (2-tailed)
VOLUME Known vs Unknown	1.498E+07	4.824E+07	4.824E+06	5.403E+06	2.455E+07	3.104	99	0.002
SQ. ERROR Known vs Unknown	-2.476E+15	1.198E+16	1.198E+15	-4.853E+15	-9.948E+13	-2.067	99	0.041

be necessary to address some of the limitations of this research, this is significant. The general implication of this study suggests that inter-agent (considering other agents as resources) availability awareness would deliver similar benefits. In terms of generalizability, this experiment illustrates that availability awareness can affect decision outcomes supported by agent-based DSS when decision-related data resources are intermittently available. However, the simulation should be expanded for a larger number of runs and include cases where the decision maker does not take the advice.

As discussed in Section 3.2, the technology to obtain availability information is mature, reducing the barriers for adoption and making practical implementations of this research feasible. As more systems are being utilized in mobile and dynamic environments, systems designers should consider the incorporation of availability awareness technologies and extending this information to system users and agents that have decision making roles. This research represents a step towards realizing the potential benefit of presence and availability awareness when utilized for decision support purposes. However, the practical implications of incorporating availability awareness may be more complex than the experimental scenario evaluated in this research.

Because the objective of this research was focused on examining the impact of availability awareness on agent-based DSS and how providing this information to decision makers would affect decision outcomes, the agent community was simplified. In a more complex system, there would be many different agents and potentially several dependent resources. Further, the study did not address the impact of resource related security or access control (e.g. dynamic security models or even collaborative file locking schemes), which may mimic the same temporal unavailability effects as network outages. In a more complex environment, the issues of availability data management and system security may have a significant impact on the support provided by the DSS and its performance.

Of particular relevance to the improvement in performance shown in this research, is the noticeable relationship between the 15% increase in accuracy and the number of data delays that were below the decision timing threshold. This would suggest that it may be possible to construct a mathematical model to represent the probability of an accurate outcome, based on the likelihood of all necessary resources being available. The incorporation of a probabilistic availability model may provide additional benefits to decision makers. Further study then, should investigate the mathematical relationship between resource availability and the temporal context of decision support provided by agent-based DSS.

CONCLUSION

As this research study illustrates, agents' awareness of resources' presence and availability can lead to different decision outcomes. In addition to presenting a theoretical and practical model that incorporates presence and availability awareness, this study examined the effects of these concepts in an operationalized agent-based DSS supporting a decision making process. The results of this study confirm that the support provided by an agent-based DSS enabled with availability awareness can improve decision accuracy when compared to outcomes supported by an agent-based DSS without it. Since the results are expressed in share volume, the findings provide an objective measure of the relative decision value of the presence and availability awareness information. The findings of this study indicate that delivering the data that availability awareness technologies provide to users and intelligent agents for decision making purposes can foster greater system utility and potentially improve overall system usability.

Technologies that can supply resource availability information are readily available and are already being used in practice. The research in this article demonstrates that the impact of providing availability awareness information to decision makers can be significant when there are issues of intermittently available essential resources. As the diversity of computing environments increases, the issue of availability awareness may be even more critical to DSS. Environments such as mobile networks are commonplace today and decision makers' dependency on computing resources in this setting is already high. Therefore, the importance of availability awareness on agent-based DSS, which are intrinsically distributed and likely mobile, is also considerable. The conceptual model and framework put forth here illustrate one solution for addressing this problem.

Although the model and framework for incorporating data resource availability awareness and the benefit of availability aware agents in general appears solid, only one decision making scenario has been investigated here. Moreover, this investigation has only examined the effects of one form of availability awareness acquisition and use. Clearly there are many situational, security, and implementation related issues to be addressed, as evidenced by the discussion of the implications of this research.

There are several limitations in this research that can be viewed as promising avenues for future work. Besides network sensing, this study did not integrate many of the potential solutions (such as QoS approaches) for quantifying a resource's availability. This was done to control and isolate the effects of availability awareness within the experiment. However, additional work should be conducted to demonstrate the applicability of these other methods of quantifying resource availability. The study also does not account for incorrect availability estimates. Although this would likely follow the same outcome as when the resource is unavailable, further study should examine this scenario. It should be further noted that unstable computing environments may suffer from complete outages and interruptions where

every disruption goes beyond the time boundaries of the decision opportunity. In this case, awareness of the availability would have a limited effect. It will be important for future studies to evaluate the implications of awareness in extreme cases of unavailable resources.

Because availability awareness may play a critical role in current and future systems, additional research is necessary to explore these aspects of availability awareness on agent-based systems. Future work is planned that will extend the system developed in this research with additional functionality such as user availability awareness components. This system will be used to expand this study, examining the limitations noted above.

REFERENCES

Abowd, G. D., Dey, A. K., Brown, P. J., Davies, N., Smith, M., & Steggles, P. (1999). Towards a Better Understanding of Context and Context-Awareness. In *Proceedings of the 1st international symposium on Handheld and Ubiquitous Computing*. Karlsruhe, Germany: Springer-Verlag.

Ajenstat, J. (2004). Virtual Decision Maker for Stock Market Trading as a Network of Cooperating Autonomous Intelligent Agents. *Proceedings of the 37th Hawaii International Conference on System Sciences*, Big Island, HI, USA.

Ali, A. S., Rana, O., & Walker, D. W. (2004). WS-QoC: Measuring Quality of Service Compliance. *International Conference on Service Oriented Computing (ICSOC04)*, New York, NY, USA.

Allbeck, J., & Badler, N. (2002). Toward Representing Agent Behaviors Modified by Personality and Emotion. *Autonomous Agents and Multiagent Systems*, Bologna, Italy

Aneiba, A., Rees, S. J., & Chibelushi, C. (2006). A Decision Support Model for Wireless Information Management Using Mobile Agents. *Proceedings of the IASTED International Conference on Artificial Intelligence and Applications (IASTED 206)* (pp. 493-498), Innsbruck, Austria.

Barron, A. R. (1986, January). Entropy and the Central Limit Theorem. *Annals of Probability, 14*(1), 336–342. doi:10.1214/aop/1176992632

Beach, L. R., & Connolly, T. (2005). *The Psychology of Decision Making: People in Organizations.* Thousand Oaks, CA, USA: Sage Publications.

Begole, J. B., Matsakis, N. E., & Tang, J. C. (2004). Lilsys: Sensing Unavailability. *2004 ACM conference on Computer supported cooperative work*, Chicago, Illinois, USA.

Benerecetti, M., Bouquet, P., & Bonifacio, M. (2001). Distributed context-aware systems. *Human-Computer Interaction Journal, 16*(1).

Brown, A., Oppenheimer, D., Keeton, K., Thomas, R., Kubiatowicz, J., & Patterson, D. A. (1999). ISTORE: introspective storage for data-intensive network services. *The IEEE Seventh Workshop on Hot Topics in Operating Systems* (pp. 32-37), Rio Rico, AZ, USA.

Brown, P. J., Bovey, J. D., & Chen, X. (1997). Context-Aware Applications: From the Laboratory to the Marketplace. *IEEE Personal Communications, 4*(5), 58–64. doi:10.1109/98.626984

Burstein, F. V., Zaslavsky, A. B., & Arora, N. (2005). Context-aware mobile agents for decision-making support in healthcare emergency applications. Proceedings of the 1st Workshop on Context Modeling and Decision Support (pp. 1-16), Paris, France.

Chakraborty, S., Yau, D. K. Y., Lui, J. C. S., & Dong, Y. (2006). On the Effectiveness of Movement Prediction to Reduce Energy Consumption in Wireless Communication. *IEEE Transactions on Mobile Computing, 5*(2), 157–169. doi:10.1109/TMC.2006.24

Crow, D., Pan, P., Kam, L., & Davenport, G. (2003). M-views: A system for location based storytelling. *ACM UbiComp 2003*, Seattle, WA, USA.

Crowe, M. (2002). *An SNMP Library for. NET Framework.* Corner. Available at http://www.c-sharpcorner.com/UploadFile/malcolmcrowe/SnmpLib11232005011613AM/SnmpLib.aspx.

Danninger, M., Kluge, T., & Stiefelhagen, R. (2006). MyConnector: analysis of context cues to predict human availability for communication. *8th international conference on Multimodal interfaces*, Banff, Alberta, Canada.

David, G., & Barry, L. N. (2001). Statistical selection of the best system. In *Proceedings of the 33nd conference on Winter simulation*. IEEE Computer Society, Arlington, Virginia, USA.

Davidson, J. (2002, February). Establishing conditions for the functional central limit theorem in nonlinear and semiparametric time series processes. *Journal of Econometrics, 106*(2), 243–269. doi:10.1016/S0304-4076(01)00100-2

Decker, K., Pannu, A., Sycara, K., & Williamson, M. (1997). Designing Behaviors for Information Agents. *First International Conference on Autonomous Agents*, Marina Del Rey, CA USA.

Dey, A. K. (1998). Context-Aware Computing: The CyberDesk Project. *Association for the Advancement of Artificial Intelligence 1998 Spring Symposium on Intelligent Environments* (pp. 51-54), Stanford, CT, USA.

Dey, A. K., Manko, J., & Abowd, G. (n.d.). *Distributed mediation of imperfectly sensed context in aware environments.* Technical Report GIJJ382R53J, Georgia Institute of Technology, Atlanta, GA, USA.

Dong, C. S. J., & Loo, G. S. L. (2001). Flexible web-based decision support system generator (FWDSSG) utilising software agents. *Proceedings of 12th International Workshop on Database and Expert Systems Applications, Munich* (pp. 892-897), Germany.

Favela, J., Navarro, C., & Rodriguez, M. (2002). Extending Instant Messaging to Support Spontaneous Interactions in Ad-hoc Networks. *The ACM 2002 Conference on Computer Supported Cooperative Work (CSCW 2002)*, New Orleans, LA, USA.

FIPA (2003). Welcome to the Foundation for Intelligent Physical Agents.

Fontanills, G. A., & Gentile, T. (2001). *The Stock Market Course.* New York, NY, USA: John Wiley & Sons.

Forgionne, G., & Russell, S. (2008a). The Evaluation of Decision-Making Support Systems' Functionality. In F. Adam & P. Humphreys (Eds.), *Encyclopedia of Decision Making and Decision Support Technologies.* Hershey, PA, USA: Information Science Reference.

Forgionne, G., & Russell, S. (2008b). The Use of Simulation as an Experimental Methodology for DMSS Research. In F. Adam & P. Humphreys (Eds.), *Encyclopedia of Decision Making and Decision Support Technologies.* Hershey, PA, USA Information Science Reference.

Goll, I., & Rasheed, A. M. (1997). Rational decision-making and firm performance: the moderating role of environment. *Strategic Management Journal, 18*(7), 583–591. doi:10.1002/(SICI)1097-0266(199708)18:7<583::AID-SMJ907>3.0.CO;2-Z

Griss, M., Letsinger, R., Cowan, D., VanHilst, M., & Kessler, R. (n.d.). *CoolAgent: Intelligent Digital Assistants for Mobile Professionals - Phase 1 Retrospective.* Hewlett-Packard Labs, Palo Alto, CA, USA.

Griswold, W. G., Boyer, R., Brown, S. W., & Truong, T. M. (2003). The activeclass project: Experiments in encouraging classroom participation. *Computer Support for Collaborative Learning)* (pp. 477-486).

Gunderloy, M. (2007). Reading and Publishing Performance Counters in. NET. *developer.com.* Available at http://www.developer.com/net/net/article.php/3356561

Holmquist, L. E., Wigstrom, J., & Falk, J. (1998). The Hummingbird: Mobile Support for Group Awareness. *Demonstration at ACM 1998 Conference on Computer Supported Cooperative Work,* Seattle, WA, USA

Hong, J., & Landay, J. (2001). A Context/Communication Information Agent. *Personal and Ubiquitous Computing, 5*(1), 78–81. doi:10.1007/s007790170037

Horvitz, E., Koch, P., Kadie, C. M., & Jacobs, A. (2002). Coordinate: Probabilistic Forecasting of Presence and Availability. *The Eighteenth Conference on Uncertainty and Artificial Intelligence* (pp. 224-233), Edmonton, Alberta, Canada.

Kwon, O., Shin, J., & Kim, S. (2006). Context-aware multi-agent approach to pervasive negotiation support systems. *Expert Systems with Applications, 31*(2), 285. doi:10.1016/j.eswa.2005.09.033

Labrou, Y., Finin, T., & Peng, Y. (1999). Agent Communication Languages: The Current Landscape. *Intelligent Systems, 14*(2), 45–52. doi:10.1109/5254.757631

Loyall, J. P., Schantz, R. E., Zinky, J. A., & Bakken, D. E. (1998). Specifying and Measuring Quality of Service in Distributed Object Systems. *First International Symposium on Object-Oriented Real-Time Distributed Computing (ISORC '98)*, Kyoto, Japan.

Luo, Y., Davis, D. N., & Lui, K. (2002). A Multi-Agent Decision Support System for Stock Trading. *IEEE Network, 16*(1), 20–27. doi:10.1109/65.980541

Menasce, D. A. (2004). Composing Web Services: A QoS View. *IEEE Internet Computing, 8*(6), 88–90. doi:10.1109/MIC.2004.57

Microsoft (2003). *Windows Server 2003 Performance Counters Reference*. Microsoft. Available at http://technet2.microsoft.com/windowsserver/en/library/3fb01419-b1ab-4f52-a9f8-09d5ebe-b9ef21033.mspx?mfr=true

Mistry, A. (2003). *Studying Financial Market Behavior with an Agent-Based Simulation*. Cornell University.

Moran, T.P., & Dourish, P. (2001). Introduction to This Special Issue on Context-Aware Computing. *Human-Computer Interaction Journal, 16*(1).

Muhlenbrock, M., Brdiczka, O., Snowdon, D., & Meunier, J. L. (2004). Learning to detect user activity and availability from a variety of sensor data. *Second IEEE Annual Conference on Pervasive Computing and Communications (PerCom 2004)* (pp. 13-22), Orlando, FL, USA.

Payton, J., Roman, G.-C., & Julien, C. (n.d.). *Simplifying Context-Aware Agent Coordination Using Context-Sensitive Data Structures*. Washington University in St. Louis, School of Engineering, St. Louis, MI, USA.

Peer, J. (2004). *Web Service Composition as AI Planning - a Survey*. University of St. Gallen.

Pistore, M., Barbon, F., Bertoli, P., Shaparau, D., & Traverso, P. (n.d.). *Planning and Monitoring Web Service Composition* (p. 106).

Plaza, E., & Arcos, J.-L. (2001). Context Aware Agents for Personal Information Services. *Lecture Notes in Computer Science*, 2182. doi:10.1007/3-540-45400-4

Power, D. J. (2002). *Decision support systems: concepts and resources for managers*. Quorum Books, Westport, CN, USA.

Rahmati, A., & Zhong, L. (2007). Context-for-wireless: context-sensitive energy-efficient wireless data transfer. *5th International Conference on Mobile systems, Applications and Services* (pp. 165-178), San Juan, Puerto Rico.

Roughan, M., Griffin, T., Mao, M., Greenberg, A., & Freeman, B. (2004). Combining routing and traffic data for detection of IP forwarding anomalies. *ACM SIGMETRICS Performance Evaluation Review, 32*(1), 416–417. doi:10.1145/1012888.1005745

Russell, S., & Yoon, V. (2005). Heterogeneous Agent Development: A Multi-Agent System for Testing Stock Trading Algorithms. *Eleventh Americas Conference on Information Systems*, Omaha, NE, USA.

Schilit, B., & Theimer, M. (1994). Disseminating Active Map Information to Mobile Hosts. *IEEE Network, 8*(5), 22–32. doi:10.1109/65.313011

Shahram, G., Shyam, K., & Bhaskar, K. (2006). An evaluation of availability latency in carrier-based vehicular ad-hoc networks. In *Proceedings of the 5th ACM international workshop on Data engineering for wireless and mobile access*. Chicago, Illinois, USA: ACM Press.

Simon, H. A. (1959). Theories of Decision-Making in Economics and Behavioral Science. *The American Economic Review, 49*(3), 253–283.

Simon, H. A. (1960). *The New Science of Management Decision.* New York, NY, USA: Harper & Row.

Teegan, H. A. (1996). Distributed performance monitoring using SNMP V2. *Network Operations and Management Symposium, 612,* 616-619. IEEE.

Telecom Italia Lab (2007). *JADE - Java Agent DEvelopment Framework* [Online].

Thio, N., & Karunasekera, S. (2005). Automatic measurement of a QoS metric for Web service recommendation. *Australian Software Engineering Conference* (pp. 202-211), Brisbane, Australia.

Wang, Y., Cuthbert, L., Mullany, F.J., Stathopoulos, P., Tountopoulos, V., Sotiriou, D.A., Mitrou, N., & Senis, M. (2004). Exploring agent-based wireless business models and decision support applications in an airport environment. *Journal of Telecommunications and Information Technology, 3.*

Weatherspoon, H., Chun, B.-G., So, C.W., & Kubiatowicz, J. (n.d.). *Long-Term Data Maintenance in Wide-Area Storage Systems: A Quantitative Approach.* University of California, Berkely, Electrical Engineering & Computer Sciences Department, Berkely, CA, USA.

Wooldridge, M. (2002). *An Introduction to MultiAgent Systems.* West Sussex, UK: John Wiley and Sons Ltd.

Yu-Chee, T., Shih-Lin, W., Wen-Hwa, L., & Chao, C.-M. (2001). Location awareness in ad hoc wireless mobile networks. *Computer, 34*(6), 46–52. doi:10.1109/2.928621

Zeidler, A., & Fiege, L. (2003). Mobility support with REBECA. *23rd International Conference on Distributed Computing Systems Workshop* (pp. 354-360), Providence, RI, USA.

This work was previously published in International Journal of Intelligent Information Technologies, Volume 5, Issue 4, edited by Vijayan Sugumaran, pp. 53-70, copyright 2009 by IGI Publishing (an imprint of IGI Global).

Chapter 9
Evaluation of Fault Tolerant Mobile Agents in Distributed Systems

Hojatollah Hamidi
University of Isfahan, Iran-Isfahan

Abbas Vafaei
University of Isfahan, Iran-Isfahan

ABSTRACT

The reliable execution of a mobile agent is a very important design issue to build a mobile agent system and many fault-tolerant schemes have been proposed. Hence, in this article, we present an evaluation of the performance of the fault-tolerant schemes for the mobile agent environment. Our evaluation focuses on the checkpointing schemes and deals with the cooperating agents. We derive the Fault-Tolerant approach for Mobile Agents (FANTOMAS) design which offers a user transparent fault tolerance that can be activated on request, according to the needs of the task. We also discuss how a transactional agent with different types of commitment constraints can commit. Furthermore, this article proposes a solution for effective agent deployment using dynamic agent domains.

INTRODUCTION

The client/server computing paradigm is today's most prominent paradigm in distributed computing. In this computing paradigm, the server is defined as a computational entity that provides some services. The client requests the execution of these services by interacting with the server.

Having executed the service, the server delivers the result back to the client. The server therefore provides the knowledge of how to handle the request as well as the required resources. The computing paradigm of mobile code generalizes this concept by performing changes along two orthogonal axes:

1. Where is the know-how of the service located?
2. Who provides the computational resources?

Depending on the choices made on the client and server sides, the following variants of mobile code computing paradigms, illustrated in Table 1, can be identified (Fuggetta, Picco, & Vigna,1998):

In the Remote Evaluation (REV) paradigm, component A sends instructions specifying how to perform a service to component B (represented by *code* in Table 1). These instructions can, for instance, be expressed in Java byte code. Component B then executes the request using its own resources, and returns the result, if any, to A. Java Servers are an example of remote evaluation (Coward, 2001).

In the Code on Demand (CoD) paradigm, the resources are collocated with component A, but A lacks the knowledge of how to access and process these resources in order to obtain the desired result. Rather, it gets this information from component B (represented by *code* in Table 1). As soon as A has the necessary know-how (i.e., has downloaded the code from B), it can start executing. Java applets5 fall under this variant of the mobile code paradigm.

The mobile agent computing paradigm is an extension of the REV paradigm. Whereas the latter focuses primarily on the transfer of code, the mobile agent paradigm involves the mobility of an entire computational entity, along with its code, the state, and potentially the resources required to perform the task. As developer-transparent capturing and transfer of the execution state (i.e., runtime state, program counter, and frame stacks, if applicable) requires global state models as well as functions to externalize and internalize the agent state, only few systems support this *strong mobility* scheme. In particular, Java-based mobile agent platforms are generally unsuitable for this approach, because it is not possible to access an agent's execution stack without modifying the Java Virtual Machine. Most systems thus settle for the *weak mobility* scheme where only the data state is transferred along with the code. Although it does not implicitly transport the execution state of the agent, the developer can explicitly store the execution state of the agent in its member attributes. The values of these member attributes are transported to the next machine. The responsibility for handling the execution state of an agent thereby resides with the developer. In contrary to REV, mobile agents can move to a sequence of machines, i.e., can make multiple hops.

A mobile agent is a software program which migrates from a site to another site to perform tasks assigned by a user. For the mobile agent system to support the agents in various application areas, the issues regarding the reliable agent execution, as well as the compatibility between two different agent systems or the secure agent migration, have been considered. Some of the proposed schemes are either replicating the agents

Table 1. Different variants of the mobile code computing paradigm (Fuggetta, Picco, & Vigna,1998). Code or computational entity transported between machines are indicated by italics. Component A accesses the services provided by component B.

	before the invocation		after the invocation	
	machine 1	machine 2	machine 1	machine 2
Client/Server	A	code,resource,B	A	code,resource,B
Remote Evaluation	code,A	resource,B	A	*code*,resource,B
Code on Demand	resource,A	code,B	*code*,resource, A	B
Mobile Agent	code,A	resource, B		*code*,resource,*A*, B

(Hamidi & Mohammadi, 2005) or checkpointing the agents (Park,Byun,Kim,&Yeom,2002;Pleisch &Schiper,2001;). For a single agent environment without considering inter-agent communication, the performance of the replication scheme In this article, we focus on the checkpoint-based schemes for the cooperating agents. For the performance analysis, a refined simulator has been developed and based on the simulation results, the performance of the schemes are discussed in the context of the influence of failures and system parameters. The suggestion for the efficient checkpointing is also made. In the area of mobile agents, only few works can be found relating to fault tolerance. Most of them refer to special agent systems or cover only some special aspects relating to mobile agents, e. g. the communication subsystem. Nevertheless, most people working with mobile agents consider fault tolerance to be an important issue (Izatt,Chan,&Brecht,1999; Shiraishi,Enoki do,&Takzawa,2003).

Johansen et al. (1995) detect and recover from faulty migrations inside the TACOMA (1995) agent system. When an agent migrates, a rear-guard agent is created that stays on the origin node. It monitors the migrated agent on the destination node. This very simple concept does not tolerate network partitioning.

In the scope of the TACOMA project, Minsky et al. (1996) propose an approach based on an itinerary concept, i. e. a plan, which nodes the mobile agent has to visit and what it has to do there. They assume that the itinerary is known at start time and the order of visited nodes is fixed. Fault tolerance is obtained by performing every itinerary step on multiple nodes concurrently and sending the results (the Mobile Agent) to all nodes of the next step. The majority of the received inputs from the last step becomes the input of the new task for this step and so on. Thus, a certain number of faults can be tolerated in each step. Disadvantages of this fault tolerance concept are the very inflexible description of the itinerary and the simple model of Mobile Agents. For example,

communication between different mobile agents is not included in this concept, so it is not suited for distributed or parallel applications.

Strasser and Rothermel present a more flexible itinerary approach for fault tolerance within the Mole system (2000). Independent items in this enhanced itinerary can be reordered. Each itinerary stage comprises the action that has be to done on one node. When the mobile agent enters a new stage by migrating to the next node of the itinerary, called a worker node, it is also replicated onto a number of additional nodes, called observers. If the worker becomes unavailable (due to a node or network fault), the observer with the highest priority is selected as the new worker by a special selection protocol. A voting protocol ensures the abortion of wrong multiple workers in case of a network fault. The voting protocol is integrated into a 2-phase commit protocol (2PC) that encloses every stage execution. These protocols cause a significant communication overhead. Just as in the work of Minsky et al(1996). nothing is said about the interaction between different mobile agents that are executed concurrently.

Vogler et al. (2002) introduce a concept for reliable migrations of mobile agents based on distributed transactions. The migration protocol is derived from known transaction protocols like the already mentioned 2PC. Besides the migrations, no other fault tolerance aspects of mobile agents are treated.

A *transactional agent* autonomously finds another object server if an object server where the agent to move is faulty. An agent leaves its *surrogate* agent which holds locks on objects in an object server when the agent leaves the object server. The surrogate agent holds locks on objects until the agent commits or aborts. The agent is faulty due to the fault of a current object server. Some surrogate agent of the agent recreates another incarnation of the agent. Furthermore, an agent can be replicated to realize parallel and fault-tolerant computation. Each replica of the agent is autonomously performed. Even if some replica agent is faulty, the agent is operational as long as at least one replica is operational. We discuss how transactional agents manipulate objects in multiple object servers in presence of server and application faults. Most distributed applications we see today are deploying the *client/server paradigm*. There are certain problems with the client/server paradigm, such as the requirement of a high network bandwidth, and continuous user-computer interactivity.

In view of the deficiencies of the client/server paradigm, the *mobile code paradigm* has been developed as an alternative approach for distributed application design. In the client/server paradigm, programs cannot move across different machines and must run on the machines they reside on. The mobile code paradigm, on the other hand, allows programs to be transferred among and executed on different computers. By allowing code to move between hosts, programs can interact on the same computer instead of over the network. Therefore, communication cost can be reduced. Besides, *mobile agent* (Fischer, Lynch,&Paterson,1983) programs can be designed to work on behalf of users autonomously. This autonomy allows users to delegate their tasks to the mobile agents, and not to stay continuously in front of the computer terminal.

MODEL

We assume an asynchronous distributed system, i.e., there are no bounds on transmission delays of messages or on relative process speeds. An example of an asynchronous system is the Internet. Processes communicate via message passing over a fully connected network.

Mobile Agent and Fault Model

A mobile agent executes on a sequence of machines, where a *place* p_i $(0 < i < n)$ provides the logical execution environment for the agent

(Pleisch&Schiper,2001,2003). Logically, a mobile agent executes in a sequence of stage actions (see Figure 1). Each stage action Sa_i consists of potentially multiple operations op_0, op_1 ,... .Agent ai $(0 < i < n)$ at the corresponding stage S_i represents the agent *a* that has executed the stage actions on places p_j $(j < i)$ and is about to execute on place p_i. The execution of ai on place pi results in a new internal state of the agent as well as potentially a new state of the place (if the operations of an agent have side effects). We denote the resulting agent a_{i+1}. Place p_i forwards a_{i+1} to p_{i+1} (for i < n). Any hardware and software component in a computing environment is potentially subject to failures.

This article addresses the following failures: crash of an agent, a place, or a machine. Clearly, the crash of a machine causes any place and any agent running on this machine **to** crash as well (Figure 2.d). A crashing place causes the crash of any agent on this place, but this generally does not affect the machine (Figure 2.c). Similarly, a place and the machine survive the crash of an agent (Figure 2.b). We do not consider programming errors in the code of the agent or the place as relevant failures in this sense.

Several types of faults can occur in agent environments. Here, we first describe a general fault model, and focus on those types, which are for one important in agent environments due to

Figure 1. Model of a mobile agent execution with three stages

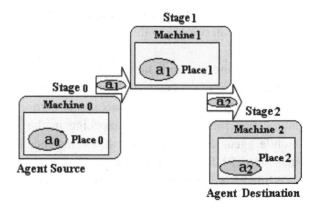

Figure 2. Failure model for mobile agents

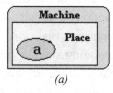 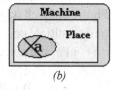 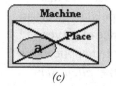 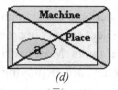

(a)   (b)   (c)   (d)

high occurrence probability, and for one have been addressed in related work only insufficiently.

- Node failures: The complete failure of a compute node implies the failure of all agent places and agents located on it. Node failures can be temporary or permanent.
- Failures of components of the agent system: Failures of agent places, or components of agent places become faulty, e. g. faulty communication units or incomplete agent directory. These faults can result in agent failures, or in reduced or wrong functionality of agents.
- Failures of mobile agents: Mobile agents can become faulty due to faulty computation, or other faults (e. g. node or network failures).
- Network failures: Failures of the entire communication network or of single links can lead to isolation of single nodes, or to network partitions.
- Falsification or loss of messages: These are usually caused by failures in the network or in the communication units of the agent systems, or the underlying operating systems. Also, faulty transmission of agents during migration belongs to this type.

We assume that link failures (and network partitions) are not permanent. The failure of a component (i.e., agent, place, machine, or communication link) can lead to blocking in the mobile agent execution. Assume, for instance that place P1 fails while executing a1 (Figure 3).While P1 is down, the execution of the mobile agent cannot proceed, i.e., it is blocked. Blocking occurs if a single failure prevents the execution from proceeding. In contrast, and execution is non blocking if it can proceed despite a single failure ,the blocked mobile agent execution can only continue when the failed component recovers. This requires that recovery mechanism be in place, which allows the failed component to be recovered. If no recovery mechanism exists, then the agents state and, potentially, even its code may be lost. In the following, we assume that such a recovery mechanism exists. Replication prevents blocking. Instead of sending the agent to one place at the next stage, agent replicas are sent to a set M_i of places $p_i^0, p_i^1, ...$ (Figure 3). We denote by a_i^j the agent replica of a_i executing on place p_i^j, but will omit the superscripted index if the meaning is clear from the context. Although a place may crash the agent execution does not block. Indeed, p_2^1 can take over the execution of a1 and thus prevent blocking.

Replication

Replication allows us to prevent blocking. However, it can also lead to a violation of the exactly–once execution property. Indeed, the exactly–once property and non-blocking are closely related. Assume, for instance, that place p_i^0 fails after having partially executed agent a_i (see Figure 3). After some time, p_i^1 detects the failure of p_i^0 and takes over the execution of a_i The agent a_i has now(partially) executed multiple times. Consequently, upon recovery, place p_i^0 needs to undo the modifications performed by agent a;" the issues if 'only an agent replica fails, but not

Figure 3. The redundant places mask the place failure, Replication potentially leads to a violation of the exactly-once property

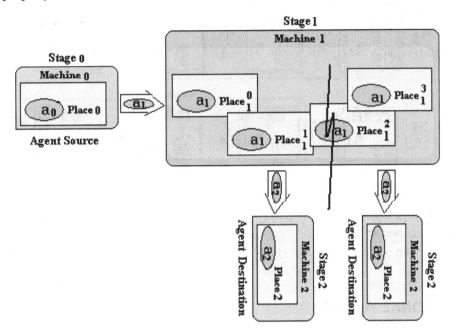

the place in this case, modifications by the failed agent to the place state survive. As the agent is then executed on place p_i^1 modifications are applied twice (to p_i^0 and p_i^1). Replication of the agent thus leads to a violation of the exactly- once execution property of mobile agents. Consequently, the replication protocol of agents has to undo the modifications if a_i to the place p_i^0. Another source for the violation of the exactly- once execution property is unreliable failure detection. Indeed, in an asynchronous system such as the Internet, no, boundaries exist on communication delays or on relative process speeds. Hence, it is impossible to detect failures reliably (Wong, Paciorek, & Moore,1999). Assume, for instance, that p_i^1 suspects p_i^0 has failed, when, in fact, p_i^0 has not (see Figure 3). This may lead to two agents a_{i+1} and a2, which are potentially sent to different places for the next stages. Clearly, this is a violation of the exactly-once execution property. In summary, a violation of the exactly-once execution property can occur: 1) in the agent replicas, and 2) at dif-

ferent places (or, rather, the services running on the places). Clearly, both instances are related in that a violation of the exactly-once execution property at the places is a consequence of multiple executions of the agent (e.g, a_i on p_i^0 and a_i on p_i^1).

Optimized Mode

In our discussion so far, we have assumed that M_{i-1} and M_i are a disjoint set of places. However, this is not a Requirement (Pleisch&Schiper,2000,2003). On the contrary, reusing places of stage S_{i-1} as witnesses for S_i improves the performance of the protocol and prevent high messaging costs; the pipelined mode thus assumes hetero-places with witnesses.At a limit , every stage S_i merely adds another place to M_{i-1}, while removing the oldest from the set M_{i-1}, In this mode , forwarding costs are minimized and limited to forwarding the agent to the new place (Figure 4).

We call this mode optimized. Note that, for set, we assume the existence of a place that acts as a

Figure 4. Model of the optimized mode

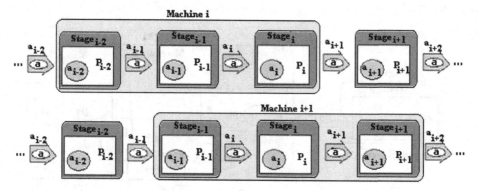

witness for The stage execution (not displayed in figure 4).The execution at stage S_0 (or Sn) is not replicated and no witnesses are needed for M_0 (Mn).

TRANSACTIONAL AGENTS

Commitment Conditions

- A transactional agent a manipulates objects in multiple object servers by moving around the object servers. A scope Scp (a) of an agent a means a set of object servers which the agent a possibly can manipulate.
- The atomic, majority, and at-least-one commitment conditions are shown in the form of $\binom{n}{r}$, $\binom{n}{(n+1)/2}$, and $\binom{n}{1}$ commitment conditions, respectively. Generalized consensus conditions with preference are discussed in a article (Shimojo, Tachikawa, & Takizawa, 1997). A commitment condition com(a) is specified for each agent a by an application.

There are still discussions on when the commitment condition com(a) of an agent a can be checked while the agent a is moving around object servers. Let H(a) be the history of an agent a, i.e. set of object servers which an agent a has so far manipulated ($H(a) \subseteq Scp(a)$). The commitment condition Com(a) can hold only if at least one object server is successfully manipulated, i.e. $|H(a)|$ =1 in the at-least-one commitment condition.

If an agent a leaves an object server S_j, an agent named surrogate of a is left on S_j (Figure 5). The surrogate agent a_i still holds objects in the object server S_j which are manipulated by the agent a.

Commitment

There are two types of agents, ordered agents and unordered agents. Every pair of ordered agents manipulate objects in a well-defined way. Each ordered agent a is assigned a precedent identifier

Figure 5. Surrogate agents

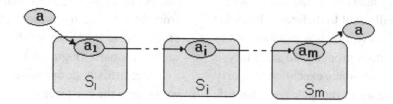

pid(a). An agent a_1 precedes another agent $a_2(a_1 \rightarrow a_2)$ if pid(a_1)< pid (a_2). For example, time stamp (Vogler, Kunkelmann, & Moschgath, 2002) can be used as identifier of an agent. That is, the identifier pid(a) of an agent a is time ts(a) when the agent a is initiated at the home server. An agent a_1 precedes another agent a_2 only if ts(a_1)<ts(a_2). An agent a_1 is concurrent with another agent $a_2 (a_1 || a_2)$ if neither a_1 precedes a_2 nor a_2 precedes a_1. Here, the agents a_1 and a_2 can be performed on an object server in any order. If a pair of the agents a_s and a_t conflict on object servers S_i and S_j the agents a_s and a_t are required to be performed in the precedence order at the object servers S_i and S_j. There are no dead locks. Like locking protocols, an unordered agent can obtain an object if no conflicting agent obtains the object.

THE FANTOMAS CONCEPT

From these considerations, we choose independent checkpointing with receiver based logging as base for our fault tolerance approach for mobile agents. Adhering to the agent paradigm, and exploiting the already available facilities of the mobile agent respect. the agent environment, an agent is used as the stable storage for the checkpointed state and the message log. For each mobile agent (called *user agent*(UA) in the following), for that fault tolerance is enabled, a *logger agent*(LA) is created. A user agent and its logger agent form an agent pair (Figure 6). The logger agent does not participate actively in the application's computation, and thus needs only a small fraction of the available CPU capacity. It follows the user agent at a certain non-zero distance on its migration path through the system. They must never reside on the same node, so that not a single fault destroys both of them. User and logger agents monitor each other, and if a fault is detected by one of them, it can rebuild the other one from its local information.

The creation of the agent pair is readily derived from the already existing migration facilities. To

Figure 6. Example for an application with three user and logger agents with checkpoints (CP) and messages (M) (Petri & Grewe, 1999)

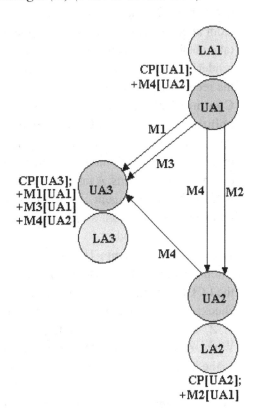

create a logger agent, the user agent serializes its state in the same way as for a migration, and sends it to a remote agent place. There, a new agent is created from this data. Different from migration, the new agent does not start the application module that was sent with the state information, and the user agent continues normal execution. Further, the communication unit of the agent is exchanged against a version that first forwards each incoming message to the logger agent before delivering it locally.

Checkpointing Schemes

The checkpointing schemes considered for the analysis are as follows:

- **Loosely Coordinated Checkpointing Coordination(LCCP) Scheme:** The checkpoints of an agent are sequentially numbered. On the receipt of a message from another agent, a forced checkpoint is taken before processing the message, if the sender's checkpoint number is larger than the receiver's checkpoint number.
- **Communication Mode Based Checkpointing Coordination(CMCP) Scheme:** An agent is either in the "sending" mode or in the "receiving" mode, regarding the communication status. A forced checkpoint is taken before the agent changes its communication status from a "sending" mode to a "receiving" mode.
- **Lazy(LAZY) Scheme:** This scheme is an extension of the LCCP scheme. The rule of the LCCP scheme is applied if the sender's checkpoint sequence number is a multiple of Z, where Z can be any integer value. When Z is one, the LAZY scheme works as the LCCP scheme. In this scheme, every Z-th checkpoint of an agent is guaranteed to be consistent, however, the others can be involved in a partial domino effect.
- **Timer Based Checkpointing Coordination(TBCP) Scheme:** The rule of the LCCP scheme is applied. However, once an induced checkpoint is taken, the timer for the next basic checkpoint is reset so that frequent checkpointing can be avoided. Among the well-known checkpointing coordination schemes, tightly coordinated schemes are excluded in this analysis, since the possibility of computation blocking required during the checkpointing coordination of these schemes is considered to be a burden for the agent.

Logging Schemes

The following three logging schemes are considered for the evaluation.

- **Pessimistic Message Logging (PML) Scheme:** On the receipt of a message from another agent, the message is logged into the stable storage before it is processed.
- **Dependency Based Message Logging (DML) Scheme:** A message received from another agent is first copied into the volatile log space. The volatile logs are flushed into the stable storage before the agent sends out any message to another agent.
- **Optimistic Message Logging (OML) Scheme:** A message received from another agent is first copied into the volatile log space.

THE FUNCTIONING OF AN AGENT

The lifecycle of an agent consists of three stages: Normal operational phase, when agents roam their domains performing the regular tasks; trading phase, where domain corrections are initiated and cloning/merging phase, where heavily loaded agents can multiply, or two under loaded agents can merge.

First we have to define the idea of logical topology. Logical network topology is a virtual set of connections stored in the hosts. If the physical topology of the managed network is rare in connections the use of logical topology can facilitate the correct functioning of the algorithm. The logical topology should follow the physical topology as setting up an arbitrary set of connections will increase the migration time.

As in most mobile agent applications the greatest reason again using them is security. Some people still look at mobile agents as a form of viruses and mobile agent platforms as security holes allowing foreign programs run on the system. Concerning the general threats of mobile agents is out of scope of this article. Instead we would like to outline the security issues concerning network management. The main difference between general mobile agents and network management agents is that the latter one cannot be closed in a separate running environment because network management agents must have the privilege to modify the configuration of the host to perform its tasks. Misusing these privileges can severely harm the nodes.

If the agent domains are not separated into distinct partitions we call the domains coherent. By keeping the coherence the migrating times can be much smaller comparing to the case when the agent domains can be partitioned into remote parts. On the other hand keeping domain coherence places limit to the trading process as the agent must know its „cutting" nodes that cannot be traded without splitting its area into distinct pieces.

BLOCKING PROBABILITY

The node needs to collect a majority of votes during processing to be able to commit the transaction of a stage. Therefore, a transaction can only be committed if more than half of the stage nodes are available. This fact can be used to give a (simple) metric for the availability As of a stage which is the probability that a majority of stage nodes is available so that an agent can finish a step and proceed with the next step. Let n be the number of the nodes of a stage and p be the availability of an individual node (i.e. the probability that the node is available). Then the probability that exactly m out of these n nodes are available can be calculated using the binomial probability function (Hughes, Grawoig, 1971).

$$f(n,m) = \binom{n}{m} p^m (1-p)^{(n-m)} \quad (1)$$

The availability $As\ (n, p)$ of a stage S can then be calculated by

$$A_s\ (n, p) = \sum_{i=\frac{n+1}{2}}^{n} \binom{n}{i} p^i (1-p)^{(n-i)} \quad (2)$$

The blocking probability is defined to be the probability that the agent is blocked in the stage. It is calculated by

$$Bs(\ n, p) = 1 - As(\ n, p) \quad (3)$$

The relative blocking probability $Br(n, p)$ is calculated by

$$Br(\ n, p) = Bs\ (n, p)\ /\ Bs\ (1, p) \quad (4)$$

Where a relative blocking probability of $Br(n, p)$=0.4 means for example that the probability of an agent blocking in a stage with n nodes (node availability p) is only 40% of the probability of an agent blocking on one node with availability p. Table 2 and Figure 7 show the relative blocking probability Br depending on the availability p of a node and the number n of stage nodes. It shows that an odd number of nodes bigger or equal to 3 reduces the relative blocking probability dramatically.

Table 2. Relative blocking probability of a stage

n	p		
	0.75	0.9	0.99
1	100%	100%	100%
2	175%	190%	199%
3	62%	28%	3%
4	105%	52%	6%
5	41%	9%	~0%
6	68%	16%	~0%
7	28%	3%	~0%

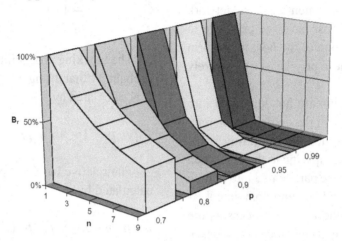

Figure 7. Relative blocking probability

EVALUATION AND SIMULATION RESULT

Evaluation

We evaluate transactional agents in terms of access time compared with client-server model. In the evaluation, three object servers S_1, S_2 and S_3 are realized in Oracle which are in sun workstation (SPARC 900MHz x 2) and a pair of Windows PCs(Pentium3 1.0GHz x 2 and pentium3 500MHz), respectively. The object servers are interconnected with 100base LAN. JDBC classes are already loaded in each object server. An application program A manipulates table objects by issuing select and update to some number of object servers at the highest isolation level, i.e. select for update in Oracle. The application program A is realized in Java on a client computer. In the transactional agent model, the application A is realized in Aglets. The computation of Aglets is composed of moving, class loading, manipulation of objects, creation of clone, and commitment steps. In the client-server model, there are computation steps of program initialization, class loading to client, manipulation of objects, and two-phase commitment.

Figure 8 shows how long it takes to perform each step for two cases, one for manipulating one

object server and another for manipulating two object servers, in client-server (cs) and transactional agent (TA) models. In the transactional agent model, Aglets classes are loaded to each object server before an agent is performed. Since Java classes are loaded to only client in the client-server model, the time for loading the classes is constant for any number of object servers. As shown in Figure 8, time to manipulate objects in a transactional agent is shorter than the client-server model because there is no communication between agent and object server. The time to load

Figure 8. Access time

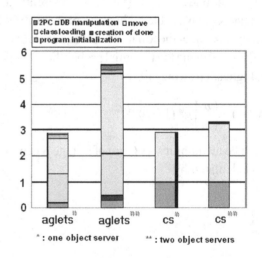

Aglets classes in each object server is about half of the total computation time in the transactional agent. The transactional agent faster manipulates objects than the client-server model. On the other hand, Aglets classes have to be loaded in the transactional agent. It takes about two seconds to load Aglets classes. Next, access time from time when the application program starts to time when the application program ends, is measured for Agents and client-server model. measured for Agents and client-server model.

Figure 9 shows the access time for number of object servers. The *non-cache Aglets* shows that Aglets classes are not loaded when an agent *A* arrives at an object server. Here, the agent can be performed after Aglets classes are loaded. On the other hand, the *cache Aglets* means that an agent manipulates objects in each object server where Aglets classes are already loaded, i.e. the agent comes to the object server after other agents have visited on the object server. As shown in Figure 9, the client-server model is faster than the transactional agent. However, the transactional agent is faster than the client-server model if object servers are frequently manipulated, i.e. cashed Aglets classes are a priori loaded.

Figure 9. Client server vs. agent

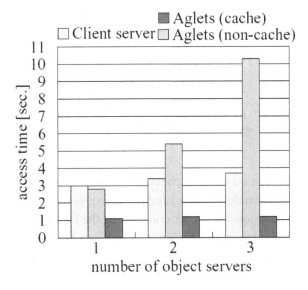

Simulation Model

A mobile agent system consisting of *Ns* sites and *Na* agents has been simulated. The working time on each site follows an exponential distribution with a mean *Tw*. The next site for the visit is selected randomly out of *Ns* sites and the migration time of *Tm* is assumed. While working on a site, an agent communicates with another agent by sending and receiving a message. The message-sending rate of each agent follows a Poisson process with a rate λc. For each message-sending event, the receiver is selected randomly and the communication delay *of Tc* is assumed. An agent takes a basic checkpoint before the migration into a volatile storage. The fixed time of *Tcp* is assumed to save an induced checkpoint into a stable storage and to log the messages into the stable storage, the fixed time of *Tl* is also assumed. A system site fails with an interval following an exponential distribution with a mean *Tf*.

When a site fails, all of the agents running on the site fail and the consistent recovery line is sought. If the local induced checkpoint or the remote basic checkpoint is selected as a consistent recovery point, the time *Tcp* is assumed to retrieve it. However, if the induced checkpoint on the remote site has to be retrieved, the time of *2* Tcp* is assumed including the round-trip communication delay.

Simulation Result

First, to measure the influence of system parameters on the checkpoint and the recovery cost, five test cases are simulated and for each case, the *checkpointing time,* the *logging time,* the *number of rollback agents,* the *lost time* and the *total overhead* are obtained.

The system environment with the following parameter values is simulated: $N_s=40$, $N_a=10$, $T_w=3000$, $\lambda c=1/400$, $T_f=320000$, $T_{cp}=100$, $T_l=10$ and $Tc=10$.

Case 1: The value of λc changes to 1/800.
Case 2: The value of T_w changes to 1500.
Case 3: The value of T_{cp} changes to 50.
Case 4: The value of N_a changes to 5.

The Cases 1-4 differs only one system parameter value compared to the Case "Basic".

From the results, it is observed that the CMCP scheme is very sensitive to the changes of the communication rate and among the logging schemes the OML scheme shows the most stable performance as the changes of the system parameters regardless of the rollback propagation.

Figure 10 analyze the influence of the communication rate in more detail, where T_f=32000, T_w=3000 and T_{cp}=100. The CMCP scheme and the DML scheme show the most drastic changes in the checkpoint cost and the lost time as the communication rate varies. However, the CMCP scheme shows very slow increases in the number of rollback agents for the communication rate increase.

Figure 11 shows experimental results of the four test cases, in which the values of T_f=320000, T_w=3000, λc=1/400 and T_{cp}=100 are used for Figure 10(a); for Figure 10(b), the value of λc changes to 1/6400 ; the value of T_{cp} also changes to 10 in Figure 10(c).

As shown in the figure 11, the LAZY schemes work well for the environment with high checkpointing overhead and low failure rate, while the CMCP scheme is good for the cases with low checkpointing overhead and high failure rate. In most of the cases, logging schemes can be a good choice except the cases where both the checkpointing overhead and the failure rate are low.

Overall, each of the checkpoint coordination and the logging scheme works well for different environments. Hence, the selection of the scheme must be taken carefully, considering the system environment. Especially, the size of the agents and the communication degree among the agents are the most important factors to choose the proper scheme. The size of an agent is related to the time

Figure 10. The influence of communication rate

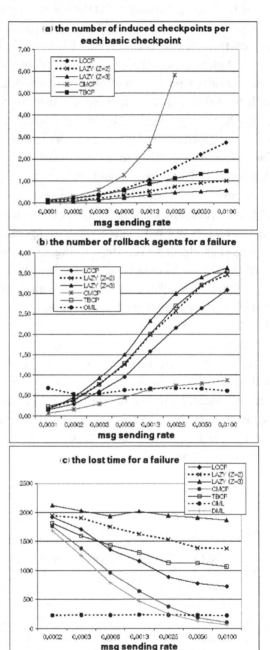

to take an induced checkpoint; and the communication degree is related to the frequency of the checkpointing. Also, considering the fact that an agent migrates from a site to another site, it is not a bad idea to take induced checkpoints into the

Figure 11. Comparison of checkpoint coordination and logging schemes

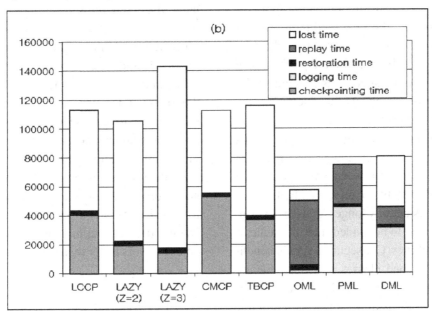

Figure 12. The size of the agent population under changing network conditions

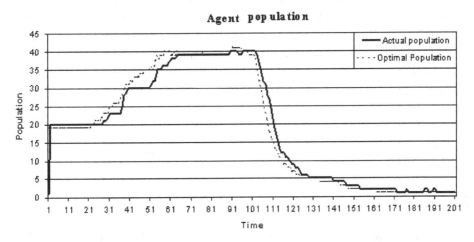

volatile storage, since an agent can retrieve any of its checkpoints from the previously visiting site. In such a case, the checkpointing overhead can be drastically decreased and then the CMCP scheme can be a good choice.

A simulator was designed to evaluate the algorithm. The system was tested in several simulated network conditions and numerous parameters were introduced to control the behavior of the agents. We also investigated the dynamic functioning of the algorithm. Comparing to the

previous case the parameter configuration has a larger effect on the behavior of the system. The most vital parameter was the frequency of the trading process and the pre-defined critical workload values. Figure 12 shows the number of agents on the network. The optimal agent population is calculated by dividing the workload on the whole network with the optimal workload of the agent.

Simulation results show that choosing correct agent parameters the workload of the agents is within a ten percent environment of the predefined visiting frequency on a stable network. In a simulated network overload the population dynamically grows to meet the increased requirements and smoothly returns back to normal when the congestion is over. To measure the performance of FANTOMAS our test consists of sequentially sending a number of agents that increment the value of the counter at each stage of the execution. Each agent starts at the agent source and returns to the agent source, which allows us to measure its round–trip time. Between two agents, the places are not restarted. Consequently, the first agent needs considerably longer for its execution, as all classes need to be loaded into the cache of the virtual machines. Consecutive agents benefit from already cached classes and thus execute much faster. We do not consider the first agent execution in our measurement results. For a fair comparison, we used the same approach for the single agent case (no replication). Clearly, this is a simplification, as the class files do not need to be transported with the agent. Remote class loading adds additional costs because the classes have to be transported with the agent and then loaded into the virtual machine. However, once the classes are loaded in the class loader, other agents can take advantage of them and do not need to load these classes again.

CONCLUSION

This article has discussed a mobile agent model for processing transactions which manipulate object servers. An agent first moves to an object server and then manipulates objects. We showed the evaluation of the mobile agent-based transaction systems for applications. If Aglets classes are a priori loaded, the transactional agents can manipulate object servers faster than the client-server model. Also, we have presented the experimental evaluation of the performance of the fault-tolerant schemes for the mobile agent environment. From the experimental results, the system environment

suitable for each of the fault tolerant schemes has been discussed and the stability of the schemes has been also discussed. General possibilities for achieving fault tolerance in such cases were regarded, and their respective advantages and disadvantages for mobile agent environments, and the intended parallel and distributed application scenarios shown. This leads to an approach based on warm standby and receiver side message logging. In the article, dynamically changing agent domains were used to provide flexible, adaptive and robust operation, and transaction systems for applications. If Aglets classes are *a priori* loaded, the transactional agents can manipulate object servers faster than the client-server model.

REFERENCES

Baumann, J., Hohl, F. & Rothermel, K. (1997). Mole - Concepts of a Mobile Agent System. Technical Report TR-1997-15, Fakultat Informatik, Germany.

Bernstein, P.A., Hadzilacos, V., & Goodman,N. (1987). Concurrency control and recovery in database systems. In Addison Wesley.

Coward, D. (2001, August). *Java Servlet Specification – Version 2.3*. Sun Microsystems.

Fischer, M.J., Lynch, N.A., & Paterson, M.S. (1983, March). Impossibility of Distributed consensus with one Faulty process. In *Proceedings of the* second ACM SIGACT-SIGMOD symposium: Principles of Database system (p. 17).

Fuggetta, A., Picco, G. P., & Vigna, G.(1998). Understanding code mobility. *IEEE Transactions on Software Engineering*, 24(5).(pp. 342–361).

Gendelman,E. & Bic,L.F., & Dillencourt, M.B. (2000). An Application-Transparent, Platform-Independent Approach to Rollback-recovery for Mobile Agent Systems. In *Proceeding of the 20th International Conference on Distributed Computing Systems*.

Hamidi, H. & Mohammadi, K.(2005, March). Modeling and Evaluation of Fault Tolerant Mobile Agents in Distributed Systems.In *Proceeding of the 2th IEEE Conference on Wireless & Optical Communications Networks (WOCN2005)* (pp.91-95).

Hamidi, H. & Mohammadi, K. (2006, January-March). Modeling Fault Tolerant and Secure Mobile Agent Execution in Distributed Systems. International Journal of Intelligent Information Technologies (IJIIT 2(1)). pp.21-36.

Hamidi, H. & Vafaei, A. (2008, May). Evaluation of Security and Fault-Tolerance in Mobile Agents. In *Proceeding of the 5th IEEE Conference on Wireless & Optical Communications Networks (WOCN2008)* (pp.1-5).

Hughes, A., & Grawoig, D. (1971). Statistics: A Foundation for Analysis. Addison-Wesley Publishing Company.

Izatt,M., Chan, P., & Brecht, T. (1999, June). Agents: Towards an Environment for Parallel, Distributed and Mobile Java Applications. In *Proceeding of the* 1999 ACM Conference on Java Grande,(pp. 15-24).

Johansen, D., van Renesse, R. & Schneider, F. B. (1995). An Introduction to the TACOMA Distributed System, Version 1.0. Report, Institute of Mathematical and Physical Science, University of Tromsf3, Norway

Johansen, D., van Renesse, R. & Schneider, F. B. (1995). Operating System Support for Mobile Agents. In *Proceeding of the 5th IEEE Workshop on Hot Topics in Operating Systems, USA*(pp. 42-45).

Minsky, Y., van Renesse, R., Schneider, F. B. & Stoller, S. D.(1996, September). Cryptographic Support for Fault-Tolerant Distributed Computing. *In Proceeding of the 7th ACM SIGOPS European Workshop,ACM Press* (pp. 109-114).

Park, T., Byun, I.,Kim,H., & Yeom, H.Y. (2002). The Performance of Checkpointing and Replication Schemes for Fault Tolerant Mobile Agent Systems. In *Proceeding of the 21th IEEE Symp. on Reliable Distributed Systems.*

Petri, S. & Grewe, C.(1999,September).A Fault-Tolerant Approach for Mobile Agents. In *Dependable Computing – EDCC-3, Third European Dependable Computing Conference, Fast Abstracts.* Czech Technical University in Prague.

Pleisch ,S. & Schiper, A. (2000). Modeling Fault-Tolerant Mobile Agent Execution as a Sequence of Agree Problems. In *Proceeding of the 19th IEEE Symposium on Reliable Distributed Systems(* pp. 11-20).

Pleisch,S. & Schiper, A.(2001, July). FATOMAS - A Fault-Tolerant Mobile Agent System Based on the Agent-Dependent Approach. In *Proceeding of the 2001 International Conference on Dependable Systems and networks* (pp.215-224).

Pleisch,S. & Schiper, A. (2003). Fault-Tolerant Mobile Agent Execution. IEEE Transactions on *Computers, 52(2).*

Shimojo, I., Tachikawa, T., & Takizawa,M. (1997). M-ary commitment protocol with partially ordered domain. In *Proceeding of the 8th International Conference on Database and Expert Systems Applications (DEXA·97)*(pp. 397-408).

Shiraishi,M., Enokido, T., &Takzawa, M. (2003). Fault-Tolerant Mobile Agents in Distributed Systems. In *Proceedings of the Ninth IEEE Workshop on Future Trends of Distributed Computer (FT-DCS·03)*(pp. 11-20).

Silva, L. Batista, V., & Silva, L.G. (2000). Fault-Tolerant Execution of Mobile Agents. In *Proceeding of the International Conference on Dependable Systems and Networks.*

Strasser, M. & Rothermel, K. (2000). System Mechanism for Partial Rollback of Mobile Agent Execution. In *Proceeding of the 20th International Conference on Distributed Computing Systems.*

Vogler, H., Kunkelmann,T., & Moschgath,L. (2002). An Approach for Mobile Agent Security and Fault Tolerance using Distributed Transactions. In *Proceeding of the* 2002 *International Conference on Parallel and Distributed Systems (ICPADS· 2002).*

Wong, D., Paciorek, N., & Moore, D. (1999, March). Java-based mobile agents. Communications of the ACM, 42(3):92-102.

This work was previously published in International Journal of Intelligent Information Technologies, Volume 5, Issue 1, edited by Vijayan Sugumaran, pp. 43-60, copyright 2009 by IGI Publishing (an imprint of IGI Global).

Chapter 10
Cognitive Parameter Based Agent Selection and Negotiation Process for B2C E-Commerce

Bireshwar Dass Mazumdar
Banaras Hindu University, India

R. B. Mishra
Banaras Hindu University, India

ABSTRACT

Multi-agent paradigms have been developed for the negotiation and brokering in B2C e-commerce. Few of the models consider the mental states and social settings (trust and reputation) but rarely any model depicts their combination. In this chapter, a combined model of belief, desire, intention (BDI) for agent's mental attitudes and social settings is used to model their cognitive capabilities. The mental attitudes also include preferences, commitments, along with BDI. These attributes help to understand the commitment and capability of the negotiating agent. In this work, we present three mathematical models. First, a cognitive computational model is used for the computation of trust, and then index of negotiation, which is based on trust and reputation. The second computation model is developed for the computation of business index that characterizes the parameters of some of the business processes, which match the buyer's satisfaction level. On the basis of index of negotiation and business, we calculate SI (selection index) to select a seller agent with the highest value of SI. The third computation model of utility is used for negotiation between seller and buyer to achieve maximum combined utility increment (CUI), which is the difference of marginal utility gain (MUG) of buyer and marginal utility cost (MUC) of seller.

INTRODUCTION

Multi-agent paradigms have been developed for the negotiation and brokering in B2C e-commerce.

Few of the models consider the mental states and social settings (trust and reputation) but rarely any model depicts their combination. By increasing the degree and the sophistication of

DOI: 10.4018/978-1-60960-595-7.ch010

the automation on both the buyer (contractee) and the seller (contractor), benefit to both can be enhanced. Various Multi-agent models have been developed; V Robu and C Jonker (Jonker, Robu, Treur, 2007) introduced component-based generic agent architecture for integrative multi-attribute negotiation, a negotiation strategy that has proved itself in experiments with human.

Some issues of engineering agents that partially automate some of the activities of information brokering in e-commerce (Mong, Sim, 2000) focuses on addressing the problem of connecting buyers and sellers. The process of matching and connecting buyers and sellers is divided in four stages: selection, evaluation, filtering and assignment. Trading agent have been developed which can either take or reject recommendations made by the broker agent (Suwu, 2001). They can also provide feedback to the brokering test bed by indicating their satisfaction level. Users' satisfaction will be used as one of the evaluation criteria of the agent-based information brokering with multiple connections for a request or an advertisement.

A multi-agent artificial market system, whose software broker agent can learn to build a relatively long-term trust relationship with their clients, the goals of these broker agents are not only to maximize the total revenue subject to their clients' risk preference as most other agents do but also to maximize the trust they receive from their clients. Social settings such as trust, reputation and mental states of buyer, seller and broker may be used individually or in combination in agent based model. In general, various trust models have been proposed with different components for different purposes. Chandrasekharan and Esfandiari (2001) model is based upon the cognitive approach in which trust and reputation are function of beliefs. Their trust acquisition network performs Bayesian learning. In the model proposed by Schillo et al. (2000), trust is based upon probability theory that deals with Boolean impression: good or bad. The trust model of Hailes (2000) is based upon

the information of witness. A trust model, based upon the most recent experiences and historic information uses probabilistic computational model of Dempster-Shafer theory Yu and Singh (2001). Castelfranchi and Falcone (1998) proposed a cognitive trust model based upon the mental background of delegation. In their trust model, trust is a set of mental attitudes which prefers another agent doing the action. It is based upon agent's intentions of doing an action. Trust is introduced into I-TRUST (Tang, Winoto, Niu, 2003) as a relationship between clients and their software broker agents in terms of the amount of money they are willing to give to these agents to invest on their behalf. Broker agents are benevolent (i.e. they will not cheat their clients!); each client can only have one broker agent at one time.

Reputation is considered on the basis of two users rating in the modal Sporas (Zacharia, 1999; Sabater, Sierra, 2005). Histos (Zacharia, 1999; Sabater, Sierra, 2005) reputation model is based upon the use witness information i.e. the most recent experience with the agent that is being evaluated. Carter et al. (2002) have calculated the reputation value for each agent by a centralized mechanism that monitors the system. Therefore, the reputation value of each user is a global measure shared by all the observers. In our model reputation is based on only broker's rating of respective seller.

Shoham defines an agent to be "an entity whose state is viewed as consisting of mental components such as beliefs, capabilities, choices, and commitments (Shoham, 1993). A generic classification of an agent's attitudes is defined as follows: Informational attitudes i.e. Knowledge and Beliefs, Motivational attitudes i.e. Desires and Intentions, Commitments (Frances, Barbara, Treur, Verbrugge, 1997).

Few attempts by researchers are made to develop a computational model which integrates social settings and mental states of agents for the performances of some processes in B2C e-commerce. For example, MAGS, a monitoring multi-agent system for the management of business process in a web services environment can be integrated with applications in the enterprise and web services provided by cross-organizational business partners. Capabilities are added to BDI agent in MAGS to offer mechanisms of monitoring process execution, carrying out alerts and access control (Zhao, Zhao, Zhang, Lin, 2004).Huang, Liang, Lai &Lin (2010) proposed a analytical hierarchy process based multiple-attributes negotiation model for B2C e-commerce, which deploys intelligent agents to facilitate autonomous and automatic on-line buying and selling by intelligent agents while quickly responding to consumers. These include a 4-phase model, information collection, search, negotiation, and evaluation.

In this work a combined model of belief, desire, intention (BDI) model for agent's mental attitudes and social settings are used to model their cognitive capabilities. The mental attitudes also include preferences, commitments along with BDI. These attributes help to understand the commitment and capability of the negotiating agent. In this work, we present three mathematical models. First cognitive computational model is used for the computation of trust and then index of negotiation which is based on trust and reputation and the second computation model is developed for the computation of business index that characterizes the parameters of some of the business processes, which match the buyer's satisfaction level. On the basis of index of negotiation and business, we calculate SI (selection index) to select a seller agent with the highest value of SI. The third computation model of utility is used for negotiation between seller and buyer to achieve maximum combined utility increment (CUI) which is the difference of marginal utility gain (MUG) of buyer and marginal utility cost (MUC) of seller. With the help of GUI intermediate and final results are shown. The organization of the chapter as follows: problem description and definitions section covers problem description and the basic definition of different types of agents. The proposed approach section provides the computational models. The prototype

implementation section provides the interaction (Communication Protocol) among agents. The major parts of algorithms to implement the models are also described in this section. Various experiments are provided in result section. Related works and comparisons of various experimentations are discussed in related works and comparison section. Finally conclusion section provides a brief concluding remarkable overview of the work.

PROBLEM DESCRIPTION AND DEFINITIONS

The process of brokering as often occurs in e-commerce involves a number of agents. A buyer agent looking for products may be supported by a broker agent that takes its buyer agents' queries and contacts other agents or looks at the web directly to find information on products with in the buyer agent's scope of interest. The model, in this chapter addresses three stages: need identification, seller selection and negotiation; where the seller selection stage is the integrated part of product brokering and merchant brokering. These three stages are related with three main problems. Firstly in the need identification, the buyer agent recognizes a need for some product through a profile. This profile may be appearing to broker agent in many different ways. Secondly the seller selection involves the broker agent to determine what product is to be bought to satisfy this need and finding the seller that offered item at desired price. The main techniques used by the brokers in this stage are (i) feature-based filtering i.e. item based on brand and quality (ii) constraint-based filtering i.e. the agent specify price range and date limit. In agent mediated e-commerce context it is common for seller agents to have capabilities, commitment and trust for processing the new business. Third stage negotiation requires negotiating the terms and conditions under which the desired items will be delivered. Automated negotiation capabilities are essential for the automated B2C e-commerce.

The buyer agent contacts with broker agent, the broker agent determines the desire (wishes) of the buyer agent. Then the broker matches products and sellers and selects one of the best proposals. The broker agent negotiates with seller agent on behalf of buyer agent to obtain best deal which satisfies both parties.

The following terms need to be defining in this context.

Buyer Agent (Buyer): the agent who needs to buy some items from another agent. The buyer gains quality when buyer buys items.

Seller Agent (Seller): the agent who sells these items to the buyer. It devotes processing time and other resources to sells these items.

Broker Agent (Broker): The agent, who acts as a mediator between buyer and sellers, is broker agent. The broker agent identifies the need of the buyer agent and then selects the best seller agent by evaluating the profile of the various seller agents and finally negotiates between buyer and seller agent.

Marginal Utility Gain (MUG): the local utility increment for the buyer by having bought items with duration and quality specified which is calculated by the buyer agent. The marginal utility gain is based upon the utility gain (UG).

Marginal Utility Cost (MUC): the local utility decrement for the seller by selling with duration and quality specified as in commitment, which is calculated by the seller agent. The marginal utility cost is based upon the utility cost (UC).

PROPOSED APPROACH

Our proposed approach consists of three computational models and an interaction model. The computational models are Cognitive computational model, business process computational model and utility computational model. The interaction

model is shown by UML diagram which depicts the various modes of interaction among different types of agents.

Cognitive Computation Model

Recently a BDI based computational model combined with QoS (quality of service)has been deployed for the selection in semantic web(Garg & Mishra, 2008) with more or less similar parameter of BDI integrate with business model and utility model. The performance, desire, intention, capability, commitment, trust, preferences, index of negotiation of contractor agent has been computed as follows (Mazumdar & Mishra ;2009):

Desire: Desires can refer to a (desired) state of affairs in the world (and the other agents), but also to (desired) actions to be performed (Frances, Barbara, Treur, Verbrugge, 1997). An agent's desires are conceived of as the states of the world that the agent wishes to bring about (Bell, 1995 Kraus, 1998).

Preference: An agent's preference plays an active role in social practical reasoning, where an action is to be selected in order for given intention to be fulfilled (Panzarasa, Jennings, Norman, 2002).

Intention: Intention is actually the goal that an agent wants to achieve; an agent's intention will give a guideline of what to do (Wu, Ekaette, Far, 2003). Intention is a fundamental characteristic that agents involve a special kind of "self commitment" to acting (Bratman 1990, Von 1980).

Commitment: An agent's individual intention towards a state of affairs entails the agent's commitment to acting to wards the achievement of that state (Panzarasa, Jennings, Norman, 2002).

Performance, capability, intention, desire, preference, commitment are multiple attribute functions, which are weighted function of the items that was sold in best, fair or defective categories. The level of trust is determined by the degree of initial success of the agent experience (He, Jennings, and Leung, 2003). The variables and the corresponding weight age in the right side of the expressions of cognitive parameters are heuristic and are based on experience in dealing with selling and buying affairs in common practices and are also used in the concerning literature. The parameters are expressed mathematically as follows (Mazumdar &Mishra,2009):

(a) The performance is calculated on the basis of number of items that are sold in best category, numbers of items that are sold in fair best category, number of items that are sold in defective category by the seller agent. This is the performance with out difficulty. Here difficulty of task indicates that storage difficulty of items i.e. there are too many risk parameters involved in the storage of items. The performance computed by the following formula has not any type of indication about the difficulty of inventory, shipping related problems related to each items. When evaluating the performance of different sellers the key factor considered the business efficiency. A total score is then calculated for each seller is based on the weight score of business efficiency constituent components (He, Jennings, and Leung, 2003).

$$P_i^j = \frac{I_i^{j,bs} \times w_{bs} + I_i^{j,fs} \times w_{fs} - I_i^{j,ds} \times w_{ds}}{w_{bs} + w_{fs} + w_{ds}}$$

where P_i^j is the performance of ith seller for jth Item with out difficulty weight, w_{bs} is weight assign for each best sold item, w_{fs} is weight assign for each fair sold item, w_{ds} is the weight assign for each defective sold item, $I_i^{j,bs}$ is the jth type best items that was sold by agent ith, $I_i^{j,fs}$ is the jth type items that was sold by ith agent, $I_i^{j,ds}$ is the jth defective items that was sold by ith agent.

In our problem we assume that w_{bs} =0.8, w_{fs} =0.3 and w_{ds} =0.9. The higher value of w_{ds} gives negative impact by the formula. The performance computed by the above formula has not any type of indication about the difficulty of tasks.

(b) The second type of performance i.e. performance with difficulty weight is calculated on the basis of difficulty weight. The difficulty weight w_d is related with level of difficulty of inventory and shipping related problem for each item. In our problem we assume that w_{dItem1}=0.1, w_{dItem2}=0.2, w_{dItem3}=0.3; w_{dItem4}=0.4, w_{dItem5}=0.5

$$p_{iw}^j = P_i^j * w_{dj}$$

p_{iw}^j is the performance with difficulty weight; Where j ε {Item1, Item2, Item3, Item4, Item5}

(c) The capability is computed on the basis of performance and difficulty weight, performance with difficulty and total number of items sold. Hence capability of ith agent is:

$$(Capability)_i = \frac{\sum_j p_{iw}^j}{Tota \ln oofItems \times \sum_j w_{dj}} \times 100$$

where $(Capability)_i$ is the capability of the ith agent; the capability shows the how much items can be sold handled by a particular seller agent.

(d) To calculate the desire of a seller agent we first calculate the factor X. The factor X is calculated on the basis of number of selected items that are sold in best category, number of selected items that are sold in fair category and number of selected items that are sold in defective category. $w_{s,bs}$, $w_{s,fs}$, $w_{s,ds}$ are relative remarks based upon the number of selected items that are sold in best category, number of selected items that are sold in fair category and number of selected items that are sold in defective category.

$$X_i^s = \frac{I_i^{s,bs} \times w_{s,bs} + I_i^{s,fs} \times w_{s,fs} - I_i^{s,ds} \times w_{s,ds}}{w_{s,bs} + w_{s,fs} + w_{s,ds}}$$

X_i^s is a parameter for calculate the desire, $I_i^{s,bs}$ is the number of selected items type s best sold item by i[th] agent, $I_i^{s,fs}$ is the number of selected items type s fair sold item by i[th] agent, $I_i^{s,ds}$ is the number of selected items type s defective sold by i[th] agent, $w_{s,bs}$ is weight assign for each selected item type s best sold, $w_{s,fs}$ is weight assign for each selected item type s fair sold, $w_{s,ds}$ is weight assign for each selected item type s defective sold. In our problem we assume that $w_{s,bs}$ =0.8, $w_{s,fs}$ =0.3 and $w_{s,ds}$ =0.9. The higher value of $w_{s,ds}$ gives negative impact. X_i^s is a parameter for calculate the desire.

(e) Desires denote states that agent wish to do the task (Frances, Barbara, Treur, Verbrugge, 1997) which is based upon the total factor X and difficulty weight. Hence desire of ith agent is:

$$(Choice)_i = (Desire)_i = \frac{\sum\limits_{s} X_i^s \times w_{d_s}}{Total\, n\, of\, Items \times \sum\limits_{s} w_{d_s}} \times 100$$

(f) The preference is calculated on the basis of number of selected items that are sold in best category, number of selected items that are sold in fair category and number of selected items that are sold in defective category i.e. an action is to be selected (Panzarasa, Jennings, Norman, 2002).

$w_{p,bs}, w_{p,fs}, w_{p,ds}$ are relative preference weight based upon number of selected items that are sold in best category, number of selected items that are sold in fair category and number of selected items that are sold in defective category respectively. Hence preference of ith agent is shown in Box 1.

$w_{p,bs}$ is preferential weight assign for each selected item type s best sold, $w_{p,fs}$ is preferential weight assign for each selected item type s fair sold, $w_{p,ds}$ is preferential weight assign for each selected item type s defective sold.

In our problem we assume that $w_{p,bs}$ =0.8, $w_{p,fs}$ =0.5 and $w_{p,ds}$ =0.7. The higher value of $w_{p,ds}$ shows negative impact.

(g) The intention computed on the basis of choice (desire) and preference (Panzarasa, Jennings, Norman, 2002). Hence intention of ith agent is:

$$(Intention)_i = \frac{(Choice)_i \times (Preference)_i}{100}$$

h) Commitment is computed on the basis of intention and capability (Panzarasa, Jennings, Norman, 2002). Hence commitment of ith agent is:

$$(Commitment)_i = (Intention)_i \times (Capability)_i$$

(i) The Trust is computed on the basis of commitment and capability of an agent (Castelfranchi and Falcone, 1998). Hence commitment of ith agent is:

$$(Trust)_i = (Commitment)_i \times (Capability)_i$$

Box 1.

$$(Preference)_i = \frac{\sum\limits_{s} w_{d_s} \times \left(\dfrac{\left(I_i^{s,bs} \times w_{p,bs} + I_i^{s,fs} \times w_{p,fs} - I_i^{s,ds} \times w_{p,ds} \right)}{w_{p,bs} + w_{p,fs} + w_{p,ds}} \right)}{Total\, n\, of\, Items} \times 100$$

(j) The index of negotiation helps to select an agent for a particular task α is a factor and $0 < α < 1$. It is computed on the basis of trust and reputation of an agent. Here reputation is based on broker's rating.

$$IN_i = α(Trust)_i + (1-α)(Reputation)_i$$

where IN_i is the index of negotiation; in our experiment we assume that $α=0.5$.

For selecting a seller agent first buyer agent find out that what type of item sold by the seller i with best quality, and then if IN_i for i seller agent is maximum then i seller agent's proposal is invited for negotiation. Social and cognitive functions of the above mathematical model we calculate the important parameters related to social state and cognitive state of different seller agents.

Business Computation Model

Business computational model depends upon the business policies of buyer and seller (Namo Kang, Sangyong Han, 2002). Through business computational model broker agent evaluates the differences between buyer's business policies and seller's business policies and informs to buyer agent. Business policies of both buyer and seller agent depends upon quality request, price request, time request, brand value and payment mode options provided by both parties. This business computational model helps to find out that whether the differences between businesses policies of both parties are going to be minimize. The business computation model is based upon two evaluations $(EV_1)_i$ and $(EV_2)_i$. Both evaluations are weighted functions of the quality, time, brand, and payment mode of both parties. Both evaluation help in feature-based filtering and constraint based filtering. EV_1 and EV_2 are based upon the concepts correlating the price, date and quality (brand) to them (He, Jennings, and Leung, 2003). The formulas to compute EV_1 and EV_2 are given in Box 2.

Where $(EV_1)_i$ is the evaluation index by which calculate the difference between initial prices, quality, time, brand provided by the buyer agent and seller agents, B_Q^j is given quality request for j^{th} item by buyer, B_{price}^j is given price request for j^{th} item by buyer, B_{time}^j is given time request for j^{th} item by buyer, $S_{i\ Q}^{\ j}$ is given quality request for j^{th} item by i^{th} seller, $S_{i\ price}^{\ j}$ is given price request for j^{th} item by i^{th} seller, $S_{i\ time}^{\ j}$ is given quality request for j^{th} item by i^{th} seller, $B_{brandvalue}^j$ is given brand request for j^{th} item by buyer,

Box 2.

$$
(EV_1)_i = \left\{ \sum_j \left(\frac{B_Q^j \times w_{quality}}{Q_{thresold}} \right) + \sum_j \left(\left(\frac{price\_\lim it_b - B_{price}^j}{price\_\lim it} \right) \times w_{price} \right) + \sum_j \left(\left(\frac{time\_\lim it_b - B_{time}^j}{time\_\lim it} \right) \times w_{time} \right) + \right.
$$
$$
\sum_j \left(\left(\frac{brand\_\lim it_b - B_{brandvalue}^j}{brand\_\lim it_b} \right) \times w_{brand} \right) \right\} - \left\{ \sum_j \left(\frac{S_{i\ Q}^{\ j} \times w_{quality}}{Q_{thresold}} \right) + \sum_j \left(\left(\frac{price\_\lim it_s - S_{i\ price}^{\ j}}{price\_\lim it} \right) \times w_{price} \right) + \right.
$$
$$
\sum_j \left(\left(\frac{time\_\lim it_s - S_{i\ time}^{\ j}}{time\_\lim it} \right) \times w_{time} \right) + \sum_j \left(\left(\frac{brand\_\lim it_s - S_{i\ brandvalue}^{\ j}}{brand\_\lim it_s} \right) \times w_{brand} \right) \right\}
$$

$S_{i\ brandvalue}^{j}$ is given brand request for j^{th} item by i^{th} seller.

In our example for the buyer has the following criteria definition $Q_{threshold}=10$, $price\_limit_b=10$, $time\_limit_b=55$, $brand\_limit_b=1$, $w_{quality}=0.7$, $w_{brand}=0.7$, $w_{price}=0.15$, $w_{time}=0.15$. The seller has the following criteria definition $Q_{threshold}=10$, $price\_limit_s=10$, $time\_limit_s=55$, $brand\_limit_s=1$, $w_{quality}=0.7$, $w_{price}=0.2$, $w_{time}=0.1$, $w_{brand}=0.7$.

$B_{brandvalue}$ Value for Brand label A =0.75; for label B=0.65, for label C=0.50.

$S_{ibrandvalue}$ Value for Brand label A =0.70; for label B=0.60, for label C=0.50.

(b)

$$(EV_2)_i = \sum_j w_{preferencepayment\,mod\,e,b}^{j} - \sum_j w_{preferencepayment\,mod\,e,si}^{j}$$

$(EV_2)_i$ is evaluation index for calculating difference between payment system desire by buyer and i^{th} seller agent. $w_{preferencepayment\,mod\,e,b}^{j}$ is the preference weight for payment mode given by the buyer agent for j^{th} item and $w_{preferencepayment\,mod\,e,si}^{j}$ is the preference weight for payment mode given by the ith seller agent for j^{th} item.

In our example the buyer $w_{preferencepaymentmode,b}$ for cheque is 0.7 and $w_{preferencepaymentmode,b}$ for Cash/Draft/Credit card is 0.3 and $w_{preferencepayment\,mod\,e,si}^{j}$ for Cheque is 0.4 and $w_{preferencepayment\,mod\,e,si}^{j}$ for Cash/Draft/Credit card is 0.6.

(c) $BI_i = (EV_1)_i + (EV_2)_i$

Business Index is based upon the $(EV_1)_i$ and $(EV_2)_i$. The main aim of BI_i is to determine the difference between the buyer choice and seller choice. If IN_i of both the agents are same then broker suggest selecting that agent whose BI is minimum.

(d) $SI_i = k_1 \times IN_i + k_2 \times \dfrac{1}{BI_i}$

where k_1, k_2 are the constant and $k_1 \times k_2 = 0.1$ and $0 < k_2 < 1$ and $0 < k_1 < 1$ SI_i is the selection Index. In our example $k_1 = 0.6$ and $k_2 = 0.1666$. k_1, k_2 are negotiation index factor.

Utility Computation Model

Over all utility for seller agent and buyer agent is determined as weighted sum of the financial utility and ease utility (Jonker, Robu, Treur, 2007; Zhang, Lesser, Podorozhny, 2005). Jonker et al. give only ease utility and financial utility where as Zhang et al. give only the concept of combined utility. The combined utility is difference of marginal utility gain and marginal utility cost. Our approach provides a mixed approach consisting of ease utility and financial utility, and the combined utility.

Financial utility for Agent

$$FU_{sagent} = \left(\sum_j CG_{s,j} \right) \times w_{cost}$$

$$CG_{s,j} = \frac{l_{cost,j} - C_{s,j}}{\sum_j l_{cost,j}}$$

where $CG_{s,j}$ the cost gain for j^{th} item by the agent at schedule s. is FU_{sagent} is the financial utility of the agent at schedule s. w_{cost} is the weight assign by the agent. $l_{cost,j}$ is the cost limit for j^{th} item from the agent side. $C_{s,j}$ is the cost at schedule s for j^{th} item.

Ease Utility for Agent

$$EU_{sagent} = \left(\sum_j Q_{s,gain,j} \right) \times w_{quality} + T_{assigngain} \times w_{time}$$

$$Q_{s,gain,j} = \frac{Q_{s,j}}{Q_{threshold}}$$

$$T_{sgain} = \frac{l_T - T_s}{l_T}$$

where EU_{sagent} is the ease utility for agent at schedule s. $Q_{s,gain}$ is the quality gain by the agent at schedule s. Q_s is the quality given by agent at schedule s. $Q_{threshold}$ is the agent's criteria function. T_{sgain} is the time gain at schedule s. l_T is the agent time limit. T_s is the agent time. The utility gain for buyer (UG) marginal utility gain for buyer MUG, utility cost for seller (UC) marginal utility cost for seller (MUC), are given as follows:

$$UG_s = FU_{sagent} + EU_{sagent}$$

$$MUG = UG_{s2} - UG_{s1}$$

$$UC_s = FU_{sagent} + EU_{sagent}$$

$$MUC = UC_{s2} - UC_{s1}$$

$$CUI = MUG - MUC$$

In our example for the buyer has the following criteria definition $Q_{threshold}=50$, $l_{cost}=50$, $l_T=55$, $w_{quality}=07$, $w_{cost}=0.15$, $w_{time}=0.15$. The seller has the following criteria definition $Q_{threshold}=50$, $l_{cost}=50$, $l_T=55$, $w_{quality}=07$, $w_{cost}=0.2$, $w_{time}=0.1$.

Interaction (Communication Protocol) Among Agents

In a multi-agent system, an agent may need to buy some items from another agent. There are several seller agents. Each seller agent can sell several types of items. In order to accomplish these items, the agent needs to negotiate with another agent about the appropriate time and approach to execute selling these items, so that the combined utility can be increased.

The buyer agent queries the broker agent to obtain the list of specification items (quality, time, price etc.) of the seller agents suggest by the broker agent, by propose a particular specification of the items of the buyer agent. According to B2C activities all the stages are described as Figure1.

i) Need Identification Support: As per Figure 1 buyer informs his needs to broker agent. Sellers advertise their items to broker for more potential buyer as possible. In more detail as shown in Figure 2 a) When buyer agent wants to buy items he has to submit own needs to broker agent and send informNeed; b) broker agent inform about the need of buyer agent as message form informNeed to seller agent; c) when a seller agent wants to make an offer about items to potential buyers, he has to submit own offer to broker agent in message form informItems; d) in the first phase on the basis of the list of items provided by the

Figure 1. Communication between buyer, broker and seller for selection a seller agent

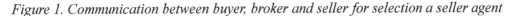

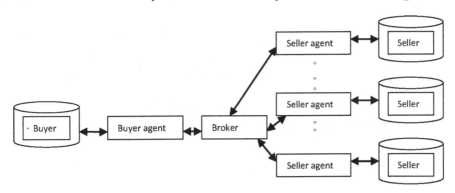

buyer agents, takes care of sending the offer to the buyer agent by broker agent as informList.

ii)Seller Selection Support: The Figure 3 depicts that at this stage occurs when a buyer receive seller agents list which are fully compatible with buyer need, then looks for suitable interest, preferences and cognitive behaviors of seller agents. In detail: a) Buyer agent can request to broker agent in message form informRequest; b) all seller agents send details of items profile which contains about their preferences, type of items deal in the previous dealing to broker agent in message informSellerProfile; c) broker agent sends cognitive values of each seller agent such as commitment, capability, trust, desire, intention, reputation, index of negotiation information of seller ; he sends a message informCog_ Value+informSeller; d) buyer agent sends his interests and preference according to each item such as quality, brand, payment mode in form of message informBusinessPolicy to broker; e)broker agent inform about the buyer's business policy to seller agent in message form inform; f) Seller agent sends his interests and preference according to each item such as quality, brand,

payment mode in form of message informBusinessPolicy to broker; g) broker agent Sends Selection Index (SI) along with informSI to buyer agent.

iii) Negotiation Support: As shown in Figure 4; in this stage a pair of buyer and selected seller agent defines the proposal details. They realize suitable strategies in a multi-round session for their respective proposal by means of messages. This stage is closed when an agreement is reached at maximum CUI in the selected multiple rounds.

In detail: a) buyer agent subscribe with broker agent in form of subscribe message; b) selected seller agent subscribe with broker agent in form of subscribe message; c) broker agent inform to both buyer and seller agent by send message inform; d)Buyer agent build initial proposal and send message to seller through broker agent in proposeInitialProposal; e)broker inform to seller agent as an informInitialProposal; f) seller agent send message to buyer through broker agent in generateCounterProposal; g)broker agent inform the utility to buyer agent in message form infor mUtility+informCounterProposal; h)buyer agent can send two type of response (i)agree or (ii)refuse; i)in both situation broker inform to seller; in case

Figure 2. Need Identification Support

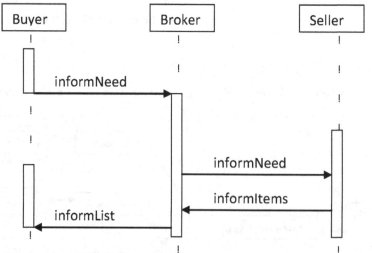

Figure 3. Seller's Selection Support

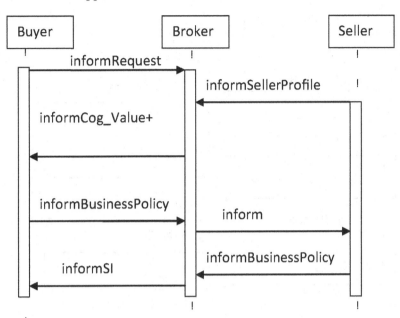

of agree broker regenerate proposal and send message informRegenProposal + informUtility; j) seller agent can send two type of response (i) agree or (ii)refuse; k) in both situation broker inform to seller; in case of agree broker refine proposal and send message

informRefineProposal + informUtility;

l)buyer agent can accept the proposal or reject proposal in message acceptProposal or rejectProposal; m) in both situation broker inform to seller; in case of accept proposal broker send message inform + informUtility. Similar message can be communicated from seller through broker to buyer

In our system agent communication is implemented using FIFA ACL messages. We have used the following messages: Subscribe, Request, Inform, Failure, Propose, Accept-Proposal, Reject-Proposal, Refuse. The Subscribe messages are used by the buyer agent and selected seller agent to register with the broker agent for

negotiate on a proposal. Request messages are used by buyer agent to query the broker agent about specification of items (quality, time, and price) on the basis of initial proposal created by buyer. Inform messages are used as responses to Subscribe or Request messages. For example after subscribing the buyer agent to broker agent the buyer agent will get an Inform message or after requesting the specification of items buyer agent gets an Inform message that contain about the seller's name and ID. Now seller agent evaluate the proposal and build a proposal and Inform to broker.Now broker agent Inform to buyer agent. Now buyer agent reevaluated the proposal and Inform to broker agent. Finally Accept-Proposal, Reject-Proposal, and Refuse messages are being used by the negotiating agents.

Figure 4. Negotiation Support

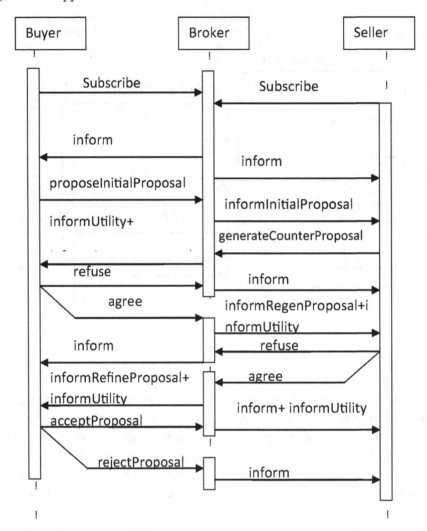

PROTOTYPE IMPLEMENTATION

The model introduced was implemented using Java in windows environment. However, the Conceptual Cognitive computational model, Business Computational model, and Utility Computational model presented in section 2 are platform independent. The Algorithm 1 is for computing maximum Selection Index value. This Algorithm 1 helps to implement the Algorithm 2 and 3. The combined utility increment obtained by using Algorithm 2 for refining the proposal and Algorithm 3 for developing the initial proposal.

We illustrate the model presented in section 2 through an example. Figure 5 depicts a visualization of the selection of a seller agent on the basis of selection index. The table of Figure 5 lists the seller agents, value of cognitive parameters, social parameters, business index (BI), index of negotiation (IN) and selection index (SI) of each seller agent. Tables 1 to Table 8 provide the complete trace of selection of a seller agent. The data of these tables are used to calculate the various

Algorithm 1. Maximum Selection Index

```
 (Input: si_agent (i): the selection index of agent  Output:  max_ si _
agent(k): the maximum selection index of agent)
       Variable: si_agent (i): the selection index of agent i
                 si_agent (j): the selection index of  agent j
                 max_ si _agent(k): the maximum selection index of agent k
    while (i<=n)
        do
      j=i+1;
 if(si_agent(i)<si_agent(j)and si _agent(j)≤max_ si_agent(k))
return max_ si _agent(k);
else if(si_agent(i)<si_agent(j)and si_agent(j)≥max_si_agent(k))
                 max_ si _agent(k) ← si _agent(j);
else if(si_agent(i)>si_agent(j) and si_agent(i)≥max_si_agent(k))
max_ si _agent(k) ←si _agent(i);
else
  return max_ si _agent(k);
```

Algorithm 2. Refining the process of proposal

```
Variable: current proposal (CP)
et:earliest serving time, lt: last serving time, min_q: minimum quality re-
quest;
dlf1(=2),dlf2(=3): a small period of time;
reduce_ratio(=0.6);
for(n=0;n≤k;n++)
        if ((n mod2)= =1)
          et←et-dlf1;
        lt ← lt +dlf2;
                 else
                   min_q←min_q*reduce_ratio;
                 if(et, lt, min_q satisfied and MUG>MUC)
                     build the proposal based on et, dl, and min_q;
                       break;
                 until proposal is built at a satisfying value of n;
                 end
```

cognitive and business parameters such as preference, desire, intention, capability, commitment, trust, IN, BI, SI of each seller agent. Table 1 provides the detail history of supplied five items by five seller agents, Table 2 provides the preference histories of five seller agents and Table 3 to

Table 8 provides details of business policies of buyer agent and five seller agents. As can be seen from the Figure 5, seller agents Ag1, Ag2, Ag3, Ag4, Ag5 with their corresponding values of cognitive parameters, social parameters, business index (BI), index of negotiation (IN) and selection

Algorithm 3. Initial proposal generating process

```
Variable: initial proposal (IP)
et0: initial earliest serving time;
lt0: initial last serving time, min_q0: initial minimum quality request;
et1: previous earliest serving time, lt1: previous last serving time;
min_q1: previous minimum quality request;
st: current serving time ;
ft: current finish time;
qa: current quality achieved;
ftf: finish time factor;
cdf: current duration factor;
etf: earliest start time factor;
if (previous proposal is acceptable)
            if (qa< avg_q_request and qa<min_q0)
                et←st;
                lt ← ft+ftf;
            min_q←avg_q_request* quality_increase_ratio;
            else if (qa>avg_q_request   and qa>min_q0)
                    et←et1;
                    lt←lt1;
                    min_q← avg_q_request*quality_reduce _ratio;
                    muc← muc*cost_reduce_ratio;
                else
                    et←et1+etf;
                     lt←et+(ft-st);
                    minq←avg_q_request*quality_reduce_ratio;
                    muc← muc*cost_reduce_ratio;
                else
                   if(first refine proposal)
                       if ((dl1-et1)< (ft-st))
                            et←et1;
                          lt←et+(ft-st)*cdf;
                          min_q←avg_q_request*quality_reduce_ratio;
                          muc←muc*cost_reduce_ratio;
                else
                        et←et1;
                          lt←et+(ft-st)+ftf;
                          min_q← avg_q_request*quality_ increase _ratio;
                        else
                          if(qa> avg_q_request)
                                    et←st;
                                    lt←ft+ftf;
                          min_q← avg_q_request*quality_ increase _ratio;
```

Algorithm 3. continued

```
else
                et←st+etf;
                lt←et+(ft-st);
        min_q← avg_q_request*quality_reduce_ratio;
        muc←muc*cost _reduce_ratio;
        evaluated new proposal with et,lt,min_q,muc)
    if(mug>muc)
            break;
    else
      if(dl<dl0)
          lt← (lt+lt0)/2;
    else
    lt←et+(ft-st)+ftf;
          muc←muc*cost_reduce_ratio;
until a good new proposal is found
end
```

Figure 5. Cognitive values of seller for calculate SI

NameOfAgent	Preference	Desire	Intention	Capability	Commitment	Trust	IN	BI	SI
Ag1	2.73	3.98	0.10	3.40	0.34	1.15	0.86	0.99	0.68
Ag2	3.49	3.43	0.11	3.17	0.37	1.17	0.87	0.69	0.76
Ag3	6.36	4.56	0.29	4.17	1.20	5.00	3.75	1.08	2.40
Ag4	5.51	4.81	0.26	4.40	1.14	5.01	3.75	0.89	2.43
Ag5	9.18	5.56	0.51	5.56	2.83	15.73	11.79	0.99	7.24

Table 1. Seller's profile

Item Type	Total Items	Total No Of Best Supplied Items					Total No Of Fair Supplied Items					Total No Of Defective Supplied Items				
		Ag1	Ag2	Ag3	Ag4	Ag5	Ag1	Ag2	Ag3	Ag4	Ag5	Ag1	Ag2	Ag3	Ag4	Ag5
Item1	100	60	80	50	70	40	20	10	30	20	40	20	10	20	10	20
Item2	100	80	60	40	50	70	10	30	40	30	20	10	10	20	20	10
Item3	100	70	50	40	80	60	00	30	40	10	40	30	20	20	10	00
Item4	100	40	50	70	60	80	40	30	30	30	10	20	20	00	10	10
Item5	100	60	30	70	60	80	20	50	10	20	10	20	20	20	20	10

index (SI) are listed in tabular form. Second, third, fourth, fifth, sixth, seventh and eighth column of this tabulate figure calculated on the basis of cognitive computation model (section 1). Ninth and tenth column of this table calculated on the basis of business computation model (section 2).

It can be seen from the figure that the seller agent Ag5 has maximum SI (as shown highlighted in Figure 5) and hence it get selected for cooperative negotiation.

The Figure 6 depicts the status of various cooperative negotiation steps between the seller

Table 2. Seller's preference profile

For Agent Ag1			
Preference Factor	Total No Of Best Supplied Items	Total No Of Fair Supplied Items	Total No Of Defective Supplied Items
Item2	80	10	10
Item3	70	0	30
Item1	60	20	20
For Agent Ag2			
Preference Factor	Total No Of Best Supplied Items	Total No Of Fair Supplied Items	Total No Of Defective Supplied Items
Item1	80	10	10
Item4	50	30	20
Item3	50	30	20
For Agent Ag3			
Preference Factor	Total No Of Best Supplied Items	Total No Of Fair Supplied Items	Total No Of Defective Supplied Items
Item1	50	30	20
Item2	40	40	20
Item5	70	10	20
Item4	70	30	0
For Agent Ag4			
Preference Factor	Total No Of Best Supplied Items	Total No Of Fair Supplied Items	Total No Of Defective Supplied Items
Item1	70	20	10
Item3	80	10	10
Item2	50	30	20
Item4	60	30	10
For Agent Ag5			
Preference Factor	Total No Of Best Supplied Items	Total No Of Fair Supplied Items	Total No Of Defective Supplied Items
Item1	40	40	20
Item2	70	20	10
Item3	60	40	0
Item4	80	10	10
Item5	80	10	10

and buyer. The new possible negotiation steps control through buyer. It can be seen from the figure that possible new proposals are generated and each step is refined multiple times and finally buyer selects that proposal whose proposal is maximum. The table of Figure 6 lists the negotiating buyer and seller agents, proposals, ServingTime, QualityRequestOfBuyer, QualityRequestOfSeller, MUG, MUC, and CUI. Third, fourth, fifth, sixth, seventh and eighth column of

this tabulate figure calculated on the basis of utility computation model (section 3). As can be seen from the figure, four new possible proposals P1, P2, P3, P4 are generated and each proposal is refined three times on the basis of ServingTime, QualityRequestOfBuyer, QualityRequestOfSeller and the proposal P4 is accepted by buyer at its third refining stage (as shown highlighted in Figure 6).

RESULT

Considering the situation where the buyer agent interact with broker agent for fulfill its needs about item 1, item 2, item3, item4 and item 5. On the basis of cognitive and business computation model (section 1 and 2) buyer agent select a seller agent through broker agent who has maximum selection index. Result from the experiment shows number of communications between buyer and various seller agents through broker agent and achieve maximum selection index (SI) 7.24 for seller agent Ag5 (as shown in Figure 5). Ag5 can effectively satisfy the buyer's need. Now for long term profit both buyer and selected seller agent tend to compromise their utilities to achieve maximum CUI (as shown highlighted in Figure 6). So buyer agent selects agent Ag5 for negotiation to perform with maximum CUI (=MUG-MUC).

Step by step generation of new proposals from both agents continues till the best CUI is obtained. For our experiments the steps are given below:

- Buyer agent gets local utility without broker agent when total quality of five items $\sum_{j} Q^{j}$ =30; total cost of five items $\sum_{j} C^{j}$

Table 3. Buyer's business policy

Item	Min. Quality Request	Price	Brand	Serving Time	Payment Mode
Item1	6	6	A	27	Cheque
Item2	6	6	B	27	Cheque
Item3	6	6	A	27	Cheque
Item4	6	6	A	27	Cheque
Item5	6	6	A	27	Cheque

Table 4. Seller Ag1's business policy

Item	Min. Quality Request	Price	Brand	Serving Time	Payment Mode
Item1	6	9	A	42	Cash/Draft/Credit card
Item2	6	9	B	42	Cheque
Item3	6	9	A	42	Cash/Draft/Credit card
Item4	6	9	A	42	Cash/Draft/Credit card
Item5	6	9	A	42	Cash/Draft/Credit card

Table 5. Seller Ag2's business policy

Item	Min. Quality Request	Price	Brand	Serving Time	Payment Mode
Item1	6	6	B	42	Cash/Draft/Credit card
Item2	6	6	B	42	Cash/Draft/Credit card
Item3	6	6	B	42	Cash/Draft/Credit card
Item4	6	6	B	42	Cash/Draft/Credit card
Item5	6	6	B	42	Cash/Draft/Credit card

=30; Serving time T=27, So Utility UG_{s1}=0.556
- Buyer agent build proposal with broker when total quality of five items $\sum_j Q^j$ =55; total cost of five items $\sum_j C^j$ =40; Serving time T=36, So Utility UG_{s2}=0.8518. Hence initial proposal build with MUG= UG_{s2} - UG_{s1}=0.295
- Seller agent review this proposal and Seller agent gets local utility without broker agent when total quality of five items $\sum_j Q^j$ =30;

total cost of five items $\sum_j C^j$ =49.5; Serving time T=42, So Utility UC_{s3}=0.446
- Seller agent build proposal with broker when total quality of five items $\sum_j Q^j$ =40; total cost of five items $\sum_j C^j$ =40; Serving time T=36, So Utility UC_{s4}=0. 635. Hence counter proposal build with MUC= UC_{s4} - UC_{s3}=0.189.
- Buyer evaluate this proposal through broker agent and MUG=0.358 and CUI=0.169. This is an acceptable proposal.

Table 6. Seller Ag3's business policy

Item	Min. Quality Request	Price	Brand	Serving Time	Payment Mode
Item1	6	9	A	30	Cheque
Item2	6	9	B	30	Cheque
Item3	6	9	A	30	Cash/Draft/Credit card
Item4	6	9	A	30	Cash/Draft/Credit card
Item5	6	9	A	30	Cash/Draft/Credit card

Table 7. Seller Ag4's business policy

Item	Min. Quality Request	Price	Brand	Serving Time	Payment Mode
Item1	6	8	A	42	Cash/Draft/Credit card
Item2	6	8	B	42	Cheque
Item3	6	8	A	42	Cash/Draft/Credit card
Item4	6	8	A	42	Cash/Draft/Credit card
Item5	6	8	A	42	Cash/Draft/Credit card

Table 8. Seller Ag5's business policy

Item	Min. Quality Request	Price	Brand	Serving Time	Payment Mode
Item1	6	9	A	42	Cash/Draft/Credit card
Item2	6	9	B	42	Cheque
Item3	6	9	A	42	Cash/Draft/Credit card
Item4	6	9	A	42	Cash/Draft/Credit card
Item5	6	9	A	42	Cash/Draft/Credit card

Figure 6. Negotiation table based on various attributes

NameOfAgent	Proposal	ServingTime	QualityReque...	QualityReque...	MUG	MUC	CUI	
buyer	P1	24	6	8	0.358	0.189	0.169	
buyer	P2	27	4.5	-	0.274	-	-	
seller	P2	19	4.5	6	-	0.163	-	
buyer	P2	19	4.5	6	0.295	0.163	0.132	
buyer	P3	27	2.5	-	0.211	-	-	
seller	P3	24	3	3.5	-	0.053	-	
buyer	P3	24	3	3.5	0.232	0.053	0.179	
buyer	P4	31	3.5	-	0.236	-	-	
seller	P4	28	3.5	6	-	0.079	-	
buyer	P4	28	3.5	6	0.293	0.079	0.214	

- Buyer refine proposal through broker agent and gets utility $UG_{s5}=0.830$ and MUG= UG_{s1}- $UG_{s5}=0.274$

- Seller agent review this proposal and gets Utility $UC_{s6}=0.472$. Hence proposal build with MUC= UC_{s6} - $UC_{s3}=0.163$.

- Buyer evaluate this proposal through broker agent and MUG=0.295 and CUI=0.132. This is an acceptable proposal.

- Buyer refine proposal through broker agent and gets utility $UG_{s7}=0.767$ and MUG= UG_{s1}- $UG_{s7}=0.211$.

- Seller agent review this proposal and gets Utility $UC_{s8}=0.582$. Hence proposal build with MUC= UC_{s8}- $UC_{s3}=0.053$.

- Buyer evaluate this proposal through broker agent and MUG=0.232 and CUI=0.179. This is an acceptable proposal.

- Buyer refine proposal through broker agent and gets utility $UG_{s9}=0.767$ and MUG= UG_{s1}- $UG_{s9}=0.236$.

- Seller agent review this proposal and gets Utility $UC_{s10}=0.556$. Hence proposal build with MUC= UC_{s3}- $UC_{s10}=0.079$.

Now, buyer evaluate this proposal through broker agent and MUG=0.293 and CUI=0.214. This is an acceptable proposal and maximum CUI (=0.214).So this proposal is accepted by the buyer as shown in Figure 6.The buyer agent purchase items to seller agent Ag5 on the basis of this proposal.

The graph is drawn between number of negotiation steps on X axis and local utility on Y-axis as shown in Figure 7. Blue line represents the buyer local utility and pink line represents seller local utility.

From graphical result it is obtained that at first round of cooperative negotiation the local utility values of both the buyer and seller agents are very low. At first round the utility gain value of buyer agent is 0.556 and utility cost of seller agent is 0.446. But at second round of negotiation both buyer and seller agents increase their local utility. At this round the utility gain value of buyer agent is 0.85 and utility cost of seller agent is 0.635. At third round of negotiation both agents decrease their local utility and at fourth round of negotiation again they increase their local utility. But their local utility values at this round are less than their individual local utility value at second round. Finally at fifth negotiation round both buyer and seller agents decrease their local utility up to some extent. In fifth round the buyer utility gain is 0.767 and seller utility cost is 0.556. So the graphical result depicts that both buyer and seller agents cooperate each other with their local utility in the sense buyer and seller increase and decrease proportionally their gain and cost. This is good sign of cooperative negotiation.

Figure 7. Utility Graph

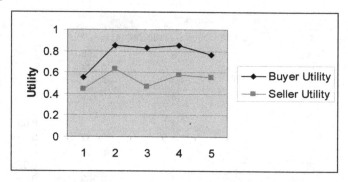

RELATED WORK AND COMPARISON

In this section we provide an overview on the existing work on selection of an agent and negotiation and by comparison we discuss different aspects from our own model. In a research approach (Jonker, Robu and Treur, 2007) characterized as cooperative one to one multi-criteria negotiation; in which agent uses the history of agents to predict his preferences. In our model broker agent helps to select a seller agent by BDI and mental state properties of seller agent and matching the business policies of seller agent and buyer agent. Then negotiation mechanism is introduced. With the help of this mechanism broker stabilize a deal between buyer and seller by maximize the CUI which satisfy both parties in multiple round of negotiations.

Various negotiation models are proposed (Gutman, Maes, 1998, Faratin, Sierra, Jennings, 2003, Fatima, Wooldridge, Jennings, 2003) but in their approach there is no view available for overall combined utility computation which satisfies both parties. In their research there is no direct concept of mental and cognitive features which help in the selection of a seller agent in B2C e-commerce. In our approach it is possible to specify overall utility and separate local utility of both parties.

In research (Kwang, 2000) also proposed algorithms for selection, evaluation and filtering using broker but they did not consider about cognitive values and mental states of an agent.

In research (Castelfranchi and Falcone, 1998) the issue of trust is third party enforcement and mixed with reputation. In our approach the agent is able to evaluate the trust by the set of formulae but the reputation is third party enforcement.

The broker based synchronous transaction algorithm (Kang, Han, 2002) for fair and satisfying best deal. The best deals are made for both sellers and buyers since the broker agent observes and compares the prices in the market and the broker agent take care after the seller and buyer agents simply just set their desired prices. Propose algorithms in our work broker agent take care about selection of seller agent and overall utility of both parties.

In the experiment values were chosen such that they provide both stable behavior of the system and assure a termination property i.e. in most instances lead the conclusion of the selection of a seller agent for negotiation on the basis of selection index and also lead to the conclusion of the negotiation in a relatively small number of negotiation steps.

In conclusion, we can say that we have been successful in meeting our stated research goal, which is to improve the efficiency of cooperative negotiations using combined utility model in electronic environments for B2C process integrated with concept of cognitive, mental and business computational model which is clear from the comparative table in this section. Table

9 shows how our proposed is better compared to other methods.

Hence from the above table it is clear that our approach can fulfill all the necessary features for B2C process.

CONCLUSION

The work has been shown the application of this method for the purchase domain in a cooperative system. The selection of seller is based upon his cognitive characteristics. The buyer agent has set of requirements of items for which it needs some seller agents. To perform this, the seller agent can choose from several alternatives that produce different qualities and consume different resources. This context requires a negotiation that leads to a satisfying solution with increasing combined utility. We first examined a search for the index of negotiation of the seller as a mechanism to find

a compromise between the histories of different sellers. This mechanism helps to evaluate a good solution to fulfill the requirements.

REFERENCES

Abdul-Rahman, A., & Hailes, S. (2000). Supporting trust in virtual communities. In *Proceedings of the Hawaii's International Conference on Systems Sciences*, Maui, Hawaii.

Bell, J. (1995). Changing attitudes in intelligent agents. In M. Woolridge & N. R. Jennings (Eds.), *Post- Proceedings of the ECAI-94 Workshop on Agent Theories, Architecture and languages*, (pp. 40-50). Berlin, Germany; Springer.

Bratman, M. E. (1990). What is intention? In Cohen, P. R., Morgan, J., & Pollack, M. E. (Eds.), *Intentions in communication* (pp. 15–31). Cambridge, MA: MIT Press.

Table 9. Comparative view with other proposed method

Method	Cognitive and mental features	Business computation features	Utility features	Role of broker agent
Proposed own method	Compute the mental and cognitive features through deterministic computational model	Yes	Overall combined utility and local utility considered for cooperative negotiation	Take care for selection of agent and overall utility of both parties.
Joneker, Robu and Treur proposed method	Only preferences are predict on the basis of history	No	Utility model proposed but no view of combined utility	Take care for bilateral negotiation of both parties
Gutman, Maes proposed method	No	No	Yes but no view of combined utility	Not specify
Faratin, Sierra, Jennings proposed method	No	No	Yes but no view of combined utility	Not specify
Fatima, Wooldridge, Jennings proposed method	No	No	Yes but no view of combined utility	Not specify
Kwang proposed method	No	No	No	For selection evaluation and filtering the sellers profile
Kang, Han proposed method	No	Yes	No	For selection of seller agent
Yin-Chen Lin Proposed model	No	No	No	Multi-attribute negotiation

Brazier, F., Dunin-Keplicz, B., Treur, J., & Verbrugge, R. (1997). *Beliefs, intentions and desire.*

Carter, J., Bitting, E., & Ghorbani, A. (2002). Reputation formalization for an information-sharing multi-agent system. *Computational Intelligence*, *18*(2), 515–534. doi:10.1111/1467-8640. t01-1-00201

Castelfranchi, C., & Falcone, R. (1998). Principles of trust for MAS: Cognitive anatomy, social importance and quantification. In *Proceedings of the International Conference on Multi-Agent Systems* (ICMAS'98), Paris, France. (pp. 72–79).

Esfandiari, B., & Chandrasekharan, S. (2001). On how agents make friends: Mechanisms for trust acquisition. In *Proceedings of the Fourth Workshop on Deception, Fraud and Trust in Agent Societies*, Montreal, Canada. (pp. 27–34).

Faratin, P., Sierra, C., & Jennings, N. (2003). Using similarity criteria to make issue trade-offs in automated negotiations. *Journal of Artificial Intelligence*, *142*(2), 205–237. doi:10.1016/ S0004-3702(02)00290-4

Fatima, S. S., Wooldridge, M., & Jennings, N. R. (2003). *Optimal agendas for multi-issue negotiation.* Second International Conference on Autonomous Agents and Multiagent Systems (AAMAS-03), Melbourne, (pp. 129-136).

Garg, S. K., & Mishra, R. B. (2008). A hybrid model for service selection in Semantic Web service composition. *International Journal of Intelligent Information Technologies*, *4*(4), 55–69. doi:10.4018/jiit.2008100104

Gutman, R., & Maes, P. (1998). Cooperative vs. competitive multi-agent negotiation in retail electronic commerce. In *Proc. of the Second International Workshop on Cooperative Information Agents* (CIA'98), Paris.

He, M., Jennings, N. R., & Leung, H. (2003). On agent-mediated electronic commerce. *IEEE Transactions on Knowledge and Data Engineering*, *15*(4), 985–1003. doi:10.1109/ TKDE.2003.1209014

Huang, C. C., Liang, W. Y., Lai, Y. H., & Lin, Y. C. (2010). The agent-based negotiation process for B2C e-commerce. *Expert Systems with Applications*, *37*(1), 348–359. doi:10.1016/j. eswa.2009.05.065

Jonker C. M., Robu, V., & Treur, J. (2007). *An agent architecture for multi-attribute negotiation using incomplete preference information, autonomous agent and multi-agent system.*

Kang, N., & Han, S. (2002). Agent-based e-marketplace system for more fair and efficient transaction. *Decision Support Systems*, *34*, 157–165. doi:10.1016/S0167-9236(02)00078-7

Kraus, S., Sycara, K., & Evenchil, A. (1998). Reaching agreements through argumentation: A logical model and implementation. *Artificial Intelligence*, *104*, 1–69. doi:10.1016/S0004-3702(98)00078-2

Panzarasa, P., Jennings, N. R., & Norman, T. J. (2002). Formalizing collaborative decision-making and practical reasoning in multi-agent system. *Journal of Logic and Engineering*, *12*(1), 55–117.

Sabater, J., & Sierra, C. (2005). Review on computational trust and reputation models. *Artificial Intelligence Review*, *24*, 33–60. doi:10.1007/ s10462-004-0041-5

Shoham, Y. (1993). Agent oriented programming. *Artificial Intelligence*, *60*(1), 51–92. doi:10.1016/0004-3702(93)90034-9

Sim, K. M., & Chan, R. (2000, November). A brokering protocol for agent-based e-commerce. *IEEE Transactions on Systems, Man and Cybernetics. Part C, Applications and Reviews*, *30*(4).

Suwu, W., & Das, A. (2001). *An agent system architecture for e-commerce*. International Workshop on Database and Expert Systems Applications (pp. 715-719).

Tang, T. Y., Winoto, P., & Niu, X. (2003). *Investigating trust between users and agents in a multi agent portfolio management system: A preliminary report*.

von Wright, G. H. (1980). *Freedom and determination*. Amsterdam, The Netherlands: North Holland Publishing Co.

Wu, W., Ekaette, E., & Far, B. H. (2003). Uncertainty management framework for multi-agent system. *Proceedings of ATS* (pp. 122-131).

Yu, B., & Singh, M. P. (2001). Towards a probabilistic model of distributed reputation management. In *Proceedings of the Fourth Workshop on Deception, Fraud and Trust in Agent Societies*, Montreal, Canada. (pp. 125–137).

Zacharia, G. (1999). *Collaborative reputation mechanisms for online communities*. Master's thesis, Massachusetts Institute of Technology.

Zhang, X., Lesser, V., & Podorozhny, R. (2005). Multi-dimensional, multi-step negotiation for task allocation in a cooperative system. *Autonomous Agents and Multi-Agent Systems, 10*, 5–40. doi:10.1007/s10458-004-5020-3

Zhao, X., Wu, C., Zhang, R., Zhao, C., & Lin, Z. A. (2004). *Multi-agent system for e-business processes monitoring in a Web-based environment*. TCL Group Corporation.

Chapter 11
User Perceptions and Employment of Interface Agents for Email Notification:
An Inductive Approach

Alexander Serenko
Lakehead University, Canada

ABSTRACT

This study investigates user perceptions and employment of interface agents for email notification to answer three research questions pertaining to user demographics, typical usage, and perceptions of this technology. A survey instrument was administered to 75 email interface agent users. Current email interface agent users are predominantly male, well-educated and well-off innovative individuals who are occupied in the IS/IT sector, utilize email heavily and reside in an English-speaking country. They use agents to announce incoming messages and calendar reminders. The key factors why they like to use agents are perceived usefulness, enjoyment, ease of use, attractiveness, social image, an agent's reliability and personalization. The major factors why they dislike doing so are perceived intrusiveness of an agent, agent-system interference and incompatibility. Users envision 'ideal email notification agents' as highly intelligent applications delivering messages in a non-intrusive yet persistent manner. A model of agent acceptance and use is suggested.

INTRODUCTION AND LITERATURE REVIEW

The purpose of this study is to empirically investigate how people utilize and perceive interface agents for electronic mail notification. Interface agents are software entities that are continuous (long-lived), reactive (adapt their actions depending on an external environment), collaborative (collaborate with users, other agents or electronic

DOI: 10.4018/978-1-60960-595-7.ch011

processes), and autonomous (independent). They act as an intermediary between a user and a system, and communicate directly with the person by offering assistance in computer-related activities (Detlor, 2004; Lieberman & Selker, 2003; Serenko, 2007a; Serenko & Detlor, 2004; Serenko, Ruhi, & Cocosila, 2007). Interface agents may be included in most software applications, including email systems (Maes, 1994; Serenko, 2006).

Email has turned into one of the most successful computer applications ever designed (Lucas, 1998; Sproull & Kiesler, 1986). However, as the volume of communication and the variety of tasks grow, today's email systems fail to provide an adequate level of user support for many routine tasks, especially for message searching and filing. People feel overwhelmed with the volume of textual information received. For example, when a person receives a new message in Outlook, he or she has to interrupt the current task to screen or read the message.

There are ways to improve email systems. One viewpoint is that a conventional text-based direct manipulation interface is a major source of users' dissatisfaction with their email tools (Ducheneaut & Bellotti, 2001) and that interface agents may provide a possible solution to address email challenges. Interface agents may potentially address some shortcomings of the contemporary email systems by meeting actual user needs, offering value-added services, implementing new approaches, automating complex or routine tasks, improving system interfaces, and enhancing an individual's experiences with email applications.

There are at least five categories of email related assistance which may be provided by agents (Gruen, Sidner, Boettner, & Rich, 1999):

1. Pre-Processing – an agent processes a message to present it in the most efficient way to the user;
2. Filtering / Prioritizing – an agent filters out incoming mail and ranks it in order of importance;

3. Adding Relevant Information – an agent supplements a message with additional relevant information; for instance, the sender's affiliation;
4. Delegating Complex Tasks – an agent performs a series of complex or repetitive steps in response to a single high-level request by directly manipulating the system; and,
5. Inferencing – an agent makes suggestions and recommendations which are based on a user's profile; for example, points out information a user might consider significant.

In addition to these types of support, agents may help users integrate their email systems into various computer applications, facilitate the use of email with new devices, trace the status of all messaging and work related activities, generate automatic responses, and add interactivity and emotions to convey equivocal information.

In spite of a number of initiatives that aimed to develop interface agents for email, there are very few end-user applications that are actually available on the software market. Most previous projects focused on the creation of models and prototypes of email interface agents rather than on the development of ready-to-use commercial products. Even though there are several successful applications, for example, CoolAgent (Bergman, Griss, & Staelin, 2002) or SwiftFile (Segal & Kephart, 2000), very few products were made freely or commercially available to all email users. Interface agents for email notification represent one of the earliest applications that have already been commercialized. The goal of these systems is to inform individuals about the current state of their email (Libes, 1997). Recently, developers have started designing add-on interface agents for some email clients.

There are several challenges that all email agents researchers currently face (Dehn & van Mulken, 2000). First, most research initiatives in this area are disparate and independent from one another which often results in the duplication of prior work. Secondly, many projects are purely technology-oriented, emphasize a technological implementation of an agent system over user evaluations, and rarely commercialize the application. Thirdly, preceding research rarely addressed the practical aspects of the usage, development, and promotion of interface agent technologies. Currently, there are few, if any, guidelines or recommendations for manufacturers of this technology. It is these problems that impede the development of this research area and delay the emergence of really useful email agent systems.

There are at least ten distinct theories that were developed to understand user acceptance and diffusion of electronic mail: 1) diffusion of innovations (Murphy & Tan, 2003; Rogers, 1995); 2) social influence (Fulk, 1993; Fulk, Schmitz, & Steinfield, 1990); 3) social presence (Rice, 1993); 4) critical mass (Markus, 1990); 5) structuration (Orlikowski, 1992; Orlikowski, Yates, Okamura, & Fujimoto, 1995; Yates & Orlikowski, 1992); 6) critical social (Ngwenyama, 1997); 7) media symbolism (Trevino, Daft, & Lengel, 1990); 8) media richness (Daft & Lengel, 1986; Daft, Lengel, & Trevino, 1987); 9) channel expansion (Carlson & Zmud, 1994, 1999); and, 10) uses and gratifications theory (Dimmick, Kline, & Stafford, 2000). None of them, however, may be utilized in the present project. First, these theories concentrate on the electronic communication itself. Second, they view email as a communications medium without taking into consideration technical aspects. Third, they ignore factors that may be associated with systems augmenting email, such as agents. Therefore, other research approaches should be investigated.

In order to fill that void, the purpose of this study is to gain insights on how individuals utilize and perceive interface agents for email notification in their electronic mail environments. This project focuses on notification agents for two reasons. First, little is known about end-user perception and employment of interface agents in general and, particularly, interface agents for

email notification. Second, there are commercially available versions of this technology that makes it possible to poll the actual users instead of conducting a laboratory experiment. On the one hand, laboratory experiments may generate valuable findings that are of interest to both scholars and practitioners. On the other hand, as hypothesized by Dehn and van Mulken (2000), adequate perceptions and behavioral intentions towards interface agents may take some time to establish; therefore, laboratory studies should be combined with user surveys.

Therefore, the study suggests an inductive research approach that polls real-life end users of this technology, via a Web-based questionnaire, on the cognitive and contextual factors surrounding the employment of email interface agents. It is hoped that by analyzing interface agents for email notification from a user perspective, a greater understanding of the factors that influence individual decisions whether to accept or reject agent technologies can be obtained.

RESEARCH QUESTIONS

An intensive Web-search for such applications was conducted, and several email interface agent-based programs that are commercially available on the market were identified. They employ the Microsoft Agent Technology and are relatively similar in terms of their functionality. Their purpose is to inform users about the state of an email system by announcing incoming messages, calendar reminders, current time, jokes, etc. They may read help files, webpages, or any text. Several offer extensive features such as teaching tutorials on email system usage and sending animated messages. Out of these products, Email Announcer developed by Blind Bat Software was randomly chosen, and agreement with the company to conduct user survey was reached (see Figure 1).

To develop the understanding of user perceptions and employment of this technology and to

Figure 1. Email Announcer by Blind Bat Software – agent interface and configuration environment

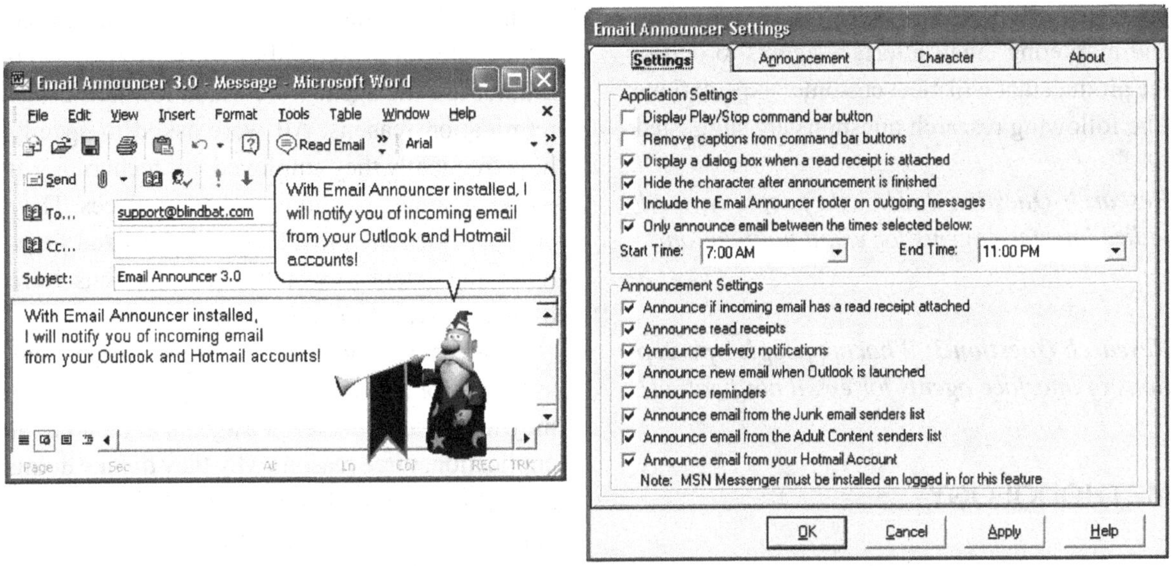

produce recommendations that may be of interest to manufacturers, three research questions were developed. Innovation research suggests that users often play a leading role in the invention and improvement of new products and services (Biemans, 1991; Lüthje, 2004). Many commercial projects have succeeded because designers and manufactures involved users in the early stages of innovation development. A strong understanding of user needs is a key factor separating new product winners from losers (Cooper & Brentani, 1991). It is crucial to collect information about consumers at each stage of a product's lifecycle (Goldsmith & Hofacker, 1991; Midgley & Dowling, 1978). The goal of most marketing surveys is to form a sound understanding of the various characteristics of product users, such as demographics, habits and inclinations.

The understanding of user attributes and personal characteristics is also important in the field of agent-human interaction (Isbister & Nass, 2000). Therefore, the following research question is proposed:

Research Question 1: *What are the characteristics of the user population who adopt interface agents for email notification? For example, age, gender, occupation, email usage experience, and country of residence.*

In addition to user attributes, the actual usage and user perceptions of interface agents are important issues that are of interest to developers. Prior experience has been found to be an important determinant of behavior in various situations (Ajzen & Fishbein, 1980), including the use of computer technologies (Taylor & Todd, 1995) and interface agents (Serenko, 2007b). There are significant differences in perceptions of applications, depending on a user's level of hands-on familiarity. For example, expert and heavy users of email interface agents may develop a stronger knowledge, special usage habits, and different perceptions of agents than individuals who use email agents less frequently. Currently, it is unknown why people like or dislike employing email interface agents, and how they envision an 'ideal' agent.

Based on this discussion, it is believed that the knowledge of agent usage patterns and people's perceptions of interface agents will help all parties involved in the process of inventing, development, and marketing email interface agents to deliver the product that will meet customer expectations. The following research questions are suggested:

Research Question 2: How do people typically utilize interface agents for email notification?

Research Question 3: What are people's perceptions of interface agents for email notification?

METHODOLOGY

This project utilized an inductive approach with the goal to investigate the contextual factors surrounding end-user employment and perceptions of email interface agents.

An inductive approach was chosen because of an exploratory nature of this study. As such, this project presented three general research questions. Based on the answers to these questions, a number of hypotheses may be suggested. An inductive method of inquiry allows new phenomena to emerge from the data, without restrictions imposed by other research techniques (Romeyn, 2004; Stolee, Zaza, Pedlar, & Myers, 1999). The purpose of inductive data analysis is similar to those of other research techniques (Miles & Huberman, 1994). Specifically, this approach is useful if the objective is to summarize open-ended data, establish links among variables, link data to research questions, and develop general models, theories or frameworks that may be further tested through deductive methods.

For research question 1, information on user background was solicited. Individuals were asked about their email usage in terms of time spent with their email, average daily number of sent and received email messages, age, gender, occupation, country of residence, and education.

To tackle research question 2, users were asked to indicate whether they were employing Email Announcer on the date of the survey. Those who did not use the agent were asked for their usage termination reasons. All were asked to specify how frequently they employed this technology at work, at home, in school, and other places. They also provided the most frequently utilized functions, the extent to which these functions were used, and period of agent usage.

For research question 3, open-ended questions asked respondents to list at least three reasons why they like to utilize interface agents in their email application, three reasons why they dislike doing so, and three tasks that they would like an 'ideal email interface agent' to perform.

The online survey included instructions, definitions, and screenshots of an agent-based notification program. A list of respondents was randomly formed from the customer database. Only those who purchased Email Announcer at least three months ago were selected. All selected individuals were sent an initial invitation and three weekly reminders. A monetary incentive of ten US dollars was offered.

RESULTS

User Background

Seventy-five usable responses were obtained at a response rate of over 30%. Eighty and twenty percent of users were male and female (Figure 2). Over 65% were between 31 and 50 years old, and the 46 – 50 age category was the most frequent user group. Two distinct occupational categories emerged: information systems / information technology-related (IS / IT), and engineering (Figure 3). The 'Other' category includes various occupations not related to IS / IT or engineering. 34% of users belonged to middle and senior management, such as a chief executive officer, vice president, department manager, or senior expert.

Figure 2. The age categories of email interface agent users

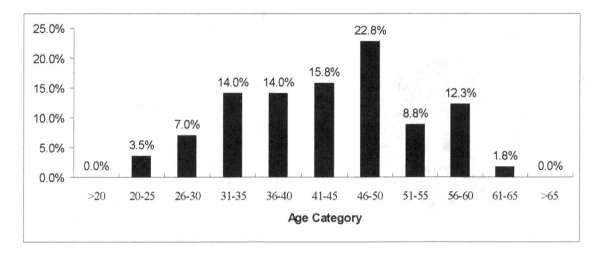

Figure 3. User occupation

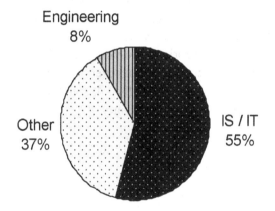

Figure 4. User education

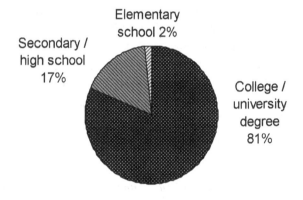

The majority of email interface agent users were well-educated and resided in the USA (Figure 4 and Figure 5).

Figure 6, Figure 7, and Figure 8 outline current email usage: the number of email messages received, the number of email messages sent, and the number of hours spent working with an email application daily. They imply that the individuals who utilized interface agents were very heavy email users.

Based on interaction with respondents, a solid understanding of users' financial position was formed. It was concluded that the respondents were financially well-off. As such, one-third of the users belonged to middle or senior management, most of them were highly educated that leads to a higher income, and 19% of the subjects kindly declined the compensations of $10.

Actual Usage of Email Interface Agents

Forty people employed the agent on the date of the survey and thirty-five did not. The current users indicated that they used it for 16 months on average, ranging from three to 36 months. The past users utilized it for 8 months on average, also ranging

Figure 5. User country of residence

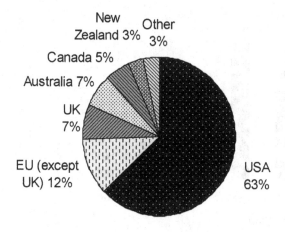

from three to 36 months. Figure 9 and Figure 10 outline the extent of the usage of interface agents at work and home. Most respondents were very heavy users of agents; they utilized agents both at work and at home.

Figure 11 and Figure 12 present the percentage of users who employed interface agents to announce messages and calendar reminders in MS Outlook. Figure 13 depicts the percentage of people who utilized interface agents to announce

messages in Hotmail, and Figure 14 offers the percentage of individuals who used interface agents to announce read receipts in any email system.

These figures demonstrate that most people used interface agents in MS Outlook. The announcement of incoming messages was the most frequently employed feature followed by the presentation of calendar messages. The announcement of read receipts was utilized less frequently; one-half of all email agent users never used it.

Figure 15 and Figure 16 present the percentage of all incoming messages and calendar announcements that were delivered by email interface agents. This confirms the earlier observation that message announcement was the most often utilized feature.

The usage categories provided by each respondent were converted into scores and a correlations matrix was constructed (see Table 1). For example, the categories corresponding to Figure 11 were converted as follows: never – 1, very rarely – 2, rarely – 3, occasionally – 4, sometimes – 5, frequently – 6, very frequently – 7.

Figure 6. Number of email messages received daily by agent users

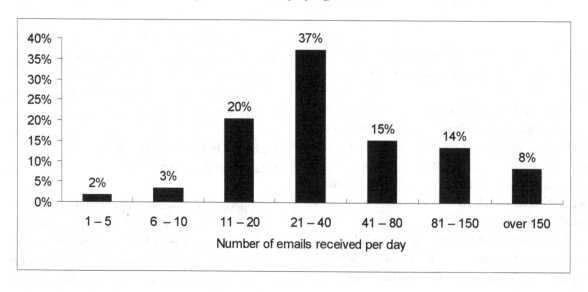

Figure 7. Number of email messages sent daily by agent users

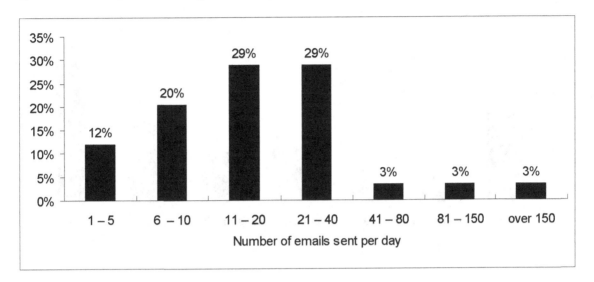

Perceptions of Email Interface Agents

The respondents were asked to provide several answers in the form of open-ended questions and classical content analysis was done. Draft *a priori* categories for a preliminary codebook were developed based on human-computer interaction, technology adoption and innovation theories. The researcher conducted successive rounds of coding, developed new codes, modified earlier codes, grouped codes together, discarded repeated codes, and aligned code labels and descriptions with concepts and definitions in the existing literature.

Figure 8. Time spent with an email system daily by agent users

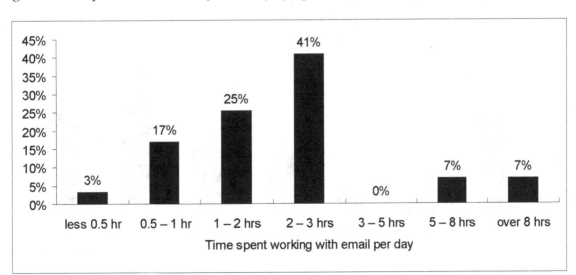

Figure 9. Actual usage of email interface agents at work

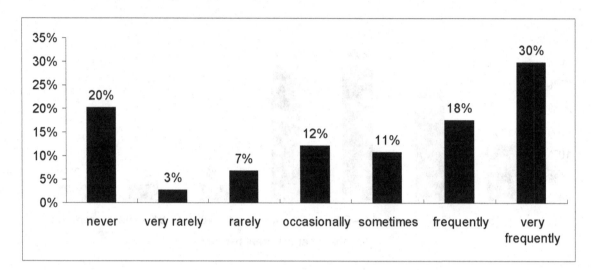

The draft version of the codebook was evaluated by an independent expert, and two rounds of revisions were made until agreement on item classification was reached. All items were coded on the lowest level by three independent coders, and only one code was assigned to a particular text unit. A training session was conducted on the use of Email Announcer and the codebook. The Krip-pendorff's (1980) agreement coefficient ranged from 0.77 to 0.84 that is acceptable (Keaveney, 1995). All discrepancies were discussed, and a final agreement on the classification of all items was reached. When the response was unclear, and the coders failed to agree on which category it belongs to, it was excluded.

Figure 10. Actual usage of email interface agents at home

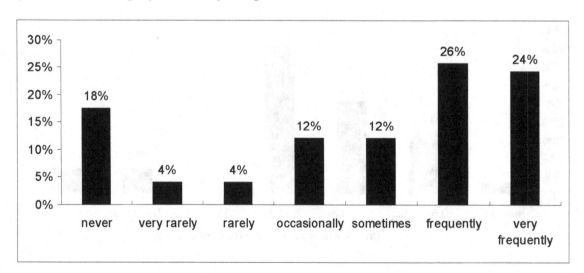

Figure 11. Users who utilize agents to announce messages in MS Outlook

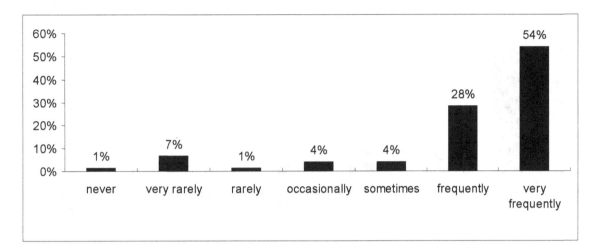

Reasons for Agent Usage Termination

The results demonstrated that 35 individuals did not use the agent on the date of the survey. Figure 17 shows the results for agent usage termination. An agent's operability, which is defined as factors pertaining to the operational characteristics of an agent, was the most frequent reason for which people stopped using the agent (37%). Negative user perceptions (high degree of perceived intrusiveness or distraction caused by the agent, low degree of perceived agent usefulness, and perceived unattractiveness of the agent interface) were the second most common reason (24%). Lack of user access, in a result of computer crash, to an agent was the third most common reason (21%). Effects of the external environment that influenced a user's adoption decision were the last category (18%). Respondents referred to their company policies that prohibited the employment

Figure 12. Users who utilize agents to announce calendar reminders in MS Outlook

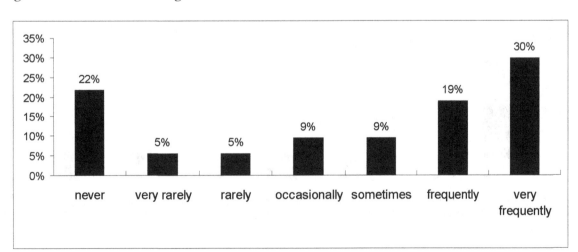

Figure 13. Users who utilize agents to announce messages in Hotmail

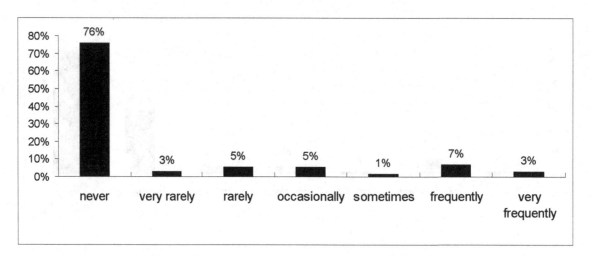

of unauthorized software, substitute software products, noise constraints, and privacy concerns. Overall, the data showed that most respondents were willing to continue using the system. Only 24% of them discontinued the usage because of their negative perceptions.

Reasons Why Users Like Email Interface Agents

With respect to the factors why people liked to use the email interface agent, 146 reasons were provided (Figure 18).

User perceptions of an agent were the major reason why people liked to utilize agents. They were followed by an agent's operability; users liked personalization, compatibility, and reliabil-

Figure 14. Users who utilize agents to announce read receipts in MS Outlook and/or Hotmail

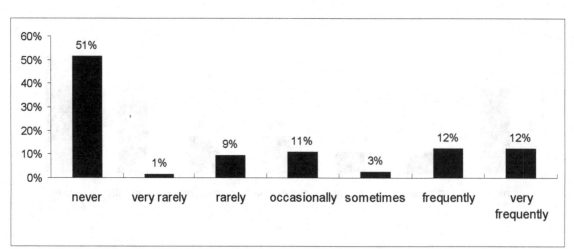

Figure 15. Incoming email messages announced by interface agents

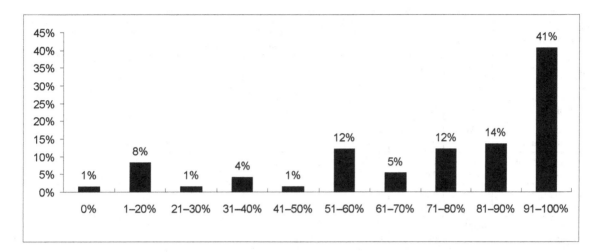

ity of this technology. External environment of an agent user represented 6% of responses. People stated they liked to utilize agents because this improved their image of being a highly innovative individual within their social group. Given that 80% of all responses related to user perceptions, a detailed review of this category was done (Figure 19).

The perceptions of an agent's usefulness (i.e., functionality) were a leading factor. Users per-

ceived themselves to become more productive with the usage of their email by engaging in multitasking. They did not have to interrupt their current non-email or even non-computer related activities. For example, when a person was working with MS Word, an agent popped up and informed her about a new message. Based on user preferences, the agent might announce a sender, a subject line, or the entire message. The individual did not have to switch from MS Word to

Figure 16. Calendar reminders announced by interface agents

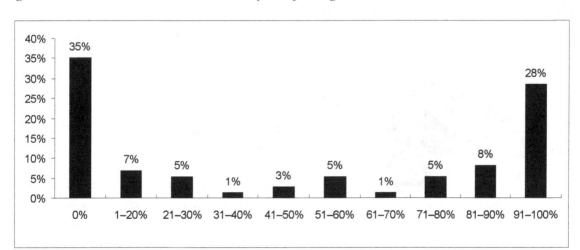

Table 1. Agent usage correlation coefficients (bold: p <.1)

Correlation/ Significance	Work Usage	Home Usage	Message Announc. Outlook	Reminder Announc. Outlook	Message Announc. Hotmail	Read Receipt Announce.	% of Messages Announc.
Home Usage	**0.282** **0.015**	1.000					
Message Announc. Outlook	**0.479** **0.000**	**0.290** **0.012**	1.000				
Reminder Announc. Outlook	**0.296** **0.010**	**0.245** **0.035**	**0.439** **0.000**	1.000			
Message Announc. Hotmail	0.029 0.805	**0.243** **0.037**	-0.045 0.703	0.188 0.109	1.000		
Read Receipt Announce.	0.179 0.128	**0.208** **0.075**	**0.276** **0.017**	**0.357** **0.002**	0.165 0.161	1.000	
% of Messages Announc.	**0.327** **0.004**	0.073 0.535	**0.611** **0.000**	**0.284** **0.014**	0.004 0.970	**0.226** **0.053**	1.000
% of Reminder Announc.	0.186 0.114	**0.206** **0.078**	**0.280** **0.016**	**0.658** **0.000**	0.096 0.415	**0.200** **0.088**	**0.422** **0.000**

an email system to be aware of incoming messages. Moreover, the user might be away from the computer and hear email, calendar, and event announcements that saved time and increased productivity.

Hedonic reasons, which were independent of the outcome of agent usage, constituted 29% of user perceptions. Most people mentioned that agent usage was fun, amusing, and entertaining. It made them laugh and gave them pleasure. Human-

Figure 17. Reasons for agent usage termination

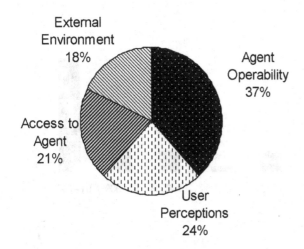

computer interaction factors comprised 22% of reasons relating to user perceptions of agents. Respondents positively perceived an agent's attractiveness, ease of use, and accessibility. Some referred to interruptions initiated by an agent; they liked when an agent interrupted their activities by initiating breaks and providing distractions from routine tasks.

Reasons Why Users do Not Like Email Interface Agents

The subjects offered 116 reasons why they did not like to use interface agents (Figure 20). Negative user perceptions of an agent (42%) were the key reason. Figure 21 outlines the breakdown of responses pertaining to this category.

Characteristics of an 'Ideal' Email Interface Agent

In terms of characteristics of an 'ideal' email interface agent, 126 answers were obtained (Figure 22).

Two distinct groups of responses emerged: items relating to an agent's operability (86%) and to human-computer interaction (7%). For an

Figure 18. Reasons why respondents like to utilize email agents

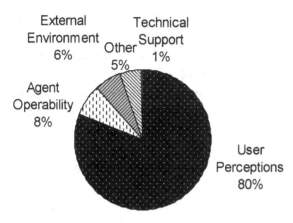

agent's operability, answers pertained to an agent's notification capabilities, which were referred to as the presentation of information, such as incoming messages, reminders, due events, etc., in a timely and persistent manner. At the time of the survey, the email interface agent by Blind Bat (as well as all other agents from other manufacturers) performed basic information notification tasks. Users wished to improve the way the agent performed some activities and to be able to utilize extra features. For instance, it should deliver more urgent notifications first, tell current time, time to take a break or go home, and due dates of critical events, such as an approaching project completion deadline. It should be more persistent, yet non-intrusive, in user notification. After announcing an important, urgent message, an agent should track task completion and remind a user if the activity was incomplete, but it should do it in a non-intrusive manner, and the user should have full control over its actions. Users also wanted agents to possess more intelligent features, including rule-based logic, machine learning capabilities, text analysis features, automatic response to simple messages, and the dynamic adjustments of an agent's behavior, voice and

appearance depending on user requirements and the type of incoming information.

In the human-computer interaction category, users wished their agents to have a lower degree of intrusiveness, better ease of use, and higher enjoyment. Overall, from the user's perspective, an 'ideal' interface agent for email should effectively, efficiently and persistently perform message and event notification tasks, be intelligent, personalizable, and incorporate several other important functions and features.

DISCUSSION, RECOMMENDATIONS AND CONCLUSION

The purpose of this study is to investigate user perceptions and employment of interface agents for email notification. For this, a Web-based survey of the actual users of an interface agent-based system was conducted, and seventy-five responses were obtained. Several interesting findings emerged as discussed below.

Figure 19. Reasons why respondents like to utilize agents (user perceptions)

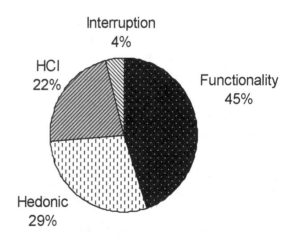

217

Figure 20. Reasons why respondents do not like to utilize email agents

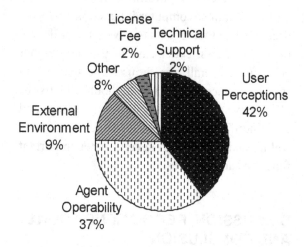

Answers to Research Questions

The purpose of the first research question is to provide characteristics of the user population based on the demographical data obtained from the survey questions. In order to develop interface agents that meet the needs of end-users and to market this product to the appropriate category of potential adopters, it is crucial to understand who the users of this technology actually are. The results of the empirical investigation show that the current email interface agent users are innovative individuals who:

- are predominantly male;
- range in age from 31 to 50 years old;
- work in the IS/IT or engineering sector;
- utilize email very heavily;
- reside in English-speaking countries, mostly in the US;
- are well-educated; and,
- are economically well-off.

According to Rogers (1995), contemporary email interface agent users may be classified as innovators who constitute 2.5% of the entire interface agent user population. These individuals

are virtually obsessed with innovating, and they are always first to try out new ideas and technologies. For them, email is the major communications medium. They are either financially well-off or have control over substantial financial resources. Recall that 34% of the surveyed agent users belonged to the middle or senior management, and that 19% of them kindly declined the compensation of $10 US for their participation in the study. Innovators are usually well-educated, have high social standing, and belong to large organizations. Again, 81% of the respondents had a college or university degree, and all of them were employed. Agent users are ready to cope with a high degree of failure, uncertainty, and risk associated with an innovation that is why they are the first to start using this technology.

Over a half of them is employed in the IS/IT field. According to a classic study by Couger and Zawacki (1980), IS/IT people are fundamentally different from non-IS/IT professionals in terms of their growth and social needs. They argue that IS/IT employees demonstrate higher growth needs; they have a stronger need for personal accomplishment, constant learning, challenge, motivation, and job satisfaction. At the same time, some IS/IT professionals exhibit low proclivity to social interaction with other people. Often, IS/IT people

Figure 21. Reasons why respondents do not like to utilize email interface agents (user perceptions)

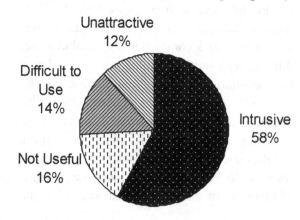

Figure 22. Characteristics of an 'ideal' interface agent

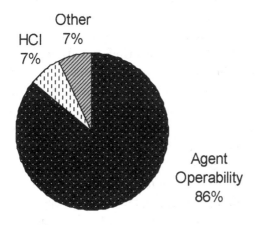

lack important communications skills and teamwork training, whereas they successfully apply different types of reasoning to problem-solving (Armour, 2002). Empirical research shows that the style of creativity of IS/IT workers differs from that of non-IS/IT people; both groups apply creativity but in slightly different ways (Miller, Couger, & Higgins, 1996).

The goal of the second research question is to understand how individuals employ interface agents in their email systems. Most innovators who started using an agent made a decision whether to continue utilizing it within several months after they first installed the product. Recall 76% of the respondents who did not utilize email interface agents on the date of the survey indicated that they abandoned this technology for the reasons they did not control. As such, most people stopped using an agent because of operability problems with an agent, lack of access to an agent, or an external environment that influenced their termination decision. Those, who terminated the usage for negative perceptual reasons, utilized an agent for only five months, whereas the current users used it for almost a year and a half on average. In other words, users form reliable perceptions soon

after they acquire an agent. In the case of positive perceptions, people continue using it in the future, and in the case of negative perceptions, individuals immediately uninstall it from their computers.

Based on the correlations table (Table 1), three key observations were made. First, given that almost all individuals utilized agents with MS Outlook, the announcement of incoming messages and calendar reminders in Outlook might potentially serve as a proxy for the degree to which the respondents utilized the technology under investigation in general. Secondly, people utilized email agents at work and at home differently. Given that the respondents to the survey were very heavy email users, they were expected to utilize a desktop email management application such as Outlook at work. The usage of a Web-based email interface would be less efficient as the volume of electronic communications increases. At the same time, the same individuals might utilize a different email application at home. In addition, the interface agent was compatible with both Outlook and Hotmail. Therefore, it may be assumed that the respondents utilized Outlook at work and Hotmail at home. The results indicated a strong positive correlation between work agent usage and message and reminder announcement in Outlook, and between home usage and message announcement in Hotmail. At the same time, no correlation between work usage and message announcement in Hotmail was found. Thirdly, email agent users tended to utilize many features of this technology simultaneously.

The third research question concentrates on understanding user perceptions of various aspects of interface agents for email notification. With respect to the reasons why individuals like to utilize interface agents in their email applications, four important points are suggested. *First and foremost*, the overall user perceptions of agents were very positive. Most people terminated the usage for the reason they did not control. According to the findings, users provided a slighter higher number of factors why they liked (146) than disliked (116) this technology. If, for example, the number of negative answers dramatically exceeded the number of positive responses, it might be assumed that user perceptions were more negative since they tended to complain about agents to a greater extent.

Second, with respect to the reasons why people like to use email agents, the key factors were perceived usefulness, perceived enjoyment, perceived ease of use, perceived attractiveness, and perceived image. This is consistent with previous individual-level technology adoption investigations. For example, the Technology Acceptance Model (Davis, 1989; Davis, Bagozzi, & Warshaw, 1989) states that users form their behavioral usage intentions based on the degree of perceived usefulness and ease of use. Serenko et al. (2007) tested a model of user adoption of interface agents in MS Office and concluded that perceived usefulness and perceived enjoyment strongly influence user adoption decisions.

Perceived attractiveness relates to user perceptions of an agent's appearance; overall, the respondents indicated that an agent's interface was cool, cute, near, or versatile. This finding emerged in pervious studies; the HCI literature labels this phenomenon as the degree of an agent's likeability (for example, see Dehn & van Mulken, 2000; Koda & Maes, 1996; Sproull, Subramani, Kiesler, Walker, & Waters, 1996).

Perceived image is the degree to which the use of an agent is perceived to enhance one's social image or status in one's social system (Moore & Benbasat, 1991). Venkatesh and Davis (2000) demonstrate that image has a positive effect on perceived usefulness of an information system. This construct may have an explanatory power only when the use of agents is visible to other people, such as co-workers or friends. For example, it may have an impact on user perceptions if people use agents at work, but it may have no effect if individuals utilize agents at home.

In addition to these five key categories, the analysis yielded three other important factors that were previously identified in the MIS and HCI

literature. These are reliability, compatibility, and personalization. Reliability is the dependability of an agent, such as the absence of bugs and crashes. Compatibility is the degree to which an agent works well with other software applications, including email clients. The reliability and compatibility constructs were already applied to other IS systems; they constitute part of a Task-Technology Fit Instrument developed by Goodhue (1998). Personalization is the degree to which an agent's actions, appearance, and voice may be tailored according to a user's requirements.

Third, with regards to the reasons why individuals do not like to utilize email interface agents, the extent of an agent's perceived intrusiveness was the top reason. It constituted 25% of all responses. The users stated that the agent distracted, annoyed, and irritated them. This frequently happened when an agent disrupted a conversation or popped up in an inappropriate time. This supports the frequent complaints of interface agent users on a high extent of an agent's perceived intrusiveness (Serenko, 2007a).

A number of users complained about agent – system interference. They stated that the agent sometimes interfered with other software applications or slowed down the entire computer. Some respondents mentioned the compatibility of an agent. Often, an agent was incompatible with other systems, especially with MS Outlook Express. Other reasons why individuals did not like to utilize email interface agents pertained to various, relatively small categories. Subjects mentioned limited usefulness, unreliability, difficulty of use, limited vocabulary, and unattractiveness.

Fourth, with respect to the characteristics of an 'ideal' email interface agent, most users wished to improve the way an agent presented message and event notifications, and the degree of an agent's intelligence. As such, an 'ideal' agent should sort out the incoming information and present it in the order of urgency and importance. It should also provide additional information and due events in a very persistent yet non-intrusive manner and track the completion of suggested activities. Extra intelligence features encompass rule-based logic, machine learning, text analysis, automatic reply, and the real-time adjustments of an agent's behavior. Other less frequent requests referred to the improvement of personalization, spam filtering, user control, compatibility, and voice recognition.

The findings above are summarized in form of a model of agent adoption and use (see Figure 23).

The constructs of this model are based on the most frequently reported categories provided by the respondents in this study. According to the model, there are two general types of factors – user perceptions and agent operability. User perceptions are either positive or negative mental reflections of several properties of an agent. They include perceived enjoyment, usefulness, ease of use, intrusiveness, and attractiveness of an agent. Perceived enjoyment, usefulness, and ease of use are well-established in the management information systems domain (Davis et al., 1989; Davis, Bagozzi, & Warshaw, 1992). Perceived intrusiveness is the degree of negatively interpreted, unwanted interactions that are initiated by an agent. When an agent is perceived to be highly intrusive, users perceive it to distract, bother, annoy or irritate them diverting their attention from current activities. For example, someone may concentrate

on a difficult task or talk over the phone when an agent pops up and interrupts this important activity. Since agent intrusiveness is the top reason why individuals dislike using an agent, it is presumed that there is a negative relationship between perceived intrusiveness and usage behavior. Perceived attractiveness is the degree to which a user finds an agent's interface and voice appealing. A positive association between perceived attractiveness of an agent and usage behavior is suggested; those individuals, who find an agent more attractive, utilize it to a higher extent.

Agent operability embraces factors pertaining to operational characteristics of an agent. During the analysis of open-ended responses, a set of factors related to agent operability was discovered that are presumed to play an important role in user adoption decisions. It is for this reason agent operability factors are included in the suggested model.

Agent operability constructs differ from perceptual constructs because they can be measured directly by a researcher rather than by surveying users. They include compatibility, system interference, reliability, and personalization. Compatibility is the ability of an agent to work well with other software applications, for example, with various email clients. It is believed that there is a positive relationship between agent compatibility

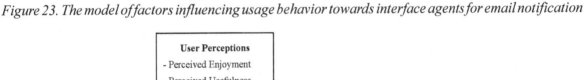

Figure 23. The model of factors influencing usage behavior towards interface agents for email notification

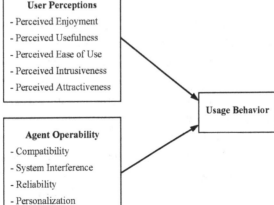

and usage; users should utilize the agent more extensively if it is compatible with a higher number of other computer applications. System interference is the hindrance of normal workflow of other applications. It occurs when an agent intrudes into the computer processes related to other systems, for example, MS Outlook or MS Word that slows down these systems and troubles users. Thus, a negative relationship between system interference and agent utilization is hypothesized. Reliability is the absence of bugs, crashes or other technical problems that take place during the employment of an agent. It is hypothesized that there is a positive relationship between agent reliability and usage; people should utilize an agent more frequently if it is more reliable. Personalization is the degree to which an agent's appearance, voice, and actions may be tailored to the needs of each user individually. It is presumed that there is a positive relationship between personalization and usage; the more personalized features and functions an agent has, the more extensively people should utilize it.

Overall, this model offers some insights on various factors of user adoption of interface agents for email that may be utilized in future investigations.

Practical Recommendations

Based on the answers to these research questions, a number of practical recommendations are presented.

First, the usage of interface agents by IS/IT professionals may be a useful way to boost their creativity and encourage imagination. Prior research shows that creativity and productivity are positively related. When people are most creative, they also become most productive that may positively contribute in the achievement of organizational goals (Miller, 1986, 1998). Therefore, under appropriate conditions, the employment of this technology may serve well the overall organizational goals.

Second, it is suggested that developers and marketers be aware of the user characteristics presented in this investigation. To reach as many of these potential customers as possible, email interface agent marketers should promote their products through appropriate communications channels, such as websites, newspapers, magazines, and journals that are read by innovative IT professionals. In addition, the study's survey showed that most users resided in an English-speaking country. Given that only one-third of all Web users speak English as their primary language, it is recommended that marketers also target IT personnel in non-English speaking countries. For this, Websites need to be translated, and agent systems should be available in other languages, besides English. Overall, it is suggested that the above strategy may be successfully utilized in the short-term. However, as interface agent technology becomes widespread in the future, other types of individuals may dominate the population of email interface agent users. In this case, it is recommended that marketers reconsider their promotional strategy.

Third, in order to facilitate the usage and adoption of this technology, designers should emphasize the creation of agent-based applications compatible with both existing email systems and everyday work applications. Currently, the implementation of highly compatible email interface agents is the central, urgent issue for agent developers. Failure to address this concern will likely result in dramatically low diffusion rates or even in the entire rejection of this technology in the future.

Fourth, agent manufacturers need to identify ways of reducing perceived agent intrusiveness. Perceived intrusiveness is a primary factor why individuals disliked email interface agents, and one of the top reasons why they entirely rejected them. Currently, the issue of perceived intrusiveness of information technologies has not been studied by the MIS research community. The extant MIS literature does not provide a clear definition of perceived intrusiveness, misses measurement instruments, and lacks recommendations on the manipulation of user perceptions of technology intrusiveness. The two first works that report on the issue of perceived intrusiveness of mobile phones were presented by Perry et al. (2001) and Love and Perry (2004). It is recommended that agent developers start investing in research projects that investigate the influence of perceived intrusiveness of interface agents and the methods to manipulate user perceptions. As a short-term solution, more personalization features need to be introduced. For example, advanced options or visual programming environments for message or event processing rules would allow individuals to precisely specify an agent's actions depending on each particular situation. They may instruct the agent to ignore messages that are automatically filed, arrive from certain people, or contain special keywords. However, the employment of such complex features should be optional.

Fifth, developers should eliminate the interference of an agent with other software applications and reduce CPU, memory, and system resources that it consumes. An agent's interference was an important factor for usage termination and the second key reason why respondents to the survey disliked using it.

Sixth, interface agent designers need to emphasize the existing facets of an agent's usefulness and to continue incorporating features that users consider important. To improve the extent of an agent's usefulness, additional features and facets should be implemented. These may include, but are not limited to, machine learning capabilities, basic text analysis with automatic message response mechanisms, run-time adjustments of an agent's behavior, appearance and voice, and rule-based logic. To implement these functions, designers should review the literature and research projects in reference disciplines, such as artificial intelligence and human-computer interaction.

Overall, it is believed that by addressing the issues above, practitioners will be able to increase the rate of user adoption of email interface agents.

CONCLUSION

The field of agent-based computing is relatively new. At the same time, it may boast a comprehensive body of knowledge with the purpose to improve the contemporary agent applications. This work represents an attempt to understand the issue of user perceptions and employment of interface agents for electronic mail notification in order to produce guidelines for technology developers. It was demonstrated that a survey of actual users is a fruitful approach to achieve the purpose of such a study.

This study had several limitations. First, users of only one email interface agent were surveyed. It is possible that users of other agents would offer slightly different insights on the usage of this technology. Second, the findings are limited to interface agents for email only. Currently, there is a variety of interface agents that may be employed with various technologies. It is likely that some of this study's conclusions may not be generalizable. Third, the survey was cross-sectional in nature. A longitudinal study design is desirable to observe changes in user behavior and perceptions over time.

It is recommended that future researchers continue investigating factors that influence user adoption decisions by conducting empirical investigations that involve real-life users. It is also suggested that agent manufacturers recognize the importance of these research projects, provide academics with necessary assistance and support, and incorporate their findings in agent-based applications.

ACKNOWLEDGMENT

I am very grateful to Dr. Brian Detlor, Dr. Nick Bontis and Dr. Milena Head for their support and guidance during my doctoral studies at McMaster University. I am sincerely thankful to Mr. Clint Batman from Blind Bat Software for his kind assistance with this project.

REFERENCES

Ajzen, I., & Fishbein, M. (1980). *Understanding attitudes and predicting social behavior.* Englewood Cliffs, N.J.: Prentice-Hall.

Armour, P. G. (2002). The business of software: The organism and the mechanism of projects. *Communications of the ACM, 45*(5), 17–20. doi:10.1145/506218.506233

Bergman, R., Griss, M., & Staelin, C. (2002). *A personal email assistant. Technical Report HPL-2002-236*: Hewlett-Packard Company.

Biemans, W. G. (1991). User and third-party involvement in developing medical equipment innovations. *Technovation, 11*(3), 163–182. doi:10.1016/0166-4972(91)90032-Y

Carlson, J. R., & Zmud, R. W. (1994). Channel expansion theory: A dynamic view of media and information richness perceptions. In Moore, D. P. (Ed.), *Academy of Management: Best papers proceedings* (pp. 280–284).

Carlson, J. R., & Zmud, R. W. (1999). Channel expansion theory and the experiential nature of media richness perceptions. *Academy of Management Journal, 42*(2), 153–170. doi:10.2307/257090

Cooper, R. G., & Brentani, U. (1991). New industrial financial services: What distinguishes the winners. *Journal of Product Innovation Management, 8*(2), 75–137. doi:10.1016/0737-6782(91)90002-G

Couger, J. D., & Zawacki, R. A. (1980). *Motivating and managing computer personnel.* New York: John Wiley & Sons.

Daft, R. L., & Lengel, R. H. (1986). Organizational information requirements, media richness and structural design. *Management Science, 32*(5), 554–571. doi:10.1287/mnsc.32.5.554

Daft, R. L., Lengel, R. H., & Trevino, L. K. (1987). Message equivocality, media selection, and manager performance: Implications for information systems. *Management Information Systems Quarterly, 11*(3), 355–366. doi:10.2307/248682

Davis, F. D. (1989). Perceived usefulness, perceived ease of use and user acceptance of information technology. *Management Information Systems Quarterly, 13*(3), 319–340. doi:10.2307/249008

Davis, F. D., Bagozzi, R. P., & Warshaw, P. R. (1989). User acceptance of computer technology: A comparison of two theoretical models. *Management Science, 35*(8), 982–1003. doi:10.1287/mnsc.35.8.982

Davis, F. D., Bagozzi, R. P., & Warshaw, P. R. (1992). Extrinsic and intrinsic motivation to use computers in workplace. *Journal of Applied Social Psychology, 22*(14), 1111–1132. doi:10.1111/j.1559-1816.1992.tb00945.x

Dehn, D. M., & van Mulken, S. (2000). The impact of animated interface agents: A review of empirical research. *International Journal of Human-Computer Studies, 52*(1), 1–22. doi:10.1006/ijhc.1999.0325

Detlor, B. (2004). *Towards knowledge portals: From human issues to intelligent agents.* Dordrecht, The Netherlands: Kluwer Academic Publishers.

Dimmick, J., Kline, S., & Stafford, L. (2000). The gratification niches of personal e-mail and telephone. *Communication Research, 27*(2), 227–248. doi:10.1177/009365000027002005

Ducheneaut, N., & Bellotti, V. (2001). E-mail as habitat: An exploration of embedded personal information management. *Interaction, 8*(5), 30–38. doi:10.1145/382899.383305

Fulk, J. (1993). Social construction of communication technology. *Academy of Management Journal, 36*(5), 921–950. doi:10.2307/256641

Fulk, J., Schmitz, J., & Steinfield, C. W. (1990). A social influence model for technology use. In Fulk, J., & Steinfield, C. W. (Eds.), *Organizations and communications technologies* (pp. 117–140). Newbury Park: Sage Publications.

Goldsmith, R. E., & Hofacker, C. F. (1991). Measuring consumer innovativeness. *Journal of the Academy of Marketing Science, 19*(3), 209–222. doi:10.1007/BF02726497

Goodhue, D. L. (1998). Development and measurement validity of a task-technology fit instrument for user evaluations of information systems. *Decision Sciences, 29*(1), 105–138. doi:10.1111/j.1540-5915.1998.tb01346.x

Gruen, D., Sidner, C., Boettner, C., & Rich, C. (1999). *A collaborative assistant for email.* Proceedings of the Conference on Human Factors and Computing Systems, Pittsburg, Pennsylvania, pp. 196-197.

Isbister, K., & Nass, C. (2000). Consistency of personality in interactive characters: Verbal cues, non-verbal cues, and user characteristics. *International Journal of Human-Computer Studies, 53*(2), 251–267. doi:10.1006/ijhc.2000.0368

Keaveney, S. M. (1995). Customer switching behavior in service industries: An exploratory study. *Journal of Marketing, 59*(2), 71–82. doi:10.2307/1252074

Koda, T., & Maes, P. (1996). *Agents with faces: The effect of personification.* Proceedings of the 5th IEEE International Workshop on Robot and Human Communication, Tsukuba, Japan, pp. 189-194.

Krippendorff, K. (1980). *Content analysis: An introduction to its methodology.* Beverly Hills, CA: Sage Publications.

Libes, D. (1997). Tcl/Tk-based agents for mail and news notification. *Software, Practice & Experience, 27*(4), 481–493. doi:10.1002/(SICI)1097-024X(199704)27:4<481::AID-SPE94>3.0.CO;2-J

Lieberman, H., & Selker, T. (2003). Agents for the user interface. In Bradshaw, J. M. (Ed.), *Handbook of Agent Technology.* The MIT Press.

Love, S., & Perry, M. (2004). *Dealing with mobile conversations in public places: Some implications for the design of socially intrusive technologies.* Proceedings of the ACM Conference on Human Factors and Computing Systems, Vienna, Austria, pp. 1195-1198.

Lucas, W. (1998). Effects of E-Mail on the organization. *European Management Journal, 16*(1), 18–30. doi:10.1016/S0263-2373(97)00070-4

Lüthje, C. (2004). Characteristics of innovating users in a consumer goods field: An empirical study of sport-related product consumers. *Technovation, 24*(9), 683–695. doi:10.1016/S0166-4972(02)00150-5

Maes, P. (1994). Agents that reduce work and information overload. *Communications of the ACM, 37*(7), 31–40. doi:10.1145/176789.176792

Markus, M. L. (1990). Toward a 'Critical Mass' theory of interactive media. In Fulk, J., & Steinfield, C. W. (Eds.), *Organizations and communications technologies* (pp. 194–218). Newbury Park: Sage Publications.

Midgley, D. F., & Dowling, G. R. (1978). Innovativeness: The concept and its measurement. *The Journal of Consumer Research, 4*(4), 229–242. doi:10.1086/208701

Miles, M. B., & Huberman, A. M. (1994). *Qualitative data analysis: An expanded sourcebook* (2 ed.). Thousand Oaks: Sage Publications.

Miller, W. C. (1986). *The creative edge: Fostering innovation where you work*. Reading, MA: Addison-Wesley Publishing Company.

Miller, W. C. (1998). *Flash of brilliance: Inspiriting creativity where you work*. Reading, MA: Perseus Books.

Miller, W. C., Couger, J. D., & Higgins, L. F. (1996). Innovation styles profile of IS personnel vs other occupations. *Creativity and Innovation Management*, *5*(4), 226–233. doi:10.1111/j.1467-8691.1996.tb00148.x

Moore, G. C., & Benbasat, I. (1991). Development of an instrument to measure the perceptions of adopting an information technology innovation. *Information Systems Research*, *2*(3), 192–222. doi:10.1287/isre.2.3.192

Murphy, J., & Tan, I. (2003). Journey to nowhere? E-mail customer service by travel agents in Singapore. *Tourism Management*, *24*(5), 543–550. doi:10.1016/S0261-5177(03)00005-0

Ngwenyama, O. K. (1997). Communication richness in electronic mail: Critical social theory and the contextuality of meaning. *Management Information Systems Quarterly*, *21*(2), 145–167. doi:10.2307/249417

Orlikowski, W. J. (1992). The duality of technology: Rethinking the concept of technology in organizations. *Organization Science*, *3*(3), 398–427. doi:10.1287/orsc.3.3.398

Orlikowski, W. J., Yates, J., Okamura, K., & Fujimoto, M. (1995). Shaping electronic communication: The metastructuring of technology in the context of use. *Organization Science*, *6*(4), 423–444. doi:10.1287/orsc.6.4.423

Perry, M., O'Hara, K., Sellen, A., Brown, B., & Harper, R. (2001). Dealing with mobility: understanding access anytime, anywhere. *ACM Transactions on Computer-Human Interaction*, *8*(4), 323–347. doi:10.1145/504704.504707

Rice, R. (1993). Media appropriateness: Using social presence theory to compare traditional and new organization media. *Human Communication Research*, *19*(4), 451–484. doi:10.1111/j.1468-2958.1993.tb00309.x

Rogers, E. M. (1995). *Diffusion of Innovations* (4 ed.). New-York: Free Press.

Romeyn, J. W. (2004). Hypotheses and inductive predictions. *Synthese*, *141*(3), 333–364. doi:10.1023/B:SYNT.0000044993.82886.9e

Segal, R. B., & Kephart, J. O. (2000, June 29-July 2). *Incremental Learning in SwiftFile*. Proceedings of the Seventh International Conference on Machine Learning, Stanford, CA, pp. 863-870.

Serenko, A. (2006). The importance of interface agent characteristics from the end-user perspective. *International Journal of Intelligent Information Technologies*, *2*(2), 48–59. doi:10.4018/jiit.2006040104

Serenko, A. (2007a). Are interface agents scapegoats? Attributions of responsibility in human-agent interaction. *Interacting with Computers*, *19*(2), 293–303. doi:10.1016/j.intcom.2006.07.005

Serenko, A. (2007b). The development of an instrument to measure the degree of animation predisposition of agent users. *Computers in Human Behavior*, *23*(1), 478–495. doi:10.1016/j.chb.2004.10.042

Serenko, A., Bontis, N., & Detlor, B. (2007). End-user adoption of animated interface agents in everyday work applications. *Behaviour & Information Technology*, *26*(2), 119–132. doi:10.1080/01449290500260538

Serenko, A., & Detlor, B. (2004). Intelligent agents as innovations. *AI & Society*, *18*(4), 364–381. doi:10.1007/s00146-004-0310-5

Serenko, A., Ruhi, U., & Cocosila, M. (2007). Unplanned effects of intelligent agents on Internet use: Social Informatics approach. *AI & Society, 21*(1-2), 141–166. doi:10.1007/s00146-006-0051-8

Sproull, L., & Kiesler, S. (1986). Reducing social context cues: Electronic mail in organizational communications. *Management Science, 32*(11), 1492–1512. doi:10.1287/mnsc.32.11.1492

Sproull, L., Subramani, M., Kiesler, S., Walker, J. H., & Waters, K. (1996). When the interface is a face. *Human-Computer Interaction, 11*(2), 97–124. doi:10.1207/s15327051hci1102_1

Stolee, P., Zaza, C., Pedlar, A., & Myers, A. M. (1999). Clinical experience with goal attainment scaling in geriatric care. *Journal of Aging and Health, 11*(1), 96–124. doi:10.1177/089826439901100106

Taylor, S., & Todd, P. (1995). Assessing IT usage: The role of prior experience. *Management Information Systems Quarterly, 19*(4), 561–570. doi:10.2307/249633

Trevino, L. K., Daft, R. L., & Lengel, R. H. (1990). Understanding managers' media choices: A symbolic interactionist perspective. In Fulk, J., & Steinfield, C. W. (Eds.), *Organizations and communications technologies* (pp. 71–94). Newbury Park: Sage Publications.

Venkatesh, V., & Davis, F. D. (2000). A theoretical extension of the Technology Acceptance Model: Four longitudinal field studies. *Management Science, 46*(2), 186–204. doi:10.1287/mnsc.46.2.186.11926

Yates, J., & Orlikowski, W. J. (1992). Genres of organizational communication: A structurational approach to studying communication and media. *Academy of Management Review, 17*(2), 299–326.

This work was previously published in International Journal of Intelligent Information Technologies, Volume 5, Issue 3, edited by Vijayan Sugumaran, pp. 55-83, copyright 2009 by IGI Publishing (an imprint of IGI Global).

Section 3
Intelligent Technologies

Chapter 12
Traffic Responsive Signal Timing Plan Generation Based on Neural Network

Azzam-ul-Asar
University of Engineering & Technology, Pakistan

M. Sadeeq Ullah
University of Peshawar, Pakistan

Mudasser F. Wyne
National University, USA

Jamal Ahmed
University of Peshawar, Pakistan

Riaz-ul-Hasnain
University of Engineering & Technology, Pakistan

ABSTRACT

This article proposes a neural network based traffic signal controller, which eliminates most of the problems associated with the Traffic Responsive Plan Selection (TRPS) mode of the closed loop system. Instead of storing timing plans for different traffic scenarios, which requires clustering and threshold calculations, the proposed approach uses an Artificial Neural Network (ANN) model that produces optimal plans based on optimized weights obtained through its learning phase. Clustering in a closed loop system is root of the problems and therefore has been eliminated in the proposed approach. The Particle Swarm Optimization (PSO) technique has been used both in the learning rule of ANN as well as generating training cases for ANN in terms of optimized timing plans, based on Highway Capacity Manual (HCM) delay for all traffic demands found in historical data. The ANN generates optimal plans online to address real time traffic demands and thus is more responsive to varying traffic conditions.

INTRODUCTION

The growth in the number of automobiles on the roads has placed a higher demand on traffic control systems to efficiently reduce the level of congestion. As such this has increased travel delays, fuel consumption, and air pollution. One of the main causes of congestion is the inherent instability in traffic flow due to the behavior of human drivers. A long-standing problem in traffic engineering has been to optimize the flow of vehicles through a given road network. Traffic control in urban networks is a nonlinear process with varying dynamic characteristics throughout the day. Accurate, reliable, and timely traffic information is therefore critical for deployment and operation of Intelligent Transportation Systems (ITSs). It is a general understanding that, traffic forecasting for travelers and traffic operators should become at least as useful, accurate and convenient as weather reports.

Increased traffic congestion and the associated pollution are forcing experts in transportation to discover new approaches in managing rapid changes in traffic and develop procedures to keep our mobility safe, comfortable, and economical. IT-driven ITSs have recently emerged to meet this challenge. This emergence is seen by many as a part of normal evolutionary adaptation to new traffic conditions and technology. They consider current ITS applications perfectly adequate, safer and a wiser response for our current and future transportation problems (Wang F. , 2005). However, technological changes and theoretical developments have created opportunities for fundamental restructuring of transportation management that could lead to significantly expanded capacity and improved efficiency. Wang in (Wang F. , 2008) presents a research that pivots around an ACP (Artificial Computational Parallel) approach, involving modeling with artificial systems, analysis with computational experiments, and operation through parallel execution for control and management of complex systems, such as transportation systems, with social and behavioral dimensions (Wang F. , 2004) (Wang F. , 2007).

Researchers have presented different approaches utilizing a multitude of different environments. For signaled intersections, Xu Jianmin (Jianmin, Ning, & Hongbin, 2000) have used waiting vehicles of the red stage and the vehicles on the link of the green stage as the inputs in obtaining the traffic timing scheme. Liu Zhiyong (Zhiyong, Jin, & al, 1999) have used the queue length of the current stage and queue length of next stage as inputs and green time extension as the output. Xu Lunhui (Lunhui, Yanguo, & Wenliang, 2005) used the queue length of current green time stage and the queue length of the next stage as the input and the current green time as the output. In the traditional signaled traffic control system, each region is considered an isolated control unit, with no coordination between regional boundaries. The aforementioned are using fuzzy control to the single or two intersections' traffic control only and not to the coordination of different regions. It is worth mentioning that regional boundary's traffic control effect has direct influence on the input traffic flow control and output traffic flow control. In (Wang, Yang, & Guan, 2008) a traffic coordination and control model of regional boundary based on fuzzy control is proposed. Two fuzzy controllers are designed to coordinate and control the regional boundary when traffic congestion occurs. The proposed method has the potential to improve traffic conditions in each region and to some extent alleviate traffic congestion.

Since the traditional actuated signal control method only considers the information of cars arriving to the current green light signal stage, it has an obvious shortcoming. In order to improve the control effect, Laichour (Laichour & al., 2001) brought forward the concept model of traffic control based on an intelligent agent. Li (Li & Huangpu, 2000) presented fuzzy traffic signal control approach for an isolated intersection and verified its validity by simulation. However, these approaches do not have the ability to self-learn. Bingham in (Bingham, 2001) improved the effect of signal control by computing certain parameters of fuzzy traffic control by neuro-network. Abdulhai in (Abdulhai & Pringle, 2000) used intelligent agent with Q-learning capacity to control a single intersection. The result of simulation has indicated that the control effects of these approaches are better than any fixed-time control method. A self-learning traffic signal control model based on fuzzy clustering and genetic algorithm is established in (Cheng & Yang, 2008). Through fuzzy clustering, the number of arriving cars and, the schemes of signal control are put into a knowledge-database in the form of rules that are set under different conditions in which cars arrive. The set of traffic control rules is divided into a set of fixed-rule and a set of variable-rule. The genetic algorithm is then used to improve the set of variable-rule during the process of traffic signal control. The article then goes on to conclude that the control effect of actuated method is better than the fixed-time method and the effect of self-learning method is better than an actuated one.

Roundabouts are also used to self-regulate traffic according to changes in traffic flows, resulting in shorter delay and lower pollutant output as the result of fewer vehicle stops and starts. However, when traffic flows exceed their capacity, operation performance of roundabouts will deteriorate. In addition, they are also not suitable for coordinated traffic signal system and sites with high volumes of pedestrians or bicycles. For these disadvantages, the English traffic engineers have attempted to introduce signal control to roundabouts since the beginning of 1970s. Subsequently scholars from China, Australia and US have joined in the research for signalized roundabouts and gradually consummated the signal control theory for roundabouts (Qian, Li, & Sun, Oct., 2008). Left-turn with two stop roundabouts resolved the congestion problem of the large conventional roundabouts

with high traffic volume in some countries. When the traffic volumes are not high enough, these modern roundabouts have the advantages of higher efficiency and less land occupation; when traffic flows fluctuate markedly, entry metering control mode can also regulate the control scheme according to the real-time traffic flows and result in lesser delays.

Ranghua in (Ronghua, 2008) states that the decision-making interactive process between governors and travelers in urban traffic coordination is a game behavior. In his paper an urban traffic coordination control system based on Multi-Agent-Game is put forward. The multi-agent mutual cooperation can strengthen the coordination degree of the traffic control and the traffic guidance, that is, the intelligent control means can effectively adjust the traffic flow. The simulation results indicate that the multi-agent cooperation based on game theory can effectively realize the coordination between urban region traffic control and traffic guidance.

The traditional way of calculating optimized timing plans is to mathematically model cost function, such as average vehicle delay, number of stops, fuel and emissions etc. and optimize these with the signal cycle length, splits and offsets using an optimization algorithm, such as Genetic Algorithm (Dotoli, Fanti, & and Meloni, 2003). Simulation softwares also use a model based approach to compute optimal plans using multiple simulation runs (SYNCHRO-6.0, 2000). To ensure that the traffic control system is responsive to the changing traffic conditions, optimization algorithm needs to be applied each time the traffic conditions change. Since traffic conditions may change after every few seconds, this demands generous computer processing power to generate real time responses. One solution to real time optimization is the closed loop system. The closed-loop system was designed for the first time in 1967 in a program called Urban Traffic Control System (UTCS) (Henry, Ferlis, & Kay, August,

1976). Closed-loop systems operate either in Time Of Day (TOD) mode or Traffic Responsive Plan selection (TRPS) mode. In TOD mode time plans are calculated for different times of the day and a plan is selected based on the current time. In TRPS mode, based on historical data, multiple traffic demand scenarios are extracted, demands with similar features are clustered and optimal timing plan is calculated for each cluster. Current traffic demand is mapped to one of the predetermined clusters and its timing plan is implemented.

Even though TRPS has been found operationally effective and the least expensive approach by the UTCS team, it still suffers from certain limitations and renders itself the less reasonable option. One major problem is the plethora of setup factors and thresholds which need to be correctly determined for the successful implementation of TRPS mode. Recent developments in the closed-loop system have improved setup methodology which has remarkably decreased misclassification errors albeit not completely eliminating them (Abbas, Chaudhary, Sharma, S, & Engelbrecht, 2003) (Abbas & Sharma, 2004). In addition to this, other problems still exist, For example, traffic demands in the same cluster always have some variation but by assigning a single time plan, these variations become flattened. Also new traffic demand patterns appear with time and old patterns become obsolete. In this paper, an Artificial Neural Network (ANN) based approach has been proposed to eliminate these problems associated with TRPS mode of operations. In this approach, a single time plan is assigned to each traffic demand and the relationship between traffic demands and their timing plans is taught to ANN. Trained ANN then generates a timing plan for the current traffic demands in real time.

Our article is organized in the following manner. Closed-loop systems are introduced in section-2. Section-3 provides a brief account of repetitive optimization, its relevance to the traffic signals control and neural network based solution

to the problem. A new approach is then proposed in Section-4 which eradicates the downsides of the closed-loop system. Experimental results for the proposed approach are presented in Section-5.

CLOSED-LOOP SYSTEMS

A closed-loop system is composed of a series of signalized intersections operated by a single master controller (Balke, Keithireddipalli, & Brehmer, 1997). The master controller issues commands to implement timing plans stored in the local controllers. Master controller coordinates the connected signalized intersections. In closed-loop systems a number of timing plans are calculated for different traffic scenarios and an appropriate plan is selected based on the current traffic conditions.

The first step in designing a closed-loop system is to determine the total number of demand states. This can be achieved by recording traffic conditions for every possible traffic scenario. Subsequently these records are presented to a clustering algorithm to extract natural grouping from it. These grouped traffic scenarios are termed "demand states". The next step is to determine an optimized timing plan for every class (demand state). This can be achieved with any commercially available software for traffic signal timing optimization e.g. SYNCHRO (SYNCHRO-6.0, 2000) or TRANSYT-7F (TRANSYT-7F, 1988). The last step is to determine TRPS weights and thresholds in order to associate the current traffic demand to one of the predetermined demand states.

Closed-loop system operates in two modes: Time Of Day (TOD) mode and Traffic Responsive Plan Selection (TRPS) mode. In TOD mode it is assumed that traffic patterns repeat themselves in a recursive manner in time by the day of week. Hence a relationship is established between time and demand. The selection function in TOD mode can be represented by equation (1).

$$TP = f(T) \qquad (1)$$

Where TP is the new timing plan and T is the Current time of day.

The major limitation with TOD mode is that the time-demand relationship is violated whenever special events, e.g. game matches, functions, convocations etc, occur. On the other hand TRPS does not require this time-demand relationship. In TRPS mode real time data is collected from the detectors and optimal timing plan is selected based on the current traffic demand. Selection function in TRPS mode can be represented by equation (2).

$$TP = f(D) \qquad (2)$$

Where D is the current traffic demand.

Since TRPS mode depends on the real time data and does not require any time-demand relationship, which may induce errors, it can operate more efficiently if properly configured.

Even though TRPS mode of operation is better than fixed timing plans and TOD mode, it also has a number of drawbacks. A major problem is to correctly determine a number of set-up factors and thresholds that are essential for the successful operations of TRPS mode (Abbas, Chaudhary, Sharma, S, & Engelbrecht, 2003) (Abbas & Sharma, 2004). Optimum plan assigned to a cluster depends on the centroid of the cluster and optimality suffers when movement is made towards the edges. Lack of software which can calculate optimal plan for a group of demand states also makes the problem more severe. It is obvious that the numbers of demand states are limited and TRPS mode does not respond to smaller variations in traffic conditions until they are above a predetermined threshold. It is also obvious that TRPS mode cannot respond correctly to a traffic scenario that does not legally fall into any of the existing classes. Lastly, traffic patterns change with the passage of time and predetermined demand states disappear, often referred to as "plan aging". Time plan aging necessitates repeating the calculation process.

REPETITIVE OPTIMIZATION

This section elaborates bases of the repetitive optimization problem and shows its relevance in adaptive traffic control systems.

Mathematical Elaboration

If f is a function of a set of n variables and m constants represented by x_i, where, $i = 1,...,n$ and c_j, where $j = 1,...,m$, respectively such that each c_i either scales a variable x_i in multiplicative manner or an additive scalar term in the function. Minor changes made to the scalars' set will not change the function landscape in a sense that no peak or valley will either disappear or change its neighborhood. That is, minor changes in the scalars' set will only shift the landscape. Minor changes exclude changes that either reverse the sign or introduce high order increase or decrease in the magnitude of any member of the scalar set. Suppose f is a unimodal function and its optimizer x_t^* at time t is found. At time $t + 1$, minor changes are introduced in the scalars' set which shift the landscape of f and invalidate x_t^*. To find correct optimizer at time $t + 1$, i.e. $x_t^* + 1$ optimization algorithm has to be applied again to f. Now suppose a set of hypothetical functions g_i, where $i = 1,...,n$, which traces x^* in the shifted landscape at time $t + 1$. Each g_i is defined on $Y^m = (y_1, y_2,..., y_m)$ such that y_j represents an offset from c_j and g_i gives the ith element of $x_t^* + 1$ at time $t + 1$. It is clear from this definition that if $Y^m = (0,0,...,0)^m$ then $x_t^* = x_t^* + 1$. If the mathematical model of each g_i could be found then x^* can be traced on the shifted landscape in case of any change introduced into the scalar set. This in turn can help us to avoid repetitive optimization of f which could save us from a lot of processing.

Neural Network Based Solution

Artificial Neural Network (ANN) in (Minsky & Papert, 1969) is a useful tool inspired by the human cognitive capability to relate dissimilar elements together and refers to a family of general mapping techniques. ANN can learn arbitrary mapping between any two datasets of real valued, discrete or vector valued, and may contain noise. Multi-Layer Perceptron (MLP), also called feed-forward networks, is a model of ANN and its distinguishing feature enables it to approximate any continuous function to any arbitrary accuracy if a large enough number of hidden units are used (Jones, 1990) (Blum & Li, 1991). In this paper, MLP network has been used to approximate each g_i by placing Y^m vectors on input and g_i values on the output. Even though a separate network for each g_i will be more efficient, a single network for all g_i will also suffice if g_i are few and do not represent highly non-linear signal. The latter approach is adopted in this article.

Repetitive Optimization in Adaptive Traffic Control

Repetitive optimization is very common in adaptive traffic signal control systems where a cost function — such as average vehicle delay or performance index — is optimized with respect to signal cycle length, splits and offsets. Cost functions also include current traffic conditions such as traffic volume counts and occupancy. Optimization process is applied periodically, usually from cycle to cycle, to the cost function to find optimum values of the cycle length, splits and offsets with respect to the changed traffic conditions. Traffic conditions are analogous to the constant set as cycle length, splits and offsets are to the variable set. The proposed approach, presented in the next section, is based on this idea.

TRAFFIC RESPONSIVE PLAN GENERATION

The Proposed Approach

Problems caused in the closed-loop system are mainly due to the number of timing plans that can be stored in the micro controller, as Naztec version 50/60 controller (Naztec Operations Manual for Closed-Loop Master Controller, 2002) can store only 48 timing plans. This necessitates grouping of demand states in a limited number of classes and calculating thresholds to map real time traffic demand to one of the classes. Besides this, generating optimized timing plans based on real time data is difficult due to the time required for the optimization process. Optimization of the timing plans involves a number of objectives e.g. average vehicle delay, number of stops, fuel consumption and emissions etc. Increasing the number of objectives complicates the cost function and hence requires large amounts of computer processing. It is very difficult, if not impossible, to build a mathematical model to represent the relationship between the traffic demands and their corresponding optimized timing plans.

The relationship between traffic demands and their timing plans can be modeled using ANN approach. A neural network is constructed for each intersection. Input for the neural network comprises of data that show current traffic conditions e.g. volume and occupancy counts etc. Constant intersection information regarding the intersection, e.g. each approach capacity, lane width, link length etc, is not needed. Results that are obtained from the optimization of the signal timing, i.e. cycle length, splits and offset, are placed on the output. A typical neural network architecture with only traffic volume V_i (volume in vph along each approach that needs a phase) is on the input and Si (Splits), C (cycle length) and Off (offset length) on the output is shown in Figure 1. In this Figure, it has been assumed that every traffic movement has a separate phase. If a

Figure 1. ANN with vehicle counts on the input and split, cycle and offset lengths on the output

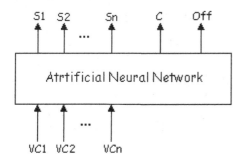

single phase is serving two or more movements, the number of split outputs (*Si*) will be reduced. Proposed ANN can contain one or more hidden layer to correctly model the relationship. Only one hidden layer with sigmoid activation function will suffice to model any arbitrary mapping — more hidden layers can make ANN over fit.

Equation (3) mentions the fact that sum of all the splits should be equal to the cycle length. This places a constraint on S_i, which the ANN cannot guarantee. SL_i is calculated, based on equation (4), to meet this constraint.

$$\sum_{i=1}^{n} S_i = C \qquad (3)$$

$$SL_i = \frac{S_i}{\sum_{j=1}^{n} S_j} \times C \qquad (4)$$

Where S_i is the split generated with trained ANN and SLi is the actual split length for phase *i*.

The proposed scheme should be applied to the real time traffic environment as follows. Traffic volume and occupancy data should be recorded for all possible scenarios including special events. Optimized cycle lengths, splits and offsets should be calculated for all scenarios. Optimization can be achieved with any commercially available software for signal timing optimization, e.g. SYN-CHRO (SYNCHRO-6.0, 2000) or TRANSYT

7F (TRANSYT-7F, 1988). A supervised ANN model can be designed by taking volume and occupancy parameters on the input and optimized cycle lengths, splits and offsets on the output. The trained ANN can then generate optimized plans in real time based on features extracted during training.

EXPERIMENTAL RESULTS

To demonstrate implementation of the proposed approach, an ANN model has been designed for a single intersection, shown in Figure 2, and HCM delay has been used as the Measure Of Effectiveness (MOE) for generating optimal plans that will be used for ANN training. Since delay is shorter for shorter cycle lengths, cycle length has been fixed, to 60 seconds in these experiments. Offset is not considered as it is the coordination between two intersections. Results have been calculated for the intersection in Figure 2. Numbering has been assigned to each movement according to the National Electronics Manufacturing Association (NEMA) (Mn/DOT Traffic Signal Timing and Coordination Manual, 2002) (McShane, Roess, & Prassas, 1998) convention. A three phase signal cycle is designed with phase 1 for the East

Figure 2. East/West Main Street

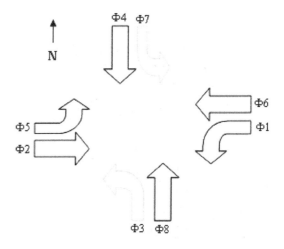

Figure 3. Ring diagram for the phases of intersection in figure 2

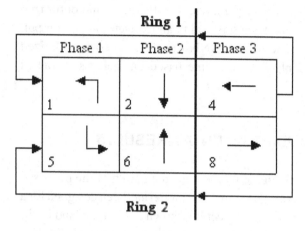

Bound Left (EBL) and West Bound Left (WBL), phase 2 for the East Bound Through (EBT) and West Bound Through (WBT) and phase 3 for the North Bound Through (NBT) and South Bound Through (SBT). Left turn movements for the North Bound Left (NBL) and South Bound Left (SBL) are permitted in phase 3. Ring diagram for the signal cycle is shown in Figure 3. For simplicity we assume that each approach is single lane and the traffic demands of NBL and SBL are not considered. Saturation flow rate for each approach is mentioned in Table 1 and assumed to be corrected for Lane Type, Environmental Class, Lane Width, Gradient and Traffic Composition Entries in Table 1 are in Through Car Units (TCU).

Table 1. Saturation flow rates for different approaches of intersection in figure 2

Approach	Adjusted Saturation flow rate (S)
WBL (Φ1)	1540
EBT (Φ2)	1620
SBT (Φ4)	1570
EBL (Φ5)	1540
WBT (Φ6)	1620
NBT (Φ8)	1570

Signal cycle lengths are optimized with respect to the Highway Capacity Manual (HCM) 2000 delay equation (Highway Capacity Manual, 2000) as given by equation (5).

$$D = \frac{0.5 \times C \times (1 - g/C)^2}{1 - \left[\min(1, X)\dfrac{g}{C} \right]} +$$

$$900 \times T \times \left[(X - 1) + \sqrt{(X-1)^2 + \frac{8kIX}{cT}} \right]$$

$$(5)$$

$$X = \frac{v}{c} \tag{6}$$

$$c = s \times \frac{g}{C} \tag{7}$$

Where C and g are respectively the cycle length and effective green time in seconds, X and v are respectively the degree of saturation and demand volume in vehicles/hour, T is the duration of analysis period in hours, k is incremental delay factor which is 0.5 for pre-timed signals, i is upstream filtering/metering adjustment factor which is 1 for isolated intersection, c is capacity in vehicles per hour and s is the saturation flow rate.

Fifty hypothetical demand scenarios have been considered, of which forty cases, mentioned in Table 2, have been used for ANN training and the remaining ten cases, mentioned in Table 3, have been selected for testing purposes. Since cycle length is fixed to 60 sec for all demand scenarios, only optimal split lengths have been calculated for all three phases with respect to HCM delay. Traffic signals plan optimization, for generating ANN training cases, has been achieved using Particle Swarm Optimizer (PSO) algorithm.

Particle Swarm Optimizer (PSO) has been used to calculate optimized splits for all the three phases - the delay equation being the objective function. PSO is a population based stochastic optimization algorithm inspired by human social behavior. It was presented by Kennedy & Eberhart (Eberhart & Kennedy, 1995) (Kennedy & Eberhart, 1995)

Table 2. Neural network training data

	Traffic Demand						PSO Optimized Splits		
S No	v1(Φ2)	v2(Φ6)	v3(Φ1)	v4(Φ5)	v5(Φ4)	v6(Φ8)	S1	S2	S3
1	344	266	151	213	215	297	24.21	15.03	20.76
2	420	318	144	194	257	279	27.23	13.11	19.66
3	321	340	189	203	210	257	25.87	15.61	18.52
4	290	285	145	192	249	302	23.11	14.14	22.75
5	412	354	138	226	195	312	26.74	14.20	19.06
6	388	215	174	210	204	289	24.89	15.31	19.80
7	432	233	138	197	176	223	29.17	14.33	16.50
8	417	274	173	205	148	173	30.34	16.14	13.52
9	281	259	187	191	201	215	24.39	17.01	18.60
10	213	195	151	162	267	219	19.84	15.28	24.88
11	269	323	189	170	251	275	23.92	14.70	21.38
12	291	354	122	115	228	239	28.89	10.57	20.54
13	261	341	176	152	318	218	24.29	13.42	22.29
14	311	416	223	137	301	251	26.03	14.12	19.85
15	326	437	185	146	235	228	29.36	13.10	17.54
16	348	423	195	171	294	267	26.89	13.36	19.75
17	210	251	102	98	131	103	32.71	12.45	14.84
18	196	323	110	120	102	59	35.76	14.18	10.06
19	102	45	51	22	71	94	23.86	8.79	27.35
20	68	74	29	49	80	105	21.13	8.91	29.96
21	320	285	140	190	230	315	23.95	13.70	22.35
22	402	298	160	215	240	309	25.49	14.29	20.22
23	340	295	212	185	230	225	25.57	16.20	18.24
24	260	318	171	175	273	290	23.16	14.06	22.78
25	379	318	180	186	177	345	25.24	13.70	21.06
26	425	192	203	245	195	259	25.50	17.15	17.35
27	391	251	148	160	212	164	29.70	13.62	16.67
28	402	282	160	215	187	140	29.79	16.24	13.97
29	311	280	177	208	174	214	26.07	16.98	16.95
30	235	190	161	152	217	230	21.44	15.56	23.00
31	281	290	175	195	302	279	22.13	14.80	23.06
32	312	280	112	132	222	342	24.70	10.53	24.77
33	280	309	156	176	340	245	22.89	13.34	23.77
34	280	390	235	160	325	255	24.02	15.03	20.95
35	318	350	215	251	245	228	24.62	17.74	17.64
36	431	380	170	180	294	302	27.21	12.47	20.31
37	235	245	75	135	170	103	30.72	12.74	16.54
38	170	280	145	122	110	70	31.73	17.12	11.14
39	70	95	55	36	105	80	23.17	9.77	27.07
40	80	45	39	55	101	95	17.33	11.13	31.54

Table 3. Results generated by trained neural network & PSO

S. No	Traffic Demand						ANN Generated Splits			PSO Optimized Splits (Desired)			Discrepancy		
	v1 (Φ2)	v2 (Φ6)	v3 (Φ1)	v4 (Φ5)	v5 (Φ4)	v6 (Φ8)	S1	S2	S3	S1	S2	S3	S1	S2	S3
1	413	329	139	179	264	285	27.35	12.34	20.31	27.38	12.37	20.25	0.03	0.03	0.06
2	379	210	178	216	198	282	24.57	15.91	19.52	24.61	15.88	19.51	0.04	0.03	0.01
3	275	218	179	178	247	268	21.22	15.50	23.27	21.54	15.63	22.83	0.32	0.13	0.44
4	288	267	182	195	196	211	25.29	16.53	18.18	25.01	16.9	18.09	0.28	0.37	0.09
5	107	51	55	27	66	103	22.84	9.74	27.42	24.24	9.42	26.34	1.40	0.32	1.08
6	410	315	155	210	225	294	26.45	13.97	19.57	26.59	14.06	19.35	0.14	0.09	0.22
7	385	309	176	195	183	329	25.68	14.54	19.78	25.51	14.02	20.46	0.17	0.52	0.68
8	292	282	171	184	311	286	22.53	14.40	23.07	22.18	14.16	23.66	0.35	0.24	0.59
9	320	365	225	255	251	219	23.98	18.44	17.58	24.79	17.91	17.3	0.81	0.53	0.28
10	155	271	151	134	158	80	27.40	17.10	15.50	28.11	17.2	14.69	0.71	0.1	0.81

in 1994. The distinguishing feature of PSO is its ease of problem modeling that motivated its selection in these experiments. Split lengths are used as parameters to the objective function. For effective learning and avoiding local minima, PSO has also been used for ANN training.

To find optimized splits, PSO algorithm was run to an extent where no further improvement was possible. Neural network that has been used as a controller, also shown in figure 4, has six input nodes, eight nodes in the only hidden layer and four nodes in the output layer. Sigmoid activation function is used for the nodes in the hidden layer and linear function is used in the nodes in output layer. Neural network was trained with 100 particles and 5000 runs of the algorithm were conducted achieving the Mean Square Error (MSE) of 1.23e-6. Since sigmoid function behaves like step function beyond (Blum & Li, 1991), both input and output data was normalized in a manner such that every value was between 0 and 1, i.e. every value was divided by 1000. Tests results are shown in Table 3. For comparison purposes, split lengths have been generated both with the trained neural network and directly through PSO. It is clear from the results that plans generated with trained ANN have only minor differences compared to the plans generated by PSO optimization. Errors mentioned in the discrepancy column are only in fractions of a second, which shows

Figure 4. Neural network used in experiments

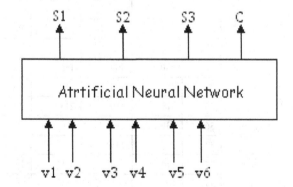

the power of ANN interpolation. More accuracy can be achieved if traffic demand cases used for ANN training are increased.

Since timing plans generated by the trained ANN in Table 3 are for those traffic demands which the ANN is watching for the first time, this can aid in better managing the previously mentioned time plan aging problem. Even though, more generalized ANN can actually completely eliminate the problem, ANN response for the newly developed patterns will drop smoothly and plans aging will never be as serious as it was in the closed loop stored timing plan method. Besides this, only weights of the trained ANN will be stored in memory, instead of storing timing plans, which makes the proposed approach, in terms of memory, "light weight".

CONCLUSION

A neural network based traffic signal controller has been presented to generate real time timing plans according to the prevailing traffic conditions. The proposed approach has eliminated most of the problems associated with TRPS mode such as clustering, correct determination of setup factors and thresholds, memory required for storage of timing plans, misclassification of current traffic demand and time plan aging. In the proposed approach, optimized timing plans for different historical demands are stored in the form of connection strengths of the neural network. New controller is more responsive to varying traffic conditions than closed loop stored timing plan methods.

REFERENCES

Abbas, M., & Sharma, A. (2004). A Robust Bayesian Approach for Setting Traffic Responsive Control System Parameters and Thresholds. *Transportation Research Records*.

Abbas, M., Chaudhary, N., Sharma, A., S, V., & Engelbrecht, R. (September, 2003). *Methodology for Determination of Optimal Traffic Responsive Plan Selection Control Parameters*. Texas Transportation Institute, College Station, Texas, USA.

Abdulhai, B., & Pringle, R. (2000). Machine Learning Based Adaptive Signal Control using Autonomous Q-Learning Agent. *The IASTED International Conference, Intelligent Systems and Control.*, (pp. 320-327).

Balke, K., Keithireddipalli, R., & Brehmer, C. (August, 1997). *Guidelines for Implementing Traffic Responsive Mode in TxDOT Closed-Loop Traffic Signal Systems*. Research Report, Texas Transportation Institute, College Station, Texas, USA.

Bingham, E. (2001). Reinforcement Learning in Neuro-Fuzzy Traffic Signal Control. *European Journal of Operational Research, 131*, 232-241.

Blum, E., & Li, L. (1991). Approximation theory and feedforward networks. *Neural Networks , 4*(4), 511-515.

Cheng, X., & Yang, Z. (2008). Intelligent Traffic Signal Control Approach Based on Fuzzy-Genetic Algorithm. *Fifth International Conference on Fuzzy Systems and Knowledge Discovery* (pp. 221-225).

Dotoli, M., Fanti, M., & Meloni, C. (2003). Real Time Optimization of Traffic Signal Control: Application to Coordinated Intersections. *IEEE International Conference on Systems, Man and Cybernetics* (pp. 3288-3295). Washington.

Eberhart, R., & Kennedy, J. (1995). A New Optimizer using Particle Swarm Theory. *Sixth International Symposium on Micro Machine and Human Science* (pp. 39-43). Nagoya, Japan.

Henry, R., Ferlis, R., & Kay, J. (1976, August). *Evaluation of UTCS Control Strategies*. Executive Summary, U.S. Department of Transportation.

Highway Capacity Manual. (2000). TRB. TRB Publications.

Jianmin, X., Ning, S., & Hongbin, Y. (2000). A New Fuzzy Control Method for Isolated Intersection Traffic Management. *Journal of South China University of Technology, 28,* 1-5.

Jones, L. (1990). Constructive Aprroximations for Neural Networks by Sigmoidal Functions. *Proceedings of the IEEE, 78,* 1586-1589.

Kennedy, J., & Eberhart, R. (1995). Particle Swarm Optimization. *IEEE International Coneference on Neural Networks, IV,* 1942-1948. Perth, Australia.

Laichour, H., & al., e. (2001). Traffic Control Assistance in Connection Nodes: Multi-Agent Applications in Urban Transport Systems. *International Workshop on Intelligent Data Application and Advanced Computing System: Technology and Application* (pp. 133-137).

Li, J., & Huangpu, Z. (2000). Design of Fuzzy Control System for City Signle Highway Intersection. *Electrical Drive Automation, 22*(2), 22-24.

Lunhui, X., Yanguo, H., & Wenliang, L. (2005). Optimized Design Traffic Signal Fuzzy Controller Based on Genetic Algorithm. *Computer and Communications, 6,* 95-98.

McShane, W., Roess, R., & Prassas, E. (1998). *Traffic Engineering* (2nd ed.). Prentice Hall.

Minsky, M., & Papert, S. (1969). *Perceptions: An Introduction to Computational Geometry.* MIT Press.

Mn/DOT Traffic Signal Timing and Coordination Manual. (2002, June).Mn/DOT Office of Traffic Engineering and Intelligent Transportation Systems.

(2002). *Naztec Operations Manual for Closed-Loop Master Controller.* Operational Manual, Naztec Inc., Texas, USA.

Qian, H., Li, K., & Sun, J. (Oct., 2008). The Development and Enlightendment of Signalized Roundabout. *2008 International Conference on Intelligent Computation Technology and Automation,* (pp. 538-542). Changsha, China.

Ronghua, D. (2008, Oct.). Urban Traffic Coordination Control System Based on Multi-Agent Game. *2008 International Conference on Intelligent Computation Technology and Automation* (pp. 817-821). Changsha, China.

SYNCHRO-6.0. (2000). Traffic Signal Timing Software and Synchro User Guide. Albany, California, USA: Traffic Corporation.

TRANSYT-7F. (1988). *User's Manual, Release 6.* U.S. Department of Transportation, Federal Highway Administration, Washignton, D.C., USA.

Wang, F. (2005). Agent Based Control for Networked Traffic Management Systems. *IEEE Intelligent Systems, 20*(5), 92-96.

Wang, F. (2004). Computational Experiments of Behavior Analysis and Decision Evaluation in Complex Systems. *Journal of Systems Simulation. , 16*(5), 893-897.

Wang, F. (2007). Towards a Paradigm Shift in Social Computing: The ACP Approach. *IEEE Intelligent Systems, 22*(5), 65-67.

Wang, F. (2008, November/December). Towards a Revolution in Transportation Operations: AI for Complex Systems. *IEEE Intelligent Systems* (pp. 8-13).

Wang, Y., Yang, Z., & Guan, Q. (2008). Traffic Coordination and Control Model of Regional Boundary Based on Fuzzy Control. *Proc. 2008 International Conference on Intelligent Computation Technology and Automation* (pp. 946-950).

Zhiyong, L., Jin, Z., & al, e. (1999). A Multi-Phase Fuzzy Control Method used for Signal Intersection. *Information and Contro, 28,* 453-458.

This work was previously published in International Journal of Intelligent Information Technologies, Volume 5, Issue 3, edited by Vijayan Sugumaran, pp. 84-101, copyright 2009 by IGI Publishing (an imprint of IGI Global).

Chapter 13

Intelligent Information Integration:
Reclaiming the Intelligence

Naveen Ashish
University of California, Irvine, USA

David A. Maluf
NASA Ames Research Center, USA

ABSTRACT

The authors present their work in the conceptualization, design, implementation, and application of "lean" information integration systems. They present a new data integration approach based on a schema-less data management and integration paradigm, which enables developing cost-effective large scale integration applications. They have designed and developed a highly scalable, information-on-demand system called NETMARK, which facilitates information access and integration based on a theory of articulation management and a context sensitive paradigm. NETMARK has been widely deployed for managing, storing, and searching unstructured or semi-structured arbitrary XML and HTML information at the National Aeronautics Space Administration (NASA). In this paper the authors describe the theory, design and implementation of our system, present experimental benchmark evaluations, and validate our approach through real-world applications in the NASA enterprise.

INTRODUCTION

This article describes an approach to achieving scalable and cost-effective information integration for large-scale enterprise information management applications. Our work is motivated by requirements in the United States National Aeronautics and Space Administration (NASA) enterprise, where many information and process management applications demand access to, and integration of information from, large numbers of information sources (in some cases up to as many as 50 differ-

DOI: 10.4018/978-1-60960-595-7.ch013

ent sources), across multiple divisions, and with information of different kinds in different formats. An example is the application of assembling an agency level annual report that requires information such as project status, division updates, budget information, personnel progress, etc., from different data sources in different departments, divisions, and centers within NASA. By the early 2000s, when we had initiated this work, intelligent information integration research projects such as SIMS, TSIMMIS, HERMES, InfoMaster, Information Manifold (Halevy, Rajaraman, & Ordille, 2006; Halevy, 2003) to name a few, that were concerned with building data integration systems based on a *mediator* architecture had reached considerable maturity. We had solutions to challenging problems such as providing efficient query processing over multiple distributed data sources, schema mapping and integration tools, wrapper technology for legacy data sources and also Internet data sources, and technologies for entity resolution and matching across multiple sources. There were also data integration start-ups such as Nimble (Draper, Halevy, & Weld, 2001), Junglee, Mergent, and Fetch, and bigger companies such as IBM touting off-the-shelf data integration technology that could address the required information integration needs. While functionally meeting the requirements, none of these technologies could provide scalable and cost-effective information integration solutions for large scale applications. The basic problem was that such middleware based technology being offered became rather "heavy-weight" in the face of large-scale applications. A significant amount of investment was required in assembling new integration applications. Particularly the effort in managing models and meta-data i.e., in describing the many sources being integrated and also in providing an integrated view over the various sources, became formidable - to the extent that this became one of the key impediments to the widespread adoption of "Enterprise Information Integration" (EII) technology in general. A

testament to this is articulated in a review of EII technology (Halevy et al., 2005) where a CTO of (a then prominent) EII start-up observes *"A connected thread to this (key impediments for EII) is to address modeling and metadata management, which is the highest cost item in the first place"*.

The above problems carried over to the area of the "Semantic-Web" (Berneres-Lee, Hendler, & Lasilla, 2001) where most applications demand a heavy investment in creating various *ontologies* and further providing semantic linkages across such ontologies. The substantial effort and complexity in ontology creation and maintenance continues to be a major impediment in realizing practical semantic-web applications.

The lack of scalable and cost-efficient data integration technologies was however not because this was something that could not be achieved, but rather because the original vision of *intelligent information integration* had gone awry. The original vision of Intelligent Information Integration (or I[3]) [1] research sponsors such as DARPA [2] was a nimble and flexible approach where clients could at will select and integrate information from different sources in a manner suited to their particular applications and the complexity of each new application was confined to the application itself (Figure 1(a)). In practice however this degenerated to a situation where the complexity of *all* applications was added on to the mediation layer (Figure 1(b)). The reason this happened was due to some flawed assumptions about how enterprise data should be managed and integrated. These assumptions, along with our alternative solutions are presented below, namely:

- *"Data must always be stored and managed in DBMS systems"* Actually, requirements of applications vary greatly ranging from data that can well be stored in spreadsheets, to data that does indeed require DBMS storage.
- *"The database must always provide for and manage the structure and seman-*

Figure 1. Intelligent information integration (III)

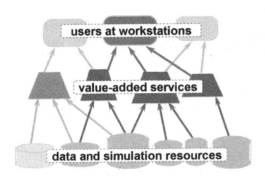 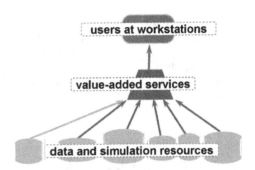

tics of the data through formal schemas" Alternatively, the "database" can be nothing more than intelligent storage. Data could be stored generically and imposition of structure and semantics (schema) may be done by clients as needed.

- *"Managing multiple schemas from several independent sources and interrelationships between them, i.e., "schema-chaos" is inevitable and unavoidable"* Alternatively, any imposition of schema can be done by the clients, as and when needed by applications.

The above philosophy in our opinion captures the *original* vision of intelligent information integration which is what we present here. The key technical contribution is the development of our NETMARK information integration and management system. NETMARK, as opposed to other data integration systems, is designed to be significantly easier to use, effectively support large-scale integration applications, and be cost-effective.

Our work in realizing such a system has involved all aspects of the spectrum from theoretical concepts to an efficient implementation to real-world deployment (Figure 2), and which is what we present in this article. In Section 2 we describe a theory of *flexible* knowledge sharing

which is the basis for making integration applications scalable. We also present a *context sensitive* query paradigm for querying enterprise data. In Section 3, we describe the architecture and system details on the NETMARK data management and integration system that is based on the above flexible knowledge sharing and context sensitive querying paradigm. In Section 4, we present performance evaluation results showing the significant advantage of NETMARK over other semi-structured and XML data management systems in the domain of enterprise data. Section 5 presents case studies of the use of NETMARK in actual NASA applications. Section 6 discusses related work and finally in Section 7 we describe ongoing work and a conclusion.

ARTICULATION MANAGEMENT AND ONTOLOGY ALGEBRA

Any information source is basically a knowledge source in more general terms. Thus information sharing and integration is, more generally, a problem of *knowledge* sharing and integration (Neches et al., 2001). The complexity of the knowledge can vary from something as simple as a list e.g., data in a single column, to a more structured associated representation such as a relational database to a richer representation such as an object-oriented

Figure 2. Theory to system realization to practice

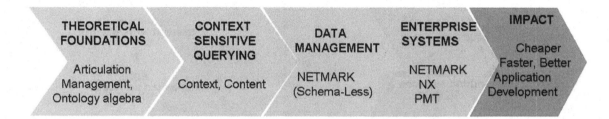

database, or a more complex knowledge representation such as LOOM (MacGregor, 1991), Classic (Brachman, McGuiness, Patel-Schneider & Borgida, 1991) or an ontology (Gruber, 1991). The theory of information integration is built upon general theories of how knowledge should be shared and integrated. This is achieved through 2 fundamental constructs: 1) Representation of knowledge – in each information source, as well as the "global" view of the integrated knowledge, and 2) *Articulations* – defining linkages across information sources and between any information source and the global view of knowledge (Collet, Huhns, and Shen, 1991). For instance the articulation associated with application A1 illustrated in Figure 3 states that the concept permanent-employees in the JPL information source *is the same* (ist) as the concept full-time-employees in the Ames information source. Literally all of the major information integration systems are based on the above constructs of describing and linking knowledge across sources, albeit the particular knowledge representation schemes may vary.

The existing approach is functional but not scalable to large applications because the knowledge and articulations in the mediator simply add on as new applications are added. Our approach generalizes the notion of articulations and provides a more flexible framework for the integration of knowledge; specifically, knowledge and articulations are incorporated on only an application specific and as-required basis. Consider a configureuration where an information integration

system i.e., mediator or other system provides integrated access to a certain (fixed) set of information sources. We refer to this as an integration configureuration; for instance, as illustrated in Figure 3 we have an integration configureuration across 3 information sources (in reality of course the number of sources is typically larger). An integration configureuration serves a number of applications, for instance the configureuration in Figure 3 serves 2 applications: A1 (say an employee payroll application), and A2 (say an agency wide project management application). The capabilities we incorporate in our approach are:

1.   The capability of selecting relevant articulations. For any integration configureuration, the existing approach is to maintain all articulations for all its associated applications at the mediator. We advocate a more scalable approach which is to maintain articulations associated with *clients* i.e., with applications (Maluf, & Tran, 2001). For example as shown in Figure 3, application A1 may require *only* the articulations between Ames and JPL budgets or application A2 may require *only* the articulations between JPL personnel and HQ personnel. Our framework provides the capability to create and select articulations that are relevant to a new application and on as as-required basis. Also, articulations are maintained at each client per application and not centralized for all

Figure 3. Knowledge representation and articulation

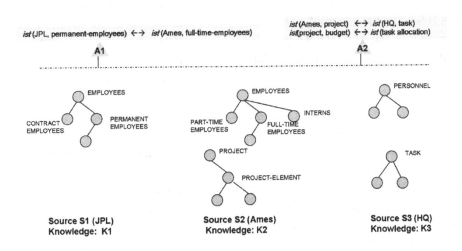

applications at the mediator. Quantitatively, if $a_1,\ldots,a_n$ are applications and if $N(a_i)$ is the number of articulation rules (an assessment of complexity) for application a_i, then with existing approaches we have a total of $\Sigma_{all\ i} N(a_i)$ articulation rules at the mediator, whereas with the application specific approach we have a maximum of $MAX(N(a_i))$ rules associated with any application. For large applications typically $MAX(N(a_i)) \ll \Sigma_{all\ i} N(a_i)$. Thus a large complexity at the mediator is now shifted to each client with the complexity at each client being much smaller than what would have been at the mediator.

2. **Algebra** for Knowledge Selection and Manipulation. In existing approaches the knowledge required for *all* applications is maintained at the mediator for a particular configureuration. Applications however require only the knowledge that is relevant to that application. For example application A1 in Figure 3 may really require only the knowledge of Budgets from the Ames and JPL sources and other available knowledge such as that related to Personnel may be irrelevant to this application.

We incorporate an ontology algebra (Mitra, & Wiederhold, 2004) that enables us to systematically select and combine and define the knowledge for each application. The primary concepts in the algebra are:

i. **Intersection:** The intersection is the first concept of the domain algebra because it allows the algebra to bring together two domains. It is equivalent to an and operator. The intersection of two knowledge sources (ontologies) results in an ontology that contains (only) the concepts that *have been articulated* as being the same concepts. For instance the intersection of the Employees ontologies from the JPL and Ames sources, i.e., that of K1 and K2, would be an ontology with the concept Permanent-Employee (or Full-Time Employee) as these are (all) the concepts that have been determined to be semantically the same by the articulation rules.

ii. **Union:** The union concept allows the algebra to bring together two domains to form a new one. It is equivalent to an OR operator. However the algebra lacks a formal approach to eliminate redundant knowledge that is common to both. This leads to several ways of establishing the unions of multiple domains. It is convenient to think of knowledge as not being redundant if not explicitly specified by the articulation rules. Similar to the natural join in relational databases, the domain algebra union joins knowledge sources when they link through shared articulation rules. The union is restricted only to the knowledge that the rules relate to. For instance, the union of the Employees ontologies in K1 and K2 would be the shared concept Permanent-Employee (or Full-Time Employee) *plus* all the other concepts such as Interns, Contract-Employees etc.

iii. **Difference:** The difference concept completes the algebra, and its presence compensates for the absence of negation. The difference operation retrieves the elements in domains that are NOT covered by another. Hence, the difference operation results in asymmetrical results and is not commutative.

The above algebraic constructs arm us with a systematic and comprehensive mechanism to select and manipulate knowledge specific to an application need. As with articulations, the complexity is thus confined to the application.

3. **Context:** The 3rd fundamental construct we use to bring scalability is the notion of context. The notion of context provides a way to define the validity of a sentence relative to a situation (Guha, 1991; Lenat, & Guha, 1991). Context logic provides the capability of translating encoding knowledge relative to its context and hence relates the knowledge to its domain. For instance one may specify the term "vision" as a query with the intent of the use of this term in the context of program management and future planning, or in an entirely different sense of vision related equipment for astronauts. We provide the ability of situating knowledge in particular contexts. When searching or querying information over large numbers of sources it is context, as we shall demonstrate, that is a simple but powerful enabler in achieving the relevance and scalability that is required.

We refer the reader to (Maluf, & Tran, 2001; Maluf, & Wiederhold, 1997) where the above summarized theories of articulation management and ontology algebra are discussed in more detail. The NETMARK system provides a practical implementation of these theories. Integration application developers have access to the algebra and articulation management capabilities described above so that they can develop scalable integration applications. Integration application users have access to a context sensitive querying capability that we now describe.

The notion of context is practically realized as a simple yet powerful primitive for querying and searching heterogeneous, distributed document collections in a context sensitive fashion in NETMARK. Any document is essentially comprised of various sections and sub-sections; for instance the project summary document in Figure 4 is comprised of a Project Summary section, and Background and Purpose sub-sections etc. These fragments such as the project summary section, background sub-section etc., are referred to as *context*. The information within the context, in this case the text within the fragment, is referred to as *content*.

These notions extend to documents beyond text documents; for instance, a spreadsheet is also comprised of different fragments such as cells, rows, and columns, and associated groups thereof; a (PowerPoint) slide comprises of a slide title (context) and the associated slides content (content), or an email message can be considered as comprising of the context of its subject and content as the actual email message text.

Figure 4. Document sections

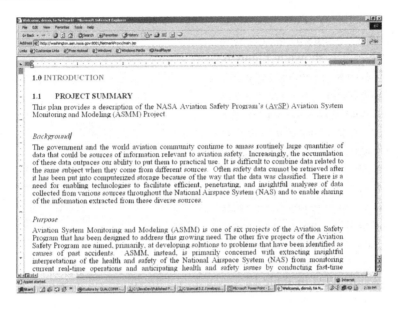

Querying

Such fragmentation into context and associated content permits context sensitive search and querying. A key capability is that of *context search*. A context search query, such as "Context=Procurement" [3] will return the content portion in the 'Procurement' sections (the text in the Procurement section) in *all* the documents in a document collection, as illustrated in Figure

6. A context query thus extracts the specified context (section) from all documents and returns it to the user. Users can also specifying *content searches*, which are essentially keyword searches that return all documents containing the specified search terms. For instance, a content query such as "Contract" will return all documents that contain the term 'Contract' anywhere in the document. One can also combine context and content searches, for instance a query such as "Context=Procurement

Figure 5. Context and content

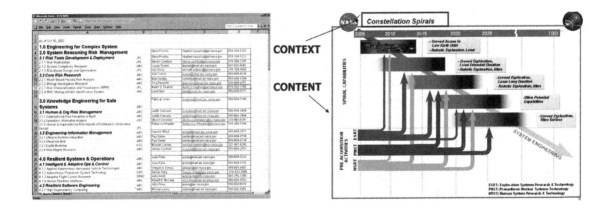

Comment&Content=Contract" returns the "Procurement" contexts (sections) of all documents where the term 'Contract' occurs *within the Procurement context (section)* as shown in Figure 6.

Essentially NETMARK provides keyword-based search over large (originally) unstructured document collections but with an added powerful capability of context sensitiveness, i.e., the user is able to ground the search terms in a particular context of interest. XDB Query is the query language for NETMARK. We will not go into the query syntax details here but the key features are that context and content search specifications are appended to a URL that is sent to NETMARK. An example of a formal XDB query, and also the XDB query syntax is illustrated in Table 1.

Context and content parameters can be specified in the query parameters of the XDB query. One can also specify additional parameters which can control the maximum number of documents returned, the (tree) depth of the result items, etc., and we refer to (Maluf, Bell, Ashish, Knight, & Tran, 2005) for details.

NETMARK: TECHNICAL DETAILS

We first briefly illustrate how integration applications are built using NETMARK and then describe the design and implementation of the NETMARK system itself. NETMARK is significantly different from other data integration systems in regards to how integration applications are assembled. Consider having to create an integration configureuration across the three information sources illustrated in Figure 3. We first create a unique resource, a URI, corresponding to this configureuration. This URI corresponds to the virtual integrated source across all three sources. Next, we load information i.e., enterprise documents corresponding to employee, project etc information into this URI. This is done by a simple drag-and-drop desktop operation at each source (JPL, Ames, and HQ) where the desktop folder is actually a remote

Figure 6. Context sensitive querying and retrieval

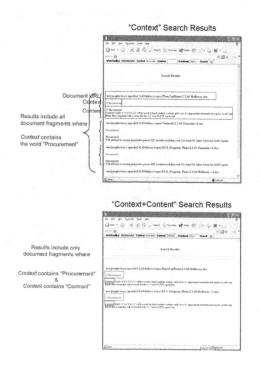

desktop folder corresponding to the URI. Now the information across all three sources can be simply queried by issuing XDB queries to the integration URI. For example a context query requesting Employee fragments will return Employee fragments in data (originally) from both JPL and Ames sources. Should any articulations be required, they are created and attached to the specific application as needed. We refer to the system documentation [4] for more details.

NETMARK System Design

As a data management engine, NETMARK is based on a "schema-less" paradigm that provides high efficiency and throughput in retrieval. Before describing the architecture and technical details we wish to highlight some additional features that we have incorporated that address key tasks in the information pipeline. These are:

Table 1. XDB query syntax

Server location	Keyword	Query parameters
http://larry.aen.nasa.gov:32080/xdbquery/context=BudgetComment&content=Ames		

```
https://<server_address>/xslt/xdbquery/{[context=<contextkeys>]|[&conte
nt=<content_keys>]}| [&scope=<relative_url_to_folder>]|[&syntax={html,
xml,ascii}]|[&sxslt=<relative_url_to_xslt_file>]
```

1. Capability of ingesting information "as-is". No data preparation or mark-up whatsoever is required from any user that wishes to provide data for incorporation and integration into NETMARK. Enterprise data in a multitude of formats ranging from Word or PDF documents to Excel spreadsheets to PowerPoint presentations is provided to the system as-is, and the system then structures the data as we shall describe shortly.

2. Information composition and presentation capabilities. XDB Query also provides for associating XSLT style-sheets with a query, the query result thus gets presented in the desired format. Integrated data collected from multiple sources is often composed (back) into common business, documents; for instance project information integration from multiple divisions and departments would be composed and presented in business document format such as report or a slide presentation. Commonly used business documents can thus be used as the *interface* to integrated data.

The NETMARK system architecture is outlined in Figure 7. All data is (ultimately) stored in a single data store which is an XML data store, implemented on top of an underlying relational database.

Clients, that is data producers and providers and data consumers (or both) access NETMARK through a Web interface, that is illustrated in the examples in Section 2. Any data, such as say a folder of several PDF or Excel documents can be provided to NETMARK by a simple drag and drop operation (into a "NETMARK Folder" on the user's desktop). The NETMARK Daemon and the SGML Parser provide functionality for loading data (documents) into NETMARK, that is a continual process (the daemon) reads in any new documents inserted into a NETMARK folder and then invokes an SGML parser for structuring it and loading it into the NETMARK XML data store.

Data Storage

Data with varying degrees of structure ranging from data that originates from a well structured database to unstructured data that is in documents and spreadsheets, is integrated into and supported by NETMARK. For data that is unstructured, some structure is automatically imposed based on fragments, sections and sub-sections in the documents. The approach to data storage is to keep the underlying representation simple, yet expressive enough to store fragment and section oriented properties and relationships in documents.

Figure 7. NETMARK system architecture

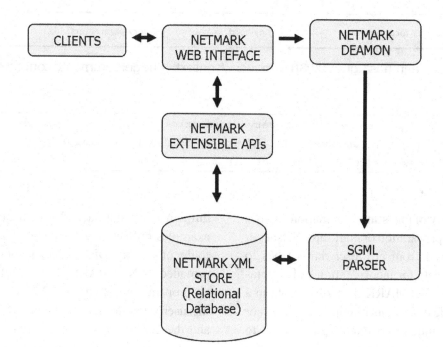

Data Fragmentation, Structuring, and Storage

Any data to be stored into NETMARK, whether originally structured or unstructured, is first fragmented into sections and sub-sections which are then marked in XML, the XML data is then stored as a tree of "nodes", finally the nodes are stored in relational tables. This pipeline is illustrated in Figure 8, where we begin with the (originally unstructured) document in Figure 4. As a first step this is fragmented into different sections and sub-sections and marked up in XML as shown in Figure 8.

Such fragmentation is done by a suite of converters that are part of NETMARK. These converters have been built on top of (text extraction) frameworks such as Apache Jakarta POI [5] and JPedal for PDF [6] and employ heuristics to automatically fragment an unstructured document into various sections, which are then marked up in XML. We next introduce the concept of a *node*,

the fundamental unit of data storage in the system. A node essentially captures the information in each context and content fragment in the document. Thus there is a node corresponding to *each* context or content fragment in the document. Every node carries in it certain information as described in Table 2 (a). As we see, this is information such as a unique identifier for that node, or a type corresponding to the particular fragment it is capturing; for instance, nodes of type 'Text' typically capture information in content fragments and nodes of type 'Context' capture information in context fragments.

Table 2 (b) illustrates a node of type 'Text' corresponding to a particular content fragment (encircled in Figure 8) where we see that the NodeData element of the node contains the text in that fragment.

Hierarchical parent-child relationships are also maintained across certain nodes, specifically the following relationships are maintained:

Figure 8. Data storage pipeline

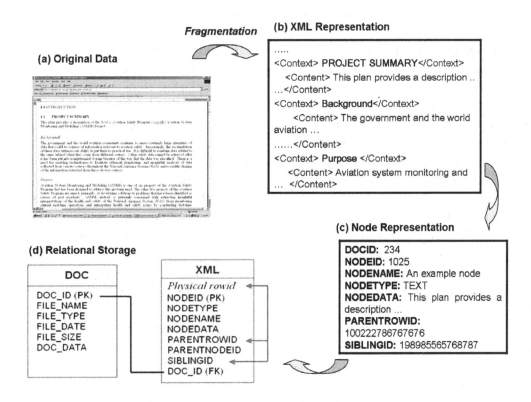

1. Any node of type 'Text' i.e., capturing a content fragment is placed as a *left* child of the node capturing its *corresponding* context.
2. Any node of type 'Context' is placed as a *right* child of the node corresponding to a context *immediately preceding* it in the document.

For the running example, some of the nodes and their parent-child relationships according to (i) and (ii) above are illustrated in Figure 9, the sharp-

Table 2. Nodes

DOCID: *A unique number assigned to the document.* **NODEID:** *A unique identifier for each node.* **NODENAME:** *A descriptive name for the node* **NODETYPE:** *Identifies the node type, which is one of a small list of mutually exclusive node types.* **NODEDATA:** *The actual content of the node.* **PARENTROWID:** *Contains the ROWID of a parent of the node (if any).* **SIBLINGID:** *Contains the ROWID of a sibling of the node (if any).*
DOCID: 234 **NODEID:** 1025 **NODENAME:** An example node **NODETYPE:** TEXT **NODEDATA:** This plan provides the … **PARENTROWID:** 100222786767676 **SIBLINGID:** 198985565768787

edged boxes representing context nodes and the rounded-edge boxes representing content nodes.

The rationale for this organization is that we wish to maintain adequate structuring information such as the association of content with particular context, and at least immediate precedence relationships amongst different contexts; however, we also wish to keep the hierarchy of relationships simple. In the nodes these relationships are captured by the 'ParentRowID' and 'SiblingID' elements which maintain pointer relationships across nodes.

XML data is ultimately stored as either tree-structures in XML databases that provide "native" XML implementations (Jagadish et al., 2002), or in an underlying relational database. In the latter approach, a variety of "shredding" algorithms exist to meaningfully convert the XML data to underlying relational tables. The number of such underlying relational tables and complexity of organization is dependent on the actual XML data in existing approaches. However in NETMARK we use just *two* relational tables to represent and store the data in *any* semi-structured document: these tables remain the same for any document or application. This is possible given the restrictions we have made on the hierarchical relationships

across nodes above. As shown in Figure 8, these two tables are called "XML" and "DOC": the XML table contains all the nodes, and the DOC table contains information about all the documents.

To summarize the above information processing pipeline from unstructured input data to storage in relational tables, we (i) Fragment an unstructured document into various sections and sub-sections and convert it to XML, this results in context and content blocks defined in XML, (ii) Create nodes corresponding to each context or content block, (iii) Capture hierarchical structure, i.e., parent-child relationships between nodes (including that of associated context and content) through pointers across nodes, and (iv) Store node and document information in two relational tables, namely XML and DOC.

Efficient Query Processing

Given an XDB query, query processing in NET-MARK basically involves locating the relevant nodes and composing the requested result form these nodes. We have exploited the availability of the RowID which is a data type available in Oracle 9i and later versions which stores either *physical* or *logical* row addresses or each record in a table. A physical RowID is the actual (absolute) address of a record through which we have the fastest access to any record in a table, with a guaranteed single-block read access. We refer to (Maluf, & Tran, 2003) for more details on the RowID format details but would like to emphasize here that the use of RowIDs is a key to efficient query processing in NETMARK. The physical RowID based technology is now patented (Gawdiak et al., 2005).

Context and content search is performed by first querying the text index for the search key. Several matching nodes may be returned. For each such node we traverse the tree structure (through the node's parent or sibling nodes) until the first

Figure 9. Tree structure

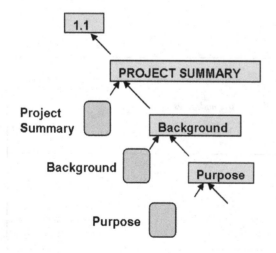

context node is found. Once a particular Context is found, traversing back down the tree structure via the sibling node retrieves the corresponding *content* text. The search result is then rendered and displayed appropriately. Accessing a record based on its physical address RowID provides an efficient, constant access time C (machine dependent; normally in the millisecond range) that is independent of the number of records or nodes in the database and regardless of maximum node depth within a node structure. The time to respond to a context or content query is thus approximately proportional to log(N) (first search time) plus a sum of the Cs for each successive search where N is the number of records or nodes.

The Schema-Less Aspect

A traditional (an object-relational) mapping from XML to a relational database schema models the data within the XML documents as a tree of objects that are specific to the data in the document. In this model, element type with attributes, content, or complex element types are generally modeled as classes. Element types with parsed character data (PCDATA) and attributes are modeled as scalar types. This model is then mapped to the relational database using traditional object-relational mapping techniques or via SQL3 object views. Therefore, classes are mapped to tables, scalar types are mapped to columns, and object-valued properties are mapped to key pairs (both primary and foreign). This mapping model is limited since the object tree structure is different for each set of XML documents. On the other hand, the NETMARK SGML parser models the document itself (similar to the DOM), and its object tree structure is the *same* for all XML documents. Thus, NETMARK is designed to be *independent* of any particular XML document schemas and is termed to be "*schema-less*".

PERFORMANCE

For any data management system, we want an assessment of its performance in query evaluation in absolute terms as well vis-à-vis other systems in its category. As emphasized, NETMARK is a really a semi-structured data management and integration system targeted towards context and content kinds of queries and with support for XML as a representation and exchange mechanism. Despite this distinction, carefully designed (and now considerably widely used) *benchmarks* for XML query processing evaluation deserve consideration for the evaluation of NETMARK. We have employed XMARK (Schmidt et al, 2001) in particular, albeit with considerations about some aspects. First, the XMARK framework generates test data in the form of an XML document in a domain of transactions, people, and auctions using a data generator called "*xmlgen*". Such generated data is indeed reasonable for evaluating NETMARK as it is representative of the kind of semi-structured data that NETMARK is designed to manage. Next however is the issue of test queries: XMARK includes a suite of 19 test queries, Q1-Q19, that are designed to evaluate a whole range of XML querying aspects ranging from aggregation to structural joins to handling of complex path expressions. NETMARK however is not designed or even intended to support such capabilities. We thus pick a relevant subset of these test queries, specifically ones that directly correspond to contextual search that NETMARK does support. We have also some added some additional contextual search test queries, at various levels of depth in the XMARK test document, for more exhaustive test coverage.

The evaluation below presents query response times for queries that correspond to context and content kinds of queries. In addition to absolute numbers, we also provide a comparison with (Oracle) Berkeley DB (which we refer to as BXML), an XML over relational system, under the same configureuration. The results are provided for a single XML document with sizes ranging from 50MB all the way to 1GB. These evaluations were conducted on an i686 machine with 4 Intel Pentium (R) 2.8 GHz processors running GNU/ Linux. We refer to (Schmidt et al., 2001) for details about the XMARK benchmark and associated data generator and test query suite.

Performance Results

We selected a subset of queries from the original test queries suite of the XMARK benchmark and also added some queries of our own for more exhaustive testing of relevant aspects. These queries are listed in Table 3. We provide the syntax for expressing these queries in both XDB Query (used for NETMARK) and XQuery (that we use for BXML).

There are a few points we wish to highlight regards the selection of queries in Table 3:

1. As mentioned above, queries in the original XMARK benchmark that relate to functionality not in XDB Query (such as complex path expressions, joins, aggregation, etc.) are not selected. We have thus selected only queries Q1, Q6, and Q14 from the original XMARK test suite.

2. Some additional queries relating to context and content have been added (NQ1-NQ4) that perform context and content searches on XML elements at various depths.

3. In XDB query for a content match we only provide the semantics of containment of which an exact match is a special case. This is different from XQuery where we make a distinction between requiring an element to exactly match a given string vs the element containing that string. Thus for the contextual search queries NQ3 and NQ4 we have considered both interpretations (i.e., exact match and containment) when expressing them in XQuery (NQ3' and NQ4')

Table 4 provides the query response times for the test queries (Table 3) for both BXML and NETMARK for varying benchmark document sizes under the same configureuration. There are two important observations to be made: (i) For context only queries, the performance of NET-MARK appears to be comparable to that of BXML; for this class of queries NETMARK appears to perform "as good as" a representative XML database system. (ii) For context+content queries (i.e., XQuery queries involving a text search within an XML element) NETMARK is significantly faster

Table 3. Test queries

Query	XDB Query	Equivalent XQuery	Result Size Ŧ
Q1	context=id & content=person0	/site/people/person/[@id='person0']	1
Q6	context=item	/continents//items/String()	21750
Q14	content=gold	//site[dbxml:contains(./*, "gold")]	1
NQ1	context=country	//country/string()	12716
NQ2	context=payment	//payment/string()	21750
NQ3	context=country & content=Tonga	//country[dbxml:contains(., "Tonga")]	12
NQ4	context=payment & content=cash	//payment[dbxml:contains(., "cash")]	10933
NQ3'	context=country & content=Tonga	//country[. = "Tonga"]	12
NQ4'	context= payment & content= Cash	//payment[. = "Cash"]	10933

Ŧ Number of XML elements in 100M XML document

compared to BXML, in fact as much as 25 times faster in some cases as demonstrated.

What we can claim to have achieved with NETMARK is a system that for the kinds of queries it is designed to support (context and content) is, depending on the type of query, comparable to or significantly faster than state-of-the-art XML database systems. Note also that such performance has been achieved with relatively much simpler query processing algorithms given the simple schema-less nature of the underlying relational database. Note also that this is just a comparison of the semi-structured and XML aspects of the system, NETMARK also provides data integration capabilities which other systems do not.

In Figure 10 we demonstrate how the query response time for NETMARK scales with document size for the various test queries (divided into 2 sets based on the actual response times). There is one other aspect to performance in NETMARK besides query response times, which is the time taken for loading documents into the system. Note that NETMARK automatically fragments and structures input data before storing it in the system and for large applications it is important that this document loading be efficient. Our earlier

work (Maluf et al., 2005) benchmarks this aspect as well demonstrating high-throughput rates for loading new input documents into the system.

APPLICATION, CASE-STUDIES

A summary of the various systems and applications in which NETMARK has been deployed at NASA is presented in Table 5.

The table summarizes the many applications and wide adoption of the system by the NASA enterprise. As the table illustrates, NETMARK has been used as-is, or as the integration engine in other applications with broader capabilities, namely "NX" and "PMT". NETMARK and the systems it is part of, have had a significant positive impact on information management in the NASA enterprise. As an example of the benefit and impact, prior to the adoption of NETMARK one of the annual project reports for NASA alone took 360 man hours per month to capture and collate necessary information from different sources to compile the report. This manual process also resulted in a high rate of transcription errors, with as much as a 40% discrepancy rate for project milestones in some cases. With the use of

Table 4. Performance results

	50M		100M		250M		500M		1G	
	BXML	**NM**	**BXML**	**NM**	**BXML**	**NM**	**BXML**	**NM**	**BXML**	**NM**
Q1	0.9	0.08*	2.3	0.91	4.7	2.4	9.2	6.9	23.1	11.3
Q6	28.1	24.9	70.0	65.1	130.3	108.1	280.4	276.5	584.3	400.1
Q14	21.3	0.01	40.2	0.02	240.0	0.32	400.1	0.7	1198.1	1.2
NQ1	25.5	21.0	60.2	61	102.1	105.4	233.4	300.1	541.4	721.0
NQ2	23.4	18.1	30.9	29	110.3	109.7	278.4	236.4	530.2	501.9
NQ3	12.2	0.1	23.0	0.83	105.6	3.8	200.6	8.4	387.2	14.4
NQ4	11.1	2.9	21.7	3.4	97.0	6.7	199.5	13.3	360.3	23.9
NQ3'	9.3	0.1	21.1	0.83	79.3†	3.8	200.1	8.4	312.4	14.4
NQ4'	7.9	2.9	14.4	3.4	88.3	6.7	151.6	13.3	287.4	23.9

* All response times are in seconds.

† No response for over 1 hour.

Table 5. System applications

System or Application	Tasks	Benefit to NASA Organization	Adoption
NETMARK	Analysis of mishap reports for aviation safety analysis.	Just 2 man days for set up and assembly. Analysis capability over thousands of unstructured reports.	NETMARK is licensed to NASA, Black Tulip, XEROX, the State of Pennsylvania, NXAR Inc., Jumpstart Inc., and UCI.
NX. Integration of NET-MARK with XEROX Docushare.	International Space Station (ISS) to mine safety assurance information. NASA Program Analysis and Evaluation (PA&E).	Content management capabilities.	Most NASA centers including ARC, LaRC, GSFC, Dryden, JPL, JSC and NASA Headquarters.
PMT. NASA Business Intelligence Tool with NETMARK engine	Many NASA project reporting, financial reporting, and inventory database applications.	End-to-end business reporting tool for NASA enterprise.	NASA Chief Engineer's Office and most Mission Directorates.

NETMARK and PMT, the effort was reduced to 52 person hours each month, with the discrepancies being virtually eliminated. We refer to (Maluf, & Tran, 2008; Maluf, 2007; Maluf, 2006) for details of many other applications and their impact, the lack of space prevents us from describing them here.

RELATED WORK

As a comprehensive system with many aspects, the NETMARK work relates to work in several areas such as knowledge sharing, XML data management and query processing, XML and text search, and information integration technology in general. All of the above have been actively investigated by academia and industry. In comparison, the distinguishing features of our work can be summarized in the following contributions.

1. The flexible and scalable approach provided to knowledge sharing and integration. Our approach has made knowledge sharing and management for information integration more scalable, by keeping it application specific and making it a client (application) responsibility as opposed to a mediator responsibility. Articulation management and an ontology algebra are the formal tools provided to do this. The merits and in fact necessity of a significantly more flexible data integration methodology, particularly with regards to managing and linking schemas, is recognized by other recent large scale data integration efforts such as (Madhavan et al., 2007). Their PayAsYouGo approach advocates moving from the more rigid traditional data integration approach of a committed global schema to a more flexible approach where multiple "schematas" are permitted describing various sources and clusters of such schemata are formed in response to particular applications.

2. A significantly optimized data management system based on a schema-less approach. Implementing XML over relational systems has been an active area of research. In all such work the underlying relational representations are document dependent and complex as they must capture the full XML structure of the document. Efficient query processing of XML queries over these underlying relational tables is then a challenge, for which there is now an impressive array of efficient algorithms and solutions (Grust, Rittinger, & Teubner, 2007; Georgiadis, & Vassalos, 2007; Bonca et al, 2006) for efficiently

Figure 10. Query performance with document size

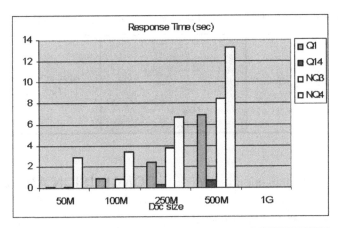

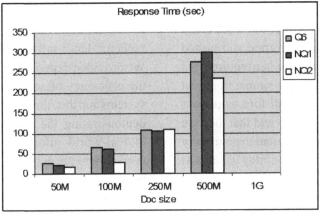

processing even rather complex queries. In NETMARK, by keeping the document structuring of enterprise data adequate yet simple, we are able to translate the XML representations to a document independent simple representation in just 2 tables. Coupled with relational database features (i.e., the availability of physical RowID s) we are able to provide very efficient query processing for XDB queries with a relatively much simpler query processing algorithm. The performance evaluation results presented validate the significantly better performance NETMARK has as compared to other XML database systems. The area of full-text search in XML (Li, Yu, and Jagadish,

2008; Xu, & Papakonstantinou 2008) has also been investigated actively in recent years. Many solutions have also advocated and developed capabilities for XML text search in context. Work such as (Li, Yu, and Jagadish, 2008) recognizes that users may in fact not have complete knowledge of the XML schema but still wish to perform text based search. They provide an approach to answering text search queries meaningfully, in appropriate XML context, using the notion of a *meaningful query focus* that provides better results as compared to a traditional least-common-ancestor (LCA) approach. Again, given our simpler representation we are able to provide high-performance text

Figure 11. Business documents to business documents

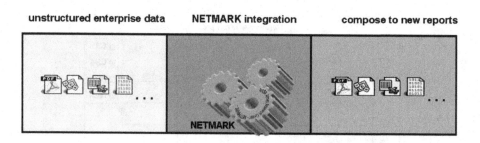

searches in context (although our notion of context is in some sense more straightforward than as investigated for more nested XML). At this point we should perhaps emphasize that the spirit of our work is not that we should not use formal and nested structuring of documents when required, but rather that structuring in a simple fragment oriented manner is adequate for a large class on enterprise applications and that then we should use simpler representations and query mechanisms given the scalability benefits as a result.

3. An end-to-end information integration system with easy desktop drag-and-drop and Web-based information ingest and retrieval capabilities. While this is mostly an engineering issue, our experience is that such capabilities have helped alleviate the 'resistance' on behalf of an owner of a particular information source to provide data to and join an integration configureuration. Such resistance is often largely due to additional investment required in brining his or her particular data to a right or agreed upon format before integration which in our case is addressed by the system. In addition, the information composition capabilities have further providing cost and time savings in that integrated data can quickly be composed into reports and presentations that it is ultimately intended for (Figure 11).

CONCLUSION AND CURRENT WORK

In this article we described the conceptualization, design, and development of the NETMARK "schema-less" information integration system. We provided experimental results demonstrating the efficiency of schema-less data management systems and then through application case-studies demonstrating the effectiveness of the system in real-world information integration applications. There are active areas of ongoing work in both research and application of the system. In research and system development we are currently investigating incorporating secure access features in the system. An equal emphasis in this effort is on the application of NETMARK in real-world applications. Beyond domains such as project and personnel management, aviation safety data management etc., that we have applied the system to in NASA, we have begun investigating applicability in other significantly different domains such as medical informatics. In fact the integration requirements in the medical and clinical informatics domain appear to pose many of the very problems that NETMARK is designed to efficiently address. As exemplified in (Anderson et al., 2007), clinical data too is present in many different kinds of sources ranging from databases to text files (notes) to spreadsheets and applications often require integrated access to all the data. The UC-Irvine Center for Medical Informatics has recently obtained a NETMARK installation and is conducting a pilot information integration study with the system in this domain. Finally, we wish to re-emphasize our commitment to making this available as open-source software for research and/or non-profit use and welcome queries regards getting a license for the software.

REFERENCES

Anderson, N., Lee, E., Brockenbrough, J. S., Minie, M., Fuller, S., Brinkley, J., & Tarczy-Hornoch, P. (2007). Issues in Biomedical Research Data Management and Analysis: Needs and Barriers. *Journal of the American Medical Informatics Association, 14*(4). doi:10.1197/jamia.M2114

Berners-Lee, T., Hendler, J., & Lasilla, O. (2001). The Semantic-Web. *Scientific American.*

Boncz, P. A., Grust, T., Keulen, M., Manegold, S., Rittinger, J., & Teubner, J. (2006). MonetDB/XQuery: a fast XQuery processor powered by a relational engine. *ACM SIGMOD Conference* (pp. 479-490).

Botev, B., & Shanmugasundaram, J. (2005). *Context-Sensitive Keyword Search and Ranking for XML* (pp. 115–120). Proceedings of WebDB.

Brachman, R. J., McGuinness, D. L., Patel-Schneider, P. F., & Borgida, A. (1991). "Reducing" CLASSIC to Practice: Knowledge Representation Theory Meets Reality. *Artificial Intelligence, 114*(1-2), 203–237. doi:10.1016/S0004-3702(99)00078-8

Collet, C., Huhns, M., & Shen, W. (1991). Resource Integration Using a Large Knowledge Base in Carnot. *IEEE Computer, 12*(24).

Draper, D., Halevy, A. Y., & Weld, D. S. (2001). The Nimble XML Data Integration System. *Proceedings of ICDE* (pp. 155-160).

Funderbunk, J. E., Kiernan, G., Shanmugasundaram, J., Shekita, E., & Wei, C. (2002). XTABLES: Bridging relational technology and XML. *IBM Systems Journal, 41*, 616–641. doi:10.1147/sj.414.0616

Gawdiak, Y., La, T., Lin, Y., Maluf, D. A., & Tran, P. (2005). US Patent **6,968,338,** Extensible database framework for management of unstructured and semi-structured documents, Awarded Nov 22, 2005

Georgiadis, H., & Vassalos, V. (2007). Xpath on Steroids: Exploiting Relational Engines for Xpath Performance *ACM SIGMOD Conference* (pp. 317-328).

Gruber, T. R. (1991). The Role of Common Ontology in Achieving Sharable, Reusable Knowledge Bases. *Proceedings of Second International Conference on Knowledge Representation and Reasoning.*

Grust, T., Rittinger, J., & Teubner, J. (2007). Why off-the-shelf RDBMSs are better at XPath than you might expect. *ACM SIGMOD Conference* (pp. 949-958).

Guha, R. V. (1991). *Context: A Formalization and Some Applications.* Doctoral Dissertation, Stanford University.

Halevy, A. Y. (2003). Data Integration: A Status Report. *Proceedings of BTW* (pp. 24-29).

Halevy, A. Y., Ashish, N., Bitton, D., Carey, M. J., Draper, D., Pollock, J., et al. (2005). Enterprise information integration: successes, challenges and controversies. *SIGMOD Conference* (pp. 778-787).

Halevy, A. Y., Rajaraman, A., & Ordille, J. (2006). Data Integration: The Teenage Years. *Proceedings of VLDB.*

Ives, Z., Halevy, A., & Weld, D. (2002). An XML query engine for network-bound data. *The VLDB Journal, 11*, 380–402. doi:10.1007/s00778-002-0078-5

Jagadish, H. V., Khalifa, S., Chapman, A., Lakshmanan, L., Nierman, A., & Paparizos, S. TIMBER: A Native XML Database. *The VLDB Journal, 11*, 274–291. doi:10.1007/s00778-002-0081-x

Lenat, D., & Guha, R. V. (1991). The Evolution of CycL, The Cyc Representation language. *Special Issue on Implemented Knowledge Representation System, ACM SIGART, 2*(3), 84–87.

Li, Y., Yu, C., & Jagadish, H. V. (2008). Enabling Schema-Free XQuery with Meaningful Query Focus. *The VLDB Journal, 17*(3). doi:10.1007/s00778-006-0003-4

Litwin, W., Mark, L., & Roussopoulos, N. (1990). Interoperability of Multiple Autonomous Databases. *ACM Computing Surveys, 22*(3), 267–293. doi:10.1145/96602.96608

MacGregor, R. M. (1991). Inside the LOOM Description Classifier. *SIGART Bulletin, 2*(3), 88–92. doi:10.1145/122296.122309

Madhavan, J., Cohen, S., Dong, X. L., Halevy, A. Y., Jeffery, S. R., Ko, D., & Yu, C. (2007). Web-Scale Data Integration: You can afford to Pay as You Go. *CIDR Conference* (pp. 342-350).

Maluf, D., & Tran, P. (2003). NETMARK: A Schema-Less Extension for Relational Databases for Managing Semi-structured Data Dynamically. *ISMIS Conference* (pp. 231-241).

Maluf, D. A. (2006). Knowledge Mining Application in an IVHM Testbed. *IEEE Aerospace Conference*, Montana.

Maluf, D. A. (2007). Searching Across the International Space Station. *IEEE Aerospace Conference*, Montana.

Maluf, D. A., Bell, D. G., Ashish, N., Knight, K., & Tran, P. B. (2005). Semi-Structured Data Management in the Enterprise: A Nimble, High-Throughput, and Scalable Approach. *Proceedings of IDEAS Conference* (pp. 115-124).

Maluf, D. A., Bell, D. G., Ashish, N., Putz, P., & Gawdiak, Y. (2006). Business Intelligence in Large Organizations: Integrating Which Data? *ISMIS Conference* (pp. 248-257).

Maluf, D. A., & Tran, P. (2001). Articulation Management for Intelligent Integration of Information. *IEEE Transactions on Systems Man and Cybernetics.*

Maluf, D. A., & Tran, P. (2008). Managing Unstructured Data With Structured Legacy Systems. *IEEE Aerospace Conference*, Montana.

Maluf, D. A., & Wiederhold, G. (1997). Abstraction of Representation for Interoperation, *Tenth International Symposium on Methodologies for Intelligent Systems*, Lecture Notes in Computer Science (pp. 441-455). Springer Verlag.

McCarthy, J. (1993). Notes on Formalizing Context. *Proceedings of the Thirteenth International Joint Conference on Artificial Intelligence.*

Mitra, P., & Wiederhold, G. (2004). *An Ontology-Composition Algebra* (pp. 93–116). Handbook on Ontologies.

Neches, R., Fikes, R., Finin, T., Gruber, T., Patil, R., Senator, T., & Swartout, W. R. (1991). Enabling Technology for Knowledge Sharing. *AI Magazine, 12*(3), 36–55.

Paparizos, S., Al-Khalifa, S., Chapman, A., Jagadish, H. V., Lakshmanan, L. V., Nierman, A., et al. (2003). TIMBER: A Native System for Querying XML. *SIGMOD Conference.*

Schmidt, A. R., Waas, F., Ketersen, M. L., Florescu, D., Manolescu, I., Carey, M. J., & Busse, R. (2001). *The XML Benchmark Project*. CWI.

Vagena, Z., Moro, M., & Tsotras, V. (2004). Twig Query Processing over Graph Structured XML Data. *Workshop on Web and Databases WebDB*, Paris, France.

Xalan, Web site: http://xml.apache.org/xalan-j/.

XML. Web site: http://www.w3.org/XML/.

Xu, Y., & Papakonstantinou, Y. (2008). Efficient LCA based keyword search in XML data. *Proceedings of EDBT* (pp. 535-546).

Docushare, Web site: http://docushare.xerox.com/ds/.

Oracle, Web site: http://www.oracle.com

MySQL. Web site: http://www.mysql.com

Apache, Web site: http://www.apache.org

WebDAV. Web site: http://www.webdav.org

ENDNOTES

[1] A US government agency sponsored R&D program in data integration.

[2] The United States Defense Advanced Research Projects Agency.

[3] We are using an informal syntax for illustration and will describe the actual query syntax shortly

[4] Technical documentation on the NETMARK system and API is available from the authors upon request.

[5] http://jakarta.apache.org/poi/

[6] http://www.jpedal.org/

This work was previously published in International Journal of Intelligent Information Technologies, Volume 5, Issue 3, edited by Vijayan Sugumaran, pp. 28-54, copyright 2009 by IGI Publishing (an imprint of IGI Global).

Chapter 14

Association Analysis of Alumni Giving:
A Formal Concept Analysis

Ray R. Hashemi
Armstrong Atlantic State University, USA

Louis A. Le Blanc
Berry College, USA

Azita A. Bahrami
Armstrong Atlantic State University, USA

Mahmood Bahar
Tabiet Moallem University, Iran

Bryan Traywick
Armstrong Atlantic State University, USA

ABSTRACT

A large sample (initially 33,000 cases representing a ten percent trial) of university alumni giving records for a large public university in the southwestern United States is analyzed by Formal Concept Analysis. This likely represents the initial attempt to perform analysis of such data by means of a machine learning technique. The variables employed include the gift amount to the university foundation as well as traditional demographic variables such as year of graduation, gender, ethnicity, marital status, etc. The foundation serves as one of the institution's non-profit, fund-raising organizations. It pursues substantial gifts that are designated for the educational or leadership programs of the giver's choice. Although they process gifts of all sizes, the foundation's focus is on major gifts and endowments. Association Analysis of the given dataset is a two-step process. In the first step, FCA is applied to identify concepts and their relationships and in the second step, the association rules are defined for each concept. The hypothesis examined in this paper is that the generosity of alumni toward his/her alma mater can be predicted using association rules obtained by applying the Formal Concept Analysis approach.

DOI: 10.4018/978-1-60960-595-7.ch014

INTRODUCTION

Data mining, extracting meaningful patterns from large quantities of information, is useful in any field where there are large quantities of data and something worth knowing (i.e., the resulting knowledge is worth more than the cost to discover). Data mining can be employed to identify the most valuable prospects, like those alumni most likely to give to their alma mater. Through the application of data mining techniques (Berry and Linhoff, 2000; Han and Kanbar, 2005), university fund raisers can potentially turn the myriad of alumni records into some sort of coherent picture.

Research Setting

A large sample (about 33,000 cases) from a very large public, land-grant university's alumni giving records was analyzed. Each state has such a land-grant institution, typically with extensive academic and research programs in agriculture and engineering. The university foundation (UF) serves as one of the institution's non-profit, fundraising organizations. The UF pursues substantial gifts that are designated for the educational or leadership programs of the benefactor's choice. Although they process gifts of all sizes, the focus of the UF is on major gifts and endowments as well as managing the donated assets for the university.

Relevant Research on Philanthropic Giving

Charitable and philanthropic organizations, including university fund raising departments, face increasing pressure to more effectively employ a variety of analytical techniques (Brown, 2004). Potential donor identification may provide one such tool (Shelley and Polonsky, 2002). As applied in other public sector or not-for-profit agencies (Johnson and Garbarino, 2001; Todd and Lawson, 2001; Wymer, 2003), data mining can assist college and university development officials in identify-

ing potential donors and help define what best to communicate to potential donors.

Research studies report various methodologies and techniques to identify giving behavior for collegiate financial development. Willemain et al. (1994) employed a general linear model to predict university alumni giving. Lindahl and Winship (1992) used logit analysis to predict rare events such as gifts over $100,000. Clotfelter (2001) utilized basic descriptive statistics (e.g., means, percentages) to portray survey results from two generations of alumni giving.

With somewhat more novel quantitative approaches, Drye et al. (2001) suggested survival analysis (based upon logarithmic charts) to better identify the most regular supporters and those most likely to repeat their support. Key (2001) recommended probit regression for building a response model to identify individuals most likely to make a major, capital or planned gift.

Two other related papers have suggested market segmentation analysis for identifying groups of potential donors in the nonprofit sector. Ewing et al. (2002) using market segmentation for identifying voluntary labor pools for nonprofit agencies. Connoly and Blanchette (1986) applied survey research and a multivariate statistical technique (i.e., discriminant analysis) to categorize individual university alumni who could be solicited for annual or major gifts.

Relevant Research on Analytical Techniques

After its introduction by Wille (1982), numerous recent applications of Formal Concept Analysis have appeared in the computing literature. FCA has been successfully applied to many different fields such as medicine and psychology, musicology, linguistic databases, library and information science, software re-engineering, civil engineering and ecology. Specific papers include Godin *et al.* (1994) and Snelting (1996) who applied this technique to software engineering and reuse, respectively. Godin *et al.* (1998) designed class objects with FCA, while Cole and Eklund (1996) employed FCA to text retrieval in medicine. Mineau and Godin (1995) and Priss (1999) utilized FCA in the related areas of knowledge engineering and lexical databases, respectively. Just recently, Belohlavek *et al.* (2004) identified hierarchically ordered attributes in FCA.

A robust feature of FCA is its capability of producing graphical visualizations of the inherent structures among the data with an exact graphical data representation. Wolf (1996) showed that only FCA transforms the original data structure without loss of information into a graphical data structure in the plane when FCA was compared to eight other graphical methods, e.g. factor analysis, principal component analysis and cluster analysis. The research reported herein represents an initial application of FCA to philanthropic giving, specifically to identify university alumni who have the ability and proclivity to make substantial gifts to their alma mater.

The research application reported herein recognizes that neither money nor time is available to solicit directly from every member of an alumni base of more than a quarter million people. Some method needs to be devised to identify those alumni who are very likely to repeatedly give substantial monies from those with significantly smaller probabilities of charitable giving. In this research effort, we examine the hypothesis that the generosity of alumni toward his/her alma mater can be predicted using association rules obtained by using the FCA approach.

The organization of the remainder of this paper is as follows. In Section 2.0, FCA is described; in Section 3.0, the methodology is presented. Section 4.0 describes the database and Section 5.0 covers the empirical results while Section 6.0 contains the conclusion and ideas for future research.

FORMAL CONCEPT ANALYSIS

The FCA is an approach introduced by R. Wille (1982) for identifying the formal concepts of a given dataset. The details of this approach may be found in Deogun et al. (1998), Ganter and Willie (1999), Hamrouni et al. (2007), and Polovina (2007).

Formal Concept Definitions

A formal concept of a dataset is identifiable based on the formal context of the dataset. A *formal context* K is a triplet (G, I, A) in which G is a set of objects, A is a set of attributes, and I is a relation between G and A (i.e. $I \subseteq G \times A$). For context K = (G, I, A), let $H \subseteq G$ and $B \subseteq A$. We define two operators of H' and B' as follows:

$$H' = \{a \in A \mid gIa \text{ for all } g \in H\} \text{ and } B' = \{g \in G \mid gIa \text{ for all } a \in B\}$$

A *formal concept* of the context K= (G, I, A) is a pair (H, B) such that $H \subseteq G$, $B \subseteq A$, H' = B, and B' = H. Let $C_1 = (H_1, B_1)$ and $C_2 = (H_2, B_2)$ be two concepts of the context K = (G, I, A). If $H_1 \subseteq H_2$ (this implies that $B_2 \subseteq B_1$), then C_1 is a *sub-concept* of C_2 and C_2 is a super-concept of C_1.

If we use the relation $\leq$ as a hierarchical order, then we can write $C_1 \leq C_2$. If all the concepts of the context K be ordered using the $\leq$ order, then the result is a *concept lattice* denoted by L(G, I, A). For two concepts C_i and C_j, (i≠j) the concepts $(C_i \wedge C_j)$ and $(C_i \vee C_j)$ are the *infimum* (also called *meet*) and *supremum* (also called *join*) concepts of C_i and C_j, respectively.

Example: Let us assume that we have a dataset, D, that has 10 records (objects) and each record has three attributes of AT_1, AT_2 and AT_3, Table 1. The set of possible values for AT_1, AT_2 and AT_3 are {a, b, c}, {d,e} and {f, g}, respectively. The context, K, for these objects is shown in Table 2.

Table 1. A set of objects and their attributes

Objects	AT$_1$	AT$_2$	AT$_3$
1	c	e	f
2	c	e	f
3	c	d	g
4	a	d	g
5	b	d	g
6	b	d	g
7	a	d	g
8	a	d	g
9	c	e	g
10	a	e	g

The *concept lattice* of Figure 1 has been created for the obtained set of concepts from the context of Table 2. The values shown under and above the concept $C_i = (H_i, B_i)$ represent H_i and B_i, respectively.

At this point, it is worth mentioning that the attributes in the context K are possible values (data items) for all the attributes of a given dataset (see Table 1). Therefore, every attribute in K has an *underlying* attribute in the dataset. For example, the attribute AT$_1$ of the dataset in Table 1, is the underlying attribute for the attributes a, b, and c of the context K.

METHODOLOGY

For a given dataset D, *a concept $C_i = (H_i, B_i)$*, in FCA nomenclature is a set of objects (H_i) and a set of attribute values (B_i) such that objects in H_i do not have any other attribute values other than those in B_i and all the attribute values (data items) in B_i appear together in every object in (H_i). If the number of objects in D that contain all the data items in (B_i) is N_{Ci} $(N_{Ci} \geq |H_i|)$, then C_i has the support value of S_{Ci} and it is defined as $S_{Ci} = N_{Ci} / |D|$.

The data items in B_i of concept C_i can be converted into a set of *association rules* (Han and Kamber, 2005). Each association rule in the set has the general form of $X_i \rightarrow Y_i$, where X_i is the condition set and Y_i is the conclusion set. The rule $X_i \rightarrow Y_i$ obeys the following constraints:

- $X_i \subset B_i$, $X_i \neq \varnothing$,
- $Y_i \subset B_i$, $Y_i \neq \varnothing$,
- $X_i \cup Y_i = B_i$, $X_i \cap Y_i = \varnothing$, and
- All data items in X_i are logically anded together as are those in Y_i.

If $|Y_i| = 1$, then the association rule $X_i \rightarrow Y_i$ is *simple*. Considering the above constraints, the total number of association rules that can be generated from a concept which contains n data items is $2^n - 2$ from which n of them are simple.

Each association rule is assigned a *support* and a *confidence*. The support for the rule $X_i \rightarrow Y_i$ that is extracted from concept $C_i = (H_i, B_i)$ is equal to S_{Ci} and the confidence K_i, is defined as $K_{(Xi \rightarrow Yi)} = S_{Ci} / S_{Xi} = N_{Ci} / N_{Xi}$ where N_{Xi} is the number of objects in the dataset D that contain all the data items in (X_i).

Example: Considering the dataset D of Table 1 and concept number 11, for example, of Figure 1, $C_{11} = (H_{11}, B_{11}) = (\{4, 7\}, \{a, d, g\})$. For this concept, $N_{C11} = 3$, that is, three objects of 4, 7 and 8 in D carry the values a, d, and g collectively. And support, $S_{C11} = NC_{11}/|D| = 3/10 = 0.34$. The support simply says that in only 34 percent of the records in D, data items of a, d, and g collectively appear.

One of the "simple" association rules generated from concept C_{11} is "a $\wedge$ g $\rightarrow$ d". The $N_{a \wedge g} = 4$, that is four objects of 4, 7, 8, and 10 in D carry values a and g collectively. The confidence, $K_{(a \wedge g \rightarrow d)} = (N_{C11} / N_{a \wedge g} = 3/4 = 0.75)$ says that 75 percent of the records in D that contain data items a and g also contain data item d.

Figure 1. The concept lattice for all concepts extracted from context of Table 2

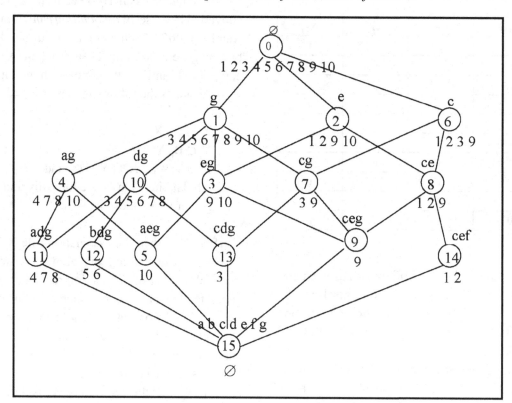

Table 2. The context of objects in Table 1

Objects	Attributes						
	a	b	c	d	e	f	g
1			x		x	x	
2			x		x	x	
3			x	x			x
4	x			x			x
5		x		x			x
6		x		x			x
7	x			x			x
8	x			x			x
9			x		x		x
10	x				x		x
Legend: x in the j-th row and i-th attribute means the object j carries attribute i.							

Reduction of Concepts and Association Rules

The application of FCA to a dataset generates a large number of concepts. The sheer volume of the concepts makes the use of them impractical. To ease this problem, we first introduce a new terminology and then present a set of criteria for pruning the concepts.

Suppose a dataset about the alumni of a university is given and we intend to analyze the alumni contributions to the university. Let us assume that one of the attributes in this dataset is the "Contribution Amount" with three possible categorical data items of zero, one and two that mean "No Contribution", "Small Contribution" and "Large Contribution", respectively. Obviously, we are only interested in those concepts that contain one of these three data items. In our analysis, we refer to these categorical data items as *designated* data items.

The pruning of the concepts is done based on the following two criteria:

1. Concepts that do not include a *designated* data item are removed, and,
2. Concepts with support less than threshold $T_{support}$ are removed.

The algorithm FilterConcepts uses the above criteria and delivers pruned concepts.

Algorithm FilterConcepts

Given: A set of concepts, $\chi = \{C_1, \ldots C_m\}$, generated using FCA. Each concept, C_i, has a support, S_{Ci}. The designated set of data items, V. The threshold value of $T_{support}$.

Objective: Pruning the concepts.
Method:
```
Step 1. Repeat Step 2 for i = 1 to |χ|;
Step 2. If ((S_Ci < T_support) || (C_i ∩ V) = ∅))
```

```
        Then remove C_i from χ;
End;
```

Upon the completion of the concepts pruning, the association rules for every concept is created and filtered using the following criteria:

1. All non-simple rules are removed;
2. All simple rules that their "conclusions" are not made up of one of the designated values are removed; and,
3. All simple rules with confidence less than a threshold value of $T_{confidence}$ are removed.

The algorithm FilterRules uses the above criteria to deliver the simple rules of interest.

Algorithm FilterRules

Given: A set of association rules, $R = \{r_1, \ldots, r_n\}$, generated from the filtered set of concepts. The threshold value of $T_{confidence}$. The confidence, K_i, for the rule r_i.

Objective Pruning the association rules.
Method:
```
Step 1. Repeat Step 2 for i = 1 to |R|;
Step 2. If ((r_i is not a simple rule) ||
        (K_i < T_confidence) ||
        (r_i.conclusion ∩ V) = ∅))
        Then remove r_i from R;
End;
```

The number of association rules is further reduced by collapsing them. To explain further, let L be a large dataset with n attributes. Each attribute has a set of possible values. In three cases, the collapse of two rules may take place. To describe the cases, let the following five association rules be samples of simple rules delivered by the algorithm FilterRules using L. All five rules have the same conclusions, f_2.

$r_1: a_1 \wedge b_3 \wedge c_4 \wedge d_2 \rightarrow f_2$

$r_2: a_1 \wedge b_3 \wedge c_4 \wedge d_2 \wedge e_1 \rightarrow f_2$

$r_3: a_2 \wedge b_3 \wedge c_4 \wedge d_2 \rightarrow f_2$

$r_4: a_3 \wedge b_3 \wedge c_4 \wedge d_2 \rightarrow f_2$

$r_5: k_3 \wedge b_3 \wedge c_4 \wedge d_2 \rightarrow f_2$

The first rule is read as "if data items a_1, b_3, c_4, d_2 are present in an object, and the data item f_2 is also present." Let AT_a, AT_b, AT_c, AT_d and AT_f be the underlying attributes for the data items a_1, b_3, c_4, d_2 and f_2, respectively. As a result, the rule r_1 may be read as "If $AT_a = a_1 \wedge AT_b = b_3 \wedge AT_c = c_4 \wedge AT_d = d_2$, then $AT_f = f_2$." Using the same analogy, rule r_5, for example, is read as: "If $AT_k = k_3 \wedge AT_b = b_3 \wedge AT_c = c_4 \wedge AT_d = d_2$, then $AT_f = f_2$."

Case 1: Let us concentrate on rules r_1 and r_2. The number of objects that can fire rule r_1 is greater than the number of objects that can fire rule r_2. The reason stems from the fact that for r_1 to be fired only four conditions need to be satisfied, whereas for r_2 five conditions need to be satisfied among which four conditions are exactly the same as the conditions in r_1. In fact, all the objects that fire rule r_2 are a subset of objects firing rule r_1. Therefore, r_2 is removed. In other words, r_1 and r_2 are collapsed into a new rule that is the same as the rule r_1.

Case 2: Let us look at rules r_1 and r_3 and concentrate only on the conditions of the two rules. Let us also assume that the underlying attribute for both a_1 and a_2 is AT_a. As a result, rules r_1 and r_3 may collapse into a new rule of r': $(a_1 \vee a_2) \wedge b_3 \wedge c_4 \wedge d_2 \rightarrow f_2$. Using the same analogy, r' and r_4 may collapse into a new rule r": $(a_1 \vee a_2 \vee a_3) \wedge b_3 \wedge c_4 \wedge d_2 \rightarrow f_2$. The first condition in r" is a complex condition. If a_1, a_2 and a_3 are the only possible values for attribute AT_a, then r" changes into $b_3 \wedge c_4 \wedge d_2 \rightarrow f_2$. In other words, rules r_1, r_3 and r_4 are collapsed into a new rule r".

Case 3: We made an observation during the process of collapsing rules that was helpful in making a heuristic rule for such a process. The heuristic rule is more appreciated when one considers the sheer size of the number of rules. As an example, if the number of concepts is 500, and each concept on average has four data items, then the number of simple rules to be dealt with is $500 * 4 = 2000$.

To present the heuristic rule, let us consider only the conditions of rules r_1 and r_5. For these two rules, $M_1 = |r_1 \cap r_5| = |\{b_3, c_4, d_2\}| = 3$, $M_2 = |r_1 - r_5| = |\{a_1\}| = 1$, $M_3 = |r_5 - r_1| = |\{k_3\}| = 1$, $M_4 = |r_1.conditions| = |\{a_1, b_3, c_4, d_2\}| = 4$, and M5 = $|r_5.conditions| = |\{k_3, b_3, c_4, d_2\}| = 4$. If the number of the common conditions between r_1 and r_5 are greater than a threshold T_{common} (i.e. $M_1 > T_{common}$) and the differences between the two rules are less than a threshold $T_{difference}$ (i.e. $M_2 < T_{difference}$ and $M_3 < T_{difference}$), then r_1 and r_5 can be collapsed into a new rule that is the same as r_1 (if $M_4 \leq M_5$) or the same as r_5 (if $M_4 > M_5$). As a result in this example, rule r_1 survives and rule r_5 is dismissed. Based on our observations, the above heuristic rule improves the performance of the analysis.

The algorithm Collapse explores the pruned set of association rules to identify the presence of the above three cases and follow the prescribed set of actions for each case.

Algorithm Collapse

Given: A set of pruned association rules, R'. The confidence K_i for rule r_i in R' (for i = 1 to |R'|). The threshold values of T_{common} and $T_{difference}$.

Objective: Collapsing the association rules and calculating the confidence of the new rules.

Method:

```
Step 1. Repeat Steps 2 to 6 for i = 1
    to |R'|;
Step 2. Repeat Steps 3 to 6 for j=
    i+1 to |R'|;
Step 3. If (r_i.conclusion ≠
    r_j.conclusion)
    Then Break;

Step 4. // Case 1.
    If (r_i.condition ⊆ r_j.condition)
    Then remove r_i;
    K_j remains the same; Break;
    If (r_j.condition ⊆ r_i.condition)
    Then remove r_j; K_i remains the
    same; Break;

Step 5. // Case 2.
    Build a new rule, r' out of r_i and
    r_j as follow:
    r' =(r_i.condition ∩ r_j.condition);
    w_1 =r_i - r'; w_2 = r_j - r';
    If (for every condition in w_1
        there is a condition in w_2 that
        belong to the same attribute)
    Then repeat for every pair of
        conditions in w_1 and w_2, (cond_i,
        cond_j), such that cond_i is in w_1
        and cond_j is in w_2 and both
        conditions belong to the same
        underlying attribute:
            r' = (cond_i ∨ cond_j) ∧ r');
        replace both r_i and r_j with r';
        K_r' = K_i + K_j;
        If (there is a complex condition
            in r' that includes all the
            possible values of its
            underlying attribute)
        Then remove the complex
        condition from r';
        Break;
    Else Delete r';
```

```
Step 6. //Case 3
    If ((r_i.condition ∩ r_j.condition)
        > T_common) &
        (r_i.condition - r_j.condition) <
        T_difference) &
        (r_j.condition - r_i.condition) <
        T_difference)
    Then If (|r_i.condition| ≤ |r_j.
    condition|)
        Then remove r_j from the
        pruned rule set; K_i remains
        the same;
        Else remove r_i from the
        pruned rule set; K_j remains
        the same;
End;
```

The resulting collapsed association rules are grouped based on the values of their conclusions. Since the conclusions are the same as the designated values, each group is a set of association rules supporting one of the designated values.

ALUMNI DATASET

A dataset with 32,901 records that carry information about alumni of a large grant university is obtained. Due to overwhelming number of missing data, use of any data imputation approach may generate artificial concepts. Therefore, we extract the association rules from only those records with no missing data and then validate the association rules by using the remaining of the data. Since a concept is made up of a subset of data items, there is a chance that it matches a number of test records.

The number of records with no missing data is 774. Each record is composed of eight attributes, see Table 3. The attribute "GiftAmount" is the designated attribute and, therefore, its data items are designated values. The designated values are 0, 1 and 2 that stand for "$0", "Greater than $0 and less than $100,000" and "Greater than or equal to $100,000" respectively.

Table 3. List of Attributes

Attribute Name	Attribute Definition	Number Categorical Data Items
Class Year	Year of Graduation	10
School	Degree Granting School	6
Gender	Gender	2
Ethnicity	Race or Ethnic Descriptor	2
Marital Status	Marital Status	2
Corps Flag	Participation in the Corps of Cadets	2
Wealth Index	Index of Wealth	4
Gift Amount	Contribution to the Foundation	3

Class Year

This variable recorded either the graduation year or a self-ascribed class year as chosen by the respective former student. There are a significant number of students who matriculated at the university and did not earn a baccalaureate degree four years later. Most typically during the 1940s, their study was interrupted by service in World War II and they graduated six or possibly eight years later. For some, they never returned to campus but selected a class year that was four years after their matriculation.

The most popular class year interval is 1990-99 with 30.5 percent of the alumni base, followed by 1980-89 with 23.8 percent. Other double digit percentile categories include 2000 and later (17.6 percent) as well as 1970-79 (13.9 percent).

School

This attributes notes the college as identified by the former students and indicated in their record. There are 17 college choices plus an unknown category. Examples of school or college choices include engineering, business, education, agriculture, etc. The most common college affiliations (double digit percentages) include engineering (25.1 percent), agriculture (18.1 percent), business administration (14.7 percent), and liberal arts (14.0 percent).

Gender

Gender attribute values can be either male or female. There were a few cell values for gender that were coded as unknown. Males constitute 65.1 percent of the alumni base, while females account for 34.2 percent.

Ethnicity

There are five specific choices for ethnicity in the database, plus a category known as other. These values include Caucasian, African American, Hispanic, Asian, etc. Caucasian alumni represent 78.1 percent of the total alumni, while Hispanic and Asian account for 9.6 percent and 8.4 percent respectively.

Marital Status

Status can be one of one of four conditions: formerly married, married, single or widowed. The most common marital status of the alumni base is married with 64.0 percent, and single status is 33.3 percent.

Corps Affiliation

This variable indicates whether an alumnus participated in the university's reserve officer training

Table 4. The result of statistical measurements of the test set

Measures	Using Only Association Rules with Conclusion = GiftAmount of Zero	Using Only Association Rules with Conclusion = GiftAmount of One	Using the Combination of Both Sets of Association Rules
Number of Hits	204	4511	4715
Number of True Positives	162 (79%)	3367 (75%)	3367 (71%)
Number of True Negatives	0 (0%)	0 (0%)	162 (3%)
Number of False Positives	42 (21%)	1144 (25%)	1144 (24%)
Number of False Negatives	0 (0%)	0 (0%)	42 (0.08%)
Prediction Quality	79.4%	74.6%	74.8%

corps. Less than 14 percent of the total sample indicated corps affiliation.

Wealth Index

The wealth index, or philanthropic potential rating, indicates to what degree that an alumnus match the characteristics of a typical U.S. philanthropist. Higher scale values indicate that an alumnus would give more frequently, give at higher levels, better respond to surveys and are more likely to volunteer.

Gift Amount

This variable is constructed by dividing the total value of all gifts to the UF by the number of gifts, yielding the average value of gift. Giving to the foundation can commence at or shortly after graduation and may continue for many years.

EMPIRICAL RESULTS

The FCA approach is applied to the test set and the resulting concepts are pruned; their association rules are generated, pruned, collapsed, and separated for designated data items using Algorithms FilterConcepts, FilterRules, and Collapse with threshold values of $T_{support} = 0.02$, $T_{confidence} = 0.6$, $T_{common} = 4$, and $T_{difference} = 1$.

Before conducting the test, we have concluded that those alumni with a wealth index less than three are not in a financial situation to make a significant contribution. Therefore, we pruned the association rules even further by removing those rules which carry a wealth index less than three. The numbers of rules in the final set for the designated values of GiftAmount = 0, 1 and 2 are 5, 75 and 1 respectively.

The association rules are applied on the test set of 32,127 (32,901 less 774) records. The total number of hits is 4,720. However, the number of hits for records with GiftAmount = 2 is five. As a result, we have removed those five records from the test set and the number of hits reduced to 4,715. The quality of prediction and the numbers of false positive (F^+), true positive (T^+), false negative (F^-), and true negative (T^-) for GiftAmount = 0, and 1 are calculated separately and in combination. The results are illustrated in Table 4.

CONCLUSION AND FUTURE RESEARCH

Charitable and philanthropic organizations, including university fund raising departments, face increasing pressure to more effectively employ a variety of analytical techniques. Identification of potential donor for any charitable and philanthropic organizations is essential because it saves considerable amounts of money, including the time of professional staff. For example, it is very costly for a university fund raising department to send a solicitation to its 400,000 alumni and solicit contributions twice a year. The postage cost alone, using as an example a U.S. Postal Service bulk rate of $0.25 per one ounce mailing, is $200,000 in U.S. dollars (400,000* $0.25 *2). (The current bulk rate is significantly more than $0.25, but less than the current first class postage rate of $0.47 for a one ounce mailing.) Any effective approach that brings this cost down is a great help to the modest budgets of university fund raising departments. If such a methodology as presented herein shortens the list of potential alumni contributors by half through identification of the more likely donors, postage cost is reduced accordingly. In addition, such a reduction also dramatically lessens the amount of related printing, material and handling expense.

We argue that the identification of the data items that frequently appear together (i.e. concepts) may be the key to the identification of the potential donors. We have examined this hypothesis and the findings in Table 4 revealed that the hypothesis is true.

Association Analysis of the alumni data generated association rules that are able to predict the generosity of the alumni to the university and on average (using the combination of both sets of association rules) the quality of the prediction is 74.8 percent with sensitivity of 98.8 percent and specificity of 12.4 percent.

In a binary prediction, all the subjects of the test may be predicted to be a part of one of the two possible cases. For the sake of generality let us refer to the two cases as Positive and Negative. If a subject of the test set is predicted as one of the positives and in reality the subject is also one of the positives, then the prediction of the subject is considered as a "true positive"; otherwise, it is a "false positive". By the same logic, the prediction

of a subject may be considered as a "true negative" or "false negative".

The "false positive" and "false negative" are considered as Type I and Type II errors of prediction that are measured by sensitivity and specificity as follow:

$$Sensitivity = (T^+) / (T^+ + F^-)$$

$$Specificity = (T^-) / (T^- + F^+)$$

where,

T^+ is the number of true positive predicted cases
T^- is the number of true negative predicted cases
F^+ is the number of false positive predicted cases
F^- is the number of false negative predicted cases

In summary, sensitivity of a test expresses the percentage of all the positive subjects that are predicted positive and specificity of a test expresses the percentage of all the negative subjects that are predicted negative.

Considering the facts that (a) the association rules conclude from only 774 records (less than 2.4 percent of the total records) and (b) the actual test set (4715/774) that is 610 percent greater than the training set, the results displayed in Table 1 are quite significant.

The creation of profiles for alumni who are "generous" and alumni who are "not so generous" represent a future line of research that has already commenced. These profiles would help the UF target the potentially "generous" graduates for possible contribution to the university.

REFERENCES

Belohlavek, R., Sklenar, V., & Zacpal, J. (2004). Formal concept analysis with hierarchically ordered attributes. *International Journal of General Systems, 33*(4), 383–394. doi:10.1080/03081070 410001679715

Berry, M. J. A., & Linoff, G. (2000). *Mastering Data Mining: The Art and Science of Customer Relationship Management.* New York: John Wiley & Sons.

Brown, D. W. (2004). What research tells us about planned giving. *International Journal of Nonprofit and Voluntary Sector Marketing, 9*(1), 86–95. doi:10.1002/nvsm.235

Clotfelter, C. T. (2001). Who are the alumni donors? Giving by two generations of alumni from selective colleges. *Nonprofit Management & Leadership, 2*(2), 119–138. doi:10.1002/nml.12201

Cole, R. J., & Eklund, P. W. (1996). The application of formal concept analysis to text retrieval in the medical domain. in *Proceedings of the 5th International Conference on Conceptual Structures.* 185-217.

Connoly, M. S., & Blanchette, R. (1986). Understanding and predicting alumni giving behavior. In Dunn, J. A. (Ed.), *Enhancing the Management of Fund Raising* (pp. 69–89). San Francisco: Jossey-Bass.

Deogun, J. S., Raghavan, J. S., & Sever, H. (1998). Association mining and formal concept analysis. *Proceedings of the Joint Conference in Information Science.* 335-338.

Drye, T., Wetherill, G., & Pinnock, A. (2001). Donor survival analysis: An alternative perspective on lifecycle modeling. *International Journal of Nonprofit and Voluntary Sector Marketing, 6*(4), 325–334. doi:10.1002/nvsm.158

Ewing, R. L., Goveckar, M. A., Govekar, P. L., & Rishi, M. (2002). Economics, market segmentation and recruiting: Targeting your promotion to volunteers' needs. *Journal of Nonprofit & Public Sector Marketing, 10*(1), 61–76. doi:10.1300/J054v10n01_05

Ganter, B., & Wille, R. (1999). *Formal Concept Analysis: Mathematical Foundations.* Berlin: Springer-Verlag.

Godin, R., Mili, H., Mineau, H., Missaoui, G. R., Arfi, M., & Chau, T.-T. (1998). Design of class hierarchies based on concept (Galois) lattices. *Theory and Practice of Object Systems., 4,* 117–134. doi:10.1002/(SICI)1096-9942(1998)4:2<117::AID-TAPO6>3.0.CO;2-Q

Godin, R., Mineau, G., Missaoui, R., Saint Germain, M., & Faraj, N. (1994). Applying concept formation methods to software reuse. *International Journal of Software and Engineering., 5,* 119–142. doi:10.1142/S0218194095000071

Hamrouni, T., Valtchev, P., Yahia, S. B., & Nguifo, E. M. (2007). About the Lossless Reduction of the Minimal Generator Family of a Context. *Proceedings of the 5th International Conference on Formal Concept Analysis.* 130-150

Han, J., & Kamber, M. (2005). *Data Mining, Concepts and Techniques.* San Francisco: Morgan Kaufmann.

Johnson, M. S., & Garbarino, E. (2001). Customers of performing arts organizations: Are subscribers different from non-subscribers? *International Journal of Nonprofit and Voluntary Sector Marketing, 6*(1), 61–77. doi:10.1002/nvsm.134

Key, J. (2001). Enhancing fundraising success with custom data modeling. *International Journal of Nonprofit and Voluntary Sector Marketing, 6*(4), 335–346. doi:10.1002/nvsm.159

Lindahl, W. E., & Winship, C. (1992). Predictive models for raising and major gift fundraising. *Nonprofit Management & Leadership, 3*(1), 43–64. doi:10.1002/nml.4130030105

Mineau, G., & Godin, R. (1995). Automatic structuring of knowledge bases by conceptual clustering. *IEEE Transactions on Knowledge and Data Engineering, 7,* 824–829. doi:10.1109/69.469834

Polovina, S. (2007). An Introduction to Conceptual Graphs. *Proceedings of the 15th International Conference on Conceptual Structures.* 1-14.

Priss, U. (1999). Efficient implementation of semantic relations in lexical databases. *Computational Intelligence, 15,* 79–87. doi:10.1111/0824-7935.00083

Shelley, L., & Polonsky, M. J. (2002). Do charitable causes need to segment their current donor base on demographic factors? An Australian examination. *International Journal of Nonprofit and Voluntary Sector Marketing, 7*(1), 19–29. doi:10.1002/nvsm.164

Snelting, G. (1996). Reengineering of configurations based on mathematical concept analysis. *ACM Transactions on Software Engineering and Methodology, 5,* 146–189. doi:10.1145/227607.227613

Todd, S., & Lawson, R. (2001). Lifestyle segmentation and museum/gallery visiting behaviour. *International Journal of Nonprofit and Voluntary Sector Marketing, 6*(4), 269–277. doi:10.1002/nvsm.152

Wille, R. (1982). Restructuring lattice theory: An approach based on hierarchies of concepts. In Rival, I. (Ed.), *Ordered Sets* (pp. 445–470). Boston: Reidel Dordecht Publisher.

Willemain, T. R., Goyal, A., van Deven, M., & Thukral, I. S. (1994). Alumni giving: The influences of reunion, class and year. *Research in Higher Education, 35,* 609–629. doi:10.1007/BF02497090

Wolff, K. E. (1996). Comparison of graphical data analysis methods. In *F. Faulbaum & W. Bandilla, SoftWat '95 Advances in Statistical Software. 5* (pp. 139–151). Stuttgart: Lucius and Lucius.

Wymer, W. W. Jr. (2003). Differentiating literacy volunteers: A segmentation analysis for target marketing. *International Journal of Nonprofit and Voluntary Sector Marketing, 8*(3), 267–285. doi:10.1002/nvsm.217

This work was previously published in International Journal of Intelligent Information Technologies, Volume 5, Issue 2, edited by Vijayan Sugumaran, pp. 17-32, copyright 2009 by IGI Publishing (an imprint of IGI Global).

Chapter 15
KStore:
A Dynamic Meta-Knowledge Repository for Intelligent BI

Jane Campbell Mazzagatti
As It Is Inc., USA

ABSTRACT

KStore is a computer data structure based on the Phaneron of C. S. Peirce (Peirce, 1931-1958). This structure, called a Knowledge Store, KStore or simply K, is currently being developed as a storage engine to support BI data queries and analysis (Mazzagatti, 2007). The first Ks being constructed handle nominal data and record sequences of field/record data variables and their relationships. These rudimentary Ks are dynamic allowing real-time data processing, ad hoc queries and data compression, to facilitate data mining. This paper describes a next step in the development of the K structure, to record into the K structure, meta data associated with the field/record data, in particular the column or dimension names and a source indicator.

INTRODUCTION

Phaneroscopy is the description of the Phaneron; and by the Phaneron I mean the collective total of all that is in any way or in any sense present to the mind, quite regardless of whether it corresponds to any real thing or not (Peirce, 1931-1958).

The Phaneron is Peirce's cognitive model. As Peirce describes the Phaneron, it contains anything that the mind requires to think, that would be experiential data and relational information,

as well as processes or strategies to manipulate and/or retrieve information. All of these elements of the Phaneron would exist within the Phaneron and in the same triadic form that Peirce describes.

A rudimentary triadic structure, K, based on the Peirce phaneron, that creates a triadic recording of basic data and relational information, has been described and implemented (Mazzagatti, 2006). The resulting K structure is truly unique and has many attributes relevant to BI. The K structure compresses the data being recorded by reusing K nodes that represent data elements.

DOI: 10.4018/978-1-60960-595-7.ch015

The locking of the K structure is at the K node level and the K structure does not contain any calculated values such as probabilities, so that the K structure remains dynamic allowing recording, building and querying to occur simultaneously.

The relationships between the data elements at all levels are recorded during the building process. All possible indexes are incorporated into the K structure, so no other data structures such as cubes are required to query for results within a context. This allows ad hoc querying at any time.

This K structure with a set of K transversal routines forms the engine for a prototype data analysis system that is very efficient for organizing and querying large field/record data sets (Mazzagatti, 2007).

Development of this K structure continues with the focus on incorporating meta data information into the K structure containing the field/record data. Some of the meta data will become an integral part of the K structure and some of the meta data will be referenced and processed by routines external to the K structure.

BASIC K STRUCTURE

Given the dataset in Figure 1, a diagram of the resulting K data structure would look like Figure 2. All possible data elements or particles, in this case the alpha-numeric character set, are represented by the K nodes at the lowest level of the K structure.

The middle level of the K structure contains the sequences of K nodes referencing the K nodes of the lower level (characters) and representing the sequences of those lower level K nodes that are the field variables. The end K nodes of middle level will be used to create top level.

Finally the top level of the K structure contains the sequences of K nodes referencing the end K nodes of the middle level (the field variables) and representing the sequences of those middle level K nodes that are the records.

Figure 1. Sample data set

Sample Data Set — Sales Team Activities
Bill Tuesday 100 sold PA
Bill Tuesday 100 sold PA
Bill Tuesday 100 sold PA
Bill Tuesday 100 sold PA
Bill Tuesday 100 sold PA
Bill Tuesday 100 sold PA
Bill Monday 103 sold NJ
Bill Monday 100 trial PA
Bill Monday 100 trial PA
Bill Monday 100 trial PA
Tom Monday 100 sold PA
Tom Monday 100 sold PA
Tom Monday 103 trial NJ
Tom Monday 103 trial NJ
Tom Monday 103 trial NJ

So the first level of the K structure contains K nodes that represent the smallest data particles, in this case the alpha-numeric character set, in other data sets it might be pixels or sound bytes for example. The second level contains the representation of a sequence of particles from the first level. All the other levels represent sequences of the sequences from the next lower level by referencing the last K node of the sequences of the next lower level.

Recording Event Sequences

As the Peirce materials suggest each level of the K structure is constructed in the same way using the basic triad (Mazzagatti, 2006).

The basic triad shown in Figure 3, shows the recording of two sequential events by a K node at a level above the two events. This recording is accomplished by establishing a set of pointers that link a pair of K nodes, called a bi-directional pointer. Each K node in the pair contains a pointer that points to the other K node.

The bi-directional pointers allow the K structure to be traversed in any direction, even changing direction if required. For example, the solid line that connects the BOT K node with the next K node is created when a pointer in the BOT K node points to the second K node and a pointer in the second K node points to the BOT K node.

Figure 2. KStore Representation of the data set

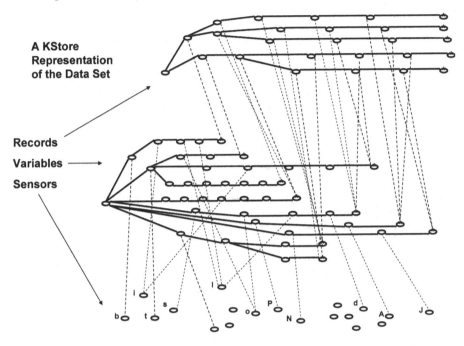

Figure 3. The basic K triad

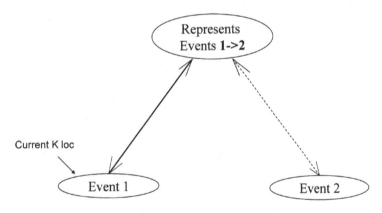

A K structure recording of the field variable event sequence 'Bill' would look like the K structure diagrammed in Figure 4. The solid lines in the diagram of the K structure show the K nodes that recorded the event sequence 'Bill'. These K nodes connected by the solid lines contain no data but instead reference the K nodes that contain the events at the lower level. A more detailed description of the construction of the K structure can be found in Zuchero (2007).

Brief Analysis of the K Structure

Both the dotted and solid lines between the K nodes represent bi-directional pointers, so that traversal routines can move in both directions between the K nodes. Solid lines are called Case paths and record a sequence of events by linking K nodes at one level that reference the K nodes of a lower level. Dotted lines are called Result paths and record the references of the Case path

Figure 4. K recording of 'Bill'

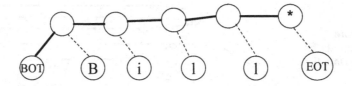

Figure 5. K recording of 'cat hat rat'

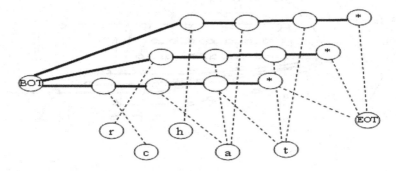

K nodes to the level below. Because each K node contains pointers along both the Case and the Result paths traversal routines can move between the two types of K paths.

Figure 5 shows a diagram of the K structure recording of three event sequences; 'cat, 'hat' and 'rat'. The BOT and EOT K nodes were created to allow coded algorithms to locate the physical beginning and end of event sequences.

The K has been patented as an interlocking trees datastore (Mazzagatti, 2005). This structure differs distinctly from the usual tree structures. Definitions of various tree structures can be found in Cormen, Leiserson and Rivest (1997).

The root nodes in a K compare to usual trees in that they have no ancestors and may have many child nodes. BOT, EOT and the K nodes of the lowest level are root nodes of the K structure.

The nodes other than root nodes in the usual tree have a single parent node. This is where the K nodes are unique, the K nodes have more than one parent node because each K node is at an intersection of more than one tree. The solid and dotted lines in Figure 5 represent different tree structures and each K node has a link to a parent

on a solid line and another link to a parent on a dotted line.

Case Paths: Solid Lines

Beginning at the BOT (beginning of thought) K node and following the top most solid line to the next K node, we see that this K node references the K node at the lower level that represent the letter 'h'. Continuing along the solid line, the Case path, the next two K nodes reference the addition of the letters 'a' and 't' to the sequence and the final K node references the EOT (end of thought) to complete the recording.

Therefore, the top most Case path records the sequence 'hat', the middle Case path records the sequence 'rat' and the lowest Case path records the sequence 'cat'.

The Case paths record the order of events in the sequence and when the initial events are the same the existing K structure is reused. This reuse of the initial section of the Case path is one way that K structure compresses the data.

For example, Figure 6 shows the Case path of a K recording of the sequences 'cat' and 'car'.

Figure 6. K recording of 'cat car'

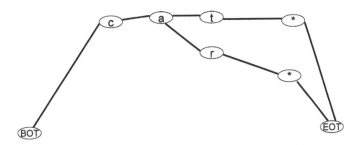

K Structure Rules

Using a combination of solid and dotted line traversals, many other 'rules' can be found (Mazzagatti, 2007). For example, referring to Figure 5, start at the K node for 'a' and traverse any one of the dotted lines into a word sequence. Then traverse the solid line along the Case path toward the EOT K node and at the next K node traverse the dotted line to determine the next sequence event, in this case a 't'. When all the dotted lines from 'a' are traversed to find the next event sequence, it can be determined that all 'a's are immediately followed by 't'.

In a similar way the set of event sequences that precede a particular event sequence can be determined, and so on.

The first two K nodes of the sequence 'cat' are reused to record the sequence 'car', then new K nodes are created to finish the recording of the sequence 'car'. Each sequence has its own unique final K node that will be used to reference the sequences individually.

The '*' in the final K node of each sequence indicates that that K node represents a complete sequence and that K node can be referenced by a higher level K node to record sequences of the sequences at the lower level.

Result Paths: Dotted Lines

Referring again to Figure 5, the dotted lines, the Result paths, then indicate the K node references to K nodes at the lower level. These Result paths record the relationships between data elements. For example, the data element 'a' is referenced by all three event sequences, therefore, as a product of the bi-directional pointers, the K node that represents 'a' contains a list or set of indexes to all the event sequences that contain 'a'.

There is only one instance of the K node that represents 'a', and it is reused each time it is needed at the next higher level, in this case to create the field variables. The same process of building relationships holds for any level, for example, each field variable will represented only once and the final K node of the sequence will contain a set of indexes to all the record sequences that contain it. This reuse of the completed sequences is another way the K structure compresses the data.

DATA ANALYZER PROTOTYPE

Figure 7 shows the typical organization of a data analysis application that uses a KStore. The KStore datastore, K, is represented by the box in the upper top. Interfacing with the K data store is the K engine, containing the K traversal routines that process the data streams from the Learn engine or the Utility routines used for queries. Both the Learn (input) and the Query (output) functions use the same K engine routines to traverse and position on the K data structure.

Figure 7. Organization of a typical KStore system

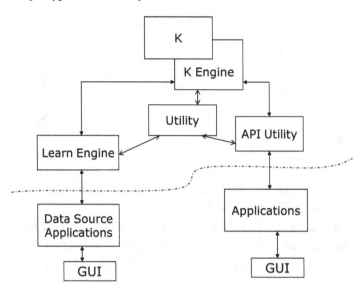

The dotted and dashed line shows the division between the KStore API and the applications softwares within the system.

During the Learn process the Learn engine receives a data stream from a data source application. As the Learn engine processes the data stream the counts within the K nodes are incremented for all repeating data sequences and new structure will be created to record new data sequences. The Query process traverses the K structure in the exactly the same way but it does not increment the counts within the K nodes or create any new structure. Both processes can run independently and simultaneously.

K Node Counts

Figure 8 shows the top level (the record level) and a few K nodes from the middle level of the K shown in Figure 2 created from the data in Figure 1. The labels outside the K nodes (ovals) represent the field variables that would be referenced by the K nodes. The numbers inside the K nodes are the K node counts.

Given the data in Figure 1 there are 10 records that contain 'Bill' in the first column and 5 records

that contain 'Tom' in the first column. Of the 10 records that contain 'Bill' in the first column, 6 of those records contain 'Tuesday' in the second column and 4 contain 'Monday' in the second column. Of the 5 records that contain 'Tom' in the first column, all 5 contain 'Monday' in the second column, and so on.

K as a Dynamic Model

The K then models the data set and can support any data analysis processes. That is the K can be traversed, constrained and return any count of any field variable in the context of any set of the other field variables. The dotted lines can be used to constrain the K to just those records of interest and then the count of the field variable can be determined by summing the counts in the constrained K nodes.

In addition to allowing queries within any context at any time even while the K is being constructed, the sequences of the K structure need a not always be a fixed length. Fields, column or dimensions can be added or deleted when necessary without interrupting processing. The data

Figure 8. Top level of the K recording of the sample data set

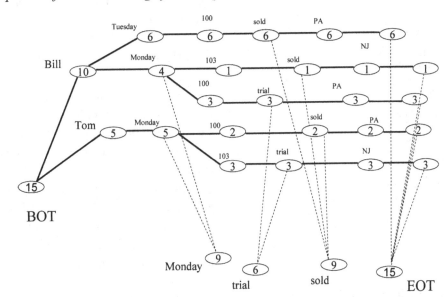

source application just begins to send the new records and they will be incorporated into the K.

In fact, multiple types of records can be recorded into a single K and each field variable will be brought into relation with every other variable via the dotted lines.

The K structure is very flexible and work continues toward recording documents and other types of data into K structure. A more detailed description of the K model can be found in Zuchero (2007).

INCORPORATING META DATA INFORMATION INTO A K STRUCTURE

One problem with the data in Figure 1 is that the indexes in the K structure will not be able to differentiate between the same field variable value in two different columns.

For example, if the there were a column for 'price' and a column for 'item number', the field variable '100' would be an appropriate value for each column. In this case the set of pointers for the field variable '100' would point to records

that contain '100' in both the 'price' and 'item' columns. To avoid this confusion each field variable needs to be related its particular column by using the column name.

Including the Column Names in the Data Stream

Figure 9 shows a .csv file of the same data in Figure 1. This .csv file however includes the column names in the first record of the file, followed by the field/record data.

To incorporate column names into the K, the data source application must save the column names and prefix them, including a delimiter, to each field variable.

Figure 10 shows the first and second level portion of the K structure that records the names "Bill" and 'Tom'. The column name for these two field variables is 'salesperson'. Using ':' as a delimiter, the data source application would concatenate the column name plus the delimiter to each field variable and in the case of 'Bill' and 'Tom', would send 'salesperson:Bill' and 'salesperson:Tom' to the Learn engine to be added to the K.

Figure 9. Sample data set including column names

```
Sample Data Set – Sales Team Activities

Salesperson,Day,Item,Disp,State
Bill,Tuesday,100,sold,PA
Bill,Tuesday,100,sold,PA
Bill,Tuesday,100,sold,PA
Bill,Tuesday,100,sold,PA
Bill,Tuesday,100,sold,PA
Bill,Tuesday,100,sold,PA
Bill,Monday,103,sold,NJ
Bill,Monday,100,trial,PA
Bill,Monday,100,trial,PA
Bill,Monday,100,trial,PA
Tom,Monday,100,sold,PA
Tom,Monday,100,sold,PA
Tom,Monday,103,trial,NJ
Tom,Monday,103,trial,NJ
Tom,Monday,103,trial,NJ
```

Column Names in the K Structure

Figure 11 shows just the solid line recording of the second level of the K recording of 'Bill' and 'Tom'. The characters in the ovals are the sequence elements referenced by K nodes.

Figure 12 shows the solid line recording of 'salesperson:Bill' and 'salesperson:Tom'. Every field variable will be preceded by its column name and ':'. The second level of the K structure then carries the column name information along with the field variables.

Figure 13 shows the K structure resulting from the data in Figure 12. Topmost sequence in the

second level is a K recording of 'salesperson:Bill' and 'salesperson:Tom'.

Queries

Because all field variables in the K are now a combination of the column name and the field variable, the query application must include the column name, field variable information within each query request.

With the column name incorporated within the K structure, queries about the number of columns, their names, the number of field variables per column, their unique names and so on, are easily resolved by traversing the K.

Adding a Source Indicator to the K

For K's that contain multiple record types, the data source application can add an additional column to the sequence as an indication of the type or source of record. The K then can be constrained using this record type to isolate one set records of the same type, or some other field variable to find related records from within all the record types.

SUMMARY

The work of C. S. Peirce has yielded a unique data structure (Peirce 1931-58). This K structure

Figure 10. Middle level K recording of 'Bill Tom'

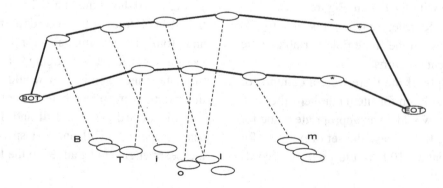

Figure 11. Solid line K recording of 'Bill Tom'

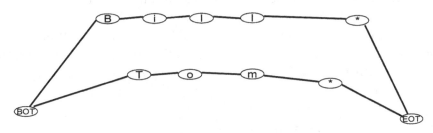

Figure 12. Solid line K Recording of 'salesperson:Bill' and 'salesperson:Tom'

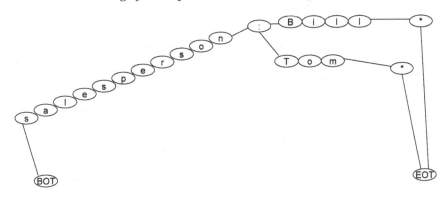

Figure 13. K recording of sample data set including column names

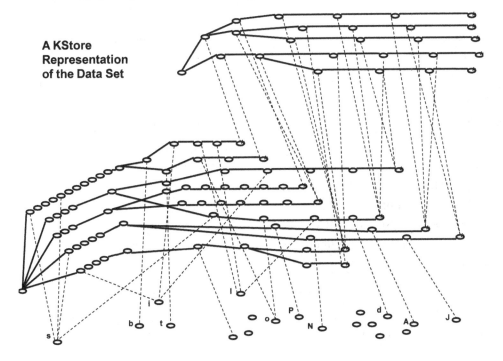

models a data set and includes relationship rules and indexes that can be used to constrain the data set to context, allowing queries that can support any type of data analysis.

The K structure is efficient, reusing event sequences to compress the data.

The K structure is also a very flexible data structure with the potential to hold information that would typically be stored in multiple data structures or as part of coded algorithms.

And, the K structure is dynamic allowing simultaneous building and querying, and variable sequence definitions.

The data analyzer prototype developed using the K structure facilitates the real-time analysis and data mining of larger datasets without the need to design or build other data structures such as cubes or indexes.

Work continues on taking advantage of these attributes to record documents into the K structure and define algorithms to process text and possibly some reasoning tasks.

REFERENCES

Cormen, T. H., Leiserson, C. E., & Rivest, R. L. (1997). *Introduction to Algorithms*. Cambridge, MA: The MIT Press.

Mazzagatti, J. C. (2005). *U.S. Patent No. 6,961,733*. Washington, DC: U.S. Patent and Trademark Office.

Mazzagatti, J. C. (2006). A Computer Memory Resident Data Structure Based on the Phaneron of C. S. Peirce. Inspiration and Application, Contributions to ICCS 2006 14th International Conference on Conceptual Structures ICCS 2006 (pp. 114-130). Aalborg, Denmark: Aalborg University Press 2006.

Mazzagatti, J. C. (2007). Adding Conceptual SIGNs to a Computer Memory Resident Data Structure Based on the Paneron of C. S. Peirce, *CS-TIW 2007, Second Conceptual Structures Tool Interoperability Workshop in Association with ICCS2007 Sheffield England (pp. 59-63)*, Bristol, UK:Research Press International.

Mazzagatti, J. C. (2007). Data Analyzer Prototype Using a K Structure Based on the Paneron of C. S. Peirce, *Proceedings of the 15th International Workshops on Conceptual Structures ICCS 2007*, Springer-Verlag London Limited.

Mazzagatti, J. C. (2007). *U.S. Patent No. 7,158,975*. Washington, DC: U.S. Patent and Trademark Office.

Mazzagatti, J. C., & Buckwalter, R. (2008). *U.S. Patent No. 7,348,980*. Washington, DC: U.S. Patent and Trademark Office.

Mazzagatti, J. C., & Claar, J. V. K. (2007). *U.S. Patent No. 7,213,041*. Washington, DC: U.S. Patent and Trademark Office.

Mazzagatti, J. C., & Claar, J. V. K. (2008). *U.S. Patent No. 7,340,471*. Washington, DC: U.S. Patent and Trademark Office.

Peirce, C. S. (1931-1958). Charles Hartshorne, Paul Weiss & Arthur Burks (Eds.), Collected Papers of Charles Sanders Peirce (8 vols.). Cambridge MA: Harvard University Press.

Zuchero, J. (2007). *The Practical Peirce – An Introduction to the Triadic Continuum Implemented as a Computer Data Structure*. New York: iUniverse.\

This work was previously published in International Journal of Intelligent Information Technologies, Volume 5, Issue 2, edited by Vijayan Sugumaran, pp. 68-80, copyright 2009 by IGI Publishing (an imprint of IGI Global).

Chapter 16

A Transaction-Oriented Architecture for Structuring Unstructured Information in Enterprise Applications

Simon Polovina
Sheffield Hallam University, UK

Simon Andrews
Sheffield Hallam University, UK

ABSTRACT

As 80-85% of all corporate information remains unstructured, outside of the processing scope of enterprise systems, many enterprises rely on Information Systems that cause them to risk transactions that are based on lack of information (errors of omission) or misleading information (errors of commission). To address this concern, the fundamental business concept of monetary transactions is extended to include qualitative business concepts. A Transaction Concept (TC) is accordingly identified that provides a structure for these unstructured but vital aspects of business transactions. Based on REA (Resources, Events, Agents) and modelled using Conceptual Graphs (CGs) and Formal Concept Analysis (FCA), the TC provides businesses with a more balanced view of the transactions they engage in and a means of discovering new transactions that they might have otherwise missed. A simple example is provided that illustrates this integration and reveals a key missing element. This example is supported by reference to a wide range of case studies and application areas that demonstrate the added value of the TC. The TC is then advanced into a Transaction-Oriented Architecture (TOA). The TOA provides the framework by which an enterprise's business processes are orchestrated according to the TC. TOA thus brings Service-Oriented Architecture (SOA) and the productivity of enterprise applications to the height of the real, transactional world that enterprises actually operate in.

DOI: 10.4018/978-1-60960-595-7.ch016

INTRODUCTION

The major benefit of adopting a structured model of a problem is so that such models draw out all the relevant parameters of a problem, from which its dynamics can be better understood and its possible solutions investigated more meaningfully. Contrast this with a written or spoken text discussion (such as word-processor document or emails), where ambiguities and obfuscations can occur easily. This 'natural language' interpretation of problems may be the most flexible and easily followed, but without at least a basis in some structured form it can be dangerously wrong. Yet it is claimed that 80-85% of all corporate information remains unstructured (Seidman & Ritsko, 2004). It is thus worryingly easy to omit or misinterpret the salient issues of a given business problem. Consequently, enterprises miss valuable business opportunities. Or they undertake transactions that they later regret, as recent financial turmoil have only too clearly shown (Borio, 2008; Kramer, 2008).

The accounting discipline provides sophisticated models for capturing the problem dynamics of economic activity in a structured way (Zimmerman, 2006). Accounting recognises the concern that "if it can't be measured then it can't be evaluated, and if it can't be measured it can't be managed". Accounting thereby offers the enterprise the tools it needs to capture and analyse otherwise unstructured data. Whilst we shall see that accounting too permits enterprises to omit or misinterpret the salient issues of a business problem, it offers a useful vehicle by which we may be able to capture unstructured information in a principled way – namely through the notion of transactions.

STRUCTURE THROUGH TRANSACTIONS

Previous work has identified how transactions might provide structure to the unstructured (Hill, Polovina, & Shadija, 2006; Polovina & Hill, 2005; Polovina & Hill, 2009). Enterprise Information Systems (EIS) echo this underpinning concept (Groenewegen, 1993). These systems model the enterprise and process its business activity based on the concept of a transaction. Such transactions may involve databases, accounting, financial/asset management, operational (e.g. payroll and pension), enterprise resource planning (ERP), decision support systems or others. These systems may only capture certain transactional elements of the domain that they represent. Accordingly, like accounting, these systems can omit or misinterpret the salient issues by making 'errors of omission or commission' (i.e. omit or misinterpret the salient issues of a business problem as we have described).

In Accounting

In order to provide a structure for modelling transactions the traditional model of accountancy, the bookkeeping model, was developed in the Middle Ages (Lee, 1986). The principle behind this model is economic scarcity. In other words for every benefit a sacrifice has to be made. For example, the benefit of a business owning its office is sacrificing £1,000,000 that could be employed elsewhere; a book prepared by its author researching a new exciting area in semantic understanding may have involved that author deciding against many complex yet important alternatives, such as the costs of not participating in his or her growing family. These 'transactions' occur because the decision-maker makes an intuitive (hence unstructured) 'value judgement' that the benefits outweigh the costs. The bookkeeping model is simple but rigorous. Fundamentally, instead of recording one amount per transaction it records two: A 'debit' and a 'credit'. Moreover these amounts are complementary to one another; hence they 'balance' against each other. An accounting 'balance sheet' is merely the aggregate of all these debits and credits. The rigorousness derives from this principled 'double entry' structure so that each benefit is accounted for by a cost and vice versa. Hence every gain is matched to a sacrifice.

Issues in Accounting Transactions

However, on deeper investigation the double entry bookkeeping model is unlikely to capture key aspects of the transactions. Say the business in the example above decides to sell its office. This transaction can be recorded easily by the elementary bookkeeping entries "DEBIT Cash £1,000,000, CREDIT Fixed Assets £1,000,000". The author preparing the book is simply too qualitative to be recorded by the bookkeeping model yet the author may want to know clearly about *all* the actual costs and benefits of such a transaction. This neglect on the part of the bookkeeping model is elaborated below.

The threshold where the bookkeeping model may break down is perhaps lower than may be thought. Reconsidering the first example about the office, the value of selling the current office may be the purchase of cheaper offices for £1,000,000. The double entry would be "DEBIT Fixed Assets £1,000,000, CREDIT Cash £1,000,000". Now say, by spending the remaining £1,000,000 elsewhere, the business generates revenue of £1,100,000. On aggregate in the balance sheet the business's money worth then increases by £100,000 (Represented by the double entry "CREDIT Profit and Loss Account £100,000, DEBIT Assets £100,000"). However if the value of the current office is retaining key employees through a comfortable work environment then, as in the author example above, the bookkeeping model is inappropriate. Therefore the double entry bookkeeping model is easily liable to make significant *errors of omission*. Whilst this example may appear rather simplistic, it is well known that office relocations can have

such dramatic adverse effects even though it 'saves money' and a whole industry has grown around this issue (Attwood, 1996).

Furthermore the bookkeeping model could mislead. Reconsidering the 'preparing the book' example the value may be viewed as the more easily quantified cost of the author ceasing to conduct consultancy work at £5,000 a week instead. This revenue would have been recorded by the bookkeeping model on an ongoing basis. However the book might bring its author the satisfaction of an enhanced reputation amongst peers. Unless this can be translated into a cash benefit the bookkeeping model would not record these judgements and thereby leave a 'loss' of £5,000. By choosing to author the book the decision-maker *qualitatively* has to justify, *against the grain of the bookkeeping model's assessment of value*, why that £5,000 each week has been forsaken even though this may be the lesser value item. Therefore the double entry bookkeeping model, taken too literally, can readily lead to significant *errors of commission*. Whilst once again this appears to be an elementary example designed to illustrate the point, Claret describes a pertinent industrial scenario where the accounting system was dysfunctional to the information needs of the organisation, causing it to make the wrong decisions even though that organisation's operations director was acutely aware of the problem (Claret, 1990).

Resource Event Accounting/Agents

The REA (Resources, Events, Accounting) model recognises these familiar problems in accounting (Geerts & McCarthy, 1991; McCarthy, 1987). The 'A' in REA has since been updated to Agents i.e. REA (Resources, Events, Agents) reflecting its on-going development (Hruby, 2006). Whichever starting point we care to choose we can note that REA, unlike the bookkeeping paradigm, attempts to capture the qualitative dimensions of economic scarcity. REA captures an exchange of resources based on the resources themselves unrestrained

Figure 1. The REA model in UML

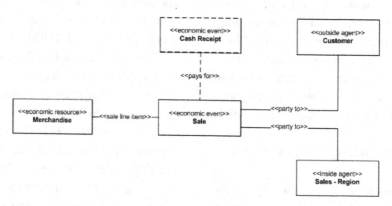

by superficial monetary measures. It drives to the heart of business transactions by recognising that "… the economic activities of an entity are a sequence of exchanges of resources - the process of giving up some resources to obtain others. Therefore, we have to not only keep track of increases and decreases in the resources that are under the control of the entity but also identify and record which resources were exchanged for which others." (Ijiri, 1967)

To achieve this, REA models are built using the following core concepts:

- *Resource* - any resource that is the subject of an exchange or transaction;
- *Event* - the activities that are required for a transaction to take place;
- *Agent* - a person, system or organisation that participates in the transaction.

Figure 1 depicts the original REA model in Hrubý's (Hruby, 2006) use of UML (www.uml. org).

REA thus represents a powerful means of recording scarcity as more than a monetary measure. Without worrying about the significance of its 'dotted' part for now, Figure 1 reveals the fundamental links between an 'economic resource', which means some exchangeable item of value, and the parties which create the 'economic event' that causes the economic resource to be exchanged.

REA as Conceptual Graphs

In subsequent work the REA model has been represented in Sowa's Conceptual Graphs (CGs) (Polovina, 2007; Sowa & Zachman, 1992). CGs provide a powerful knowledge representation environment, whilst exhibiting the familiar object-oriented and database features of contemporary enterprise and web applications. CGs capture the nuances in natural language whilst being able to be implemented in computer software. CGs were devised by Sowa from philosophical, psychological, linguistic, and artificial intelligence foundations in a principled way (Sowa, 1984). Furthermore CGs are core to the recent ISO Common Logic standard (http://cl.tamu.edu/). CGs are attractive as they are built upon such a strong theoretical and wide-ranging base. There are industrial examples using CG such as Sonetto (Sarraf & Ellis, 2006) and Erudine (www.erudine. com/products-data-visualisation-tool). Numerous examples support the case for capturing the REA model in CG (Gerbé, Keller, & Mineau, 1998; Hill et al., 2006; Hill, 2010a; Launders, 2009).

The REA UML model of Figure 1 is thus transformed into the REA CGs model, Figure 2. This figure captures the duality in the 'dotted part' of Figure 1 referred to earlier. In other words, the 'cash receipt pays for the sale' in Figure 1 is really a shorthand to make that diagram concise. For instance 'party to' should also connect to 'cash receipt' because it is also part of the exchange.

Figure 2. The Transaction Concept

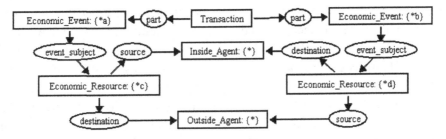

By completing REA's representation in conceptual graphs as shown by Figure 2, this duality is revealed in full.

The Transaction Concept

Transaction in this sense is thus a high-level declarative statement that conceptualises the enterprise itself rather than a number of lower-level transactions that support its business processes. This Transaction Concept (TC) restates the enterprise's mission statement, but in a balanced way that shows what an enterprise is willing to sacrifice ('pay') to satisfy the desires in its mission statement. It therefore sets the value of the mission statement, which is essentially qualitative in nature. Many enterprises, such as charities, universities, government, do not seek to maximise their profit in purely monetary ways. Even many outwardly profit-oriented enterprises present their mission statements in qualitative ways (e.g. quality of service, duty to all stakeholders, society, and reputation).

Figure 2 is the generic TC. The TC has also been referred to as the Transaction Model (TM) e.g. (Polovina & Hill, 2009). Both sides of duality are shown in the TC by linking the economic events to the same transaction. This, like REA, gives the same notion of balance as in the double entry bookkeeping model. As such it continues REA's capture of the essence of accounting by providing abstract constructs to model organisational transactions, including the bookkeeping notion of duality *and* drawing on the power of CGs. The

duality relationship permits two economic events to be represented as a mirror-image exchange of resources, thereby forming the basis of a transaction. As one value describes the benefit in the transaction, the other value depicts what had to be sacrificed for that benefit.

Like REA, the TC comprises two *Economic Event* concepts, denoted by {*a} and {*b}. The transaction is complete when both economic events balance, which indicates that {*a} always opposes {*b}, representing debits and credits. The 'event subject' of these events are related to the two *Economic Resource* concepts, {*c} and {*d}, each having independent source and destination agents. Note that here we have refined the 'party-to' relations in the original REA model to 'source' and 'destination' relations to describe the actual movement of the resources. The *Inside Agent* and *Outside Agent* refer to the parties involved with the transaction. The Inside and Outside prefix denotes the relative perspective of the transaction for each party. The braces '{}' denote plurality, indicating that each concept can represent a number of aggregated resources, events or agents.

The TC allows us to support the computation of these qualitative concepts and capture hitherto hidden transactions that would otherwise be a lost opportunity for an enterprise. Put simply, the TC has the ability to structure the previously unstructured aspect of transactions. As such it structures more of that remaining 80-85% of corporate information that we identified at the beginning of this discussion in a computer-based organisational memory. Accepting that the TC is a model of the enterprise, it offers a common basis by which an enterprise's knowledge of itself and its environment can be accessed and manipulated across all its divergently encoded data, information and knowledge bases according to this fundamental concept.

This generic TC with its generic concepts of 'Economic Resource', 'Economic Event' and 'Inside/Outside Agent' may be appropriately specialised to any quantitative or qualitative concept describing more specific items of interest. In Figure 1 the specialisations of 'Merchandise', 'Cash Receipt', 'Sale', 'Sales – Region' and 'Customer' were illustrated. The simple but illuminating case study that now follows reveals a more expressive use of the TC.

A SIMPLE EXAMPLE: P-H UNIVERSITY

P-H University is a fictional higher education institution that has a student population of 15,000 and an annual turnover of £15m (15,000,000 British pounds). It specialises in technological subjects, with centres of excellence in certain areas. Due to the uncertain impact arising from reduced government financial support, students' anxieties in paying higher fees, increased staff and equipment costs, and an increasingly competitive higher educational market it has had a difficult year and is expected to remain so for the next three years. Indeed this year the university will make a loss of £1m.

The university's staff members are concerned about keeping their jobs, not helped by the equivocal statements given by management who are in turn pressed by the financial statements that paint a grim picture. Consultants to the university have advised that it will revert to profit, as there is an increasing trend by industry to recruit technological graduates, as well as a significant increase in interest by schoolchildren in technology after a number of successful initiatives by government

and industry. The university's management are nonetheless concerned that the university will not survive until then, which they view as uncertain anyway, and has suspended all staff development and is seriously considering applying the same to the research budget for emerging researchers who do not yet generate income. The university is beginning to lose key staff who simply choose to leave, and risks losing credibility amongst its community and its profile in higher education overall. But by saving these costs a net surplus of £1m can instead be made, further increased by the salaries saved (allowing for pay-offs such as redundancy or other associated costs) of those staff leaving.

Many of P-H's staff are research active. This means they pride themselves on the quality of their research. 20% of the staff generate 80% of the research output. They bring in a substantial amount of research income that contributes £7m to the bottom line. A further 40% are emerging researchers contributing the remaining 20% of the research output but little that is income generating presently. It is this group that are most affected by the proposed research budget cut and although most of these staff are resigned to this fate, it will have a significantly adverse impact on their motivation. This will have an effect on P-H that presently cannot be calculated but is worryingly adverse. The other 40% of staff are interested in teaching only and do not contribute to research, but are already de-motivated by the loss of staff development. As many of them aspire to be research active, the loss of psychical enjoyment offered by this career path, like those already engaged in research is incalculable. Would the loss of its staff's psychical stimulation reflected in key staff leaving and the rest being demotivated, undermine the very purpose of the university, let alone its return to profit?

The university's Director of Research and representatives of the research staff meet to decide what the best course of action should be. They have distilled the situation as that captured by Figure 3,

Figure 3. The TC for P-H University

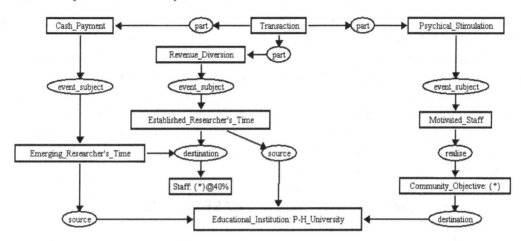

which is the specific TC for this enterprise. The basis of this CG was Figure 2, the generic TC we have already encountered.

From P-H University's TC we can observe the following:

- The transaction reveals its validity through the costs being outweighed by the benefits of the university achieving its community objectives by undertaking this transaction. As we know the *{*}* in *Community Objective* above denotes a plural, thus stating that we are referring to community objective*s*.

- The balancing of these debits and credits denotes the exchange of resources but over and above the simple monetary aspects, thus in a conventional system this could not be captured leading to errors of omission or commission.

- The TC shows that *Cash Payment* and *Revenue Diversion* versus *Psychical Stimulation* are the two complementary sets of economic events that trigger the transaction. In CG theory they are hierarchical subtypes of *Economic Event*. The terms subtype (and supertype) are analogous to subclass (and superclass) in Object-Orientation (OO) (Fowler, 2004).

- The *event subject* relations (i.e. the states altered by the economic events) highlight the salient time and staff motivation resources (being subtypes of *Economic Resource*).

- The *source* and *destination* relations (i.e. providers and recipients) of the resources are the agents in the transaction. The subtype of *Inside Agent* in this scenario being the educational institution, with the *Outside Agent* being the staff involved as its corresponding subtype.

- The *{*}@40%* once again describes a plural of staff, but in particular the 40% who are the emerging researchers.

- P-H University is shown as a referent of *Educational Institution* (a subtype of *Inside Agent*), thus denoting it as a particular instance of the educational institution type. This corresponds to an object of a class in OO, or the value of a field in a database (Connolly, 2005; Fowler, 2004).

The meeting thus has the information presented in a structured way that enables them to recommend that the 'top 20%' are allowed to divert some of their revenue generating activities (hence the term 'revenue diversion') to mentor the other 'up-and-coming 40%'. This 40% in turn has managed to retain a research budget, which the director knows that the university's governing board will ratify. The top 20% have the research income generating activities from which they can sustain their existence. The meeting agrees that this provides the most conducive environment to motivate the staff (who are thus more appreciative of the difficult environment), sustain the university in the present difficult climate and grow it in the future according to its community objectives. The university will show a net loss of £0.5m (500,000 British pounds) but this is now considered the optimal worthwhile investment for achieving its community objectives whilst retaining its sound financial management. Through the TC we have overcome the need to rely on unstructured brute-force judgements or too-narrowly structured accounting measures that, unlike the TC, do not accord with the intuitive purpose of P-H University.

Missing Agent?

Whilst the P-H case study makes a number of assumptions for the sake of simplicity of this illustration, a careful examination of even this simplified example reveals that P-H University's TC is missing one key aspect. If we look again at *Community Objective* in this TC (Figure 3), we see that it lacks a source, and in the generic TC (Figure 2) every economic resource has a source and a destination. It is evident that this requirement is needed as part of balancing this transaction. Thus we have captured a potential error of omission – there is a stakeholder in our transaction that we have not explicated! Who might this 'new' outside agent be? It might be argued that this agent may not need to be explicated as it is immaterial; it's likely however that given P-H University's emphasis on satisfying its community objectives it would be key to explicate who is supplying this economic resource (being its supertype) that P-H is enjoying as a destination. It forces P-H University to consider its TC and bring this agent

into it. The meeting decides that agent it is simply *Community*, reflecting the role that the community plays in P-H University's transactions. It would not have been captured in its existing (accounting or otherwise-based) information system, and left implicit in any natural language description, but it is in the structure of the TC and demonstrates another value of this approach. Figure 4 demonstrates the correctly balanced TC.

CASE STUDIES

The following experiences demonstrate the validity of the TC across a variety of domains and application areas, highlighting its general applicability:

Community Healthcare

A TC was identified and explored for the complex realm of home-based community healthcare services to frail and disabled people. This domain provides a complex set of challenges for UK Local Authority Managers. Defining the agents was an involved process and there was a continual temptation to introduce redundant resources, thus contributing to high levels of cost (errors of commission). The TC was able to identify the relevant agents in a hierarchical way, and identify a new *Purchase Agent* role that had hitherto prevented progress on this work (error of omission) (Hill et al., 2006; Hill, 2006).

Emergency Healthcare

The provision and management of emergency care consumes considerable economic resources, which must be balanced against the potential increase in lives lost. One of the challenges of this domain is to identify the key performance indicators (Key PIs, or KPIs) that have a direct influence upon the monetary balance sheet, in order that they can be managed appropriately

Figure 4. The balanced TC for P-H University

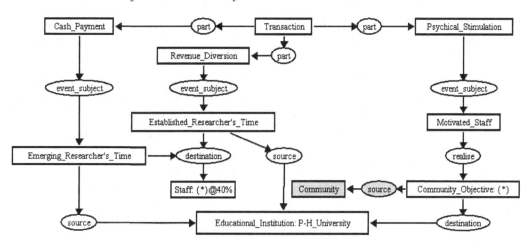

without the PI measures themselves losing sight of the economic resources they are meant to measure (e.g. an unacceptable loss of lives for saving money in hard-pressed budgets). In this case the TC identified problematic qualitative concepts and enabled measures to be derived to simplify the management of these difficult issues. As such, the PIs for qualitative measures became indexes rather than the objects (economic resources) in themselves thus avoiding errors of commission (Hill et al., 2006).

Learning Environments

Mobile learning (or m-learning) presents new opportunities for learners to interact with materials using their smart phones or personal digital assistants. Analysis with the TC highlighted how this particular mode of learning raised the tensions between study-time, employment and leisure time that typical m-learners experience. As such the TC enabled learners to make an informed judgement about the costs (e.g. time sacrificed) and rewards (e.g. psychic or career benefits of qualification) in place of an ill-considered surface level desire that leads to their dropping out and wasting their energies (errors of omission and commission) (Hill, 2010a).

Early Requirements Elicitation

The combination of a rich, lucid modelling notation, foundations in formal logic through CGs and the TC has been adopted as a means of capturing and expressing ontologies at a very early stage of preliminary requirements gathering. Since the TC requires concepts to be specified, this approach also serves to identify types and their associated hierarchical relationships, thus forming the ontological basis for a domain such as those applied to above. This approach is referred to as Transaction Agent Modelling (TrAM) as a pre-early (or 'embryonic') requirements technique for multi-agent systems and the enterprise applications that can be built upon them (Hill et al., 2006; Hill, 2007).

Enterprise Architectures

The above early requirements elicitation work is being extended in the sphere of enterprise architectures, which comprise of complex transactional Information Systems that perform repetitive and bespoke business transactions to meet business goals. Contemporary enterprise architecture frameworks such as TOGAF (www.opengroup. org/togaf) and Zachman (www.zifa.com) have been widely adopted to organise design thinking about the architectural components as well as to provide a description of architecture artefacts. Like these frameworks, the TC is core to enterprise architecture, The TC and TrAM is therefore being related with these existing enterprise architecture frameworks to explore the value-add that the TC brings to these frameworks (Launders, Polovina, & Hill, 2010; Sowa & Zachman, 1992). Allied to this work is the Open Semantic Enterprise Architecture (OpenSEA), bringing the previously referred-to ISO Common Logic (Bridges & Polovina, 2010) through CGs into these frameworks (Bridges & Polovina, 2010).

Multi-Agent Systems

An initial implementation of TrAM as a multi-agent system (MAS) now exists. In this implementation, enterprise agents take advantage of new scenarios by understanding the ontologies of other enterprises. Coupled with the belief, desire and intention (BDI) model, the TC is used as part of an agent's model for reasoning on a particular course of action. The work shows how the TC can be implemented using CGs and MAS software tools such as Amine, Jason and JADE (Hill, 2010b).

Research-Informed Learning and Teaching

Given the issues discussed thus far, it is not surprising that learning about the designing of robust, expressive software for the enterprise is a perennial challenge for students too. The TC been used for learning, teaching and assessment (LTA) to enable students to make tangible links between enterprise architectures and the needs of robust enterprise applications that reflect the issues that the TC addresses. Using a number of case studies that relate to healthcare, financial services and manufacturing, the TC has enabled learners to consider enterprise architectures that focus on the business rather than just the technology. At the outset it forces them to consider the 80-85% of

unstructured information as well as the 15-20% that they see as the being the total problem with the serious levels of errors of omission and commission that can entail. The TC drives them to consider use cases for enterprise applications at the kite (business) level rather than the sea (system) level view (Fowler, 2004), and that reflect the balance the stakeholders and their transactions with the enterprise e.g. like the P-H University case demonstrated. These 'transactional use cases' are rather unconventional compared to mainstream approaches, and together with the TC enable students to engage on a path of enquiry around the real issues in contemporary architectures for enterprise applications as we have described (Launders, Polovina, & Khazaei, 2010a, 2010b).

FORMAL CONCEPT ANALYSIS

The TC can also be defined through a technique related to CGs known as Formal Concept Analysis (FCA) (Ganter, Stumme, & Wille, 2005). In FCA, formal objects and formal attributes in a domain are identified and their (un-named) binary relations are shown as crosses in what is termed in FCA as a formal context. Figure 5 shows the formal context for P-H University's original TC that was shown by Figure 3. The type labels in CGs become formal attributes in FCA and the referents in CGs become formal objects. Thus *Educational Institution* becomes a formal attribute and *P-H University* becomes a formal object. For anonymous cases (i.e. where the referent is not shown), a token is used to represent this instance, e.g. in Figure 5, *CP* is an instance of *Cash Payment*.

Figure 6 shows the concept lattice that results from the P-H University formal context. In FCA, the concept lattice depicts the hierarchy of formal objects in the context. The hierarchy can be found in the context, but it is more visible in the lattice. For example, it is clear that the transaction, T, is at the top of the hierarchy and that there is a hierarchical order in the object instances $T, PS, MS,$

Figure 5. Formal Context of P-H University scenario

A	B	C	D	E	F	G	H	I	J	K
	Cash Pay...	Emerging ...	Staff	Transaction	Revenue D...	Establishe...	Education...	Physical St...	Motivated ...	Communit...
CP	X			X						
EMRT	X	X		X						
S	X	X	X	X	X	X				
T				X						
RD				X	X					
ESRT				X		X				
P-H University	X	X		X	X	X	X	X	X	X
PS				X				X		
MS				X				X	X	
CO				X				X	X	X

Figure 6. The P-H University scenario concept lattice

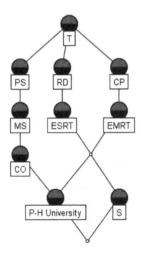

CO and *P-H University* that depicts the dependency between such objects in the TM.

By incorporating the TC's relations into the formal attributes, shown by Figure 7, it becomes possible to see the complete TC hierarchy in the corresponding concept lattice, Figure 8.

Looking at the lattice, it is clear that emerging and established researchers are conceptually similar, having the same source and destination and only differing in their instantiation; one by a revenue diversion and the other by a cash payment. It is also again clear that CO (Community Objective) does not have a source. The obvious source would be the community. Adding this to the formal context results in the revised, now balanced TC shown in Figure 9.

An interesting natural 'layering' of concepts in the lattice is apparent, with event subjects forming an upper layer and sources and destinations forming a lower layer. The lattice provides an intuitive and easily readable representation of the CG. In figures 6 and 7, a further piece of information is given by the size of the node: the larger the node the more objects are reachable from that node. So, for example, *PS event subject* involves more objects than *RD event subject*.

Unlike the CGs that were drawn by hand (using in our case CharGer, http://sourceforge.net/projects/charger/) the FCA concept lattice is machine-generated (using Concept Explorer, http://sourceforge.net/projects/conexp/). Thus FCA offers an automated vehicle by which the hand-drawn TC in CGs can be checked by the machine-drawn TC in FCA to see if it balances, as the concept lattice automatically clusters the components of the TC (resources, events, agents i.e. REA) captured by CGs. Extending this to a fully-automated scenario, as the CG is developed it is dynamically updated in the concept lattice feeding back into the CG that is in turn re-drawn by, for example, an enterprise architect for the added clarification that FCA's concept lattice offers.

TRANSACTION-ORIENTED ARCHITECTURE (TOA)

Given the evidence thus far, it is possible to foresee the emergence of a Transaction-Oriented Architecture (TOA) (Polovina & Stalker, 2010).

Figure 7. The P-H University context incorporating the relations in the TC

A	B	C	D	E	F	G	H	I	J	K
	CP event s...	EMRT sour...	EMRT dest...	T part	RD event s...	ESRT dest...	ESRT sour...	PS event s...	MS realise	CO destin...
CP				X						
EMRT	X			X						
S	X		X	X	X	X				
RD				X						
ESRT				X	X					
Education...	X	X		X	X		X	X	X	X
PS				X						
MS				X				X		
CO				X					X	

Figure 8. The P-H University lattice incorporating TM relations

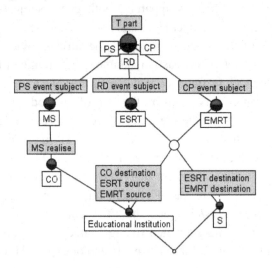

Figure 9. A balanced CG for the P-H University scenario

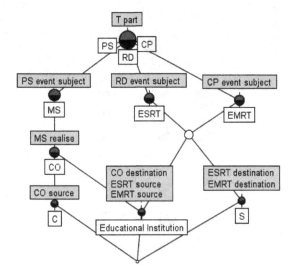

As we have seen, the TC structures the unstructured information for enterprise applications. The notion of a TOA captures the TC within an enterprise architecture that can be aligned with contemporary developments in Service-Oriented Architecture (SOA) (Sweeney, 2010). In particular, the TOA can give direction and purpose to SOA, which provides the components for an enterprise system according to business rather than technical concepts but not the overarching direction that the TC provides. Rather SOA relies on providing tools for business process experts and a governance structure as part of useful enterprise architecture frameworks such as TOGAF or Zachman referred to earlier. It can therefore be envisaged that TOA could similarly be integrated into these frameworks, hence adding the value

of the TC. Process-Oriented Architecture (POA) aligns SOA towards processes rather than services, thus addressing why the services are provided (Manasco & Schurter, 2005). The TOA can also give direction and purpose to POA as processes too are subject to the overarching direction that the TC provides. The TOA thus provides the direction for SOA and POA, as illustrated by Figure 10.

CONCLUSION

In the quest to identify how enterprises may be able to structure their unstructured information to enable them to engage in the right transactions, the relevance of REA and its effectiveness through the TC was explored and demonstrated across a

Figure 10. TOA, POA and SOA

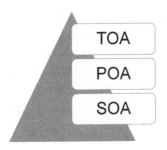

variety of domains. Using a worked example it was shown how the TC could most usefully be expressed in CG and FCA. The TC was then advanced into the TOA, setting the scene for its integration with SOA and POA in meaningful enterprise architectures.

Enterprise applications built upon the TOA would discover otherwise hidden business opportunities available to an SOA-enabled business enterprise as it transacts electronically with other enterprises. TOA captures the semantics of the intrinsic transactions that symbolise the enterprise and its aims i.e. the TC. With this knowledge the TOA can automatically orchestrate the enterprise's business processes according to these key, high-level business transactions. TOA thus brings SOA and the productivity of computers to the height of the real, transactional world that enterprises actually operate in. With TOA, enterprise systems become transformed into an informed, mediating artefact for integrating an enterprise across its numeric, data, information and knowledge-based dimension and identifying its transactions with other enterprises. Whilst there is no doubt more work to be done to fully evaluate its validity, we foresee that the TOA will become an inherent part of future architectures for enterprise applications.

REFERENCES

Attwood, D. A. (1996). *The office relocation sourcebook: A guide to managing staff throughout the move. Europe.* Wiley.

Borio, C. (2008). *The financial turmoil of 2007–? A preliminary assessment and some policy considerations* (BIS Working Papers No. 251). Basel, Switzerland: Bank for International Settlements.

Bridges, S., & Polovina, S. (2010). *An OpenSEA framework using ISO24707 common logic.* Paper presented at the 2010 International Conference on Intelligent Networking and Collaborative Systems, Thessaloniki, Greece. (pp. 335-336). DOI 10.1109/INCOS.2010.92

Claret, J. (1990). Why numbers are not enough. *Accounting Technician: The Journal of the Association of Accounting Technicians UK,* (October), 24-25.

Connolly, T. M. (2005). *Database systems: A practical approach to design, implementation, and management* (Begg, C. E., Ed.). 4th ed.). Harlow, UK: Addison-Wesley.

Fowler, M. (2004). *UML distilled: A brief guide to the standard object modeling language* (3rd ed.). Boston, MA: Addison-Wesley.

Ganter, B., Stumme, G., & Wille, R. (2005). *Formal concept analysis: Foundations and applications* (Stumme, G., & Wille, R., Eds.). Berlin, Germany & Great Britain: Springer.

Geerts, G., & McCarthy, W. E. (1991). Database accounting systems. In B. Williams, & B. J. Sproul (Eds.), *Information technology perspectives in accounting: An integrated approach* (June ed., pp. 159-183). London, UK: Chapman and Hall Publishers.

Gerbé, O., Keller, R. K., & Mineau, G. W. (1998). Conceptual graphs for representing business processes in corporate memories. In M. Mugnier, & M. Chein (Eds.), *Conceptual structures: Theory, tools and applications: 6th International Conference on conceptual structures, ICCS'98, Montpellier, France, August 1998 (Proceedings)* (pp. 401-415). Heidelberg, Germany: Springer-Verlag.

Groenewegen, J. (Ed.). (1993). *Dynamics of the firm: Strategies of pricing and organisation.* Cambridge, UK: Edward Elgar Publishing Ltd.

Hill, R. (2006). Capturing and specifying multi-agent systems for the management of community healthcare. In Yoshida, H., Jain, A., Ichalkaranje, A., Jain, L. C., & Ichalkaranje, N. (Eds.), *Advanced computational intelligence paradigms in health-care - 1, studies in computational intelligence* (48th ed., pp. 127–164). Berlin, Germany: Springer.

Hill, R. (2007). *A requirements elicitation framework for agent-oriented software engineering.* PhD thesis, Sheffield Hallam University (pp. 1-244).

Hill, R. (2010a). *Agency and the virtual campus: The TrAM approach.* Paper presented at the 2010 International Conference on Intelligent Networking and Collaborative Systems, Thessaloniki, Greece (pp. 8-15). doi:DOI 10.1109/INCOS.2010.95

Hill, R. (2010b). Conceptual structures for reasoning enterprise agents. In Croitoru, M., Ferré, S., & Lukose, D. (Eds.), *Conceptual structures: From information to intelligence* (pp. 191–194). Berlin/Heidelberg, Germany: Springer. doi:10.1007/978-3-642-14197-3_20

Hill, R., Polovina, S., & Shadija, D. (2006). Transaction agent modelling: From experts to concepts to multi-agent systems. In H. Schärfe, P. Hitzler & P. Øhrstrøm (Eds.), *Conceptual structures: Inspiration and application, lecture notes in artificial intelligence* (LNAI 4068, pp. 247-259). Heidelberg, Germany: Springer.

Hruby, P. (2006). *Model-driven design using business patterns* (1st ed.). Springer.

Ijiri, Y. (1967). *The foundations of economic accounting.* UK: Prentice Hall.

Kramer, J. (2008, 18 September 2008). Financial turmoil. Retroieved from http://uk.youtube.com/watch?v=Sanr9kx3Mq4

Launders, I. (2009). Socio-technical systems and knowledge representation. In Whitworth, B., & de Moor, A. (Eds.), *Handbook of research on socio-technical design and social networking systems* (pp. 558–574). Hershey, PA: IGI Global. doi:10.4018/9781605662640.ch037

Launders, I., Polovina, S., & Hill, R. (2010). *Semantics and pragmatics in enterprise architecture through transaction agent modelling.* Paper presented at the The 12th International Conference on Informatics and Semiotics in Organisations, Reading, UK. (pp. 285-291). Retrieved from http://www.scitepress.org/DigitalLibrary/

Launders, I., Polovina, S., & Khazaei, B. (2010a). *Case studies as simulation of industrial practice.* Paper presented at the CPLA Enquiry, Autonomy & Graduateness Conference, Sheffield Hallam University, UK (pp. 73-88). Retrieved from http://extra.shu.ac.uk/cetl/cpla/resources/CPLA_Conference_Proceedings.pdf

Launders, I., Polovina, S., & Khazaei, B. (2010b). *Learning perspectives of enterprise architectures through TrAM.* Paper presented at the First Conceptual Structures - Learning, Teaching and Assessment Workshop (CS-LTA) at the 18[Th] International Conference on Conceptual Structures (ICCS 2010), Kuching, Malaysia (pp. 29-41). Retrieved from http://extra.shu.ac.uk/cetl/cpla/cslta2010/publication.html

Lee, G. A. (1986). *Modern financial accounting.* UK: Van Nostrand Reinhold.

Manasco, B., & Schurter, T. (2005). POA or SOA? *ZDNet.* Retrieved March 1, 2010, from http://blogs.zdnet.com/service-oriented/index.php?p=206

McCarthy, W. E. (1987). On the future of knowledge-based accounting systems. In M. Vasarhelyi (Ed.), *The D. R. Scott memorial lecture series, University of Missouri, and published in artificial intelligence in accounting and auditing: The use of expert systems* (October ed., pp. 19-42). USA: Markus Wiener Publishing.

Polovina, S. (2007). An introduction to conceptual graphs. In U. Priss, S. Polovina & R. Hill (Eds.), *Proceedings of the 15th International Conference on Conceptual Structures (ICCS 2007): Conceptual structures: Knowledge architectures for smart applications, July 2007, Sheffield, UK* (Lecture Notes in Artificial Intelligence 4604, pp. 1-15). Berlin/Heidelberg, Germany & New York, NY: Springer.

Polovina, S., & Hill, R. (2005). Enhancing the initial requirements capture of multi-agent systems through conceptual graphs. In F. Dau, M. Mugnier & G. Stumme (Eds.), *Conceptual structures: Common semantics for sharing knowledge, lecture notes in artificial intelligence* (LNAI 3596, pp. 439-452). Heidelberg, Germany: Springer.

Polovina, S., & Hill, R. (2009). A transactions pattern for structuring unstructured corporate information in enterprise applications. *International Journal of Intelligent Information Technologies,* *5*(2), 34–47. doi:10.4018/jiit.2009040103

Polovina, S., & Stalker, I. D. (2010). *TOASTIE: Transaction-oriented architecture for structuring the totally integrated enterprise.* Paper presented at the 2010 International Conference on Intelligent Networking and Collaborative Systems, Thessaloniki, Greece. (pp. 333-334). DOI 10.1109/INCOS.2010.93

Sarraf, Q., & Ellis, G. (2006). Business rules in retail: The tesco.com story. *Business Rules Journal, 7*(6)

Seidman, D. I., & Ritsko, J. J. (2004). Preface. *IBM Systems Journal, 43*(3), 449. doi:10.1147/sj.433.0449

Sowa, J. F. (1984). *Conceptual structures: Information processing in mind and machine.* Boston, MA: Addison-Wesley.

Sowa, J. F., & Zachman, J. A. (1992). Extending and formalizing the framework for Information Systems architecture. *IBM Systems Journal, 31*(3), 590–616. doi:10.1147/sj.313.0590

Sweeney, R. (2010). *Achieving service-oriented architecture: Applying an enterprise architecture approach.* Hoboken, NJ: Wiley.

Zimmerman, J. L. (2006). *Accounting for decision making and control* (5th ed.). Boston, MA: McGraw-Hill Irwin.

Chapter 17
Virtual Organisational Trust Requirements:
Can Semiotics Help Fill the Trust Gap?

Tim French
University of Bedfordshire-Luton, UK

ABSTRACT

It is suggested that the use of the semiotic ladder, together with a supportive trust agent can be used together to better explicate "soft" trust issues in the context of Grid services. The contribution offered here is intended to fill a gap in current understanding and modelling of such issues and to support Grid service designers to better conceptualise, hence manage trust issues. The semiotic paradigm is intended to offer an integrative viewpoint within which to explicate "soft" trust issues throughout the Grid life-cycle. A computationally lightweight trust agent is described that can be used to verify high level trust of a Virtual Organisation. The potential benefits of the approach that is advocated here include the reduction of risk and potential improvements in the quality and reliability of Grid service partnerships. For these benefits to accrue, explicit "soft" as well as "hard" trust management is essential as is an integrative viewpoint.

INTRODUCTION

Computational models of trust mechanisms based on explicating notion of trust in the context of Grid services have only recently emerged from the research literature (Eymonn, Konig, & Matros, 2008; Song, Hwang, & Kwok, 2005). One reason for this is that traditional security mechanisms are being increasingly challenged by open, large scale and decentralized environments. Specifically, the Grid is specifically characterized by *ad hoc* collaborations (sharing of computing resources) as between geographically distributed Virtual Organisations (VO's). Explicit trust management should ideally aim to go well beyond "hard" tangible security aspects of Grid services (Matthews, Bicarregui, & Dimitrakos, 2003). Rather, at a higher level of organizational abstraction, wider trust dimensions inherent within Grid partnerships such as partner reputation and organizational culture, quality of service issues such as reliability, provenance, values and ethical concerns need to be examined. Emergent research work is only beginning to seek to address these "soft" trust issues and seeking to integrate these with more fine-grained Grid service security concerns (Wilson, Arenas, & Schubert, 2007).

Since Grid standards are grounded on Web-Services, it might at first appear to be reasonable to assume that various Web-Service standards that are still under development will together, create a suitably structured framework within which to address both "hard" and "soft" Grid trust and security concerns. Indeed, initiatives are now underway, having the aim of ensuring that emergent Grid computing paradigms are based on a fully articulated set of trust and security protocols and standards (Cahill et al., 2003). However, it is becoming increasingly apparent that there is a gap in our current understanding of "soft" trust aspects of Grid services. The remainder of this paper seeks to show the potential for filling the trust gap with respect to agent-to-agent Grid services through use of the semiotic paradigm.

GRID COMPUTING: A BRIEF OVERVIEW

Grid computing is a computational network of tools and protocols for coordinated resource sharing and problem solving among pooled assets. These pooled assets are known as Virtual Organizations (VO). They can be distributed across the globe and are heterogeneous in character. The Grid is a type of a parallel and distributed system that enables the sharing, selection, and aggregation of resources distributed across multiple administrative domains based on their availability, capability, performance, cost, and users' quality of service requirements. Grid computing uses many computers connected via a network simultaneously to solve a single scientific or business related problem. Whereas current initiatives have focused on the needs of the scientific community, in the future the business community is expected to benefit too. Indeed, Grid computing is expected to become a mainstream business-enterprise topology during the rest of the current decade. In the most common case, the type of application most likely to benefit from the blurring of the binding as between application and host is one that usually require substantial amounts of computer power and/or produce or access large amounts of data. That is to say, execution of an application in parallel across multiple host machines distributed within or between enterprises can increase performance substantially and also make use of the spare capacity of existing nodes too.

Grid applications often typically involve large volumes of data produced by data-intensive simulations and experiments. The Grid can be conceived as a huge network of VO's which have coordinated their resource node sharing capabilities. The Global Grid Forum (GGF) has been formed to standardize the growth of the Grid. The GGF has embraced the Open Grid Services Architecture (OGSA) as the industry blueprint for standards-based grid computing. "Open" refers to both the process to develop standards and the standards themselves. It is "service-oriented" because it delivers functionality as loosely-coupled, interacting services aligned with industry-accepted Web service standards. The "architecture" defines the components, their organizations and interactions, and the design philosophy used. A basic premise of OGSA is that everything is represented by a service: a network enabled entity that provides some capability through the exchange of messages. Computational resources, storage resources, networks, programs, databases, and so forth are all services. This adoption of a uniform service-oriented model means that all the components of the environment are virtual. More specifically, OGSA represents everything as a Grid service: a Web service that conforms to a set of conventions and supports standard interfaces for such purposes as lifetime management. The general reader is encouraged to refer to the work of Ian Foster, one of the pioneers of the Grid, (see: Foster and Kesselman, 2004), where definitions and explanations of Grid standards, tools, architectures, techniques and methods such as OGSA, GGF *et al.*, can be found, together with an extensive Glossary of grid-specific terminology.

Consumer and Provider Trust Issues

Most of the attention has thus far been placed on fine-grained service level trust and security issues. Little attention comparatively speaking appears to have been invested in coarse grained VO level reputation trust issues to date. The work that has emerged (Matthews et al., 2003) claims to deal with high-level reputation issues but upon closer examination appears to mainly address tangible security GSI (Grid Service Infrastructure) aspects and performance aspects. This work has however clearly established the validity of the need to examine trust issues. For example, Song goes on to describe a trust *index* that is calculated using a mixture of inputs including the site's defence capabilities (anti-virus protection) and reputation, defined as a performance track record (Song et al., 2005). A highly diverse nature of mainly XML (Extensible Markup Language) based "Open" Standards that have hitherto sought to address trust, security and related topics in the context of Web and Grid Service based architectures. Indeed, one of the key issues is the lack of any overall viewpoint or intellectual paradigm to encompass this entire area.

How Can Semiotics Seek to Fill the Trust Gap?

Semiotics has been called the "science of signs". More specifically it is the discipline which connects meaning, meaning making, communication and culture through an understanding of acts of signification (Liu, 2000). The fundamental notion is that stakeholders give meanings to 'signs' through acts of signification called semiosis and that this (highly variable) process of meaning making serves to mediate all acts of human communication. Within an organisational context these acts of communication typically comprise communication patterns, social rituals and norms, speech-acts, and social constructs of various kinds. Signs typically take the form of tangible visual concrete stimuli (such as icons, images, hypertext cues etc) as well as be expressed as social constructs (shared knowledge) often known as social affordances. Signs can also take form of more abstract meaning making such as beliefs, culture and trust. The field of organisational semiotics is a diverse field of enquiry that has developed in order to relate semiotics to both IT systems and their organisational business contexts. Much of this work has been hitherto directed towards gaining insights into the development of socio-technical systems using various "soft" methodologies, frameworks and tools (Liu, 2000).

It may be helpful in the context Grid trust specifically, to view trust issues through an integrative *semiotic lens*. This lens is derived mainly from Ronald Stamper's pioneering work (Stamper, 1973) in which the classical division of semiotics into syntactics, semantics and pragmatics is extended so as to include extra layers that comprise a complete semiotic framework (Liu, 2000). The added layers comprise empirics, physics and the social world. The aim of the classic semiotic framework is to provide a complete account of sign processes and sign exchange and meaning making at all of these levels so as to provide a complete

Figure 1. Classic semiotic ladder (Stamper, 1973)

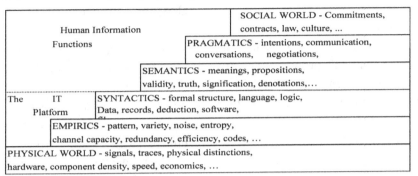

semiotic picture of the human, organisational, and social contexts within which IT platforms and their human actors are typically embedded. For each level, it is possible and indeed necessary to identify the actors and agents involved and to select an appropriate investigative technique matched to the type of communication acts that typically take place within that level. The choice of technique is not defined as such by the ladder. Rather, the ladder defines the level of system abstraction within which the information system and its various constituent elements are being described. The vision is that information systems and organisations and their human actors form an integrative whole.

Within this whole, the ladder provides a lens within which particular activities can be investigated in more detail. Table 1 below shows a classical semiotic ladder derived from Stamper's work (Stamper, 1973). Brief explanatory headings for each of the layers are embedded within Table 1 and some explanatory notes are also given. Further details can be found in Liu (Liu, 2000).

• Physical Level & Empiric Level

These levels are concerned with information. Signs are modelled by physical signals, their sources and destinations and the routes over which they are transmitted. Information is seen as a collection of physical tokens.

Table 1. Macro-dimensions of virtual organisation and the semiotic trust ladder

Exemplar Grid service trust issues	Semiotic trust ladder	Applicability (VO Grid Lifecycle)	Signs
To what extent does the Service conform to desired VO cultural/ cross-cultural norms? Legal safeguards?	**Social world:** trust beliefs and expectations	Planning stage	Cultural/Social trust Policy signs
Reputation of Grid service provider/consumer? Any ethical conflicts?	**Pragmatics:** goals, intentions, trusted negotiations, trusted communications	Planning, build, run time	Reputation signs
How reliable, valid are the services and will they meet quality norms?	**Semantics:** meanings, truth/ falsehood, validity	Build and run time	Authentication/ validity signs
Secure agents: how trusted are they?	**Syntactics:** formalisms, trusted access to data, files, software	Build and run time	Trusted access signs
Intrusion detection/prevention adequate?	**Empirics:** entropy, channel capacity	Run time	Messaging/traffic management signs

- Syntax Level

Here, signs correspond to logical tokens that stand for some physical token or tokens that are often called symbols. Concepts such as complexity, ambiguity and structural richness are typically the objects of research.

- Semantic Level

Semantics is concerned with the meaning of signs. At the semantic level communication is fully successful only if the intended transmitted meaning and the received meanings are the same, according to an operational procedure reflecting one of the semantic principles. This is rarely the case in practice due to mediating influences such as culture as well as individual differences in human cognition.

- Pragmatic Level

Pragmatics is the level of semiotics concerned with the relationship between signs and the potential behaviour of responsible agents, in a social context. Intentions and beliefs are central.

- Social Level

Communication at the social level requires the message sender and receiver share social norms. There are several different kinds of norms, which determine the way a social member sees the world. For example behavioural norms are rules that not only constrain individual behaviour but also guide individual behaviour according to social and organisational goals. Meaning, at the social level, refers to the relations of signs to the norm structures specific to the social context.

Grid Trust: Role of Semiotics as a Conceptual Tool

There is evidence to support the view that human trust formation is a far more elusive and subtle process than implied by existing OGSA XML dialects, models and initiatives or indeed trust (security) oriented architectures. In particular, human trust formation involves wider trust contexts: organizational, social, and human cultural factors pre-determine human trust formation and expectations and beliefs (Komiac & Benbasat, 2005). Furthermore, human trust is also ultimately not merely a rational cognitive construct but has a strong emotional component. For this reason, we propose that the current models and approaches to autonomic trust formation within the emergent Grid computing paradigm should seek to endow agents and entities with these wider more subtle "soft" contexts.

As will be seen later, an agent based solution is outlined in which objective measures of corporate governance are used as a proxy for trust signification at the organisational level. Thus, the agents can be considered to support the social and pragmatic layers of the semiotic trust ladder previously outlined. Hence the relevance of this work to conceptual structures and applications: the *semiotic paradigm* (more specifically the semiotic trust ladder presented later) provides the conceptual framework within which *agent based enablers* are used to discover and report back trust metrics that are seen to operate mainly at the higher levels of the generic semiotic ladder introduced earlier. The added-value of such an approach lies mainly in the potential risk reduction amongst Grid partners, engaged in often complex patterns of E-Service provision and consumption.

A SEMIOTIC MODEL OF TRUSTED GRID SERVICES

Human trust is an elusive and subtle concept that involves reference not merely to local contexts but also wider organizational and social settings within which E-Service transactions of all kinds typically take place (Gambetta, 1998.) Existing approaches to the trusted Grid Services which emphasis the value of establishing secure communications between autonomic entities do not appear to attempt to explicitly seek to verify local events, and credentials against wider social, cultural and organizational dimensions.

In Table 1, for each layer of the semiotic trust ladder, some exemplar trust issues are identified and aligned to the Grid Service lifecycle. By extending this approach it is possible to develop a fully comprehensive account of trust issues during the entire Grid Service lifecycle. Indeed, by attempting to identify and map trust issues to the trust ladder, it is hoped that previously implicit or poorly understood or articulated trust issues may be more clearly revealed to VO partners at an earlier stage in the Grid Service lifecycle than hitherto.

The ladder currently exists as a kind of meta-model, within which VO Grid partners can seek to better conceptualise trust issues within a typical Grid partnership, from its earliest inception to design and implementation. The intention is for Grid partners to use the high-level model as a reference point for trust issues at each stage of the evolution of a grid partnership, thus making the issues fully explicit to all concerned. For example, at the planning and building stages of the Grid, any mismatches between partners (in terms of trust thresholds, expectations or trust service level policies) will need to be resolved by on-going negotiation. During run-time execution, partners will need to continuously check with one another that the agreements previously entered into are being implemented in the expected manner. Typically, validation of security aspects and quality of service agreements will be the major concerns.

It is later suggested that one recommended method of validating the agreements entered into during the earlier stages of the ladder, might well take the form of trust agent(s). These agents will ideally be enabled with knowledge sufficient so as to check high level norms, and policies as well as low level access rights. In a sense therefore these 'semiotic' agents will act as the self-validators of the agreements and policies identified in the earlier stages of the ladder itself. An open question at present is the detection of intrusion into Grids via vulnerabilities of various kinds. Little is known about intrusion at the present time. To validate this part of the ladder, partners will however, need to anticipate intrusion (hence vulnerabilities) and will need to carry out a vulnerability analysis that is relevant to the particular security standard chosen (e.g. SSL/TLS, proxy X509 certificates, Shibboleth). It is expected that for any given Grid partnership, the ladder will become refined and indeed tailored by the partners themselves, so as to best meet their needs. The main idea therefore is to use the ladder as a generic framework within which the Grid partners themselves can seek to validate and negotiate agreements, with each other. That is to say the ladder is designed to be self-tailored to each and every Grid partnership.

Role of the Trust Agents and Semiotics

A means of enabling an agent with human like rational reasoning concerning trust and irrational (emotional) human like responses to trust is ideally needed to fully simulate human trust formation. Pioneering work has already been carried out by researchers in developing and applying various mathematical formalisms that can be used to design and implement trust models within autonomic systems. Many of these formalisms (Marsh, 1994) rely on the calculation of local trust thresholds of various kinds and their subsequent propagation across nodes via graph-theoretic models. This approach is currently being extended so as to seek to enable MAS (Multi-agent Systems) with the power to investigate trust credentials, provenance and reputation. However, it may be the case that a more lightweight approach is needed to assessing VO high-level reputation using a computationally and analytically lightweight methodology. This approach together with the use of the semiotic trust ladder has the potential to look beyond 'mere' security concerns, to assessing VO level trust domain concerns. In the longer term a richer model and approach may well be needed, but as yet the whole area of "soft" trust is still an emergent one emergent within E-systems with many conflicting models and solutions, (Josang, Ismail, & Boyd, 2007).

The contribution described below can be regarded as a lightweight, pragmatic model that does not seek to be fully comprehensive. Rather, the model though simplistic, is intended to offer a pragmatic means to leverage current technologies to address VO "soft" trust, without inducing latency into the Grid.

A High-Level Semiotic Trust Agent Model

Following on from the review of trust and related security issues (Olmedilla, Rana, Matthews, & Nejdi, 2006) the key issues that an agent based approach should seek to satisfy is related to the extent to which a service requested should (or should not) trust in the ability, of a service provider to fulfil a particular request to a given level of service quality. From the preceding discussion it is clear that some kind of dynamic trust verification process is needed. The approach that is adopted below seeks to provide information about the service provider's "real" organization (reputation) whilst also seeking to access any previous service history (reliability) data, so as to partially fill the trust "gap". The approach is top-level and what is now presented is a design (a set of requirements) for an agent-based solution

rather than a fully working system. The intention is to show from a top level viewpoint, that agent-to-agent systems (such as Grid and also web-services) can be accounted for and perhaps better designed by a semiotically informed trust model. On this basis, the proposed multi-agent system encompasses the following stages (1-8 below) of local and global trust management in the context of a Virtual Organisation (VO) seeking to check trust credentials just prior to invoking a request for a generic Grid-service. For the purposes of this model two agents working co-operatively are assigned to support the task, which are named as Agent-1 ["Local trust agent"] and Agent-2 ["Global trust agent"].

1. A service request is made originating within a given VO, named service requestor, which seeks to request and invoke a given service originating from outside that VO. The request is sent to Agent-1 in terms of a message.
2. Agent-1 responds to the request by looking up the service in a "Yellow Page" registry of VO's and their services that are accessible by all existing VO's in the Grid.
3. Agent-1 finds the service (if not found or not available a suitable error message is sent back to the requestor). Every available service is mapped to at least one VO, named service provider.
4. Agent-1 passes the name of the service provider to Agent-2. Agent-2 then looks up a Global VO Trust Table for their rating details by calculating a trust score for that VO. The Global VO Trust Table contains a series of ratings that, when combines, are used to calculate a trust rating based on various "Corporate Governance" scores.
5. Agent-2 calculates the sum of the scores and returns a single integer value to Agent-1.
6. Agent-1 compares the received global trust rating to see if it lies within the acceptable range of the service requestor. If not, the

service request is terminated with a suitable diagnostic message sent to the service requestor. The procedure can go to Stage 3 to check if the requested service can be available by another VO. If not, the procedure is terminated. If the trust rating is acceptable within the acceptable range of the service requestor, Agent-1 proceeds with Stage 7 by sending a message to Agent-2.

7. Agent-2 looks up another VO Previous Performance table for the recent real time performance (Previous Performance Measure) of the VO providing the service and passes the value back to Agent-1. If minimal acceptable performance criteria are met (e.g. history of node failures is within an acceptable boundary value) then Agent-1 flag's as "low-risk" so as to allow the service request to continue. If not, the service request is flagged as being of "high-risk" of failure before invocation.

8. Finally, Agent-1 check the service requestor's access rights and privileges, by a Access Right table, to see if the requestor has the necessary permission (as defined by role, security and time delimiters) to access the required service and hence local data sets residing outside the current VO.

Role of Global Trust Table

Stephen Marsh (Marsh, 1994) made an early attempt to formalise the notion of the trust for computational use in interactions between two autonomous agents. This approach takes into account many of the widely accepted aspects of trust as seen in the literature, defining basic or dispositional trust, general trust in another entity and situational trust in another entity, combined with the notions of utility, risk and importance. From this, simple linear equations allow the formation of trust values, which are represented in the range [-1, 1) to allow for reasoning about distrust. Trust information (values representing payoff)

from past interactions of an agent is stored, allowing evolution of trust, albeit in a rather arbitrary manner. The concept of a threshold for trusting behaviour based on the perceived risk and competence in the situation, demonstrates the important relationship between trust and risk. One of the basic requirements of a computational trust model is that it should provide a metric for comparing the relative trustworthiness of different agents.

An agent can be considered to be trustworthy if it has a high probability of performing a particular action which, in our context, is to fulfil its obligations during an interaction. This probability can be related to a wide variety of inputs. The function of the Global Trust Table is to provide a set of inputs that can increase the confidence level (the probability whether subjectively or objectively determined) that a VO will perform a task successfully, reliably and which meets an agreed quality of service. The approach adopted here is to advocate the use of trust scores which although simplistic, are computationally lightweight enough to be used within realistic dynamic Grid contexts. A lightweight approach is ideally suited to the need to reduce latency time within demanding high-performance environments.

The only assumption made is that of the availability of data for the calculation of VO high-level reputation and perhaps a more questionable premise also, that such 'scores' are reliable proxies for high-level VO trust. Organisations such as the Investors Shareholder Services (ISS) now regularly publish data for Corporate Governance scores for major corporations, so it would seem reasonable to assume that such data can be readily accessed. We propose a scoring system provided by a trusted third party in which it is assumed that "reputation" can be scored using one or more Corporate Governance metrics. This approach to quantifying organisational reputation (hence trust) and associating this with company valuations appears to be widely accepted in the relevant literature (Brown & Caylor, 2006).

The role of the Global VO Trust table is to verify the trustworthiness of the owner of the service provider (expressed as a set of Corporate Governance scores) as a proxy for trust in the service itself. In the human world it is a commonplace observation that we invest our trust in entities that are known to us through brand identity and reputation. Corporate Governance indexes and scores are publicly available and have been shown to correlate well with firm performance. Similar indexes have been generated for E-Government (Blakemore & Lloyd, 2007). An exemplar scoring model is presented below so as to illustrate how, at a top level of abstraction the lightweight model operates. The process is essentially a two-stage model: VO reputation trust is measured and compared to a threshold value (*Trust Threshold Score*), followed if available by any previous service performance history (*Previous Performance Measure*). If no-history is available then the service is invoked and a service log is then generated accordingly in real-time.

Agent Scoring Model

i. Service requestor sends Agent-1 two values: a *Trust Threshold Score* (TTS) for VO "reputation" and a *Previous Performance Measure* (PPM) that quantifies trust as past history (trust as reliability). Both TTS and PPM are scaled for convenience to a real number that lies in the range [0..1];

ii. The service requestor will only "trust", hence invoke the service from the service provider if the THS = 0.8; PPM = 0.9 (these being two arbitrary values for illustrative purposes);

iii. Agent-2 locates an entry in the Global VO Trust Table for the provider of the requested service i.e. "Basepoint Ltd";

Table 2 presents an exemplar table instantiated with five Corporate Governance values as used by Agent-2.

iv. Agent-2 sums up the available values:

$$\sum_{i}^{n} Sc_n / T$$

where $T = \sum_{1}^{n} Sc_n$ for all known (available) values of **S**. That satisfies the condition: $\forall S_n = 1$

That is to say, Agent-2 sums up the values for entry "Basepoint Ltd" for every non-null value. In Table 3 only five values are shown for illustrative purposes, however in practice up to 51 or so Corporate Governance values might be potentially available to generate a given TTS for any given organization. (The case of a VO being owned by many "real" organizations is not considered here for reasons of clarity, but the model supports this case by simple extension).

v. Agent-2 compares the TTS for "Basepoint Ltd" (let us assume this is > 0.8). Agent-2

Table 2. Agent Scores – an exemplar

Corporate Governance Criteria/Metrics[1]	CG Metric Availability for "Basepoint Ltd" (S)	Score (1-5) – supplied by trusted third party (Sc)
All directors > I yr of service own shares in Basepoint Ltd	1	0.4
> 1 member of the Board has participated in an accredited director education program	(no value/not known)	0.1
Basepoint Audit committee comprises solely of independent outside directors	1	0.1
CEO[2] of Basepoint serves on < 2 additional company boards	1	0.1
All directors have attended > 75% of board meetings	1	0.2

[1] *Derived from Brown & Caylor (2004)*   [2] *Chief Executive Officer*

now attempts to establish any previous experience (service invocation history) for the requested service by examining a history log.

vi. The service history log contains a service history (analogous to a credit check for a human agent) that records failure points or service non-availability per unit time. If the service log does not exist then the service is invoked, if the TTS exceeds the minimum value required.

Essentially, the history log needs to be "mined" using well established approaches to the intelligent data mining of consumer credit transactions such as regression analysis, statistical analysis and the use of neural network methods (Hand & Crowder, 2005; Mohammadian, 2004; Xiaohua, 2005). As a result of these mining activities a particular service provided by a VO may be regarded as being "low" or "high" risk and a variety of actions could be taken in response to this categorisation, depending on the expressed preferences of the service requestor. The connection of the proposed agent-based solution to the semiotic paradigm lies in the ability of the proposed agent based solution to derive trust values from raw reputation data and to reference these values back to internal trust models and thresholds that match consumer VO norms and attitudes to risk. Furthermore, the proposed agent based solution accepts implicitly that trust at the VO level needs to (perhaps somewhat crudely) quantify *reputational trust* at the social semantic and pragmatic levels of the trust ladder, as well as to reference tangible security aspects at the lower syntactic and empiric levels. It is generally acknowledged that up until now, the attention of the Grid trust community of interest has hitherto focussed perhaps rather too narrowly upon the syntactics and empirics of trust. This contribution seeks to remedy that imbalance, without of course implicitly neglecting or mitigating the very real security issues raised by collaboration amongst VO's.

CONCLUSION

Trust aspects of the Grid and indeed E-service architectures are in general are gaining momentum as "soft" issues are being increasingly seen to as relevant to the roll-out of Grid services as "hard" issues. At present the approach to ensuring secure and trustworthy Grid services has emphasized hard security aspects and associated XML based standards, such as WS-Trust, within the OGSA model. This initiative suggests that to achieve clarity of vision the semiotic paradigm may well prove a useful conceptual tool within which to view and conceptualize about trust issues in the context of Grid services. In particular, it has been demonstrated that the "soft" trust 'gap' can be partially filled through using a semiotic trust ladder to aid better conceptualization of trust issues at the VO level of abstraction. Additionally, it can be seen that by using one unified paradigm to describe VO level trust as well as (in the future) Grid Service level trust, trust issues will be considerably better clarified and articulated more explicitly that at present: where trust issues too often remain ambiguous or poorly articulated and separated from tangible security concerns.

Clearly, much further work is needed to develop the approach i.e. richer models of conceptualizing trust at the VO level of abstraction are needed. Later, these models ideally need to lead to the design and deployment of "richer" semiotic trust agents that can more fully and richly simulate human trust cognition, emotional and rational dimensions of trust formation at the Grid Service level of granularity whilst also referencing wider trust domains, not merely simply checking and verifying local tangible security credentials.

It is necessary to further refine the semiotic trust ladder itself, to seek to fully test and validate the agent enabled solution that has been described earlier and to seek to further develop ways of assessing the value and reliability of Corporate Governance scores as a proxy for high-level organisational trust within Grid contexts of use. It will later be necessary, to construct a large scale simulation using a realistically sized data sets, and to enable a semiotic trust agent with an appropriate set of behavioural constraints in respect to trusted VO Grid Service invocation and trusted resource scheduling operating within a variety of heterogeneous VO simulated settings involving different kinds of bi-lateral and multi-lateral simulated VO partnerships. This simulation is in-progress, and a working agent solution has been implemented using a small scale test-bed in Java. The remaining challenge is to scale up the test-bed and to address performance issues within more realistic Grid contexts of use.

ACKNOWLEDGMENT

The author would like to acknowledge the informal assistance of the following academic colleagues at the University Of Bedfordshire Department of Computing & Information Systems in relation to formalising the link between semiotics and the Grid: Dr O Adjei, Dr N Bessis and Dr W Huang. I would also like to acknowledge the role of Professor Kecheng Liu (Informatics Research Centre, Reading University) in relation to his own continuing inspirational contribution to the field of Organisational Semiotics and also with respect to my own ongoing part-time PhD research.

REFERENCES

Blakemore, M., & Lloyd, P. (2007). Trust and transparency: pre-requisites for effective eGovernment, Retrieved May 30th, 2008, from http://www.ccegov.eu/

Brown, L., & Caylor, M. (2006). Corporate governance and firm valuation, *Journal of Accounting Policy*, 25, 409-434.

Cahill, V., Gray, E., Seigneur, J., Jensen, C., Chen, Y., Shand, B., Dimmock, N., Twigg, A., Bacon, J., English, C., Wagealla, W., Terzis, S., Nixon, P., Serugendo, G., Bryce, C., Carbone, M., Krukow, K., & Nielsen, M. (2003). Using trust for secure collaboration in uncertain environments, *IEEE Pervasive Computing Magazine*, 52-61.

Eymonn, T., Konig, S., & Matros, R. (2008). A Framework for trust and reputation in Grid environments, *Journal of Grid Computing*, 6, Retrieved May 29th, 2008, from http://www.springerlink.com/content/111140/?Content+Status=Accepted

Foster, I., & Kesselman, C. (2004). *The Grid 2: Blueprint for a New Computing Intrastructure*, Elsevier Publications.

Gambetta, D. (1988). Can we trust trust? In D. Gambetta, (Ed.), Trust: Making and Breaking Cooperative Relations, (pp. 213–237). Basil Blackwell.

Hand, D.J., & Crowder, M.J. (2005). Measuring customer quality in retail banking. *Statistical Modelling: An International Journal*, 5, 2, 145-158.

Josang, A., Ismail R., & Boyd, C. (2007). A Survey of trust and reputation systems for on-line Service Provision, *Decision Support Systems*, 43(2), 618-644.

Komiak, S., & Benbasat, I. (2004). Understanding customer trust in agent-mediated electronic commerce, web-mediated electronic commerce, and traditional Commerce, *Information Technology and Management*, 5, 181-207.

Liu, K. (2000). *Semiotics in Information Systems Engineering*, Cambridge University Press.

Marsh, S. (1994). Formalizing Trust as a Computational Concept, (Doctoral Dissertation, Glasgow University, UK).

Matthews, B., Bicarregui, J., & Dimitrakos, T. (2003). Building trust on the Grid: trust issues underpinning scalable Virtual Organizations, CLRC Rutherford Appleton Laboratory, UK. Retrieved May 29th, 2008, from http://epubs.cclrc.ac.uk/bitstream/643/trustedgridERCIM.pdf

Mohammadian, M. (2004). *Intelligent Agents for Data Mining and Information Retrieval*. IGI Publishing, Hershey, PA, USA.

Olmedilla, D., Rana, O., Matthews, B & Nejdi, W. (2006). Security and Trust Issues in Semantic Grids, *Proceedings from The Semantic Grid: The Convergence of technologies*, Retrieved May 30th, 2008, from http://epubs.cclrc.ac.uk/bitstream/757/05271.OlmedillaDaniel3.Paper.pdf

Song, S., Hwang, K., & Kwok, Y. (2005). Trusted Grid computing with security binding and trust integration, *Journal of Grid Computing*, 3, 1-2, 53-73.

Wilson, M., Arenas, A., & Schubert, L. (2007). TrustCOM Framework Version 4, Retrieved May 29th, 2008, from http://www.eu-trustcom.com

Stamper, R. (1973). *Information in Business and Administrative Systems*, John Wiley and Sons, New York.

Xiaohua, H. (2005). A Data Mining Approach for Retailing Bank Customer Attrition Analysis. *Journal of Applied Intelligence*, 22, 1, 47-60.

Compilation of References

Abdul-Rahman, A., & Hailes, S. (2000). Supporting trust in virtual communities. In *Proceedings of the Hawaii's International Conference on Systems Sciences*, Maui, Hawaii.

Abowd, G. D., Dey, A. K., Brown, P. J., Davies, N., Smith, M., & Steggles, P. (1999). Towards a Better Understanding of Context and Context-Awareness. In *Proceedings of the 1st international symposium on Handheld and Ubiquitous Computing*. Karlsruhe, Germany: Springer-Verlag.

Agichtein, E., Lawrence, S., & Gravano, L. (2001). *Learning search engine specific query transformations for question answering*. Paper presented at the Tenth International World Wide Web Conference.

Ahmed, F., & Nürnberger, A. (2010). *Multi searcher: Can we support people to get information from text they can't read or understand?* Paper presented at the ACM Special Interest Group of Information Retrieval (SIGIR) Conference, Geneva, Switzerland.

Ajenstat, J. (2004). Virtual Decision Maker for Stock Market Trading as a Network of Cooperating Autonomous Intelligent Agents. *Proceedings of the 37th Hawaii International Conference on System Sciences*, Big Island, HI, USA.

Ajzen, I., & Fishbein, M. (1980). *Understanding attitudes and predicting social behavior*. Englewood Cliffs, N.J.: Prentice-Hall.

Ali, A. S., Rana, O., & Walker, D. W. (2004). WS-QoC: Measuring Quality of Service Compliance. *International Conference on Service Oriented Computing (ICSOC04)*, New York, NY, USA.

Allbeck, J., & Badler, N. (2002). Toward Representing Agent Behaviors Modified by Personality and Emotion. *Autonomous Agents and Multiagent Systems*, Bologna, Italy

Amati, G., & Ounis, I. (2000). Conceptual graphs and first order logic. *The Computer Journal*, *43*(1), 1–12. doi:10.1093/comjnl/43.1.1

Amershi, S., & Morris, M. R. (2008). *CoSearch: A system for co-located collaborative Web search*. Paper presented at the Computer and Human Interaction Conference, Florence, Italy.

Anderson, N., Lee, E., Brockenbrough, J. S., Minie, M., Fuller, S., Brinkley, J., & Tarczy-Hornoch, P. (2007). Issues in Biomedical Research Data Management and Analysis: Needs and Barriers. *Journal of the American Medical Informatics Association*, *14*(4). doi:10.1197/jamia.M2114

Aneiba, A., Rees, S. J., & Chibelushi, C. (2006). A Decision Support Model for Wireless Information Management Using Mobile Agents. *Proceedings of the IASTED International Conference on Artificial Intelligence and Applications (IASTED 206)* (pp. 493-498), Innsbruck, Austria.

Apache, Web site: http://www.apache.org

Arasu, A., Cho, J., Garcia-Molina, H., Paepcke, A., & Raghavan, S. (2001). Searching the Web. *ACM Transactions on Internet Technology*, *1*(1), 2–43. doi:10.1145/383034.383035

Argyris, C., & Schön, D. A. (1992). *Theory in practice: Increasing professional effectiveness*. Jossey Bass Higher and Adult Education Series.

Armour, P. G. (2002). The business of software: The organism and the mechanism of projects. *Communications of the ACM, 45*(5), 17–20. doi:10.1145/506218.506233

Attwood, D. A. (1996). *The office relocation sourcebook: A guide to managing staff throughout the move. Europe.* Wiley.

Baader, F., Calvanese, D., McGuinness, D., Nardi, D., & Patel-Schneider, P. F. (2003). *The Description Logic Handbook: Theory, Implementation and Applications.* Cambridge: Cambridge University Press.

Bainbridge, D., Novak, B. J., & Cunningham, S. J. (2010). *A user-centered design of a personal digital library for music exploration.* Paper presented at the ACM/IEEE-CS Joint Conference on Digital Libraries, Surfer's Paradise, Australia.

Bakos, Y. (1998). The emerging role of electronic marketplaces on the Internet. *Communications of the ACM, 41*(8), 35–42. doi:10.1145/280324.280330

Barron, A. R. (1986, January). Entropy and the Central Limit Theorem. *Annals of Probability, 14*(1), 336–342. doi:10.1214/aop/1176992632

Bartell, B. T., Cottrell, G. W., & Belew, R. K. (1994, 3-6 July). *Automatic combination of multiple ranked retrieval systems.* Paper presented at the 17th Annual International ACM-SIGIR Conference on Research and Development in Information Retrieval, Dublin, Ireland.

Bast, H., Majumdar, D., & Weber, I. (2007). *Efficient interactive query expansion with CompleteSearch.* Paper presented at the Conference on Information and Knowledge Management, Lisbon, Portugal.

Bateson, G. (1979). *Mind and nature: A necessary unity* (1st ed.). New York, NY: Dutton.

Beach, L. R., & Connolly, T. (2005). *The Psychology of Decision Making: People in Organizations.* Thousand Oaks, CA, USA: Sage Publications.

Begole, J. B., Matsakis, N. E., & Tang, J. C. (2004). Lilsys: Sensing Unavailability. *2004 ACM conference on Computer supported cooperative work*, Chicago, Illinois, USA.

Bell, J. (1995). Changing attitudes in intelligent agents. In M. Woolridge & N. R. Jennings (Eds.), *Post-Proceedings of the ECAI-94 Workshop on Agent Theories, Architecture and languages*, (pp. 40-50). Berlin, Germany: Springer.

Belohlavek, R., Sklenar, V., & Zacpal, J. (2004). Formal concept analysis with hierarchically ordered attributes. *International Journal of General Systems, 33*(4), 383–394. doi:10.1080/03081070410001679715

Bendersky, M., Gabrilovich, E., Josifovski, V., & Metzler, D. (2010). *The anatomy of an ad: Structured indexing and retrieval for sponsored search.* Paper presented at the World Wide Web Conference, Raleigh, NC.

Benerecetti, M., Bouquet, P., & Bonifacio, M. (2001). Distributed context-aware systems. *Human-Computer Interaction Journal, 16*(1).

Beneventano, D., Guerra, F., Magnani, S., & Vincini, M. (2004). A Web service based framework for the semantic mapping amongst product classification schemas. *Journal of Electronic Commerce Research, 5*(2), 114–127.

Bennett, J. (1970). Culture. In Schindler, S. (Ed.), *Encyclopedia international* (*Vol. 5*, pp. 395–397). New York, NY: Grolier, Inc.

Bergman, R., Griss, M., & Staelin, C. (2002). *A personal email assistant. Technical Report HPL-2002-236*: Hewlett-Packard Company.

Berners-Lee, T., Hall, W., Hendler, J. A., O'Hara, K., Shadbolt, N., & Weitzner, D. J. (2006). A framework for Web science. *Foundations and Trends in Web Science, 1*(1), 1–130. doi:10.1561/1800000001

Berners-Lee, T., Hendler, J., & Lassila, O. (2001). The Semantic Web. *Scientific American, 284*, 34–43. doi:10.1038/scientificamerican0501-34

Berry, M. J. A., & Linoff, G. (2000). *Mastering Data Mining: The Art and Science of Customer Relationship Management.* New York: John Wiley & Sons.

Bertels, T., & Savage, C. (1998). Tough questions on knowledge management. In von Krogh, G., Roos, J., & Kleine, D. (Eds.), *Knowing in firms* (pp. 7–25). London, UK: Sage Publications.

Biemans, W. G. (1991). User and third-party involvement in developing medical equipment innovations. *Technovation*, *11*(3), 163–182. doi:10.1016/0166-4972(91)90032-Y

Boncz, P. A., Grust, T., Keulen, M., Manegold, S., Rittinger, J., & Teubner, J. (2006). MonetDB/XQuery: a fast XQuery processor powered by a relational engine. *ACM SIGMOD Conference* (pp. 479-490).

Borio, C. (2008). *The financial turmoil of 2007–? A preliminary assessment and some policy considerations* (BIS Working Papers No. 251). Basel, Switzerland: Bank for International Settlements.

Botev, B., & Shanmugasundaram, J. (2005). *Context-Sensitive Keyword Search and Ranking for XML* (pp. 115–120). Proceedings of WebDB.

Brachman, R., & Levesque, H. (2004). *Knowledge representation and reasoning.* San Francisco, CA: Elsevier, Inc.

Brachman, R. J., McGuinness, D. L., Patel-Schneider, P. F., & Borgida, A. (1991). "Reducing" CLASSIC to Practice: Knowledge Representation Theory Meets Reality. *Artificial Intelligence*, *114*(1-2), 203–237. doi:10.1016/S0004-3702(99)00078-8

Brachman, R. (1985). On the epistemological status of semantic networks. In Brachman, R., & Levesque, H. (Eds.), *Readings in knowledge representation* (pp. 91–215). Los Altos, CA: Kaufmann.

Brank, J., Grobelnik, M., & Mladenic, D. (2005). A survey of ontology evaluation techniques. *Proceedings of the Conference on Data Mining and Data Warehouses (SiKDD 2005)*.

Bratman, M. E. (1990). What is intention? In Cohen, P. R., Morgan, J., & Pollack, M. E. (Eds.), *Intentions in communication* (pp. 15–31). Cambridge, MA: MIT Press.

Brazier, F., Dunin-Keplicz, B., Treur, J., & Verbrugge, R. (1997). *Beliefs, intentions and desire.*

Brewster, C., Alani, H., Dasmahapatra, S., & Wilks, Y. (2004). Data driven ontology evaluation. *Proceedings of the International Conference on Language Resources and Evaluation (LREC-2004)*.

Bridges, S., & Polovina, S. (2010). *An OpenSEA framework using ISO 24707 common logic.* Paper presented at the 2010 International Conference on Intelligent Networking and Collaborative Systems, Thessaloniki, Greece. (pp. 335-336). DOI 10.1109/INCOS.2010.92

Brin, S., & Page, L. (1998). *The anatomy of a large-scale hypertextual Web search engine.* Paper presented at the Seventh International World Wide Web Conference.

Brinkmeier, M. (2006). PageRank revisited. *ACM Transactions on Internet Technology*, *6*(3), 282–301. doi:10.1145/1151087.1151090

Broglio, J., Callan, J. P., & Croft, W. B. (1994). *INQUERY system overview.* Paper presented at the TIPSTER Text Program (Phase I).

Brown, J. S., & Duguid, P. (2001). Knowledge and organization: A social-practice perspective. *Organization Science*, *12*(2), 198–213. doi:10.1287/orsc.12.2.198.10116

Brown, P. J., Bovey, J. D., & Chen, X. (1997). Context-Aware Applications: From the Laboratory to the Marketplace. *IEEE Personal Communications*, *4*(5), 58–64. doi:10.1109/98.626984

Brown, D. W. (2004). What research tells us about planned giving. *International Journal of Nonprofit and Voluntary Sector Marketing*, *9*(1), 86–95. doi:10.1002/nvsm.235

Brown, A., Oppenheimer, D., Keeton, K., Thomas, R., Kubiatowicz, J., & Patterson, D. A. (1999). ISTORE: introspective storage for data-intensive network services. *The IEEE Seventh Workshop on Hot Topics in Operating Systems* (pp. 32-37), Rio Rico, AZ, USA.

Bruza, P., McArthur, R., & Dennis, S. (2000). *Interactive Internet search: Keyword, directory, and query reformulation mechanisms compared.* Paper presented at the 23rd Annual International ACM SIGIR Conference on Research and Development in Information Retrieval.

Bucchiarone, A., Pelliccione, P., Polini, A., & Tivoli, M. (2006). *Towards an architectural approach for the dynamic and automatic composition of software components.* Paper presented at the 2nd International Workshop on the Role of Software Architecture in Testing and Analysis Portland, Maine.

Burstein, F. V., Zaslavsky, A. B., & Arora, N. (2005). Context-aware mobile agents for decision-making support in healthcare emergency applications. Proceedings of the 1st Workshop on Context Modeling and Decision Support (pp. 1-16), Paris, France.

Burton-Jones, A., Storey, V. C., Sugumaran, V., & Ahluwalia, P. (2005). A semiotic metrics suite for assessing the quality of ontologies. *Data & Knowledge Engineering*, *55*(1), 84–102. doi:10.1016/j.datak.2004.11.010

Callan, J. P., Croft, W. B., & Harding, S. M. (1993). *The INQUERY retrieval system.* Paper presented at the International Conference in Database and Expert Systems Applications.

Carlson, J. R., & Zmud, R. W. (1999). Channel expansion theory and the experiential nature of media richness perceptions. *Academy of Management Journal*, *42*(2), 153–170. doi:10.2307/257090

Carlson, J. R., & Zmud, R. W. (1994). Channel expansion theory: A dynamic view of media and information richness perceptions. In Moore, D. P. (Ed.), *Academy of Management: Best papers proceedings* (pp. 280–284).

Carter, J., Bitting, E., & Ghorbani, A. (2002). Reputation formalization for an information-sharing multi-agent system. *Computational Intelligence*, *18*(2), 515–534. doi:10.1111/1467-8640.t01-1-00201

Castelfranchi, C., & Falcone, R. (1998). Principles of trust for MAS: Cognitive anatomy, social importance and quantification. In *Proceedings of the International Conference on Multi-Agent Systems* (ICMAS'98), Paris, France. (pp. 72–79).

Chakraborty, S., Yau, D. K. Y., Lui, J. C. S., & Dong, Y. (2006). On the Effectiveness of Movement Prediction to Reduce Energy Consumption in Wireless Communication. *IEEE Transactions on Mobile Computing*, *5*(2), 157–169. doi:10.1109/TMC.2006.24

Chau, D. H., Myers, B., & Faulring, A. (2008). *What to do when search fails: Finding information by association.* Paper presented at the Computer and Human Interaction Conference, Florence, Italy.

Chein, M., & Mugnier, M.-L. (1992). Conceptual graphs: Fundamental notions. *Revue d'Intelligence Artificielle*, *6*(4), 365–406.

Chen, H. (1995). Machine learning for information retrieval: Neural networks, symbolic learning, and genetic algorithms. *Journal of the American Society for Information Science American Society for Information Science*, *46*(3), 194–216. doi:10.1002/(SICI)1097-4571(199504)46:3<194::AID-ASI4>3.0.CO;2-S

Chen, C. (1999). Visualising semantic spaces and author co-citation networks in digital libraries. *Information Processing & Management*, *35*, 401–420. doi:10.1016/S0306-4573(98)00068-5

Chen, H. L. (2004). *An intelligent broker architecture for pervasive context-aware systems.* PhD Thesis, University of Maryland.

Chen, Z., & Zhu, B. (2000). *Some formal analysis of Roccio's similarity-based relevance feedback algorithm.* Paper presented at the International Symposium on Algorithms and Computation.

Chomsky, N. (2006). *Language and mind* (3rd ed.). Cambridge, UK: Cambridge University Press. doi:10.1017/CBO9780511791222

Choudhury, V., Hartzel, K., & Konsynski, B. (1998). Uses and Consequences of Electronic Markets: An Empirical Investigation in the Aircraft Parts Industry. *MIS Quarterly*, *22*(4), 471–507. doi:10.2307/249552

Chui, M. (1999). *Pattern, procedurality and pictures: Factors affecting Boolean query interface design for the Web.* Paper presented at the SIGIR Conference.

Claret, J. (1990). Why numbers are not enough. *Accounting Technician: The Journal of the Association of Accounting Technicians UK,* (October), 24-25.

Clarke, R. (2001). Studies in organisational semiotics: An introduction. *Australasian Journal of Information Systems*, *8*(2), 75–82.

Clotfelter, C. T. (2001). Who are the alumni donors? Giving by two generations of alumni from selective colleges. *Nonprofit Management & Leadership*, *2*(2), 119–138. doi:10.1002/nml.12201

Coates, J. (1995). Customization promises sharp competitive edge. *Research in Technology Management*, *38*(1), 6–7.

Cole, R. J., & Eklund, P. W. (1996). The application of formal concept analysis to text retrieval in the medical domain. in *Proceedings of the 5th International Conference on Conceptual Structures*. 185-217.

Collet, C., Huhns, M., & Shen, W. (1991). Resource Integration Using a Large Knowledge Base in Carnot. *IEEE Computer, 12*(24).

Coluccia, S., Di Noia, T., Di Sciascio, E., & Donini, F., &Mongiell0, M. (2005). Concept abduction and contraction for semantic-based discovery of matches and negotiation spaces in an e-marketplace. *Electronic Commerce Research and Applications, 4*(4), 345–361. doi:10.1016/j. elerap.2005.06.004

Connolly, T. M. (2005). *Database systems: A practical approach to design, implementation, and management* (Begg, C. E., Ed.). 4th ed.). Harlow, UK: Addison-Wesley.

Connoly, M. S., & Blanchette, R. (1986). Understanding and predicting alumni giving behavior. In Dunn, J. A. (Ed.), *Enhancing the Management of Fund Raising* (pp. 69–89). San Francisco: Jossey-Bass.

Cooper, R. G., & Brentani, U. (1991). New industrial financial services: What distinguishes the winners. *Journal of Product Innovation Management, 8*(2), 75–137. doi:10.1016/0737-6782(91)90002-G

Copeland, D. G., & McKenney, J. L. (1988). Airline Reservation Systems: Lessons from History. *MIS Quarterly, 12*(3), 353–372. doi:10.2307/249202

Cordeiro, J., & Felipe, J. (2004, July 19-20). *The semiotic pentagram framework - a perspective on the use of semiotics within organisational semiotics*. Paper presented at the 7th International Workshop on Organisational Semiotics, Escola Superior de Tecnologia, Setúbal, Portugal.

Cormen, T. H., Leiserson, C. E., & Rivest, R. L. (1997). *Introduction to Algorithms*. Cambridge, MA: The MIT Press.

Couger, J. D., & Zawacki, R. A. (1980). *Motivating and managing computer personnel*. New York: John Wiley & Sons.

Croft, W. B. (2000). *Combining approaches to information retrieval. Advances in information retrieval: Recent research from the Center for Intelligent Information Retrieval* (pp. 1–36). Kluwer Academic Publishers.

Crow, D., Pan, P., Kam, L., & Davenport, G. (2003). M-views: A system for location based storytelling. *ACM UbiComp 2003*, Seattle, WA, USA.

Crowe, M. (2002). *An SNMP Library for. NET Framework*. Corner. Available at http://www.c-sharpcorner.com/UploadFile/malcolmcrowe/SnmpLib11232005011613AM/SnmpLib.aspx.

Daft, R. L., & Lengel, R. H. (1986). Organizational information requirements, media richness and structural design. *Management Science, 32*(5), 554–571. doi:10.1287/mnsc.32.5.554

Daft, R. L., Lengel, R. H., & Trevino, L. K. (1987). Message equivocality, media selection, and manager performance: Implications for information systems. *Management Information Systems Quarterly, 11*(3), 355–366. doi:10.2307/248682

Dang, T.-T., & Shirai, K. (2009). *Machine learning approaches for mood classification of songs toward music search engine*. Paper presented at the International Conference on Knowledge and Systems Engineering.

Danninger, M., Kluge, T., & Stiefelhagen, R. (2006). MyConnector: analysis of context cues to predict human availability for communication. *8th international conference on Multimodal interfaces*, Banff, Alberta, Canada.

Dashofy, E. M., Hoek, A. d., & Taylor, R. N. (2005). A comprehensive approach for the development of modular software architecture description languages. *ACM Transactions on Software Engineering and Methodology, 14*(2), 199–245. doi:10.1145/1061254.1061258

Dau, F. (2004). Types and tokens for logic with diagrams. In K. E. Wolff, H. Pfeiffer, & H. S. Delugach (Eds.), *12th International Conference on Conceptual Structures: Lecture Notes in Computer Science, 3127* (pp. 62-93). Berlin, Germany: Springer-Verlag.

David, G., & Barry, L. N. (2001). Statistical selection of the best system. In *Proceedings of the 33nd conference on Winter simulation*. IEEE Computer Society, Arlington, Virginia, USA.

Davidson, J. (2002, February). Establishing conditions for the functional central limit theorem in nonlinear and semiparametric time series processes. *Journal of Econometrics, 106*(2), 243–269. doi:10.1016/S0304-4076(01)00100-2

Davis, F. D. (1989). Perceived usefulness, perceived ease of use and user acceptance of information technology. *Management Information Systems Quarterly*, *13*(3), 319–340. doi:10.2307/249008

Davis, F. D., Bagozzi, R. P., & Warshaw, P. R. (1989). User acceptance of computer technology: A comparison of two theoretical models. *Management Science*, *35*(8), 982–1003. doi:10.1287/mnsc.35.8.982

Davis, F. D., Bagozzi, R. P., & Warshaw, P. R. (1992). Extrinsic and intrinsic motivation to use computers in workplace. *Journal of Applied Social Psychology*, *22*(14), 1111–1132. doi:10.1111/j.1559-1816.1992.tb00945.x

De Angeli, A., Coventry, L., Johnson, G., & Renaud, K. (2005). Is a picture really worth a thousand words? Exploring the feasibility of graphical authentication systems. *International Journal of Human-Computer Studies*, *63*(1-2), 128–152. doi:10.1016/j.ijhcs.2005.04.020

Decker, K., Pannu, A., Sycara, K., & Williamson, M. (1997). Designing Behaviors for Information Agents. *First International Conference on Autonomous Agents*, Marina Del Rey, CA USA.

Dehn, D. M., & van Mulken, S. (2000). The impact of animated interface agents: A review of empirical research. *International Journal of Human-Computer Studies*, *52*(1), 1–22. doi:10.1006/ijhc.1999.0325

Demartini, G., Saad, M. M., Blanco, R., & Zaragoza, H. (2010). *Entity summarization of news articles*. Paper presented at the ACM Special Interest Group of Information Retrieval (SIGIR) Conference.

Deogun, J. S., Raghavan, J. S., & Sever, H. (1998). Association mining and formal concept analysis. *Proceedings of the Joint Conference in Information Science*. 335-338.

Detlor, B. (2004). *Towards knowledge portals: From human issues to intelligent agents*. Dordrecht, The Netherlands: Kluwer Academic Publishers.

Dey, A. K. (1998). Context-Aware Computing: The CyberDesk Project. *Association for the Advancement of Artificial Intelligence 1998 Spring Symposium on Intelligent Environments* (pp. 51-54), Stanford, CT, USA.

Dey, A. K., Manko, J., & Abowd, G. (n.d.). *Distributed mediation of imperfectly sensed context in aware environments*. Technical Report GIJJ382R53J, Georgia Institute of Technology, Atlanta, GA, USA.

Di Noia, T., Di Sciascio, E., Donini, F., & Mongiello, M. (2004). A System for Principled Macthmaking in an Electronic Marketplace. *International Journal of Electronic Commerce*, *8*(4), 9–37.

Dillon, A. (2000). Spatial semantics and individual differences in the perception of shape in information space. *Journal of the American Society for Information Science American Society for Information Science*, *51*(6), 521–528. doi:10.1002/(SICI)1097-4571(2000)51:6<521::AID-ASI4>3.0.CO;2-5

Dimmick, J., Kline, S., & Stafford, L. (2000). The gratification niches of personal e-mail and telephone. *Communication Research*, *27*(2), 227–248. doi:10.1177/009365000027002005

Ding, Y., & Foo, S. (2002). Ontology research and development part 1 – a review of ontology generation. *Journal of Information Science*, *28*(2), 123–136.

Docushare, Web site: http://docushare.xerox.com/ds/.

Dolog, P., Henze, N., Nejdl, W., & Sintek, M. (2003). *Towards the adaptive Semantic Web*. First Workshop on Principles and Practice of Semantic Web Reasoning, (pp. 51-68).

Dominik, H., Schwartz, T., & Brandherm, B. Schmitz, M., & Wilamowitz-Moellendorff, M. V. (2005). Gumo – the general user model ontology. *Proceedings of The 10th International Conference on User Modeling*, Edinburgh, Scotland, UK, (pp. 24-29).

Dong, C. S. J., & Loo, G. S. L. (2001). Flexible web-based decision support system generator (FWDSSG) utilising software agents. *Proceedings of 12th International Workshop on Database and Expert Systems Applications*, Munich (pp. 892-897), Germany.

Doring, S., Kiebling, W., Preisinger, T., & Fischer, S. (2006). Evaluation and optimization of the catalog search process of e-procurement platforms. *Electronic Commerce Research and Applications*, *5*(1), 44–56. doi:10.1016/j.elerap.2005.08.004

dos Santos-Mello, R., & Heuser, C. A. (2001). *A bottom-up approach for integration of XML Sources.* Paper presented at the Workshop on Information Integration on the Web.

Doumpos, M., Zopounidis, C., & Pardalos, P. M. (2000). Multicriteria sorting methodology: Application to financial decision problems. *Parallel Algorithms and Applications, 15*(1-2), 113–129.

Draper, D., Halevy, A. Y., & Weld, D. S. (2001). The Nimble XML Data Integration System. *Proceedings of ICDE* (pp. 155-160).

Dreilinger, D., & Howe, A. E. (1997). Experiences with selecting search engines using metasearch. *ACM Transactions on Information Systems, 15*(3), 195–222. doi:10.1145/256163.256164

Drye, T., Wetherill, G., & Pinnock, A. (2001). Donor survival analysis: An alternative perspective on lifecycle modeling. *International Journal of Nonprofit and Voluntary Sector Marketing, 6*(4), 325–334. doi:10.1002/nvsm.158

Ducheneaut, N., & Bellotti, V. (2001). E-mail as habitat: An exploration of embedded personal information management. *Interaction, 8*(5), 30–38. doi:10.1145/382899.383305

Duric, Z., Gray, W. D., Heishman, R., Li, F., Rosenfeld, A., & Schoelles, M. J. ... Wechsler, H. (2002). Integrating perceptual and cognitive modeling for adaptive and intelligent human-computer interaction. *Proceedings of the IEEE, 90*(7), 1272–1289.

eCl@ss. (2008). *International standard for the classification and description of products and service*, V8.0. Retrieved September 30, 2010, from http://www.eclass-online.com

Edmonds, B. (2002). Learning and exploiting context in agents. *First International Joint Conference on Autonomous Agents and Multi-agent Systems: Proceedings Part 3* (pp. 1231-1238). New York, NY: ACM Press.

Efthimiadis, E. N., & Biron, P. V. (1993). *UCLA-Okapi at TREC-2: Query expansion experiments.* Paper presented at the Text REtrieval Conference.

Eitz, M., Hildebrand, K., Boubekeur, T., & Alexa, M. (2010). *Sketch-based 3D shape retrieval.* Paper presented at the ACM Special Interest Group on Graphics (SIGGRAPH) Conference, Los Angeles, CA.

Engel, J. F., Blackwell, R. D., & Miniard, P. W. (1995). *Consumer behavior* (8th ed.). Fort Worth, TX: Dryden Press.

Esfandiari, B., & Chandrasekharan, S. (2001). On how agents make friends: Mechanisms for trust acquisition. In *Proceedings of the Fourth Workshop on Deception, Fraud and Trust in Agent Societies*, Montreal, Canada. (pp. 27–34).

Ewing, R. L., Goveckar, M. A., Govekar, P. L., & Rishi, M. (2002). Economics, market segmentation and recruiting: Targeting your promotion to volunteers' needs. *Journal of Nonprofit & Public Sector Marketing, 10*(1), 61–76. doi:10.1300/J054v10n01_05

Eyambe, L., & Suleman, H. (2004). *A digital library component assembly environment.* Paper presented at the South African Institute for Computer Scientists and Information Technologies.

Fagan, M. E. (1976). Design and code inspections to reduce errors in program development. *IBM Systems Journal, 15*(3), 182–211. doi:10.1147/sj.153.0182

Faloutsos, C., & Oard, D. W. (1996). *A survey of information retrieval and filtering methods.* University of Maryland College Park.

Faratin, P., Sierra, C., & Jennings, N. (2003). Using similarity criteria to make issue trade-offs in automated negotiations. *Journal of Artificial Intelligence, 142*(2), 205–237. doi:10.1016/S0004-3702(02)00290-4

Fatima, S. S., Wooldridge, M., & Jennings, N. R. (2003). *Optimal agendas for multi-issue negotiation.* Second International Conference on Autonomous Agents and Multiagent Systems (AAMAS-03), Melbourne, (pp. 129-136).

Favela, J., Navarro, C., & Rodriguez, M. (2002). Extending Instant Messaging to Support Spontaneous Interactions in Ad-hoc Networks. *The ACM 2002 Conference on Computer Supported Cooperative Work (CSCW 2002)*, New Orleans, LA, USA.

Fensel, D., McGuinness, D. L., Schulten, E., Ng, W. K., Lim, E.-P., & Yan, G. (2001). Ontologies and electronic commerce. *IEEE Intelligent Systems, 16*(1), 8–14. doi:10.1109/MIS.2001.1183337

FIPA(2003). Welcome to the Foundation for Intelligent Physical Agents.

Firat, A., Madnick, S. E., & Grosof, B. (2004). *Contextual alignment of ontologies for semantic interoperability*. Retrieved from http://papers.ssrn.com/sol3/papers.cfm?abstract_id=612472

Fontanills, G. A., & Gentile, T. (2001). *The Stock Market Course*. New York, NY, USA: John Wiley & Sons.

Forgionne, G., & Russell, S. (2008a). The Evaluation of Decision-Making Support Systems' Functionality. In F. Adam & P. Humphreys (Eds.), *Encyclopedia of Decision Making and Decision Support Technologies*. Hershey, PA, USA: Information Science Reference.

Forgionne, G., & Russell, S. (2008b). The Use of Simulation as an Experimental Methodology for DMSS Research. In F. Adam & P. Humphreys (Eds.), *Encyclopedia of Decision Making and Decision Support Technologies*. Hershey, PA, USA Information Science Reference.

Forgy, C. L. (1982). Rete: A fast algorithm for the many pattern/ many object pattern match problem. *Artificial Intelligence, 19*, 17–37. doi:10.1016/0004-3702(82)90020-0

Fowler, M. (2004). *UML distilled: A brief guide to the standard object modeling language* (3rd ed.). Boston, MA: Addison-Wesley.

Fox, M. S., Barbuceanu, M., Gruninger, M., & Lin, J. (1997). An organization ontology for enterprise modelling. In Prietula, M., Carley, K., & Gasser, L. (Eds.), *Simulating organizations: Computational models of institutions and groups* (pp. 131–152). Menlo Park, CA: AAAI/MIT Press.

Fulk, J. (1993). Social construction of communication technology. *Academy of Management Journal, 36*(5), 921–950. doi:10.2307/256641

Fulk, J., Schmitz, J., & Steinfield, C. W. (1990). A social influence model for technology use. In Fulk, J., & Steinfield, C. W. (Eds.), *Organizations and communications technologies* (pp. 117–140). Newbury Park: Sage Publications.

Funderbunk, J. E., Kiernan, G., Shanmugasundaram, J., Shekita, E., & Wei, C. (2002). XTABLES: Bridging relational technology and XML. *IBM Systems Journal, 41*, 616–641. doi:10.1147/sj.414.0616

Gaifman, H. (2002). *Vagueness, tolerance and contextual logic* (Philosophy Dept., unpublished paper). New York, NY: Columbia University. Retrieved November 6, 2010 from http://www.columbia.edu/~hg17/VTC-latest.pdf

Gajos, K. Z., Everitt, K., Tan, D. S., Czerwinski, M., & Weld, D. S. (2008). Predictability and accuracy in adaptive user interfaces. *Proceedings of the 28th Annual SIGCHI conference on Human Factors in Computing Systems*, (pp. 1271-1274).

Ganter, B., & Wille, R. (1999). *Formal Concept Analysis: Mathematical Foundations*. Berlin: Springer-Verlag.

Ganter, B., Stumme, G., & Wille, R. (2005). *Formal concept analysis: Foundations and applications* (Stumme, G., & Wille, R., Eds.). Berlin, Germany & Great Britain: Springer.

Garcia-Castro, R., Vrandecic, D., Gomez-Perez, A., Sure, Y., & Huang, Z. (2007). *Evaluation of ontologies and ontology-based tools*. Retrieved from http://km.aifb.uni-karlsruhe.de/ws/eon2007

Garg, S. K., & Mishra, R. B. (2008). A hybrid model for service selection in Semantic Web service composition. *International Journal of Intelligent Information Technologies, 4*(4), 55–69. doi:10.4018/jiit.2008100104

Gawdiak, Y., La, T., Lin, Y., Maluf, D. A., & Tran, P. (2005). US Patent **6,968,338,** Extensible database framework for management of unstructured and semi-structured documents, Awarded Nov 22, 2005

Gazendam, H. (2004, March 23). Organizational semiotics: A state of the art report. *SemiotiX, 1*. Retrieved July 5, 2010 from http://www.semioticon.com/semiotix

Gazendam, H. (2010, April 11-12). *From subject databases to flow of responsibility*. Paper presented at 11th International Conference on Informatics and Semiotics in Organisations, IFIP WG8.1 Working Conference. Reading, UK.

Gazendam, H. W. M., & Liu, K. (2004). The evolution of organisational semiotics. In J. Filipe, & K. Liu (Eds.), *7th International Workshop on Organisational Semiotics: Proceedings* (pp. 1-11). Setubal, Portugal: INSTICC Press.

Geerts, G., & McCarthy, W. E. (1991). Database accounting systems. In B. Williams, & B. J. Sproul (Eds.), *Information technology perspectives in accounting: An integrated approach* (June ed., pp. 159-183). London, UK: Chapman and Hall Publishers.

Georgiadis, H., & Vassalos, V. (2007). Xpath on Steroids: Exploiting Relational Engines for Xpath Performance *ACM SIGMOD Conference* (pp. 317-328).

Gerbé, O., Keller, R. K., & Mineau, G. W. (1998). Conceptual graphs for representing business processes in corporate memories. In M. Mugnier, & M. Chein (Eds.), *Conceptual structures: Theory, tools and applications: 6th International Conference on conceptual structures, ICCS'98, Montpellier, France, August 1998 (Proceedings)* (pp. 401-415). Heidelberg, Germany: Springer-Verlag.

Gibson, J. J. (1982). A preliminary description and classification of affordances. In Reed, E. S., & Jones, R. (Eds.), *Reasons for realism* (pp. 403–406). Hillsdale, NJ: Lawrence Erlbaum Associates, Inc.

Glover, E. J., Lawrence, S., Birmingham, W. P., & Giles, C. L. (1999, 1999-11). *Architecture of a metasearch engine that supports user information needs.* Paper presented at the Eighth International Conference on Information and Knowledge Management (CIKM'99), Kansas City, MO.

Godin, R., Mili, H., Mineau, H., Missaoui, G. R., Arfi, M., & Chau, T.-T. (1998). Design of class hierarchies based on concept (Galois) lattices. *Theory and Practice of Object Systems.*, *4*, 117–134. doi:10.1002/(SICI)1096-9942(1998)4:2<117::AID-TAPO6>3.0.CO;2-Q

Godin, R., Mineau, G., Missaoui, R., Saint Germain, M., & Faraj, N. (1994). Applying concept formation methods to software reuse. *International Journal of Software and Engineering.*, *5*, 119–142. doi:10.1142/S0218194095000071

Goldsmith, R. E., & Hofacker, C. F. (1991). Measuring consumer innovativeness. *Journal of the Academy of Marketing Science, 19*(3), 209–222. doi:10.1007/BF02726497

Goll, I., & Rasheed, A. M. (1997). Rational decision-making and firm performance: the moderating role of environment. *Strategic Management Journal, 18*(7), 583–591. doi:10.1002/(SICI)1097-0266(199708)18:7<583::AID-SMJ907>3.0.CO;2-Z

Goodhue, D. L. (1998). Development and measurement validity of a task-technology fit instrument for user evaluations of information systems. *Decision Sciences, 29*(1), 105–138. doi:10.1111/j.1540-5915.1998.tb01346.x

Green, S. J. (1998). Automated link generation: Can we do better than term repetition? *Proceedings of the 7th International World-Wide Web Conference*, Brisbane, Australia.

Greenberg, J. (2001). Automatic query expansion via lexical-semantic relationships. *Journal of the American Society for Information Science and Technology, 52*(5), 402–415. doi:10.1002/1532-2890(2001)9999:9999<::AID-ASI1089>3.0.CO;2-K

Griss, M., Letsinger, R., Cowan, D., VanHilst, M., & Kessler, R. (n.d.). *CoolAgent: Intelligent Digital Assistants for Mobile Professionals - Phase 1 Retrospective.* Hewlett-Packard Labs, Palo Alto, CA, USA.

Griswold, W. G., Boyer, R., Brown, S. W., & Truong, T. M. (2003). The activeclass project: Experiments in encouraging classroom participation. *Computer Support for Collaborative Learning)* (pp. 477-486).

Groenewegen, J. (Ed.). (1993). *Dynamics of the firm: Strategies of pricing and organisation.* Cambridge, UK: Edward Elgar Publishing Ltd.

Grover, V., & Teng, J. (2001). E-Commerce and the information market. *Communications of the ACM, 44*(4), 79–86. doi:10.1145/367211.367272

Gruber, T. (1993). A translation approach to portable ontology specifications. *Knowledge Acquisition, 5*(2), 199–220. doi:10.1006/knac.1993.1008

Gruber, T. R. (1991). The Role of Common Ontology in Achieving Sharable, Reusable Knowledge Bases. *Proceedings of Second International Conference on Knowledge Representation and Reasoning.*

Gruen, D., Sidner, C., Boettner, C., & Rich, C. (1999). *A collaborative assistant for email.* Proceedings of the Conference on Human Factors and Computing Systems, Pittsburg, Pennsylvania, pp. 196-197.

Grust, T., Rittinger, J., & Teubner, J. (2007). Why off-the-shelf RDBMSs are better at XPath than you might expect. *ACM SIGMOD Conference* (pp. 949-958).

Guha, R. V. (1991). *Context: A Formalization and Some Applications.* Doctoral Dissertation, Stanford University.

Gunderloy, M. (2007). Reading and Publishing Performance Counters in. NET. *developer.com.* Available at http://www.developer.com/net/net/article.php/3356561

Gutman, R., & Maes, P. (1998). Cooperative vs. competitive multi-agent negotiation in retail electronic commerce. In *Proc. of the Second International Workshop on Cooperative Information Agents* (CIA'98), Paris.

Halevy, A. Y. (2003). Data Integration: A Status Report. *Proceedings of BTW* (pp. 24-29).

Halevy, A. Y., Ashish, N., Bitton, D., Carey, M. J., Draper, D., Pollock, J., et al. (2005). Enterprise information integration: successes, challenges and controversies. *SIGMOD Conference* (pp. 778-787).

Halevy, A. Y., Rajaraman, A., & Ordille, J. (2006). Data Integration: The Teenage Years. *Proceedings of VLDB.*

Hamel, G. (1991). Competition for Competence and Inter-Partner Learning with International Strategic Alliances. *Strategic Management Journal, 12,* 83–103. doi:10.1002/smj.4250120908

Hamrouni, T., Valtchev, P., Yahia, S. B., & Nguifo, E. M. (2007). About the Lossless Reduction of the Minimal Generator Family of a Context. *Proceedings of the 5th International Conference on Formal Concept Analysis.* 130-150

Han, J., & Kamber, M. (2005). *Data Mining, Concepts and Techniques.* San Francisco: Morgan Kaufmann.

Hansen, M. H., & Shriver, E. (2001). *Using navigation data to improve IR functions in the context of Web search.* Paper presented at the Conference on Information and Knowledge Management.

Hartley, R., & Barnden, J. (1997). Semantic networks: Visualizations of knowledge. *Trends in Cognitive Sciences, 1*(5), 169–175. doi:10.1016/S1364-6613(97)01057-7

Hartmann, J. (2005). *Methods for ontology evaluation.* (Knowledge Web Deliverable D1.2.3). Retrieved from http://knowledgeweb.semanticweb.org

Hayes-Roth, B., Pfleger, K., Lalanda, P., Morignot, P., & Balabanovic, M. (1995). A domain-specific software architecture for adaptive intelligent systems. *IEEE Transactions on Software Engineering, 21*(4), 288–301. doi:10.1109/32.385968

He, M., Jennings, N. R., & Leung, H. (2003). On agent-mediated electronic commerce. *IEEE Transactions on Knowledge and Data Engineering, 15*(4), 985–1003. doi:10.1109/TKDE.2003.1209014

Hepp, M. (2007). Possible ontologies: How reality constrains the development of relevant ontologies. *IEEE Internet Computing, 11*(1), 90–96. doi:10.1109/MIC.2007.20

Hepp, M., Leukel, J., & Schmitz, V. (2007). A quantitative analysis of product categorization standards: Content, coverage, and maintenance of eCl@ss, UNSPSC, eOTD, and the RosettaNet technical dictionary. *Knowledge and Information Systems, 13*(1), 77–114. doi:10.1007/s10115-006-0054-2

Hepp, M. (2006). *eClassOWL 5.1. Products and services ontology for e-business, user's guide.* Retrieved from http://www.heppnetz.de/eclassowl

Hetzler, B., Whitney, P., Martucci, L., & Thomas, J. (1998). Multi-faceted insight through interoperable visual information analysis paradigms. *Proceedings of IEEE Information Visualization '98.*

Hill, R. (2010b). Conceptual structures for reasoning enterprise agents. In Croitoru, M., Ferré, S., & Lukose, D. (Eds.), *Conceptual structures: From information to intelligence* (pp. 191–194). Berlin/Heidelberg, Germany: Springer. doi:10.1007/978-3-642-14197-3_20

Hill, R. (2006). Capturing and specifying multi-agent systems for the management of community healthcare. In Yoshida, H., Jain, A., Ichalkaranje, A., Jain, L. C., & Ichalkaranje, N. (Eds.), *Advanced computational intelligence paradigms in healthcare - 1, studies in computational intelligence* (48th ed., pp. 127–164). Berlin, Germany: Springer.

Hill, R. (2007). *A requirements elicitation framework for agent-oriented software engineering.* PhD thesis, Sheffield Hallam University (pp. 1-244).

Hill, R. (2010a). *Agency and the virtual campus: The TrAM approach.* Paper presented at the 2010 International Conference on Intelligent Networking and Collaborative Systems, Thessaloniki, Greece (pp. 8-15). doi:DOI 10.1109/INCOS.2010.95

Hill, R., Polovina, S., & Shadija, D. (2006). Transaction agent modelling: From experts to concepts to multi-agent systems. In H. Schärfe, P. Hitzler & P. Øhrstrøm (Eds.), *Conceptual structures: Inspiration and application, lecture notes in artificial intelligence* (LNAI 4068, pp. 247-259). Heidelberg, Germany: Springer.

Hofstede, G. (1997). *Cultures and organizations: Software of the mind.* New York, NY: McGraw-Hill.

Hofstede, G. J., Pedersen, P., & Hofstede, G. (2002). *Exploring culture: Exercises, stories and synthetic cultures.* Yarmouth, ME: Intercultural Press.

Holmquist, L. E., Wigstrom, J., & Falk, J. (1998). The Hummingbird: Mobile Support for Group Awareness. *Demonstration at ACM 1998 Conference on Computer Supported Cooperative Work,* Seattle, WA, USA

Hong, J., & Landay, J. (2001). A Context/Communication Information Agent. *Personal and Ubiquitous Computing,* 5(1), 78–81. doi:10.1007/s007790170037

Horvitz, E., Koch, P., Kadie, C. M., & Jacobs, A. (2002). Coordinate: Probabilistic Forecasting of Presence and Availability. *The Eighteenth Conference on Uncertainty and Artificial Intelligence* (pp. 224-233), Edmonton, Alberta, Canada.

Hruby, P. (2006). *Model-driven design using business patterns* (1st ed.). Springer.

Hu, M., Lim, E.-P., Sun, A., Lauw, H. W., & Vong, B.-Q. (2007). *On improving Wikipedia search using article quality.* Paper presented at the Web Information and Data Management Conference, Lisbon, Portugal.

Huang, C. C., Liang, W. Y., Lai, Y. H., & Lin, Y. C. (2010). The agent-based negotiation process for B2C e-commerce. *Expert Systems with Applications,* 37(1), 348–359. doi:10.1016/j.eswa.2009.05.065

Huang, N., & Diao, S. (2006). Structure-based ontology evaluation. *Proceedings of the IEEE International Conference on e-Business Engineering (ICEBE 2006)* (pp. 132-137).

Ijiri, Y. (1967). *The foundations of economic accounting.* UK: Prentice Hall.

Isbister, K., & Nass, C. (2000). Consistency of personality in interactive characters: Verbal cues, non-verbal cues, and user characteristics. *International Journal of Human-Computer Studies,* 53(2), 251–267. doi:10.1006/ijhc.2000.0368

Ishita, E., Agata, T., Ikeuchi, A., Yosuke, M., & Ueda, S. (2010). *A search engine for Japanese academic papers.* Paper presented at the ACM/IEEE-CS Joint Conference on Digital Libraries.

Ives, Z., Halevy, A., & Weld, D. (2002). An XML query engine for network-bound data. *The VLDB Journal,* 11, 380–402. doi:10.1007/s00778-002-0078-5

Iyer, L. S., Singh, R., & Salam, A. F. (2005). Collaboration and Knowledge Management in B2B eMarketplaces. *Information Systems Management,* 22(3), 37–49. doi:10.1201/1078/45317.22.3.20050601/88744.6

Jacquet-Lagreze, E. (1995). An application of the UTA discriminant model for the evaluation of R&D projects. In: Pardalos, P.M., Siskos, Y., Zopounidis, C. (Eds.), *Advances in Multicriteria Analysis* (pp. 203-211). Dordrecht: Kluwer Academic Publishers.

Jagadish, H. V., Khalifa, S., Chapman, A., Lakshmanan, L., Nierman, A., & Paparizos, S. TIMBER: A Native XML Database. *The VLDB Journal,* 11, 274–291. doi:10.1007/s00778-002-0081-x

Janecek, P., & Pu, P. (2002). *A framework for designing fisheye views to support multiple semantic contexts*. In the 6th International Working Conference on Advanced Visual Interfaces, Trento, Italy.

Jansen, B. J., Spink, A., Bateman, J., & Saracevic, T. (1998). Real life information retrieval: A study of user queries on the Web. *ACM SIGIR Forum, 32*(1), 5–17. doi:10.1145/281250.281253

Jasper, R., & Uschold, M. (1999). A Framework for Understanding and Classifying Ontology Applications. *Proceedings of the IJCAI-99 Workshop on Ontologies and Problem-Solving Mehtods*, Stockholm, Sweden.

Jennings, N. R., & Wooldridge, M. (1998). *Agent Technology: Foundations, Applications, and Markets,* Springer, London.

Jiang, D., Pei, J., & Li, H. (2010). *Search and browse log mining for Web information retrieval: Challenges, methods, and applications*. Paper presented at the ACM Special Interest Group of Information Retrieval (SIGIR) Conference.

Johnson, M. S., & Garbarino, E. (2001). Customers of performing arts organizations: Are subscribers different from non-subscribers? *International Journal of Nonprofit and Voluntary Sector Marketing, 6*(1), 61–77. doi:10.1002/nvsm.134

Jonker C. M., Robu, V., & Treur, J. (2007). *An agent architecture for multi-attribute negotiation using incomplete preference information, autonomous agent and multi-agent system.*

Jung, J. H., Schneider, C., & Valacich, J. (2010). Enhancing the motivational affordance of Information Systems: The effects of real-time performance feedback and goal setting in group collaboration environments. *Management Science, 56*(4), 724–742. doi:10.1287/mnsc.1090.1129

Kahneman, D. (2003). A perspective on judgment and choice. *The American Psychologist, 58*(9), 697–720. doi:10.1037/0003-066X.58.9.697

Kalfoglou, Y., & Schorlemmer, M. (2003). Ontology mapping: The state of the art. *The Knowledge Engineering Review, 18*(1), 1–31. doi:10.1017/S0269888903000651

Kaner, M., & Karni, R. (2004). A capability maturity model for knowledge-based decisionmaking. *Information Knowledge Systems Management, 4*(4), 225–252.

Kang, N., & Han, S. (2002). Agent-based e-marketplace system for more fair and efficient transaction. *Decision Support Systems, 34*, 157–165. doi:10.1016/S0167-9236(02)00078-7

Keaveney, S. M. (1995). Customer switching behavior in service industries: An exploratory study. *Journal of Marketing, 59*(2), 71–82. doi:10.2307/1252074

Keeney, R. (1994). Using values in operations research. *Operations Research, 42*(5), 793–814. doi:10.1287/opre.42.5.793

Key, J. (2001). Enhancing fundraising success with custom data modeling. *International Journal of Nonprofit and Voluntary Sector Marketing, 6*(4), 335–346. doi:10.1002/nvsm.159

Khatri, V., Vessey, I., Ram, S., & Ramesh, V. (2006). Cognitive fit between conceptual schemas and internal problem representations: The case of geospatio-temporal conceptual schema comprehension. *IEEE Transactions on Professional Communication, 49*(2), 109–127. doi:10.1109/TPC.2006.875091

Kirn, S. (2008). *Individualization engineering*. Goettingen, Germany: Cuvillier.

Kishore, R., Sharman, R., Zhang, H., & Ramesh, R. (2004). Computational Ontologies and Information Systems: I. Foundations. *Communications of the Association for Information Systems, 14*, 158–183.

Klahr, D., & Kotovsky, K. (1989). *Complex information processing. The impact of Herbert A. Simon*. New Jersey: Lawrence Erlbaum Associates Publishers.

Klein, M., Fensel, D., van Harmelen, F., & Horrocks, I. (2001). The Relation Between Ontologies and XML Schemas," *Electronic Transactions on Artificial Intelligence (ETAI), Linköping Electronic Articles in Computer and Information Science, 6*(4).

Kleinberg, J. (2002a). *Local approximation of centrality measures*. Pages linking to www.epa.gov. http://www.cs.cornell.edu/Courses/ cs685/2002fa/data/gr0.epa

Kleinberg, J. (2002b). *Pages matching the query "California"*. Retrieved from http://www.cs.cornell.edu/ Courses/cs685/2002fa/data/gr0.California

Koda, T., & Maes, P. (1996). *Agents with faces: The effect of personification.* Proceedings of the 5th IEEE International Workshop on Robot and Human Communication, Tsukuba, Japan, pp. 189-194.

Kogler, M., & Lux, M. (2010). *Bag of visual words revisited - an exploratory study on robust image retrieval exploiting fuzzy codebooks.* Paper presented at the 10th International Workshop on Multimedia Data Mining Washington, DC.

Kramer, J. (2008, 18 September 2008). Financial turmoil. Retroieved from http://uk.youtube.com/watch?v=Sanr9kx3Mq4

Kraus, S., Sycara, K., & Evenchil, A. (1998). Reaching agreements through argumentation: A logical model and implementation. *Artificial Intelligence, 104*, 1–69. doi:10.1016/S0004-3702(98)00078-2

Kreiner, K. (2002). Tacit knowledge management: The role of artifacts. *Journal of Knowledge Management, 6*(2), 112–123. doi:10.1108/13673270210424648

Krippendorff, K. (1980). *Content analysis: An introduction to its methodology.* Beverly Hills, CA: Sage Publications.

Kuntz, C. (2005). An integrated approach for semantics-driven information retrieval. *Proceedings of the 11th International Conference on Human-Computer Interaction*, Las Vegas, Nevada, USA, (pp. 22-27).

Kwon, O., Shin, J., & Kim, S. (2006). Context-aware multi-agent approach to pervasive negotiation support systems. *Expert Systems with Applications, 31*(2), 285. doi:10.1016/j.eswa.2005.09.033

Labrou, Y., Finin, T., & Peng, Y. (1999). Agent Communication Languages: The Current Landscape. *Intelligent Systems, 14*(2), 45–52. doi:10.1109/5254.757631

Lam, K. F., Choo, E. U., & Moy, J. W. (1996). Minimizing deviations from the group mean: A new linear programming approach for the two-group classification problem. *European Journal of Operational Research, 88*, 358–367. doi:10.1016/0377-2217(95)00183-2

Launders, I. (2009). Socio-technical systems and knowledge representation. In Whitworth, B., & de Moor, A. (Eds.), *Handbook of research on socio-technical design and social networking systems* (pp. 558–574). Hershey, PA: IGI Global. doi:10.4018/9781605662640.ch037

Launders, I., Polovina, S., & Hill, R. (2010). *Semantics and pragmatics in enterprise architecture through transaction agent modelling.* Paper presented at the The 12th International Conference on Informatics and Semiotics in Organisations, Reading, UK. (pp. 285-291). Retrieved from http://www.scitepress.org/DigitalLibrary/

Launders, I., Polovina, S., & Khazaei, B. (2010a). *Case studies as simulation of industrial practice.* Paper presented at the CPLA Enquiry, Autonomy & Graduateness Conference, Sheffield Hallam University, UK (pp. 73-88). Retrieved from http://extra.shu.ac.uk/cetl/cpla/resources/CPLA_Conference_Proceedings.pdf

Launders, I., Polovina, S., & Khazaei, B. (2010b). *Learning perspectives of enterprise architectures through TrAM.* Paper presented at the First Conceptual Structures - Learning, Teaching and Assessment Workshop (CS-LTA) at the 18[Th] International Conference on Conceptual Structures (ICCS 2010), Kuching, Malaysia (pp. 29-41). Retrieved from http://extra.shu.ac.uk/cetl/cpla/cslta2010/publication.html

Leake, D. B., & Scherle, R. (2001). *Towards context-based search engine selection.* Paper presented at the International Conference on Intelligent User Interfaces.

Lee, H. G., & Clark, T. H. (1996). Impacts of the electronic marketplace on transaction cost and market structure. *International Journal of Electronic Commerce, 1*(1), 127–149.

Lee, G. A. (1986). *Modern financial accounting.* UK: Van Nostrand Reinhold.

Lee, J. H. (1995). *Combining multiple evidence from different properties of weighting schemes.* Paper presented at the ACM SIGIR Conference on Research and Development in Information Retrieval.

Lee, S. (1972). *Goal Programming for Decision Analysis.* Philadelphia, PA: Auerbach.

Lenat, D., & Guha, R. V. (1991). The Evolution of CycL, The Cyc Representation language. *Special Issue on Implemented Knowledge Representation System, ACM SIGART, 2*(3), 84–87.

Lesser, E. L., & Storck, J. (2001). Communities of practice and organizational performance. *IBM Systems Journal, 40*(4), 831–841. doi:10.1147/sj.404.0831

Leukel, J. (2004). Standardization of product ontologies in B2B relationships – on the role of ISO 13584. *Proceedings of the 10th Americas Conference on Information Systems (AMCIS 2004)* (pp. 4084-4091).

Leukel, J., & Sugumaran, V. (2007). Evaluating product ontologies in e-commerce: A semiotic approach. *Proceedings of the 6th Workshop on e-Business (WeB 2007)* (pp. 240-249).

Leung, K. W.-T., Ng, W., & Lee, D. L. (2008). Personalized concept-based clustering of search engine queries. *IEEE Transactions on Knowledge and Data Engineering, 20*(11), 1505–1518. doi:10.1109/TKDE.2008.84

Lewis, D. D., Shapire, R. E., Callan, J. P., & Papka, R. (1996). *Training algorithms for linear text classifiers.* Paper presented at the 19th Annual International ACM SIGIR Conference on Research and Development in Information Retrieval.

Li, J., & Wang, J. Z. (1997). Automatic linguistic indexing of pictures by a statistical modeling approach. *IEEE Transactions on Pattern Analysis and Machine Intelligence, 25*(9), 1075–1088.

Li, Y., Wang, Y., & Huang, X. (2007). A relation-based search engine in Semantic Web. *IEEE Transactions on Knowledge and Data Engineering, 19*(2), 273–282. doi:10.1109/TKDE.2007.18

Li, L., & Horrocks, I. (2004). A Software Framework for Matchmaking Based on Semantic Web Technology. *International Journal of Electronic Commerce, 8*(4), 39–60.

Li, Y., Yu, C., & Jagadish, H. V. (2008). Enabling Schema-Free XQuery with Meaningful Query Focus. *The VLDB Journal, 17*(3). doi:10.1007/s00778-006-0003-4

Libes, D. (1997). Tcl/Tk-based agents for mail and news notification. *Software, Practice & Experience, 27*(4), 481–493. doi:10.1002/(SICI)1097-024X(199704)27:4<481::AID-SPE94>3.0.CO;2-J

Lieberman, H., & Selker, T. (2003). Agents for the user interface. In Bradshaw, J. M. (Ed.), *Handbook of Agent Technology*. The MIT Press.

Lin, X. (1997). Map displays for information retrieval. *Journal of the American Society for Information Science American Society for Information Science, 48*(1), 40–54. doi:10.1002/(SICI)1097-4571(199701)48:1<40::AID-ASI6>3.0.CO;2-1

Lindahl, W. E., & Winship, C. (1992). Predictive models for raising and major gift fundraising. *Nonprofit Management & Leadership, 3*(1), 43–64. doi:10.1002/nml.4130030105

Lindsey, D., Cheney, P. H., Kasper, G. M., & Ives, B. (1990). TELCOT: An Application of Information Technology for Competitive Advantage in the Cotton Industry. *MIS Quarterly, 14*(4), 347–357. doi:10.2307/249781

Linguistic Data Corporation. (1993). *TIPSTER complete text corpus*.

Litwin, W., Mark, L., & Roussopoulos, N. (1990). Interoperability of Multiple Autonomous Databases. *ACM Computing Surveys, 22*(3), 267–293. doi:10.1145/96602.96608

Love, S., & Perry, M. (2004). *Dealing with mobile conversations in public places: Some implications for the design of socially intrusive technologies.* Proceedings of the ACM Conference on Human Factors and Computing Systems, Vienna, Austria, pp. 1195-1198.

Loyall, J. P., Schantz, R. E., Zinky, J. A., & Bakken, D. E. (1998). Specifying and Measuring Quality of Service in Distributed Object Systems. *First International Symposium on Object-Oriented Real-Time Distributed Computing (ISORC '98)*, Kyoto, Japan.

Lucas, W. (1998). Effects of E-Mail on the organization. *European Management Journal, 16*(1), 18–30. doi:10.1016/S0263-2373(97)00070-4

Luo, Y., Davis, D. N., & Lui, K. (2002). A Multi-Agent Decision Support System for Stock Trading. *IEEE Network, 16*(1), 20–27. doi:10.1109/65.980541

Lüthje, C. (2004). Characteristics of innovating users in a consumer goods field: An empirical study of sport-related product consumers. *Technovation, 24*(9), 683–695. doi:10.1016/S0166-4972(02)00150-5

MacGregor, R. M. (1991). Inside the LOOM Description Classifier. *SIGART Bulletin*, *2*(3), 88–92. doi:10.1145/122296.122309

Madhavan, J., Cohen, S., Dong, X. L., Halevy, A. Y., Jeffery, S. R., Ko, D., & Yu, C. (2007). Web-Scale Data Integration: You can afford to Pay as You Go. *CIDR Conference* (pp. 342-350).

Maes, P. (1994). Agents that reduce work and information overload. *Communications of the ACM*, *37*(7), 31–40. doi:10.1145/176789.176792

Magennis, M., & Rijsbergen, C. J. v. (2000). *The potential and actual effectiveness of interactive query expansion.* Paper presented at the Twentieth Annual International ACM SIGIR Conference on Research and Development in Information Retrieval.

Malhotra, Y. (2004). Why do knowledge management systems fail? Enablers and constraints of knowledge management in human enterprises. In Koenig, M. E. D., & Srikantaiah, T. K. (Eds.), *Knowledge management lessons learned: What works and what doesn't* (pp. 87–112). Silver Spring, MD: American Society for Information Science and Technology Monograph Series, Information Today Inc.

Malone, T., & Crowston, K. (1994). The Interdisciplinary Study of Coordination. *ACM Computing Surveys*, *26*(1), 87–119. doi:10.1145/174666.174668

Malone, T. W. (1987). Modeling Coordination in Organizations and Markets. *Management Science*, *33*(10), 1317–1332. doi:10.1287/mnsc.33.10.1317

Maluf, D. A. (2006). Knowledge Mining Application in an IVHM Testbed. *IEEE Aerospace Conference*, Montana.

Maluf, D. A. (2007). Searching Across the International Space Station. *IEEE Aerospace Conference*, Montana.

Maluf, D. A., & Tran, P. (2008). Managing Unstructured Data With Structured Legacy Systems. *IEEE Aerospace Conference*, Montana.

Maluf, D. A., & Wiederhold, G. (1997). Abstraction of Representation for Interoperation, *Tenth International Symposium on Methodologies for Intelligent Systems*, Lecture Notes in Computer Science (pp. 441-455). Springer Verlag.

Maluf, D. A., Bell, D. G., Ashish, N., Knight, K., & Tran, P. B. (2005). Semi-Structured Data Management in the Enterprise: A Nimble, High-Throughput, and Scalable Approach. *Proceedings of IDEAS Conference* (pp. 115-124).

Maluf, D. A., Bell, D. G., Ashish, N., Putz, P., & Gawdiak, Y. (2006). Business Intelligence in Large Organizations: Integrating Which Data? *ISMIS Conference* (pp. 248-257).

Maluf, D., & Tran, P. (2003). NETMARK: A Schema-Less Extension for Relational Databases for Managing Semi-structured Data Dynamically. *ISMIS Conference* (pp. 231-241).

Maluf, D. A., & Tran, P. (2001). Articulation Management for Intelligent Integration of Information. *IEEE Transactions on Systems Man and Cybernetics.*

Manasco, B., & Schurter, T. (2005). POA or SOA? *ZDNet*. Retrieved March 1, 2010, from http://blogs.zdnet.com/service-oriented/index.php?p=206

Mandala, R., Tokunaga, T., & Tanaka, H. (1999). *Combining multiple evidence from Different types of thesaurus for query expansion.* Paper presented at the 22nd Annual International ACM SIGIR Conference on Research and Development in Information Retrieval.

Mao, Y., & Tian, W. (2009). *A semantic-based search engine for traditional medical informatics.* Paper presented at the Fourth International Conference on Computer Sciences and Convergence Information Technology.

Markus, M. L. (1990). Toward a 'Critical Mass' theory of interactive media. In Fulk, J., & Steinfield, C. W. (Eds.), *Organizations and communications technologies* (pp. 194–218). Newbury Park: Sage Publications.

Matsokis, A., & Kiritsis, D. (2010). An ontology-based approach for product lifecycle management. *Computers in Industry*, *61*(8), 787–797. doi:10.1016/j.compind.2010.05.007

Mazzagatti, J. C. (2005). *U.S. Patent No. 6,961,733.* Washington, DC: U.S. Patent and Trademark Office.

Mazzagatti, J. C. (2006). A Computer Memory Resident Data Structure Based on the Phaneron of C. S. Peirce. Inspiration and Application, Contributions to ICCS 2006 14th International Conference on Conceptual Structures ICCS 2006 (pp. 114-130). Aalborg, Denmark: Aalborg University Press 2006.

Mazzagatti, J. C. (2007). Adding Conceptual SIGNs to a Computer Memory Resident Data Structure Based on the Paneron of C. S. Peirce, *CS-TIW 2007, Second Conceptual Structures Tool Interoperability Workshop in Association with ICCS2007 Sheffield England (pp. 59-63)*, Bristol, UK:Research Press International.

Mazzagatti, J. C. (2007). Data Analyzer Prototype Using a K Structure Based on the Paneron of C. S. Peirce, *Proceedings of the 15th International Workshops on Conceptual Structures ICCS 2007*, Springer-Verlag London Limited.

Mazzagatti, J. C. (2007). *U.S. Patent No. 7,158,975*. Washington, DC: U.S. Patent and Trademark Office.

Mazzagatti, J. C., & Buckwalter, R. (2008). *U.S. Patent No. 7,348,980*. Washington, DC: U.S. Patent and Trademark Office.

Mazzagatti, J. C., & Claar, J. V. K. (2007). *U.S. Patent No. 7,213,041*. Washington, DC: U.S. Patent and Trademark Office.

Mazzagatti, J. C., & Claar, J. V. K. (2008). *U.S. Patent No. 7,340,471*. Washington, DC: U.S. Patent and Trademark Office.

McCarthy, J. (1993). Notes on Formalizing Context. *Proceedings of the Thirteenth International Joint Conference on Artificial Intelligence.*

McCarthy, W. E. (1987). On the future of knowledge-based accounting systems. In M. Vasarhelyi (Ed.), *The D. R. Scott memorial lecture series, University of Missouri, and published in artificial intelligence in accounting and auditing: The use of expert systems* (October ed., pp. 19-42). USA: Markus Wiener Publishing.

McCreadie, R. M. C. (2010). *Leveraging user-generated content for news search*. Paper presented at the ACM Special Interest Group of Information Retrieval (SIGIR) Conference.

McElroy, M. (1999, October). The second generation of knowledge management. *Knowledge Management Magazine*, 86-88.

McNab, R. J., Smith, L. A., Bainbridge, D., & Witten, I. H. (1997). The New Zealand digital library MELody inDEX. *d-Lib Magazine, 3*(5), 288-301.

Medvidovic, N., & Taylor, R. N. (2000). A classification and comparison framework for software architecture description languages. *IEEE Transactions on Software Engineering, 26*(1), 70–93. doi:10.1109/32.825767

Meier, W. M. (2002). *eXist open source database*. Retrieved from http://exist.sourceforge.net/

Melnik, O., Vardi, Y., & Zhang, C.-H. (2007). Concave learners for Rankboost. *Journal of Machine Learning Research, 8*(1), 791–812.

Menasce, D. A. (2004). Composing Web Services: A QoS View. *IEEE Internet Computing, 8*(6), 88–90. doi:10.1109/MIC.2004.57

Meng, W., Wu, Z., Yu, C., & Li, Z. (2001). A highly scalable and effective method for metasearch. *ACM Transactions on Information Systems, 19*(3), 310–336. doi:10.1145/502115.502120

Meng, W., Yu, C., & Liu, K.-L. (2002). Building efficient and effective metasearch engines. *ACM Computing Surveys, 34*(1), 48–89. doi:10.1145/505282.505284

Merkl, D., & Rauber, A. (1999). *Uncovering associations between documents.* Paper presented at the International Conference on Artificial Intelligence.

Microsoft (2003). *Windows Server 2003 Performance Counters Reference*. Microsoft. Available at http://technet2.microsoft.com/windowsserver/en/library/3fb01419-b1ab-4f52-a9f8-09d5ebeb9ef21033.mspx?mfr=true

Midgley, D. F., & Dowling, G. R. (1978). Innovativeness: The concept and its measurement. *The Journal of Consumer Research, 4*(4), 229–242. doi:10.1086/208701

Miles, M. B., & Huberman, A. M. (1994). *Qualitative data analysis: An expanded sourcebook* (2 ed.). Thousand Oaks: Sage Publications.

Miller, W. C. (1986). *The creative edge: Fostering innovation where you work*. Reading, MA: Addison-Wesley Publishing Company.

Miller, W. C. (1998). *Flash of brilliance: Inspiriting creativity where you work*. Reading, MA: Perseus Books.

Miller, W. C., Couger, J. D., & Higgins, L. F. (1996). Innovation styles profile of IS personnel vs other occupations. *Creativity and Innovation Management, 5*(4), 226–233. doi:10.1111/j.1467-8691.1996.tb00148.x

Mineau, G., & Godin, R. (1995). Automatic structuring of knowledge bases by conceptual clustering. *IEEE Transactions on Knowledge and Data Engineering, 7,* 824–829. doi:10.1109/69.469834

Mishra, R. K., & Prabhakar, T. V. (2000). *KhojYantra: An integrated MetaSearch engine with classification, clustering, and ranking.* Paper presented at the International Database Applications and Engineering Symposium.

Mistry, A. (2003). *Studying Financial Market Behavior with an Agent-Based Simulation.* Cornell University.

Mitra, P., & Wiederhold, G. (2004). *An Ontology-Composition Algebra* (pp. 93–116). Handbook on Ontologies.

Moore, G. C., & Benbasat, I. (1991). Development of an instrument to measure the perceptions of adopting an information technology innovation. *Information Systems Research, 2*(3), 192–222. doi:10.1287/isre.2.3.192

Moran, T. P., & Dourish, P. (2001). Introduction to This Special Issue on Context-Aware Computing. *Human-Computer Interaction Journal, 16*(1).

Mørch, A. I., Stevens, G., Won, M., Klann, M., Dittrich, Y., & Wulf, V. (2004). Component-based technologies for end-user development. *Communications of the ACM, 47*(9), 59–62. doi:10.1145/1015864.1015890

Muhlenbrock, M., Brdiczka, O., Snowdon, D., & Meunier, J. L. (2004). Learning to detect user activity and availability from a variety of sensor data. *Second IEEE Annual Conference on Pervasive Computing and Communications (PerCom 2004)* (pp. 13-22), Orlando, FL, USA.

Muramatsu, J., & Pratt, W. (2001). *Transparent queries: Investigating users' mental models of search engines.* Paper presented at the Twenty-Fourth Annual International ACM SIGIR Conference on Research and Development in Information Retrieval.

Murphy, J., & Tan, I. (2003). Journey to nowhere? E-mail customer service by travel agents in Singapore. *Tourism Management, 24*(5), 543–550. doi:10.1016/S0261-5177(03)00005-0

MySQL. Web site: http://www.mysql.com

Nakayama, H., & Kagaku, N. (1998). Pattern classification by linear goal programming and its extensions. *Journal of Global Optimization, 12*(2), 111–126. doi:10.1023/A:1008244409770

Neches, R., Fikes, R., Finin, T., Gruber, T., Patil, R., Senator, T., & Swartout, W. R. (1991). Enabling Technology for Knowledge Sharing. *AI Magazine, 12*(3), 36–55.

Newell, A., & Simon, H. A. (1972). *Human problem solving.* New Jersey: Prentice Hall, Inc.

Newell, A. (1982). The Knowledge Level. *Artificial Intelligence, 18,* 87–127. doi:10.1016/0004-3702(82)90012-1

Nguyen, P., & Corbett, D. (2006). A basic mathematical framework for conceptual graphs. *IEEE Transactions on Knowledge and Data Engineering, 18*(2), 261–271. doi:10.1109/TKDE.2006.18

Ngwenyama, O. K. (1997). Communication richness in electronic mail: Critical social theory and the contextuality of meaning. *Management Information Systems Quarterly, 21*(2), 145–167. doi:10.2307/249417

Nonaka, I., & Takeuchi, H. (1995). *The knowledge-creating company: How Japanese companies create the dynamics of innovation.* New York, NY: Oxford University Press.

Noy, N. F., & McGuinness, D. L. (2001). *Ontology development 101: A guide to creating your first ontology,* (pp. 1-25). (Stanford Knowledge Systems Laboratory Technical Report KSL-01-05).

Noy, N. F., & McGuinnss, D. L. (2002). *Ontology Development 101: A Guide to Creating Your First Ontology.* Stanford University, Stanford, CA, Stanford Medical Informatics Report SMI-2002-0880.

Oh, S., & Park, S. (2003). Task-role-based Access Control Model. *Information Systems, 28*(6), 533–562. doi:10.1016/S0306-4379(02)00029-7

O'Leary, D. (1998). Enterprise knowledge management. *Computer, 31*(3), 54–61. doi:10.1109/2.660190

Oracle, Web site: http://www.oracle.com

Orlikowski, W. (2002). Knowing in practice: Enacting a collective capability in distributed organizing. *Organization Science, 13*(3), 249–273. doi:10.1287/orsc.13.3.249.2776

Orlikowski, W. J. (1992). The duality of technology: Rethinking the concept of technology in organizations. *Organization Science, 3*(3), 398–427. doi:10.1287/orsc.3.3.398

Orlikowski, W. J., Yates, J., Okamura, K., & Fujimoto, M. (1995). Shaping electronic communication: The meta-structuring of technology in the context of use. *Organization Science, 6*(4), 423–444. doi:10.1287/orsc.6.4.423

Page, L., Brin, S., Motwani, R., & Winograd, T. (1998). *The PageRank citation ranking: Bringing order to the Web*. Stanford University.

Panzarasa, P., Jennings, N. R., & Norman, T. J. (2002). Formalizing collaborative decision-making and practical reasoning in multi-agent system. *Journal of Logic and Engineering, 12*(1), 55–117.

Paparizos, S., Al-Khalifa, S., Chapman, A., Jagadish, H. V., Lakshmanan, L. V., Nierman, A., et al. (2003). TIMBER: A Native System for Querying XML. *SIGMOD Conference*.

Papazoglou, M. P., & van den Heuvel, W.-J. (2007). Service oriented architectures: Approaches, technologies and research issues. *The VLDB Journal, 16*(3), 389–415. doi:10.1007/s00778-007-0044-3

Parsons, J., & Cole, L. (2005). What do the pictures mean? Guidelines for experimental evaluation of representation fidelity in diagrammatical conceptual modeling techniques. *Data & Knowledge Engineering, 55*(3), 327–342. doi:10.1016/j.datak.2004.12.008

Paulk, M., Weber, C., Curtis, B., & Chrissis, M. B. (1994). *The capability maturity model: Guidelines for improving the software process*. Reading, MA: Addison-Wesley Longman, Inc.

Payton, J., Roman, G.-C., & Julien, C. (n.d.). *Simplifying Context-Aware Agent Coordination Using Context-Sensitive Data Structures*. Washington University in St. Louis, School of Engineering, St. Louis, MI, USA.

Peer, J. (2004). *Web Service Composition as AI Planning - a Survey*. University of St. Gallen.

Peirce, C. S. (1931-1958). Vol 2, paragraph 228. In C. H. vols. 1-6, P. Weiss; & A. W. Burks vols. 7-8 (Eds.), *The collected papers of C. S. Peirce*. Cambridge, MA: Harvard University Press.

Peirce, C. S. (1931-1958). Charles Hartshorne, Paul Weiss & Arthur Burks (Eds.), Collected Papers of Charles Sanders Peirce (8 vols.). Cambridge MA: Harvard University Press.

Pepper, S. (2000). The Tao of topic maps. *XML Europe 2000, Paris: Palais des Congres, Paris, June 12-16: Proceedings*. Retrieved November 5, 2010, from http://www.gca.org/papers/xmleurope2000/papers/s11-01.html

Perry, M., O'Hara, K., Sellen, A., Brown, B., & Harper, R. (2001). Dealing with mobility: understanding access anytime, anywhere. *ACM Transactions on Computer-Human Interaction, 8*(4), 323–347. doi:10.1145/504704.504707

Peuschel, B., & Schafer, W. (1992). Concepts and implementation of a rule-based process engine. *Proceedings of the 14th International Conference on Software Engineering*, Melbourne, Australia, (pp. 262-279).

Pietarinen, A.-V. (2009, July 19-21). *On the conceptual underpinnings of organizational semiotics*. Paper presented at 11th International Conference on Informatics and Semiotics in Organisations, IFIP WG8.1 Working Conference. Beijing.

Pirolli, P., & Card, S. (1999). Information foraging. *Psychological Review, 106*(4), 643–675. doi:10.1037/0033-295X.106.4.643

Pistore, M., Barbon, F., Bertoli, P., Shaparau, D., & Traverso, P. (n.d.). *Planning and Monitoring Web Service Composition* (p. 106).

Plaza, E., & Arcos, J.-L. (2001). Context Aware Agents for Personal Information Services. *Lecture Notes in Computer Science, 2182*. doi:10.1007/3-540-45400-4

Polanyi, M. (1966). *The tacit dimension*. Garden City, NJ: Doubleday and Company, Inc.

Pollock, J., & Hodgson, R. (2004). *Adaptive Information: Improving Business Through Semantic Interoperability, Grid Computing, and Enterprise Integration*, Hoboken, NJ: John Wiley & Sons, Inc.

Polovina, S., & Hill, R. (2009). A transactions pattern for structuring unstructured corporate information in enterprise applications. *International Journal of Intelligent Information Technologies*, *5*(2), 34–47. doi:10.4018/jiit.2009040103

Polovina, S. (2007). An Introduction to Conceptual Graphs. *Proceedings of the 15th International Conference on Conceptual Structures*. 1-14.

Polovina, S. (2007). An introduction to conceptual graphs. In U. Priss, S. Polovina & R. Hill (Eds.), *Proceedings of the 15th International Conference on Conceptual Structures (ICCS 2007): Conceptual structures: Knowledge architectures for smart applications, July 2007, Sheffield, UK* (Lecture Notes in Artificial Intelligence 4604, pp. 1-15). Berlin/Heidelberg, Germany & New York, NY: Springer.

Polovina, S., & Hill, R. (2005). Enhancing the initial requirements capture of multi-agent systems through conceptual graphs. In F. Dau, M. Mugnier & G. Stumme (Eds.), *Conceptual structures: Common semantics for sharing knowledge, lecture notes in artificial intelligence* (LNAI 3596, pp. 439-452). Heidelberg, Germany: Springer.

Polovina, S., & Stalker, I. D. (2010). *TOASTIE: Transaction-oriented architecture for structuring the totally integrated enterprise*. Paper presented at the 2010 International Conference on Intelligent Networking and Collaborative Systems, Thessaloniki, Greece. (pp. 333-334). DOI 10.1109/INCOS.2010.93

Porter, M. (1980). An algorithm for suffix stripping. *Program*, *14*(3), 130–137.

Power, D. J. (2002). *Decision support systems: concepts and resources for managers*. Quorum Books, Westport, CN, USA.

Priss, U. (1999). Efficient implementation of semantic relations in lexical databases. *Computational Intelligence*, *15*, 79–87. doi:10.1111/0824-7935.00083

Quillian, M. R. (1968). Semantic memory. In Minsky, M. (Ed.), *Semantic information processing* (pp. 216–270). Cambridge, MA: MIT Press.

Rahmati, A., & Zhong, L. (2007). Context-for-wireless: context-sensitive energy-efficient wireless data transfer. *5th International Conference on Mobile systems, Applications and Services* (pp. 165-178), San Juan, Puerto Rico.

Ram, S., & Park, J. (2004). Semantic Conflict Resolution Ontology (SCROL): An Ontology for Detecting and Resolving Data and Schema-Level Semantic Conflicts. *IEEE Transactions on Knowledge and Data Engineering*, *16*(2), 189–202. doi:10.1109/TKDE.2004.1269597

Ramesh, R., & Zionts, S. (1997). Multicriteria Decision Making. In Gass, S. & Harris, C. (Eds.), *Encyclopedia of Operations Research* (pp. 419-425). Operations Research Society of America.

Rice, R. (1993). Media appropriateness: Using social presence theory to compare traditional and new organization media. *Human Communication Research*, *19*(4), 451–484. doi:10.1111/j.1468-2958.1993.tb00309.x

Richens, R. H. (1956). Preprogramming for mechanical translation. *Machine Translation Archive*, *3*(1), 20–25.

Robertson, S., Walker, S., Jones, S., Hancock-Beaulieu, M., & Gatford, M. (1993). *Okapi at TREC-2*. Paper presented at the Second Text REtrieval Conference (TREC).

Rodhain, F. (1999). Tacit to explicit: Transforming knowledge through cognitive mapping - an experiment. In R. Agarwal & J. Prasad (Eds.), *1999 ACM SIGCPR Conference on Computer Personnel Research: Proceedings* (pp. 51-56). New York, NY: ACM Digital Library.

Rogers, E. M. (1995). *Diffusion of Innovations* (4 ed.). New-York: Free Press.

Romeyn, J. W. (2004). Hypotheses and inductive predictions. *Synthese*, *141*(3), 333–364. doi:10.1023/B:SYNT.0000044993.82886.9e

Roughan, M., Griffin, T., Mao, M., Greenberg, A., & Freeman, B. (2004). Combining routing and traffic data for detection of IP forwarding anomalies. *ACM SIGMETRICS Performance Evaluation Review*, *32*(1), 416–417. doi:10.1145/1012888.1005745

Russell, S., & Yoon, V. (2005). Heterogeneous Agent Development: A Multi-Agent System for Testing Stock Trading Algorithms. *Eleventh Americas Conference on Information Systems*, Omaha, NE, USA.

Ruthven, I. (2003). *Re-examining the potential effectiveness of interactive query expansion*. Paper presented at the Twenty-sixth Annual International ACM SIGIR Conference on Research and Development in Information Retrieval.

Saaty, T., Vargas, L., & Dellmann, K. (2003). The allocation of intangible resources: the analytic hierarchy process and linear programming. *Socio-Economic Planning Sciences*, *37*(3), 169–185. doi:10.1016/S0038-0121(02)00039-3

Saaty, T., & Vargas, L. (2000). *Methods, Concepts and Applications of the Analytic Hierarchy Process*. Boston, MA: Kluwer Academic Publishers.

Sabater, J., & Sierra, C. (2005). Review on computational trust and reputation models. *Artificial Intelligence Review*, *24*, 33–60. doi:10.1007/s10462-004-0041-5

Sadowski, P. (2010). Towards systems semiotics: Some remarks and (hopefully useful) definitions. *Semiotix, 1*. Retrieved November 5, 2010, from http://www.semioticon.com/semiotix/issues/2010-issue-2011/

Salter, A. (2001). *Semantic modelling and a semantic normal form*. (School of Computing Technical Report SOCTR/01/01): Staffordshire University.

Salton, G., & Buckley, C. (1990). Improving retrieval performance by relevance feedback. *Journal of the American Society for Information Science American Society for Information Science*, *41*(4), 288–297. doi:10.1002/(SICI)1097-4571(199006)41:4<288::AID-ASI8>3.0.CO;2-H

Salton, G., Buckley, C., & Fox, E. A. (1983). Automatic query formulations in information retrieval. *Journal of the American Society for Information Science and Technology*, *34*(4), 262–280. doi:10.1002/asi.4630340406

Sarraf, Q., & Ellis, G. (2006). Business rules in retail: The tesco.com story. *Business Rules Journal, 7*(6)

Saussure, F. (2001). *Course in literary theory: An anthology*. Hoboken, NJ: Blackwell Publishers.

Schärfe, H., Petersen, U., & Øhrstrøm, P. (2002). On teaching conceptual graphs. In Priss, U., Corbett, D., & Angelova, G. (Eds.), *Conceptual structures: Integration and interfaces: Lecture Notes in Computer Science 2393* (pp. 285–298). Heidelberg/ Berlin, Germany: Springer. doi:10.1007/3-540-45483-7_22

Schiffel, J. (2008). *Improving knowledge management programs using marginal utility in a metric space generated by conceptual graphs*. ProQuest Theses: Doctoral Dissertation, Nova Southeastern University, Fort Lauderdale.

Schilit, B., & Theimer, M. (1994). Disseminating Active Map Information to Mobile Hosts. *IEEE Network*, *8*(5), 22–32. doi:10.1109/65.313011

Schmidt, A. R., Waas, F., Ketersen, M. L., Florescu, D., Manolescu, I., Carey, M. J., & Busse, R. (2001). *The XML Benchmark Project*. CWI.

Schmitt, I., & Saake, G. (1996). *Schema integration and view generation by resolving intensional and extensional overlappings*. Paper presented at the 9th ISCA Int. Conf. on Parallel and Distributed Computing Systems (PDCS'96), Dijon, France.

Schön, D. A. (1983). *The reflective practitioner: How professionals think in action*. Basic Books.

Segal, R. B., & Kephart, J. O. (2000, June 29-July 2). *Incremental Learning in SwiftFile*. Proceedings of the Seventh International Conference on Machine Learning, Stanford, CA, pp. 863-870.

Seidman, D. I., & Ritsko, J. J. (2004). Preface. *IBM Systems Journal*, *43*(3), 449. doi:10.1147/sj.433.0449

Senge, P. (1990). *The fifth discipline: The art and practice of the learning organization*. New York, NY: Currency Doubleday.

Serenko, A. (2006). The importance of interface agent characteristics from the end-user perspective. *International Journal of Intelligent Information Technologies*, *2*(2), 48–59. doi:10.4018/jiit.2006040104

Serenko, A. (2007a). Are interface agents scapegoats? Attributions of responsibility in human-agent interaction. *Interacting with Computers*, *19*(2), 293–303. doi:10.1016/j.intcom.2006.07.005

Serenko, A. (2007b). The development of an instrument to measure the degree of animation predisposition of agent users. *Computers in Human Behavior*, *23*(1), 478–495. doi:10.1016/j.chb.2004.10.042

Serenko, A., Bontis, N., & Detlor, B. (2007). End-user adoption of animated interface agents in everyday work applications. *Behaviour & Information Technology*, *26*(2), 119–132. doi:10.1080/01449290500260538

Serenko, A., & Detlor, B. (2004). Intelligent agents as innovations. *AI & Society*, *18*(4), 364–381. doi:10.1007/s00146-004-0310-5

Serenko, A., Ruhi, U., & Cocosila, M. (2007). Unplanned effects of intelligent agents on Internet use: Social Informatics approach. *AI & Society*, *21*(1-2), 141–166. doi:10.1007/s00146-006-0051-8

Shaft, T. M., & Vessey, I. (2006). The role of cognitive fit in the relationship between software comprehension and modification. *Management Information Systems Quarterly*, *30*(1), 29–55.

Shahram, G., Shyam, K., & Bhaskar, K. (2006). An evaluation of availability latency in carrier-based vehicular ad-hoc networks. In *Proceedings of the 5th ACM international workshop on Data engineering for wireless and mobile access*. Chicago, Illinois, USA: ACM Press.

Shaw, W. M., Wood, J. B., Wood, R. E., & Tibbo, H. R. (1991). The Cystic Fibrosis database: Content and research opportunities. *Library & Information Science Research*, *13*(4), 347–366.

Shelley, L., & Polonsky, M. J. (2002). Do charitable causes need to segment their current donor base on demographic factors? An Australian examination. *International Journal of Nonprofit and Voluntary Sector Marketing*, *7*(1), 19–29. doi:10.1002/nvsm.164

Shim, J., & Shim, S. S. Y. (2006). Ontology-based e-catalog in e-commerce: Special section. *Electronic Commerce Research and Applications*, *5*(1), 1. doi:10.1016/j.elerap.2006.01.001

Shishkov, B., Dietz, J. L. G., & Liu, K. (2006, May 23-27). *Bridging the language-action perspective and organizational semiotics in SDBC*. Paper presented at the Eighth International Conference on Enterprise Information Systems, Paphos, Cyprus.

Shoham, Y. (1993). Agent Oriented Programming. *Journal of Artificial Intelligence*, *60*(1), 51–92. doi:10.1016/0004-3702(93)90034-9

Shoham, Y. (1993). Agent oriented programming. *Artificial Intelligence*, *60*(1), 51–92. doi:10.1016/0004-3702(93)90034-9

Silverstein, C., Henzinger, M., Marais, H., & Moricz, M. (1999). *Analysis of a very large Altavista query log*. Paper presented at the ACM SIGIR Forum.

Sim, K. M., & Chan, R. (2000, November). A brokering protocol for agent-based e-commerce. *IEEE Transactions on Systems, Man and Cybernetics. Part C, Applications and Reviews*, *30*(4).

Simon, H. A. (1996). *The sciences of the artificial* (3rd ed.). Cambridge, MA: MIT Press.

Simon, H. A. (1959). Theories of Decision-Making in Economics and Behavioral Science. *The American Economic Review*, *49*(3), 253–283.

Simon, H. A. (1960). *The New Science of Management Decision*. New York, NY, USA: Harper & Row.

Singh, R., Iyer, L. S., & Salam, A. F. (2005). Semantic eBusiness. *International Journal on Semantic Web and Information Systems*, *1*(1), 19–35.

Singhal, A., Choi, J., Hindle, D., Lewis, D. D., & Pereira, F. (1998). *AT&T at TREC-7*. Paper presented at the Seventh Text REtrieval Conference (TREC-7).

Sivashanmugam, K., Miller, J. A., Seth, A. P., & Verma, K. (2004). Framework for Semantic Web Process Composition. *International Journal of Electronic Commerce*, *9*(2), 71–106.

Slowinski, R., & Zopounidis, C. (1995). Application of the rough set approach to evaluation of bankruptcy risk. *International Journal of Intelligent Systems in Accounting Finance & Management*, *4*(1), 27–41.

Snelting, G. (1996). Reengineering of configurations based on mathematical concept analysis. *ACM Transactions on Software Engineering and Methodology*, *5*, 146–189. doi:10.1145/227607.227613

Sowa, J. (2000). *Knowledge representation: Logical, philosophical, and computational foundations*. Pacific Grove, CA: Brooks/Cole.

Sowa, J. F. (1984). *Conceptual structures: Information processing in mind and machine*. Boston, MA: Addison-Wesley.

Sowa, J. F., & Zachman, J. A. (1992). Extending and formalizing the framework for Information Systems architecture. *IBM Systems Journal*, *31*(3), 590–616. doi:10.1147/sj.313.0590

Sproull, L., & Kiesler, S. (1986). Reducing social context cues: Electronic mail in organizational communications. *Management Science*, *32*(11), 1492–1512. doi:10.1287/mnsc.32.11.1492

Sproull, L., Subramani, M., Kiesler, S., Walker, J. H., & Waters, K. (1996). When the interface is a face. *Human-Computer Interaction*, *11*(2), 97–124. doi:10.1207/s15327051hci1102_1

Stal, M. (2002). Web services: beyond component-based computing. *Communications of the ACM*, *45*(10), 71–76. doi:10.1145/570907.570934

Stamper, R., Liu, K., Hafkamp, M., & Ades, Y. (2000). Understanding the roles of signs and norms in organizations – a semiotic approach to Information Systems design. *Behaviour & Information Technology*, *19*(1), 15–27. doi:10.1080/014492900118768

Stamper, R. (2004, July 18). *MEASUR – Semiotic tools for IS development*. The 7th International Workshop on Organisational Semiotics. Retrieved July 15, 2010, from http://www.orgsem.org/sedita.htm

Stamper, R. (2008). *Posting to Ontolog forum on October 6, 2008*. Retrieved October 6, 2008, from http://ontolog.cim3.net/forum/ontolog-forum/2008-10/msg00044.html

Stevens, G. (1989). Integrating the supply chain. *International Journal of Physical Distribution & Materials Management*, *19*(1), 3–8.

Stolee, P., Zaza, C., Pedlar, A., & Myers, A. M. (1999). Clinical experience with goal attainment scaling in geriatric care. *Journal of Aging and Health*, *11*(1), 96–124. doi:10.1177/089826439901100106

Suchman, L. (1987). *Plans and situated action*. New York, NY: Cambridge University Press.

Suwu, W., & Das, A. (2001). *An agent system architecture for e-commerce*. International Workshop on Database and Expert Systems Applications (pp. 715-719).

Sweeney, R. (2010). *Achieving service-oriented architecture: Applying an enterprise architecture approach*. Hoboken, NJ: Wiley.

Sycara, K., Lu, J., Klusch, M., & Widoff, S. (1999). Dynamic Service Matchmaking among Agents in Open Information Environments. [Special Issue on Semantic Interoperability in Global Information Systems]. *SIGMOD Record*, *28*(1), 47–53. doi:10.1145/309844.309895

Sycara, K., Widoff, S., Klusch, M., & Lu, J. (2002). LARKS: Dynamic Matchmaking Among Heterogeneous Software Agents in Cyberspace. *Autonomous Agents and Multi-Agent Systems*, *5*, 173–203. doi:10.1023/A:1014897210525

Tallman, S., Jenkins, M., Henry, N., & Pinch, S. (2004). Knowledge, Clusters, and Competitive Advantage. *Academy of Management Review*, *29*(2), 258–271.

Tan, S., & Liu, K. (2004, April 14-17). *Requirements engineering for organisational modelling*. Paper presented at the 6th International Conference on Enterprise Information Systems, Porto, Portugal.

Tang, T. Y., Winoto, P., & Niu, X. (2003). *Investigating trust between users and agents in a multi agent portfolio management system: A preliminary report*.

Taylor, S., & Todd, P. (1995). Assessing IT usage: The role of prior experience. *Management Information Systems Quarterly*, *19*(4), 561–570. doi:10.2307/249633

Teegan, H. A. (1996). Distributed performance monitoring using SNMP V2. *Network Operations and Management Symposium*, *612*, 616-619. IEEE.

Telecom Italia Lab (2007). *JADE - Java Agent DEvelopment Framework* [Online].

Thelwall, M., & Hasler, L. (2007). Blog search engines. *Online Information Review*, *31*(4), 467–479. doi:10.1108/14684520710780421

Thio, N., & Karunasekera, S. (2005). Automatic measurement of a QoS metric for Web service recommendation. *Australian Software Engineering Conference* (pp. 202-211), Brisbane, Australia.

Thomas, M., Redmond, R., Yoon, Y., & Singh, R. (2005). A semantic approach to monitor business process performance. *Communications of the ACM*, *48*(12), 55–59. doi:10.1145/1101779.1101809

Thomas, M., Redmond, R. T., Yoon, V., & Singh, R. (2005). A semantic approach to monitoring business process performance. *Communications of the ACM.*

Todd, S., & Lawson, R. (2001). Lifestyle segmentation and museum/gallery visiting behaviour. *International Journal of Nonprofit and Voluntary Sector Marketing, 6*(4), 269–277. doi:10.1002/nvsm.152

Trevino, L. K., Daft, R. L., & Lengel, R. H. (1990). Understanding managers' media choices: A symbolic interactionist perspective. In Fulk, J., & Steinfield, C. W. (Eds.), *Organizations and communications technologies* (pp. 71–94). Newbury Park: Sage Publications.

Tsikrika, T., & Lalmas, M. (2001). *Merging techniques for performing data fusion on the Web.* Paper presented at the Conference on Information and Knowledge Management.

Turban, E., & Aronson, J. (2001). *Decision support systems and intelligent systems.* Upper Saddle River, NJ: Prentice-Hall, Inc.

UNSPSC. (2010). *The United Nations Standard Products and Services Code.* Retrieved September 30, 2010, from http://www.unspsc.org

Uschold, M., & Grüninger, M. (1996). Ontologies: Principles, methods, and applications. *The Knowledge Engineering Review, 11*(2), 93–155. doi:10.1017/S0269888900007797

Vagena, Z., Moro, M., & Tsotras, V. (2004). Twig Query Processing over Graph Structured XML Data. *Workshop on Web and Databases WebDB*, Paris, France.

van Ommering, R. (2002). *Building product populations with software components.* Paper presented at the International Conference on Software Engineering.

van Rijsbergen, C. J. (1979). *Information retrieval* (2nd ed.). Butterworths.

Venkatesh, V., & Davis, F. D. (2000). A theoretical extension of the Technology Acceptance Model: Four longitudinal field studies. *Management Science, 46*(2), 186–204. doi:10.1287/mnsc.46.2.186.11926

Vessey, I. (1991). Cognitive fit: A theory-based analysis of the graphs versus tables literature. *Decision Sciences, 22*(2), 219–240. doi:10.1111/j.1540-5915.1991.tb00344.x

von Wright, G. H. (1980). *Freedom and determination.* Amsterdam, The Netherlands: North Holland Publishing Co.

Vrandecic, D. (2009). Ontology evaluation. In Staab, S., & Studer, R. (Eds.), *Handbook of ontologies* (pp. 293–313). Berlin, Germany: Springer. doi:10.1007/978-3-540-92673-3_13

Vrandecic, D. (2010). *Ontology evaluation.* Doctoral dissertation, Karlsruhe Institute of Technology. Retrieved September 30, 2010, from [INSERT FIGURE 001]http://www.aifb.kit.edu/web/Phdthesis3008/en

Wang, X., Fang, H., & Zhai, C. (2007). *Improving retrieval accuracy for difficult queries using negative feedback.* Paper presented at the Conference on Information and Knowledge Management, Lisbon, Portugal.

Wang, X., Tao, T., Sun, J.-T., Shakery, A., & Zhai, C. (2008). DirichletRank: Solving the zero-one gap problem of PageRank. *ACM Transactions on Information Systems, 26*(2), 10:11-10:29.

Wang, Y., Cuthbert, L., Mullany, F.J., Stathopoulos, P., Tountopoulos, V., Sotiriou, D.A., Mitrou, N., & Senis, M. (2004). Exploring agent-based wireless business models and decision support applications in an airport environment. *Journal of Telecommunications and Information Technology, 3.*

Weatherspoon, H., Chun, B.-G., So, C.W., & Kubiatowicz, J. (n.d.). *Long-Term Data Maintenance in Wide-Area Storage Systems: A Quantitative Approach.* University of California, Berkely, Electrical Engineering & Computer Sciences Department, Berkely, CA, USA.

WebDAV. Web site: http://www.webdav.org

Weber, R. (2003). Conceptual modelling and ontology: Possibilities and pitfalls. *Journal of Database Management, 14*(2), 1–20. doi:10.4018/jdm.2003070101

Weisteoffer, H. R., Wooldridge, B., & Singh, R. (1999). A Multi-criteria Approach to Local Tax Planning. *Socio-Economic Planning Sciences, 33*, 301–315. doi:10.1016/S0038-0121(99)00015-4

Wexelblat, A. D. (1999). *Footprints: Interaction history for digital objects.* PhD Thesis, Massachusetts Institute of Technology.

Wille, R. (1982). Restructuring lattice theory: An approach based on hierarchies of concepts. In Rival, I. (Ed.), *Ordered Sets* (pp. 445–470). Boston: Reidel Dordecht Publisher.

Willemain, T. R., Goyal, A., van Deven, M., & Thukral, I. S. (1994). Alumni giving: The influences of reunion, class and year. *Research in Higher Education, 35*, 609–629. doi:10.1007/BF02497090

Wilson, T. D. (2002). The nonsense of knowledge management. *Information Research, 8*(1), paper no. 144.

Winston, W., & Albright, S. (2007). *Practical Management Science* (3rd ed.). Mason, OH: Thomson South-Western.

Wolff, K. E. (1996). Comparison of graphical data analysis methods. In *F. Faulbaum & W. Bandilla, SoftWat '95 Advances in Statistical Software. 5* (pp. 139–151). Stuttgart: Lucius and Lucius.

Wooldridge, M. (2002). *An Introduction to MultiAgent Systems*. West Sussex, UK: John Wiley and Sons Ltd.

Wu, W., Ekaette, E., & Far, B. H. (2003). Uncertainty management framework for multi-agent system. *Proceedings of ATS* (pp. 122-131).

Wymer, W. W. Jr. (2003). Differentiating literacy volunteers: A segmentation analysis for target marketing. *International Journal of Nonprofit and Voluntary Sector Marketing, 8*(3), 267–285. doi:10.1002/nvsm.217

Xalan, Web site: http://xml.apache.org/xalan-j/.

XML. Web site: http://www.w3.org/XML/.

Xu, G., Yang, Z., & Huang, H. (2004). A basic model for components implementation of software architecture. *ACM SIGSOFT Software Engineering Notes, 29*(5), 1–11. doi:10.1145/1022494.1022522

Xu, J., & Croft, W. B. (1998). Corpus-based stemming using cooccurrence of word variants. *ACM Transactions on Information Systems, 16*(1), 61–81. doi:10.1145/267954.267957

Xu, Y., & Papakonstantinou, Y. (2008). Efficient LCA based keyword search in XML data. *Proceedings of EDBT* (pp. 535-546).

Yang, K. (2002). *Combining text-, link-, and classification-based retrieval methods to enhance information discovery on the Web*. Unpublished PhD Thesis, University of North Carolina-Chapel Hill, Chapel Hill, NC.

Yang, Z., Zhang, D., & Ye, C. (2006). Evaluation metrics for ontology complexity and evolution analysis. *Proceedings of the IEEE International Conference on e-Business Engineering (ICEBE 2006)* (pp. 162-169).

Yao, H., Orme, A. M., & Etzkorn, L. (2005). Cohesion metrics for ontology design and application. *Journal of Computer Science, 1*(1), 117–113.

Yates, J., & Orlikowski, W. J. (1992). Genres of organizational communication: A structurational approach to studying communication and media. *Academy of Management Review, 17*(2), 299–326.

Yoo, S. B., & Kim, Y. (2002). Web-based knowledge management for sharing product data in virtual enterprises. *International Journal of Production Economics, 75*, 173–183. doi:10.1016/S0925-5273(01)00190-6

Yu, B., & Singh, M. P. (2001). Towards a probabilistic model of distributed reputation management. In *Proceedings of the Fourth Workshop on Deception, Fraud and Trust in Agent Societies*, Montreal, Canada. (pp. 125–137).

Yu-Chee, T., Shih-Lin, W., Wen-Hwa, L., & Chao, C.-M. (2001). Location awareness in ad hoc wireless mobile networks. *Computer, 34*(6), 46–52. doi:10.1109/2.928621

Zacharia, G. (1999). *Collaborative reputation mechanisms for online communities*. Master's thesis, Massachusetts Institute of Technology.

Zeidler, A., & Fiege, L. (2003). Mobility support with REBECA. *23rd International Conference on Distributed Computing Systems Workshop* (pp. 354-360), Providence, RI, USA.

Zhang, J. (1997). The nature of external representations in problem solving. *Cognitive Science, 21*(2), 179–217. doi:10.1207/s15516709cog2102_3

Zhang, X., Lesser, V., & Podorozhny, R. (2005). Multidimensional, multi-step negotiation for task allocation in a cooperative system. *Autonomous Agents and Multi-Agent Systems, 10*, 5–40. doi:10.1007/s10458-004-5020-3

Zhang, Y., Zheng, Z., & Lyu, M. R. (2010). *WSExpress: A QoS-aware search engine for Web services*. Paper presented at the Proceedings of the IEEE International Conference on Web Services.

Zhao, X., Wu, C., Zhang, R., Zhao, C., & Lin, Z. A. (2004). *Multi-agent system for e-business processes monitoring in a Web-based environment*. TCL Group Corporation.

Zhdanova, A. V., Krummenacher, R., Henke, J., & Fensel, D. (2005). Community-driven ontology management: DERI case study. *Proceedings of the 2005 IEEE/WIC/ACM International Conference on Web Intelligence* (pp. 73-79).

Zhou, J., Pakkala, D., Perala, J., & Niemela, E. (2007). *Dependency-aware service oriented architecture and service composition*. Paper presented at the IEEE International Conference on Web Services.

Zhu, K. (2002). Information Transparency in Electronic Marketplaces: Why Data Transparency May Hinder the Adoption of B2B Exchanges. *Electronic Markets*, *12*(2), 92–99. doi:10.1080/10196780252844535

Zimmerman, J. L. (2006). *Accounting for decision making and control* (5th ed.). Boston, MA: McGraw-Hill Irwin.

Zuchero, J. (2007). *The Practical Peirce – An Introduction to the Triadic Continuum Implemented as a Computer Data Structure*. New York: iUniverse.\

About the Contributors

Vijayan Sugumaran is Professor of Management Information Systems in the Department of Decision and Information Sciences at Oakland University, Rochester, Michigan, USA. He is also a Visiting Professor in the Department of Service Systems Management and Engineering at Sogang University, Seoul, South Korea. He received his PhD in Information Technology from George Mason University, Fairfax, VA. His research interests are in the areas of service science, ontologies and Semantic Web, intelligent agent and multi-agent systems, component based software development, and knowledge-based systems. His most recent publications have appeared in *Information Systems Research, ACM Transactions on Database Systems, IEEE Transactions on Education, IEEE Transactions on Engineering Management, Communications of the ACM, Healthcare Management Science,* and *Data and Knowledge Engineering.* He has published over 140 peer-reviewed articles in Journals, Conferences, and Books. He has edited eight books and two journal special issues. He is the editor-in-chief of the *International Journal of Intelligent Information Technologies* and also serves on the editorial board of seven other journals. He was the program co-chair for the *13th International Conference on Applications of Natural Language to Information Systems* (NLDB 2008). In addition, he has served as the chair of the *Intelligent Agent and Multi-Agent Systems* mini-track for Americas Conference on Information Systems (AMCIS 1999 - 2010) and *Intelligent Information Systems* track for the Information Resources Management Association International Conference (IRMA 2001, 2002, 2005 - 2007). He served as Chair of the E-Commerce track for Decision Science Institute's Annual Conference, 2004. He was the Information Technology Coordinator for the Decision Sciences Institute (2007-2009). He also regularly serves as a program committee member for numerous national and international conferences.

* * *

David Al-Dabass is Emeritus Professor and occupies the personal chair of Intelligent Systems in the School of Science & Technology, Nottingham Trent University, United Kingdom. He is a graduate of Imperial College, London University, holds a PhD and has held post-doctoral and advanced research fellowships at the Control Systems Centre, UMIST, Manchester University. He is member of IEEE and ACM and Fellow of the IET, IMA and BCS. He is founder and editor-in-chief of the International Journal of Simulation: Systems, Science and Technology, currently serves as chairman of the UK Simulation Society and has previously served on the European Council for Modelling and Simulation as director of the European Simulation Multi-conference series. He has authored or co-authored over 170 scientific publications in intelligent systems modelling and simulation and served as general chair for over 20 international conferences.

Manish Agrawal is an Associate Professor of Information Systems and Decision Sciences at the University of South Florida in Tampa. His current research interests include software quality, electronic intermediaries, and the development of agent-based systems for negotiations and fraud detection. His articles have appeared in IEEE Transactions on Software Engineering, INFORMS Journal on Computing, Communications of the ACM, Journal of Management Information Systems, Decision Support Systems, and the Journal of Organizational Computing and Electronic Commerce. Agrawal teaches classes on computer networks and distributed Information Systems at both the graduate and undergraduate levels. He completed his PhD at SUNY Buffalo. Agrawal is a member of AIS and INFORMS.

Jamal Ahmed received his MS in computer science from Peshawar University and is currently working as a lecturer at FAST-National University of Science & Technology, 160-Hayatabad Industrial Estate, Peshawar. His area of expertise is artificial neural networks and MANETS.

Simon Andrews is a Senior Lecturer in Software Engineering within the Department of Computing at Sheffield Hallam University, co-leader of the Conceptual Structures Research Group and an international expert on Formal Concept Analysis (FCA). Originating from his PhD, awarded in 1996, his first interest was in writing and animating Z specifications. That work had turned theoretical mathematics into a practical software development tool for software engineers in safety-critical systems. These interests lead him to FCA; again applying advanced mathematical theory to contemporary industrial practice. He was a key participant at the FCA Algorithm Performance Competition at the 2009 International Conference of Conceptual Structures (ICCS) in which his FCA algorithm (In-Close) was the close runner up. He is currently a Principle Investigator for a prestigious European Commission 7th Framework Programme project, called CUBIST: http://www.cubist-project.eu/, were he is working on leading-edge, large-scale, data analysis techniques that include knowledge discovery, visual analytics, data optimisation and semantic conversion. Working with a range of public and private data sets, including those from local government, biomedical research, satellite telemetry and human resources, he is developing algorithms, techniques and software to elicit hidden meaning from data that is not accessible using traditional data analysis techniques.

Azzam ul Asar received his PhD and MSc degrees from the University of Strathclyde Glasgow, UK. He did his Bachelor's degree in electrical and electronic engineering from the N.-W.F.P. University of Engineering and Technology (UET), Peshawar, Pakistan. His areas of interest in research are intelligent systems, neural networks, Petri nets, and supply chains with application to industrial systems. He has over 40 publications in international journals and conference proceedings and has presented numerous papers in the IEEE international conferences abroad. He has been a recipient of several fellowships and scholarships to conduct research in USA and UK. He has also served as a visiting Professor in the New Jersey Institute of Technology, USA. He is currently serving as Professor in the Dept. of Electrical and Electronic Engineering, and dean, Faculty of Engineering, NWFP University of Engineering and Technology, Peshawar. He acted as a referee for IEEE, USA and IEE UK technical journals. He has organized several international conferences both at home and abroad. Asar is a member of IEEE.

Naveen Ashish is a senior computer scientist with Calit2 at UC-Irvine. His research interests and expertise are in areas such as information integration, Semantic-Web, information extraction, and semi-structured data management. His current work is in the application domains of IT for emergency response, and medical informatics. He received a PhD in computer science from the University of Southern California, Los Angeles in 2000, and a BTech in Computer Science from IIT, Kanpur, India in 1993. Prior to UC-Irvine, he worked at NASA Ames Research Center.

Mahmood Bahar is Assistant Professor of Physics at Tarbiat Moallem University, Tehran, Iran. He received his PhD in medical physics, MS in nuclear technology and BS in physics. Dr. Bahar has authored and translated 40 books in physics, published over 40 journal and peer reviewed conference papers, and supervised over thirty MS theses. Dr. Bahar is a member of the Iran's Physics Association and serves as a member of the association's scientific committee.

Azita A. Bahrami is Assistant Professor of Information Technology at Armstrong Atlantic State University. She earned her PhD in curriculum and instruction and her MEd in Educational Technology from University of Missouri-Columbia. She has served as founding chair of General Education Department, founding director of Preparatory Program, director of Learning Development Center, founding president/chair/director of several associations, and president of her own company. Her areas of research are information retrieval, Web mining, e-commerce, and e-learning. Bahrami has authored several books, book chapters, journal articles, essays, and peer reviewed conference papers. She has served as co-chair of the 2008 International Conference on E-Learning, E-Business, Enterprise Information Systems, E-Government, and Outsourcing as well as co-editor and vice chair of other international conferences. Dr. Bahrami has also served as Program Committee member of over twenty international conferences.

Kaushal Chari is a Professor and the Chair of Information Systems & Decision Sciences department at the University of South Florida. Previously he served as the director of research for the College of Business Administration at the University of South Florida. He obtained a BTech. in mechanical engineering from the Indian Institute of Technology Kanpur, followed by an MBA and PhD from the University of Iowa. His research has been published in various journals including INFORMS Journal on Computing, Information Systems Research, IEEE Transactions on Software Engineering, Telecommunication Systems, Decision Support Systems, European Journal of Operational Research, and the Communications of the ACM. His research interests include software engineering, business intelligence, information security & risk management, and distributed systems. He currently serves as the associate editor of MIS for Interfaces Journal, and vice chair of the INFORMS Information Systems Society. He previously served as the co-chair for the Seventeenth Workshop on Information Technology & Systems (WITS) 2007, co-chair for the Sixth INFORMS Conference on Information Systems & Technology (CIST) 2001, and program co-chair for the Fourth Workshop on E-Business (WeB) 2005. Chari currently teaches a course on distributed systems.

Roger H. L. Chiang is an Associate Professor of Information Systems at the College of Business, University of Cincinnati. He received his B.S. degree in Management Science from National Chiao Tung University, Taiwan, M.S. degrees in Computer Science from Michigan State University and in Business Administration from University of Rochester, and a Ph.D. in Computers and Information Systems from the University of Rochester. His research has been published in a number of journals including ACM Transactions on Database Systems, Communications of the ACM, The DATA BASE for Advances in

Information Systems, Data & Knowledge Engineering, Decision Support Systems, Journal of American Society for Information Science and Technology, Journal of Database Administration, Journal of Management Information Systems, and Very Large Data Base Journal.

Cecil Eng Huang Chua is an Associate Professor at the University of Auckland. He received a PhD in Information Systems from Georgia State University, a Masters of Business by Research from Nanyang Technological University and both a Bachelor of Business Administration in Computer Information Systems and Economics and a Masters Certificate in Telecommunications Management from the University of Miami. Cecil's published research has focused on the design of intelligent systems, and control and coordination in technology organizations. Cecil has several publications in such journals as *Decision Support Systems, Journal of the AIS, MIS Quarterly,* and the *VLDB Journal.*

Fergle J. D'Aubeterre is the Application Services & Architecture Team Lead at Flint Transfield Services Ltd (FT-SERVICES), Canada. He obtained his PhD in Information Systems from The University of North Carolina at Greensboro and his MBA from Central Michigan University. His research interests include electronic commerce, business processes, Semantic Web, IT security and privacy, and global IT management. Fergle has published papers in journals such as Journal of the Association for Information Systems, European Journal of Information Systems, Information Systems Journal; Electronic Government an International Journal; the International Journal of Electronic Commerce Research; Encyclopedia of E-Commerce; E-Government, and Mobile Commerce; the Proceedings of the International Conference on Information Systems; the Proceedings of Americas Conference on Information Systems; the Proceedings of Global Information Technology Management; the Proceedings of the Design Science Research in Information Systems and Technology; and the Proceedings of the Decision Sciences Institute.

Richard Ehrhardt is a Professor in the Department of Information Systems and Operations Management, Bryan School of Business and Economics at The University of North Carolina at Greensboro. He holds an MA and PhD in Administrative Sciences from Yale University. At the Bryan School, he has held the positions of Department Head and MBA Program Director. His research interests are in stochastic models of operations research, logistics systems, materials management and production control systems. He has published in Management Science, Operations Research, IIE Transactions, Naval Research Logistics, International Journal of Production Research, Journal of the Operational Research Society, and other journals.

Tim French obtained a BA from the Open University whilst working in industry, later completing a Master's degree (MA) in Computer Studies at Nottingham University. He is a Fellow of the College of Preceptors (FCollP) and a Member of the British Computing Society, (MBCS) with a specialist interest in usability and trust issues. He has published extensively on trust issues and is currently an industrial Fellow. He has undertaken extensive freelance industrial consultancy activities to businesses of all sizes ranging from SME's to large "blue-chip" PLC's and has most recently has engaged in part-time PhD studies in Computer Semiotics (E-Trust aspects) at Reading University.

Hojaollah Hamidi received BSc, MSc, and PhD in electronic & computer engineering, respectively, from the Mazandaran University, Babol Iran (1999), Iran University of Science & Technology, Teheran

Iran (2000), and Iran University of Science & Technology, Teheran Iran (2005). His main research interest areas are fault-tolerant systems and applications and reliable and secure distributed systems and mathematical aspects of computing.

Ray R. Hashemi is Yamacraw Professor of Computer Science at the Armstrong Atlantic State University. He has earned his PhD in Electrical Engineering-Computer Science from the University of Missouri-Columbia. His MS is in Computer Science, and his BS is in Physics. Dr. Hashemi has published over 100 journal articles, book chapters, and peer reviewed conference papers and his research interest is in the area of data mining. Dr. Hashemi has served as co-chair of several international conferences, co-editor of several conference proceedings, and consultant to both governmental and non-governmental organizations. Dr. Hashemi is the owner of two patents, has presented his research in more than ten countries, and has served as a program committee member of more than thirty national and international conferences.

Syed Riaz ul Hasnain received his MS and BSc degrees from N-W.F.P. University of Engineering and Technology, Peshawar, Pakistan, where he currently serving as an Assistant Professor. He is also working on his PhD degree. His field of research is intelligent systems, neural networks, and alternative sources of energy. He has number of publications in international and national journals and conference proceedings.

Lakshmi Iyer is an Associate Professor in the Information Systems and Operations Management department at The University of North Carolina, Greensboro. She obtained her PhD from the University of Georgia, Athens. Her research interests are in the area of e-business processes, e-commerce issues, IS privacy and security, intelligent agents, decision support systems, and knowledge management. Her research work has been published or accepted for publication in Journal of the Association for Information Systems, European Journal of Information Systems, Communications of the ACM, eService Journal, Annals of OR, Decision Support Systems, Information Systems Management, International Journal of Semantic Web and Information Systems, Electronic Government, Journal of Global Information Technology Management, and others. Iyer has served as a Guest Editor for Communications of the ACM and the Journal of Electronic Commerce Research. She is a board member of Teradata University Network and AIS SIG on Semantic Web and Information Systems (SIGSEMIS) and serves on the editorial board for the International Journal of Information Security and Privacy.

Louis A. Le Blanc is Professor of Business Administration at the Campbell School of Business, Berry College, Mount Berry, Georgia, USA. He received a PhD from Texas A&M University, followed by postdoctoral study at the University of Minnesota and Indiana University. His publications have appeared in the MIS Quarterly, Decision Sciences, Journal of Organizational and End User Computing, Transportation Journal, European Journal of Operational Research, Group Decision and Negotiation, and the Journal of Decision Systems. Dr. Le Blanc teaches courses in strategic use of Information Technology and operations management.

Joerg Leukel is a Senior Researcher and Lecturer in the department of Information Systems 2 at the University of Hohenheim, Stuttgart, Germany. There he leads the Supply Chain Management & Logistics Research Group. He obtained a Ph.D. degree in Business Information Systems from the University of Duisburg-Essen. His research interests are in the areas of inter-organizational Information Systems, supply chain management, product lifecycle management, semantic interoperability, business ontologies, and standardization. He has initiated the 1st and 2nd International Workshop on Service-Oriented Computing in Logistics (SOC-LOG 2009, 2010) and served as the chair of 4th International Workshop on Data Engineering Issues in E-Commerce and Services (DEECS 2009).

David Maluf is a principal investigator in information sciences at NASA Ames Research Center. His expertise is in data and knowledge management, particularly information and service integration in heterogeneous environments. His work has particularly impacted NASA process management and data centric operations. He received a PhD in electrical engineering and an M.Eng from McGill University, Canada in 1995 and 1991, respectively. From 1995-1996 he was a post-doctoral scholar at Stanford University.

Bireshwar Dass Mazumdar obtained his MCA degree from UP Technical University, Lucknow, India in the year of 2004. He completed his Ph.D. from Department of Computer Science and Engineering IT, BHU Varanasi India in May 2010. He has 4 years experience of teaching and research in the field of computer science and engineering. Presently he is an Assistant Professor in Department of Computer Science, School of Management Sciences, Varanasi India. His research interest is multiagent system and its application in e-commerce, e-governance, intelligent tutoring system, and data mining.

Jane Campbell Mazzagatti is the Chief Knowledge Engineering Officer for Ai3 (As It Is Inc.). Her focus is developing the Phaneron technology, a new data organization system inspired by the cognitive model of C. S Peirce. As technical lead she is responsible for interpreting the Peirce materials and designing algorithms to create increasingly more sophisticated Phaneron structures. Mazzagatti and her team are currently creating Phaneron structures that record all the knowledge within field/record datasets. These field/record Phaneron structures are proving valuable for commercial applications. Mazzagatti was employed at UNISYS as a systems software engineer from 1972 to 2008, developing operating systems, language compilers, linkers, and loaders across many hardware platforms. Prior to that, she was employed as a math tech at the GE Re-entry Systems in King of Prussia, PA where her primary role was data reduction of large amounts of wind tunnel data, and at UNISYS developing commercial applications. Mazzagatti's formal education has been focused on the study of intellectual development and human computer interaction. Areas of study include the reduction of the complexity of program code to facilitate code maintenance and reduce coding errors, and design of GUI interfaces to increase the amount of information on a computer screen while keeping the screen space requirements at a minimum.

R. B. Mishra (BSc, Eng.; MTech; PhD) is a reader with the Department of Computer Engineering, Institute of Technology, Banaras Hindu University (IT-BHU), Varanasi, India. He has around 30 years of experience in teaching and research. He has published more than 100 research papers and articles in journals and conferences. He has supervised 8 PhD and 21 M.Tech. dissertations. He has also visited as faculty to the University of Bath, UK. His current areas of interest include AI and its application to medicine, robotics, the Semantic Web, and e-commerce.

Taha Osman is a Senior Lecturer at the College of Science and Technology, Nottingham Trent University. He gained his PhD in Fault-Tolerance of Distributed Computing Systems from the same university in 1998 and immediately joined its academic staff. Dr. Osman leads the Semantic Web research network at the Department of Computing and Informatics, and his research interests include multi-agent systems, Semantic Web, knowledge engineering, and intelligent information retrieval.

Simon Polovina is a Senior Lecturer in Business Computing within the Department of Computing at Sheffield Hallam University, UK. He is the founder and co-leader of the Conceptual Structures Research Group in the university and a steering group committee member of the Communication and Computing Research Centre of the University's Cultural, Communication and Computing Research Institute (C3RI, www.shu.ac.uk/research/c3ri). He has eight years of industrial experience in accounting and information and communication technologies (ICT). Arising from his PhD, awarded in 1994, his interests are in the use of ICT to help enterprises discover novel transactions that would otherwise remain as lost business opportunities. A particular theme of his work is Conceptual Structures (CS), which harmonises the creativity of humans with the productivity of computers. CS recognise that while organisations work with concepts, machines like structures. CS advances the theory and practice in connecting the user's conceptual approach to problem solving with the formal structures that computer applications need to bring their productivity to bear in solving these problems. He has over 70 learned publications to date. He provides educational and consultancy services to SAP, and is a Principal Investigator for the prestigious European Commission 7th Framework Programme project CUBIST (www.cubist-project.eu), where he is applying CS and co-managing the project. Simon has expertise in SAP NetWeaver Portal, SOA, business process management with ARIS, object-oriented analysis and design, conceptual modelling of businesses as multi-agent systems, and in interaction design.

Richard Redmond is Chairman and Associate Professor, of the Department of Information Systems in the School of Business at Virginia Commonwealth University. His publications and research have been in the areas of software engineering, database systems, expert systems, agent-based systems, and applications of AI to business. More recently, his focus has turned toward the Semantic Web and multi-agent based systems.

Stephen Russell is currently a visiting Assistant Professor in the School of Business at the George Washington University. He teaches in the Department of Information Systems & Technology Management and instructs courses under the Federal CIO Certificate Program, Management, and Information Systems subject areas. He received a BSc in Computer Science and MS and PhD degrees in Information Systems from University of Maryland Baltimore County. His primary research interests are in the area of decision support systems, Information Systems development, systems architectures, and intelligent systems. His published research articles appear in Expert Systems with Applications, Decision Support Systems Journal, the Encyclopedia of Decision Making and Decision Support Technologies, and Frontiers in Bioscience, amongst others.

Jeffrey A. Schiffel is a systems and software engineer with the Boeing Company. He currently leads a team of airplane-level integration engineers for USAF aerial refueling development, and has previously lead independent verification and validation studies to review software development processes, requirements traceability, and software testing for the B-52 weapons modernization; he has lead the interface control working group for the 767 Tankers program, and has taken part in various architectural and planning activities for the E-6B and E-4B airplanes and the Future Combat System. His 35 years experience includes hardware and software integration, process improvement and evaluation, computer operations, network and data communications, and project management. His Ph.D. from Nova Southeastern University is in Information Systems, specializing in knowledge management and conceptual structures. He received a M. Sc. in Industrial Engineering at Wichita State University, and a B. Sc. in Mathematics from The Ohio State University. Jeff is a member Upsilon Pi Epsilon, a computer science honorary society. He has been adjunct lecturer in engineering, computer science, and business departments at the Wichita State University. His research interests include formalization in requirements engineering, reasoning in argumentation, and the effects of culture on organizations.

Alexander Serenko is an Associate Professor of Management Information Systems in the faculty of Business Administration, Lakehead University, Canada. He holds an MSc in Computer Science, an MBA in Electronic Business, and a PhD in Management Information Systems. Serenko's research interests pertain to user technology adoption, knowledge management, and innovation. His articles have appeared in various refereed journals, and his papers have received awards at Canadian and international conferences. In 2007, he received the Lakehead University Contribution to Research Award that recognized him as one of top three university researchers.

Rahul Singh is an Associate Professor in the Department of Information Systems and Operations Management, Bryan School of Business and Economics at The University of North Carolina at Greensboro. He obtained his PhD in Business from Virginia Commonwealth University. His research interests include semantic e-business, security of systems, secure business process design, knowledge management, intelligent agents, data mining, and machine learning. He is the editor-in-chief for the Journal of Information Science and Technology (JIST). Singh is a member of the editorial board for the International Journal of Semantic Web and Information Systems, the International Journal for Intelligent Information Technologies, the Journal of Information Technology Theory and Applications, and the International Journal of Information Security and Privacy. His research work has been published in leading IS journals including Journal of the Association for Information Systems, European Journal of Information Systems, IEEE Transactions on Systems, Man and Cybernetics, Communications of the ACM, Information Systems Management, eService Journal, International Journal of Semantic Web and Information Systems, International Journal of Intelligent Information Technologies, Information Resources Management Journal, International Journal of Production Engineering, and Socio-Economic Planning Sciences.

Veda C. Storey is the Tull Professor of Computer Information Systems, J. Mack Robinson College of Business Administration, Georgia State University. She has research interests in intelligent systems, the Semantic Web, and design science research. Her research has been published in *Information Systems Research, ACM Transactions on Database Systems, IEEE Transactions on Knowledge and Data Engineering,* and *Journal of Data Management*. She has served on the editorial board of several journals including *Information Systems Research, MIS Quarterly, Data Base*, and *Decision Support Systems*.

Dhavalkumar Thakker is a research & development specialist working for Press Association, UK. Dhavalkumar was awarded a PhD from the Nottingham Trent University, UK in Semantic Web Services. His work focuses on areas of Semantic Web and its application in intelligent search engines. His research interests include semantic technologies, digital image libraries, NLP techniques, and Web services.

Manoj A. Thomas is the Director of Technology in the Department of Information Systems at Virginia Commonwealth University. He holds a Ph.D in Information Systems, a Masters of Information Systems, a Masters of Business Administration as well as a Bachelor of Engineering. His current research interests focuses on context aware computing, Semantic Web, knowledge engineering, and distributed computing. He has published in many practitioner and academic journals and presented at various Information Systems conferences and technical panels.

M. Sadeeq Ullah received his MS in computer science from Peshawar University and is currently working as a lecturer in the Institute of Information Technology, Kohat University of Science & Technology, Kohat, Pakistan. His area of expertise is artificial neural networks.

Abbas Vafaei received his BSc in electrical engineering from Amir Kabir University Teheran Iran, his MSc from Polytechnic of Toulouse, and his PhD from Paul Sabatier University Toulouse France (all with honours). Since 1988, he has been a faculty member at the computer group of Isfahan University, Isfahan Iran. His research interests include computer architecture and mathematical aspects of computing.

Mudasser F. Wyne received his PhD from University of Birmingham, UK. He has also received degrees in BSc in Electrical Engineering and MS in Engineering. He is currently serving as a Professor of Computer Science at National University, San Diego, USA. He has served at different positions in academia for the last 20+ years at various universities in USA and other countries. He is currently serving on the editorial boards of various journals and program committees for many international conferences. He is also the co-chair for ICSTC-2009 conference. His research interests include database, intelligent systems, Information Systems, and health informatics. He is the author of numerous journal and conference publications. He has managed numerous projects for various private companies and government organizations. Wyne is a member of ASEE and ACM.

Victoria Yoon is a Professor in the Department of Information Systems at University of Maryland Baltimore County. She received her MS from the University of Pittsburgh and her PhD from the University of Texas at Arlington. Her primary research interest lies in the application of intelligent technologies to business decision making in organizations. She has been involved in building various multi-agent systems for space missions at NASA Goddard Space Flight Center. Yoon has published many articles in a number of journals, including MIS Quarterly, Decision Support Systems, Journal of Management Information Systems, Information and Management, Journal of Operation Research Society, and others.

Index

Symbols